The Lost World of Socialists
at Europe's Margins

The Lost World of Socialists at Europe's Margins

Imagining Utopia, 1870s–1920s

Maria Todorova

BLOOMSBURY ACADEMIC
LONDON • NEW YORK • OXFORD • NEW DELHI • SYDNEY

BLOOMSBURY ACADEMIC
Bloomsbury Publishing Plc
50 Bedford Square, London, WC1B 3DP, UK
1385 Broadway, New York, NY 10018, USA
29 Earlsfort Terrace, Dublin 2, Ireland

BLOOMSBURY, BLOOMSBURY ACADEMIC and the Diana logo are trademarks of
Bloomsbury Publishing Plc

First published in Great Britain 2020
This paperback edition published 2022

Copyright © Maria Todorova, 2020

Maria Todorova has asserted her right under the Copyright, Designs and Patents Act, 1988,
to be identified as Author of this work.

Cover design: Anna Toshkova
Cover Image: (©) Collage by Anna Toshkova based on a 1911 New Year's card
(in private collection)

All rights reserved. No part of this publication may be reproduced or transmitted in any form or by any means, electronic or mechanical, including photocopying, recording, or any information storage or retrieval system, without prior permission in writing from the publishers.

Every effort has been made to trace copyright holders and to obtain their permissions for the use of copyright material. The publisher apologizes for any errors or omissions and would be grateful if notified of any corrections that should be incorporated in future reprints or editions of this book.

Bloomsbury Publishing Plc does not have any control over, or responsibility for, any third-party websites referred to or in this book. All internet addresses given in this book were correct at the time of going to press. The author and publisher regret any inconvenience caused if addresses have changed or sites have ceased to exist, but can accept no responsibility for any such changes.

A catalogue record for this book is available from the British Library.

Library of Congress Cataloging-in-Publication Data
Names: Todorova, Maria Nikolaeva, author.
Title: The lost world of socialists at Europe's margins: imagining utopia,
1870s-1920s / Maria Todorova.
Description: New York: Bloomsbury Academic, 2020. |
Includes bibliographical references and index. | Identifiers: LCCN 2020019748 (print) |
LCCN 2020019749 (ebook) | ISBN 9781350150331 (hardback) | ISBN 9781350150348 (ebook) |
ISBN 9781350150355 (epub)
Subjects: LCSH: Socialism–Europe, Eastern–History–19th century. |
Socialism–Europe, Eastern–History–20th century.
Classification: LCC HX240.7.A6 T63 2020 (print) | LCC HX240.7.A6 (ebook) |
DDC 335/.02094709034–dc23
LC record available at https://lccn.loc.gov/2020019748
LC ebook record available at https://lccn.loc.gov/2020019749

ISBN: HB: 978-1-3501-5033-1
PB: 978-1-3502-0183-5
ePDF: 978-1-3501-5034-8
eBook: 978-1-3501-5035-5

Typeset by Deanta Global Publishing Services, Chennai, India

To find out more about our authors and books visit www.bloomsbury.com and
sign up for our newsletters.

*To the memory of my grandparents,
Maria Krusheva and Virban Angelov,
realist idealists.*

Contents

List of Illustrations	viii
Acknowledgments	x
List of Abbreviations	xi
Map of Bulgaria	xiii
Introduction	1
Part I Centers and Peripheries	11
1 Accommodating Bulgarian Social Democracy Within the Socialist International	17
2 Metropolitan Nationalists and Provincial Cosmopolitans	48
Part II Generations	79
3 The Prosopography of the Bulgarian Socialist Left	87
4 Tales of Formation	117
5 Socialist Women or Socialist Wives	147
Part III Structures of Feeling	171
6 Dignity and Will: The Odyssey of Angelina Boneva	179
7 Love and Internationalism: The Diary of Todor Tsekov	201
8 Romanticism and Modernity: Koika Tineva and Nikola Sakarov	229
Coda	251
Notes	255
Bibliography	327
Index	355

Illustrations

Figures

1	New Year's card, 1911	2
2	Maria Krusheva as a schoolgirl, second from left	3
3	Georgi Kirkov in 1887 after his return from Russia and as a student at the Cartographical Institute in Vienna in 1892	26
4	Blagoev and Sakŭzov, 1899	27
5	Blagoev in the 1890s	29
6	Blagoev's translation of Marx's *Capital*, 1909 edition	34
7	Trotsky, passport photo in 1915, and Rakovski, June 1909	37
8	Karl Kautsky	57
9	First Balkan Social Democratic Conference, Belgrade, January 1910	60
10	Georgy Plekhanov in 1917	68
11	Georgi Kirkov in 1903	75
12	Cohorts by Date of Birth	90
13	Blagoev's *What is Socialism and Do We Have a Basis for It?*	93
14	Bulgarian Socialists by Occupation	96
15	Georgi Dimitrov in 1905	99
16	Bulgarian Socialists by Specialization in Higher Education	103
17	Higher Education of Bulgarian Socialists by Location	104
18	Blagoev in the 1920s	108
19	Death in 1923–25 by Cohorts	111
20	Geo Milev	113
21	Spiro Gulabchev as a student in Russia, 1880	128
22	Balabanov, Nokov, Rakovski, Riabova, Bakalov–Geneva circa 1890–91	135
23	Bakalov, Rakovski, Milanov, Balabanov (sitting)–Geneva 1892	136
24	Ianko Sakŭzov, 1930	142
25	Title page of the Bulgarian translation of Bebel's *Woman and Socialism*	148
26	Conference of women social democrats, Sofia, July 1914	154
27	Anna Karima, 1920	156
28	Vela Blagoeva, 1887	158
29	Tenth Congress of the BWSDP, 1903	161
30	Marxist circles in women's high schools, Plovdiv 1907 and Shumen 1912	163
31	Stella and Natalia Blagoevi in 1914	167
32	"Short Biographical Notes"	183
33	Angelina Boneva at 32	197
34	Poster "The Bulgarian–Macedonian Worker Wakes Up"	203
35	Todor Tsekov with his friends Kosta Nikolaev and Georgi Goranov, 1900	210

36	The Board of Trustees of the "Liberation" Society—February 25, 1901	211
37	Manuscript page	217
38	The Radomir social-democratic teachers' group, 1904/05	220
39	Katia and Todor Tsekov, 1907	224
40	In the editorial office of *Siznanie*, 1928	227
41	The wedding and divorce certificates	230
42	Berlin, June 1903	231
43	In Istanbul as newlyweds	231
44	Koika standing with her parents and younger siblings, Varna 1893	233
45	With her brother Tiniu Tinev in Berlin 1902	234
46	Koika Tineva in Varna, 1904	236
47	Kharlakov and Tineva, Moscow 1926	239
48	Koika Tineva, 1960s	241
49	Pages from the herbarium	243
50	Nikola Sakarov, 1917	244

Tables

1	Socialist publications in the Balkans (1880–1914)	31
2	Translations of socialist texts from different languages	32
3	Translations of books, brochures, and articles by the author, 1880–1916	33
4	Membership in the BWSDP (Narrow)	97
5	Education of members of the BWSDR (Narrow)	102

Acknowledgments

More than a decade ago, while leading an international project on "Remembering communism," I discovered an amazing unused cache of documents at the Central State Archives in Bulgaria. My appreciation to the VolkswagenStiftung for securing a fruitful year in the Sofia archives and libraries. The next few summers I was dutifully in the archive under the care of its competent staff, from the ever-changing guards and directors to my permanent guardian angels, Marieta Tzanova and Varban Todorov. My endless gratitude goes to them, as well as to the staff of the National Historical Museum and the Archive of the Ministry of Interior. A few years after my paradisiacal stay at the Wissenshaftskolleg, I was again hosted for a brief stay, when I was exploring the libraries of Berlin and Leipzig. I wish to acknowledge the help and inspiration of my friend and colleague Augusta Dimou. Veneta Ivanova and Anca Mandru, my talented graduate students, helped me with the digitization of the date-base. The illustrations would have been unthinkable without Anna Toshkova's meticulous work; she also did the cover design. My heartfelt thanks to all of them.

The writing was facilitated by a semester at the Illinois Program for Research in the Humanities where I profited from the comments of my colleagues. Parts of this work have been presented at fora in Switzerland, Germany, Greece, and the United States and if some places are improved and richer, it is thanks to the engagement of many attentive colleagues. I would also like to extend my thanks to the internal reviewers and to the superb editors at Bloomsbury. Finally, the book was finished in the serene atmosphere of the ivory tower at the Remarque Institute of NYU with its perfect host Larry Wolff. Ironically, the book's subtitle could have been "Socialists on Fifth Avenue." This sounds like "imagining utopia," but why not?

Abbreviations

BANU	Bulgarian Agrarian National Union (Bulgarian acronym БЗНС)
BCP	Bulgarian Communist Party (Bulgarian acronym БКП)
BRCC	Bulgarian Revolutionary Central Committee
BSDP	Bulgarian Social Democratic Party (Bulgarian acronym БСДП)
BSDU	Bulgarian Social Democratic Union (Bulgarian acronym БСДС)
BSLF	Bulgarian Socialist Labor Federation
BTU	Bulgarian Teachers' Union (Bulgarian acronym БУС)
BWSDP	Bulgarian Workers' Social Democratic Party (Bulgarian acronym БРСДП)
BWSDP (b)	Broads, Bulgarian acronym БРСДП (о) or БРСДП (ш)
BWSDP (n)	Narrows, Bulgarian acronym БРСДП (т.с.)
BWU	Bulgarian Women's Union (Bulgarian acronym БЖС)
CC	Central Committee
Comintern	Communist International
CPA	Central Party Archive (Bulgarian acronym ЦПА)
CPUSA	Communist Party of the United States
FTUF	Free Trade Union Federation (Broads)
GFTU	General Federation of Trade Unions (Narrows)
IESBH	International Encyclopedia of Social & Behavioral Sciences
IMRO	Internal Macedonian Revolutionary Organization (Bulgarian acronym ВМРО)
ISB	International Socialist Bureau
IWW	International Workers of the World
Krestintern	Peasant International (Крестьянский Интернационал)
MOSDG	Macedono-Odrin Social-Democratic Group
RCP (b)	Russian Communist Party (Bolsheviks), Russian acronym РКП (б)
SAG	Social Democratic Working group (Sozialdemokratische Arbeitsgemeinschaft)

SDTO	Social-Democratic Teachers' Organization (Bulgarian acronym УСДО)
SLP	Socialist Labor Party of America
SPD	Sozialdemokratische Partei Deutschlands (German Social Democratic Party)
USDP	Unabhängige Sozialdemokratische Partei Deutschlands (Independent Social Democratic Party of Germany)

* * *

Архив на МВР	Archive of the Ministry of Internal Affairs
ДА	Държавен архив, State Archive
ИИИ	Известия на Института по История на БКП
ЦДА	Централен Държавен Архив, Central State Archives in Sofia

Map of Bulgaria

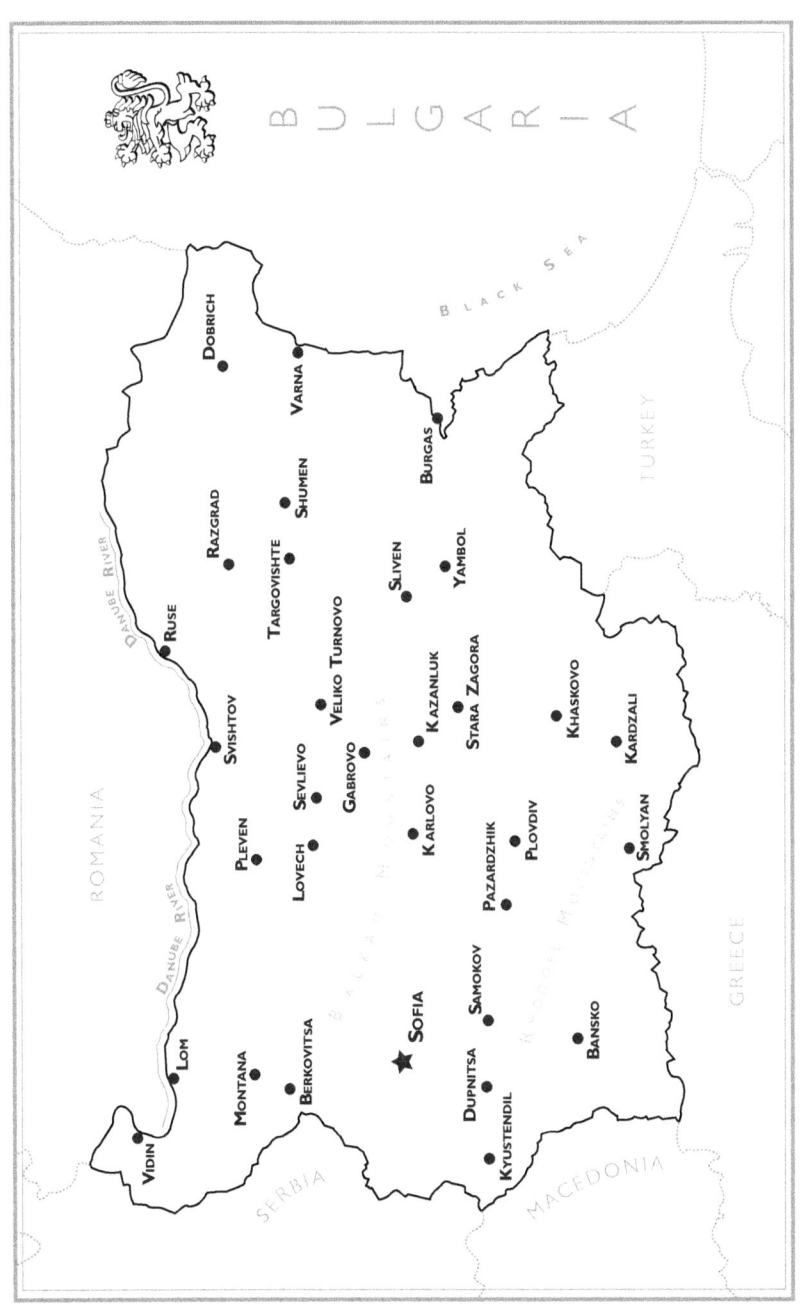

Introduction

A map of the world which does not include Utopia is not even worth glancing at, for it leaves out the one country at which Humanity is always arriving.
        Oscar Wilde, "The Soul of Man under Socialism" 1891

A lovely New Year's card was sent in December 1910 by one fourteen-year-old girl to another fourteen-year-old girl. The postcard had been produced in Ruse, Bulgaria, and was sent from Tîrnovo to the village of Obchelare. It is executed in the fashionable *Jugendstil* of the times. The allegory of the three graces has been known since antiquity when they depicted beauty, charm, and grace, but by the beginning of the twentieth century it had passed through its Christian hypostasis of faith, hope, and charity to personify the symbols of the French Revolution: liberty, fraternity, and equality. Liberty in a light blue dress is breaking the chains of bondage; Fraternity and Equality in deep red and gold, and in light green are holding hands, and between them are the scales of justice. In three corners of the card are small cameo portraits of (counterclockwise) Karl Marx, August Bebel, and Ferdinand Lassalle (Figure 1).

Writing at the close of the twentieth century, Jacques Attali lamented that "the French Revolution is a sequence of failed utopias."[1] The Paris Commune in 1871, which adopted the revolutionary calendar, counted itself as year I of Equality and year IV of Liberty (believing that liberty existed only from 1792 until the coming of the Directory in 1795). And Fraternity, which had been envisaged by Robespierre as the end of nations, lost its universality almost immediately and eventually became the basis for the engineering of the nation.[2] But at the beginning of the twentieth century, these utopias were very much alive, and they inspired young girls.

Perhaps they would not call their dreams utopias, especially not if they were inspired by the then dominant Marxism which liked to think of itself as non-utopian, to distinguish itself from the so-called utopian socialism that was not based on a scientific analysis of the dynamics of capitalist society. But, of course, Marxism is "utopia which is presented under the guise of anti-utopia."[3] The addressee of the New Year's card Maria Krusheva (Figure 2) wrote later: "I don't remember what we read, but we considered ourselves socialists. I only recall that the following year, when the teacher in Bulgarian assigned to us an essay about a great personality in world history, Stanka wrote about Karl Marx, and I wrote about Wilhelm Liebknecht. By then, I had already liberated myself from religion and demonstrated it openly."[4]

Utopias change with time and social change. They are not the same for different individuals or groups: it has been wisely observed that "every utopia comes with its implied dystopia."[5] The Paris Commune was hailed as the utopia of the dispossessed

Figure 1 New Year's card, 1911.

and the dystopia of the rabble, and both views were not merely fictional representations. The twentieth century dealt several profound blows on utopia. The First World War not only put an end to the elites' illusion (or utopia) that the civilized world could preserve peace (and an end to the illusion that it was a civilized world) but also dispelled the illusion of working-class solidarity. Out of the war emerged a deeply traumatized and utterly disillusioned but also impatient and radicalized population. The Bolshevik Revolution became for millions the great achievement of socialist utopia, but this utopia was qualitatively different from the previous one. Before 1917 socialists were striving for it but saw it in rather nebulous terms and far ahead in the time horizon; "after the October Revolution, utopia ceased to be the abstract representation of a liberated society projected into a far, unknown future; it became the unchained imagination of a world to be built in the present."[6] In the following decade it was the vanguard of utopian experimentation in practically all aspects of social life despite all the uncertainties and doubts. Even with the onset of Stalinism, utopia receded only gradually, still inspiring millions for decades.[7] Yet, 1917 also gave rise to a warring view that considered, and fought, it as the pinnacle of tragedy and dystopia.

Ernst Bloch's *The Spirit of Utopia*, published in 1918, was written during the great turmoil of the war and the beginning of revolution. It irritated many contemporary critics but remained nonetheless immensely influential. While it may sound alien today with its exalted and occult style, biblical metaphysics, and messianic eschatology, it captured the spirit of the time with its stress on unfulfilled dreams, and the journey toward an unattained goal through an organized movement:

Figure 2 Maria Krusheva as a schoolgirl, second from left.

> In this book, a new beginning is posited, and the unlost heritage takes possession of itself; that glow deep inside, over there, is no cowardly "as if," no pointless commentary; rather, what rises above all the masquerades and the expired civilizations is the one, the eternal goal, the one presentiment, the one conscience, the one salvation: rises from our hearts, unbroken in spite of everything, from the deepest part, that is, the realest part of our waking dreams: that is the last thing remaining to us, the only thing worthy to remain. . . . To find it, to find the right thing, for which it is worthy to live, to be organized, and to have time: that is why we go, why we cut new, metaphysically constitutive paths, summon what is now, build into the blue, and build ourselves into the blue, and there seek the true, the real, where the merely factual disappears—*incipit vita nova*.[8]

It is important here to recall Marx's stress on movement when he spoke of communism in *The German Ideology* in 1845: "Communism is for us not a *state of affairs* which is to be established, an *ideal* to which reality [will] have to adjust itself. We call communism the *real* movement which abolishes the present state of things. The conditions of this movement result from the premises now in existence."[9]

Between 1937 and 1949, Bloch wrote his magnum opus, *The Principle of Hope*.[10] Hope had appeared discreetly in 1918 in *The Spirit of Utopia* but not yet as a central category; hope had still not been lost.[11] It was also a very fragile category: "Hope is the opposite of security. It is the opposite of naïve optimism. The category danger is always within it.... [H]ope is critical and can be disappointed. However, hope still nails a flag on the mast, even in decline, in that the decline is not accepted, even when this decline is still very strong."[12] Writing during the high period of fascism and Stalinism, and the horrors of the Second World War, Bloch was confronted with the deep pessimism that paralyzed all action, and he tried to revive the idea of utopia: "Unconditional pessimism . . . promotes the business of reaction. . . . That is why the most dogged enemy of socialism is not only . . . great capital, but equally the load of indifference, hopelessness."[13] Rehabilitating "utopia as a neglected Marxist concept," Bloch made a distinction between abstract (compensatory) and concrete (anticipatory) utopia. Ruth Levitas remarks that it is difficult to distinguish between the two, except in the element of praxis and Marxism that Bloch introduced.[14] Indeed, as Bloch had it, "[the] road is and remains that of socialism, it is the practice of concrete utopia. . . . It means a world which is more adequate for us, without degrading suffering, anxiety, self-alienation, nothingness. . . . Marxist knowledge means: the difficult processes of what is approaching enter into concept and practice."[15]

As Peter Thompson remarks, Bloch pointed out that the process of attaining utopia was a self-generating one. He therefore restored honor to the idea of utopia by treating it "not as a pre-existing programmatic state which had to be reached under wise and all-knowing leadership either of the party or the church, but as an autopoietic process driven by the laboring, creating and producing human being driven on by their material hunger as well as their dreams of overcoming that hunger. The society we ended up with would therefore be the product of the process of getting there. This turns on its head the traditional understanding of utopia as a Telos, a pre-existing ideal state. In this he agreed explicitly with Marx's rejection of utopian communism."[16]

Utopias are not only socialistic/communistic in character, and Bloch had a lot to say about music, painting, literature, especially the fairy tale, philosophy, religion, medicine, architecture, and technology, but social utopias predominated and among them these were the major ones in the nineteenth and twentieth centuries, even as after the Second World War the utopia of the free market, already existing from the previous century, gained momentum and rose to a victorious ascendancy after 1989.[17] Writing in 1945, Martin Buber directly linked utopia to the socialist ideal. Concerned with the central value of community as "the inner disposition or constitution of life in common," he was critical of developments in the USSR but still willing to give it a chance: "So long as Russia has not undergone an essential inner change . . . we must designate one of the two poles of Socialism between which our choice lies, by the formidable name of 'Moscow.' The other, I would make bold to call 'Jerusalem.'"[18] He turned out to be overly optimistic on both counts.

By the 1960s, utopia was a problematic notion.[19] Adam Ulam pronounced a moratorium on utopia and "perhaps this is not altogether a bad thing."[20] Accepting that "the essential function of utopia is a critique of what is present," in 1964 Adorno suggested that "the idea of utopia has actually disappeared completely from the conception of socialism." He was speaking of state socialism, especially after the horrors of Stalinism had been laid open. Bloch agreed with this verdict but added that it had done so also in the West: "West and East are *d'accord*. They are sitting in the same unfortunate boat with regard to this point: nothing utopian should be allowed to exist."[21]

Leszek Kołakowski, writing after his exile from Poland in 1968 and bitter about the wasted decades he had spent in service of what now looked like a doomed and disappointing idea, was dismissive of Bloch who, he thought, had inflated the concept to a degree that made it of little use. Kołakowski, on the other hand, restricted the concept by applying it only to projections that are supposed to be implemented by human effort and to those that believe in a definitive and unsurpassable condition, a final state, ignoring entirely Bloch's insistence on the processual and limitless character of utopia, but also the fact that most utopias have not been written of as reaching a finite perfection. This second condition, however, allowed him to conveniently critique utopia as potentially stagnant, reduced to immobile mediocrity, inhumane, and tending to totalitarian despotism.[22] Still, dialectician as he was, Kołakowski also saw the limits of this reasoning and the dangers from the death of utopia: "The victory of utopian dreams would lead us to a totalitarian nightmare and the utter downfall of civilization, whereas the unchallenged domination of the skeptical spirit would condemn us to a hopeless stagnation, to an immobility which a slight accident could easily convert into catastrophic chaos. Ultimately, we have to live between two irreconcilable claims, each of them having its cultural justification."[23]

Then came 1989 when in the words of Ralf Dahrendorf, communism collapsed and social democracy was exhausted.[24] The communist utopia had been already long drained of any strength and the "free world" announced the end of utopia and the end of history, most often gloatingly and sometimes melancholically.[25] Given the defeat of the "real socialist" experiment, the mood today is at best to forget about it, at worst to criminalize it entirely. Approaching the history of socialism and Marxism through the prism of melancholy, Enzo Traverso summarized the significance of the event as announcing the general eclipse of utopias:

> When, after 1989, we became "spiritually roofless" and were forced to recognize the failure of all past attempts to transform the world, the ideas themselves which had tried to interpret the world were put into question. . . . Instead of liberating new revolutionary energies, the downfall of State Socialism seemed to have exhausted the historical trajectory of socialism itself. The entire history of communism was reduced to its totalitarian dimension, which appeared as a collective, transmissible memory. . . . After having entered the twentieth century as a promise of liberation, communism exited as a symbol of alienation and oppression.[26]

As Beverley Best observes, debates about the mechanics of an alternative society, which had animated the public sphere in the nineteenth and early twentieth centuries, have been replaced by debates "around why visions of an alternative society seem to have stalled altogether or, at least, gone underground, or why they can be detected only in allegorical forms such as science fiction that can travel incognito as 'entertainment.'"[27] Nonetheless, as Lyman Tower Sargent aptly notes, the "end of utopia" industry was wrong on at least three counts: first, by equating utopia with communism; second, by assuming that communism had ended, ignoring the world beyond Europe; and finally, by missing the utopian potential of capitalism itself. He accordingly pleads that utopian thinking, however problematic, is the only way to challenge dystopia.[28] Debates on whether utopia is possible or impossible, whether it is necessary or whether it is better dead, will continue, but in academia, at least, utopia continues to be affirmatively on the agenda, as "culture's unrest."[29]

What needs to be addressed is the relationship between ideology and utopia, namely the utility of approaching utopia via ideology and vice versa. With the exception of Karl Mannheim who proposed a model in which ideology and utopia were strongly decoupled and implicitly opposed, most other sociologists accept the dialectical unity of the two concepts. For Mannheim, who considered both complexes of ideas, the crucial distinction between them was that ideologies sustain the status quo, whereas utopias strive to bring about change.[30] Moreover, they are attached to specific social classes; "ideology is linked to dominant but declining classes, utopia to oppressed (or at least subordinate) and rising ones."[31] This binary distinction was heavily criticized at the time and first Bloch produced an alternative by arguing about the interpenetration of these concepts.[32]

Paul Ricoeur refined the understanding of ideology not by discounting its function as "distortion" (Marx) or "legitimation" (Weber) but by insisting on its fundamentally integrative function: "Even if we separate off the two layers of ideology—ideology as distortion and as the legitimation of order or power—the integrative function, the function of preserving an identity, remains."[33] Utopia, on the other hand, is a disruptive but productive imagining, a breakthrough, a glance from nowhere, which "introduces a sense of doubt that shatters the obvious."[34] Both ideologies and utopias deal with power, although from different ends and with different goals, and they are mutually correcting: "We must try to cure the illness of utopia by what is wholesome in ideology—by its element of identity, which is once more a fundamental function of life—and try to cure the rigidity, the petrification of ideologies by the utopian element."[35]

For Sargent ideology is "a system of beliefs regarding the various institutions of society that is accepted as fact or truth by a group of people. An ideology provides the believer with a picture of the world both as it is and as it should be. . . . As such every ideology contains a utopia, and the problem arises when it becomes a system of beliefs rather than what it is in almost all cases, a critique of the actual through imagining a better alternative."[36] And Levitas is categorical that "both conventional sociology and critical social theory have unavoidable utopian character" and that the method of utopia is "the Imaginary Reconstitution of Society, the construction of integrated accounts of possible (or impossible) social systems as a kind of speculative sociology."[37]

This book seeks to recuperate something of the appeal of the socialist ideology and the utopia implicit in it. I want to do this by going back to the *experience* of people who thought and *dreamed* of utopia and *struggled* to achieve it. It does not matter how they called their dreams—"liberty," "equality," "fraternity," "justice," "happiness," "hope," "revolution," "socialism," "communism," "social democracy"—the important thing is that they were involved in a movement that worked toward their ideal. Again, it is worth quoting Bloch at length, because of his emphasis on "striving," "path," "dream," and "goal," in a language that captures the Zeitgeist:

> The seemingly more remote revolutionary *concept* is not "rootless" after all, or "impossible" or "abstract" in the capitalist age: rather, since the thinking subject is located not only in its time, and the collective from which it speaks is not only socially collective, it can be achieved absolutely eccentrically to time as the inventory of Oughts (that is, of out tasks even beyond the historically given) and thus in a suprahistorically concrete way, as an absolutely constitutive presentiment of the goal, knowledge of the goal. As a whole, in any case, we have here reached the place to strive—instead of for the mere self-way, the pure soul-expanse of the self-encounter, even the most direct shape of the moment and the question—for another, practical-exemplary level of concretion. To shape a path from the lonely waking dream of the inner self-encounter to the dream that goes out to shape the external world at least to alleviate it, at least as *locus minoris resistentiae* or even as the instrumentation for the goal.[38]

Chronologically, I am restricting my analysis roughly to the half-century when the social-democratic movement was at its peak, from the 1870s to the 1920s. Utopian visions and emancipatory movements in this era were obviously not restricted to socialism and I deal with some of them, but socialism, especially with the Second International, was the hegemonic one.[39] I end with the aftermath of the October Revolution not because I want to gloss over, let alone smear, the interwar period of communism by insisting that it had an earlier and nobler, less militant prehistory. This would be an entirely different project but also a nonhistorical one displaying little sensitivity to the specificities of the historical moment. I do think, however, that there is a qualitative difference between a "utopia of the future" and a "utopia on earth," and it has to do with the effects of generational shifts, encompassing everything from approximate demographic clusters and specific social habitus to the consequences of singular dramatic events serving as a rupture, like the Great War and the Bolshevik Revolution. It was, especially, the latter that allows for the distinction of "utopia of the future" from "utopia on earth," insofar as contemporaries believed that they had brought their strivings to fruition in 1917 even as they continued to strive for the final construction of their utopia. For them, the future was no longer desirable and nebulous; it had just arrived and had to be defended.

The selection of the European periphery as the space of my account is not simply because it is less known but because I hope to fracture and recalibrate the dominant narrative of social democracy which is confined to Western Europe and insists on the exclusive authenticity of industrial environment and working-class milieu. Within this periphery I am choosing a topos that is even less known, Bulgaria, which had one of the largest (if not the largest) and most influential social-democratic movements in Eastern Europe with a unique relationship to both German and Russian social democracy. What was socialism's unique appeal in a young nation-state with an overwhelmingly rural population and an incipient proletariat? Using different optical ranges of observation, I shift the focus from aerial views of the large-scale movement of ideas to closer pictures of characteristics of groups and, finally, to close-ups of individuals. The study looks at different intersections or entanglements: of spaces, generations, genders, ideas and feelings, and different flows of historical time.

Part I, *Centers and Peripheries*, focuses on the intersection between center and periphery by looking at the history of social democracy from the posited margins of Europe. Chapter 1 challenges the established typology of two modes of socialism, Western (European) and Eastern (Russian/ Soviet) until the First World War. Insofar as we can speak of a binary *model*, it would be applicable only for the period after the 1920s, after the schism that occurred with the creation of the Third International in 1919 and the developments in the interwar period. The passionate debates within the Second International were not played out on a West-East axis. I then situate Bulgarian social democracy within this bickering but still family formation and demonstrate how this problematizes the notion of transfer of ideas. Chapter 2, "Metropolitan Nationalists and Provincial Cosmopolitans" highlights the attitudes toward the national question, the particular case of the Balkan Federation, and, especially, the divergent positions toward the First World War, which proved the central issue and the undoing of the movement. Nowhere was the national idea more dominant than in the southeastern corner of Europe, where the newly created nation-states were locked in a struggle over the last dominions of the retreating Ottoman Empire. How did socialists navigate between the Scylla of genuine patriotism as citizens of young states and the Charibdis of equally genuine condemnations of nationalism?

Part II, *Generations*, addresses the intersection or interplay of several generations of leftists, looking at the specifics of how socialist ideas were generated, received, transferred, and transformed. This period and its agents remain relatively unknown, even in the local historiography. The three chapters of this part offer, consecutively, three ways of approaching groups. Chapter 3 is a quantitative prosopographcial analysis of several demographic cohorts unified in a specific political generation. It is based on the digitized database of close to 3,500 individuals harnessing material from existing biographical dictionaries, encyclopedias, published sources, documents, and archival documentation. These include, first and foremost, self-defined social democrats of different, often passionately opposed factions, but also anarchists, anarcho-liberals, populists, left-wing agrarians, and left-wing members of different nationalist organizations. It allows to establish patterns of social provenance, types and place of education, professional and political networks, involvement in crucial events, etc. The analysis then moves to a qualitative account in Chapter 4, where representative cases are singled out to create a narrative around the notion of formation, that is, to offer several mini-*Bildunsroman(s)* in the effort to reveal the different experiences of becoming socialist. Finally, Chapter 5 sheds light on the "invisible" women of the movement by questioning the opposition between socialist women and socialist wives. I am especially intrigued by how early socialists approached gender issues, how they dealt with the conundrum of professed ideas of equality but practiced it in a society of unequal footing.

Part III, *Structures of Feeling*, focuses the lens on individual experience. It investigates the intersection between subjectivity and memory as reflected in (and inflected by) written sources: published and unpublished memoirs, diaries, personal correspondence, biographies and autobiographies, written down oral interviews, all of which allow the reconstruction of the world of the first socialist generations. It introduces several unknown biographies by highlighting their emotional world: of an extraordinary peasant teacher (Chapter 6, "Dignity and Will: The Odyssey of Angelina Boneva"); of a lawyer who also happened to be a love-stricken graphomaniac (Chapter 7, "Love and Internationalism: The Diary of Todor Tsekov"); and of a brilliant economist and bank director and his stunning partner (Chapter 8, "Romanticism and Modernity: Koika Tineva and Nikola Sakarov"). In doing all this, I want to pick up and resurrect what has been considered to be historical debris and serve as the transmitter-translator of human visions and emotions, and, broadly, the human condition. In "The Task of the Translator" Walter Benjamin had observed:

> One might, for example, speak of an unforgettable life or moment even if all men had forgotten it. If the nature of such a life or moment required that it be unforgotten, that predicate would imply not a falsehood but merely a claim unfulfilled by men, and probably also a reference to a realm in which it *is* fulfilled: God's remembrance.[40]

Of course, I am not pretending to play the role of the divine remembrancer; mine is the simple one of the historical remembrancer: "History is that certainty produced at the point where the imperfections of memory meet the inadequacies of documentation."[41]

Part I

Centers and Peripheries

All things were together, infinite both in number and in smallness; for the small too was infinite.

Anaxagoras

Scale has become an important category in the present debate about the meaning of the historical profession. When explored analytically by Jacques Revel some twenty years ago in *Jeux d'échelles*, it dealt mostly with microhistory and the gains we acquire from the intensive study of limited objects. Recognizing the crisis in the classical paradigms with which we analyze the social, it explored the relative significance of the big versus the small, of detail versus the whole, of the local versus the global, of the value of exception versus generalization.[1] By 2013, when the *American Historical Review* housed a debate on the question of scale in history, it dealt almost exclusively with macrohistory, although with some nostalgic nods in the direction of the assaulted area studies.[2]

One is tempted to ascribe this to a European versus an American debate, reflecting the scale of the geopolitical ambitions and practices of the spaces that these respective academics inhabit. Yet, a more careful scrutiny belies this dichotomy. It is true that area studies are especially challenged in the United States where the trend in historical thinking is geographically on the scale of the world and temporally in large periods, from the human (200,000 to 4 million years) to the planetary (Gaian), and the cosmological, as illustrated in the work of its chief practitioner David Christian, who borrowed Revel's title to use as a foil: "Macrohistory: The Play of Scales."[3] However, only some area studies are affected (East European in particular) whereas others are booming (Islam and the Middle East, or Asian studies).

European historians, on the other hand, are equally engaged in the global turn, both with individual contributions and in transatlantic publications.[4] In both the American and European cases, the focus on macrohistory can easily slip into the marketing of world history teaching and a happily celebrated monolingualism (often bordering on monoglossia) but, at the same time and constructively, also in the new and deserved interest in environmental studies, and several stimulating big turns: the Atlantic, the oceanic, borderland history, and so on, even as much of this was prefigured by the *Annales* school, specifically the work of Fernand Braudel and by the pioneering scholarship and journalism of C. L. R. James.[5] Despite the appearance that global is taking over, smaller scale initiatives and interesting work continue to be generated on the micro and intermediate levels. Inconveniently, specificity does not want to disappear.

European historiography has gone methodologically through several turns in the past decades—from comparative history and transfer studies to an emphasis on *histoire croisée*, entangled history, or connected histories.[6] But both the American and European endeavors have been equally inspired by the striving to supersede the nation-state, to shed the swaddling bands in which modern historiography was born in the nineteenth century, and which nowadays are perceived as its original sin. To what extent they succeed in this endeavor is still open: it is a work-in-process with contradictory results and with serious side effects.

So, what happens if we use the change of the optical range on an object of research that, although belonging to the nineteenth and twentieth centuries, by definition superseded national boundaries and reached global dimensions (although in the parlance of the day, and if we are to stick to emic categories, it referred to itself as "international" which, being a secondary category, still binds it to the "national," just as it does the "transnational"). We are speaking, of course, of socialism. To Eric Hobsbawm, the birth of socialism and its spread, together with the rise of the workers' movement, was the pivotal moment of the nineteenth century, especially after 1848.[7]

The new technologies that revolutionized Europe in the second half of the nineteenth century, and especially after 1870—the train, the steamship, electricity, the telegraph, industrial chemistry, and also photography, cinema, and radio—resulted in massive industrial growth and an enormous surge in international trade, which reached 9 percent of the global GDP. This level was reached only in the 1970s (today it is around 18 percent), and scholars are speaking of the first wave of globalization (ours being the second).[8] This was accompanied by the growth of disruptive political developments, the enfranchisement of the majority of male citizens, and the rise of mass movements, mostly inspired by nationalism and socialism as well as international solidarity. While socialist internationalism came into being in the framework of early industrialization and the formation of nation-states, enforced by demands for democratic participation and labor protection, "it was only just before and after the revolutionary wave of 1848 that leagues and committees with international aspirations began to be formed."[9] In the words of Patrizia Dogliani, this internationalism of oppressed peoples "was based, however, on the 'sacredness of nationality' and a notion of brotherhood inherited from masonry, mutualism and proto-syndicalism."[10]

Logistically, the International Workingmen's Association, known later as the First International, failed as an organizational structure. Formed in 1864, it was torn between different factions, most prominently between Marx's followers who favored parliamentary agitation and the anarchists around Bakunin who focused on economic struggle. It finally split in 1872, and the First International was officially dissolved in 1876. It left, however, a powerful legacy, both in the concept of internationalism as "the ideal of universal emancipation and of activities linked to the struggles of the popular and working classes" and, more concretely, in "The Internationale," the song written by Eugène Pottier to the melody of the Marseillaise.[11]

The new and current melody of "The Internationale," composed by Pierre De Geyter in 1888 coincided with the foundation of the "Nouvelle Internationale" (to distinguish it from the "Vieille Internationale") in 1889, although there had been attempts already from the early 1880s. Known as the Second International after its dissolution, it operated with periodic international congresses of which there were nine before the outbreak of the First World War. All of them were held in cities of Western Europe (France, Germany, England, Belgium, the Netherlands, Denmark, and Switzerland), reflected also in the numbers of delegates, overwhelmingly from these countries. According to Moira Donald, 58 percent of the delegates at the nine congresses came from three countries: France (26 percent), Germany (16 percent), and the United Kingdom (16 percent). Belgium had 9 percent, Switzerland 5 percent, Austria 4.5 percent, and Russia 3.5 percent. Italy, Sweden Bohemia, Poland, Denmark, and the Netherlands hardly made 3 percent, and the rest even less.[12] After 1900, the International operated in a more regular and centralized way, under the coordinating oversight of the International Socialist Bureau (ISB), with a permanent executive council in Brussels.

By general consent, the era of the Second International, from the last quarter of the nineteenth century to the First World War, was the acme of social democracy as a movement. What made it the Golden Age in the words of Leszek Kołakowski was the spread of parliamentary institutions over most of Europe and the radical extension of male suffrage, which allowed for the creation of socialist political parties. Kołakowski himself attributed the Golden Age to the fact that the Marxist doctrine was not so rigidly codified and allowed for discussions of theoretical and practical problems.[13] For James Joll, "socialism, from being a doctrine of economic and political theorists, became the creed of mass parties."[14] The institutionalization of socialism was thus in the form of autonomous parties based on the national principle. As Stephen Bronner notes: "Neither the First International led by Marx nor the Second International of the socialist labor movement was ever conceived to supplant the positive functions of the nation-state."[15]

Some thirty parties were founded in Europe between 1871 and 1905, variously describing themselves as "social democratic," "socialist" or "labor": the German Socialist Workers' Party in 1875 (preceded by the workers' association in 1863 and the Socialist Democratic Workers' Party in 1869), the Portuguese in 1871, the Danish in 1876, the Czech in 1878, the French and Spanish in 1879, the Dutch in 1881, the Belgian in 1885, the Norwegian and the Armenian Hanchaks in 1887, the Swiss in 1888, the Austrian and Swedish in 1889, the Hungarian in 1890 (with a predecessor in the General Workers Association), the Bulgarian in 1891, the Italian and Serbian in 1892, the Polish and Romanian in 1893, the Croatian in 1894, the Slovenian in 1896, the Russian in 1898 (preceded by the Russian Group for the Emancipation of Labor in 1883), the Finnish Labor Party in 1899, the Ukrainian social-democratic party in Galicia in 1899, the United Kingdom Labor Party in 1900 (which was a Social Democratic Federation in 1883), and the Latvian in 1904.[16] As of 1889, they were united in the Socialist International, which held regular congresses, coordinated, from 1900 on, by the ISB in Brussels. With few exceptions, in which they are unevenly represented, one can read about the constituent parties almost solely in national accounts. This period also saw the gradual expansion of socialist ideas over the globe but until after the First World War international socialism was mostly a European enterprise.

Of the non-European socialist movements, by far the most significant in this period was the American movement, and it had a direct influence with the adoption of May 1 as International Workers' Day by the Second International in 1891, in recognition of the Haymarket affair of 1886. While organized socialism had its roots in the 1876 Workingmen's Party with strong Lassallean and anarchist influences, the Socialist Party of America was formed in 1901. In other aspects, American socialism was characterized by its strong populist and Christian roots, as a whole not preoccupied by doctrinal issues and with practically no parliamentary representation, unlike its European counterparts. Like the British Labor Party, it "remained somewhat incomprehensible to most European Socialists, and . . . lay outside the main stream of the movement."[17] The other movement that was held in disproportionally high esteem in the Second International even as it was unable to have deep roots in its own country was Japanese socialism, characterized by factionalism and a few ephemeral formations in the early 1900s.[18] The Chinese socialist party was formed in 1911 and had exclusively educational activities.[19] India saw practically no socialist influence until the end of the First World War and the effects of the Russian Revolution.[20] The influence of socialist ideas in the Arab world and Modern Turkey remained limited among select intellectuals and embryonic until the 1920s.[21] Iran's social-democratic movement dated from the Persian Constitutional Revolution, 1905–1907, under the direct Russian organizational influence from Transcaucasia.[22]

Zooming out to world history, in one of its latest impressive iterations of the period from 1870 to 1945, the emerging social-democratic parties are confined to the West, juxtaposing them to the "primitive and dark" forces of the peasant masses in southern and Eastern Europe.[23] As for the Second International, it is deemed worthy of mention on two half-pages of an 1,160-page tome and, in what is surely an idiosyncratic choice and interpretation, exemplified by a brief biographical sketch of Jean Jaurès and the assertion that "his [sic!] 'Second International'" "sought evolution, country by country, toward a transnational democratic socialist state."[24] But socialism rendered irrelevant seems to be a trend in the new world/global history. In the equally impressive achievement of Jürgen Osterhammel, who offered a sweeping survey and rethinking of the nineteenth century, socialism merits less than five pages in its 1,167, even if in the concluding chapter it is called "the most important nineteenth-century current of dissident ideas."[25] As Enzo Traverso in his critical review essay rightly observes, "Anxious to avoid the pitfall of historical teleology—socialism having been one of its main figures—he [Osterhammel] sketches a picture in which socialism simply vanishes."[26] Big surveys are often barometers of the latest fashionable trend, of contemporary moral geopolitics, and of the unsurprisingly eclectic and unavoidably incomplete knowledge of their authors.

This is the place to tackle the notions of *core* and *periphery*. Introduced in the 1950s in the vocabulary of the United Nations, specifically the Economic Commission on Latin America, they were theorized later by Immanuel Wallerstein in several works.[27] Wallerstein and other proponents of world-system theory stressed the processual character of these concepts: "In world-system analysis, core-periphery is a relational concept, not a pair of terms that are reified, that is, have separate essential meanings."[28] Standing on but critically complicating dependency theory, world-system theory was mostly used to describe the international division of labor and its repercussions on the social system. Within this framework, Christopher Chase-Dunn has developed a comparative theory of the semi-periphery, to which Eastern Europe is often (but not always) added.[29] For Chase-Dunn, the semi-periphery favors the development of interesting social and political phenomena and therefore can be said to occupy "a structural position which often has developmental (or evolutionary) significance."[30]

While criticized for its excessive economism and neglect of social class and culture, the influence of world-systems analysis is undisputed, and the notions *core* and *periphery* have entered everyday use, so much so that a "peripheral" status is accorded to all aspects of life in economically peripheral territories. But, as Osterhammel has argued, "political geography does not coincide with economic geography, and the global distribution of cultural cores is different from that of the concentrations of military power."[31] Likewise, Susan Gal has warned that a number of cultural categories, among them center-periphery, alongside East-West or public-private, are "indexical signs that are always relative: dependent for part of their referential meaning on the interactional context in which they are used."[32] Not only does core-periphery indicate a relation, but it always indicates an asymmetrical relation and "what matters is the self-understanding of the actor: does (s)he think that her or his opinion is in the 'catch up' part of the yardstick, or does (s)he experience being part of an ascendant or even dominant culture?"[33] I will employ "periphery" and "peripheral" in quotation marks to indicate that I am using them in their common sense (and questionable) usage, and to differentiate them from the strict meaning that they have in world-systems theory, even as I concede that the concept continues to have salience "as both critical concept and media shorthand for (relative) backwardness."[34]

In what follows, I want to argue for the crucial importance of scale. The category of scale here has to be distinguished from scalability, which has a different meaning, despite both having the same etymological roots. As Anna Tsing has insightfully argued, scalability blocks the ability to notice the heterogeneity of the world, whereas the change of scale helps precisely to highlight this heterogeneity.[35] I do not posit that there exists a privileged scale; in the end what counts is the variation and the discrete questions that different scales can answer. However, changing the scale is not an innocent exercise: it alters radically the narrative that emanates from it. Using different lenses, in the following two chapters I first comment on the deeply seated stereotype of two models of socialism through a brief excursus in the history of concepts. I then deal with three instances in which a "peripheral" case, that of Bulgarian social democracy, problematizes the question of transfer of ideas, underscores the entangled history of the national question, and insists on a comparative account of the attitude to war, which became the central issue of the International's debates and the litmus test of its internationalism. In doing so, I seek to achieve a fracturing or recalibrating of the dominant European narrative from the inside.

1

Accommodating Bulgarian Social Democracy Within the Socialist International

Two Socialist Models?

Zooming slightly in, from world history to the general accounts of socialism, it is German social democracy that is usually the most heavily represented.[1] There is, of course, good reason for this: a party with a following of over one million members by 1913, it towered over all others who had a significant following but counting in the tens of thousands, with the exception of the Czechs who reached a quarter million, and the Swedes at over 130,000. The German party served as the recognized model for the rest, and especially for Eastern Europe.[2] It achieved the "merger of socialism and the worker movement," sealed in the Erfurt Program of 1891, providing the whole period with Lars Lih's apt designation of Erfurtianism.[3] More importantly, the Second International was dominated intellectually by the two crown princes of Marx and Engels, Kautsky and Bernstein, and Kautsky was affectionately referred to as the Red Pope.[4] This German hegemony was not necessarily resented, except by the French.[5] I am using hegemony here in the classical sense as a form of leadership based on consent, but not entirely dismissing the coercive element; as Perry Anderson reminds us, "hegemony . . . was inherently interventionist."[6] Gramsci, who developed and refined this classical understanding as well as Lenin's notion of the hegemony of the proletariat, transformed the idea of hegemony "from a merely political to a moral and intellectual form of leadership" by pointing out that "the subject of hegemony could not be any socio-economically pre-constituted class, but had to be a politically constructed collective will—a force capable of synthesizing heteroclite demands that had no necessary connection with each other, and could take sharply different directions."[7]

For the rest of the social-democratic parties, German hegemony was rather inspiring, even as on the national level there was substantial diversity among the individual parties. This diversity, however, is recognized in the big surveys in the usual one-sentence lip-service acknowledgment. Thus, the main questions that occupied the Second International—the revisionist crisis and parliamentary tactics, the national question, the colonial question, the questions of war and peace—are exemplified mostly by the German debates.

The main premise of all these works is that socialism was a response to the challenges of modern mass industrial society, with an emphasis on *industrial*. This triggered the perpetual surprise at the "paradox" of socialism's spread in the agricultural lands of Eastern Europe, notwithstanding the fact that outside of England proper, Germany and Bohemia, the industrial working class was everywhere in the making in societies with the numerical preponderance of small proprietors, urban but most often rural, and even in Germany where the industrial working force in the period between 1882 and 1895 rose by 40 percent from 7.3 million to 10.2 million, the waged labor was predominantly employed in small enterprises.[8] As Tony Judt reminds us in his exquisite study of the close identification of the socialist movement with the peasantry in Provence, French Socialists "'missed' their chance in their early years not through the lack of a large social base, in the countryside especially, but through their *political failure to seize power in the centre*."[9] Extending this configuration to other "backward" societies in Latin southern Europe, he points out that "we should avoid the easy temptation to mock the popularity of 'Marxism' in Africa, Asia or central and southern America. The concept of a socialist revolution was, indeed, born of the nineteenth-century experience of industrial capitalism in Europe. But it can seem an irrelevance in non-European contexts only if we persist in understanding it exclusively on its own terms . . . based on the class consciousness of an industrial proletariat and dependent upon a high level of industrial progress and production."[10]

This easy temptation to mock has actually been avoided successfully in the politically correct parlance about the so-called Third World, and especially with the advent of postcolonial studies and the discourse on "alternative modernities." Sophisticated work on "peripheral" labor history has criticized the reductive understanding of "proletarians" as property-less males compelled to sell their skills for money and the labor movement consisting of trade unions and workers' parties supported by "genuine" proletarians as industrial workers. When E. P. Thompson stressed the social variety and heterogeneity of the working class, this was allowed only for England. For the Third World, Robin Cohen and Peter Worsley have been instrumental in shedding the stereotype and showing the presence of ambivalent class positions of "semiproletarians," "semipeasants," and other fluid categories as part of the labor force, including also other types of labor relations outside or alongside "free wage labor."[11] But the stereotype continues to be applied to Eastern Europe. Even the latest iteration of East European history, which aims "to globalize the history of East Central European political thought, while at the same time to 'renegotiate' the European intellectual canon," explains the popularity of socialism merely with its utopianism: "The utopianism of socialism, and of the political left in general, allowed for the crossing of regional and national boundaries. It may, in particular, explain the popularity of socialism in agrarian societies, where it otherwise could seem to be a contradiction in terms (having no basis in an urban working class)."[12] There is genuine surprise that when in 1912 social democrats in Germany won 34 percent of the vote, "even in relatively backward Bulgaria they captured over 20 percent in 1913."[13] There is no surprise, however, that social democrats in Switzerland garnered the same percentage (actually a little less), that in "backward" Italy and Belgium it was comparable (circa 22 percent), that the Netherlands (18.6 percent), France (16.8 percent) and Britain (7 percent) won less, and that predominantly rural Finland trumped the German victory with its 43 percent of the vote.[14]

Not bothering to look at figures, George Cole boldly concluded that "in the Balkan countries . . . the Socialist movement remained small right up to 1914. In none of these countries was there a large enough industrial proletariat to provide a basis for any considerable growth of Trade Unions" while benignly conceding that "*some sort* [italics mine] of Socialist movement had developed before 1914 in all the Balkan countries except perhaps Montenegro; but nowhere had Socialism become a major influence, nor had any Socialist thinker of first stature emerged. The nearest approach was Dr. Christian Rakovsky," whose biography fills the next two pages of the meager twenty pages dealing with the Balkans in a volume of 1042 pages devoted to the Second International.[15] Even Augusta Dimou in what is arguably the most sophisticated and careful "thick" reading of the beginnings of socialism in the Balkans writes about "the absence of *objective conditions* [italics mine] for the reception of socialism in the nineteenth and early twentieth centuries," reproducing a doctrinaire conceit of Marxism.[16]

In what has become the easiest substitute for profound analysis, namely creating classifications and typologies, the complexity of European socialisms is folded into models or types. The most distinguished collective history of socialism offers a fourfold typology. There is the dominant German brand, characterized by the tension between "revolutionary appearance and reformist reality," to which belong also Austria-Hungary, the Netherlands, the Scandinavian countries and Finland. Then, there is France, with its "amazing diversity," from its revolutionary socialism to its "ministerialism," and the strong influence of anarchism, where Marxism never could take deep roots. The French type was even more pronounced in its adherence to anarchism in Italy and Spain; Belgium and Switzerland form a transitional sphere between Germany and France. The third type is the British linked to a long history of workers' struggle and distinguished by its weak adherence to Marxism and strong syndicalism. And, finally, the fourth type is the Russian, where the beginning of socialism "was not linked to the existence of a revolutionary class," but was inspired by the populism of an intelligentsia which maintained that, because of its past history and peasant institutions, Russia had a revolutionary calling. The same populist attitudes, according to the authors, characterized the Balkan countries, except that there the national question was overwhelming.[17] The overall conclusion, though, contracts this model even further into a bipolar one: "There is general consensus that at the moment when the world war erupted, because of its political and economic lag, the path of socialism in Russia would be different than that of the great Western countries."[18]

It is my contention that this bipolar schema is anachronistic and retrospectively applies to the late-nineteenth and early-twentieth century the schism, which had occurred only after the First World War and particularly with the foundation of the Third International in 1919, between "socialism" and "communism" and only subsequently acquired the garb of a "western" versus an "eastern" model. Of course, prejudice against the East in general and Russia in particular had existed before, both in politics and in the public sphere, and it inevitably affected the views of socialists, but socialist thought readily and even enthusiastically accommodated the Russian revolutionary movement. Famously, Marx began studying Russian in order to follow the rising revolutionary wave coming out of Russia in the 1870s. While his celebrated dictum that "the country that is more developed industrially only shows, to the less developed, the image of its own future,"[19] remained the guiding principle of the Second International (and specifically among Russian social democrats grouped around Georgy Plekhanov until the rise of Lenin), Marx himself was moving in the direction of different roads to socialism, even as he overemphasized the role of the Russian village commune, the *mir*, as "the fulcrum for social regeneration."[20]

For all the mistrust toward Russian official policies, especially under the banner of Slavophilism, Russian socialists (most of them in exile) were not seen in this period as different, as part of another civilization. On the contrary, they were sharing the same goals and struggle against Russian absolutism. Plekhanov was second only to Kautsky in keeping the torch of Marxist orthodoxy alive. There was even a certain division of labor, where Kautsky was the main theoretician on economic and social issues, leaving philosophy and aesthetics to Plekhanov.[21] Moreover, the Russian Revolution of 1905 and its use of the mass strike, especially promoted in the speeches and writings of Rosa Luxemburg, gave an impetus to passionate theoretical debates around the practice of the mass strike, and is a prime example of entangled history. And yet, most subsequent historical works promote the idea of the existence of two models of socialism that had crystallized in this period: the Western or European, and the Russian model.

To explain this, we have to look back and recall the long common history the concepts of socialism, communism, and Marxism have had. This is also important for providing the background for understanding the famous interparty splits and reunions that pestered the movement. The saga of the semantic peregrinations of these concepts is fascinating and certainly merits close and detailed scholarly analysis. Luckily, this has been broached not only by a respectable literature, but has also been synthesized, among other works, in the magisterial *Geschichtliche Grundbegriffe*, which charted the turn from the history of ideas to conceptual history.[22] We thus possess an exemplary *Begriffsgeschichte* of the three concepts in the languages in which they were first articulated.

Both socialism and communism have an etymological pedigree in Latin (*communion, communis, socialis, socialibis*). In their modern usage they are neologisms from the time of the late *ancien régime*. Their widespread use in practically all European languages dates from the 1840s. Both were future-oriented concepts, and although there were substantive differences more in the perception rather than in the contents of these two terms, until the Great War they were often used interchangeably. *Communism* has had a theological tradition in the German-speaking realm reaching back to the sixteenth and seventeenth centuries among the Anabaptists, many of whom called themselves *communistae* and defied private property. In eighteenth-century France and Italy, *communistes, communisti* was an ascriptive judicial term describing the common use of land property by a village commune. When it entered the vocabulary of the late Enlightenment thinkers (Nicolas Edmé Restif de la Bretonne), the revolutionary language of Babeuf and his disciples, and the terminological apparatus of Etienne Cabet and Théophile Thoré, it was oriented to the future, and subsumed all kinds of theories that aimed to achieve an equitable society on the basis of the abolition of private property, and in most cases, through revolutionary means. In was in this sense that it was adopted in Germany where Wilhelm Weitling can be identified as "the first German communist," but also alongside such figures as Moses Hess, Friedrich Engels, and Karl Marx.[23] The official judicial overreaction against Weitling, and the perceived danger from communism in the German space, created an actual "Communist Scare" (*Kommunistenfurcht*) in the 1840, culminating in the revolutions of 1848–49 and thereafter. It is in this atmosphere that Marx and Engels ironized the fear of the communist specter in the *Communist Manifesto* and laid a monopolizing claim to the use of the concept.[24] Looking back forty years later, Engels wrote: "We could not have called it a *Socialist* manifesto. In 1847, Socialism was a middle-class movement. Socialism was, on the continent at least, respectable; Communism was the very opposite."[25]

In an interesting twist, in England at the time communism was the tamer word. Robert Owen preferred to use socialist which suggested the secular reorganization of society as a whole, whereas communism, at least until the Paris Commune, had a religious tinge and was not associated with atheism, as socialism was.[26] On the continent, however, communism had acquired the sense of a militant movement and, although not denounced by the Left, was cautiously eschewed. Ferdinand Lassalle, while accused of being a communist, was careful to avoid it as a designation. He never referred to himself as a communist, and only once as a socialist.[27] Both August Bebel and Wilhelm Liebknecht avoided the term, although they tried to emancipate it in speeches and writings from its alarming reputation. Even Engels and Marx showed a frustrating ambivalence. They did use the term sparsely, referring mostly to the Vormärz period. After the death of Marx, Engels spoke of "the dialectical method" and the "communist worldview" but used the concept "scientific socialism" not "scientific communism."[28]

Like *communism*, *socialism* also had an earlier tradition. The accusation of being *socialistae* was leveled against Hugo Grotius and his followers, especially Samuel Pufendorf in Germany and John Locke in England, who developed the system of natural law in the seventeenth century. In its modern sense, however, the concept took root around the social reforms of Robert Owen in England. Interestingly, it was not the Owenists themselves, but their adversaries who put the concept *socialism* on the national agenda, bemoaning "the abominable and atrocious system known by the disgusting name of Socialism."[29] By the late 1830s Saint-Simon, Fourier, and Owen were understood to be "socialistes modernes."[30] As already remarked earlier, in England, unlike on the continent, socialism was considered to be the tougher word. And yet, even from the outset, *socialism* as a concept had a life outside the revolutionary critique of society, and thus as a concept proved more acceptable and tamable.

The reason for this may have been purely semantic as the term *social* could also be used in a purely descriptive and neutral way and, in this sense, politically it could be understood as a continuation of liberalism, that is, social, including radical, reform in the name of the main liberal values—political freedom and social justice—but not upsetting the base of capitalist society, the private ownership over the means of production that was at the center of the revolutionary reading.[31] The reception of the term in Germany goes back to the key role played by the publication of Lorenz Stein's book in 1842 on French socialism and communism.[32] Stein privileged socialism as a positive force and communism as a destructive one, but his book, in fact, served to couple the two concepts together. The link between the two notions, which should not be taken for granted given their different pedigree, had already been made in France in 1840.[33] And while Marx and Engels opted for *communism* over *socialism*, their typology of socialism in the *Communist Manifesto* was less than clear. There were three types of socialism: there was reactionary socialism, and there was bourgeois socialism, but there was also critical-utopian socialism and communism as sub-species of the general phenomenon.[34]

During the revolutionary years of 1848–49, the evangelical church articulated a version of Christian socialism which was to save throne and altar from the social revolution.[35] This was a first step to imbuing socialism with the national spirit. In 1895, Friedrich Naumann, whose views were close to Christian socialism, coined the locution "national socialism": "We need a socialism that is capable of governing. Such socialism must be German national."[36] Naumann's liberal version was not carried through, but the phrase has been forever bound to designating Hitler's ideology. The Paris Commune sealed the militant reputation to communism, although there is a continuing debate whether *communard* is equivalent to *communiste*. And, of course, one should not forget Otto Weininger's 1903 dictum in *Geschlecht und Charakter* that socialism is Aryan (Owen, Carlyle, Ruskin, Fichte), while communism is Jewish (Marx).[37] As a result, the preferred self-designation for the workers' parties from the 1870s until the end of the First World War everywhere was "socialist" and even more so "social democratic."

It was only after Lenin consciously appropriated the word "communist" that it came into widespread use again. He had done so already in December 1914 after the outbreak of the war, when most social-democratic parties supported their governments, when he wrote "whether it would not be better to avoid the stained and abased word social-democrat and go back to the old Marxist designation communist," and the following year he started, with Bukharin and Pyatakov, publishing the journal *Kommunist* in Geneva.[38] After the war and the creation of the Third Communist International, all participating former socialist or social-democratic parties changed their names to communist. From 1925, when the *Comintern* started an official campaign for bolshevization, Bolshevism became synonymous with communism.[39] The interwar period saw an unmitigated and often bloody struggle between socialists and communists, abating only during their common struggle against fascism. After the end of the Second World War the trend to identify communism with the Soviet experience and that of its satellites continued. Within the reigning orthodoxy of the time, the system was one of "real socialism" as a step toward the as-yet-unattained communist society. This is the basis for the presently existing historiographical debate, whether one should speak about a "socialist system," "socialist heritage," "socialist or postsocialist nostalgia" and the like, or, respectively, about a communist system, heritage, and nostalgia.

The Soviet domination was interrupted only in the 1960s when China broke its monopoly over communism, and again in the 1970s with the emergence of Eurocommunism, which opened the possibility to rescue it from its dependence on Soviet communism.[40] Less than a decade later, "real socialism" ended in the dustbin of history, and the communist parties of Eastern Europe, just as in 1919, switched en masse to a new name—*socialist*—and entered the Socialist International. Communism has been relegated almost exclusively to the role of a *Schimpfwort*, a generalized term of abuse in Europe and North America. And yet, its future may still be open, judging from the persistence of communist parties in the world (in Asia in particular, but also in Latin America, and in Europe itself), and also because of its polysemic nature.[41]

Marxism was a relative latecomer to this triad of concepts. While it was occasionally used to narrowly describe followers of Marx within the socialist movement or in conjunction with derogatory attributes by their opponents,[42] its general notion as a systematic theory slowly entered the vocabulary of social democracy and was sealed only in the 1890s. This was mostly triggered by the famous polemic of Engels against Eugen Dühring in the late 1870s. The verdict on Dühring nowadays is of an eclectic thinker, who criticized Marx's political economy and specifically the labor theory of value, adopting the views of one of the major figures of the American school, Henry C. Carey, in his *Harmony of Interests*, who preached fierce protectionism, was an aggressive opponent of religion, and an ardent nationalist and notorious anti-Semite. His work, however, had a growing influence among the German social democrats, and Engels undertook a thorough criticism in his *Anti-Dühring*,[43] in which he produced the first systematic survey of the philosophical, natural-science, and historical views that, according to Engels' claim, they shared with Marx.[44] In the words of Franz Mehring, written already in 1877, it was not *Kapital* but *Anti-Dühring* that became the communist [sic!] Bible and Engels boasted that not even the *Communist Manifesto* or *Kapital* was so often translated and reprinted.[45]

The oft cited adage of Marx that "all I know is that myself, I am not a Marxist" is completely decontextualized: it was pronounced after a visit to his son-in-law Paul Lafargue in Paris and addressed concretely the economic part of the program of Guesde and Lafargue's *parti ouvrier*, not a putative obscurantist comprehensive theory.[46] When Kautsky wrote about a Marxist school and Marxism in his correspondence with Bebel and Engels in the 1880s, Engels corrected him to speak only of Marx himself.[47] It was only after the repeal of Bismarck's anti-socialist legislation in 1890 that the works of Marx and Engels began to be published and disseminated in Germany in large quantities, and in 1892 German social democracy adopted "Marxism" as its official theoretical party foundation.[48] Marxism also became the official doctrine of the Second International after the definitive expulsion of the anarchists.[49]

Marxism was, of course, hotly debated, interpreted, sanctified, and vilified. It was approached as an economic theory, as a social system, as a particular method, as a philosophy of history, as a science, as a worldview, as a socialist theory, and as a social movement. Kautsky was the recognized premier exegete of Marxism in the Second International. His popularizing exegesis of Marxian ideas became its official doctrine and dogma, marked by its critics for its excessive economic determinism and lack of flexibility.[50] Nevertheless, until his death in 1938 Kautsky was revered as the keeper of the orthodoxy. The one serious contending current from within Marxism in the era before the First World War came from Eduard Bernstein, whose effort to update and revise Marxism in light of the new economic developments at the end of the nineteenth century translated into a new reformist tactic for the party, generating one of the central debates within the International over "revisionism." After 1905, to a great extent under the influence of the Russian Revolution, the left wing of German social democracy under Karl Liebknecht, Rosa Luxemburg, Clara Zetkin, and others advocated a more activist politics and espoused an alternative concept about the formation of class consciousness, achieved spontaneously during the struggle. There exists an overall consensus that these, as well as the theoretical works of the Austro-Marxists, were challenges from within the orthodoxy, although there are well-argued opinions that Bernstein, in particular, "was not revising Marx; he was advocating a completely different point of view."[51]

Lenin, who closely followed orthodox Marxism in all theoretical aspects until the war, was an authentic "Russian Erfurtian."[52] Still, he brought in his own imprint in the theory of revolution and especially in the organizational practice of a centralized revolutionary party. And, as Lindemann aptly remarks, "Prior to 1917, many non-Russian socialists had entertained ideas similar to those which would later be called Leninist."[53] Lenin's sharp departure from Kautsky came only in the aftermath of the breakup of the international socialist movement because of the attitude toward the war, and the creation of the *Comintern* in 1919. The schism was irreversible. Shortly after Lenin's death, the Soviet monopoly over Marxism was sealed with the concepts of Marxism–Leninism under Stalin and soon after frozen into a dogma. This is not the place to review all other currents and appropriations of Marxism during the interwar and postwar period—from Trotskyism to Maoism, from the critical theory of the Frankfurt school to the New Left, the *Praxis* group, and the Situationist International. What is important, however, is that the notion of a Western Marxism stemmed from the interwar period. The publication in 1923 of György Lukács's *History and Class Consciousness* and Karl Korsch's *Marxism and Philosophy*, although written at the time by devoted Leninists, was seen as an ultra-leftist western European deviation and denounced by the *Comintern* in 1924.[54] Only later, in 1953, was the term "Western Marxism" coined and appropriated as a self-designation by Maurice Merleau-Ponty.[55]

One can conclude that as a self-designation, "Western Marxism" was adopted after the Second World War to set it apart and rescue Marxism from the stifling straitjacket of the Stalinist Marxism–Leninism that crystallized in the 1930s and was imposed thereafter on the Soviet Union and its satellites. It bears thus the imprint of the Cold War. Ironically, however, as a phenomenon its roots go back to the 1920s from within the ranks of committed Leninists, and in the interwar period many were part of the left wing of social democracy and communists (Lukács, Korsch, Antonio Gramsci, Erich Fromm, Ernst Bloch, Bertold Brecht). It covers efforts to creatively develop the insights of a humanist and dialectical Marxism and geographically encompasses Western, Central and Southeastern Europe (the *Praxis* group) as well as "eastern" Marxists who were marginalized, repressed, or exiled. Insofar as we can speak of a binary *model*, a Western/European Marxism and an Eastern/Russian/Soviet one (and even this is debatable), it would be applicable only for the period after the 1920s.[56]

In his synthesis of the *biennio rosso* (the red two years, 1919–21), Albert Lindemann concludes that the Great War and the Bolshevik Revolution were the catalysts, but not the reason, for the split within the socialist movement. The polemics during these radical years show "the many possible varieties of Marxism, Leninist and non-Leninist" that "occurred according to prewar factions of the International, to social divisions within the working class, to generational divisions, and to divisions relating to previous experience in organized parties and other working-class institutions."⁵⁷ Some of the Western socialists became uncritical admirers of the Bolsheviks; others, like Ernst Däumig, Antonio Gramsci, or Alfred Rosmer, while admiring the revolution, were hoping for a more humane and democratic outcome; still others were suspicious and hostile. "The prewar doyens of Marxian orthodoxy, such men as Karl Kautsky, Filippo Turati, and Jules Guesde . . . were forced to reformulate carefully what they believed to be the fundamental theoretical verities of Marxism against what seemed to them an eastern, anarchist corruption of Marx's thought."⁵⁸

The point to stress is that this binary enters later. During the era of the Second International, the Golden Age of social democracy, and before, at the time of the First International, there were passionate debates and conflicts within the movement, but they were not played out on a West-East axis. The one exception may be the debate around the nature and applicability of the general strike advocated by Rosa Luxemburg and her wing, clearly inspired by the success of the 1905 Russian Revolution. Some opponents advanced the argumentation that the Russian experience cannot be applied to the conditions of Western Europe. It is in this atmosphere of a common socialism, but one housing a broad spectrum of competing, often incompatible, trends, opinions, and local specificities and under the unquestioned hegemony (and often condescension) of the German social-democratic party as far as the spread of Marxism to the north, east, and southeast of Europe is concerned, that one has to accommodate the "peripheral" social democracies of the end of the nineteenth century until the First World War.

How Are Ideas "Transferred"?

"The Communist Party of Bulgaria was shaped by the Socialist movement from which it evolved. The distinctive factor in the history and development of the Bulgarian Socialist tradition was that it was the offspring of the Russian, not the German or French one."⁵⁹ So starts the most authoritative (and detailed) history of the Communist Party of Bulgaria in its early period by Joseph Rothschild. This was Rothschild's first book published when he was twenty-eight (his doctoral dissertation) for which he received tenure at Columbia University to become one of the most important scholars on East-Central European history. Rothschild goes on further to illustrate his opening sentence with examples of the leaders of the socialist movement:

> Dimitar Blagoev, one of the half-dozen important leaders of Bulgarian Socialism, had, as a student at St. Petersburg University, founded in the winter of 1883-84, the first known Marxist circle in Russia. Georgi Kirkov and Yanko Sakazov, who were to become leaders of the Bulgarian Communist and Socialist Parties, respectively, received their political education in the Populist and Socialist student circles at the gymnasia of Nikolaev and Odessa in the early 1880s. Nikola Gabrovski and Nikola Kharlakov, who both repeatedly transferred their allegiance from one to the other wing of Bulgarian Marxism before being finally reconciled to Communism, had likewise studied in Russia, the latter at Kiev University. The Communist leaders Vasil Kolarov and Khristo Kabakchiev were initiated into the Marxist movement

by Plekhanov while studying in Geneva in the 1890s, as was Georgi Bakalov, who in 1900 organized the smuggling of Lenin's *Iskra* into Russia. Georgi Dimitrov, indeed, is exceptional in having achieved a prominent position in the Bulgarian Communist movement without a period of apprenticeship in a Russian Socialist organization, but he rose out of the ranks of the trade unions and not the political Socialist movement. It is not surprising that these men, on returning to Bulgaria, should organize the Socialist movement of their native country along lines similar to those of the Russian model.[60]

Almost everything on the first page of this otherwise important work is untrue, if not entirely false. Georgi Kirkov (b.1867) was sent to study in a Russian gymnasium at the age of twelve, and five years later was expelled not because of any political leanings but for undisciplined behavior.[61] He completed high school in Gabrovo and was sent on a state fellowship for his higher education in Vienna, at the Cartographic Institute. His encounter with socialist ideas occurred there, between 1892 and 1895, and he was an active participant in the Austrian labor movement (Figure 3). Upon his return from Vienna, he joined the Bulgarian Workers' Social Democratic Party (BWSDP, Bulgarian acronym БРСДП).

Ianko Sakîzov (b.1860) also finished gymnasium in Russia, but in 1881 went to study natural sciences, philosophy, and history in Germany; biology in England; and literature and art criticism in France.[62] Nikola Gabrovski (b.1864) received his law degree in Geneva (1884–1887) without spending any time in Russia. Likewise,

Figure 3 Georgi Kirkov in 1887, after his return from Russia and as a student at the Cartographical Institute in Vienna in 1892.

Vasil Kolarov (b.1877) was a member of the BWSDP from 1897 before he went to study law, first in Aix-en-Provence, and then in Geneva. Khristo Kabakchiev (b.1878) became a member of the BWSDP as a high school student in Bulgaria at the age of nineteen, before he went to France to study medicine, and then transferred to law in Geneva. Georgi Bakalov (b.1873) was the president of his high school socialist society and became a member of the Bulgarian Social Democratic Party (BSDP, БСДП) in 1891, before he left for Geneva to study natural sciences. None of them were "initiated into the Marxist movement by Plekhanov." They came to Geneva not with some mute socialist leaning but were committed Marxists and organizationally involved in the BSDP. None of them, upon their return, organized the socialist movement in Bulgaria following a putative Russian model, because the movement existed before they left the country.

Given the numerous splits within Bulgarian social democracy and their complicated acronyms, this is the place to bring in some initial clarity. BSDP is the acronym used between 1891 and 1894. In 1892 the group under Sakîzov split to form the Bulgarian

Figure 4 Blagoev and Sakîzov, 1899.

Social Democratic Union (BSDU, БСДС). The differences were over the appropriateness of overt political activity, the Unionists arguing that it was premature, and that at this stage the work should be confined to educational and economic activities.[63] The two formations merged in 1894 to form the BWSDP. They experienced a final split in 1903 over the issue of collaboration with bourgeois parties and differences in their attitude toward the peasantry. In the aftermath of 1903, Bulgaria had two bickering social-democratic parties, both recognized by the International and both known as BWSDP but with qualifications in parentheses. The broads around Sakîzov, that is, the ones working for a broad common cause, called themselves broads (*shiroki*, широки) or workers for the common cause (*obshtodeltsi*, общоделци) using (о) or (ш) alternatively; thus БРСДП (о) and БРСДП (ш). The Narrows (*tesni*, тесни), the Blagoev faction advocating no collaboration, used (т.с.). Further in the text I will use the accepted acronyms in English: BWSDP (b) and BWSDP (n) or will refer to them as Broads and Narrows. The Geneva group around Christian (Krîstiu) Rakovski (1873–1941),[64] which had initially advocated adopting the Russian example, whereby émigrés in Switzerland would lead the Bulgarian socialist movement, eventually joined the different wings of the BWSDP. The Geneva circle, in particular, became very close to Plekhanov and was undoubtedly influenced by him, decisively in the case of Bakalov's work on literary criticism and Marxist aesthetics.

Only Dimitîr Blagoev (b.1856) and Nikola Kharlakov (b.1874) were entirely formed in Russia. But even in the latter case, they do not prove Rothschild's main points, which can be summarized as follows: first, that the Bulgarian movement was copying the Russian one, down to the "peculiar rhetoric and phraseology," and was characterized by the "narrow intensity so characteristic of the Russian intelligentsia," and second, that unlike Western Europe, both Russia and Bulgaria were backward countries and "only shadows of future social classes existed in Bulgaria at the turn of the century," creating an atmosphere that bred "doctrinairism and fanaticism and a spirit of schism."[65] Anyone who has seriously studied Marx and the whole rhetoric of nineteenth- and twentieth-century socialist polemic will shy away from depriving it of its archetypal intensity and intolerance, its routine use of disrespectful, not to say rude, epithets. Moreover, the schism was typical of the socialist movement as a whole. Beyond this the link between doctrinairism and "incomplete societies" with "shadows of future social classes" seems to be a sociological leap of faith. But it conforms to the doctrinairism that socialism is possible, workable, normal, and objective only in developed industrial societies.

If doctrinairism, an authoritarian streak, and I would also add puritanism, but certainly not fanaticism, can be attributed to Blagoev, Kharlakov defies any such classification. After having received his degree in natural sciences in Kiev, he became a teacher and prominent leader of the BSDP, but left it as an "anarcho-liberal," then merged with Sakîzov's "broads," and between 1913 and 1919 was a member of parliament as an independent socialist, before joining the Bulgarian Communist Party (BCP) in 1920, disappointed by the right swing of the broads.[66] Even in the case of Blagoev, who de facto organized the first Marxist group in Russia, it is difficult to argue that he bears the imprint of a "Russian tradition," whatever this means. In view of the historic (although often justified) condescension both from the West and from Russia about Bulgaria that dismisses Blagoev's pioneering organization as a mere curiosity, it is well worth remembering that Plekhanov valued Blagoev's "Program of the party of Russian social-democrats" higher than the program of his own group "Liberation of Labor," founded the same year in Geneva.[67] Blagoev's name can be substituted effectively in an assessment of Daniel De Leon, his contemporary and the leading North American socialist, never accused of being a Russian minion:

> Even De Leon's opponents were usually willing to concede that he possessed a tremendous intellectual grasp of Marxism. Those who had suffered under his editorial lashings looked on him as an unmitigated scoundrel who took fiendish delight in character assassination, vituperation, and scurrility. But most of De

Figure 5 Blagoev in the 1890s.

> Leon's contemporaries, and especially his critics, misunderstood him, just as he himself lacked understanding of people. He was not a petty tyrant who desired power for power's sake. Rather, he was a dogmatic idealist, devoted brain and soul to a cause, a zealot who could not tolerate heresy or backsliding, a doctrinaire who would make no compromise with principles. For this strong-willed man, this late nineteenth-century Grand Inquisitioner of American socialism, there was no middle ground. You were either a disciplined and undeviating Marxist or no socialist at all. You were either with the mischief-making, scatterbrained reformers and "labor fakirs" or you were against them. You either agreed on the necessity of uncompromising revolutionary tactics or you did not, and those falling into the latter category were automatically expendable as far as the Socialist Labor Party was concerned.[68]

My purpose here is different from simply "decentering" the role of Russia and Russian connections, let alone negating them, and maintaining that Western ones trumped Russia's. In the previous section I showed that for the period under study the whole notion of different and polarized models of socialist tradition that has been the dominant framework of the general surveys of socialism, mostly through binaries such as Western Marxism–Eastern or Russian Marxism, liberal socialism–authoritarian socialism, are inadequate. Here I want to achieve two things: to examine the utility of the transfer paradigm, and to reach a general characterization of the Bulgarian socialist movement in the period until the end of the First World War.

The spread of Marxism is usually described in a specific language: it "penetrates," it "exerts influence," it is being "diffused," it is "transmitted." The socialism of the countries that were the object of this diffusion was, accordingly, imitative and derivative. With the advent of transfer studies, this vocabulary became somewhat subtler: knowledge was "circulated," "appropriated," ideas were "translated," "transplanted," adapted in a communicative action, stressing the processual character of the transfer, cultural mixing, and hybridization. Transfer studies, sometimes too strongly contrasted to comparative studies, were supposed to overcome the assumption inbuilt in comparison about static units of analysis and, instead, study processes in transformation. An additional advantage was that while comparison tended to focus on synchrony, inquiry into transfer favored a diachronic perspective.[69]

For the Balkans, with the honorable exception of Augusta Dimou, other accounts do not care to apply this framework. Most embarrassing is the great Eric Hobsbawm (who is still my hero). In a huge book about the spread of Marxism, he has a few lines on Bulgaria: "*Capital* was not translated in any southeastern European language except Bulgarian before 1914. Perhaps it is more significant that some Marxism did penetrate these backward regions —even, in a way, the remote valleys of Macedonia—rather than that its impact (outside of Russia-influenced Bulgaria) remained relatively modest." The same paragraph has the following jewel of a phrase: "The appeal of Marxism to intellectuals in southeastern Europe was limited chiefly by the scarcity of *any kind of intellectuals* [italics mine] in some of the more backward countries (as in part of the Balkans)."[70] One is bound to ask what the syntagm "some Marxism" should signify. Is it Marxism's "lesser" part? Or one easier to understand for natives?

The trope of "Russia-influenced Bulgaria" is ubiquitous and, as shown further, has a later provenance, again mostly from the interwar period, but has been unquestioningly applied to all of Bulgaria's modern history.⁷¹ Even Dimou insists on a two-step process of transfer, from the West to Russia, and thence to the Balkans: where "chunks of Western socialist thought infiltrated the Balkans in a roundabout way, often mediated, that is, through Russian channels."⁷² Geoff Eley, more carefully, speaks of the diffusion of Marxist writings: "The countries of weakest diffusion were those of the Iberian Peninsula, where anarchism dominated, and the Balkans and parts of Eastern Europe where there was no labor movement yet and little popular literacy." However, this conclusion follows the previous sentence where he asserts that the liveliest interest for the Manifesto was displayed in East-Central Europe and Tsarist Russia, with seventy editions in Russian, eleven in Polish, nine in Hungarian, eight in Czech, seven in Yiddish and Bulgarian, six in Finnish, five in Ukrainian, four in Georgian, and two in Armenian. The Balkan country par excellence, Bulgaria, is elevated to an East-Central European one, not to damage the neat conclusion.⁷³ Indeed, in the Balkans (but also in East-Central Europe, Bulgaria stands apart with the very high reception of socialist ideas as can be seen in Table 1.⁷⁴

Contrary to the received wisdom of Russia being the main bridge and channel of socialist ideas, the translations were made predominantly from German as evidenced in Table 2.

In terms of translated authors, Kautsky had the premier place, followed in the Bulgarian case by Plekhanov, Marx and Engels, and Lafargue (Table 3). For Bulgaria, this was followed by Roland-Holst, Schulz, Tugan-Baranovsky, Vandervelde, Wilhelm Liebknecht (five each), Pannekoek, Dietzgen (two each), and Clara Zetkin (one). All this is not to minimize the importance of Russian contacts and especially the Russian language as an accessible medium; it was formative in many ways. While the first documented encounter with Marx and socialism was in French,⁷⁵ the bulk of translations well into the 1880s was from Russian, to be then superseded with ones from German. It was mostly Russian translations of Marx, Engels, and other socialists, published in the Russian émigré presses that were imported in huge numbers in

Table 1 Socialist publications in the Balkans (1880–1914)

Country	Publications Total number	Translations* N	%	Socialist translations** N	%
Bulgaria	1,151	710	64.7	404	57
Serbia	675	164	24.4	130	79.3
Romania	198	42	21.2	34	81
Hungary	[300]	—	28.5	—	50
Croatia	103	17	16.5	16	15.5
Slovenia	86	18	20.9	16	18.6

*These include not only theoretical texts on socialism but also translations of belles-lettres, and books and brochures on popular science.
**This is the number of translations exclusively on socialist themes, and the percentages in this column are not calculated from the total but from the number of translations in column 2.

Table 2 Translations of socialist texts from different languages

Country	Total	German		Russian		French		Polish		Serbian		English		Italian	
		N	%	N	%	N	%	N	%	N	%	N	%	N	%
Bulgaria	405	162	40	106	26	70	17.3	38	9.4	13	3.2	5	1.2	1	0.2
Serbia	130	62	48	21	16	19	15	1	1	—	—	2	1.5	2	1.5
Romania	34	17	50	4	12	9	27	—	—	—	—	2	—	2	—
Hungary	—	—	28	—	9	—	30	38	9.4	—	—	—	20	—	—
Croatia	16	10	62.5	—	—	—	—	—	—	3	18.75	—	—	2	12.5
Slovenia	16	14	87.5	—	—	1	6.25	—	—	—	—	—	—	1	6.25

Table 3 Translations of books, brochures, and articles by the author, 1880–1916

Author	Bulgaria		Serbia		Romania	
	Books	Articles	Books	Articles	Books	Articles
Kautsky	51	49	14	54	3	13
Marx	21	6	5	16	3	12
Engels	17	12	6	10	7	24
Lafargue	19		6		4	
Bebel	11		5		4	
Rühle	10		4			
Plekhanov	42		3			
Bogdanov	8					
Kropotkin	8				2	
Lassalle	7		3			
Vasa Pelagić	7					
Jaurès	6		1		1	
Guesde	5		2		1	

Bulgaria. In fact, many Bulgarian socialists ordered their literature directly from the Elpidin Russian émigré bookstore in Geneva.[76] At the same time, Marx's 1883 German edition of *Das Kapital* was already in the Plovdiv public library by 1885.[77]

True, *Capital* was first translated into Bulgarian from Russian in two separate translations in 1909 and 1910, but does Marx translated from Russian become less Marxist and more "Russian," especially keeping in mind that the first translation of *Capital* in any European language was in Russian?[78] The 1909 translation by Blagoev took several years to complete, and the preface specifies: "This translation is made from Russian, but in fact it can be said that it was made equally from German and French. We had at our disposal all four Russian editions, but the basic text was Struve's translation, closest to the original. We still had to compare it, line by line, with the original, following the latest, fourth German edition of Friedrich Engels, and also according to the French translation edited by Marx himself."[79] Equally, the 1910 translation of Bakalov was made from the Russian translation of Bazarov and Stepanov, compared to the fifth German edition.[80]

The Bulgarian socialists took the work of translating their Bible seriously and executed it meticulously. With Marx, Bulgarian socialists were reading—in original or in translation—a German text written in London by a cosmopolitan atheist who also happened to come from a converted Jewish background and had strong opinions on the Jewish question, so much so that he is not even claimed as part of the Jewish pantheon of prominent figures (unlike similar characters like Trostky or Heine). Why is this a West-East transfer or transmission, when these ideas were equally "transmitted" to the West European intellectuals and working classes through a popularizing and often reductionist propaganda? One never speaks of the "transfer" of Marxism in France although it never took deep roots in this country, nor in England where it was technically conceived, but was never popular in the labor movement. Even in the German context, where it became the official doctrine, it had to be "transmitted" and imposed. It also had to be "translated" from German into German, in a more accessible language by a whole troop of Marxian exegetes. Kautsky's popularized version (paraphrase) of 1887 alone had thirty-five editions in German until 1930.[81]

Even though "transfer" introduced a greater flexibility and dynamism in the analysis, transfer studies came with their inbuilt problems, the most important being the fixed frames of reference that included the points of departure and arrival. This unwittingly restores "through a sort of boomerang effect, the national references that were to be put in question."[82] It is a sublime irony that the universalist Marx (no matter how one deconstructs his universalist claims) has to be "nationalized" (for Germany) or "regionalized" (for Western Europe) where he is deemed authentic, but "transferred" to the rest of Europe and the world. It is for this reason, and while never minimizing the role of literal and figurative translation of these ideas in the Bulgarian context, that I prefer to speak about the *formation* (in the sense of the German *Bildung*) of a Marxist or broadly socialist worldview. This will be my operating concept in the next chapters.

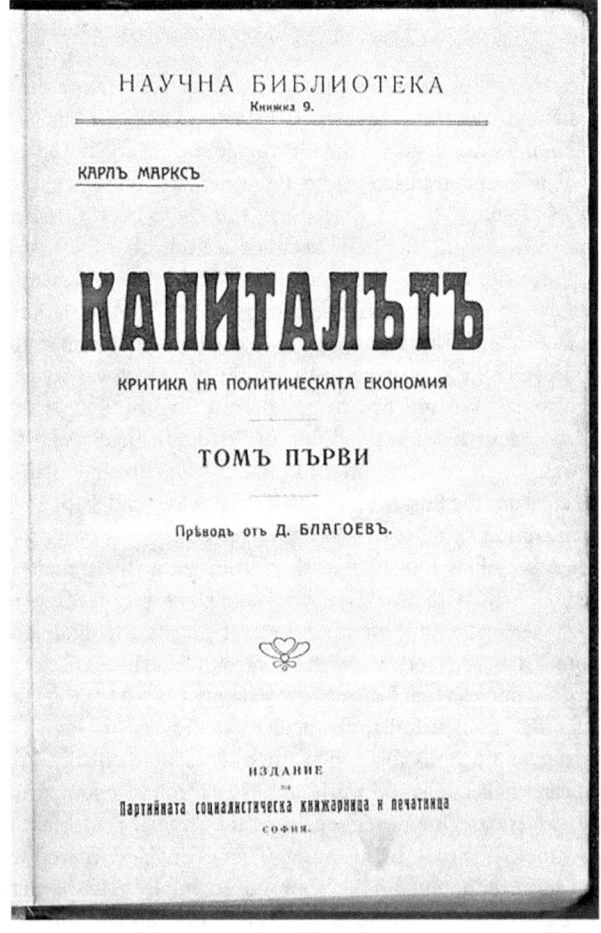

Figure 6 Blagoev's translation of Marx's *Capital*, 1909 edition.

How Are Ideas Represented?

Yet, how did it come to the deep-seated conviction of Russia's exclusive influence? The cultural proximity between Russia and Bulgaria is unquestionable. It stems from the linguistic closeness as well as from their shared Orthodoxy. The latter circumstance did not play any role in the case of the socialists but, interestingly, nor did Slavophilism based on the linguistic kinship. By the time the Slavophile idea was harnessed by the Russian imperial mission, the Bulgarian social democrats were its virulent critics and opponents, so much so that in July 1910, the Narrows invited to their congress delegates from several Slavic social-democratic parties—Poles, Russians, Serbs, Czechs, and Ruthenians—as a counterweight to the all-Slav congress, this "all-Slav comedy" that had been convened a couple of weeks earlier in Sofia.[83] Trotsky was the Russian delegate and he heaped praise on the Bulgarian socialists for their stance and endorsed their views that "the only way out of the national and state chaos and the bloody confusion of Balkan life is a union of the peoples of the peninsula in a single economic and political entity, on the basis of national autonomy of the constituent parts."[84] This was the only way to rebuff the "shameless pretensions of tsarism and European imperialism" and enjoy the advantages of a common market of the Balkans. Given the fact that Trotsky lived at that time in Vienna, the place of the blossoming of a sophisticated (if controversial) Austro-Marxism, his own views on the rise of the national ideal were deterministic, not to say dogmatic: "Economic development has led to the growth in national self-awareness and along with this a striving for national and state self-determination."[85]

But Trotsky had also come with another mission. He was sent by the Socialist International alongside Rakovski to mend the split within the socialists' ranks. This mission is described in detail in Bulgarian historiography; suffice it to say that it proved completely unsuccessful.[86] This failure prompted Trotsky's dismissive critique of the Narrows in an article published in August 1910. He first expressed his surprise that the badges of the Bulgarian congress had pictures of Marx and Bebel but explained this off as an outward mark of gratitude to the great German teachers and as a sign of protest against the anti-German agitation of the all-Slav chauvinists. He immediately followed this by a lengthy paragraph in which he described the Bulgarian socialist movement as essentially a division of the Russian. I am providing a long excerpt as I believe that this is the Urtext from which the subsequent Western writings (with all their tiny errors) stem:

> The Bulgarian language is in general very close to Russian, and furthermore, it must be remembered that the Bulgarian Social democrats have been brought up on Russian Marxist literature. Not only "Granddad"[87] Blagoev, the founder of Bulgarian and cofounder of Russian Social Democracy; not only Georgi Kirkov, who attended grammar school in Nikolaev and already at that time moved in Narodnaya Volya circles; but also the younger generation of the Bulgarian revolutionary intelligentsia, who studied in Swiss universities and there passed through the Russian school of Marxism, under the direct guidance of Plekhanov or of his closest pupils. The advanced workers of Bulgaria, even if they have never left

> the country, follow Russian party literature and understand the Russian language. The Bulgars sing Russian revolutionary songs, it must be admitted, better than we Russians do.... In brief, one could say that, as regards its ideas, the Bulgarian movement is merely a branch of the Russian. This is shown, unfortunately, in negative phenomena: like the Russian Social Democrats, the Bulgars are split into two factions which have no link except the fierce struggle between them.
>
> In full conformity with the backwardness of capitalist development, the intelligentsia plays a disproportionately large role in the Bulgarian labor movement. It brings into the proletarian ranks ideological fervor, an intense desire for socialist knowledge; but also, along with these, its characteristic negative features—on the one hand, the striving to play a political role at any cost, which, when the proletarian base is inadequate, leads to dangerous combinations and opportunistic vacillations; on the other, fanaticism and doctrinaire intransigence, which leads to continual splits and breakaways. In these phenomena must be seen the disorders of youth and growth.[88]

This article produced an immediate and equally heated riposte by Blagoev who wrote that "our party has developed and continues to develop not under the influence of the Russian party, but under the influence of the German party. It is not the *Iskra*, but the *Neue Zeit* and German socialist thought that is a living concept for us."[89] Incidentally, even the theoretical journal of the BWSDP (n) was *Novo vreme*, named after *Die Neue Zeit*. In a second article, commenting on the efforts to impose the unification of the two parties, Blagoev concluded: "It is wrong to impose the unification of the proletariat everywhere following a template, without knowing the concrete circumstances in which the working-class movement develops in the separate countries. . . . In the end, it is not very smart to consider yourself smarter that all those who do not find it possible to advocate to everyone and in all circumstances the unification of all socialist fractions."[90] This angry rebuttal seems at first glance to be in stark contrast to previous acknowledgments of the close links to the Russian socialists. Thus, at its report to the Stuttgart Congress, the Bulgarian socialists had written that

> the principal source from where our early socialists drew their ideas, came from the Russian socialist literature. Comrade Plekhanov can be justifiably said to be the father of Bulgarian socialism. His influence on the Bulgarian socialists was and continues to be considerable. The ones among the Bulgarian socialists, for whom the western socialist literature, primarily the German, was not accessible because they did not know the language, studied socialism through Russian works, first and foremost Plekhanov's. The explanation is in the similarity of the Bulgarian and Russian languages and the strong influence of Russian literature in the first years after our Liberation.[91]

Paradoxically, though, many Bulgarian socialists corresponded with Plekhanov in French![92] In fact, what all of this tells us is that influences or stimuli coming from the German or Russian (mostly in translation) literature are neither incompatible nor mutually exclusive. Even more importantly, the Bulgarians were making a distinction between the linguistic sources from where they studied Marxist literature and organizational issues.

Trotsky remained in Bulgaria only briefly, but Rakovski stayed behind for over a year, attempting to heal the split as "a latter-day Don Quichote, the sorrowful figure of socialist unification" in the words of Simeon Radev.[93] Engaging in bitter polemics principally with the Narrows, he published the newspaper *Napred*, which was fully funded by him, where he advocated reconciliation, republicanism, and a Balkan federation. The paper became the platform of the left wing of the Broads, consisting of the two waves of expellees from the Narrow Party. Notorious for their purges aimed at retaining doctrinal purity, the Narrows had expelled a group of prominent intellectuals whom they accused of individualism and branded as "anarcho-liberals" in 1905. The latter formed the tiny but influential Liberal Socialist Party (LSP), referring to themselves as liberals or, more often, as "proletartsi" after their organ "Proletarii."[94] In 1908 another group was expelled, the Progressives, close to Rakovski, who demanded negotiations with the Broads and eventual union. The LSP and the Progressives merged with the Broads at the end of 1908, but by 1915 they had left the Broad party and eventually most of them became communists, protesting the Broads' open "ministerialism" and attitude toward the war.[95] At first siding with the Broads, Rakovski was eventually disillusioned by their policy of collaboration which led, according to him, to the "mongrelization" of the party and lack of "honesty and dignity," and he turned his support to the Narrows.[96] In early 1912 he left the country and for all intents and purposes effectively ceased to be a decisive factor in the Bulgarian movement.[97] Being Trotsky's chief informer on things Bulgarian, his close friend and future collaborator in the Soviet Union, Rakovski himself did, indeed, become an important "branch" of Russian social democracy (Figure 7).

Figure 7 Trotsky, passport photo in 1915, and Rakovski, June 1909.

It is my belief that the explanation for Rothschild's assertion that the Bulgarian socialist movement "was the offspring of the Russian, not the German or French one" lies not only and even not so much in the Cold War atmosphere during which his work was written in 1959 but, rather, in his close and uncritical reliance on Trotsky who was especially popular among American leftists.[98] The split of 1903 left Bulgaria with two, and at times with three and more, socialist formations. Narrows and Broads were recognized as member parties of the Second International in 1904, much to the displeasure of both.[99] The disagreements have been differently explained in the historiography, from views that see them as negligent and the result of personal, often temperamental, distinctions and rivalries, to others who stress principled divergences both in theory and in tactics. As a whole, however, the boundaries between the two formations remained porous and were sealed only with the attitude toward the First World War. In this sense, the rift was analogous to the reformist (Bernsteinian) versus the orthodox wing of the German party, except that there the cosmetic unity was preserved until the war. The so-called Broads corresponded to and shared the philosophy of Bernstein, especially on the issue of collaboration with the bourgeois parties and revolutionary tactics. The Narrows espoused the Plekhanovite/Kautskian, that is, the Marxian orthodoxy of the Second International.

One of the reasons for the parallels between the Russian and Bulgarian parties was the coincidence of the split in 1903 (the Bulgarians split in July and the Russian Menshevik–Bolshevik split occurred in November). However, they fought over completely different issues. While the Russian conflict was over the organization of the party, the Bulgarians, as pointed out earlier, fought over the issue of collaboration with bourgeois parties and this was an issue they had debated for over a decade. As rightfully summarized by Stefan Troebst, "there was no affinity between the Bulgarian Narrow socialists and the Bolsheviks, respectively between the Bulgarian Broad socialists and the Mensheviks. The Bulgarian socialists of either ilk looked at the German Social Democratic Party as their object of identification, and followed neither Vladimir I. Lenin, nor Julij O. Martov."[100]

Besides, neither the Bulgarian nor the Russian splits were exceptions to the rule. The most notorious schisms were, in fact, between the several socialist parties of France, which merged only in 1905 to split again in the wake of the World War. There were three socialist parties in Britain, and the International made efforts to unite them as late as 1914, with a promise that did not materialize. There were also several small Polish socialist parties. And the German party itself was held together almost exclusively by the centrist position of Kautsky. As Lukács put it eloquently in 1924, Kautsky was "utterly consistent in attempting at all times to blur theoretically the decisive problems of revolution; he was never prepared to sacrifice organizational unity with the reformists for a single moment, and he was willing to pay any price to preserve that unity" adding that had Bernstein's "arguments really been discussed and their consequences properly analyzed, the Social Democrats would inevitably have been split."[101] Thus, when Kautsky pontificated condescendingly that it was particularly socialists in economically and socially backward countries, singling out Russia and Bulgaria, that "are easily inclined to splits," this was sheer hypocrisy.[102] The point here is not to take sides in the reformist debate, but to stress that the cleavage was present and was barely contained. To maintain that the split in the BWSDP "exemplifies an instructive theoretical dispute over the limits of Social Democracy in the context of a 'backward' egalitarian society" is a hazardous oversimplification.[103]

The German revisionist debate between Bernstein and Kautsky was over party tactics and the attitude toward the revolution. The German workers' movement had become a decisive force, but workers were not developing a revolutionary consciousness, according to Bernstein. Accordingly, he advocated an evolutionary approach, a focus on trade union work, and eventually a struggle to ameliorate capitalism rather than work toward its revolutionary annihilation. The Orthodox position upheld by Kautsky continued to insist on revolution, even as the interpretation of "revolution" was ambivalent.[104] In Bulgaria, Narrows and Broads roughly corresponded to the philosophical positions of Kautsky and Bernstein, but both doggedly espoused "revolution" as their final goal and both claimed that they were the legal representatives of Bulgarian socialism and authentic interpreters of Marxism, not revisionists. In addition, the Bulgarians were unfamiliar with the conflicts in the Russian movement.[105] The Russian split, personal rivalries aside, was over the structure of the party, with Lenin insisting on a conspiratorial organization. This was never on the agenda of the Bulgarian social democrats on either side of the divide. From the outset, the social-democrats were firmly set on legality and both parties adhered to this principle until the 1920s: "The Bulgarian social-democratic party considers the open and legal struggle the most natural one. Any other work the BSDP considers unnatural leading to a distortion of the ideas and aspirations of the social-democrats."[106] Bernsteinian revisionism was possible in the Bulgarian context but impossible in the Russian "because trade unionism and constitutionalism remained illegal."[107]

Another comparison was the economic backwardness, which generated analogies about the societal response. But the Bulgarian social structure was notoriously different from the Russian, having had a distinct social tradition in the Ottoman Empire. Most importantly, a fundamental difference was that, unlike its Russian counterpart, Bulgarian social democracy functioned legally, in a very imperfect, constrained, and unstable, but still democratic, parliamentary regime, and this had a direct effect on its lack of militancy well into the early 1920s.[108] Bulgaria had enjoyed universal male suffrage since 1878, with the adoption of the so-called Tîrnovo constitution, one of the most liberal at the time in Europe.[109] In this, it was on par with the most progressive electoral systems: France and Switzerland had adopted universal male suffrage in 1848, Greece in 1844, and Germany in 1871 (the North German Federation since 1867). It was ahead of Serbia (1888), Norway (1898), Italy (1912 for males over 30, and 1918 for male voters over 21), and Austria-Hungary (1896, but with multiple voting until 1907, when equal male suffrage was adopted at last). The United Kingdom had to wait until 1918. All of this does not mean, of course, that Bulgaria was more "developed" and "progressive." It does mean, though, that the Bulgarian social democrats did not need to spend time and effort on reforming the electoral system like their Austrian comrades who saw "suffrage as revolutionary utopia,"[110] but could concentrate on the inequities of capitalism.

There is an interesting (and rare) instance where Bulgarians clashed openly with Trotsky on the issue of Bulgarian political culture and its democratic traditions. Petko

Yurdanov Todorov (1879–1916) was a major romantic poet, dramatist, and writer. As a high school student he was influenced by socialist ideas and was in contact with Jean Jaurès. He studied law in Bern and literature in Leipzig and Berlin. In 1905 he became a cofounder of the Radical-Democratic Party (a center-left party formed by the left wing of the Democratic Party). In 1912 he was on Capri where he befriended Maxim Gorky. He died in 1916 of tuberculosis. Trotsky knew him from 1910 when they both were protesting the Pan-Slav Congress in Sofia. At the time of the Balkan Wars, Todorov, who had advanced tuberculosis, was serving in the office of the military censorship. As a war correspondent, Trotsky wrote several fiery articles against the stupidity of the censorship and the compliant press which "is tuned to make a cheerful sound," while the "opponents of the war have been reduced to complete silence."[111]

However, his blanket pontification about the war censorship, in a rhetoric almost lifted from present-day liberal think tanks, provoked the wrath of Petko Todorov who sent him a letter that Trotsky published in *Kievskaya Mysl* on November 30, 1912, alongside his own response. Todorov protested that "all reproaches that you level against Bulgarian democrats, and me in particular, are due to the misunderstanding that constantly arises between us and the Russians who come to Bulgaria, and which results from the facts that all of you, to employ a splendid Russian saying, try to apply your own rule in someone else's monastery."[112] In a style paralleling Trotsky's own liberal pathos, he further extolled Bulgaria's democratic traditions, its constitutionalism, rule of law, and civic discipline. In a war that had been viewed widely as a patriotic enterprise, even by the anti-war parties and individuals, foremost among them the socialists and agrarians, Todorov saw his participation as the fulfillment of his duty as a citizen: "Just as hundreds of thousands of my fellow countrymen have been sent, some to fight at Chataldja, others to besiege Odrin, so I have been placed in a position where I am entrusted with the safeguarding of our task of liberation from all those conscienceless spies and marauders with whom the press organs of Europe's usurers have now inundated our country."[113] He further accused Trotsky of irresponsibility and intransigence and contrasted this to a sense of proportion, which was the most valuable legacy bestowed by the Ancient World: "You see how far we Bulgarians are from your Russian flight from responsibility. We, unlike you, see in this the very foundation of our civic spirit, and it with this sentiment that we, like European democracy, seek to secure our rights as men and citizens. Similarly alien to us is your uncompromising attitude, which we are inclined to see as an anomaly that has been fortified in you by the regime under which you are obliged to live without rights; though also, it seems to me, behind this intransigence of yours you hide from yourself your social impotence and lack of any practical sense."[114] Trotsky dismissed this as "a very primitive level of political culture."[115] These encounters pose the question about the production and acceptance of hegemony. Writing in another context (about the British Empire), Antoinette Burton asks "under what conditions hegemony obtained; when it did not; how it did not; and how it was scripted as ascendant at the very moment when it was not."[116] One can discern here the "residual cultural explanation, of the type favored by Weber, and still the ghost in many machines."[117]

The assertion of the mimetic character of Bulgarian socialism thus stems from different sources and reasons, but it results in a curious, although not specially coordinated consensus. In the few Western writings one can trace this directly to Trotsky's irritation at the Narrows' refusal to bend to his mission. Nor is this assertion denied in the Bulgarian communist historiography but for entirely different reasons. To the contrary, it went out of its way to stress the early kinship with Lenin and Bolshevism. But there was a serious motive for this zealousness and it goes back to the specific events that shaped the destiny of the socialist movement. Two ostensibly "revolutionary situations" put the BWSDP (n) to the test.

One was the so-called Radomir rebellion or Soldiers' Uprising in September 1918. With the breaking of the front lines in Macedonia, the Bulgarian army fell in disorder. Alexander Stamboliiski, the leader of the Bulgarian Agrarian National Union (BANU), imprisoned for his anti-war views, was released from prison in order to contain the soldiers' rebellion. He used the opportunity to proclaim a republic and invited the Narrows to co-operate with him. Blagoev refused, citing the weakness of the party and the unfavorable international situation. Indeed, this decision was made after the attempt of the Narrows to get in touch with the deserting soldiers, who clearly wanted simply peace, threw away their arms, and went back to their homes. It was inconceivable to effectuate a successful coup with a deserting army and with German military units in Sofia.[118] While sympathetic to the demands of the soldiers, the Narrows retreated back to their official stance that the peasant masses could not be consistently revolutionary and that the revolution in Bulgaria could happen only after the successful revolution in the developed capitalist countries. This was Blagoev's famous formula that the revolution "depends three quarters on external circumstances, and only one quarter on internal ones" which he developed in several pamphlets.[119] The following year, in 1919, he warned that the revolution in small countries like Bavaria, Hungary, and the Ukraine is doomed, and that for Bulgaria a socialist revolution is possible only as part of a general Balkan revolution.[120] This episode was held, however, as proof and reproof that Blagoev and the BWSDP were not sufficiently Leninist. As John Bell nicely summarizes it, "if Blagoev was no Lenin, Stamboliiski was no Chernov or Kerenski."[121]

The more serious event came a few years later. Whereas elsewhere the revolutionary wave inspired by the October Revolution was quelled by 1919, in Bulgaria, sole among the European countries, a left-wing agrarian government with a bold foreign policy and radical social reformist program held the reins of power from 1919 until 1923. At the height of his rule, the Bulgarian prime minister Alexander Stamboliiski summed up the significance of his policies not simply for Bulgaria but also for European and for world history: "Today there are only two interesting social experiments: the experiment of Lenin and my own."[122] His was definitely not a socialist experiment but one seeking to find a third way between capitalism and Bolshevism. This not only exacerbated relations with the communists, the rival leftist formation, but also precipitated a huge counterrevolutionary wave that resulted in a bloody coup against Stamboliiski in June 1923. Even the Broads supported the coup and the crushing of the abortive September Uprising, and participated in the subsequent dictatorships in analogy to the Eberts and Noskes, although in secondary roles.

The Narrows (by 1919 renamed the Bulgarian Communist Party, BCP, and a member of the Third International) proclaimed a policy of neutrality over the overthrow of a government of the "peasant bourgeoisie." Khristo Kabakchiev reported to the *Comintern* that the masses met the coup "with indifference and even a certain amount of relief."[123] Within the ranks of the party, the motivation was clear: the party was too weak, it was basically unarmed, and the coup, accomplished by an effective army, was successful. Any militant move would be adventurous, jeopardizing the organization.[124] This decision was met with strong disapproval by the *Comintern* and Vasil Kolarov and Georgi Dimitrov were dispatched to implement the *Comintern* line for an armed rebellion. In September, Kolarov and Dimitrov unilaterally made the decision for an armed uprising. The idea was to stir revolutionary enthusiasm, weaken the ruling regime, and prepare the ground for the worldwide socialist revolution. The result of September 1923 and the following terrorist act of April 1925 was the decimation of the Communist Party, triggering a huge emigration of agrarians and communists (in the latter case, mostly to the Soviet Union, where the Bulgarians were numerically second only to the Poles, but proportionately first).[125]

It was from among these émigrés that the earliest works on Bulgarian socialism were written in the interwar period in the Soviet Union, with the explicit goal of positing the direct influence of Lenin's ideas, mostly in the writings of Bakalov.[126] It was a period of acute and ugly (often fatal) struggle between different factions of the Bulgarian immigrants, reflecting, among others, a generational shift.[127] The ones who had been radicalized, especially by 1917, to embrace violent revolution and had thoroughly accepted the Bolshevik ideology (later designated as "left sectarians") were accusing the former leaders of the BWSDP (n) of having been essentially an unreformed party of the Plekhanov type. In retrospect this allegation seems to be ironically true, but at the time it meant a serious denunciation with immediate, often existential, consequences, given the atmosphere in the Soviet Union in the 1930s.

The "old guard" had good reason to be afraid because in 1915 Blagoev had warned Kolarov, the Bulgarian delegate to the Zimmerwald conference, to be vigilant, because "Lenin exhibited some elements of Blanquism."[128] While the BWSDP (n) voted against the war credits in 1915, it never raised the Leninist slogan to turn the imperialist war into a civil war, held later as an accusation of its insufficient bolshevization.[129] In 1915, even after his patriotic turn in the wake of the war, Plekhanov was still the great authority for the Bulgarians. In 1906, he had accused Lenin of Blanquism, which was then considered a great sin and a deviation from the Marxist orthodoxy. This was based on the analysis of Engels who considered Blanqui as simply a man of action who believed "that a small and well organized minority, who would attempt a political stroke of force at the opportune moment, could carry the mass of people with them by a few successes at the start and thus make a victorious revolution." Engels then charged the Blanquists that what followed from this view was the imposition of a dictatorship "not of the entire revolutionary class, but of the small minority that has made the revolution, and who are themselves organized under the dictatorship of one or several individuals."[130] As a result, the Bulgarian vote was given to the united resolution and not to Lenin's minority position. This was something that Stalin would never forget, and he blackmailed the Bulgarians for not having been true disciples. Already in 1931 Stalin had criticized in writing all communist parties who had not voted with Lenin in 1915 for their unsatisfactory bolshevization.[131] Later he would maintain that the Bulgarian Narrows should not be considered a movement akin to the Bolsheviks, but, rather, to Plekhanov, "since repeatedly the Narrows have been against Lenin and the Bolsheviks," having in mind the particular vote at Zimmerwald.[132]

Among the Bulgarian communists, Vasil Kolarov (1877–1950), a complex and controversial figure, was probably the most celebrated after Dimitrov and Blagoev. After graduating from high school, he became a teacher for a short period and joined the BWSDP in 1897. A university student at Aix-en-Provence and Geneva, upon his return to Bulgaria he became a lawyer. Highly intelligent, educated, and cultivated, proficient in eight languages, he was the preferred delegate to the congresses of the Second International. In 1903, during the split of the party, he joined the Narrows and headed the organization in the second largest Bulgarian city, Plovdiv. After 1905 he became a member of the Central Committee (CC) of the party, a position he held to the end. In 1913 he was elected to Parliament, where he sat until 1923. He was secretary of the BCP after 1919 and played a crucial role in imposing the *Comintern* decision to start the ill-fated armed revolt in 1923. After the bloody crackdown of the September rising, he emigrated to Moscow, and spent the next two decades as a high functionary in the Soviet Union: general secretary of the *Comintern* from 1922 to1924 and a top official until its dissolution in 1943, head of the *Krestintern* (1929–31), and director of the Moscow-based International Agrarian Institute (1931–40). After his return to Bulgaria in 1945 he was consecutively chairman of the National Assembly, deputy prime minister and foreign minister, and served as prime minister for a few months before his death in 1950. As late as 1949 Stalin warned the BCP against their prime minster who was seventy-two at the time: "Do the Bulgarians know that Kolarov has taken right-wing positions in the past? We considered him an opportunist. At the time, he harmed Lenin badly. Later Kolarov improved. But he used to have an affinity to the right. He is unquestionably our man, but relapses are not to be ruled out."[133]

Kolarov left an enormous archive and wrote carefully crafted memoirs that have to be often read between the lines. His memoirs were published posthumously in 1961, eleven years after his death. This huge volume of 640 pages, printed by the publishing house of the BCP, was almost immediately sequestered from the bookstores, on account of a few lines about the Second International and Zimmerwald.[134] The Zimmerwald conference was described on only five pages, in vivid but highly predictable prose, and it dealt mostly with Lenin. According to Kolarov, Zimmerwald was the first international meeting, which singled out Lenin as the future leader of the international proletariat. Lenin was praised for his deep analysis and foresight in pleading for a new International: "This idea, however, seemed so bold as to perturb the conference, which in its majority was still permeated with the traditions of the Second International."[135]

Despite his proverbial and judicious caution, Kolarov had let slip a phrase in his otherwise bland account of Zimmerwald, which triggered the confiscation of his volume. He started his description with the official invitation by the Swiss socialist Robert Grimm, sent to the CC of the BWSDP (n). He also mentioned that a letter had been sent by Lenin, insisting that the Bulgarians take part. And he added: "We wanted to clarify Lenin's position toward the concrete issues around the war and the International. Blagoev said only that he did not know for sure, but it seemed that Lenin's views contained some elements of Blanquism." In a later document from his archives dating from 1938, when he was preparing for a commemorative celebration for Blagoev (who had died in 1924), he specified Blagoev's admonitions: "You will stick to the decisions of the Second Balkan conference. . . . He [i.e., Blagoev] thought that Lenin exhibited some elements of Blanquism. Blagoev warned me to be very vigilant. This is why in Zimmerwald we voted for the united resolution, and not for the minority one."[136] Kolarov's vote with the majority against the draft resolution of the Zimmerwald Left was a well-known fact, and he was always on the alert for the possible price he had to pay. In Moscow, his activities and contacts in the Second International were seen as a liability, and although he escaped the critique of the "left sectarians" because of his stance in 1923, he always felt vulnerable. Of the ones who ended up in the Soviet Union, he was the only Zimmerwalder who survived the Great Purge.[137]

After the Second World War, the communist historiography emphasized the crucial role of 1917 and of Bolshevism, effectively downplaying the history of early socialism in the countries of Eastern Europe who after 1945 became Soviet satellites. Concretely in the Bulgarian case, more attention was paid to the interwar and postwar generations that were considered already "bolshevized." The earlier ones were accorded due respect but were seen as not entirely enlightened and were altogether given short shrift. The BWSDP (b) was dogmatically excised, replicating the often vicious rhetoric between Narrows and Broads, and as for the BWSDP (n), huge efforts were made to portray them as more pro-Bolshevik or at least, receptive to Bolshevik ideas in order to preserve the earlier pedigree.[138]

No wonder that Soviet historiography would also insist on the formative influence of Russia, but without necessarily making the claim of exclusive impact. In an early scholarly article, A. Shnitman focused on the role of Blagoev and the reception of Plekhanov's and Lenin's works. One has to read this article knowing the logistics of writing in the communist period. It is thoroughly respectable in its main body, but flanked with the necessary lip-service formulae, like the ending that should not be taken for a conclusion: "Bulgarian Marxists are indebted to Lenin and Stalin, to the Bolshevik party, to the Russian revolutionary movement, which gave Bulgarians ideas, experience, and the key to solving the problems facing the Bulgarian proletariat."[139] In the text, Shnitman accurately quoted Blagoev when in 1886 he wrote about the main influences on his ideas: "I read Marx, Lassalle, Darwin, Bagehot, Chernyshevsky, and even Plekhanov."[140] Plekhanov did, indeed, become a major influence in the spreading of Marxism in Bulgaria, so much so that when Lenin published his famous article "Что делать?" ("What is to Be Done?") in 1902, it was assumed that this was a pseudonym for Plekhanov. Once the Bulgarians were disabused of this, they continued to refer to Lenin as Lyonin.[141] There exists, thus, collusion between communist and Western writings in which the agency of the early Bulgarian socialists thoroughly disappears.

To reiterate, from the subsequent viewpoint of achieving bolshevization, considered to be the peak of communist tactics, the Blagoev Narrow party, even in its early communist incarnation, can be said to have been, indeed, essentially an unreformed party of the "Plekhanov type," doctrinally (and dogmatically) following the Second International's precepts (with the exclusions of its principled and consistent anti-militarist stance, which pushed in the direction of the Third International). It held strictly to "the Second International's commitment to historical stagism and to the achieved completion of bourgeois revolution as a necessary condition in the final transition to proletarian socialism."[142] But its position can also be interpreted, at least from the point of view of tactics, as an unconscious practical precursor of national roads to socialism.

In their aspiration to achieve socialism, both Bulgarian socialist parties espoused a revolutionary ideology. "Revolution" was understood as a fundamental transformation of the social order, the overthrow of capitalism, but not necessarily through a violent and militant rupture. In this they adopted, literally, the interpretation of "revolution" as understood by the Second International. As summarized by Gerassimos Moschonas, the goals of social democracy in the period until 1914 can be grouped into five major thematic categories: democratization and the expansion of the rules of law; cultural radicalism; improving the conditions of labor; social equality through redistribution; and socialism. In most of these demands there "prevailed a parliamentary-centered vision of democracy."[143] In the words of Stefan Berger, "Kautskyism, Bersteinian revisionism, Fabianism and most variants of continental Marxist thought were united in this belief in statism."[144] The revolutionary aspiration was not empty rhetoric; the ideology was profoundly anti-capitalist, but the aspiration was for "a peaceful revolution, but a revolution all the same."[145] Until the First World War social democracy was a revolutionary project, "but revolutionary in a specific way: revolutionary with powerful reformist pillars."[146] This is how it was articulated in the Bulgarian case in an editorial authored by Georgi Kirkov:

> We have to define what we understand under the term "revolution." As is well known, in our country revolution usually implies brutality, carnage, violence and a whole string of terrible atrocities. We think this is completely natural but also wrong. It is natural, because our bourgeois writers cannot imagine the revolution in any other way but as terrible atrocities. As usual, they think by analogy. They always have in mind the old bourgeois revolutions in France, Germany, Austria and elsewhere, which were indeed characterized by atrocities. Their protagonist, however, was the Third estate, i.e. today's bourgeoisie.... This is where they have formed their idea of the term revolution and its character.... But this is wrong. It is wrong because there is a great difference between a bourgeois and a workers' revolution, namely, that the laboring class employs different tools. The bourgeois class had no other weapons but violence, the dagger and guns. Nowadays the labor class has thousands of other means that can be much more effective than the crude violence of the bourgeois revolution. Now it has an economic and political organization, it can resort to strikes, it has class consciousness, and can use the voting ballot. Wherever it does not have these tools, like in Russia, it struggles to attain them.... The class of hired labor is revolutionary because through its very appearance in public life it creates a radical change in society.... [It] represents organized public labor, the source of all wealth, without being able to take advantage of it.... The present order allows for the fruits of public labor to go into private hands, in the hands of only one class which does not directly participate in the labor process but holds the means of production and gathers the profit.... The working class is revolutionary in the sense that it requests the abolition of the private property derived from public labor and its transformation into public property. This radical change, however undesirable for the bourgeoisie,

has to happen, because on it hinges not only the condition of the working class but of the whole society.... Only such a radical change can abolish the dreadful chasm between labor and capital which threatens to engulf all society.[147]

Another editorial in *Rabotnik* (*Работник*) proclaimed that "the social-democratic party has no intention to come to power tomorrow with any means. Coming to power would mean to proclaim the socialist transformation which is the end goal of social democracy. But it cannot come to power other than when the largest part of the people embraces the ideas and program it seeks to pursue. Until this time, it will work through all legal means to develop the consciousness of the working class and attract it to its ideas."[148] It should be unequivocally stated that both Broads and Narrows acceded to this understanding of the revolution, both described themselves as revolutionary parties, although with important differences in the understanding of the practice of the legal political struggle. This is important to emphasize because even in the most recent specialist historiography in Bulgaria there is the tendency to describe the Narrows as revolutionary and the Broads as (wrongly) nonrevolutionary and (correctly) reformist or revisionist.[149] This is a legacy of the communist period when even in the most eulogizing accounts of Blagoev's activity, one can detect a defensive tone of forgiveness when describing his adherence to legal forms of struggle.[150]

This is not the place to characterize the ideology of the Broads, which preceded by several years the articulation of the ideas of Bernstein to which it was no doubt very close, although Sakîzov made it a point of principle to profess his closeness to Kautsky and distance himself from the "extreme teaching of Bernstein."[151] As late as 1932 Sakîzov insisted that both Broads and Narrows were Marxist parties, because "with us the actual western revisionism found no ground" ("der eigentliche westliche Revisonismus keinen Boden bei uns fand").[152] Even after the split of 1903, the Broads did not change their program until 1924.[153] This program underscored their tactics of class struggle but allowed for temporary alliances with bourgeois parties. It considered itself a party of the revolution, but also of reforms and there were vigorous debates and eventual ruptures between the different factions.[154] It was only in the aftermath of the Russian Revolution of 1917 that there was ambivalence in the ranks of the Broads about the term. Thus, Petîr Dzhidrov (1876–1952), one of its leaders and theoreticians, already in 1919 had posed the question: How would the proletariat gain state power, through revolutionary or evolutionary means? He then, however, positively cited, and sided with, Bebel and Liebknecht who insisted on the term revolution but through organization, not violence.[155] Since this presented a logical problem, he differentiated between social revolution espoused by the social democrats, which aimed at a social transformation, and "political revolutions which do not happen in democratic countries."[156] If the bourgeoisie violently resisted this peaceful transformation achieved through parliamentary means, "the proletariat would be forced to resort to revolution, its historical right."[157] This, however, was a sentence that did not receive further elaboration. Instead, we hear a lot about the catastrophe brought by the Bolshevik revolution, which would never achieve any socialist transformation.[158]

It has to be understood that Dzhidrov came to these ideas at a time when the Broads entered into a coalition government with the bourgeois parties and he himself served as justice minister in 1918–1919. This had cost them public support and by 1921 just before the electoral victory of BANU, Dzhidrov lashed out with intemperate wrath, smearing his political opponents and ardently seeking to disengage the Broads of any attempts to identify them with the Bolsheviks. On April 17, 1921, Dzhidrov and Asen Tsankov gave two public lectures on the topic "Imperialism, Bolshevism, and Socialism." There was a new orientalist element in Dzhidrov's speech, namely that Bolshevism appealed only to uncultured backward societies consisting of half-wild tribes in Asia.[159] For the prominent lawyer that he was, Dzhidrov committed a logical fallacy, on the one hand accusing the Bolsheviks of voluntarism and violent revolution and, on the other hand, ironizing them that their revolution was no revolution at all, since it was realized without a drop of blood.[160] But his shell fire was reserved for the Bulgarian "Bolsheviks—communists—and the agrarians, the national Bulgarian Bolsheviks" who had managed to attract the ignorant masses.[161] This was amplified by his friend and colleague Asen Tsankov who directly spoke of the oriental character of Bolshevism (ориенталщина) and the Bolshevism of the agrarians (дружбаши) and the Narrows who were spreading this "modern disease, this spiritual epidemic."[162]

All in all, however, one can say that the prewar generations shared the belief (or illusion) that parliamentarianism allowed for a fundamental social transformation, a belief that was irretrievably lost in most of the world in the interwar period. In all aspects, Bulgarian social democracy shared the characteristics of the other parties of the Second International so ably synthesized by Eley: these parties reached their ceiling by mustering the support of between a quarter and a third of the electorate; nonparticipation in "bourgeois governments" remained the norm but "this policy of abstention implied enormous confidence in the future, a steadfast belief in the inevitable working-class majority and the ever-expanding power of socialism's working-class support"; because of their feverish focus on industrial workers, they remained poorly equipped to handle other identities, especially peasant ones; and, finally, these "were parties of the organized and respectable male working class."[163] A specificity of the Bulgarian parties was that this latter feature was in the making. At the outset they were parties of the organized, predominantly male, progressive, and respectable (even if this respectability was not recognized in the eyes of the regime) intellectual class, and only gradually but very consciously were they working to increase their working-class component.[164] To this I would add that the Bulgarian social-democratic parties were essentially self-described propaganda machines, intent on "raising the workers' class consciousness through the powerful and tireless propaganda of the new teaching, socialism."[165] Georgi Kirkov, in an editorial of *Rabotnicheski vestnik* (Worker's gazette), the organ of the BWSDP, defined its tasks thus: "The modest, but clearly defined mission of our newspaper will be: the spiritual enlightenment of the Bulgarian workers of all occupations and the all-round defense of their general interests. An incessant stimulus toward education and class self-consciousness; tireless agitation and encouragement for mutual support and united struggle for attaining human justice and preventing arbitrariness and violations on the fruits of the honest worker's labor: these are the main points of the program of our newspaper."[166] One is tempted to define Bulgarian social democracy before the war as a pedagogical venture.

2

Metropolitan Nationalists and Provincial Cosmopolitans

The National Question and the International

There was a basic incongruity in the International between the ideology and rhetoric of international solidarity, based on a "worldwide community of autonomous men united apart from, and even against, their nations and governments" and its organizational structure and performance based on national units that did not form "a potential political community, but rather one resembling the League of Nations."[1] The rhetoric was powerful and as we shall see later (in Parts II and III) it exerted a formidable emotional pull in attracting people to the socialist cause, at least in the "periphery." The International operated under the coordinating oversight of the ISB but day-to-day activities were left to the constituent parties. This meant that the only time "internationalism for all" was on display was at the regular congresses, which met every two to four years. These were carefully staged and orchestrated theatrical affairs. One of the most effective mise-en-scène was the handshake between Plekhanov and Katayama at the Sixth Congress in Amsterdam in 1904. Japan and Russia were at war in the previous six months, and the handshake, accompanied by the jubilant applause of the delegates, symbolized that socialists transcended the rivalries of their home governments. For all its beauty, this was also an innocuous and inconsequential handshake: Plekhanov was in exile since 1880, and Katayama who represented the miniscule socialist party of Japan, was en route to the United States where he stayed until 1907, engaged in rice farming.

Beyond this, internationalism remained as a whole confined to speeches and resolutions. As Bebel famously quipped in 1891, "a great number of our comrades if they so much as hear about foreign policy prefer to shrug their shoulders. With some justification."[2] Still, there were a few questions that were debated broadly and taxed relations between socialists. One such was the Polish question. Despite the commonly held liberal sympathy for the restoration of Polish independence, German socialists proved insensitive to the demands of their Polish counterparts in Prussia and insisted that the interests of the proletariat could be served best by a uniform centralized democratic party. To the complaints of Polish socialists that candidates in their constituencies did not know Polish, Bebel responded: "A good comrade who only knows German is more use than an incompetent Polish speaking one."[3]

Rosa Luxemburg's position on the issue, which supported Bebel's, contributed to the numerous splits within Polish social democracy. Still, the Germans were happy that they "were not obliged to labor under the confusion of languages which our comrades in Austria have to deal with."[4]

Indeed, the Austrian situation was complex, and Adler claimed at the Fifth Congress in Paris in 1900 that "we in Austria have a little International ourselves, we are the ones who know best the difficulties which have to be overcome."[5] Especially acute was the trade union question with Czech trade unionists demanding separate unions analogous to the autonomous socialist political organizations. That they were denied this and the International tried unsuccessfully to impose single unions only demonstrated the extent to which social democracy was unable to solve national tensions. The attempt to forge a *Gesamtpartei* that would work "to find a way to prevent the collapse of Austria and to enable its natives to live together" proved futile.[6]

The financial support of the organization produced tensions. The meeting of the ISB in Brussels in 1908 discussed the issue of a potential creation of a socialist telegraph agency that would better coordinate international efforts. When it came to the funding, the Bulgarian delegate Stefan Avramov said that each party should contribute according to its means. He gave the example of the support sent to the striking Swedish workers in 1907, in which France contributed 3,000 gold francs, small agricultural Bulgaria gave 1,500, and Germany, the strongest, most disciplined, and organized party contributed 3.5 million. Kautsky immediately took the floor and thanked Avramov for his high opinion of the SDP but added in French: "Le parti social-démocrate allemand ne veut pas jouer le rôle de vache au lait de l'interantionale socialiste" (The German Social Democratic Party does not want to play the role of a milk cow for the Socialist International).[7]

Another stormy issue that the socialists in the International discussed and on which they passionately disagreed, was the colonial question, particularly at the Seventh Congress in Stuttgart in 1907. Colonialism was confined naturally and primarily to the British, Dutch, Belgians, Germans, and French. The positions ranged from a complete disavowal of imperialism by the left wing to calls by Bernstein for a "positive socialist colonial policy. We must relinquish the utopian idea of simply abandoning the colonies. The ultimate consequence of such a view would be to give the United States back to the Indians."[8] Symbolically this coincided with the ongoing German genocide of the Herero and Nama people in Namibia that had produced "a paroxysm of imperialistic enthusiasm" in the words of Rosa Luxemburg, but the majority of German delegates at the congress supported Bernstein's view.[9] Germany, in particular, had begun its colonial policy belatedly in the 1880s but by the early 1890s colonial themes were included in the school curriculum, and after 1906 with the adoption of a dynamic colonial policy by the Reichstag, the introduction of *Kolonialkunde* became a central pillar in the socialization of future German citizens.[10] The debates at the Stuttgart Congress with their overwhelming tendency to justify colonial policies from a *mission civilisatrice* point of view seem awkward and embarrassing from today's point of view, but they come a long way to explain the nationalist turn on the eve of the war. Eventually, the draft motion reflecting these views was defeated, but only by 128 votes against 108 with 10 abstentions, and mostly due to the combined vote of the small nations.[11]

However, "the one point on which all socialists could unite in feeling strongly was hatred of Russia."[12] This was the overwhelming attitude among liberals in the nineteenth century, triggered mostly by the Polish Question, but in general because of the rise of yet another Great Power in Europe and the world. Marx and Engels shared this hatred because of the events in 1848 when Russian troops suppressed the Hungarian revolt. They concluded that the independence movements among the Slavs in the Habsburg and Ottoman Empires had to be opposed at any cost, since they played into pan-Slav sympathies and the danger of "the creation of a Slav state under Russian domination."[13] The unfortunate but plentiful and at times openly racist pronouncements of Marx and Engels about the national struggles of the small Slavic nations in the Ottoman and Habsburg Empires are well known, and there have been numerous and unsuccessful attempts to explain them away.[14] Yet, they are worth emphasizing because, as a *basso continuo*, to borrow Troebst's felicitous phrase,[15] they shaped the attitudes of most Western social democrats in the era of the Second International, even if they were not always voiced so openly and bluntly by the politically correct internationalist rhetoric after the 1890s.

Surprisingly little had changed in Marx and Engels's views after 1848, when German unification remained one of their prime concerns. They declared war on the slogan of national self-determination (the Poles gallantly excluded) for "the Serbians, Croats, Slovaks, Czechs, and other remnants of bygone Slavonian peoples in Turkey, Hungary and Germany" and wrote that "at a time when great monarchies were a 'historical necessity' what a 'crime' it was that the Germans and the Magyars should have bound these tiny, crippled, powerless little nations together in a great empire, and thereby enabled them to take part in an historical development which would have remained alien to them!"[16] This was a further development of their 1849 conviction that a general war "will destroy all these little, bullheaded nations so that their very name will vanish. The coming world war will cause not only reactionary classes and dynasties to disappear from the face of the earth, but entire reactionary peoples, too. And this will also be progress."[17] During the Crimean War, they were critical of the Western powers' "sham war," hoping that they would destroy Russia. During the decisive Russo-Turkish war of 1877–78 (known in Bulgaria as the Liberation War), Marx praised the "gallant Turks" and wrote to Wilhelm Liebknecht that "we are most decidedly espousing the Turkish cause."[18] Liebknecht himself dismissed the oppression of the South Slavs as "99 per cent a Russian lie" and "one per cent a Russian manufacture."[19]

I am evoking this not to expose Marx and Engels' prejudices, which were widely shared at the time, their inconsistencies, Russophobia, and emotional great-power chauvinism, but simply to make the point that internationalism was mostly a rhetorical device already at the time of the First International and it remained so, always at the service of the "civilized" nations and the inexorable march of History. As Carl Schorske notes, the model party of the German social democrats took over two ideas from their masters, Russophobia and the idea of the citizens' army. But while in the mid-nineteenth century it could be safely argued that Russia was the "bastion of reaction," this became tenuous by the 1890s and especially with the 1905 revolution. What remained, however, was an inflated idea of national defense which "prepared a justification for Social Democratic support of the state in the event of war."[20]

What is even more important is that Balkan socialists were painfully aware of the condescending and outright dismissive attitude toward their nations, which did not make them less passionately and consistently Marxist. Thus, Dimitrije Tucović, the cofounder of the Serbian Social Democratic party, wrote in a letter to Dragiša Lapčević, the other founder of the party:

> Ever since the 1870s when Marx and Engels spoke of the Herzegovinian uprising as a revolt of "horse-thieves" provoked by the "rolling Russian roubles," Social Democracy in Germany has continued and still continues to determine its standpoint on the Eastern Question by one *external* factor: the struggle to the death with the Russian Panslavic danger! It is true that today no one dares write about that danger as they once did, but it pervades the very soul of the German socialists. [. . .] The danger of Balkan conquest is no longer threatened by Russia, but by Austria; the straining of relations following the disturbance of the balance of power no longer originates from Nicholas, but from Franz Joseph, which merely confirms our standpoint that the conquering policy of the bourgeoisie is based on *class* and not on *race*. Today, no one believes anymore in Panslavic danger, which anyway never represented a real force. And what is especially regrettable, the socialist ranks are full of people who decide this question of capitalist conquest according to *circumstances, practically*, and defend the *right of conquest of the uncultured by the cultured*. It goes without saying that we in the Balkans are also counted amongst the "uncultured" whom Austria has to civilize. Of course, no one actually says this (except for what Bernstein wrote about Bosnia).[21]

Tucović wrote this letter to his friend lamenting the fact that *Vorwärts*, the organ of the German Social Democratic Party, had refused to publish his article on the Balkan railway. He had received a response that the article was well written and its standpoint was correct, and that the editors were "sorry for the small states and peoples in the Balkans . . . but the question is thorny and we have to be reserved. . . . I am telling you this," Tucović concluded, "because this kind of attitude from a socialist organ has affected me rather badly. *But given my beliefs, where else can I turn?*"[22]

The imposition of Marxism as the doctrine of the Second International came with this ambiguous heritage about the national question.[23] Marx himself had famously brushed away nationality as an explanatory tool: "The nationality of the worker is neither French, nor English, nor German, it is *labor, free slavery, self-huckstering*. His government is neither French, nor English, nor German, it is *capital*. His native air is neither French, nor German, nor English, it is *factory air*. The land belonging to him is neither French, nor English, nor German, it lies a few feet *below the ground*."[24] However, the declarative and categorical tone of this statement has been overblown in the general insistence that Marxism ignored or underestimated nationalism. Both Marx and Engels were extremely sympathetic to Irish nationalism and published numerous articles in support of the Irish movement. They were in favor of the right of the Irish to organize independently within the British working-class movement, thus anticipating some of the major tenets of Austro-Marxism.[25] However, they were inconsistent in the way they legitimized their choices for support.

Well into the 1880s, Engels persisted in dividing the European nations into historic and non-historic ones, the ones viable and the others immature for independence. On February 7, 1882, in a letter to Kautsky, Engels wrote: "And now you ask me whether I do not sympathize at all with the small Slavic peoples? In fact, damn little."[26] In the same letter he explained that "only after the collapse of Tsardom, when the national aspirations of these dwarf-peoples cease to be mixed up with pan-Slavic tendencies to world domination, only then can we allow them to be free."[27] In 1885 he continued to refer to them as "pathetic debris of nations," "robber rabble," and "lousy Balkan peoples."[28] In a letter to Bernstein from October 9, 1882, Engels suggested: "For the Bulgarians, and *for us* [emphasis mine] it would have been infinitely better, had they stayed under the rule of the Turks until the European revolution; their communal institutions would have been a splendid starting point for further evolution toward communism."[29] In the same letter he specified that socialists could support the South Slavs but only insofar as they opposed Russia: "If they go against the Turks, however, and demand the annexation of the few Serbs and Bulgarians who are still left under Turkish domination, they consciously or unconsciously work for Russia and in that case we cannot be with them."[30]

We see here the conflation of two ideas. One was the long-term and widespread suspicion of the rise of Russia as a geopolitical power after the last quarter of the eighteenth century, re-enforced for the socialists by what was perceived as its counterrevolutionary role, especially in 1848, and the fact that this was the last absolute monarchy in Europe. The other was the growing interest in the uneven spread of capitalism and the rising revolutionary movements in the East. Since knowing all the intricacies of social and cultural development of so many new nations was an uphill task, it was easier to lump them all together with Russia as agrarian communal societies. The South Slavs could be supported but only insofar as they were against Russia; otherwise their struggle against the Turks unconsciously worked in Russia's favor. Encouraged by the critical, in fact hostile, attitude of the Bulgarian socialists against Russian politics and Slavophilism, Engels by the early 1890s had slightly changed his opinion.

A young twenty-year-old Bulgarian student had been introduced to him at the Zurich Congress of the International in 1893, and shortly after that he received an issue of *Sotsialdemokrat* (Социалдемократ) published in Sevlievo that triggered a brief correspondence with Engels from 1893, a couple of years before his death. Stoian Nokov (1872–1959), had been born in the small town of Kotel in 1872 in the family of a wealthy merchant. After finishing high school in Gabrovo, an industrial center and site of the premier high school in the country, the "Aprilov gymnasium," he proceeded to Geneva, where he pursued natural sciences between 1889 and 1894. He was the cofounder and secretary of the so-called Geneva group of Bulgarian socialist students. In those years there were hundreds of Bulgarian students studying abroad, and they had founded socialist circles in Zurich, Brussels, Liège, and other Swiss, Belgian, French, and German cities.[31] Geneva alone had more than 150 Bulgarian students, many sent on state fellowships. The majority were organized in a patriotic brotherhood and rarely used their meetings for self-education. The socialist group, thirty-five in number, organized reading groups and lectures in sociology, socialism, the history of the workers' movement, ethnography, and natural sciences.³² Nokov was very close to Plekhanov, who accepted him almost as a family member, and it was Plekhanov who introduced him to Engels.

Nokov, despite his early prominence in the socialist movement and his close relations with Plekhanov, Rosa Luxemburg, and personal acquaintance with Wilhelm Liebknecht, Jules Guesde, and other important figures, has remained a subaltern in the Bulgarian communist historiography. This is mostly because in 1892 he became a co-founder of the Social Democratic Union, which had seceded from the Social Democratic Party of Blagoev, formed the previous year. Nokov sided with the Broads but was always on the left of the party, continuing his contacts with Blagoev, and in 1920 joined the newly formed Communist Party. He had returned to Bulgaria in 1894 when a fire had devastated Kotel and ruined his father and was left responsible for the well-being of the family. A high school teacher in biology and natural sciences, he secured a respectable place as a devoted and outstanding local educator, never abandoning his ideology and party affiliation, but not as a professional revolutionary. All his life he spent in Kotel. His brother Khristo Nokov (1884–1925), a construction engineer, educated in Germany, and likewise a communist, was killed by the police in 1925 during the deadly wave of the White Terror.³³

In his first letter written in French from June 1893, Engels thanked Nokov, and asked whether Sevlievo was another name for Philipopol as he did not have a dictionary or atlas handy.³⁴ (Imagine someone asking whether Rouen is another name for Lyon or Glasgow for Birmingham!). In his second letter written in German on the same day and addressed to the editorial board of *Sotsialdemokrat*, Engels noted that until 1848 it was enough for the international socialists to know the main Western and Central European languages, "but now things are different and at my old age, I have to learn Rumanian and Bulgarian, in order to be able to follow the movement of socialism to the East and Southeast" and he rejoiced at this "southeast European outpost to the Asian borders" [*sic*!] which carries Marx's flag.³⁵ The third letter from April 1895 was addressed to a student in Nancy (most likely Rakovski) apologizing for declining at this moment to write a special address to the Bulgarian socialists. Engels had been diagnosed with cancer in March and died in July 1895.³⁶

At the same Zurich Congress of the Second International, Ianko Sakîzov, the leader of the Bulgarian Social Democratic Union (BSDU) asked Kautsky why he had not published his article against Stefan Stambolov in *Die Neue Zeit*. Stambolov was a major political figure in the newly independent Bulgaria,³⁷ serving as government minister, president, regent, and finally prime minister (1887–94). While today his elevated standing in Bulgarian historiography is secured by his indefatigable efforts to strengthen the Bulgarian state and the national cause, and especially his particular brand of enmity toward Russia (between 1886 and 1896 diplomatic relations between Russia and Bulgaria were broken off), he was notorious for his authoritarian regime and crude suppression of political opponents. This was the theme of Sakîzov's article. Kautsky's answer was that the article implicitly supported Tsarist Russia and was against the policies pursued by Germany.³⁸ Political prudence trumped considerations of democracy, even as Kautsky was one of the rare exceptions from the automatic Russophobia and anti-Slav stance among Western social democrats. In his memoirs he emphasized that it was perhaps his Czech origins and his understanding of Slavic life and culture that opened him to seek active contacts with Russian socialists. Under their influence he read and highly valued Chernyshevsky as well as Lavrov.[39]

The Balkan Federation Idea

All throughout this period, Balkan socialists were seeking the involvement of the international social democracy in the Macedonian Question and more broadly, in the Eastern Question, but with very little success. This was not because their thoughts and writings were linguistically inaccessible. In 1894, a League for a Balkan Confederation was constituted in Paris, organized by the Greek–French socialist Paul Argyriadès (1849–1901). A native of Macedonia, Argyriadès settled in Paris after 1870 to study law. As one of the leaders of the Paris Commune and a prominent lawyer, he defended communards, anarchists, and socialists. He was a member of the *Parti socialiste révolutionnaire* of Édouard Vaillant, which eventually merged in 1905 with the socialists of Jean Jaurès and the Marxists of Jules Guesde to form the Socialist Party of France. His idea for the solution of the Eastern Question was the creation of a confederation of autonomous states: Greece with Crete; Bulgaria; Romania; Serbia; Bosnia-Herzegovina; Montenegro; Macedonia and Albania; Thrace with Constantinople as a free city and the center of the confederation; Armenia; and finally, the coastal regions of Asia Minor. While their full autonomy would be guaranteed, their foreign affairs would be regulated by a body of delegates in Constantinople.[40] Little is known of the League and it apparently exerted little influence, but two circumstances merit mention. Its foundation in Paris and publications in French could easily have attracted the attention of the functionaries of the Second International if they were interested. The second is that their publication was immediately noticed and translated into Bulgarian.[41]

In fact, the idea of a Balkan federation had had a long pedigree among nineteenth-century Balkan national revolutionaries already in the 1860s, and was immediately taken up by the Bulgarian socialists from the 1880s on.[42] Building on this legacy, Blagoev in 1885 published an article "Balkan Federation" in *Macedonian Voice*.[43] He even met the highly popular Bulgarian unification in September 1885 with skepticism, fearing the strengthening of the dynasty. He believed that the Constitution of Eastern Rumelia was more progressive and recommended a federal republican arrangement. That this was unrealistic at the moment does not distract from the fact that the issue was very much on the agenda.[44] In a Balkan federation Blagoev sought the means to regulate inter-Balkan relations. In 1886, he even foresaw the driving force for his project: "an international union of the intelligentsia of the Balkan countries" that should work through printed propaganda and activism.[45] Calling the future federation variously Balkan or "Balkan United States," he adamantly opposed dynastic interference and advocated a republican solution.[46]

At the London Congress of the International in 1896, the Bulgarian delegates Rakovski and Bakalov handed in a report in French but because of lack of funds, they could not reproduce and disseminate it broadly. The report itself has not been preserved but parts of it were printed in the French and German press. In his autobiography,

Rakovski wrote that they wanted to correct the "ignorance and lack of understanding of Eastern Questions," which "were one of the deficits of the international socialist movement."[47] In February 1897 Rakovski sent Guesde six articles on the Eastern questions, which were published in three consecutive issues of *La Petite République*.[48] Likewise, Kautsky published in *Die Neue Zeit* Rakovski's article under the title "The Bulgarian social democracy and the Eastern Question."[49] A significant part of Rakovski's article was dedicated to condemning Russian policy and this is the part he stressed in his accompanying letter to Kautsky. His most interesting contribution, however, was the solution he proposed to the problem of the national struggles in the Ottoman Empire, in the wake of the Armenian (or Hamidian) massacres of 1894-96. He suggested that the International support the demand to give the "eastern peoples" political freedom and autonomy, which would allow them to develop their economic life and create favorable conditions for the dissemination of socialist propaganda and would be the best way to avoid foreign intervention. This was in categorical support of the views of the Armenian socialists who had appealed to the International to endorse their efforts toward autonomy and independence.[50]

With hindsight, these demands seem anodyne but in the context of the 1890s they sounded radical and novel. The grisly outcome of the Armenian massacres shook public opinion and produced different reactions, from humanitarian outcry and charitable help to attempts to use the Armenian issue to promote the Zionist cause.[51] But the Great Powers were adamant about their defense of the integrity of the Ottoman Empire and continued to apply the reform card that they unsuccessfully employed in the Macedonian case. Socialists did not go further than that, Jean Jaurès appealing to the powers to "ensure the security of the Armenians and to reconcile the nations in Turkey no matter what religion or race they belong to, by general guarantees of freedom, prosperity and progress."[52]

When, a few years later, the Macedonian issue was again on the agenda of international diplomacy, and BWSDP at the beginning of 1903 pleaded for the ISB to take a stand, Victor Serwy, the then secretary of the Bureau, sent a circular to poll the opinions of the member parties. Both Serbian and Bulgarian social democrats were united in their views that the declaration should support "complete autonomy" for Macedonia and Armenia and the end of the absolutist regime of Abdul Hamid II. They were tentatively supported by the Spanish and Czech socialists, the latter making the parallel with the position of the Czechs in the Habsburg Empire. The rest were against the idea. The Dutch socialists opined that the stories about Turkish atrocities in Macedonia were grossly exaggerated. Expressing the opinion of the French socialist revolutionary party, Vaillant, usually sympathetic, thought that it was not the business of the ISB to organize campaigns for the defense of the Macedonian population; this should be at the discretion of the national parties in their own countries. One faction among the Polish socialists was firmly against it, the others thought the question was complicated. The German SPD agreed in principle to sign a resolution but was quick to point out that the main danger came from Russian tsarism. And Harry Quelch, the British Marxist, one of the leaders of the Social Democratic Federation and British representative to the International bluntly summarized what was on the mind of the others: "In reply to your enquiry, I do not think that the Macedonian question is one which calls for the intervention of the ISB. We have simply to choose between two despotisms of Russia and Turkey, and the former, in my opinion, is the worse."[53]

A few months later, when the Bulgarian party again insisted that the Macedonian question be included in the agenda of the next international congress, the majority expressed their "regret of not being aware of the exact situation."[54] Eventually, after the bloody suppression of the Ilinden Uprising in August 1903, at its meeting in February 1904, the ISB came out with a brief resolution in favor of "complete autonomy" for Macedonia.[55] In the preceding debates, however, the position of Victor Adler, the charismatic leader of the Austrian Social Democratic Party, was noteworthy: "The Bulgarian socialists do not generally understand our position, which is the basis of the misunderstanding [i.e., of the position defended in the *Arbeiter Zeitung* on the Macedonian question-MT]. We recognize the right of the Macedonians to independence just as we recognize this right for any other nation. But we have another more important and more immediate interest, that of the proletariat, whose representatives we are. An intervention of the great powers, which would result in a war, would hamper the interests of the Austrian proletariat in the first place, and of European socialism in general. Our workers are the first who would march; this is why the problem for us is of a different order than platonic declarations of solidarity. Moreover, things in the Balkans are very murky; there are also other national groups there who claim the right of autonomy."[56] This spirited defense of the interests of the Austrian proletariat did not deter Adler from enthusiastically blessing its march against the Serbs in 1914.

The outbreak of the Young Turk Revolution in July 1908 and the restoration of the Ottoman constitution, greeted with enthusiasm by the European governments and the socialist parties alike, shelved the reform program of the great powers. The question of Macedonia's autonomy was seen as no longer urgent, and the Bulgarian social democrats revived different projects for a Balkan federation, this time including Turkey. The BWSDP (n) advanced the idea of a Balkan federation but included only the European parts of the Ottoman Empire. Blagoev specified that by confederation or federation (the two terms were indiscriminately used) he understood "a union, in which the constituting states retain their independence in all respects, except the commitment to common defense."[57] He foresaw a common constitution, joint parliament, common foreign policy, collective military, and common finances.[58] Especially popular in this respect was the 1907 book by the Marxist economist Georgi Toshev on a Balkan customs union, which was seen as the first step in the long process of Balkan unification.[59] Some in the BWSDP (b) on the other hand, extended the federation to the Asia Minor territories, setting their hopes on the democratic success of the constitutional movement.[60] There were also differences about the compatibility of the Balkan monarchies with the federation process but these did not neatly follow party lines.[61]

It is within this conjuncture that in 1908 Kautsky was asked by the BWSDP (n) to contribute a preface to the Bulgarian translation of his work "Republic and Social Democracy in France" that had appeared in 1905. He wrote "The National Tasks of the Socialists among the Balkan Slavs."[62] In his understanding Kautsky was amazingly close to the views of the Bulgarian socialists, especially the Narrows.[63] This should

Figure 8 Karl Kautsky.

come as no surprise. His translator Drenski had furnished him with a detailed synopsis of Bulgaria's recent history, and he was aware of the continuous and unsuccessful efforts of the Bulgarian social democrats to put the national issue on the agenda of the International. He was also in close correspondence with Rakovski who had published his articles on the Balkan union and the Eastern Question in *Revue de la Paix*.[64]

This was not the first time that Kautsky was engaged in the Eastern Question. In 1896–97 he had participated in a heated and rather ungracious exchange with Rosa Luxemburg, Liebknecht, and Bernstein on the fate of Crete.[65] But it was the first time that he was engaging in the self-defined Balkan national question. The emphasis of his article was on the relationship of social democracy to the issues of national unification and independence. Kautsky addressed the Macedonian question and concluded that a Bulgarian annexation of Macedonia would solve the problem of unification but would exacerbate relations with the other Balkan countries: "There is only one way to unify fully the Bulgarian nation without the outside help of Bulgaria and without the ever-present quarrels with Serbs, Greeks and Turks, and this is through the union of all nations of the Balkan Peninsula in a federal republic."[66] He further pointed out that the main obstacle to the federative idea were the local monarchies.[67] The defense of internationalism was more important than national interests and Balkan socialists should be particularly hostile to the aims of Russian Pan-Slavism.[68] He finally warned the socialists from countries with underdeveloped capitalist relations and a small organized proletariat to advance their own understanding of the national question distinct from bourgeois democracy, and be careful not to be absorbed by it.[69] The one thing that can be said about the latter warning is that the Balkan social democrats heeded this advice some six years later in 1914, while Kautsky apparently thought internationalism was territory-specific and valid only for the "underdeveloped." Compared to the other debates within the Socialist International on revisionism, colonialism, and imperialism, and the question of war, the national question remained of secondary importance. As Annie Kriegel puts it, "the question of war and peace was a *strategic* question, whereas the national question was derivative, rather one of *tactics*."[70] At no time did the International elaborate or ratify any general document on the national question despite a number of resolutions and proclamations.

It goes without saying that no general theory of the national question was offered. The one exception strictly for the Habsburg realm was Austro-Marxism.[71] For the twenty-six-year-old Otto Bauer, socialism was "drawing the people as a whole into the national community of culture, achieving full self-determination by the nation, growing intellectual differentiation between the nations."[72] For Karl Renner, there were three approaches to solving the national question: First, through assimilation by a dominant unifying group; these were the cases of Germany and Italy, where minorities would eventually disappear. Second, through the concept of territorial federation and the creation of a multinational state; this solution was deemed unacceptable for Central Europe because of the entanglement between different nationalities and the impossibility to create small territorial units. Third, and this is what he and Bauer offered, was the detachment of the nation from its territorial basis, the creation of national autonomous cultural entities akin to religious communities within the same state.[73] They eventually called it a "democratic federation of nationalities" in their 1899 program but one that would preserve the Empire's territory as a larger economic region and guarantee progressive development. The new democratized imperial state would give cultural self-determination uncoupled from territorial independence. This was offered as a model for the rest of the International and Adler identified the project as a "little International."[74] When Stalin, who had been sent to study the Austro-Marxist vision, published his *Marxism and the National Question* in 1913, he was critical of the Austro-Marxists for having emphasized nationalism at the expense of class struggle. And yet, Lenin and the Bolsheviks as a whole distinguished between oppressors and oppressed nationalities and as a result supported national self-determination.[75] Only Rosa Luxemburg remained adamantly opposed to national self-determination.[76]

Apart from the great sophistication of the Austro-Marxist theorists, cynically put, this was a way to defend the territorial integrity and the *mission civilisatrice* of the Habsburg Empire. This is how it was seen by Serbian socialists, especially in the aftermath of the Austro–Hungarian annexation of Bosnia-Herzegovina in

1908. It even came to a scandal and public apology, when the Austrian socialists, while critical of the annexation of Bosnia-Herzegovina, protested at the same time against the position of the Serbian government, which ostensibly made it difficult for Austria to fulfill its mission. Tucović submitted a memorandum to the ISB, and at the Copenhagen Congress in 1910 Renner made a public apology and there was a theatrical reconciliation.[77] What Kautsky did was to legitimate the second option, the federative territorial one, given that the Balkans already had a plethora of independent small national states which had seceded from the Ottoman Empire in the course of the previous century. In the few instances that this is reflected in general accounts outside of the national historiographies of the Balkans, it is attributed to the theoretical wisdom of Kautsky. Thus Georges Haupt wrote that "this article has to be seen as the starting point for a Marxist approach to the national question in the Balkans and a framework for a socialist solution."[78] Leo van Rossum asserts that when Kautsky "openly supported the idea of a democratic Balkan federation, this contributed to the fact that this solution was adopted by the social democrats in the Balkans."[79] Fišera adds that in 1908, Rakovski "picked up the idea of a Balkan Federation, defended in the International by Parvus, Longuet, Kautsky, and Bernstein."[80]

As we have seen, this idea had long been developed and espoused by the Bulgarian, and broadly, the Balkan socialists, and Kautsky simply endorsed it. So, how do we qualify Kautsky's contribution in light of this detailed reading? We can hardly evaluate it in terms of transfer/translation of a theoretical insight that influenced the views and behavior of the Balkan social democrats once it was adapted locally, although this is how it is rendered in the general accounts. Closer to the point, is it not an unacknowledged summation of the views of Bulgarian social democracy developed over the previous quarter-century? This is not meant as an unkind putdown of Kautsky. By the turn of the twentieth century he most genuinely inhabited the role of the infallible "Red Pope." In this he was facilitated by the reverence, adulation, indeed almost obsequiousness, that streams from the letters sent to him over the course of several decades, especially from the small "peripheral" parties.[81] What his great accomplishment was, and this should not be underestimated, was to anoint the Balkan Federation idea. It is not by coincidence that Kautsky first published his article in *Der Kampf*, the theoretical journal of the Austrian party. By giving it the official imprimatur of his office, he legitimized it within the international world of Marxism, where to this point it had a completely subaltern status. The paternalism of the German SPD can be taken for granted and, as Georges Haupt aptly noticed, "it was nothing more than ignorance about the problems of the subjugated peoples."[82] There were minor exceptions though, among them Bernstein, Hermann Wendel, but most of all Kautsky. His attitude evolved from complete skepticism about the ability of agrarian societies to form a socialist party to a genuine and sympathetic interest.

Perhaps a more proper framework is that of entangled history, *histoire croisée*, with its insistence on "a multidimensional approach that acknowledges plurality and the complex configurations that result from it. Accordingly, entities and objects of research are not merely considered in relation to one another but also *through* one another, in terms of relationships, interactions, and circulation."[83] This does not evade the asymmetry of the relationship, not only in the sense of an unequal starting point but also in the sense of not being affected in the same manner by the interaction. The important point, however, is that the two sides of the intercrossing remain active. A last point about intercrossings: they are inherent not only in the object, but are also a result of a theoretical and methodological choice: "Intercrossing never presents itself as an 'already given' that need only to be observed and recorded. It requires an active observer to construct it and only in a to-and-fro movement between researcher and object do the empirical and reflective dimensions of *histoire croisée* jointly take shape."[84]

In the following years, despite different and contending interpretations, having received the highest blessing, the Balkan federative idea became a practical goal and entered the organizational efforts of Balkan socialists. In January 1910 the First Balkan Social Democratic Conference was convened in Belgrade. It represented different social-democratic organizations from six states—Austria-Hungary (Croatian, Slovenian and Bosnian socialists), Bulgaria (the Narrows), Montenegro, the Ottoman Empire (represented by the Armenian Social Democratic Hunchakian Party), Romania, and Serbia. Since the Narrows insisted on the exclusion of the Broads, as well as of the Workers' Federation of Salonica, Rakovski and the Romanian socialists boycotted the conference, but entrusted their mandate to the Serbs.[85]

In his report to the conference, Blagoev upheld the basic Marxist premise that socialists are for the affirmation and reinforcement of capitalism, because only developed capitalism could guarantee the independence of the Balkan countries and the rise of a conscious working class. Accordingly, he expected that the Balkan bourgeoisies would inevitably take the path to federation but under the immediate pressure of the proletariat. Thus, the Balkan Federation would not be a socialist state from the outset, but a bourgeois one, since the conditions for a socialist revolution were not yet mature.[86]

Figure 9 First Balkan Social Democratic Conference, Belgrade, January 1910.

The joint Resolution reflected these views. It laid the blame for the territorial fragmentation of the peninsula, the particularism, and insularity on European diplomacy, "the instrument of the political expansion of European capitalism." The national bourgeoisies, with the help of the local dynasties, exacerbate national tensions and "prevent the resolution of the Balkan Question by way of the unification of the peoples." Therefore, the conference takes the position that the legitimate aspirations of the Balkan nations can be achieved only by "combining their economic forces into one whole, abolishing artificially drawn borders, and enabling them to live together in full reciprocity and in united defense against the common danger." This could be realized by militarist policies, and the conference declared: "As the political representative of the working classes, which are not divided by the national antagonisms of the ruling classes, Social Democracy has the important role of being the most conscious and the most resolute proponent of the idea of solidarity between the nations of south-eastern Europe and of the strengthening, through the class struggle of the proletariat, the powers of resistance of the peoples towards the policy of conquest of European capitalism."[87]

In the next years, Bulgarian socialists developed a differential attitude toward the idea of federation, conditioned by their assessment of the evolution of the Young Turk regime. Both Broads and Narrows were critical toward the nationalist and Turkifying turn among the Young Turks, and their actions against the young socialist and working-class movements. The Narrows, however, definitively embraced the idea of a federation, arguing that supporting autonomy would, in fact, exacerbate the inter-Balkan tensions and would inevitably lead to war. While they thought that "the political ideals of the Young Turks do not go beyond the constitution of Midhat Pasha," they advocated a minimal program for the social democrats in Thrace and Macedonia, including the following:

1. The right of free self-determination for the nationalities in the Turkish Empire and a federation of nations unified in one Balkan state.
2. Universal, direct, equal, and secret suffrage for all elected bodies—the imperial parliament; the national popular assemblies; the regional and local councils.
3. Abolition of the senate.
4. Complete self-government for regions and local communities.
5. Full rights of workers' association.
6. Absolute freedom of conscience and belief, speech, press, and association.
7. Workers' legislation, including wide-ranging protection of the interests of the working class and especially of female and child labor in the factories, mines, workshops, agricultural estates, etc.
8. Secular education in the schools and instruction in the appropriate national language.
9. A people's militia instead of a standing army.
10. Abolition of taxes of kind, indirect taxes, and the introduction of a progressive income tax and property tax.[88]

They thus advocated bringing the revolution to its logical end and not having it "stopped half way."[89] What is remarkable is their shying away from the notion of

Macedonian autonomy, which at the time was believed to be a shorthand for the future unification with Bulgaria, on the pattern of Eastern Rumelia in 1885. They did not endorse autonomy or the right to secession, but self-government within a larger federation, including Turkey. Nevertheless, it has to be said that their ideas of what exactly "Turkey" would comprise were not clearly specified, at times including only the European domains of the empire. For example, Vasil Glavinov (1869–1929), the recognized pioneer of socialism in Macedonia and member of BWSDP (n) wrote in an editorial: "A Balkan federation means the creation of a state from the peoples that populate the Balkan Peninsula in which all the nations have equal rights. Thus, for example, European Turkey, Bulgaria, Serbia, Greece and Romania united to form one state in which all would enjoy equal rights—this would be a Balkan federation."[90]

On the other hand, Dimo Hadzhidimov (1875–1924), one of the leaders of the left wing of the Internal Macedonian Revolutionary Organization, IMRO, and member of the BWSDP (n) was speaking of a Balkan federation that would be an "association of the Turkish Empire and all the remaining Balkan statelets in one political and economic union, which would guarantee the political and economic freedom of each state through mutual concessions, strengthen industry, utilize all the natural resources and facilities for trade and commerce, stimulate the cultural progress of each of them, cease to spend large sums beyond the means of the people on militarism, and eliminate every cause for wars between them."[91] Fikret Adanir, in his otherwise pioneering and thoughtful assessment of the socialist idea in Macedonia exaggerates, according to me, the differences in Hadzhidimov's position from the mainstream Narrow socialist one by claiming that Hadzhidimov, who was himself a leading Narrow "considered the idea of a Balkan federation an abstract and illusory goal, not fit to solve the real problems in Macedonia. Instead, he tried to restructure the IMRO on federalist principles: in other words, the Macedonia he envisaged was not an autonomous Macedonia forming part of a socialist Balkan federation, but a Macedonia of federated peoples enjoying autonomy within the framework of the Ottoman state."[92] Adanir is conflating here the views of Hadzhidimov on the structure of the IMRO with his views on the future structure and fate of the province as a whole.[93] To be sure, Hadzhidimov was in a minority in his views about the particular organization of the IMRO, but the Narrows had all rejected the idea of a Macedonian autonomy, precisely on the grounds that this "would mean asking for the partition of the province among the neighboring states."[94]

Thus, the allegation that the "Narrow's idea of a Balkan federation presupposed the destruction of the Ottoman state.... [Hence] we can establish a close parallelism between the policies of the Bulgarian nationalist bourgeoisie on the one hand and the Narrow social democrats on the other. They willingly accepted the risk of a Balkan war which would lead to the partition of Macedonia" is clearly off the mark.[95] It is not off the mark for the Broads, however, who gravitated toward the idea of Macedonian autonomy, which they hoped to achieve in collaboration with some of the bourgeois parties. While Sakŭzov was rightly critical of the notion of federation that was not sufficiently and concretely developed and which he called a "Fata Morgana,"[96] the Broads were already bitten by "the bug of nationalism" to use Maehl's useful phrase apropos the Germans.[97]

On the ground, the most remarkable, albeit short-lived, episode was the active involvement of Bulgarian socialists in the Young Turk movement. Already in 1894 Vasil Glavinov, as a member of the BWSDP and on the instruction of Blagoev, had founded the Macedono-Odrin Social Democratic Group or Union (MOSDG) as a regional group of the BWSDP in Veles. The next year, together with Dimo Hadzhidimov, he started a short-lived (10 issues) newspaper *Revolution* (Револющия) in Sofia.[98] Both were members of the left wing of the IMRO and of the BWSDP and later the Narrows (Glavinov since 1893, Hadzhidimov since 1901) espousing its political stance on federalism.[99] Creating a network of socialist groups in Macedonia, especially strong in Bitola and Krushevo, the members of MOSDG were closely cooperating with the other left-wing cadres of the IMRO, among them the leader of the Krushevo Republic of 1903, Nikola Karev (1877–1905). In the summer of 1908, Glavinov settled in Thessaloniki, where he created a social-democratic group and trade union, as an offshoot of BWSDP (n).[100]

At the same time, Thessaloniki had attracted the so-called group of the "anarcho-liberals." Most prominent among the "anarcho-liberals" were Pavel Deliradev (1879–1957) and Nikola Kharlakov (1874–1927) who organized another Bulgarian social-democratic group in Thessaloniki. By October 1908, the two groups (Glavinov's and Deliradev's) decided to unite and began issuing the newspaper *Worker* (*Работник*). It was a short-lived venture and factionalism took over. Both groups entered the Socialist Workers' Federation (*Federacion socialista laboradera*) under the leadership of Avram Benaroya (1887–1979), the future founder of the Greek Communist Party. Benaroya was born in Vidin and had become a member of the BWSDP (n): "It is necessary to correct some misconceptions regarding my early year. I . . . became 'converted' to socialism in Bulgaria, joining the 'Narrow' wing. In 1907, when this group split into the 'liberals' (or democrats) and the 'conservatives' (or centrists), I became one of the liberal militants. I must, nevertheless, admit that I retained great respect for the 'conservative' socialist leaders of Bulgaria, my original mentors."[101] The reason for Benaroya's dissent was his insistence on taking ethnic differences into consideration, whereas BRDSP (t.s.) opposed the federative principle within the workers' movement. As a teacher in Plovdiv, he was in the Supervisory Board of the Jewish workers' society *Consciousness* (*Съзнание*) and had published in Bulgarian his work *The Jewish Question and Social Democracy* (1908). After the Young Turk Revolution, Benaroya moved to Thessaloniki and founded the Sephardic Circle of Socialist Studies, which became the basis for the Federation and whose backbone were the Jewish tobacco workers.[102]

The Federation published in 1909 a *Workers' Paper (Journal del Labourador - Работнически вестник - Amele gazetesi - Εφημερίς του Εργάτου)* in Ladino, Bulgarian, Ottoman Turkish, and Greek, of which only the last issue (out of nine) has been preserved.[103] However, most of the membership of the organization was Jewish and Bulgarian, and a Greek and Turkish section failed to form, so that after issue 5 the newspaper came out only in Ladino and Bulgarian.[104] Due to problems with the censures, the paper was renamed to *Workers' Solidarity* (*La Solidaridad Ovradera-Работническа солидарност*) and came out in 1911.[105]

In his memoirs about the founding of the Federation, Benaroya writes about the tensions among its members. Mostly they concerned how they envisioned the form of the organization. The Macedono-Odrin Social Democratic Group around Glavinov, as well as some Jewish members, were aiming at a united socialist party, while Benaroya planned for a federative organization along ethnic lines.[106] After the split, the "anarcho-liberals" merged with the Federation, while the Macedono-Odrin Social-democratic Group opened an international socialist bookstore in Thessaloniki and began publishing a new paper, *Workers' spark (Работническа искра)* from January 1909 to May 1911.[107] Its position on the Young Turk Revolution was essentially the abovementioned platform of BWSDP (n) arguing for a Balkan socialist federation and was critical of the Young Turks' policy toward the working class. Relations between the two groups soured, and in August 1910 Glavinov sent a report to the Copenhagen Congress about the socialist movement in European Turkey. It gives a detailed and valuable analysis of the situation of the working class but is unjustly offensive of "un certain" Benaroya and "un certain" Vlahov with whom he had recently collaborated. He resorts to a veritable smear campaign in asking the International Bureau to not admit the Socialist Federation because it has nothing to do with socialism and is a simple subsidiary of the Young Turks.[108] With the coming of the Balkan Wars, the members of this group moved back to Sofia.

The other prominent member of the Federation, besides the Sephardic Circle and the "anarcho-liberals," was the People's Federative Party–Bulgarian Section (Народна федеративна партия–българска секция). The latter was founded in April 1909 by IMRO members who actively participated in the Young Turk Revolution and the "Army of Freedom" march on Istanbul to quell the countercoup in 1909. It was strongly divided along ideological lines and different strategic choices around social democrats like Dimitîr Vlahov (1878–1953), nationalists with socialist leanings like Iane Sandanski (1872–1915), and nationalists like Khristo Chernopeev.[109] The circle around Vlahov remained active within the Federation and he became a socialist MP in the Ottoman parliament, representing the People's Federative Party–Bulgarian Section. His party, however, was banned by the Young Turks in August 1910 and after its dissolution he once more entered the parliament in 1912 as an MP, this time from the short-lived Ottoman Socialist Party (OSP).[110] The Young Turks launched a massive clampdown on socialist groups and the OSP was disbanded during the Balkan Wars. Benaroya himself was jailed three times and deported to Serbia in 1911 and Greece in 1912.

Even after the suppression of the socialist movement in the Ottoman Empire, Rakovski and his "Progressists" were inclined to lay more hopes on the Young Turk regime, even as they were disappointed by its evolution. With Rakovsky being the chief spokesperson of this faction in his daily newspaper *Napred*, which he published in 1911–12 (184 issues), he, like the Narrows, refuted autonomy as a viable solution, but insisted mostly on an internal democratic struggle and against the rapacious intentions of the great powers and the neighboring countries. Rakovski published several programmatic articles, in which he advocated a defensive military alliance of the Balkan states and the Ottoman Empire organized in a Balkan confederation.[111] In this, he may have espoused a nebulous and "strange 'popular front,' based on the idea of a Balkan confederation and including mutually opposed political forces such as the Young Turks, the bourgeoise and the reformist parties in the Balkan states as well as the progressive and socialist forces in the West."[112] Rakovski was following the generally favorable attitude of the International toward the Young Turk regime, and its support of the integrity of the Ottoman Empire as a guarantee for peace. The chief exponent of these views in the West was Jean Jaurès who, critical as he was of the antisocialist policy of the Young Turks, maintained that only the consolidation of their regime could bring stability to the East and avoid war.[113]

The defense of the territorial integrity of the Ottoman Empire by Rakovski, the left wing of the IMRO in the face of Vlahov and the Jewish Workers' Federation of Salonika has led to the somewhat exaggerated claim of a Turko-Marxist tendency, in analogy to the Austro-Marxist one.[114] It has been suggested that Benaroya named his organization *Federacion*, since he had built it on the federative model of the Austrian Social Democratic Party, consisting of separate sections representing the four main ethnic groups of Thessaloniki.[115] However, Benaroya's own memoirs dispel this claim. He never mentioned a putative Austro-Marxist connection or inspiration: "I was guided only by my socialist conscience and by my understanding of local conditions. . . . [T]he principle embodied in the Socialist Federation . . . endorsed the recognition of local circumstances and ethnic groups as the basis of socialist activity in Turkey. The Serb, Turkish and Jewish delegates supported this principle, which was also accepted by the Bulgarians born in Turkey, and the Greeks were not absolutely opposed."[116]

All in all, the Bulgarian socialist parties and factions on the eve of the Balkan Wars espoused the pacifist orientation of the International in support of the *status quo* as a guarantee against a general conflagration. In this they underestimated the determination of the ruling Balkan monarchies and governments to look for a military solution, but overestimated their ability to do so while confining the conflict to the Balkans.[117] In a remarkable passage in his war correspondence from the Balkan Wars, Trotsky quotes disparagingly the opinion of a Bulgarian bourgeois politician: "For you, all this is simple: you reject war altogether, at any time and under any circumstances. A war in the Balkans or a war in Patagonia, aggressive or defensive, for liberation or for conquest—you make no distinction. But *we* consider it necessary to investigate the real historical content of the war, the given war, the war in the Balkans, and we can't just shut our eyes to the fact that what is involved here is the liberation of the Slav people from Turkish rule."[118] Socialists were dismissive of this view in theory, but when it came to their own countries, the leading parties of the Second International proved more accommodating to their own bourgeoisies.

The Coming of the Great War

The Young Turk Revolution, the subsequent annexation of Bosnia-Herzegovina by the Habsburgs, the formal proclamation of Bulgarian independence, the Second Moroccan crisis, the Tripolitanian War between Italy and the Ottoman Empire (1911–12), and the Balkan Wars (1912–13), raised the specter of a general war. The question of war, of course, had been one of the central issues preoccupying the International since its inception, and the first resolution against war was passed as early as 1889. How this imposing international body came to support the war efforts in 1914 has been bemoaned as treason and failure, but with hindsight the roots were discernible already from the beginning, and especially in the "model" German party. The attitude of the SPD can be easily understood given the successful development of capitalism in Germany coupled with the spectacular growth of the party and the trade unions. The SPD was becoming an important factor in political life and "in their eagerness to escape from isolation, social democrats accepted the proposition that they were much the better patriots who would allow nobody to outdo them."[119] More specifically, the SPD leadership was averse to losing its popularity after the spectacular electoral victory in 1912. By 1914, the modus operandi was not the representation of an oppressed class, but a powerful vested interest in the state.[120]

Alongside the widespread belief that capitalism inevitably bred war, there was a sincere effort to avoid it. From the outset socialists had to tackle the age-old debate of just war and the right to self-defense. The Golden Age of socialism was also the era of rising and triumphant nationalism and the two, while enjoying a complex relationship, were most often not at cross-purposes. In 1891 Engels declared that "if Russia, the hotbed of cruelty and barbarism, the enemy of all human culture, should attack Germany in order to partition and destroy her . . . then we are as much concerned as those who rule Germany and we shall resist."[121] The following year he warned the French socialists that "if France, in alliance with Russia, should declare war on Germany, she would be fighting against the strongest social-democratic party in Europe; and that we would have no choice but to oppose with all our strength any aggressor that was on the side of Russia."[122] A year later, at the 1893 congress of the International in Zurich, Plekhanov rejected the idea of mass strikes against imminent war, arguing that it would "disarm above all the cultured nations and deliver Western Europe into the hands of the Cossacks. Russian despotism would sweep away our entire civilization, and in lieu of the freedom of the proletariat we would get the rule of the Russian knout."[123]

The issue of war was intimately related to that of mass strikes, and it came to a head at the Stuttgart Congress in 1907 where a resolution on war was adopted, and approved at the subsequent meetings in Copenhagen in 1910 and Basel in 1912. At the Stuttgart Congress, August Bebel, the august leader of the SPD, proclaimed the *Communist Manifesto* outdated in its view of patriotism. The debates between the French and German delegates became acrimonious, and the Germans refused to support the French resolution brought in by Gustave Hervé, Jean Jaurès, and Édouard Vaillant which declared that "a country that has been attacked is entitled to count upon the aid of the working class of all lands and that to prevent war all means were legitimate."[124] The final resolution, reflecting the primacy of the German section, should be seen as a compromise between the German determination on the right to defend the fatherland and the French insistence on social revolution.[125] As Maehl accurately observed, "the ultimate Stuttgart resolution obligated all socialist parties to refuse support for increased armaments and spoke of preventing war by every means, but it neglected to specify by just what means. . . . The resolution spread confusion and consternation in the ranks of the European socialists."[126]

Nevertheless, doctrinal purity was preserved at the expense of clarity. At what was effectively the last congress of the International in Basel (November 1912), the "Balkan Question" became the focus of the anti-war declarations against the possibility that the Balkan Wars would provoke the intervention of the great powers and spark a general war. It was also the first time it was called a "Balkan Question": in all previous deliberations of the ISB and congresses, Balkan issues were debated (if at all) under the rubric of Eastern Question or Turkish Question after July 1908. The manifesto, prepared by Kautsky and adopted by the congress, stated that the interests of the working class also included the issue of national self-determination. This should be achieved not through war but through progressive democratization as well as the unification of the Balkan peoples, Turkey inclusive, into a democratic federation. There was special mention of Albania which was to be given autonomous status in the framework of the federation.[127] Yet neither the International, nor the separate Balkan parties elaborated on the mechanism, structure, and functions of the future political entity. It mostly remained a wishful slogan. This should not deter us from appreciating the profound analysis that Balkan socialists gave the federal idea in this period, the work of Khristo Kabakchiev, *Towards a Balkan Federation*, standing out with its insightful examination of the Balkan League and the two Balkan Wars.[128]

In addition, Western and Balkan socialists approached the national question in fundamentally different ways, because of the question of tactics. For the Western socialists it was imperative to maintain the *status quo* in the Balkans, lest war should spill over from the region to engulf the whole continent. For the Balkan socialists, on the other hand, the *status quo* was in the interest of the capitalist powers whose aim was "to preserve the existing condition in the Balkans, conditions which would be a perpetual source of discontent, disorder, revolution and war."[129] The *status quo* therefore condemned the Balkans to immobility and far from being a guarantee for peace, it was, in fact, a permanent source of war. The Balkan Wars did not provoke a European conflagration but a year later the Balkans, through the Sarajevo crisis, were used as a pretext for a general war that involved the world in the biggest bloodshed heretofore. Socialist leaders in most European countries embraced the logic of just war and persuaded themselves they were acting in self-defense. The SPD, voting for the war credits, said in its declaration: "In this respect we feel ourselves in accord with the International, which has always conceded the right of every people to national independence and self-defense, even as we agree in denouncing every war of conquest."[130] In the German case, this was sold not only as a self-defense against Russia, but also as a fight against Europe's most reactionary power. Haupt adds an additional interesting circumstance for the SPD: "Beyond the seduction of patriotism, the devotion to the national state, and the mentality of a 'loyal' opposition, the party's morbid fear of its own left wing plays its part."[131]

Contrast this to the position of the Bulgarian Narrows who adamantly refuted what they saw essentially as sophism: "Social democracy cannot apply the criteria of a defensive war without the risk to fall into disadvantage. Today the boundary between aggressive and defensive wars is obliterated."[132] Ironically, the Balkan socialists who had been consistently disregarded by the International were rediscovered with the outbreak of the war, especially by the right wing of the SPD, the so-called "social patriots," who began a campaign to persuade the socialists of the neutral countries to support the entry of their countries on the side of Germany. Two missions were sent: Albert Südekum in Rome and Bucharest, and Alexander Parvus in Sofia and Bucharest.[133] The mission in

Bucharest became clearly quixotic because of the traditional French orientation of the Romanian socialists.[134] On January 10, 1915, Parvus arrived in Sofia, hoping for better success. The sympathies of the Broads were gravitating toward the Entente whose victory was seen as a catalyst for European democratization. On the other hand, the Narrows advocated firm neutrality, and Blagoev wrote that "whoever wins, one thing is certain: both victors and vanquished will come out of the war exhausted, devastated, and heartbroken in all respects. Millions of people would be thrown into misery. All of this the European proletariat and the European nations are not going to endure in resignation. After the general war comes a general revolution in Europe."[135] However, the general revolution was expected to erupt in the large industrial countries and therefore the question as to who wins was considered crucial for the small countries. For the BWSDP (n) the victory of the Central Powers was the lesser evil: "It is true that in either case there is the danger that smaller countries may lose their independence, but the greatest danger both for the smaller countries but, above all, for the proletarian liberation movement in all of Europe and, in general, for the delay of the revolution, can come from a Russian victory."[136]

This position and the well-known and long documented hatred of Blagoev for Tsarist Russia encouraged Parvus. Already in October of 1914, Blagoev had lashed out against Plekhanov who had sent a letter, asking the Narrows to use their influence to throw the country on the side of the Entente. The letter was published in *Novo vreme*, accompanied by Blagoev's powerful rebuke "Magister dixit."[137] The significance of this criticism is all the greater, given the enormous authority that Plekahnov had among Bulgarian social democrats, equal only to Kautsky's, and reflected in the title of Blagoev's article, referring to the *magister*. Especially interesting is Blagoev's rebuttal of Plekhanov's argumentation that the defeat of Russia would harm the cause of democracy in France, Belgium, and England, that it would weaken the Russian revolutionary movement

Figure 10 Georgy Plekhanov in 1917.

and strengthen German imperialism, and that, conversely, a Russian victory would be beneficial for the development of capitalism in Russia and thus for the development of the working class and the revolutionary movement. Blagoev countered that the defeat of big nations brings in the defeat of the ancien regime and the possibility for revolution, and that history has furnished us with numerous examples, namely the Russian Revolution of 1905 and the French Commune, which were triggered after the military defeat of the Russo-Japanese and Franco-Prussian war.[138]

When Parvus arrived in Sofia, he still had the reputation of a leading social democrat and was invited by the Narrows to give a speech in front of their mass meeting the next day in the largest theater in Sofia. Parvus's fiery speech "was met with stony silence" by an assembly of over 4,000.[139] A few days later Blagoev came out with another famous article "Plekhanov and Parvus," where he accused the two prominent social democrats of becoming patriots and chauvinists (one of the rare critical analogies that does not distinguish between the two). He also stated his admiration for the Karl Liebknecht–Rosa Luxemburg–Franz Mehring faction that had consistently upheld their anti-war beliefs.[140] In February 1915, the Narrows convened a conference with their Serbian and Romanian counterparts in Sofia repeating their previous admonitions to their governments to mediate and end the conflict. In March Georgi Kirkov, the Secretary-General of the BWSDP (n), protested in a letter to the Secretary of the ISB, Camille Huysmans, against the support of the French and German socialists for their governments, and against the inactivity of the International. The Bulgarian Narrows demanded that the International convene a conference to reestablish the disunited organization: "Today, to the shame of the International, its most progressive and trustworthy sections are taking part in the bloody work of the bourgeoisie, in which millions of proletarians fall prey, with an enthusiasm that is typical only for the social democracy, and with an energy that is worthy for any other cause but this."[141] Huysmans berated the Narrows as "the old incorrigibles."[142]

In July 1915, this was followed by the Second Balkan Socialist Conference in Bucharest, where the BWSDP (n) (the Broads were not present), in conjunction with the Greek, Romanian, and Serbian socialists, issued a manifesto in which they denounced the imperialist war and again called for federation as the only safeguard for the liberty and integrity of the Balkan nations: "Balkan Social Democracy fights for a federal Balkan Republic based on national autonomy, which will ensure the independence of peoples, cause the hate that animates them to disappear, unite them through their federal organization, and give them their surest means of defense by setting up of national militias in place of standing armies."[143] Interestingly, the Broads sent a letter to the International Bureau stigmatizing the Narrows as "a faction which in its practical politics is on the verge of anarchism" and denouncing their association with Rosa Luxemburg and Karl Liebknecht: "The Bucharest conference calls for the creation of a new international which would include only spotless individuals and parties, and they see these only in themselves and people like Luxemburg and Karl Liebknecht.... We consider it our duty to warn our western comrades, that Balkan socialism has nothing in common with such decisions. It is not the task of the smaller parties to denounce the big ones whose final word has not yet been heard."[144]

When on October 1, 1915, Bulgaria finally broke its neutrality and entered the war on the side of the Central Powers, the Narrows voted against the war credits. The Broads abstained from the vote, but participated in the plans for economic mobilization and later accepted important ministerial seats as "sons of this sinful earth who by education and psychology yield to the great national idea and cannot oppose it."[145] To be fair, Sakŭzov, like Kautsky and Bernstein in Germany, later developed doubts about the wisdom of supporting the war but he was isolated within his own party.[146] The BWSDP (n) were one of an honorable foursome who consistently opposed the war. When on August 4, German and French socialists voted for the war credits and embraced *Burgfrieden* and *Union sacrée*, they were soon followed by the socialists in Austria, Hungary, Belgium, Britain, Switzerland, the Netherlands, Sweden, and Denmark, who adopted "national defensism." Of the belligerent countries, only the Serbian social democrats and the left coalition in the Russian Duma (the Bolsheviks consistently, and Kerensky's *Trudoviki* and the Mensheviks at first) opposed the war, and in the neutral countries, it was the Italians and the Bulgarians, who remained opposed even after their governments entered the war in 1915. Madeleine Rebérioux raises the interesting question of the correlation between the numerical growth of the socialist movement and the ensuing ideological transformation, especially the attitude toward the war. Explaining away the Serbian and Russian opposition with the weakness of the parties and the trade unions, and the lack of a national democratic tradition, however, minimizes their accomplishment, and sounds almost like a tacit justification of the *Union sacrée*. The Italians and the Bulgarians are not even deigned worthy of mention.[147]

Lindemann, too, earlier gave a quasi-economic explanation for the paroxysm of patriotism or lack thereof in asserting that "socialist opposition to war was first taken up by those socialists whose countries were incompletely engaged by the dynamics of mass industrial warfare" and that "mobilizing the rural, illiterate, backward, politically passive masses" in Italy into active and ardent support for war was more difficult than in France or Germany.[148] One is bound to side with Lenin who not only spread the blame equally to all imperialisms—German, Russian, French, Austro–Hungarian—but also proclaimed that imperialism, through its creation of a workers' aristocracy in the economically advanced West, was also the reason for "patriotism" among socialists.[149]

There is a poignant account in the memoirs of Vasil Neichev of a meeting between Vasil Kolarov and Victor Adler in 1916. Neichev was in Vienna on other business and met Kolarov, an old friend, by chance. In early May, returning from the Kienthal Conference, Kolarov was having a meeting with the Austrian comrades and had taken him along much to the delight of Neychev who venerated Adler as someone who had personally known Marx and Engels. They were speaking in French, Adler haltingly as he did not know the language well, Kolarov fluently as he had studied in France. After informing Adler of the decision of the conference, a debate ensued. The main issue at the moment, so said Adler, was to defeat Russia and the Entente, and only then turn to the international ties of the workers' parties. According to him this was a "progressive war, a struggle against the ignorant masses of the East." On Kolarov's remarking that they should begin propaganda among the prisoners of war, Adler retorted that not only was any contact with enemy POWs forbidden but "a pitiful people as the Serbs should be obliterated for the peace of my country and the whole world." The Bulgarians protested that such a phrase should not be pronounced by a leader of the International. Adler eventually agreed but thought it was not worth the risk. He was relieved when his son Friedrich entered the room: "You'll get along better with him: he shares your views."[150] This was just a few months before Friedrich's famous assassination of the Austrian minister-president, Count Karl von Stürgkh.

The least one can do is agree with Augusta Dimou's poetic tribute to Balkan socialists, *"for daring to dream otherwise in an age that thought and acted otherwise is what Balkan socialists should be given credit for and for which they should be paradigmatically remembered."*[151] If anything, the Narrows could be reproached for being "doctrinaire" and taking at face value the internationalism preached by the International. Georgi Pîrvanov's latest book, *Bulgarian social democracy and the Macedonian Question* (already cited as Първанов. *Българската социалдемокрация*), written after 1989, takes an interesting stance. This is the latest and most up-to-date work on a problem that has produced an enormous, although uneven, historiography in Bulgaria. Pîrvanov himself was a party historian who, between 2002 and 2012 became president of Bulgaria and enjoyed reasonable popularity. On the one hand, he seeks to shield the socialists, especially the Narrows, from allegations of national treachery, common in the interwar period and ubiquitous after 1989.[152] On the other hand, he often describes their stance, and especially Rakovski's, who was an unabashed cosmopolitan, as verging on national nihilism. He may be partly right about Rakovski, whose horizons of practice and expectations were, indeed, transnational,[153] but hardly about the Narrows as a whole, who were residing in Bulgaria and were intimately involved in the intricacies of the national predicament. Pîrvanov clearly embraces the position of the Broads whom he tacitly characterizes as taking a more realistic view of the national question. In any case, the Narrows took seriously the rhetoric of the International. But, as Haupt pointed out, "rhetorical internationalism was not equal to this test" and C. L. R. James remarked in 1937 that "the leaders of great parties judge history from the necessities of their organizations and not their organizations from the necessities of history."[154] Eley ruefully concludes that "despite these exceptions, for all practical purposes the old internationalism was buried."[155]

But was there actually an "old internationalism" at all? Geoff Eley may have been overly generous in assigning internationalist culture as one of the key aspects of socialist culture in this period: "Among the Second International's leading activists, socialist culture was nothing if not internationalist," and quoting Hobsbawm he concludes that they were "a body of men and women conscious of being engaged on the same historical task, across national and political differences."[156] The examples he gives are Kautsky's being born in Prague, Filipo Turati having the Russian exile Anna Kuliscioff as his lifelong companion, Rosa Luxemburg and Leo Jogiches, Christian Rakovski, and Anton Pannekoek. With the exception of the last, who was at home in both the Dutch and German parties, the rest came from Eastern Europe.[157] This is not to say that the leaders of the East European socialists carried more of the "internationalist gene," but to point out that both they and their Western counterparts were products of the milieu they came from: the Western leaders representing consolidated and rising powerful nation-states and colonial empires, the Eastern ones coming from the imperial background of the Ottoman, Habsburg, and Romanov empires that were in the last decades of their existence. As Sabine Rutar has shown in her study of the social democrats in Trieste before the First World War, they were operating in a mixed ethnic milieu, where they had to give concrete practical expression to the internationalist rhetoric. This can be extended to Eastern and, especially, Southeastern Europe as a whole. The German social democrats were spared this. Their internationalism with the French remained purely imaginary, on a rhetorically formalist level, and had never to be put to the test of everyday practice.[158]

The local, everyday internationalism in the east was accompanied by a remarkable multilingualism, a fact that awaits its researcher, and should be analyzed beyond the predicament of small nations being forced to learn to communicate in the hegemonic tongues of the period. To take the Bulgarian case, Rakovski was fluent in at least eight languages, but he was not the exception. Vasil Kolarov (1877–1950) was also proficient in eight. Of the lesser known socialists (not outside, but in Bulgaria proper), many were polyglots: Aleksandŭr Atanasov (1879–1925) knew nine, Vŭrban Angelov (1887–1974) six, Stella Blagoeva six, Georgi Dobrev (1893–1966) ten, Avram Benaroia (1887–1972) at least six, Roman Avramov (1882–1937) at least five, Koika Tineva (1880–1969) at least four, Nikola Sakarov (1881–1943) at least four, Georgi Andreichin (1884–1950) four, Boris Stefanov (1883–1969), and Ivan Stefanov (1899–1980) five, and this is to mention but a few. In fact, four languages is the routine number, including German, French, and Russian (English being rare at this time), and it comes not only from formal university training abroad. Polyglossia does not guarantee internationalism but compared to monolingualism, it certainly does not hurt.

Epilogue: Eggs for Comrade Kautsky

Let us now drastically zoom in and look through a magnifying glass. On February 10, 1917, through his nephew, Mikhail Kantardzhiev, the son of his sister, Kirkov sent Kautsky "on the part of our comrades here, a modest gift that could be useful in the present circumstances, namely 100 eggs and some other things to eat." The gift was accompanied by a brief letter in which Kirkov reiterated the position of the BWSDP (n) to "remain unwavering in the old position of the international revolutionary socialism" and it informed Kautsky of the brutal censorship and the difficulties the Bulgarian socialists were encountering during the war.[159] Kautsky, who at first had tacitly supported the position of the SPD, had become disillusioned by the summer of 1915, and had denounced the annexation aims of the German government in an appeal that he issued together with Bernstein and Hugo Haase. In the meantime, the left pacifist opposition in parliament had formed the Social Democratic Working group (SAG, *Sozialdemokratische Arbeitsgemeinschaft*) around Haase and Liebknecht. The SAG members were expelled from the SPD in January 1917 by Friedrich Ebert, the then co-chairman of the SPD (the other co-chairman being Haase). In April 1917 they formed the Independent Social Democratic Party of Germany (USDP) under the leadership of Haase, uniting the socialists who opposed the war, including the Spartacus League. Thus, the German party eventually ended up with a split that the

Bulgarians had lived through a little over a decade earlier. Kautsky joined the USPD in 1917. The important thing to emphasize here is that the letter of Kirkov, as well as the following two, are all dated before Kautsky left the SPD. This is not to imply any influence, but simply to stress that the Bulgarians did not know about the events within the SPD at the time of this correspondence.

The next much longer letter by Kirkov is from March 6, 1917. Kirkov acknowledged the letter of Kautsky sent with his nephew and added: "I am happy that I could contribute, through my modest gift, to the material basis of your world of ideas, especially now, when the international proletariat, brought to confusion by the events, betrayed and almost without leadership, needs urgently the bold, committed and, above all, consistent word of its old, trusted, and faithful master and leader."[160] If the tease in the first sentence can be taken for a doctrinaire recitation of historical materialism, readers should be disabused. Kirkov (1867–1919) was celebrated for his inimitable sense of humor. His feuilletons were printed in the press and in a separate book, and he was the preferred and beloved orator at public meetings. Twice elected to Parliament, his speeches were so popular that the MPs of the governing parties came to listen to him because of his wit. When one of them, the future prime minister and leader of the People's Party, Teodor Teodorov, teased him over the negligibility of the socialists, Kirkov's response was: "Gentlemen, members of parliament. One gadfly is enough for one hundred asses."[161] The redoubtable journalist and diplomat Simeon Radev valued Kirkov as one of the best speakers, second only to Genadiev, the leader of the National-Liberal Party. When asked why he ranked him second, he responded that Genadiev was the chief of his own party.[162] Radev also added: "His language is unique in our literature, inimitable, astonishing, an incredible and pleasant mixture of scientifically sounding socialist phrases, used without any pedantism but with the air of an ironic apology, of popular witticisms that can reach buffoonery, of literary quotes, of proverbs, fables, parables, words taken from the coffee house, phrases encountered only in specialized works, something colorful, picturesque, impish, almost always intelligent and always funny. Never has a socialist suggested suicide to the bourgeoisie in such a pleasant manner, like citizen Kirkov."[163]

In his letter, Kirkov wrote about the consternation of the Bulgarian socialists over the volte-face of their German comrades: "Should I tell you with what grief we have followed the sad spectacle of what was happening within the ranks of the German social democracy in these two and a half years? The magnificent building that the German workers erected in a stubborn fifty-year-old struggle with innumerable victims is now shaken to its foundations and threatens to bury under its ruins all the achievements and results reached with such costly exertions and so much innermost idealism and sacrifice. The International offers the same gloomy picture."[164] He then went on the offensive: "We know well what caused this result. We have been struggling against these causes for the past 15 years and for this we often received brusque and unjust treatment from the ISB, whose chairman is now a government minister,[165] as well as from foreign comrades, who wanted to fold revolutionary socialism and opportunism under the same roof." He praised the socialist minority in the German parliament for not forgetting the important historical goal of the struggle: "To forgo this goal to a feigned unity of the organization means to sacrifice the goal to the means and namely to such means that are no longer serving the goal." He thus saw a vindication of the split of the Bulgarian social democrats that had been so deeply deplored by the International, and called on all socialist minorities to come together, to sever their ties with the ISB and unite again in a new international.[166] This is the first time the Bulgarians raised this issue when they implicitly, although not yet explicitly, sided with Lenin.

The third letter was penned on April 14, 1917.[167] Responding to Kautsky's comment that the Russian (February) revolution would speed up the end of the war, Kirkov agreed but added that the German proletariat entered the war under the slogan "against Russian tsarism": "Now that the Russian proletariat has brought down tsarism, the question is what should the attitude of the German proletariat be, since the position of 'the backbone of reaction' has been ceded to the German monarchy?" And he aired the final disenchantment of the Bulgarians who continued to ask themselves how it was possible that such a transformation happened within the "mightiest, most decisive and best organized party in the International."

"It seems that our perceptions—the perceptions of the social democrats in the small, still underdeveloped countries—of the German social democracy were very exaggerated, and that German monarchism was stronger and thus, more dangerous for socialism and democracy, than the Russian." The letter ended with a polite sentence stating Kirkov's hopes that the German proletariat would rise to its task, and that everyone awaited Kautsky's "powerful word and energetic call for the consolidation of the revolutionary struggle of the proletariat in Germany and the whole world." Immediately following was a P.S.: "This letter will be passed to you by comrade Mikhov. He is also going to hand you 150 eggs, and would you please kindly give 50 of them to comrade R. Luxemburg and comrade K. Liebknecht together with the warmest greetings of the Bulgarian comrades." Thus, the whole correspondence, despite the serious issues discussed, was tactfully bookended not by reproach but by eggs (of which only ten arrived broken).[168]

Here one is drawn to apply the now fashionable lens of "materiality": "Like words in the postmodern 1980s, things today are shaking our fundamental understandings of subjectivity, agency, emotions, and the relations between humans and nonhumans."[169] Yet, one should resist the temptation to ascribe the things in question—eggs—to their symbolism and some putative sexual innuendo. Of course, the egg's symbolism has an ancient pedigree, standing for birth, life, fertility, resurrection, and creative magical power. But one can hardly expect socialists to play with the traditional egg symbolism. Besides, in Bulgarian "eggs" are not used in the respective profanities, which utilize the Turkish word *tashak* (testicle). Even if they were used as an obscenity, eggs in this manner would certainly not have been forwarded to Rosa Luxemburg and Karl Liebknecht. But, as Trentmann reminds us, stressing the organic relationship between things and practices, "[t]he life of objects . . . is not prior to or independent of social practices but codependent. This also means that value is not based in a product or its meanings but in how it is put to use."[170] Eggs have always been considered one of the most nutritional foods and in poor societies a rare and coveted ingredient on a festive table. Alongside meat and butter, eggs were also considered if not a remedy, at least providing a strengthening resistance to tuberculosis. Romanticized by poets, writers, and composers in the nineteenth century, the disease was seen as the ultimate scourge of the century, the *mal du siècle*. Especially virulent among the urban working-class poor, tuberculosis began to rise from the seventeenth century on and reached pandemic status in the nineteenth century when it caused a quarter of all deaths in the industrializing countries of Europe. The mortality rate among the working classes reached 40 percent and by the end of the century, public health officials estimated the infection rates in some cities to be nearly 100 percent.[171] Even as it was correctly diagnosed by the end of the century and as mortality started to decline due to heightened sanitary measures, improved nutrition, sanatoria, and maybe epidemiological reasons beyond human intervention, the disease was tamed only by the mid-twentieth century. It was thus considered an overwhelmingly urban disease and one accompanying the process of industrialization. A good number from among the early Bulgarian socialists died of tuberculosis. In times of war especially, but also during peacetime, it was

Figure 11 Georgi Kirkov in 1903.

common that rural relatives would send eggs to their city kin, which would be usually reserved for the children as a strong preventive nutrient. Ironically, by sending eggs to their German comrades, the Bulgarian socialists were playing the role of the rural relatives and were reproducing their country's status as agricultural supplier to the industrialized German center.

What does this multiscopic[172] survey of the place of Bulgarian social democracy within the Socialist International leave us with? Does it upset the history of socialism? Is there an East European or Balkan contribution to socialism? What is the price of excising the "periphery"? There are several conclusions that can be drawn from this narrative. First, it questions the prejudices/stereotypes about how Marxism in "peripheral" societies, specifically agrarian societies with a weak or incipient working class, has been formed. And for that we do not necessarily have to wait for the "discovery" of the so-called Third World and postcolonial theory to show that this formation is not paradoxical, but possible and normal. This is not to minimize the fundamental contribution of postcolonial theory as a critique of Marxist teleological developmentalism.[173] Where the Balkans are evocative is that they show this alternative as not in line with the argument of different paths to modernity in different spaces and different time-periods but happening synchronically and within the same space. The Balkans, and Bulgaria in particular, despite the condescension, have never been questioned as a European space and their path to modernity has been described as lagging but not systemically different. Theoretically, the Russian example, which has been more studied and to which Western historians are bound to pay at least minimal attention, should be sufficient. Yet, in practice, with Russia there is always the fallback to deviation because it is often described (and self-described) as "essentially" non-European, "really" different, and because Western Marxism had excised it neatly, and now, with the new Cold War, it is difficult to use as a foil. But Bulgaria can be used; its inclusion fractures the normative story about socialism from within.

Second, this narrative shows intersections, the intercrossing of ideas, even if rare and rarely reciprocal. To imply that Balkan socialists contributed to the theory of socialism with their take on the Balkan federative idea might seem overstated not only because it was not acknowledged, but also because it was a failure and can be deemed utopian. At least Bulgarian (and Balkan socialists at large) were consistent in their support of the idea and did not vacillate when harshly accused of national disloyalty. Yet no other theoretical attempt of Marxism in the sphere of nationalism has endured and borne any fruit, including the highly (and justly) praised contribution of Austro-Marxism. In actuality, the detailed deliberations of the Bulgarian socialists, creating a federative structure beginning with a customs union and preserving independent territorial entities was original, and ran against the predominant views even after it was adopted only in 1908 by Kautsky.

Third, this analysis addresses the challenging problem of historical significance. This is, of course, a philosophical question, and historians notoriously avoid it when they choose the significant items with which to weave their explanatory narrative. Altogether, and even when not being explicit about it, they assign importance in terms of causal significance, but they often forget that assigning causality itself is a function of a value-orientation, as Max Weber eloquently reminds us:

The significance of a configuration of cultural phenomena and the basis of this significance cannot be derived and rendered intelligible by a system of analytical laws, however perfect it may be, since the significance of cultural events presupposes a value-orientation toward these events. [. . .] We cannot discover, however, what is meaningful to us by means of a "presuppositionless" investigation of empirical data. Rather, perception of its meaningfulness to us is the presupposition of its becoming an object of investigation. [. . .] [I]n every case only a part of concrete reality is interesting and significant to us, because only it is related to the cultural values with which we approach reality. Only certain sides of the infinitely complex concrete phenomenon, namely those to which we attribute a general cultural significance, are therefore worthwhile knowing. They alone are objects of causal explanation.[174]

Did Bulgarian (or for that matter Serbian or Italian) social democracy change the general drift into "patriotism"? No, it didn't. So, the standard narrative of socialism having failed and having caved in before the more powerful ideology is not necessarily incorrect. What the corrective of a close reading does, of zooming in from the smooth generalized account into the complexity of detail, is not to change the relative significance (or non-significance) of the outliers: that depends on the "presuppositions" of the researcher. What it does do, is *transform* the sweeping and, by necessity, reductive narrative that has excised the "periphery." I want to insist on the transformative quality, not simply on recovering subaltern voices, salvaging "peripheral" visions, and showing the irreducible property of locality and its resistance to the flattening processes of globalization. All this makes us go back again and look, among other things, into the relationship between socialism and nationalism, rework the generalized and generalizing statements, and look at existing alternatives.

Besides, significance is fickle. Just a reminder: in 1998, Zbigniew Brzezinski gave an interview to the *Nouvel Observateur*, in which he revealed that the CIA had coaxed the Russians into invading Afghanistan by starting a secret operation in the country six months earlier. When asked whether he had any regrets over giving support to Islamic fundamentalism, he responded: "Regret what? That secret operation was an excellent idea. It had the effect of *drawing the Russians into the Afghan trap* and you want me to regret it? . . . What is more important in world history? The Taliban or the collapse of the Soviet empire? Some agitated Moslems or the liberation of Central Europe and the end of the cold war?"[175]

Eugen Weber may have been right in asserting that "history is the tale of what happened, not of what might have happened; and that does a great deal to narrow our field."[176] But what do we do when it actually happened, and we choose not to write about it, because we decide that it is not "representative" or "typical" or "significant"? By excising these parts, we pay a price both epistemologically and ethically. To borrow from the philosophy of language, Saul Kripke distinguishes between rigid and non-rigid designators, and that allows us to think of our actual world as just one of many possible worlds. A rigid designator inflexibly connects to the same referent in all possible worlds. The classical example is "the square root of 4" referring to 2 in all possible worlds.[177] But, if we say, "the winner in the contest between different ideologies on the eve of the First World War was nationalism," this is a non-rigid designator, because nothing about this victory is necessarily true; linguistically, there are possible worlds in which it could have been otherwise, not simply by reversing the equation and making internationalism the winner. The *winner*'s connection to nationalism is pliable and can be attached to other referents. Ironically, in real history such worlds actually did exist, as this text emphasizes, even if they were in a minority.

We should be thinking of the International (and socialism at large) as an intersection in time, where different outlooks meet, held together by a shared worldview, a polyphonic contrapuntal chorale. It is only normal (and sometimes inbuilt) that we hear a dominant voice —it may even have a solo part—but the other voices make a difference. Do they change the basic melody? Hardly. But they change the rhythm, the harmony, and how we hear it, and the difference is that between a Gregorian chant and Bach.

Part II

Generations

Generalization is necessary to the advancement of knowledge; but particularity is indispensable to the creations of the imagination. In proportion as men know more and think more they look less at individuals and more at classes. They therefore make better theories and worse poems.

Thomas B. Macaulay

Evils which are patiently endured when they seem inevitable, become intolerable when once the idea of escape from them is suggested.

Alexis de Tocqueville

"Young" and "old" were monikers inherited from the Bulgarian national-liberation movement of the 1860s–70s when they were used to characterize the adherents of an armed revolutionary struggle against the supporters of a gradualist opposition to the Ottoman Porte focused on the enlightenment of the nation. If there was some demographic truth to it, it was definitely not absolute. Many of the "young" were old, just as many, if not most, of the "old" were young. After independence, this nomenclature remained only in history books and fiction, while their followers formed the first two political parties. The Liberals dominated the political scene during the 1880s as advocates of broad democratic rights and a parliamentary regime and, as a whole, were recruited from among the "young," and the Conservatives championed a centralized monarchy and came from the wealthy elites and upper clergy, linked to the "old." In the late 1880s and 1890s, these parties disintegrated into several new political formations, often with porous boundaries and involved in coalition governments. The passionate opposition between so-called Russophiles and Russophobes that dominated Bulgarian politics (virtually until today) was linked to different visions of Bulgaria's international standing and foreign policy and cannot be neatly delineated as strictly corresponding to the political divisions. The point is that "young" and "old" during the half-century after independence remained only a historical classification, no longer used as a living political taxonomy, although it was employed effectively in the programmatic book of Bulgarian modernism *Young and Old* (1907).[1]

When in the early 1920s a bitter debate started within the newly created (or renamed) Communist Party, it revived the opposition between "old" and "young." Already at the First inaugural congress in 1919, a group of the so-called "left communists" called on the party to abandon legal activities. Organized around the newspaper *Lich (Ray)* under the leadership of Ivan Ganchev, Ivan Klincharov, and Sider Todorov, they refused to participate in elections, advocated the creation of Soviets, and embraced armed struggle.[2] They were soon expelled from the BCP but continued their attack against Blagoev and the leadership as blind followers of the West European countries and legal forms of struggle. Blagoev and the so-called "old" responded with a vehement critique against the "narrow socialists with anarchic heads," warning against "the blindest and most uncritical following of the Russian and Hungarian Bolshevism and German Spartakism."[3] With the decimation of the party in 1923–25, the physical annihilation, and emigration of thousands, the underground BCP passed entirely into the hands of the ultra-left who declared the Blagoev party as opportunistic and demanded that "Narrow socialism" be uprooted. Only with the rise of Georgi Dimitrov in the *Comintern* and the adoption of the Popular Front strategy were the "left sectarians" removed from the leadership after 1935–36.[4]

The use of "old" versus "young" introduces implicitly the notion of generations, although not literally. In the Bulgarian context, generation (поколение) was not used in the dramatic fashion in which it was employed in Russia where it was a powerful operative term. As Stephen Lovell convincingly argues in his fascinating article, the Russian generational rebellion of the mid-nineteenth century "has been frequently cited as the first of its kind anywhere in Europe" and Russian intellectuals "all found in the generational concept a powerful source of self-definition—more powerful than class, culture, or nationality."[5] In Bulgaria in the nineteenth century, "поколение" was employed mostly in its biological/genealogical sense and rarely as an emic designation of a political or cultural group, as a preferred collective distinction over other qualifiers. It was later used, indeed, to define two literary generations, the so-called September generation of writers shocked by the bloody quashing of the 1923 uprising, many of whom themselves were murdered then and in the subsequent years, and the April generation of writers in what was defined as the literary thaw of post-Stalinism after 1956, alongside some retrospective ascriptive designations of a "revolutionary generation" in different time-periods.

Generational awareness has been known since antiquity and the term generation is so common in everyday speech, yet also so elastic and difficult to specify, that some have attempted to disqualify it altogether as a heuristic scholarly category. Yet, it is widely employed in academia and productively theorized in the past two centuries, although in a variety of meanings and with different weights in separate disciplinarian traditions.[6] It is "a basic unit of social reproduction and social change—in other words, of stability over time as well as renewal (or sometimes revolution)."[7] It is widely recognized as a basic building block of social structure, alongside social class, ethnicity, race, and gender.[8] It is also equally inflected by these other categories; clearly the members of the same age group but with differing class provenance or gender will have different characteristics, consciousness, and behavior.[9] Like gender, age is a cultural construct and a system of power relationships but compared to gender, it is more malleable and fluid, its variations are wider and it does not define individual identity in such an encompassing way.[10] Just like class that happens, gender that needs doing, nations that are imagined communities, "historical generations need the same sort of treatment as other claims of collective identity which they cut across in particular circumstances and for particular purposes."[11]

Generally, there are two different connotations to the concept, one in a biological-genealogical sense with an emphasis on reproduction and continuity, the other in a historical one, with an emphasis on change and discontinuity.[12] The first pertains mostly to family history in the sense of lineage and the calendrical use of age, and some authors insist that this should be the only proper employment of the concept.[13] In its different use over the ages, generation has been measured at a broad quantitative array serving a variety of purposes, from three years (in modern demographic studies), to fifteen years (Ortega y Gasset, the stages of life perspective), to thirty-three years (Herodotus).[14] As mentioned, it has different articulations but mostly around biological reproduction, kinship, and socialization within the family. It is used in genealogies descriptively and legally, but also as an economic factor, securing social continuity and progress.[15] In both family history and, especially, in historical demography with its operation of mass data and quantitative analysis, the notion of cohort is of central significance, mostly as some kind of age cohort (birth, age, marriage, fertility) but also cohorts with any other demographic characteristics (professional profile, property transfer, disease).[16]

The other connotation, in terms of a social generation in history, without discounting the significance of age-groups, adopts as its main criterion the common historical context, lifestyle, and experience. In the revolutionary nineteenth century, generation became a category of intellectual and political history, harnessed to explain the sweeping changes that occurred in society, and the concept of generation was focused on intellectual and political history, so that by the end of the century it had acquired mostly a political–cultural sense. Research agendas were mostly directed to conflict, traumatic ruptures, and the disproportionate study of youth in contrast to historical family studies with their interest in the gradual change of relatively stable structures and an emphasis on old age.[17] There also exists a serviceable distinction between political, economic, and cultural generation introduced by Mark Szydlik.[18] Political generation has been differently defined as a "politically distinctive age group delimited by their years of birth or some major political event, such as their years of entry into the electorate," "a group of human beings who have undergone the same basic historical experience during their formative years," or "an age group in history that mobilizes to work for a political change" but could work also for the status quo.[19] Research on the German working-class movement has introduced an additional typology based on the central figure in a generation; thus one speaks of "generation Bebel," "generation Ebert," and so on, even as the opposition between "young" and "old" existed from the very beginnings of the movement.[20] There is also a tendency to overcome the dichotomy between the concepts of social and family generation. After all, generation implies relations in time: "Whether we think of intergenerational links within families or across historical periods, generation is about connections and contrasts—and often conflicts—in a temporal perspective."[21] Fruitful in this respect is the input from cultural history, especially memory studies, and interfamilial and intergenerational dialogue.[22]

While all surveys on generation begin with and profess the continuing relevance of the generational theory of Mannheim, they often misrepresent his sophisticated distinctions and usually pay lip-service merely to his most general definition: "The social phenomenon 'generation' represents nothing more than a particular kind of identity of location, embracing related 'age groups' embedded in a historical-social process."[23] Mannheim himself warned that if we speak simply of generations without any further differentiation, "we risk jumbling together purely biological phenomena and others which are the product of social and cultural forces: thus we arrive at a sort of sociology of chronological tables (*Geschichtstabellensoziologie*), which uses its bird's-eye perspective to 'discover' fictitious generation movements to correspond to the crucial turning-points in historical chronology."[24] He introduced several other notions that help refine the concept of generation. Basing himself on Wilhelm Dilthey, he first spoke of interior time and contemporaneity which cannot be measured but can be experienced and expressed only in qualitative terms:

> The same dominant influences deriving from the prevailing intellectual, social, and political circumstances are experienced by contemporary individuals, both in their early, formative, and in their later years. They are contemporaries, they constitute one generation, just because they are subject to common influences. This idea that, from the point of view of the history of ideas, contemporaneity means a state of being subjected to similar influences rather than a mere chronological datum, shifts the discussion from a plane on which it risked degenerating into a kind of arithmetical mysticism to the sphere of interior time which can be grasped by intuitive understanding. . . . The time-interval separating generations becomes subjectively experienceable time; and contemporaneity becomes a subjective condition of having been submitted to the same determining influences.[25]

Secondly, Mannheim distinguished generation from what he called concrete groups that are based on physical proximity and community of life, where he names the family, tribe, sect, and organizations for specific purposes. A generation, like class, is not a concrete group. Although its members are bound in certain ways, they do not need the concreteness of the link. He considered them location groups, where class position is determined by the existing economic and power structures, and generational location depends on the biological rhythm, "by the way in which certain patterns of experience and thought tend to be brought into existence by the natural data of the transition from one generation to another."[26] They create "a link between spatially separated individuals who may never come into personal contact at all."[27] Mannheim here anticipated the notion of imagined communities avant la lettre.

In addition, generation is not merely immersed in the cultural process, it is a continuous process itself. Each newborn individual comes into contact with the accumulated heritage handed down by its predecessors who gradually withdraw. In the course of this contact some features of the heritage are lost, while others are retained and reevaluated, thus securing the flow of social rejuvenation and creative transmission of the accumulated heritage. Mannheim especially warned against a mechanistic tendency to correlate biological factors (youth/age) to intellectual and political orientation, for example positing that youth is automatically progressive. At the same time, Mannheim stressed the formative period of youth. While both older and younger generations can experience a certain historical process together, they do not share the same generation location, something that is explained by the notion of stratification of experience (*Erlebnisschichtung*). There is an inner dialectic in the way consciousness is formed by experience, from the decisive first impressions, to later second, third, fourth, and other strata:

> [I]n estimating the biographical significance of a particular experience, it is important to know whether it is undergone by an individual as a decisive childhood experience, or later in life, superimposed upon other and early impressions of the world. Early impressions tend to coalesce into a natural view of the world. All later experiences tend to receive their meaning from this original set, whether they appear as that set's verification and fulfilment or as its negation and antithesis. Experiences are not accumulated in the course of a lifetime through a process of summation or agglomeration but are dialectically articulated.[28]

For Mannheim "the possibility of really questioning and reflecting on things only emerges at the point where personal experimentation with life begins—round about the age of 17, sometimes a little earlier and sometimes a little later."[29] Of utmost importance is the distinction that Mannheim made between "generation as actuality" and "generation-unit." Taking the example of the post-1800 German youth, he pointed out that while belonging to the same actual generation, the romantic-conservative and liberal-rationalist youth comprised two polar responses to the same historical stimulus. He therefore concluded that the generation-unit represented a much more concrete bond than the actual generation as such: "Youth experiencing the same concrete historical problems may be said to be part of the same actual generation; while those groups within the same actual generation which work up the material of their common experiences in different specific ways, constitute separate generation-units."[30] Within the same "generation as actuality" there can exist, thus, a number of different, including antagonistic, generation-units.

While not a concrete group itself, the generation-unit does have a concrete group as its nucleus which has formulated the basic new conceptions that are subsequently appropriated and developed by the unit. Often these new attitudes can be formed and practiced by older people isolated in their own generation (forerunners) just like the forerunners of a particular class ideology can belong to an alien class.[31] Mannheim also adopted but creatively reworked two further concepts, entelechy and *Zeitgeist*, mostly based on the work of the art historian Wilhelm Pinder, that subsequently have fallen out of favor in academia because of their broad misuse and Pinder's own Nazi involvement. Entelechy is the actualization of a potentiality, the expression of the "inner aim" of experiencing life and the world in a generation. Yet, not every generation location or age group creates new collective impulses or formative principles; this seems to be connected to the tempo of social change:

> When as a result of an acceleration in the tempo of social and cultural transformation basic attitudes must change so quickly that the latent, continuous adaptation and modification of traditional patterns of experience, thought, and expression is no longer possible, then the various new phases of experience are consolidated somewhere, forming a clearly distinguishable new impulse, and a new center of configuration. We speak in such cases of the formation of a new generation style, or of a new generation entelechy.[32]

The Zeitgeist, the "spirit of an epoch" or the "mentality of a period," is not an organic unity and does not pervade the whole society:

> The mentality which is commonly attributed to an epoch has its proper seat in one (homogeneous or heterogeneous) social group which acquires special significance at a particular time and is thus able to put its own intellectual stamp on all the other groups without either destroying or absorbing them.[33]

If Zeitgeist as a unitary category is to make sense, this is possible only if it is seen as a dynamic-antinomical unity of an epoch in which polar opposites interpret their world in terms of one another, in their different attempts to master the same destiny and solve the same social and intellectual challenges. The spirit of the age would thus be the "outcome of the dynamic interaction of actual generations succeeding one another in a continuous series."[34]

A further terminological clarification is needed, concerning the category "cohort" mentioned earlier. Mannheim himself did not use it, but it is often employed as a synonym for social generation, above all in American social science.[35] Thus Tamara Hareven keeps "generation" strictly for the realm of kinship, whereas cohort is a specific age group with a common historical experience.[36] This is not the case elsewhere, where "cohort" is understood as simply aggregates of individuals born at the same time. Cohort in this case is mostly a technical tool used primarily in mass data, especially computerized storing, to describe distinctive birth groups, usually in ten-year, but also in smaller (three-, four-, eight-year) or larger (twenty-five-, thirty-year) categories.[37]

In this book I am dealing with social generation, mostly in its political hypostasis. Of course, one could have avoided this lengthy excursus on generational theory and simply spoken of ideological groups or political communities, constellations, organizations, or parties, but for the analysis I want to offer, generation has a superior heuristic value over other categories.[38] Not only does it allow to better emphasize and visualize the group transformations over time, but it was also used as a self-description, even if not exclusively. And I definitely do not want to substitute it for class analysis, aware of Jürgen Kocka's quip: "After ceasing to think of class structure, we have begun to divide society into generations."[39]

I posit the existence of two large political generations in the "space-time" within which I work. The first encompasses people socialized in the first several decades of the de facto independent Bulgarian state after 1878. What characterized the political atmosphere of these decades, despite the existing socioeconomic conflicts, bitter political animosities and reprisals, and dictatorial encroachments on democracy, was the fact of a peaceful existence and an intense political life dominated by a general feeling of the possibility for progress within an imperfect but still functioning parliamentary institutional system.

The other political generation was the one formed in its adolescence and youth by the experience of the wars of the early twentieth century: the Balkan Wars and the First World War. It has been widely accepted that especially in Europe the Great War served as a radical break in mentality and behavior between the prewar political generation and the ones coming of age during the interwar period, without the experience of the prewar peacetime political scene.[40] This was amplified by the example of the Bolshevik Revolution in Russia and the experience of the de facto civil war in Bulgaria after 1923. Large segments of this generation were impatient with and disappointed by the parliamentary institutions and in the interwar period were radicalized so as to advocate and impose right-wing dictatorships, or monarchical authoritarian rule (from the right), or revolution and proletarian dictatorship (from the left).

Obviously both these political generations consisted of different generation-units, often hostile, spanning the whole ideological spectrum from right to left. Here I focus on the ones espousing leftist, mostly socialist, ideas. For convenience, I have selected 1900 as a conditional boundary between the two consecutive leftist political generation-units. Individuals born before 1900 were as a whole already mature followers of the socialist idea by the First World War in which most of them participated, and they were socialized within a limited and often repressive but still existing parliamentary system in which they forwarded their views and organized their struggle. While this generation consisted of, stricto sensu, several demographic age cohorts, it comprised a single political generation-unit, from the founders, born in the mid-nineteenth century to the ones born before the turn of the century. It was comprised of several, often bitterly bickering, but interweaving factions whose members often crisscrossed. Taking cue from the abovementioned work on the German working-class movement, one can tentatively speak of a "Blagoev" generation in a broader sense, not simply confined to the Narrows, but encompassing all socialists in this period. The funeral of Blagoev on May 9, 1924, two days after his death, began with an imposing procession of over 50,000 people in a city of about 200,000,[41] and was honored by his political rivals. Despite the inner divisions and often uncompromising fights and mutual incriminations, there were many more connections that held them together in an interwoven texture, in a "we-stratum" (Wir-Schicht) which operated as a differentiator from other, larger "we-strata" in the nation and humanity.[42]

This socialist "we-stratum" also included the second generation-unit which, despite a different generational self-understanding, belonged to the same general ideological configuration. It serves as a foil to the first, and comprises individuals born between 1900 and 1930. They are no longer a "Blagoev" generation and for lack of a better label, one can name them "the Bolshevized generation." Another option would have been to select 1891 as a provisional boundary, so that it would cover the twenty-one-year-olds (the age of military service), deployed during the Balkan Wars in 1912. But this is as mechanical as 1900. And, indeed, the most important rupture was 1917–1918, the Bolshevik revolution, Bulgaria's defeat in the war, and the subsequent soldiers' Radomir rebellion (Владайско or Войнишко въстание). The year 1900 is obviously an arbitrary, but not illogical, choice; it comprises the age cohort in the last decade of the nineteenth century, which is in many ways a transitional one and the database can reflect the generational "radicalization." It is this second generation that was radicalized by the wars, impatient, militant, and eager to emulate the Russian Revolution. They were the ones that took over the leadership of the socialist movement by the mid-1920s and effectuated what is known as its bolshevization. This generational shift was not only a local peculiarity: it happened elsewhere, for Great Britain described "that generational displacement which was part of what bolshevization represented, occurring at a moment of extravagant and sometimes brutal disregard for the movement's traditions and its older layer of activists."[43] As already pointed out, this "war generation" shifted its allegiances from its own avant-garde (socialized in the prewar arrangements) toward the new prophetic avant-garde of the Bolshevik revolution.

3

The Prosopography of the Bulgarian Socialist Left

The Database

All available material for these generations that can be harnessed for prosopographical analysis has been assembled from the existing encyclopedias, biographical dictionaries, published documentary sources, published and unpublished memoirs, archival documentation, and historical monographs. These include the two multivolume Bulgarian encyclopedias published from the 1960s to the 1990s: *Кратка българска енциклопедия* (five volumes, София: БАН, 1963–69) and *Енциклопедия "България"* (seven volumes, София: БАН, 1878–1996).[1] Usually people who have been entered in encyclopedias are considered "reputational elites." In this case, I am not treating them as such, because in their effort to increase the representation of leftists, principally of members of the BCP, the compilers had erred in the direction of very broad inclusion; besides, there was also pressure from contemporaries to be recognized and included. In addition, these were supplemented by the two valuable handbooks of documentation and memoirs from the former Institute for the History of the Bulgarian Communist Party, today in the Central State Archive (*Пътеводител по мемоарните документи за БКП, съхранявани в Централния държавен архив*, София, 2003 and *Пътеводител по фондовете на БКП, съхранявани в Централния държавен архив*, София, 2006), as well as by the indexed seven-volume collection of documents of the central governing bodies of the BCP (*БКП. Документи на централните ръководни органи.* София: Партиздат, vols. 1–7, 1972–89). The latter publication also includes hundreds of names as delegates to one or more party congresses. These names have been omitted in the creation of the database, since they figure only as a name without any other characteristic. Interestingly, there is a broad swath of individuals who had perished in 1923–25 but had not made it into the encyclopedias. They have been recovered from the card catalog of the photo-archive of the former Museum of the Revolutionary Movement. This museum was closed and physically wiped out, but the card catalog was luckily rescued and is today in the basement storage of the National Historical Museum.[2] The only reason I can think of for why these individuals were not included in the encyclopedias is lack of coordination and the fact that most of the omitted ones were from the "provinces."[3] Finally, the list was augmented by names mentioned in personal memoirs, and archival or secondary sources, whenever they had enough biographical data to allow prosopographical comparison.

For this project, I am analyzing in greater depth the first generation-unit (the cohorts born between the 1850s and 1900). The database encompasses comparable data for about 3,500 individuals who were part of or close to the socialist movement. These include, first and foremost, self-defined social democrats of different, often passionately opposed factions, but also some anarchists, *narodniks*,[4] left-wing agrarians, members of different nationalist organizations, most notoriously the Macedonian. In general, however, social democrats of both ilk dominated the left. Until 1903 they were united, after which there was rather intensive flow from one formation to the other and back. The names of agrarians in the database are numerically few and in no way representative, because while some began as early socialists—most notably Tsanko Tserkovski[5]—by the turn of the century the newly created BANU harnessed the countryside politically. Mostly, these names come from socialist sources about individuals who fought and were killed in 1923. The IMRO members are more numerous and they all belong to the Macedonian left, some with double affiliations to the socialist parties. Others, like anarchists or *narodniks*, are represented only randomly, although by exceptional individuals. Thus, while my ambition was to create a database of the "left" broadly speaking, a meaningful analysis is possible only for the socialists whose representation in the database is fairly comprehensive.

The list is strongly biased in the direction of Narrow socialists and communists, given the publication period of the sources from which it was compiled. This bias, however, does not distort other characteristics, such as places and type of education and occupation, especially for the earlier cohort, as will be argued below. Had the broad socialists been equally represented, the numbers would have been increased by at least a third because, at the time of the split in 1903, Narrows and Broads had an almost equal following: the membership in the Broad party, 1,210 in 1904, grew to just over 3,000 in 1912; the Narrows were 1,195 in 1904 and by 1912 had reached 2,923.[6] The Trade Unions they created also had, at first, comparable membership: 1,500 in the General Federation of Trade Unions (GFTU) against the 1,200 in the Broad Free Trade Union Federation (FTUF) in 1904; but the Narrow GFTU had seriously outnumbered the FTUF by 1915: 7,590 members against 4,900.[7] The number would not double, however, because the database reflects also the cohorts from the 1890s and the avalanche-like influx of the demobilized soldiers into the BWSDP (n.) and the BCP after the wars. Thus, the BWSDP (n.) increased its membership from 3,435 in 1915 to 22,533 in 1919 (in the May elections, already as BCP) and to 38,686 in 1920.[8] Still, while the Broad socialists had lost working-class control to the communists, the elections in August 1919 gave them 82,826 votes (13 percent) against the 118, 671 (18 percent) for the communists, together outnumbering the victorious BANU at 180,648 votes (28 percent). Altogether, these three but unfortunately quarreling left-wing parties controlled close to 60 percent of the vote in the country.[9]

In this chapter, the material is subjected to two types of analysis. The first is quantitative using the digitized data to discover possible patterns of social provenance, types and place of education, professional and political networks, and involvement in crucial events. The second is qualitative, where representative cases are singled out to illustrate these trends. In the next chapter I seek to create a narrative around the notion of formation, that is, to offer several mini-Bildunsroman(s) in an effort to bring to light the different experiences of becoming socialist. The database is wide-ranging although, as mentioned, dozens if not hundreds have been left out, either because they exist only by name or because of inevitable but not deliberate omissions. This database continues to be a work-in-progress: I find new names all the time and many have been omitted in the initial database for the calculations.[10] I still think that it is far above what Daniel Bertaux would call the point of saturation, meaning the point when a series of regularities and patterns emerge.[11]

The "Larks"

Today all are speaking of socialism and socialists, everywhere they see socialists. If someone leads a private life, does not frequent coffeehouses, seeks out books to read, he is called a socialist. If someone takes a critical view of affairs and speaks up, he is immediately declared to be a dangerous socialist. If a teacher treats his students humanely and teaches his subjects unconstrained, he is pronounced to be a disseminator of socialism. Someone does not like my views on nature, life and (physical) phenomena, my personal sympathies and antipathies; as a revenge this someone proclaims that I am a socialist.[12]

Socialists were given a number of derogatory epithets, mostly godless people, hoodlums, hooligans, ruffians, louts, drunkards, and robbers, but the sobriquet that stuck closest to the early socialists was "larks" (in Bulgarian *chuchuligi*, чучулиги). When walking through the streets, children would run after them and mock them (often throwing stones at them) with this name.[13] Filip Panaiotov, who wrote a spirited book about the early years of socialism, commented that "the venerable citizens of philistine Bulgaria were naïve to think that they offended them with this name. They were larks indeed. The new time, just like the new day, has its messengers."[14] Early socialists were, indeed, rare and exotic birds, but larks are not exotic. Not only are they one of the most widely spread birds in the world, but they were also highly praised for their melodious singing and were the object of numerous songs and folktales. In fact, "Sweetsinging lark" (Сладкопойна чучулига) is to this day one of the most popular songs in Bulgaria, as well as the name of a nationwide popular competition for children's songs. The song was written by the composer Panaiot Pipkov in 1903, with lyrics by Tsonio Kalchev, and was included in one of his operas.[15]

Most likely, *chuchuligi* was a homophone to a corrupted pronunciation of socialists, possibly combined with *chuchelo* (dummy, scarecrow). The early socialists stood apart not only by their behavior but also by their dress, especially the women among them with their short hair and long man's coats "as if coming from an alien world, in order to upset this one, grey and pedestrian like the grey ash in the streets."[16] Indeed, the socialist movement began with very modest numbers. Figure 12 gives the age cohorts of the complete list. There is data for the birthdate of 2,864 individuals. Another 599 have no date of birth indicated. The last column, comprising the ones born in the

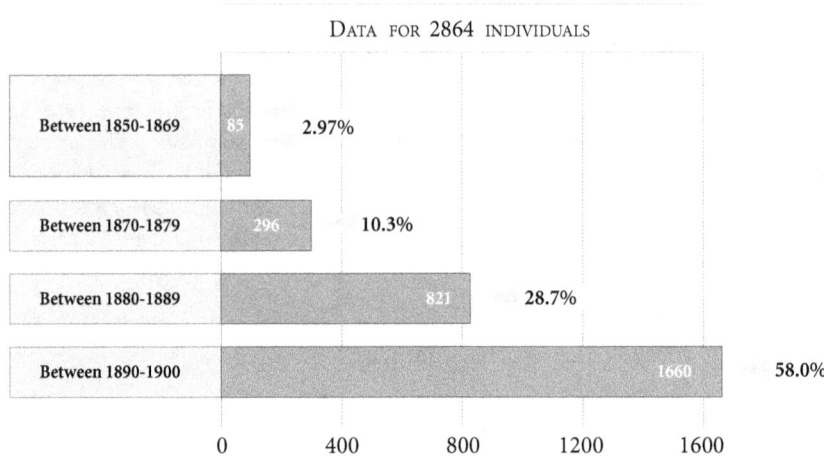

Figure 12 Cohorts by Date of Birth.

last decade, is almost two-thirds of the whole number, containing 1,662 persons, of whom 186 were born in the year 1900. The rest are distributed as follows: born in the 1850s—18; born in the 1860s—67; born in the 1870s—296; born in the 1880s—821. In the graph, the first column is presenting the two oldest cohorts, born between 1850 and 1869, 85 individuals. Clearly, there is an exponential growth in the numbers.

Even more striking are the figures about "early socialists" in the database. I have defined early socialists as those individuals for whom data exists about their socialist (including a few with *narodnik*) activity before 1903. They could be members of the BSDP (later BWSDP), delegates to a congress, or simply indicated as participants, like Iordan Kinev (1880-1904) who frequented the factory owned by his maternal uncle and was close to the workers. He became a socialist as a high school student, acted in a theater troupe, studied in Prague but came back in bad health and died of tuberculosis at the age of twenty-four.[17] Many are without an indicated date of birth but since some form of affiliation is given during the 1890s, one can safely assume that most were born in the 1870s or earlier. Others with more extensive bibliographic data, including year of birth, had been active in the movement and later would join the Narrows, the Broads, or other parties. Altogether, there are 279 individuals that form the group of "early socialists," essentially belonging to the first two columns of Figure 12. Three were born in the 1840s, eight in the 1850s, thirty-seven in the 1860s, 226 in the 1870s (of whom 127 were without date of birth, so some could have been born in the 1860s), and only five in the early 1880s.[18]

There were certainly others from the same cohort who cannot be characterized as "early socialists," such as Angelina Boneva who became an active socialist only after the turn of the century (see chapter 6) or the very attractive Bulgarian Armenian lawyer Tigran Ismian (late 1850s–1931). He had become secretary to Alexander (Aleko) Bogoridi, the Ottoman governor-general of Eastern Rumelia, and in the 1890s studied law at the Sorbonne. He opened law offices in Plovdiv where Vasil Kolarov became his partner. Not a public tribune, Ismian was a profound thinker, lecturing on political economy, history, and philosophy, and insisting on systematic education and reading. In 1919, he entered the BCP in his sixties, and was arrested twice in 1923 and 1925.[19] There were also others who were close to, but not part of, the movement, like Todor Ionchev (1859–1940), who studied chemistry in Vienna and Zurich, and became a major figure in the cooperative and gymnastic movements, and was a pioneer of the Olympic idea in Bulgaria.

We do not know much about the three oldest members born in the 1840s. One, Hadzhi Dimitîr Stoilov (1840–1927), was the first chairman of the party circle "Solidarity" in Varna. Petîr Nikolov Draganov (1844–1913?) was perhaps the most colorful among them. In his youth he had gone to Wallachia as a gardener, a frequent occupation among Bulgarian seasonal laborers. There he became a priest and joined the nationalist revolutionary committees. He was an insurgent in the famous detachments (*cheti*) of Bacho Kiro and Pop Khariton during the April Uprising of 1876, and the next year joined the Bulgarian volunteers within the Russian army. He was the one who consecrated the legendary Samara flag and fought the Ottomans at Shipka, the most famous battle of the war for Bulgarians. After the war, he joined, first, the Liberal Party but then left it and founded a socialist party organization in his village. Excommunicated from the church, often arrested, he was consecutively Broad and Narrow. The third, Trifon Bogoev, a bookbinder and founder of the Stara Zagora organization, has no birth and death dates, but was the father of two prominent later socialists: Georgi Bogoev (1863–1933), a future leader of the Broads, and Tina Kirkova (1872–1947), who was a Narrow socialist and wife of Georgi Kirkov (see Chapter 5). This and the fact that the number of people who would join either the Broads or the Narrows was not so divergent (40 and 72) leads to the conclusion that in the coverage of the early socialists the abovementioned bias in favor of the Narrows is not that acute.

The eight "early socialists" born in the 1850s can be named. They include Dimitîr Blagoev (1856–1924, see Part I and passim), Vela Blagoeva (1858–1921, see chapter 5), Spiro Gulabchev (1852–1918, see chapter 4), Teofana Popova (1856–1929, see chapter 5), Gavril Balamezov (1857–97), Todor Postompirov (1854–1940), Mikhail Boichinov (1859–1934), and Georgi Kîrdhiev (1854–1907). With the exception of Blagoev, who was the most recognized of the prewar generation of socialists and on whom there is considerable literature, including a collected edition of his works, the others are less known, if at all. Three among them (the Blagoevs and Boichinov) were Narrows and later communists; Postompirov, a teacher and the oldest delegate at the Buzludzha founding congress of the party in 1891, later withdrew from active political life but remained a dedicated socialist until his last days;[20] Teofana Popova renounced the movement altogether. The other three were *narodniks*. Both Kîrdhiev and Balamezov, who became writers and journalists, were heavily influenced by the Russian *narodniks* and Balamezov in particular was offended by Blagoev's characterization of them as reactionary. He thought they had the same goals as the social democrats and believed in close work among people for their moral upliftment.[21] Kîrdhiev later joined the Liberal Party and was an MP. Without any doubt, the most impressive figure among the *narodniks* and anarchists was Spiro Gulabchev.

"Early socialists" cannot be confined to these 279 individuals, let alone to the eight from the 1850s, nor even to the group of forty-eight born between 1840 and 1869.

Before the nationwide consolidation of socialists in the early 1890s, there were about twenty socialist societies or groups (дружинки). In his memoirs, Konstantin Bozveliev (1862–1951), one of the most attractive socialist veterans, gives the list of the twenty-eight members of the Kazanlŭk organization, one of the oldest, making the probable number of active "early socialists" around 1891 at over 500, in this case excluding most of the ones born after the mid-1870s.[22] Their "lark" period was relatively short. The limitation of democratic rights inflicted by the Stambolov regime with the revision of the constitution in late 1892 pushed the socialists (then in the BSDP) among the most active fighters for their restoration. This increased their popularity and a letter from February 6, 1893, sent to *Rabotnik* stated: "In our town Gabrovo the attitude towards the socialists is changing. It seems that the opinion changed suddenly, so that recently most everyone is saying that they wrongly judged the socialists and that the socialists are saying the truth."[23] This social acceptance also prompted the socialists to participate with their own lists in the 1893 elections.[24]

Intellectuals and Proletarians

That the social-democratic parties consisted mostly of intellectuals as self-described defenders of the interests of the proletarian class is not a retrospective assessment. The early socialists were very conscious of this and had to respond to the challenge of organizing themselves in a country that was overwhelmingly rural and where the industrial working class was incipient. In 1900 the population had reached almost 3,750,000 according to the official census (4,850,000 in 1920 and 5,400,000 in 1926), but only twenty percent were residing in urban areas that consisted overwhelmingly of small towns, with the exception of Sofia, Plovdiv, Varna, and Ruse. The divide between city and village was a constant tension and would prove decisive in the socialist debates and the ensuing split. Indeed, at the time of political independence in 1878, there were less than 2,000 industrial workers. By 1894, their number had risen to 5,732, some of them employed in 501 factories and mills. Half of them worked in textile, ceramics, and tobacco-processing factories, many more in other light industries.[25] Blagoev, who wanted to make the case for the need of a party representing the class that would inevitably grow, calculated that by 1900 there were already 276,687 workers of whom 20,250 were in the industrial sector and the rest were occupied in agriculture and the crafts.[26] Later scholars gave a more modest number for workers, 188,000 in 1900.[27] Of this hired labor, 41 percent were employed in agriculture, 19 percent were domestic servants (consisting mostly of village girls), 18 percent in crafts, 9 percent in commerce, 5 percent in transport and communications, and only 5 percent in industry.[28] It was still a staggering growth in just two decades, and by 1905 it had increased to 268,000 and to 332,000 by 1910.[29] One important conclusion is that the notion of "workers" encompassed not only the industrial proletariat but also "hired laborers" as a whole. In the whole literature, including the secondary literature after World War II, there is no analytical clarity and industrial workers, laborers, servants, proletariat, the exploited, the oppressed, the poor, the toiling masses, the working people, etc. were, and are, often used interchangeably, often subservient to the ideological point that is being made.

In 1891, under the name Bratanov, Blagoev published a small book, just over 100 pages, entitled *What is Socialism and Do We Have a Basis for It?* (*Що е социализъм и има ли той почва у нас?*), which has been characterized as the Bulgarian Communist Manifesto (Figure 13).[30] It was provoked by articles, both from the government press (most notably Zakhari Stoianov) and the Russian *narodniks* (especially Vladimir Debogory-Mokrievich and Boris Mintses) denying the basis for socialism in an egalitarian rural country like Bulgaria.[31] Analyzing the developments in the countryside and the growing industrialization, Blagoev argued for the differentiation and polarization of the old social structure: "Poverty is growing and our people are being divided in two classes: capitalists, in whose hands wealth is centralized, and the poor, in rags and hungry, in a word the proletarians, whose numbers increases by the day, and who are competing with each other so that their situation worsens even

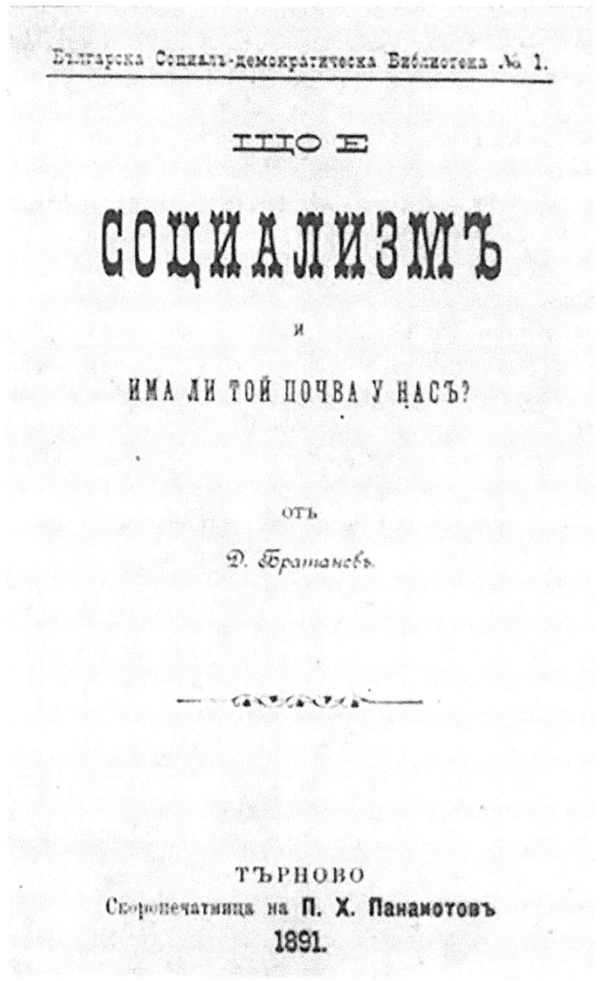

Figure 13 Blagoev's *What is Socialism and Do We Have a Basis for It?*

further."³² In 1893 Nikola Gabrovski spoke about the need to unite workers with what he called the "all oppressed" (всички угнетени) in a political party which would win parliamentary majority and eventually proclaim socialism, and this was the unanimous position of the BSDP.³³ It was unclear who exactly among the "all oppressed" would be the preferred political partners, but it was clear that "workers" were the nucleus. If they were dogmatic, they were following the dogma of Kautsky that "the task of social democracy is to support all the oppressed and exploited, not only the industrial workers. Their significance for a Marxist consists in the fact that the other toiling strata are incapable of liberating themselves without the help of the industrial workers."³⁴

It is usually the moniker "poor" (*siromakh, pl. siromasi,* сиромах/сиромаси) that encompasses the ones to whom intellectuals were devoted. Even the Bulgarian version of *narodnik* socialism was not in the name of the "people" (*narod*, hence, *narodniks*) but in the name of the "poor," hence *siromakhomilstvo* (сиромахомилство), that is, literally love for the poor, translated also as pauperophilia. Here again we see the difference from the Russian social structure where members of the privileged classes had "to go to the people" whereas in the relatively egalitarian Bulgarian society with the absence of a gentry and a small bourgeoisie, intellectuals were part of the people faced often with poverty in an increasingly destabilizing economic climate. A similar tendency was observable in Croatia, where "Workers of the world, unite!" was rendered in the sense of "Poor (i.e., proletarians) of the world unite!"³⁵ Yet, the similarities ended there. While in the last decades of the nineteenth century the Croatian socialists insisted on representing broad social strata except for the wealthy, and thus played the role of a bourgeois-democratic party in the absence of other parties, Bulgarian socialists were adamant about their class commitment to workers, understood broadly as hired labor, while privileging the emergent industrial proletariat. The social milieu in which the party would work consisted of "workers and candidates for workers, like craftsmen, peasants, petty merchants and educated people who are able to understand the drive of historical development," who are all tomorrow's proletariat.³⁶ An additional difference was the fact that workers' organizations in Croatia existed prior to the socialist movement while the situation in Bulgaria was the reverse, with one early short-lived exception of an organization of printers and typographers.³⁷

When the group around Blagoev insisted on the creation of a party, they were motivated by the desire to save the working-class movement the vacillations, errors and suffering it had experienced in other countries before the advent of workers' political parties: "it is a moral offense not to learn from the historical experience" of others.³⁸ "People's happiness depends on the solidarity of interests. When it is absent, it has to be created." The people who understand this "are usually called *intelligentsia*" but they cannot alone achieve anything in this struggle, because the power is among the workers; thus, the intelligentsia is going to unite with them.³⁹ This was a clear program of "enlightenment" and it sounded promising at the outset. With hindsight, already in 1929 Nikola Sakarov (chapter 8) and Naiden Nikolov were more critical. That the workers' movement postdated the socialist one meant that from its outset it was led by socialism: "This saved it from the many confusions typical of the early workers' movements but its extremely tight connections to the socialist party compelled it unflinchingly to follow its fate."[40] The split in 1903 also divided the workers' movement and as a result until the war both parties were small with limited influence.

The effects of the war mobilized the people and inspired by the success of the West European proletariat and especially the Russian Revolution, "these laboring masses were looking for quick revenge and the satisfaction of their immediate needs without being able to appraise the possible real achievements. With such dispositions they burst into the two socialist fractions with the ardent belief that these would ensure a new life and will preserve them from a return to their past trials."[41] Both parties committed huge errors in these circumstances. The Broads entered the government in coalition with the bourgeois parties that were compromised during the war: "Its participation in the regime in 1918-1919 turned out disastrous and disappointed the working masses. They began leaving it and, after the exit of its left wing, its influence among the workers dwindled."[42] On the other hand,

> the Narrow socialist party until the wars avoided active involvement in the political life and focused on educational and propaganda work. All of a sudden, it was forced to start political struggle on a grand scale, moreover not simply with its small but well-disciplined old cadres, but with large resentful and undisciplined masses. It was utterly unprepared for such a struggle and allowed itself to be carried along into the abyss. Renamed a Communist party, the Narrow social-democratic party joined the newly formed communist international and *nominally* [italics in the original] adopted the methods of Bolshevism. Until the September Uprising in 1923, however, it remained a social-democratic party that, in its attempt to retain the impatient masses, mostly rural and petty bourgeois, transformed its former sober educational work into an empty revolutionary demagogy, filled with impossible promises of an imminent social revolution.[43]

From the outset, there was unease in the midst of this socialist intelligentsia that they were not authentic workers and they worked unceasingly to instill class consciousness among the "real workers" and bring them into the organized movement. Both parties held meticulous statistics about their working-class membership. After the split, the BWSDP (n) started with a membership of 1,174 of whom 480 were workers (41 percent). By then, the working class had grown and there was an organized strike movement, so that working-class membership swelled and by 1907 had reached 66 percent. The figures for the Broads are comparable: in the same year 1907, their working-class membership was 65 percent.[44]

Very interesting is the breakdown of the membership of the BWSDP (b) for 1909 which they sent to the Bureau of the Socialist International. It reveals the way they classified their followers. The 2,427 are grouped in the following categories: 774 civil servants and state employees, 720 apprentices, 285 merchants, 196 members of the liberal profession (chiefly lawyers), 157 peasants, 156 master artisans, and 139 workers. These categories reflected the official state statistics at the time. Thus, the largest category of civil servants and state employees included a large proportion of railwaymen, who for all intents and purposes should belong to the category of workers, but here "workers" was clearly identified only with industrial labor. Equally, the apprentices and a large part of the merchants and artisans could be reclassified as "proletariat" in its broad meaning. The report also gives a breakdown by age. The party was young: 1,114 members were between the ages of twenty-one and twenty-five; 1,150 between twenty-six and forty; and 163 over forty.[45] So was the Narrow party: 1,647 of its members were between the ages of twenty and thirty, and only 459 over thirty.[46] On the other hand, the internal statistics of the BWSDP (n) clearly distinguished between industrial and other workers, starting with the less numerous but most cherished category. In its annual report for 1913/1914, it gave aggregate figures for its membership during the whole period from 1908 to 1914.[47] (Table 4)

Figure 14 presents a breakdown of the database by occupation. There is information for 1,576 people: 305 are teachers, 246 artisans, 233 urban workers (the seven miners have been added to this category), 197 agricultural laborers, 162 lawyers, and 157 civil servants. The rubric "others" includes fifty-eight journalists, forty-nine military personnel, forty-eight occupied in trade, thirty-four doctors and nurses, twenty-four engineers, and the rest in single digits were agronomists, writers, chemists, artists, and others. Altogether, one can group together urban and rural workers and artisans to get to the somewhat escalated figure of 676 for the "proletariat" (since part of the artisans could be middle class and educated) and the rest, with the possible exception of the forty-eight who were involved in commerce, can be termed "intelligentsia," but with them they would all comprise the educated class, 900 of them. These figures correspond to the ratios from the party statistics.

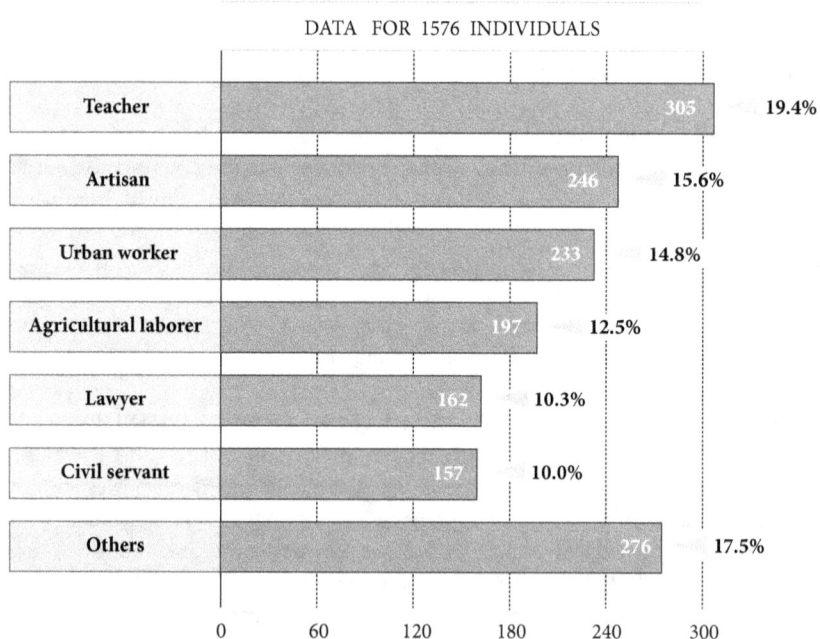

Figure 14 Bulgarian Socialists by Occupation.

Table 4 Membership in the BWSDP (Narrow)

Year	Total	Industrial workers	Workers in commerce, crafts, etc.	Agricultural workers	State employees	Liberal professions	Owners
1908	1,665	257	741	12	248	48	235
1909	1,870	298	1,090	18	260	64	240
1910	2,126	316	1,171	32	273	69	265
1911	2,510	442	1,265	54	356	98	398
1912	2,923	607	1,382	67	402	110	355
1914	3,645	711	1,221	268	515	84	846

While the influx of workers was altogether a post-1905 and, especially, post-1915 phenomenon, there had been individual workers already among the "early socialists," although more as an exception. Stoian Kazandzhiev (1870–1926), a coppersmith from Kazanlŭk, was one of the first handicraft workers to become a socialist. He was twenty-one as a delegate at the Buzludzha congress and is considered one of the prototypes for Kirkov's short story heroes.[48] Another interesting case, who nominally belongs to the workers as he was a railwayman, was Nikola Penev (1879–1955), the older brother of the great literary critic Boian Penev (1882–1927). He joined the BWSDP in 1896, and then was consistently Narrow and communist. He founded the railway workers' trade union in 1904, was a member of the CC of the BCP, and member of parliament. Imprisoned in 1923, he emigrated to the USSR between 1925 and 1933. Upon his return, he was active in the trade union movement, including after 1944. Very articulate, he was regularly writing in the press and left intelligent memoirs.[49]

The figure that stands out among the workers is, without any doubt, Georgi Mikhailov Dimitrov (1882–1949), the future leader of the Comintern and prime minister of Bulgaria after World War II. This is perhaps the one Bulgarian name that is internationally widely known because of Dimitrov's heroic conduct at the Leipzig trial in 1933. There is a vast literature on him and for this reason in this work he is mentioned in passim, not proportionate to his historical significance, which anyway lies in the period following the span of this book.[50] Suffice it to say that in the period before the wars, Dimitrov was a central figure of the trade union movement. A tireless organizer, he was the secretary-treasurer of the GFTU between 1909 and 1923, besides being a member of the CC of the BWSDP (n). A self-taught man, Dimitrov had become a typesetter, joining "the ranks of the quasi-intelligentsia" in the patronizing locution of Rothschild.[51] In fact, the journalist Petko Velichkov, who was editing the newspaper *The Workers Printer* (Работнически печатар) was impressed by Dimitrov's first contribution, which he thought was written by an intellectual not a worker.[52] In 1913, Dimitrov became the first worker elected in any Balkan parliament.[53]

The tension that was felt in the attempts of both parties to increase the numbers of workers was real and it also reflected relationships between intellectuals and workers that were not necessarily harmonious. These were, of course, carefully hushed up, but they crop up in some of the archival memoirs. Stoian Dzhorov (1878–1950), born in a village in the region of Ikhtiman near Sofia, entered the party in 1901 and then joined the Narrows. As a worker in Varna, he organized the workers' opposition in the party organization in a bitter anti-intellectual campaign protesting the perceived privileging of intellectuals as delegates to the party congress in 1903 and was instrumental in the removal of Anna Stefanova, the only woman secretary of a party organization at the time (see Chapter 5). This can be recovered from the memoirs of Koika Tineva (see Chapters 5 and 8) who, while critical of Dzhorov for his petulant and undisciplined character, was adamant about his unflinching devotion to the workers' movement.[54] Dzhorov did not reciprocate with the same generosity in his own memoirs, where Tineva was depicted with much hostility as "overrated from above, " "picking her nails and blushing" when criticized, and turning the workers' club with her cultural activities into a musical salon because of her "aristocratism."[55] As is to be expected,

Figure 15 Georgi Dimitrov in 1905.

aristocratism would be the ultimate accusation in a non-aristocratic society, but given the makeup of the party at the time, it did not have dire consequences for her.

Dzhorov eventually left the Narrows and became an anarcho-liberal in 1905. In 1907, he left the country and worked in Egypt, France, and Russia. Arrested by the Tsarist police in 1910 together with Georgi Dimitrov's brother Nikola, he was exiled to Siberia. He took part in both the February and October Revolutions, and in 1918 became chair of the Central Bureau of the Bulgarian communist groups as part of the Russian Communist Party (Bolsheviks), RCP (b). He participated in the founding congress of the Comintern in 1919. In the secondary literature Dzhorov is heroicized as the main protagonist of a book describing Bulgarian participants in the Bolshevik revolution.[56] In 1920 he returned to Bulgaria as part of the Military Organization, organizing illegal armed groups.[57] He later settled in his village of Gorna Vasilitsa. In the brief biographical entry in the archival guide, as well as in his copious memoirs, the period between 1920 and 1943 is missing, when Dzhorov, already in his sixites, joined the Ikhtiman partisan detachment.[58]

Dzhorov's own memoirs are self-serving and boastful, written in an affected, even pompous, style to the point of discomfort for the reader. His motivation for writing them was to put down what he had done during fifty years for "the great cause of the working class and laboring humanity."[59] He had been accused of being a Trotskyite so he wanted to set the record straight. This did not prevent him from approaching Koika Tineva after her return from the USSR in 1946, presenting himself as a follower of her uncle Rakovski and Trotsky. After she rebuffed his attempts at closeness, he started spreading rumors against her and Rakovski, who was still considered "an enemy of the people."[60] He also left scores of unpublished poems, short stories, and essays whose quality, unfortunately, hardly allows them to be elevated to the rank of the "proletarian imagination," aptly described by Mark Steinberg.[61] Despite his profound enmity against intellectuals, he was someone who fancied himself as one. While his case exemplifies the ambivalent relationship between proletarians and intellectuals, it should not be generalized to other workers. Stefan Bîchvarov (1888–1969), another working-class communist, a typographer, had also been in Varna in 1905 and had only positive comments about Tineva, referring to Dzhorov as frivolous and a prattler.[62] The tension between the two groups was not because they came from different milieus. The main difference was education. In many cases, of course, poverty prevented further education, but it was not a prohibitive hindrance. A poor or modest family background was typical for most socialist intellectuals. One of the most hotly debated issues in the first decade of the twentieth century was whether teachers and the intelligentsia as a whole belonged to the proletariat or to the petty bourgeoisie.[63]

The Education of the Intelligentsia

The place of intellectuals as a social group was a question that bothered not only Bulgarian socialists and it has remained an open question until today. Some of the most insightful socialist thinking came in the interwar period. Gramsci asked in his *Prison Notebooks*: "Are intellectuals an autonomous and independent social group, or does every social group have its own particular specialized category of intellectuals? The problem is a complex one."[64] He objected to the stark opposition between physical and mental labor, between *homo faber* and *homo sapiens*, noting that there is a minimum of creative intellectual activity even in the most degraded and mechanical physical work, and famously concluded that non-intellectuals do not exist: "All men are intellectuals, one could therefore say: but not all men have in society the function of intellectuals."[65] For Gramsci, intellectuals cannot be understood as a distinct social category outside of class, every class produces its own "organic" intellectuals, and he was arguing for the development of "organic" intellectuals coming out of and belonging to the working class.

Class theory, beginning with Marx and continuing to this day, is one of the main traditions that inform the sociological understanding of intellectuals. The classlessness thesis, first elaborated by Karl Mannheim and having illustrious proponents like Talcott Parsons among others, forms another powerful tradition. Today, critical of the class theory that tends to dismiss or downplay the ideological heterogeneity of intellectuals and of the classlessness theory which allegedly tends to minimize the social significance on the shaping of ideas, it is network theory that has become dominant, reflecting the influence of Pierre Bourdieu, Randall Collins, and Robert Brym.[66] Still, it is useful to listen again to Mannheim who asserted that intellectual activity in the modern period "is not carried on exclusively by a socially rigidly defined class, such as a priesthood, but rather by a social stratum which is to a large degree unattached to any social class and which is recruited from an increasingly inclusive area of social life."[67] Mannheim was careful not to dismiss status and class and warned that intellectuals are not "suspended in a vacuum into which social interests do not penetrate"; on the contrary, they are shaped by them and the more complex a society and the more classes and strata from which they are recruited, the greater the "multiformity and contrast in the tendencies operating on the intellectual level."[68] Despite its heterogeneity, the bond that brings this stratum together, even if in antagonistic relations, is education:

> Although they are too differentiated to be regarded as a single class, there is, however, one unifying sociological bond between all groups of intellectuals, namely, education, which binds them together in a striking way. Participation in a common educational heritage progressively tends to suppress differences of birth, status, profession, and wealth, and to unite the individual educated people on the basis of the education they have received.[69]

One of the defining features of the intelligentsia, according to Mannheim, was its ability to attach itself to classes to which it did not originally belong, because of its capacity to think in a totality, to take into consideration every point of view, and because it was in a position to choose this affiliation, a luxury that other groups bound by class affiliations rarely possessed: "This voluntary decision to join in the political struggles of a certain class did indeed unite them with the particular class during the struggle, but it did not free them from the distrust of the original members of that class."[70]

In the relatively egalitarian Bulgarian society of the nineteenth century but especially in the more dynamic atmosphere in the newly created and modernizing state at the turn of the century, education was a most valued cultural capital and the principal meritocratic means for advancement. Bulgaria came out of the Ottoman framework as an overwhelmingly peasant society, poor but not entirely impoverished, with very few landless peasant households. At the same time, it did not have a wealthy landowning class. As a rule, and with few exceptions, large estates were not typical for the Balkans. The large estates that existed in Bulgaria were in Muslim hands, and after the emigration of tens of thousands of Muslim landowners after the Russo-Turkish war of 1877–78, their land was seized, distributed, confiscated, or bought by Bulgarians.[71] The social profile of the Bulgarian countryside was made up of petty and middling landowners. The roughly 15 percent urban population at mid-century, with the exception of three or four larger cities, lived in semi-agrarian towns, and the contrast, let alone abyss, between city and village set in only a few decades later, by the turn of the century. The

Table 5 Education of members of the BWSDR (Narrow)

Year	Total	Elementary education	Middle school	High school	University
1908	1,665	823	581	224	37
1909	1,870	1,075	552	234	39
1910	2,126	1,311	584	285	46
1911	2,510	1,468	648	302	78
1912	2,923	1,562	931	345	85
1914	3,645	1,826	1,143	429	117

thin layer of a relatively wealthy commercial and incipient industrial elite as well as the newly formed state bureaucracy was removed, if at all, only one generation from its peasant roots. Education was considered by the educated strata as one of the most important modernizing tools and was valued by the uneducated or semi-educated as the most important instrument for upward social mobility.

Education has not been regularly recorded in the biographical information of the database. There are only 660 individuals with a definite record and of them 541 acquired a university education (including thirteen with a dissertation and one in a "semi-high" institution), ninety-six went to high school, five to secondary school, sixteen had elementary education, and two were self-taught. There is a clear bias in the direction of university education. More reliable figures come from the yearly reports of the social-democratic parties. Table 5 presents the figures for BWSDR (n).[72] The numbers for the Broads are comparable: in 1909 there were 102 members with a university education, 645 had completed high school, 638 primary school, and ten were illiterate.[73]

Where the database is indispensable is in giving a breakdown of the fields of university study. These are called "specialization" in the database and given that students changed their fields or were educated in several, they have been entered as first, second, and third specialization. Of the total of 541 people with university education, "law" was indicated as the first specialization of 251 individuals, nine had it as their second specialization, and another two as their third specialization, 262 altogether. There were forty medical students and thirty-two engineers (twenty-nine as a first specialization and another three as a second specialty). There were thirty-eight people who received military education, ten individuals who studied history, five pedagogy, and fourteen studied unspecified "social and natural sciences." We do not know the specialty of sixty-two individuals. In terms of a possible correlation between age and higher education, the results are balanced and correspond to the relative share of the age cohorts. If we group together every other discipline except law (217 people), the overwhelming proportion of lawyers is obvious (Figure 16).

What explains this preference for law? There is an explicit description in one of the memoirs that is worth citing in extenso:

> Once the party started its broad propaganda and political work and the government began to persecute socialists, teachers and other state employees began to retreat and were no longer active as leading figures. These then became the professional

The Prosopography of the Bulgarian Socialist Left   103

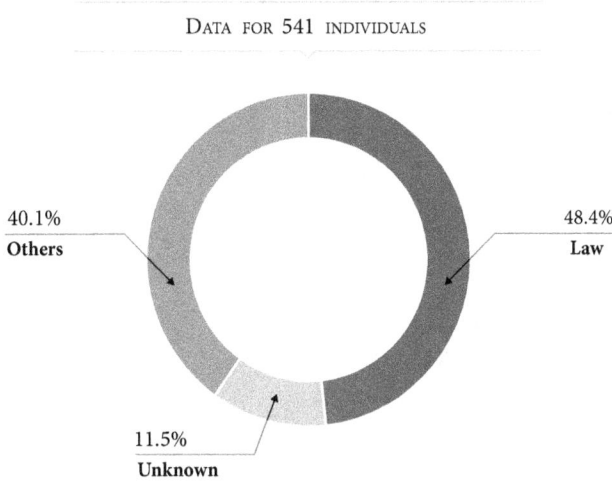

Figure 16 Bulgarian Socialists by Specialization in Higher Education.

revolutionaries, intellectuals in and around the party leadership: members of the Central Committee, editors of newspapers and journals, etc. Alongside this small number of the leading core of the socialist movement, there was another group of intellectuals, much more numerous, constantly growing and scattered over all the big cities in the country, the lawyers. The law profession is independent, i.e. it is materially independent from the direct control of the state. Lawyers cannot be fired. They can be deprived of their rights only under exceptional circumstances anticipated in the law. This guaranteed lawyers not only their material existence but allowed them to undertake social and specifically political work. . . . Every idealist intellectual (идеалист интелигент) who in the past desired to devote himself to social work, wanted to study law and become a lawyer. This naturally did not mean that only idealists became lawyers. Many bourgeois politicians and political careerists chose this path. This field offered favorable conditions to all kinds of speculators who manipulated the ignorance of the people. It is not by chance that lawyers in general were held in low esteem among the people.[74]

Angelov, himself a lawyer, adds that the group of dedicated socialist lawyers was constantly growing, and they were trained either in the student group attached to the party in Sofia or in the socialist student groups abroad, primarily in Geneva.[75] This latter remark leads us to consider the places of higher education for Bulgarians in this period. Of the 412 socialist individuals with explicit information about the place of study, 162 received their education in Bulgaria (at the University of Sofia after 1888), seventy-seven in Switzerland, thirty-one in Russia, twenty-eight in Germany, twenty in Austria, thirteen in France, and thirty in other places (Italy, Belgium, Czechoslovakia, Serbia, the Ottoman Empire, Romania, England, and the United States). The number of fifty-one for the USSR encompasses the émigrés to the Soviet Union after the events of 1923–25. What is striking is that the numbers for Russia—thirty-one—pale compared

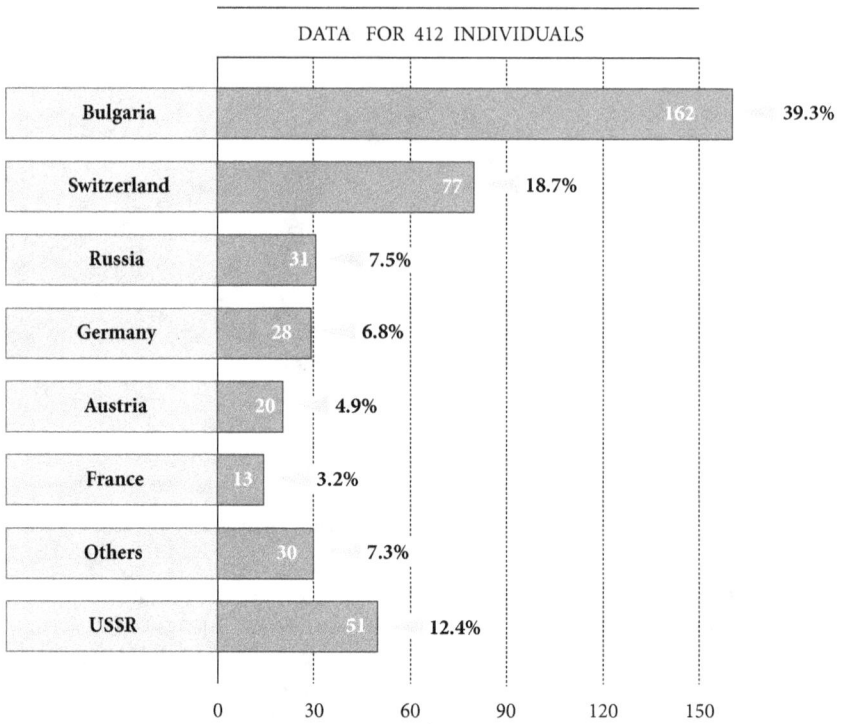

Figure 17 Higher Education of Bulgarian Socialists by Location.

to the aggregate number of students who studied in West European universities (Switzerland, Germany, Austria, and France)—138 or 168 if we add the rubric "others," a number which is higher than even the number of students matriculating in Bulgaria. In any case, Figure 17 puts to rest the theory of the exclusive Russian educational formation of socialists, which was already addressed in Part I, without in any way denying the immense role of the personal and cultural ties to Russia.

This downscaling of Russia was, however, a new phenomenon. In his excellent monograph on Bulgarians studying abroad, Ivan Tanchev explains this new tendency. During the 1850s and 1860s, while still Ottoman subjects, Bulgarians overwhelmingly went to Russia to receive their high school and university education, mostly supported by different charitable organizations: 627 out of the total 1,636, followed by the Ottoman Empire, Romania, Greece, and Austria-Hungary. Two-thirds of this intelligentsia studied medicine, law, and theology.[76] The preference for Russia lasted only a few years after the creation of the Bulgarian Principality. Already by the early 1880s, relations were extremely tense because of the heavy-handed and inept Russian diplomacy and the alienation of Prince Battenberg, and with the Unification of the Principality with Eastern Rumelia in 1885 that Russia opposed, they reached a breaking point. What followed during the regency and premiership of Stambolov and the reign of Ferdinand was a decade of severed diplomatic relations, when Russia lost its most faithful client state in the Balkans to the point that politically Bulgaria fought in the anti-Russian camps in the two World Wars despite a general positive attitude toward Russian culture.

During this period Bulgaria followed a pro-Western policy and students were sent on state-supported fellowships primarily to Austria-Hungary (the universities of Vienna, Prague, and Zagreb), but also to France, Germany, Switzerland, and Belgium.[77] It was also in this period that the issue of legalizing foreign diplomas and other educational certificates was solved.[78] Interestingly, these state-supported fellowships were mostly in the sphere of engineering and different technical fields, followed by medicine (including veterinary) and pharmacology while law ranked only third.[79] The non-state-supported students converged in Geneva, studying mostly medicine, because of the low fare and acceptance of women.[80] Very few, if any of the socialists, received state fellowships; at least, there were none in the long lists published in Tanchev's book, but these lists reach only until 1892 whereas the bulk of university socialists were born after the mid-1870s and would not be reflected there. They supported themselves with savings and family aid, most often from their working wives, like Petîr Dzhidrov who was fired from his teacher's position for his socialist ideas alongside another forty to fifty teachers in 1896. His friend Ivan Kolarov went to Berlin and persuaded his mother to assist him by selling some property, but this was not possible in Dzhidrov's case. To amass the needed 100 levs needed to sustain him very modestly in Berlin, where he studied law, friends and family came together. Three of his teacher friends supplied fifty levs, and the other fifty came from the teacher's salary of his twenty-year-old wife Maria who was left behind with a one-year-old son. When she too was fired, his further education was in jeopardy and only the lucky intervention of a family acquaintance saved her (and his) position.[81]

The Generational Rupture

The radicalization of the Bulgarian socialists came with the depravities of the wars. Before and during the wars (both Balkan Wars and the Great War), socialists of every ilk embraced the anti-militarist propaganda and worked ceaselessly for it, especially (and illegally) within the army, risking imprisonment. Especially among the younger generation, crucial was the influence of 1917, which immensely broadened the horizon of expectations almost to the point of delirium, expecting the revolution to arrive "tomorrow." What happened was that the war generation (the ones socialized during the war decade) shifted its allegiances from its own avant-garde (socialized in the prewar arrangements) toward the new prophetic avant-garde of the Bolshevik revolution, which had opened an endless (if teleological) perspective. This perspective was offering not immediate earthly hopes and goals, but a fabulous, heavenly, and closer "horizon of expectations."

I want to explicitly address the notion of "radicalism." All socialists were radical in the sense that all advocated a radical social transformation. The difference lay in the methods with which this was to be achieved, either working within the institutional framework (but with the goal of radically overturning it) or by a violent upheaval. Thus, when I speak of "radicalized," I mean this latter kind. It was only when the BCP was formed in May 1919 by renaming the former BWSDP (n) that it called for the first time for the establishment of a dictatorship of "workers and poor peasants" and, behind closed doors, adopted the strategy of arming the masses and the creation of secret armed groups attached to the party organizations.[82] Earlier Blagoev had acknowledged the adoption of some illegal, next to legal, forms of struggle, like clandestine work in the army, fraternization at the front, the creation of soldiers' councils, etc.[83] Yet, even as a leader of the Communist Party, he was dedicated to legal struggle.

Petko Smilov (1890–1967) emigrated in 1912 to avoid mobilization as an opponent of the war. After years in Austria, Germany, and France, reaching even New York, he ended up in Russia and participated in the Bolshevik Revolution. As a member of the RCP (b), he was its delegate to the First Congress of the BCP to present officially Lenin's congratulations but clearly to coordinate the future strategy. He had just arrived from Germany where he had been on the barricades during the Spartacist Uprising, and passing through Budapest, had met Bela Kun. Smilov described the enthusiasm of the Bulgarian leadership and the separate meetings he had with Blagoev, Kabakchiev, the ailing Kirkov, Kolarov, and Dimitrov. Blagoev "interrogated me about my impressions from Soviet Russia and about the events I had lived through in Germany. He listened to me attentively with a thoughtful look and turned his big eyes with even greater attention when I started to give the directives (поръчения) of the RCP (b). Our conversation was long and at the end without any comment he asked me to meet the other members of the CC."[84] A few days later Blagoev and Kabakchiev were even more careful and restrained in their responses. They said that in Bulgaria things should not be rushed, that they were with the RCP (b) and would do everything possible to help the comrades in Soviet Russia, but then added: "We are a legal party and will remain so." Smilov countered that he disagreed, and that any practical resistance would be in the service of Soviet Russia and the world proletariat.[85]

But it took some time before the slogan for armed struggle was turned into practice. In the meantime, there were hot debates and harsh, impatient accusations on the part of "the young" against the party leadership, denounced for "blindly following the West European countries in their legal forms of struggle" and Blagoev, on his part, warned against "the blindest and most uncritical following of the Russian and Hungarian Bolshevism and German Spartacism." [86] Matthias Neumann draws attention to the fact that this was a common European experience: "The communist movement associated itself from its beginnings with the image of 'youth'... Indeed, the idea of generational conflict was a recurring theme in contemporary conceptualizations of the legacy of the war."[87] The opposition between "young" and "old" mirrored the monikers of the revolutionary versus the conservative wings in the national-liberation struggle of the nineteenth century, but there was also some demographic truth about it. In the next two years the party leadership began secret discussions on how to organize an illegal military structure and, finally in 1921, a Supreme Military Revolutionary Association (Върховна военна революционна колегия, referred to in this text as the Military Organization) was created, attached to the CC. All of this was closely correlated with the *Comintern* and reflected the generational shift in the leadership of the Bulgarian party, especially after Kirkov's death in 1919 and Blagoev's serious illness after 1920 but was put to the test only in 1923.[88]

Following the June coup against BANU, the BCP proclaimed a policy of neutrality. Although the official explanation was that this was a skirmish between two bourgeois camps, town versus peasant bourgeoisie, within the ranks of the basically unarmed party it was understood that any militant move against an effective army, which had just accomplished a successful coup, would be suicidal. Still, it was an utterly misfortunate formulation whose motivation was simply to conceal the impotence of the party to contribute anything in the struggle against the military coup, all the more as it had in the past two years constantly asserted that it would fight against a possible overthrow of the government.[89] The highly intelligent Ivan Klincharov to whom Bulgarian historiography is in great debt, summarized it thus:

> The ones who had taken the movement in their hands believed that June 9 put the question of seizure of power on the agenda [but] the *historic task*, both on June 9 and after that was not the seizure of power by the Bulgarian proletariat. The *concrete task* for the Bulgarian workers was very simple and could be achieved with very simple means: the *concrete* and therefore the *historic task* consisted in preserving the political freedoms necessary for the movement, so that it could preserve its strength for the decisive battle that awaits it![90]

The decision of the BCP was met with strong disapproval by the *Comintern* and Karl Radek delivered a scathing critique, accusing it of narrow sectarianism, "the greatest defeat ever suffered by a communist party" and announcing that the party should be thoroughly reorganized.[91] Radek's report is a curious (not to say sinister) mixture of dogmatisms and voluntarism. He blamed the Bulgarian communists for not making the move from propaganda and agitation to practical opposition and taking power. His analysis pointed to Bulgaria's social structure, having a small working class but one of the best organized parties in Europe: of about 100,000 workers, 40,000 were members of the BCP. On the one hand, he claimed, a union between communists and agrarians could prevent the coup; on the other hand, he accused the communists of indecisiveness in their attempt to win over or at least split up the agrarians. "Our fault," Radek concluded, "was that we were afraid to meddle in the internal affairs in a longstanding communist party."[92] And he was eager to correct this fault. Zinoviev dispatched Vasil Kolarov and Georgi Dimitrov to implement the *Comintern* line for an armed rebellion. This was rejected by the Party Council in July by a vote of forty-two to three.[93]

By August, with Blagoev ailing and absent, and four new members irregularly coopted to the CC, the *Comintern* line was reluctantly adopted. In September, Kolarov and Dimitrov unilaterally made the decision for an armed uprising and imposed it on a rump CC over the strong objections of the then organizational secretary of the party, Todor Lukanov. What was amazing was that this decision was taken just a few days after the mass roundup of 2,000 party members on September 12, including Blagoev and Kabakchiev.[94] What followed was an abortive revolt, exclusively in rural areas and small towns, without the participation of the working class. In no major city was there an uprising, and only Ferdinand in northeast Bulgaria was held for a few days by the insurgents. The choice of northeast Bulgaria as the center of the uprising was knowingly conceived by its leaders who prudently moved themselves close to the Serbian border and within five days of the bloody suppression emigrated to Yugoslavia, and subsequently to Vienna and the USSR.[95] From there they dictated a permanent "course for armed struggle," culminating in a major terrorist act in April 1925. The idea was to stir revolutionary enthusiasm, weaken the ruling regime and prepare the ground for the worldwide socialist revolution.[96]

In light of this, the September Uprising of 1923 and the bombing of the "Sveta Nedelia" Cathedral in April 1925 can be seen as one of the last practical experiments and implementation of the concepts of "export of revolution" and "permanent revolution" that otherwise stayed on the level of theory, and served as a scarecrow and justification for the White Terror and periodical Red Scares.[97] The result for Bulgaria was the decimation of the Communist Party and its disappearance from the political scene for a considerable period of time.[98] Its leadership was taken over by younger cadres, militant and deeply conspiratorial. A few days before his death, Klincharov

Figure 18 Blagoev in the 1920s.

maintains, Blagoev revised his famous formula that the revolution depended three-quarters on external circumstances, and only one-quarter on internal ones. Now, he said, the three-quarters are equal to nine-tenths![99]

Blagoev died a crushed man in May 1924, saying: "They destroyed (razstroikha) my lovely party."[100] This became the epitaph to the experience of Bulgarian social democracy from its founding in 1891 until its demise in the 1920s. Had he lived another two years, he would have probably agreed with the remarkable Amedeo Bordiga's speech at the Sixth Plenum of the *Comintern* in 1926, when he parted ranks and confronted Stalin and Bukharin (after all, Italy's "liberal-parliamentary capitalist State" was less than twenty years older than the Bulgarian one):

> Russian development does not provide us with an experience of how the proletariat can overthrow a liberal-parliamentary capitalist State that has existed for many years and possesses the ability to defend itself. We, however, must know how to attack a modern bourgeois-democratic State that on the one hand has its own means of ideologically mobilizing and corrupting the proletariat, and on the other can defend itself on the terrain of armed struggle with greater efficacy than could the Tsarist autocracy. This problem never arose in the history of the Russian Communist Party.[101]

It might be perhaps an exaggeration to shift the entire responsibility to the *Comintern* and explain the events in the 1920s as solely an outside manipulation. There was, indeed, an already radicalized cohort as a result of the consecutive wars and the Russian Revolution. Here is a letter from a member of BANU following the June coup d'état, not even as a response to the September events. Written by Petko Nichev in Munich and sent to Iurdan Nenchev in Berlin on June 23, 1923, it never reached the addressee, but it is unclear how it made its way to the police archives:

> We went through many wars, we overcame lots of problems, but we have never witnessed today's ruthlessness. . . . I am disgusted, my friend, I am on the verge of going back to Bulgaria, to raise the flag of salvation, to lead the masses against the bandits. I do not know what you think, but their viciousness and malice have driven me to hate every officer and anyone from another party and from the city. Hatred is growing within me, revengefulness has appeared.[102]

The mishandled response to the June coup with the bizarre formulation of neutrality engendered an energetic left-wing critique within the party, attacking the CC for its stance. Ivan Koichev (1896–1979), a member of the Military Organization, explicitly worded this as a clash between the "younger" and "older" party members. In his reckoning, the left wing (левица) comprised perhaps a quarter of the party leadership and included communists like Kosta Iankov (1888–1925), Petîr Iskrov (1891–1938), Iako Dorosiev (1890–1925), Marko Fridman (1892–1925), Ivan Manev (1887–1925), and Georgi Lambrev (1899–1937).[103] There were many others, enthused and proud to take up arms, although even amid the ranks of the critics there were reflections on the impossibility of this uprising.[104] Traicho Kostov would later add: "Like any pioneering activity, there was something new, fascinating and romantic in this illegal activity."[105]

And yet, without the outside push and the willingness of the new Bulgarian *Comintern* operatives to stir the people who had been critical of the party's policy of neutrality and were ready to take up arms with the agrarians, the uprising would not have happened. These people all died as heroes: Nikola Avramov (1898–1924) who was the secretary of the district committee in Lom and who led the uprising in Medkovets, alongside the legendary priest Andrei Ignatov Ivanov (1979–1923) who was caught and hanged by the authorities; Alexander Karastoianov (1886–1923) a dentist, who had participated in the 1905 Russian Revolution, and after the arrests of September 12 went underground and organized an armed group; Asen Velchev (1894–1923), a lawyer and the son of the general-major Vîlko Velchev (1859–1935), a hero of the Serbian and Balkan Wars who was tortured by the police because of his son; Stoiko Stoianov Lashov (1899–1923); Damian Lazarov (1891–1923); Lazar Lazarov (1884–1923); the brothers Toniu (1899–1923) and Tsviatko (1898–1923) Lekov; the "red lawyer" Nikola Lisichev (1886–1923); Dimitîr Milchev (1891–1923); Ivan Stamboliiski (1895–1923, no relation of the prime minister); Ilia Stanchev (1900–1923); Georgi Stanev (1887–1923); Petko Lechev (1897–1923); Manol Stanev (1887–1923); Pavel Stanev (1897–1923); Boian Statev (1891–1923); Filip Stefanov (1890–1923); Rusi Stefanov (1891–1923); Krîstiu Stoev (1896–1923); Vasil Stoichev (1899–1923); Lazar Stoimenov (1894–1923); Spas Todorov Kîrpachev (1888–1923); Stoimen Stoimenov (1900–1923); Koiu Uvaliev (1882–1923), Vîlcho Uzunov (1892–1923); Daniu Vasilev (1895–1923); and many others. These are random names out of a long list of communists and agrarians killed only in 1923, and they were followed by the bloodbath of 1925. Most of the ones killed in 1923–25 did not have an illustrious biography and have only their date of birth and party allegiance recorded. Most were young, in their twenties and thirties. A list of more than 140 people killed in the 1920s from the villages of Belogradchishko and Vidinsko and another 150 who emigrated, mentioned in the memoirs of Vîlko Nakov Davidov, shows most born in the 1890s.[106] In the database, we have 1751 individuals whose death is indicated as "killed" and of them 1275 were killed in the 1923–25 interval (767 in 1923, 59 in 1924, and 449 in 1925). Of the 1213 for whom we have the birth data, the ones born in the 1890s number 757 (see Figure 19).

To this day, the numbers of the killed are disputed. Immediately after the defeat, the victors suggested two-, three-, or five-thousand for just the victims of 1923.[107] When Émile Vandervelde visited Bulgaria in 1924, the government figure he was given was 1,500; the agrarians claimed 16,000; and members of the diplomatic corps thought that 10,000 was the reliable estimate.[108] Khristo Stoianov, the agrarian leader, spoke of 3,000 killed during the Soldiers' Uprising in 1918, and 13,000 in September 1923.[109] The army, especially the paramilitary forces, IMRO groups, and the White Russian troops indulged in a White Terror that increased after April 1925. A 1925 police report put the numbers of emigrants at 60,000.[110] Another one from 1927 reported that Bulgarian students in Berlin maintained that 20,000 were killed in 1923–25.[111] This was an exaggerated figure, as was the number of 30,000 often appearing in the historiography of the 1950s and later popular works.[112] Equally, the present officially accepted number

The Prosopography of the Bulgarian Socialist Left 111

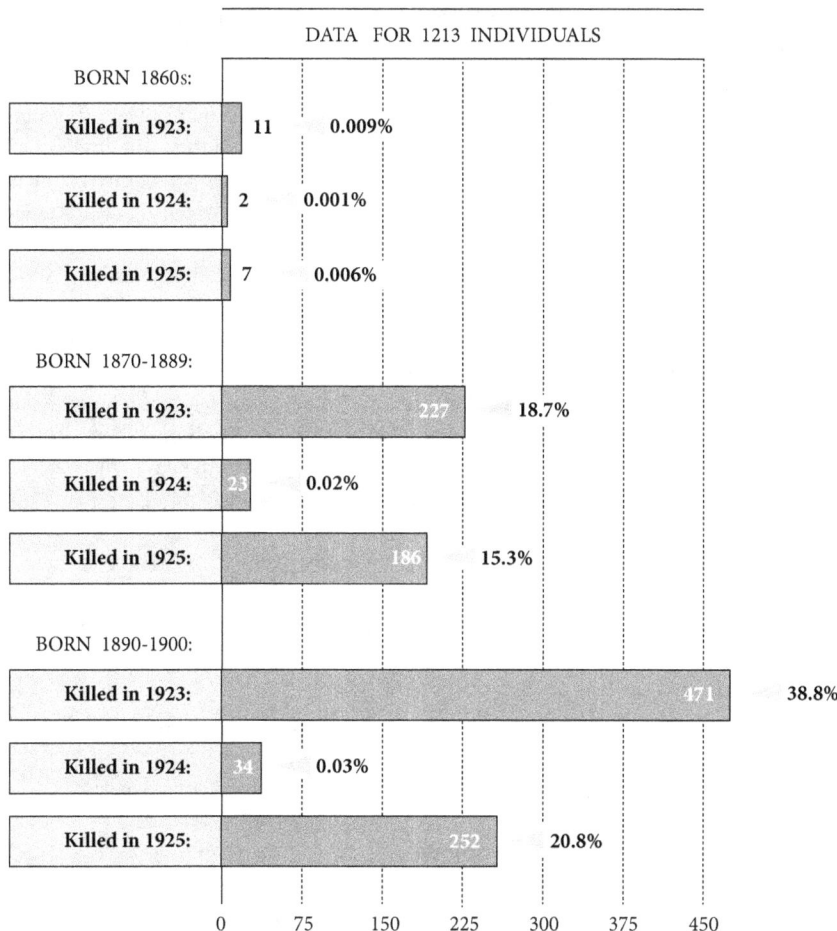

Figure 19 Death in 1923–25 by Cohorts.

of 5,000 is a low guesstimate.[113] John Bell was right to write that "at best, the September Uprising was a blood sacrifice through which the party gained expiation for its past sins in the eyes of the Comintern, and it provided its survivors with reputations of revolutionary heroes."[114] The ones who died were heroes but as a communist wrote in his memoirs that could be published only after 1989: "We are always ready to glorify heroic acts, even when they are in the name of noble but unattainable goals. It is however our duty to inquire whether the idealism, enthusiasm and bravery of the best in our party did not simply serve as a pretext to slaughter so many fine people?"[115] It was a "dearly paid lesson in Bolshevism."[116]

After the wars, the generation of the "early socialists" frittered away. Some died of old age, others lost their lives in the wars, many more were massacred in the civil war of 1923–25 and many emigrated. Dozens died young of diseases, especially tuberculosis.

The teacher Gina Zlatkova described tuberculosis as a particular scourge among the malnourished teachers; the newspaper *Rabotnik* had numerous obituaries.[117] Several young promising socialist intellectuals dying of the disease in their twenties were much lamented and irreplaceable losses for the movement, but their names were forgotten subsequently. Dimitîr Dimitrov (1876–1902), pivotal in gestating the theoretical foundations of the BWSDP(b), was not followed by others with his clarity of mind. Dimitîr Ivanchev Bakîrdzhiev (1864–89) came from a wealthy family and studied social sciences in Zurich where he became a socialist. The Bulgarian representative in the Slavic Socialist Club, he also founded a Balkan Federation Society and the Marxist student group "Ralo." A volunteer in the Serbo-Bulgarian war of 1885, he was close to Blagoev's circle around "Sîvremennii pokazatel" in Sofia and obsessed with the plight of fellow Bulgarians in the unredeemed lands.[118] Another young man, Khristo Stoianov from Tîrnovo, had studied in Germany, France, and Belgium where he had founded a Bulgarian student society "Worker." He died in 1888 of bone tuberculosis.[119] Ivan Zagubanski (1875–1904) came to Marxism as a student in the navy. As a teacher and hardware worker, he was the illegal courier of the Russian *Iskra* but died of TB at twenty-nine. The musician Georgi Goranov (1882–1905) lived on through his "Labor Song," to a great extent the hymn of the socialists (see Part III). Khristo Smirnenski (1898–1923), one of the most talented and innovative Bulgarian poets, a bard of urban and revolutionary poetry, was a committed communist, and wrote a moving poem about Rosa Luxemburg:

[T]here's a memory in our hearts,
Oppressive in its weight,
Wrapped in a flame of grief that smarts
And never shall abate.
    See the volcanic pillar loom
    Of dream and action brave!
    The world has not sufficient room
    To find this heart a grave.[120]

Death can at times be wretched, life –
Insufferably hard,
But on this funeral carriage lies
No corpse, but a great star.

Smirnenski's death from tuberculosis spared him an almost certain assassination. This fate did not avoid the symbolist poet Khristo Iasenov (1889–1925), a member of the BCP. Not being a communist was not a safety guarantee, even membership in the political elite did not secure immunity. Iosif Herbst (1875–1925) was born in Adrianople in a Jewish family from Austria that had taken refuge in the Ottoman Empire after 1848 and in 1879 came to Sofia. He finished military school in Sofia in 1893 and became a leading journalist, editing the mainstream liberal *Dnevnik*, *Svobodna tribuna*, and *Vreme*, and serving as foreign correspondent for the *Daily Mail*, *Die Zeit*, and others. A member of the Democratic Party (of Petko Karavelov), he was wounded in the Balkan War and appointed the first Press Director in 1913–18, and later of the Bulgarian Telegraph Agency. In 1921 he married Viola Karavelova, the daughter of the former prime minister. After September 1923 he joined the "Committee of the Victims of the Events," edited several papers that were closed (*Vik, ABV, Ek, Dnes*) and wrote devastating critiques of the Tsankov government. On an accusation that he was helping communists, he was arrested and "disappeared" in police custody.[121]

The outrage of left-leaning intellectuals over the bloody suppression also doomed the premier avant-garde figure in Bulgarian culture at the time, the expressionist poet Geo Milev (1895–1925). This was a versatile talent: artist, theater director, literary and music critic, theoretician of expressionism, editor, translator, and publisher. He grew up in Stara Zagora and studied Romance languages and literature at Sofia University, philosophy in Leipzig, worked on a thesis on Richard Dehmel, and studied English literature in London, where he met the exiled Émile Verhaeren. Mobilized in 1916, in 1917 Geo Milev was severely wounded and lost his right eye. A contributor to *Die Aktion* and *Der Sturm*, he published the two most important modernist cultural magazines *Scales* (Везни, 1919–22) and *Flame* (Plamîk, Пламък, 1924–25). It was in *Flame* in 1924 that he printed his poem "September."[122] The issue was confiscated, the magazine closed in January 1925, and on May 14 the poet was fined, sentenced to one year in prison, and deprived of civil and political rights for two years. The next day, he was summoned for a "brief investigation" and disappeared. He had been strangled and his remains, recognized by the artificial eye that he had implanted after an operation in Germany in 1919, were discovered in a mass grave in the late 1950s.[123] It took a highly cultivated aesthete to become the bard of the crowd.[124]

Figure 20 Geo Milev.

From the dead womb of night
The age-old spite of the slave is born:
His passionate hate
Is great . . .

- Bearing no roses,
No songs,
No music, no gongs,
No clarinet, sidedrum and drone,
No trumpet and horn, no trombone:
Shouldering bundles in tatters,
Gripping – not glittering sabres,
But common stocks,
Peasants with stakes,
Cudgels,
Goads,
Choppers,
Pitchforks,
Hoes,
Scythes
And sunflowers
      Young and old –
Down from every direction behold
They came
      A blind herd
Of beasts let loose,
Numberless
Thundering bulls –
Calling,
Bawling
(Behind them a stoneblack sky)
Without order
Forward
They flew
Irresistible
Terrible,
Great:
THE PEOPLE!
. . .
Peasants,
Workers,
Commonfolk,
Landless,
Illiterate,
Boors,

Hooligans,
Boars
A rabble like cattle:
>Thousands,
>Masses,
>The people:
Thousands of faiths
>One faith in the people's cause.
Thousands of wills
>One will to obtain better laws,
Thousands of turbulent hearts
>In the reddening range of expanse
Eagerly raising on high
Red
Banners
Which spread
Far
And wide
Over a land in the grip of alarm and revolt,
Ferocious fruit of the storm:
>Thousands -
>Masses -
>The people.

...

Death, murder and blood –
For how long must it be?
All-powerful Zeus,
Jupiter
Ahura Mazda,
Indra,
Tot, Ra,
Jehovah,
Sabaoth!
>*Reply*!
From the smoke of the fires
Rise
Assailing the ears,
The cries of the killed,
The roars
Of the numberless martyrs
On blazing wood pyres:
>Who
Has betrayed our faith?
Reply!

You say nothing?
Don't know?
    We do!
Look:
With one bound
We leap into heaven:
DOWN WITH GOD!
From your throne
Send you dead
Down to the starless
Ironclad depths
Of the world's great abyss –
    DOWN WITH GOD!
From the boundless high
Bridge of the sky
With levers and ropes
We'll bring down Heaven.
The land of our hopes,
Down
To the sorrowing
Blood-soaked
Earth.
All that the poets and philosophers wrote
Shall come true!
    No god! No master!
The month of September shall turn into May
The life that men lead
From that day shall proceed
Ever upward, upward!
Earth shall be Heaven –
It shall.

4

Tales of Formation

The prominent literary critic Dr. Krîstiu Krîstev wrote in 1896: "One thing cannot be denied to the socialist ideas that, no matter how achievable, they bring in ideals and promote undoubtedly a better social order and thus captivate the souls of the youth."[1] Dr. Krîstev was no socialist but he evaluated calmly the appeal of socialism. This was not so generously met by the authorities who were sending confidential inquiries to school directors. The respected pedagogical high school in Kazanlîk was giving yearly reports on this issue, beginning in 1892. In 1900, the director of the school sent yet another report, this time in a defensive tone:

> I cannot avoid the question of socialism, which is constantly raised and reported to the honorable ministry and which serves to harm the school entrusted to me. . . . We know well that, like any enticing and new teaching, this idea was spread rapidly by its first propagators in a certain period in different towns, in boys' and girls' schools alike. At first, it was passionately embraced, but with the flow of time passions have cooled down, because its followers became convinced, openly or discretely, in the unsuitability of this idea in our country. The cooling is more intensive in places where the idea appeared earlier. This is an organic process in the spiritual life and the fermentation was intensive at first, but now it is weakening.[2]

It was an overly optimistic report, because the next director of the same school, in 1911 lamented that the socialists who were quite numerous in Kazanlîk succeeded in alienating students from the program, persuading them that the literature they were reading was reactionary and focused on supporting the regime: "Landlords, guardians, restaurant owners, apprentices and journeymen who are friends of our students, almost all primary school teachers and part of the high-school ones have decided to paint us as enemies of progress and draw in our students into the social-democratic organization."[3] For several years they would organize a ceremony at the end of the school year, in which they would solemnly "baptize" the graduates into socialism.

The even more famous Aprilov High School (the Gabrovo high school founded in 1835 by Vasil Aprilov as the first modern secular school) reported in 1900 that in the past few years, there was a student circle that gathered regularly at nights at students' homes and discussed historical, political, and economic issues. The director suspected some of the teachers of socialism whom he named but without definitive proof.[4] The most bizarre plea came from the same school in 1898, which reported that students frequented the municipal library where they would read without any control, including political papers: "It would be good if the Honorable Ministry would forbid high school students to visit municipal libraries; the school libraries are almost complete."[5] And as late as 1922, in a brochure dedicated to Metropolitan Methodius, Ivan Drumev wrote that the leadership of schools is almost half in the hands of socialists who corrupt the youth.[6]

Socialisms

Not only was socialism enticing, but it was also not altogether new, and was understood differently by separate people and groups. Educated Bulgarians had been informed through their press already in Ottoman times. The very first and brief mention was in 1851 in *Tsarigradski vestnik*, an educational and altogether conservative weekly, about socialist propaganda in France, followed by a report about the banning of socialist literature by the Pope.[7] The same paper had reported extensively in 1848–49 about the fate of the Frankfurt Assembly, praising Prussia and Russia on their position.[8] There was an avalanche of substantive information on socialism in the 1870s. The most widely read paper at the time was the weekly *Makedonia*, edited by the poet Petko R. Slaveikov and printed in Istanbul between 1862 and 1872 when it was banned and discontinued for its liberal stance and passionate polemics with the semi-official *Pravo* and *Turtsiia*. It dedicated three consecutive issues to "socialism and communism" in 1870, explaining that socialism was a teaching about the social-economic structure of people. Born in France, the place of revolutions, it was a reaction against the dire situation of workers and peasants. Introducing its readers to the teachings of Babeuf, Saint-Simon, Proudhon, and, especially, Fourier, the paper concluded the if Fourierism does not succeed, the blame will lie not in the will of the people, nor in the virtues of socialism but only in the privileged strata. *Makedonia* differentiated between socialism, which preserved private property but advocated collaborative labor for the common good in a somewhat vague formulation, and the dangerous egalitarian communism that would abolish private property and limit freedoms, to which the paper strongly objected.[9] *Turtsiia*, on the other hand, devoting five of its issues to socialism, flatly denounced it as a militant, violent, and perfidious teaching, arguing that inequality was normal and unavoidable and that workers can be as corrupt as capitalists. Socialism was not democracy but a despotism in the name of the people.[10] The official *Dunav*, coming out bilingually in Bulgarian and Ottoman Turkish, praised Russia for its stern justice system that was against these ideas aimed at the destruction of the world.[11]

Den, a liberal educational weekly, edited by Stefan Bobchev, the future founder of Sofia University and leader of the People's Party, also devoted a whole issue to socialism and communism. Socialism was the child of the great revolution in France, "the mother of human-loving ideas useful for the whole world" (*родителка на човеколюбиви и всесветскополезни идеи*). With this revolution, the people realized their own sovereignty, but soon, "delivered from one bondage, they fell into another, the bondage of capital." The question was who was culpable: the peasants who reproduced unrestrainedly or the social order that kept the people in ignorance. Many theories were advanced by well-meaning and noble people, based both on Christianity and natural rights, among them Babeuf, Saint-Simon, and the "great mind" Proudhon, arguing for the redistribution of property, the abolition of birth privileges, etc. These ideas, however, were misused by others who turned the socialist ideas into the "heinous communism" that seeks to abolish private property, family, and marriage and allows for all types of violence.[12] In another issue *Den* informed about the working-class movement and especially the role of German social democracy. Far from being socialist papers, *Makedonia* and *Den* had the whole conceptual apparatus already in place: "In contemporary society the instruments of labor have been monopolized by the capitalists. This dependence of the working class causes poverty and all kinds of enslavement."[13] At the time and after the Paris Commune, communism had already become the preferred scarecrow.

One of the most interesting articles came out in the journal *Chitalishte*. It was written by Lazar Iovchev (1840–1915) who had completed his studies at the French Catholic College in Istanbul, and aided by the Kalofer municipality, pursued first literature and then law at the Sorbonne (1864–70). Two years later he became a monk under the name Iosif and swiftly rose through the Orthodox hierarchy to become a metropolitan in 1876. In 1877 he was elected Exarch, and became the third and longest serving leader of the independent Bulgarian church (1877–1915), bar Patriarch Maxim (1971–2012). His article "International" was written after the demise of the Paris Commune and aimed to give information on the International Workingmen's Association which occupied the attention of the European public.[14] Workers felt betrayed that the promise of liberty, equality, fraternity never materialized. They lacked religious ideas that make people patient and were full of hatred toward the powers that did not defend them, the clergy that taught them only to endure, and the capitalists who exploited them.[15]

Iovchev had followed the origins of the association since 1862, especially its official foundation in Geneva in 1866, and presented its views and goals: "The main issue is the relationship between capital and labor, which it wants to change so that capitalists will earn less, and workers more. . . . It also demands that education should be affordable for the poor, asks for just taxation, and the liquidation of the standing army which is worthless and serves despotism."[16] All these points were considered reasonable but with time the association embraced communism, "a theory which is pure utopia because it contradicts liberty and human nature."[17] Iovchev then went into a comparison of the plight of European workers and Bulgarians as a whole. While he found the demands of European workers justified, he pointed out that all Bulgarians, with rare exceptions, worked harder, lived worse and less, dressed poorer, ate less, paid higher taxes, and got loans not with 5 to 6 percent interest, but with 15 to 20 percent. Iovchev finished with a startling conclusion: "The European worker finds it redundant that the people pay millions to support a standing army which however serves to defend its glory and honor. On this point I leave it to the reader to make his own comparison."[18]

In fact, this conclusion was not surprising given the fermentation of a heightened national spirit in the 1860s and 1870s seeking both religious and political sovereignty. Another young man from Kalofer, a few years younger, who embraced both the national cause as a revolutionary and can be undoubtedly classified as an "early socialist" was Khristo Botev (1848–76). Given his iconic stature in Bulgarian history, second only to Vasil Levski's, Botev has been the object of bitter controversies of ideological appropriation. Because of his more explicit ideological commitments, he was claimed principally by the left. After 1989 in particular, there has been a cleansing of Botev, so that his anti-Russian views are overexposed, and his radicalism described but never named "socialist."[19] The greatest dispute was around the often cited "Symbol-Creed of the Bulgarian Commune" that Botev allegedly wrote in 1871 in Galați from where he also sent a congratulatory telegram to Paris. That Botev welcomed the Paris Commune is proven, but the question of whether he hailed it in the particular words of the "Creed," which exists solely as a copy and was published only in 1934, has given rise to reasonable and judicious doubts over its authorship.[20]

Botev was raised on a literary diet including Nikolai Chernyshevsky, Charles Darwin, Thomas Huxley, Herbert Spencer, Ferdinand Lassalle and, yes, Karl Marx, although his close friend Nikolai Konstantinovich Sudzilovsky wrote that their interest was "only theoretical."[21] What was not theoretical at all was that they both had close links to the ideas and personality of Petr Lavrov (1823–1900), philosopher and sociologist, considered a theoretician of *narodnichestvo* and a self-described socialist and Marxist. A member of the First International, he was intimately involved in the Paris Commune. Where he parted ways with his younger Marxist co-exile Plekhanov was in believing in the revolutionary potential of the peasantry and especially the intelligentsia in the particular circumstances of Russia as part of the worldwide socialist revolution. Botev was equally insistent on the peculiarity of Bulgarian society, on the promise inherent in its decentralized communities, guilds, and educational societies.[22] In 1875 Sudzilovsky was tasked by Lavrov to organize a channel for the distribution of his journal *Forward!* (Вперед!) and other revolutionary literature; the headquarters became the editorial office of Botev's newspaper *Banner* (Знаме).[23] It was in *Banner* that Botev reflected on the inaugural congress of German social democracy in Gotha in 1875, ending his editorial with a poem extolling the struggle.[24]

The Bulgarian revolutionaries had been in contact with the Russian emigration. Liuben Karavelov, the chairman of the Bulgarian Revolutionary Central Committee (BRCC), and an admirer of Switzerland, had visited the country and met with Bakunin. As followers of Herzen and Bakunin, he and several other members of the BRCC (Botev was the most zealous) served as channels of transmission and dissemination of illegal Russian literature, in addition to providing shelter for Russian revolutionaries. Botev had in his library issues of *Bell* (Колокол), of *Polar Star* (Полярная звезда), and the works of Polish émigrés with whom he was in close connection after the crushing of the Polish Uprising in 1863–64. This latter circumstance is not denied but gets short shrift in Botev's biographies at the expense of the overblown link to Sergey Nechayev. Botev met Nechayev through Karavelov and hid him while he was on his way to Russia in 1869. For this he was imprisoned for several months by the Romanian authorities. This casual meeting, no doubt between people who thought alike, turned in the historiography into an exclusive formative friendship for Botev, stressing the nihilist, anarchist, conspiratorial elements, but especially the Russian connection.[25]

If the subsequent claims of Botev's professed Marxism and communism were attempts at exclusive appropriation by the communists and are undoubtedly anachronistic, Botev's socialism (qualified with anarchism) is equally undoubted. Sudzilovsky who participated directly and actively in the preparation of the April Uprising of 1876 wrote in a letter to Geneva in March 1876: "There will be an uprising in Bulgaria very soon. It is in the hand of socialists. . . . One can hope that it would come out differently than in Herzegovina. Nowadays there is socialist propaganda throughout all Bulgaria and, as I understand, it is very successful." This was somewhat exaggerated but the important point to make here is that Sudzilovsky considered Botev's revolutionary propaganda socialist.[26] And he was not alone. Ivan Vazov, the "Patriarch of Bulgarian literature," whom no one accuses of socialism, wrote that under the influence of Botev, he wrote "a bunch of socialist poems" but later cooled down.[27] There is, of course, an additional credible reason for Sudzilovsky's letter. He had intended to join the *cheta* of Botev as a surgeon and he wrote to Geneva passing the Bulgarians' request to send them leaders with practical military experience. The response was negative. The Lavrov circle objected to political struggles and they insisted on confining their participation only to socialist movements. It was well known that not only the *narodniks* around Lavrov but also other Russian groups were against participating in the Herzegovinian Uprising the previous year. Before the creation of *Narodnaya Volya* in 1879, they were dedicated exclusively to social struggle, and objected to political struggle and political revolutions that would only strengthen the existing regime. This would also explain the mention of Herzegovina and the emphasis on socialism in Sudzilovsky's letter. After the rebuttal, Sudzilovsky cut off his links to Lavrov, although he never joined Botev in his tragic expedition.[28]

Sudzilovsky, known also by his pseudonym Nicholas Russel (1850–1930), brings us to an important theme, namely the influence of Russian *narodnichestvo* in the Balkans and in Bulgaria in particular. It is widely recognized that in Serbia it was formative: "Of all Balkan countries to have come under the influence of the ideas of Russian populism (*Narodničestvo*), only in Serbia was this to initially materialize as a genuine political and social movement and, subsequently, into a mighty and hegemonic party formation."[29] It was central in the gestation of Svetozar Marković's worldview and it served "as the core constitutive doctrine" of the *Omladina* and the People's Radical Party that dominated the political scene in the Kingdom of Serbia.[30] It was equally decisive in Romania where Constantin Stere codified it as *poporanismul* and where it became the foundation of Romanian peasantism in the interwar period but was also directly at the roots of early socialism through the Russian exiles, among them Constantin Dobrogeanu-Gherea, Nicolae Zubcu Codreanu, Zamfir Arbore-Ralli, and Sudzilovsky himself, and where one could follow up the interesting transformation of *narodnik* ideas into Marxist ones.[31]

In Bulgaria, however, the situation was different and Augusta Dimou recognizes that "Russian populists . . . did not play such an influential role there as in neighboring Romania and were not instrumental in the foundation of the Socialist Party, which was exclusively the achievement of Bulgarian intellectuals [but] they formed part of the broader revolutionary network of exiles operative outside Russia."[32] Still, she is so wed to the model of "passage from populism to Marxism" that, despite the contrast to Serbia and Romania, she concludes that "by the early 1890s, the Bulgarians had slowly accomplished the passage from populism to Marxism, a circumstance testified by the early institutionalization of the Socialist Party (1891)."[33]

The problem is that none of the socialists who founded the party had been *narodniks*, unless anyone who had read, and was inspired by, Chernyshevsky was automatically one. Characterizing the early views of Nikola Gabrovski (1864–1925) as "a resourceful amalgamation of the basic tenets of Lavrov and Chernyshevsky, admixed with pauperophilia themes and distant echoes of Lassalleanism and French radical thought" raises eyebrows.[34] After, indeed, finishing high school in Russia, Gabrovski received his law education in Geneva (1884–87) where French thought was not that distant and he participated in the 1889 Paris Congress of the Second International. The characteristics that Dimou identified as residues of populist (her preferred term) catalysis in the gestation of Bulgarian socialists, like their belief in close work among the people, a popular language for propaganda and their self-understanding as engaged political human beings, were not a *narodnik* monopoly, but typical for most nineteenth-century democratic and revolutionary movements.[35] Bulgarian *narodniks* did exist but most did not end up as Marxists and the role of the Russian émigrés (but not Russian thought, which was, indeed, immense) was rather limited.

To start with the latter, the only one directly involved with Bulgarians before 1878, and highly valued for that, was Sudzilovsky. He was expelled from Romania in 1881 and after brief periods of stay in the Ottoman Empire, Switzerland, France, and Belgium, settled in Plovdiv in Eastern Rumelia in 1882, where he was a respected surgeon. His stay in Bulgaria was short, only four years. He and his friend Vladimir Lutskii were the channel for the distribution of Russian revolutionary literature printed in Geneva to the Bulgarian principality and Serbia. Both also contributed financially to the *Emancipation of Labor Group* of Plekhanov, Zasulich, Axelrod, Lev Deutsch, and others.[36] The circle of Sudzilovsky was frequented by Zakhari Stoianov, a national revolutionary of great repute, who was then working in the Office of Justice and headed the Bulgarian Secret Revolutionary Committee working for the Unification of Bulgaria. This was a goal that both official Tsarist Russia and its exiled revolutionaries supported. However, when Unification was proclaimed unilaterally by the Bulgarians on September 6, 1885, without Russian blessing and with Prince Battenberg at the helm to whom the Tsar was hostile, Russia withdrew military support from Bulgaria. The ensuing Serbo–Bulgarian war, greatly at the instigation of Austria-Hungary, was unexpectedly won by the Bulgarians and led to an unprecedented national enthusiasm but cemented the breach with Russia.

The act of unification, cherished by the Bulgarians as a revolution, was dismissed by Sudzilovsky as a simple coup d'état that would subordinate Bulgaria to Austria, alienate it from its natural protector, Russia, and that would fall short of a broad social program. To paint Sudzilovsky as in league with Russian tsarism is wrong and yet, this is exactly what happened in the eyes of the Bulgarians: he was accused of being a Russian spy and plotting against Battenberg, which prompted a spirited defense by Plekhanov.[37] Sudzilovsky's thinking can be reconstructed from several articles and two unpublished drafts in his personal archive. Sympathetic as he was to Bulgaria's national integration in principle, he subordinated it to a broader revolutionary tenet of a general popular democratic effort, not through a military revolt. Most importantly, he thought that this could be achieved only in coordination and with the support of the Russian revolutionary movement. With the crisis of this movement after the Tsar's assassination in 1881, the promise of a successful Bulgarian unification that would not alienate it from Russia and would not bring it in the Austrian and German camp, faded. Sudzilovsky accordingly accused Zakhari Stoianov who had become one of the leaders of the People's Liberal Party and future chairman of the Bulgarian National Assembly, of forfeiting his revolutionary internationalism.[38] In the rather murky ideas in these articles and drafts, one can hear reverberations of the previous *narodnik* suspicions of the purely national political struggle in the Balkans in combination with some, probably unconscious, condescending subordination to Russian interests, albeit revolutionary. In one of the drafts Sudzilovsky even wrote that a Russian occupation of Eastern Rumelia would be preferable as it would save Bulgaria for the near socialist future.[39] Little wonder that Sudzilovsky had to leave Bulgaria, although a few of his Russian friends and co-exiles participated in the Bulgarian army and stayed in the country.[40] He had a subsequent colorful and illustrious career as a doctor, scientist, and revolutionary, including a stint as the first president of the Hawaii Senate, and ended his life in China in 1930.

It was also in 1882 that Vladimir Karpovich Debogory-Mokriyevich (1848–1926) settled in Eastern Rumelia in the town of Pazardzik close to Plovdiv where he was employed as an architect, much to the amusement of Plekhanov who knew he had no such qualifications.[41] Under the name Prokopiev he is best known for his polemic with Blagoev that came out in *Lîcha* (Лъча) in 1891–92, immediately after Blagoev's publication of *What is Socialism and Do We Have a Basis for It?*[42] The argument essentially concerned the applicability of socialism in a rural milieu and the lack of correspondence to the experience of capitalism in Western Europe. Debogory-Mokriyevich, however, disappears subsequently from the Bulgarian annals although he died in 1926 in Chirpan, Bulgaria. We only know that his daughter, Natalie De Bogory (Debogory-Mokriyevich, 1887–1939) was born in Geneva and ended up as Sol Hurok's publicity person and correspondent to the *International Herald Tribune* in Paris, but she is more famous for the first anonymous English translation of the *Protocols of the Elders of Zion*.[43] Both his recollections published in Russian in Paris in 1894, and a later German edition in 1905 "The Memoirs of a Nihilist," say nothing of the Bulgarian episode of his life. They are concerned exclusively with his revolutionary activities in Russia and the Siberian exile, and reaffirm his belief that the 1870s movement had inexorably declined since its peak in 1881. He criticized social democracy for its exclusively propagandist nature and insisted on the virtues of revolutionary terrorism.[44] Even less is known about Boris Mintses who for a time was a professor at the University of Sofia but ended in Vienna as an editor of the liberal *Die Zeit* and committed suicide in 1904.[45] No wonder that Bulgarian historiography, until 1989 characterized by its obsequiousness to the notion of Russian influence, pays little if any attention to the role of the Russian *narodniks*, even if only to highlight Blagoev's eventual victory over them.

Some Russian émigrés may have been more influential in the spread of anarchist ideas alongside Bulgarian students who had returned from their studies in France and Switzerland.[46] Khristo Botev with his newspapers *Duma na bŭlgarskite emigranti*, *Nezavisimost*, and *Zname* is credited by the anarchist movement as an implicit beginning. Interestingly, early Bulgarian socialists did not distinguish between *narodnichestvo* and anarchism. Blagoev, who met Debogory-Mokriyevich earlier in 1883 during his summer vacation, had referred to him as "this pleasant Russian émigré, a well-known Russian Narodnik and Bakuninist."[47] Mikhail Gerdzhikov (1877–1947) was directly influenced by Sudzilovsky who had stayed in their house in Plovdiv. During his law studies in Lausanne and Geneva he participated in the Geneva group and the anarchist IMRO alongside Petŭr Mandzhukov (1878–1966) and Ivanka Boteva (1876–1906), the daughter of Khristo Botev.[48] In Geneva the group published a sole issue of the newspaper *Revenge* (Отмъщение) as well as several issues of the *Voice of the Macedonia Secret Revolutionary Committee* (Глас на Македонския таен революционен комитет).[49] Upon his return to Bulgaria he became a teacher in Bitola, and a renowned leader of the IMRO close to Gotse Delchev who participated actively in the Ilinden Uprising.

Anarchism had made more serious inroads into Bulgaria's neighbors to the west, especially in Slovenia and Croatia through the works of Johann Most, although it is difficult to distinguish between the reception of anarchist and socialist literature at the time, which reached the same audience.[50] In the 1890s several anarchist student circles existed in Plovdiv, Kazanlŭk, Lom, Gabrovo, and Pleven and a few anarchists, like Gerdzhikov, were involved in the revolutionary organizations in Macedonia, forming circles in Skopje, Thessaloniki, and Edirne. In this period the self-designation for their ideas was "without authority" (*bezvlastie*, безвластие, безвластничество). The movement faded out by the end of the century but was revived after 1905, with a few publishing centers for anarchist literature in Razgrad, Ruse, and Sofia, which brought out translations, mostly by Peter Kropotkin, Mikhail Bakunin, Pierre-Joseph Proudhon, Jacques Élisée Reclus, Errico Malatesta, and others. A few papers were also printed: *Rabotnicheska misŭl, Bezvlastie, Vŭzrazhdane, Uchenicheska probuda*, and *Oscobozhdenie*. Attempts at uniting the diverse groups failed, however, and it was only after the wars that the First Conference of the Federation of Anarcho-Communists in Bulgaria (FACB) was convened in Sofia in 1919, which issued a "Program and tactic of the anarchists in Bulgaria" replete with the classical anti-statist and federalist ideas of anarchism, the belief in direct action through strikes and armed action, often advocating terrorism, anti-parliamentarism, and hostility to the dictatorship of the proletariat.

A particularity of the Bulgarian anarchists was the preponderance of the anarcho-communists, promoting the decisive role of ideological groups against the anarcho-syndicalists centering their efforts on the trade unions.[51] Thus, Mikhail Gerdzhikov, who after the wars still remained an IMRO member, became a cofounder of FACB.[52] By 1923 anarcho-syndicalism was effectively wiped out as apolitical, and at its Fifth Congress in 1923, the program adopted as its tactics "boycott, sabotage, strikes, general strike, social revolution . . . and as a variation terror against authority and capital."[53] The anarchist press was also revived with new but, again, short-lived publications: *Komuna* (1919), *Probuda* (1918–19), *Bunt* (1920), *Anarchist* (1920), *Svobodno obshtestvo* (1923–24), *Zov* (1924), *Svobodna misŭl* (1924), and others.

The Bolshevik revolution produced ambivalent attitudes among the anarchists but with time a strong anti-Bolshevik position crystallized. In the period of agrarian rule they actively opposed BANU and the BCP, although at times they cooperated in certain actions, like the protests against the Treaty of Neuilly, against the deployment of White Army troops in Bulgaria, and especially during the period between 1923 and 1925. In a country where the two social-democratic parties had great influence, anarchists could achieve a high profile but were less numerous. In 1924–25 when their numbers swelled, the police records listed 848 in number, and Daskalov estimates that there were around 2,500.[54] Russian revolutionary ideas also came mediated. Thus, Georgi Kîrdhiev, a famous teacher and journalist already before 1878, was the editor of *Rabotnik* which was declared by the government as the "organ of Bulgarian nihilists." Kîrdhiev later edited *Bratstvo* in which he disseminated the ideology of the early Serbian socialist and anarchist Vasa Pelagić (1833–99).[55]

More consequential was the influence of the ideas of Tolstoy. While Tolstoyism cannot be categorized as socialism, it was close to it in many of its overall tenets and was embraced by many of the early socialists. In 1928, the literary critic Georgi Konstantinov wrote that "after 1900, Tolstoy had only one rival among the Bulgarian intelligentsia: Karl Marx."[56] One among the intelligentsia was Dimo Kiorchev (1884–1928) who studied law in Leipzig, Zagreb, and Sofia and was a well-known lawyer and literary critic. A prominent student of Nietzsche, he was considered a theoretician of Bulgarian symbolism and his work was promulgated in the 1930s, after his untimely death in Paris, by the philosopher Yanko Yankov.[57] As behooves today's sanitized biographical versions, only his later right-wing ideas are reflected, while the fact that he had been consecutively a Tolstoyist, Narrow, and Broad socialist, before joining the pro-German National-Liberal Party as one of its leaders in 1920, is redacted.[58]

Another interesting case is Petîr Taushanov (1881–1960s?), a lifelong communist, born in the Ottoman Empire, who became a member of the IMRO and after an assassination attempt fled to Russia. Enrolled in the Odessa seminary he was expelled as a Tolstoyist and socialist. He later joined the Bolsheviks.[59] Dimitîr Blagoev's own younger brother Khristo (1865–96) was described as a Tolstoyist by his closest friend Matei Ikonomov, although there is no question that as a schoolboy he was also under the influence of the Russian *narodniks*. He studied geology and botany in Zurich and Lausanne where he joined the Marxists around Plekhanov. For a year he was at the medical faculty of Moscow University from where he was expelled for revolutionary activities in 1890. Soft-spoken and highly sensitive, he had married very early and had a child, Mladen, whose godfather was Dimitîr. Aware of his fateful disease, he left his wife and child with the sturdy and vivacious Matei Ikonomov (1871–1960), later a famous actor, theater director and author who, with his equally successful actress wife Mania (Maria), the widow of Khristo, founded the well-known *Contemporary Theater*, staging Maxim Gorky, Henrik Ibsen, William Shakespeare, Lev Tolstoy, Alexander Ostrovsky, and Gerhardt Hauptmann. A dedicated Narrow, Ikonomov offered the theater he was working at the time, *Crown* (Korona), for the First Congress of the BCP in 1919 without the permission of the trustees.[60] His stature as a great actor saved him from persecutions in the interwar period and also secured him a place in today's encyclopedias, although there is no word there of his political affiliations.[61]

A defining feature of Bulgarian Tolstoyism in contrast to the Russian movement was its political presence in several political parties but especially within the BANU, where many of its politicians shared its principles of peasant defense in the face of the state and the church. Khristo Stoianov (1892–1970), minister of internal affairs and public health in the agrarian government wrote that "as a student I was roving between Russian nihilism and the Christian anarchism of Tolstoy and Kropotkin" before embracing the ideology of Stamboliiski.[62] Its most prominent representative was the great BANU leader, lawyer, and writer Iordan Kovachev (1895–1966) who became a follower of the economic teachings of Henry George (Georgism) and was known as the Bulgarian Mahatma Gandhi. There were several successful Tolstoyist communes from 1908 and throughout the interwar period, and the influence of their ideas was strengthened by the popular journal *Vŭzrazhdane* (1907–35) and the activities of the Vegetarian Association (1914).[63] The myth (probably starting with Tolstoy's daughter Alexandra) that Tolstoy undertook his last voyage with the intention to settle in Bulgaria is extremely potent in Bulgaria to this day.[64]

As a whole *narodnichestvo* in Bulgaria was not so much a social as a cultural movement, with an especially substantive role in literature, which was understood first and foremost to have a social function, including an elevated role for the social mission of the intellectuals, mostly teachers and writers, a critical attitude toward the new bourgeois transformations, and a retrospective utopian idealization of tradition family and community values, principally in the village and small towns.[65] As already mentioned, of the Bulgarian *narodniks* Gavril Balamezov died young in 1897 and Georgi Kŭrdhiev joined the Liberal Party. Among the *narodnik* writers and scholars, the names of Tsanko Tserkovski, Vasil Kŭnchov, and Khristo Maksimov (Mircho) stand out. The premier figure in the cohort of Bulgarian *narodnik* litterateurs was Todor Vlaikov (1865–1943) who studied Slavic philology in Moscow and came under the influence of the ideas of Tolstoy and, especially, Nikolay Mikhailovsky. On his return to Bulgaria, he became a teacher and founded the first village cooperative in Mirkovo. His prose was "a eulogy of traditional Bulgarian virtues: hard work, devotion to home, family, and kin, simplicity and warmth in human relationships, emotional reticence, stoicism in suffering."[66] One of the founders of the Bulgarian Teachers' Union, Vlaikov joined the Democratic Party in 1900 and became the leader of the Radical-Democratic Party in 1905 alongside Naicho Tsanov, Anton Strashimirov, and Petko Todorov.

The latter three names are symptomatic for the often-convoluted relationship to socialism. Naicho Tsanov (1857–1923), a prominent lawyer and leader of the Liberal Party of Karavelov, whose left wing created the Democratic Party in 1896 and the Radical-Democratic Party in 1905, was a fierce opponent of the Stambolov regime and its assault on democracy. This led him in 1891 to be in the same electoral list as Blagoev, and their friendly relations continued. When in 1898 he survived an ill-fated duel with the arrogant Hungarian consul in Vidin, Blagoev sent a congratulatory letter to "my dear friend Naicho." And this, after an editorial by Tsanov in which he accused the socialists of "unconsciously undermining the foundations of the newly created Democratic Party," since there was no room for socialism in Bulgaria.[67]

Anton Strashimirov (1872–1937), a complex and turbulent figure, spanning all major literary trends from social realism to individualist modernist avant-gardism in his prolific oeuvre, studied geography, literature, and philosophy in Bern. A fiery nationalist, he was active in the Macedonian organization and as a leader of the radical-democrats was several times MP. He espoused socialist ideas in his youth but did not participate in the socialist movement. His brother Todor Strashimirov (1880–1925), on the other hand, was an early socialist and member of the Broads, who in 1920 joined the BCP. He was assassinated in 1925 as an opposition MP. Anton published the briefest obituary—"They also killed my brother Todor. God save Bulgaria"—followed by the culmination of his works, the novel *Round Dance* (Хоро), which gave a tragic expressionist portrait of the violence of the civil war. Banned immediately, the novel reached the Bulgarian public only after 1944, despite its many translations in the interwar period.[68]

The celebrated poet Petko Todorov (1879–1916, see Part I) was influenced by socialism in his high school years, and during his studies in France, Switzerland, and Germany read French and Russian literature and modern drama (Ibsen, Schnitzler, Chekhov). While there is some influence of *narodnik* motives in his work, his idylls and dramas have an inordinate place in the beginnings of Bulgarian modernist literature.[69] Other writers and poets, Peiu Iavorov (1878–1914), Kiril Khristov (1875–1944), Stoian Mikhailovski (1856–1927), Elin Pelin (1877–1949), had brief but deep encounters with socialism in the 1890s which left indelible traces in their works.[70] Petko Todorov's death from tuberculosis in a sanatorium in Switzerland sheds light on the untimely end of these first generations of Bulgarian intellectuals.

As already mentioned, the towering figure in what has been defined as the Bulgarian version of *narodnichestvo* and dubbed the father of Bulgarian anarchism but also the most influential personality in the 1880s before the rise of the BSDP, was Spiro (Spiridon) Gulabchev (1852–1918). The son of a priest actively involved in the national struggle in Macedonia, Spiro was sent to the Bulgarian schools in Istanbul, Edirne (together with Blagoev), and Plovdiv before he went to Russia in 1878 on a fellowship from Eastern Rumelia to study theology in Odessa, then law in Moscow and history in Kiev. Besides his dedication to the Macedonian cause he was deeply interested in Slavic folklore and philology. Already during his student years he urged for the democratization of language, the utilization of the richness supplied by different dialects, and the adoption of a phonetic orthography.[71]

In Kiev he came under the influence of the ideas of Mikhail Dragomanov (Mykhailo Drahomanov) and was arrested in 1885 for smuggling the illegal journal *Hromada* and socialist books. The influence of Dragomanov was immense and Gulabchev continued his personal contacts with him after Dragomanov accepted a position at Sofia University in 1889, until his death from heart failure in 1895.[72] While characterizing Gulabchev's ideas broadly as *narodnichestvo*, this should be strongly qualified. Dragomanov himself declared his adherence to non-Marxist socialism as an ethical system for social justice. While his socialism was oriented toward the peasantry because of the specific social structure in the Ukraine, he rejected the *narodniks*' disregard for liberal institutions and the glorification of peasant revolts. A central tenet of his thought was the federative idea of self-ruling socialist communes, which in his struggle for Ukrainian sovereignty he also extended to international relations.[73] Gulabchev's embrace of the Balkan Federation as a way to reach the "federative decentralized ideal" had a local pedigree, but it also had the imprint of Dragomanov.[74]

The peak of Gulabchev's activities and propaganda, mostly in northeast Bulgaria (Gabrovo, Varna, and Tîrnovo) was in the later 1880s when he gained wide popularity with his teaching of *siromakhomilstvo* (pauperophilia). An eclectic mixture of

Figure 21 Spiro Gulabchev as a student in Russia, 1880.

revolutionary democratic, *narodnik*, and anarchic ideas, it also had a purely Bulgarian tonality, reminiscent of the medieval Bogomils.[75] He organized so-called "friendly societies" (приятелски дружинки) in several cities—Gabrovo, Sevlievo, Tîrnovo, and maybe Sofia) between 1887 and 1889.[76] These societies were entirely devoted to educational activities and Gulabchev opened a library with the name "Read, brother, read," where people could consult the poetry of Botev, Rakovski, and Lermontov, the works of Proudhon, Adam Smith, Spencer, John Stuart Mill, Karl Marx, Nikolai Dobroliubov, Nikolai Shelgunov, and, above all, the works of Pisarev, Gulabchev's favorite writer.[77]

The one thing that defined his organization as idiosyncratic was its conspiratorial character. The members of the societies consisted of groups that did not know each other and were coordinated solely by Gulabchev who had the lists of all members. They used secret scripts and were discouraged from forming close friendships.[78] Physically hypnotizing, with intense eyes and white hair even in his twenties, reticent and withdrawn, hostile to fashion and dressed simply, a true ascetic, Gulabchev was able to fire up his students and followers.[79] And yet, this strict conspiracy was not dictated by any clandestine preparation for violent acts. On the contrary, Gulabchev was a firm believer in nonviolence and the transformative effect of education. According to Panaiotov, Gulabchev was doing this solely for the psychological impact: "If the fervent imagination of the youth could not be attracted with risky and romantic revolutionary deeds, why not fascinate them with the masonic mystery of his organization, with the dark mystery of the acceptance ritual?"[80]

In his so-called *Diary* from 1888, in fact, a notebook with casual notes written in a microscopic illegible handwriting and consisting mostly of summaries for his history lessons, Gulabchev defined the main concepts he would introduce, such as revolution, state, religion, war, law, reforms, republic, equality, liberty, property, progress, reaction, pessimism, and optimism. He also indicated the sources he was using: the liberal historian of law Alexander Gradovskii's *On the State System* and excerpts from the French journals *Philologie* and *Sociologie*.[81] Revolutions are manifold, political or economic, abrupt or gradual, bloody or peaceful, involving the whole society or the individual: "The best lesson one can take from the French Revolution is that revolutions should not be made in the name of an idea, unless this idea has matured in at least half the population, until the soil is prepared. One thing was intended, something else resulted."[82] Freedom is the ability to do everything one needs or wants, but "this all should be such as not to harm others (all humanity) ... and be in accordance with nature. ... The only condition for freedom is the equality of labor."[83] Today's idea of nationalism was nothing else but a form of the idea of national dignity and national pride. The idea of freedom for the people developed in the late-eighteenth century naturally and logically from the idea of freedom for the individual.[84] And nationalism is the idea that individuals belonging to the same people should also belong to a separate body of political, literary, and cultural sovereignty. Since today people are so mixed, however, under "nationalism one should understand individuals from different nationalities (народност), who comprise a separate body of political (and partly common cultural) sovereignty."[85] So much for an Eastern/Balkan type of organic nationalism!

During the 1880s, Gulabchev thought of himself as a socialist and was considered by the authorities as one of the most dangerous.[86] Yet, he became a fierce opponent of the social democrats. In 1890 in Ruse, with the financial support of the socialist circles Gulabchev founded a press. This became one of the most important publishing centers for socialist and anarchist literature, which functioned between 1890 and 1905. Its first publication was the first issue of *Novo Vreme*, but Gulabchev personally meddled in its editing, rearranging the materials and even threatening to preface it with a note stating his disagreement with Blagoev's editorial.[87] This was the end of Gulabchev's collaboration with the social democrats, and after the creation of the party which he vehemently opposed, especially on the issue of its adherence to the international movement dominated by Marxism, the breach was complete.[88] The second book printed by his press was Edward Bellamy's *Looking Backward* in the translation of Bozveliev.[89] After 1890, Gulabchev turned entirely to anarchism, arguing for spontaneous activity, against party discipline, for full personal freedom, and against the right of the majority to impose its will.[90] He published translations of Bakunin, Kropotkin, Reclus, and Jean Grave, wrote polemical brochures against social democracy, but after 1905 the press was closed and to the end of his life he had to pay off his enormous debts.[91]

Marxisms

The *narodniks* were socialists, but there was among them no "passage to Marxism," slowly or otherwise. There did exist a "passage to Marxism" but it was almost directly from the revolutionary national movement via the disappointment with Bulgaria's independent development. After the heightened hopes with San-Stefano in March 1878 and the subsequent dismemberment of the country in Berlin in July of the same year, only partial national sovereignty was achieved, and unification and irredenta were on the agenda. The Bulgarian revolutionary democrats of the 1860s and 1870s were republicans and the imposition of a monarchical arrangement with a foreign prince who aimed at absolute powers brought the first blow. More serious were the structural social transformations following the gradually intensifying capitalist development, rising inequalities, and the blatant exploitation of a new class of *nouveax riches* that shocked a deeply egalitarian society harboring ideas of social justice. There was an array of critical reactions, from a barricading within a nostalgic patriarchal traditionalism, through a stoic acceptance of the status quo as inevitable or a brazen embrace of nationalism, to the support and struggle for a broad humanistic and democratic ideal, of which socialism was a variety.

It is not that Bulgarians were more resistant to the "bug" of Russian *narodnichestvo*. It simply reached them after its zenith in the 1870s when they were completely preoccupied with their national cause. The disappointments in the 1880s coincided with the rethinking of *narodnik* tactics that no longer served as a role model. Even Gulabchev's peak period coincided with the growing interest in Marxism, especially in the teachers' milieu. Moreover, the first socialists pointed to this direct link themselves. Blagoev's *Our Apostles* (Нашите апостоли) written in 1886 directly accused the new elites of betraying the ideas and ideals of Liuben Karavelov and Khristo Botev, and in his later reminiscences he noted:

> During my youth I was shaped in the spirit of nationalism, but it was not merely nationalist but also revolutionary. By absorbing the national idea from the Bulgarian agitators of the time, I also took in their revolutionary spirit. . . . When I went to Russia, I already had the revolutionary yeast in me. The political and social relations provided this yeast with the proper condition to mature and helped me develop a clear revolutionary consciousness. Moreover, the political conditions and struggles in Bulgaria after the Liberation demonstrated very clearly the bankruptcy of that path to the realization of the national idea.[92]

Many others also saw or acted out this direct link, like Christian (Krîstiu) Rakovski, born Krîstiu Georgiev Stanchev, who adopted the name of his uncle on his mother's side, the illustrious revolutionary and literary figure Georgi Stoikov (Sava) Rakovski (1821–67). There were also direct existential links. Totiu Daalov (1864–1925) who as a child had fought with the Russian army and the Bulgarian volunteers at Shipka in 1877, became a cobbler and participated at the Buzludzha congress. Siding with the Broads in 1903, after 1915 he left politics.[93] Rakovski's teacher in Gabrovo was Evtim Dabev

(1864–1946), the first translator and publisher of Marxist literature, who had formed his socialist outlook under the direct impact of Botev's journalism. Born in Gabrovo in a poor potter's family, he attended the Aprilov High School but was kicked out for his atheism and finished in Plovdiv. He was a teacher in Sevlievo for a year whence he returned to Gabrovo and stayed in Bulgaria all his life. In June 1886 at the age of twenty-two, he started the first socialist newspaper *Rositsa* of which twenty issues came out until the end of the year and where he published Marx's early and accessible *Wage Labor and Capital*, translated from the Russian edition of Plekhanov's "Emancipation of Labor" group by Lev Deutsch. It is unclear how he got hold of this edition but most likely it was through Blagoev who was already in touch with Plekhanov or maybe even directly, as attested by another socialist in Gabrovo at the time, Andrei Konov (1865–1933) who wrote: "We provided books directly from Russia and the Geneva émigré bookstore which stored all the works of the free-spirited Russian writers forbidden in Russia."[94]

Arguing for the need of a workers' party whose aim would be to end the present division of society into exploiters and exploited and distribute equitably the products of labor, Dabev wrote that such a party has existed from Ottoman times (от турско време) and "its member and founder is Khristo Botev who died for the realization of its goal. Even today this party has dozens of decent members."[95] In 1888, Dabev translated what became the most widespread and admired popularization of Marxism, the Polish socialist Szymon Dickstein's *By What Do We Live?* (1881, *Kto z czego żyje?*) rendered in Bulgarian as *Who Lives At Whose Expense?* (Кой на чий гръб живее?). Altogether he published more than a dozen Marxist books of translation as well as his own poetry under the pseudonym Druzheliubov. A participant at the Buzludzha congress in 1891 and siding at first with Blagoev, he later joined the Broads, but after 1905 retreated from political work and stayed a social democrat without a party allegiance, lamenting the split in the movement.

Iurdan Rashenov (1884–1966?), the son of a provincial lawyer, was a spirited boy and participated in different gangs, mostly imitating Botev's armed company. Already in middle school, his friends were devouring Botev's and Levski's biographies written by Zakhari Stoianov, and reciting Botev's poems. Once in the Aprilov High School in Gabrovo, he joined the reading socialist circles, adding to the diet of Bulgarian literature Russian authors—Pushkin, Nekrasov, Turgenev, Gorky, and the Russian revolutionary democrats Chernyshevsky, Dobroliubov, Belinsky, and Pisarev. The socialist circle in Gabrovo had links to other societies in Varna and Tîrnovo, where a student paper was published. There was a strict reading regime. The first year was devoted to the evolution of society from antiquity, through feudalism, urban society with its guilds, and so on. In the next years, a stronger political element was added, through the study of militarism and wars, criminality, Christianity and socialism, revolutionary movements, etc. They read Plekhanov, Marx, and, most prominently, Dickstein. The meetings were held at the homes of students and since they were forbidden, the members would always come with a mug and sugar pretending they had gathered for a tea party, in case of the regular teachers' inspections.[96] Rashenov later studied law in Geneva and was a member of the BWSDP (b) in Kharlakov's group, the so-called "anarcho-liberals." In 1920 he joined the BCP.

The direct "passage" was also prominent in the later generation of socialists inspired and/or involved in the Macedonian struggle who "tamed" their militancy through the embrace of socialist ideas. Such was the case of Todor Tsekov (see chapter 7) or of Vladimir Dimchev (1887–1954) who started out as a fiery Macedonian patriot. During his school years, mostly attracted to mathematics and physics, he read Ludwig Büchner's *Force and Matter* (*Kraft und Stoff: Empirisch-naturphilosophische Studien*, 1855), which shook his religious beliefs. The scientific materialism led him to socialist literature, supplied by one of his close school friends. He started frequenting lectures and meetings, but his encounter with a workers' demonstration in 1906 from the tobacco factory in Plovdiv was formative. "It was the first time I heard about strikes and the first time I saw workers as a separate class. Until this moment, especially when I was preoccupied with the Macedonian movement, we used to speak about the people, the masses, the enslaved Bulgarians, and the like. Now for the first time I heard that workers had their own demands and interests, different from the owners of the factories, the bourgeoisie."[97]

The ritual of the reading circles leads us directly to Michel de Certeau who theorized reading as an everyday practice of wandering and poaching and sought to nuance the gloomy Foucauldian disciplinary society by emancipating the reader as an active consumer. Acknowledging "how the violence of order is transmuted into a disciplinary technology," he nonetheless "brings to light the clandestine forms taken by the dispersed, tactical, and make-shift creativity of groups or individuals already caught in the nets of 'discipline.' Pushed to their ideal limits, these procedures and ruses of consumers compose a network of an antidiscipline."[98] The reader is not a passive recipient but uses the act as a strategy of non-conformity. His "place is not here or there, one or the other, but neither the one nor the other, simultaneously inside and outside, dissolving both by mixing them together, associating texts like funerary statues that he awakens and hosts, but never owns. In that way, he also escapes from the law of each text in particular, and from that of the social milieu."[99] The intensity of reading reminds us also of what Robert Darnton described as the fabrication of a romantic sensitivity through the Rousseauian concept of intensive reading emulating religious texts transposed onto secular works.[100]

At his high school, students were allowed to receive free of charge the government paper *Svoboda*, but Stoian Nokov and his friends were reading Shelgunov, Chernyshevsky, Pisarev, Belinsky, Turgenev, and Gogol not only in Bulgarian translation but also in the Russian original. Since they were using textbooks in disciplines that did not yet have Bulgarian counterparts, their Russian was well developed.[101] Later in Geneva, Nokov entered the books he had bought in 1889–90: Victor Hugo's *Angelo, Tyrant of Padua*, and *The Hunchback of Notre-Dame* and Hernani, Alexander Dumas' *Les Blancs et les Blues* on the death of Marat, Tolstoy's *Confession*, Vasil Drumev's play *Ivanko*, Vazov's poems, Schiller's *Kabale und Liebe*, Shakespeare's *Macbeth* and *Romeo and Juliet*, Zola's *La mort d'Olivier Bécaille*, Pushkin's *Boris Godunov* and *Mozart and Salieri*, Molière's *Le Bourgeois gentilhomme*, the Christian socialist Émile de Laveleye's *Luxury* and other works, Shelgunov's articles and brochures, surveys on medieval European history, modern history, intellectual history, and textbooks on French grammar, physics, and trigonometry, a truly "poaching" enterprise.[102]

As a rule, the fascination with socialism came with an equally strong attraction to science. Blagoev had arrived in Russia with the sole desire of studying mathematics and natural sciences in order to be useful to the fatherland. When a few years later he wrote *What is Socialism and Do We Have a Basis for It?* he concluded: "Socialism is above all a science, the fruit of the enormous development of natural sciences and philosophy. And do we not really have a basis for science?"[103] The step from Darwin to Marx was natural. Ianko Sakŭzov (1860–1941), Blagoev's closest friend before they became bitter opponents, had studied biology in London, listening to Thomas Huxley and reading Herbert Spencer and Henry George. It seems that it was the latter's *Progress and Poverty* that turned his attention to social issues.[104] In Paris he listened to Hippolyte Taine and studied the works of Auguste Comte, Louis Blanc, and Proudhon but when he returned, he came with a degree in natural sciences. His first difficulties as a teacher were not because of his social views but because he introduced anatomical experiments, dissecting frogs, birds, and lambs with his students.[105]

In his unpublished memoirs *On a secret path to the forbidden sciences* written in 1962, Ivan Marinov (1893–1980) describes how in the Shumen high school he was attracted to science but was reading unsystematically and as a result with little comprehension. With a few friends, he decided to form a circle and approached a teacher for a reading list and advice on how to make reports and proceed with self-education. The teacher was "the young and handsome Ilia Iankulov" who had the reputation of a socialist.[106] The first book on the list was the French astronomer Camille Flammarion's *What is the Heaven?*, translated from his best-selling *Astronomie Populaire*. Books were expensive, and they were waiting in line in the library. If someone owned a book, it was "executed" and the chapters handed out among the group, something that befell Flammarion. Marinov started distributing socialist literature, and the English poet Edward Carpenter's *Sex and Marriage* proved to be the bestseller. Other books they read and discussed were Lewis H. Morgan's *Ancient Society*, Darwin's *On the Origin of Species*, Marx's *A Contribution to the Critique of Political Economy* and *Wage Labor and Capital*, Jules Guesde's *Collectivism* and, of course, *The Communist Manifesto*. Crucial was Alexander Bogdanov's *A Short Course in Economic Science*.[107] After four years of intense self-education, in which they analyzed 112 reports on their readings, they decided to join organized social democracy and began with the Social-Democratic Teachers' Organization (SDTO) as members of the BWSDR (n).[108] Marinov became a teacher and after 1923 emigrated to Romania and Austria, ending up in the USSR where he studied medicine and was a military doctor in the Red Army. He finished his career as a general and professor of the Military Medical Academy in Plovdiv.

If in this text little attention is given to religion and atheism, it is not that it was absent. On the contrary, atheism was a given and the first accusation hurled against the socialists was that they were godless (*bezbozhnitsi*). As already mentioned, Pisarev, whom Victoria Frede describes as making "doubt the permanent condition of all human beings" and advocating "a life of total independence, stripping their minds of all preconceptions and attempting to discover a new set of principles and way of life on their own," was one of the most widely read authors among the Bulgarians.[109] And yet, the obsessive atheism and frenetic anti-clericalism typical of the Russian movement was absent from the Bulgarian and, as a whole, from the Balkan socialist movements.

This had probably to do with the relative weakness of the church as an institution alongside the role Orthodoxy had played as a national pillar in opposition to the status quo in the Ottoman period, as well as the egalitarian ethos not only among the lower clergy but penetrating even the higher echelons, especially in the first decades after independence. This also set Bulgaria and the Balkans apart from the south of Europe, particularly Spain and Italy, where both socialism and anarchism were directed primarily against the powerful Catholic church.[110]

All in all, one can say that it was several prominent high schools that were the principal disseminators of socialism, especially the famous Gabrovo high school, and the ones in Plovdiv, Sofia, Tîrnovo, and others, as well as the most active socialist circles in Sevlievo, Drianovo, Kazanlîk, and elsewhere. Ivan Kutev (1863–1933), the first translator of the *Communist Manifesto*, was from Kazanlîk, studied law in Switzerland, and was a lawyer in Stara Zagora, Khaskovo, and Pazardzhik. Described by Bozveliev as a good orator but highly eccentric, in 1897 he refused to be on the same list with Sakîzov, and as a result tore away eighty-one votes for which he was expelled from the party for six years. After 1903 he retreated from politics.[111] The "dozens of decent members" mentioned by Dabev were probably just a few dozens. In Gabrovo they were five—Evtim Dabev, Todor Postompirov, Petio Mustakov, Tincho Khristov, and Nikifor Solnikov, and they were the soul of the first socialist circle organized among students and some workers.[112] These were all homebred socialists, as was Sava Mutafov (1864–1943) who had studied at the Aprilov High School and became a teacher and secretary in the Sevlievo regional court. In 1889 he founded the socialist group in Sevlievo where he opened a printing press and bookstore. In 1891 at Buzludzha he joined the opponents of Blagoev arguing for a continuation of the enlightenment work and against premature participation in the political struggle. In 1894 he went to Bern to study law and was close to Plekhanov and Rakovski. In the 1890s, as editor of *Drugar* and *Social-Democrat*, he published mostly materials from the Geneva group. After 1903 he joined the Broads but two years later retreated from political life, and practiced law in Sevlievo, Sofia, and Stara Zagora.

The Geneva circle, although relatively small and not long-lived, had a disproportionate influence in the early years of Bulgarian social democracy, not least because of its closeness to Plekhanov but also because of the pronounced talents of its members. Three of its founding members were classmates from the Aprilov High School and under the direct influence of Evtim Dabev: Slavi Balabanov (1872–93), Stoian Nokov (1872–59), and Christian (Krîstiu) Rakovski (1873–1941). Nokov left detailed memoirs about the Geneva period and his archive has the correspondence of the four Geneva golden boys together with Georgi Bakalov (1873–1939) who joined them after he had finished the Plovdiv high school.[113] Balabanov and Rakovski left for Geneva in 1889 to study medicine, and Nokov (see Part I) and Bakalov (see Part I and III) joined them the same year in the Faculty of Natural Sciences. There were around 150 Bulgarian students in Geneva of different political allegiances and many more Russian ones, but the Russian students, mostly *narodniks*, were negative toward Plekhanov whom they accused of possessing insufficient knowledge of the Russian conditions. By contrast, the young Bulgarian socialists gravitated toward Plekhanov and invited him to present lectures for their group on *The Development of*

Figure 22 Balabanov, Nokov, Rakovski, Riabova, Bakalov–Geneva circa 1890–91.

the Monist View of History, the book he had just completed.[114] The "Group of Bulgarian Student Socialists" around the core of the abovementioned four, had thirty-five members and it held weekly meetings dedicated to themes from sociology, natural sciences, ethnography, and the history of the workers' movement.[115] With the help of Plekhanov, Nokov was instrumental in bringing Gules Guesde as a speaker to the May 1, 1893, demonstration.[116] Nokov left vivid portraits of Guesde, Wilhelm Liebknecht, Vera Zasulich, Rosa Luxemburg, and, of course, Plekhanov, with whom he was especially close.[117]

In March 1893, Slavi Balabanov ended his twenty-one-year-old life after a long period of physical suffering, although there have been unproven but persistent theories that this was the result of his unrequited love for Elisaveta Riabova, the future wife of Rakovski.[118] His death was a shock for the movement and widely bemoaned because of the promise he had shown of becoming a leading theoretician of socialism. A few months before his suicide, he wrote to Nokov, explaining his views. This is important, since it sheds a nuance on the widely spread opinion that from the outset the Geneva group was against the formation of a social-democratic party:

> We should first of all create our own physiognomy as social-democrats, form our specific characteristics. And only then, if necessary, as a social-democratic party enter in accord with other "dissatisfied" social elements. And what is characteristic for the social-democrat, what forms his physiognomy? That he expresses the interests mostly of the workers, that this is a purely workers' movement. . . . It means that first and foremost, we have to create a workers' movement, to organize

the workers, however small their number may be, to create a social-democratic nucleus in real life, and thus bring social democracy from literature to life, from the journals and brochures to the factory and the street, where its real place should be.[119]

For this to be achieved, they should begin with pushing for the immediate interests of the workers: regular wages, labor legislation, etc.: "Once they begin being active about their economic demands and the government begins prosecuting them, [workers] themselves will see the need for a political party."[120] The Geneva group accordingly supported the BSDU around Sakŭzov in 1892. When the BSDU and BSDP merged in 1894 to form the BWSDP, Balabanov was no more. The rest were consecutively Broads, Narrows, and anarcho-liberals, and all ended up as communists.[121]

Rakovski (see Parts I and III) is the best-known figure among the first Geneva socialist generation because of his international role in several socialist movements, most notably the Romanian, Bulgarian, Russian, and the Balkan in general (he was the

Figure 23 Bakalov, Rakovski, Milanov, Balabanov (sitting)–Geneva 1892 (ЦДА, C-II-7024).

representative of the Balkan Communist Federation in the *Comintern* of which he was one of the cofounders). Nokov remembered him as a student in Kotel and Gabrovo, a fiery orator and passionate actor, playing the title role in Schiller's *The Robbers*. In 1894, after Nokov returned to Bulgaria, Rakovski visited him in Kotel but would not settle there: "For me Bulgaria is narrow." He wanted to receive French citizenship and when Nokov countered that this would be impossible, Rakovski assured him that Jaurès and Clemenceau would vouch for him.[122] His regular letters to Nokov between 1891 and 1913 sparkle with wit. His writing style, linguistic capacities, cultural allusions, vivacity, even his handwriting distinguish him from his equally talented compatriots, and one could easily forgive the slightly narcissistic quality of his persona.[123]

Rakovsky received his medical degree in 1897 from the University of Montpellier with a dissertation on "The Cause of Crime and Degeneration." In 1902, after the death of Riabova in childbirth, which he experienced as a devastating blow, he worked as a physician in France but was denied naturalization. When he was summoned back to Romania where he inherited his father's estate in 1904, he became entirely dedicated to revolutionary work. A leader in the Romanian socialist movement, he was a prominent figure in the Second International. After 1917 Rakovski had a high-profile status in the USSR as chairman of the Provisional Revolutionary Government and Commissar for Foreign Affairs of the Ukraine, and an illustrious career as the Soviet Ambassador in London and Paris. One of Trotsky's closest friends, after 1927 he was ousted from the *Comintern* and expelled from the party, to live in internal exile. In 1934 he "admitted his mistakes," was sent as ambassador to Japan in 1935, but following his second arrest in 1937 during the Great Purge and the 1938 show trials, he was sentenced to twenty years of hard labor. That he escaped the immediate liquidation to which Bukharin, Rykov, Krestinsky, and the others from the Trial of the Twenty-One was due to the broad international outcry, "Save Krîstiu from the bullet! Since Russia is boiling, it would not be surprising to see him freed soon and heading this unfortunate land which is now ruled by a virtually crazy type and satrap."[124] Rakovski outlived Bukharin by three years, but was shot alongside Trotsky's sister, Anna Kameneva, Maria Spiridonova, and others in the Medvedev Forest Massacre in September 1941. He was rehabilitated only in 1988. The literature on Rakovski is enormous.[125]

Another two later Geneva graduates were also closely linked to the Russian movement. Pavel Nonchev (1876–1950) came to Geneva to study finance after finishing the pedagogical school in Kazanlik. He arrived in 1896 after the dissolution of the Geneva group and became very close to Plekhanov, but later was captivated by Lenin. He was elected secretary of the Russian group "Collaboration with the Russian social-democratic party" and managed the printing of *Iskra*. Entrusted with the archive, he preserved full runs of *Iskra* (1900–05), *Zaria* (1901–02), *Vpered* (1904–05) and *Proletarii* (1905). In 1909 he returned to Bulgaria where he became the director of the commercial school in Plovdiv and disseminated socialist ideas.[126]

Roman Avramov (1882–1937/1938?) came from a rich merchant's family in Svishtov. At the age of sixteen, he joined the BWSDP in 1898, and in 1900 moved to Geneva to study law. Married to a Russian medical student, he later wrote: "Since 1901 I started a double party life. Involved all the time in the life of the Bulgarian social democracy, I also started working actively for the Russian social democracy abroad."[127]

Fluent in French, German, English, and Russian, he was asked by Lenin to take part in the founding of a Bolshevik group in Berlin. A co-editor of *Vpered*, he was secretary of the committee of the Bolshevik organizations abroad and became vice-manager of the publishing house *Demos*, whose revenues went for arms. In 1909 he returned to Bulgaria for his military service. Although he had joined the Narrows in 1903, he felt the stifling atmosphere of the hyper-centralization imposed by Blagoev. In 1905 Bakalov had written to him, complaining of the intolerance of Blagoev who could not stand alternative opinions: "I will tell you that, because of this excessive 'tightness', the party will soon tear at its tightest point."[128] Yet, Bakalov refused to start an open polemic: "I have only strength to fight the enemy, but when it comes to deliver a blow to a friend who has forgotten himself, the hand dies down."[129] Together with Bakalov and Kharlakov, Avramov joined the group "Proletarii" (the anarcho-liberals) and eventually the Broads in 1910 as their left wing. Like Rakovski, Bulgaria's horizons seemed narrow. In 1911 he wrote to Gorky, whom he had befriended, in Russian: "I feel very bored in Bulgaria. In the small town it is impossible to participate actively even in the Lilliputian political struggles typical for the country."[130] His only solace was writing for the Rakovski-edited newspaper *Napred*. An able officer during the war, he was part of the Soviet mission to negotiate the armistice in Petrograd in 1918. In 1920 he entered the BCP and the following year, with the agreement of the BCP, was asked by the Soviet government to work in the Soviet trade mission in Berlin. By 1924 he was also a member of the RCP (b). Between 1925 and 1929 he was the Soviet commercial representative in France, Germany, and Great Britain. From 1929 to 1937 he chaired the All Russian Syndicate "Khlebstroi." His horizons shrank in 1937 when he was arrested and executed.[131]

Others from poor workers' or peasants' backgrounds found different and often colorful paths to socialism. Konstantin Poprusinov (1879–1948), dubbed the Red Priest, was born near Plovdiv, and supported by a state grant finished the seminary, becoming a village priest in 1903. Sensitive to poverty and injustices, he began preaching against the wars and the ones in power (чорбаджиите). In 1919 he blessed the railway workers' strike and for a year was a "cassocked communist." When reprimanded, he countered that Jesus wore a red mantle, and the communists have a red flag, and invited all to join them. In 1922 he formally joined the party and left the church in 1923. His wife (попадията) had been a member of the party since 1920 and had organized the women's hunger riots in Pazardzhik during the war. Arrested and tried in the interwar period, he became an MP after the Second World War.[132]

Dimitŭr Pandov (1888–1962) was eleven when he heard the word socialism and the name of Blagoev from his father, a stonecutter who would go for seasonal work to Plovdiv. This made him proud as none of his friends had heard of it and he was no longer ashamed of his poverty, his bad clothes, and the fact that he walked barefoot until the snow fell. He did not know much about socialism except that it defended the poor. It also left him with an immense desire to be educated. He was a servant for a few years but managed to finish middle school. In 1904, he decided to attend high school in Plovdiv and walked the 37 kilometers (23 miles) from Peshtera to Plovdiv on foot with a walking stick on which he had suspended his shoes to preserve them for the winter and a long red ribbon on which he had written "Proletarians of the world, unite!" He managed to pass the exams and was accepted on a fellowship. He immediately entered the two running socialist circles which studied philosophy and political economy. In 1906 he had an interesting meeting with Exarch Iosif who was passing through Plovdiv and wanted to meet the young people that he spotted in the park. Pandov obviously looked a socialist with his long hair, rubashka, torn coat, and beaten shoes. The Exarch told him: "You are too young to be a socialist. It is too early. I too was a socialist when I was in Paris and saw the bourgeoisie promenade in landaus." They conversed for over an hour about Spinoza, Hegel, Kant, Marx, and Engels and the Exarch gave him a golden Turkish lira to buy trousers and shoes. The first share of the Exarch's gift went to buy sweets for the socialist circle from the best pastry shop in town where they had long admired the cakes through the window.[133] Pandov eventually became a lawyer and member of the BWSDP (n) and BCP but after 1923 retreated from the movement as he opposed the illegal means of struggle.

Still others entered the movement through the classical method of agitation. Georgi Dimov, born in 1880, had his reminiscences dictated in his dialectal speech in May 1960. He had received an irregular primary education in the school attached to the local village church after he turned nine but after a few years the school was closed. He worked the fields and looked after the cattle of the extended family and then went to work in the Pernik mines before he was twenty. In 1906, coming back from a night shift, they were told by another miner to go and listen to someone from Sofia. This was Georgi Dimitrov who urged them to form a syndicate for the defense of their interests, explaining the logic of strikes, and Dimov joined the BWSDP (n) in 1908. In 1910 he briefly flirted with the idea of going to America but Dimitrov reproached him for leaving his coworkers.[134] Nenko Hadzhistoianov (1882–1946) was in middle school in Stara Zagora and entered the school choir. One day while walking in the market with a friend, he was approached by a tailor who asked for help to organize a workers' choir. The choir consisted of young men who had left middle school and had become apprentices, because Stara Zagora had no high school and their parents could not afford to send them elsewhere. But their conscious baptism occurred after the visits and lectures in political economy by Georgi Kirkov who explained the notion of labor and surplus value. Nenko himself became a train conductor and was active in the railway workers' syndicate and the party.[135] Some were attracted out of curiosity. Khristo Georgiev Petrov, born in 1889, came from the very religious family of a furrier craftsman and venerated the church services. However, he was made uncomfortable by the hatred with which the priest spoke against the godless socialists which was contrary to the teaching of Christ for love among people. So he went to see these hateful people and in 1907, at the age of eighteen, joined the party.[136]

A unique case of the press as a formative experience comes from Traicho Kostov (1897–1949), a victim of Stalinist repression who received posthumous fame for insisting on his innocence at the final public trial (a rare case in the history of show trials). He came from an exceptionally poor family of eight children with two illiterate parents, and lost his brother to tuberculosis. A precocious child, he ended up in the elite classical gymnasium as a straight-A student but who was excessively shy. At high school he had no idea of socialism, although some of his classmates, especially the Jewish ones, hinted that he should become one. He was not, however, invited to any meeting and did not participate in, or outside, school in any activity. When he was mobilized, he witnessed how the sergeants were cruelly beating up soldiers, especially the Roma. Persuaded by some socialist officers, he subscribed to *Rabotnicheski vestnik*: "I could be taken as an example of how a socialist newspaper has played a definite formative influence."[137] It was in this same year 1916 that he wrote in the album of an unidentified girl:

> I was given your album by accident, unknown Miss, and I thought I would write something. To wish you happiness is redundant as every page of your album does it and this would hardly make you happier, but mostly because the whole notion of happiness is so general and undefined that everyone invests it with his own meaning and often what passes for happiness for one is the unhappiness of another; besides there are heretics who doubt that happiness is possible at all on this sinful earth. And indeed, I would like to know how one can be happy if one is hungry or what happiness can be felt by the ones unceremoniously thrown far away to shed their blood for alien ideals? Even in the best of circumstances, it is enough to have a toothache to wipe out your happiness. And would it not be too egotistical to dream of personal happiness when an endless and bottomless sea of misery and destitution is around you? . . . If life cannot be happy, it can be at least meaningful, and the meaning of life is labor. Its goal can be only the fulfilment of the sacred principles of liberty, fraternity and equality . . . Look carefully at the life around you, try to understand its foundations, find the source of evil and do spare your energy to destroy it. Today this is a thousand times more urgent. The peoples, choked by the uselessly shed blood of millions, disgusted with the meaningless mutual destruction, rise and with powerful efforts attempt to break the heavy chains of capitalism. . . . Only in the struggle for common happiness is it possible to reach the personal one, and only there can one find the meaning of life.[138]

Some of these coming-of-age stories are written with an immense sense of humor and give a vivid picture of the atmosphere of the period and place. Vŭrban Angelov (1887–1974) was born in the village of Samovodene close to Tǔrnovo, in the family of a high school teacher at the Jewish school in Shumen. He entered middle school in Tǔrnovo but many teachers were hostile to the village boys, reproaching them for running away from rural work in order to become state employees. The constant nagging and taunting of the town boys over their clothes made him quit school, and he told his father he wanted to become an apprentice and learn a craft. At age twelve he was apprenticed in Ruse in a Jewish tailor's shop where he was used solely as a servant around the house and often beaten. Religious at the time, he was afraid that on Passover they would suck Christian blood: "My blood was sucked indeed not by Jews, but by lice." From his stint there he came with an unforgettable ammunition for his future studies in law. Once he was sent by the master to fetch some "chai sin lemon," and to him this sounded like "blue lemon tea." Accordingly, when he brought back the tea with a lot of lemon, he received so many expletives over his ignorance of Ladino that from then on terms like "sine qua non," "sine die," and "sine causa" always evoked this early lesson.[139]

Eager to learn the trade properly, he went to another famous tailor's firm "Dinkov and Hermann" where the workers were a veritable international mixture: an Armenian, a Czech, a Jew, and two Bulgarians. The apprentices were again used mostly as servants, but Frau Hermann was gentle and would often treat them to sweets and tea. In the workshop the languages most spoken were Turkish and Vlach. It was cold and they had to secure their own heating, mostly by stealing planks from the wooden fence around the monument in the park which contributed to its early inauguration. One of the workers was a socialist, a good man who treated the apprentices nicely: "I loved him and so I came to love socialism." Between meetings at the worker's club and the protestant church, which was warm, by 1900 he thought he was a socialist and stopped going to church.[140] After two years of apprenticeship, Vîrban decided it was better to attend school, wrote to his father, and enrolled in the pedagogical high school in Shumen where he immediately joined the socialist circle, reading Darwin and Bogdanov.[141] He eventually studied law in Berlin, Jena and Sofia and joined the Narrows in 1907.

It is inescapable that one should address the issue of the different Marxisms within the Bulgarian movement. Much has been written and little can be added to the substance of the ideational conflict, except to balance out some of the verdicts. The best, most detailed, and evenhanded treatment to date belongs to Augusta Dimou.[142] She carefully weighs in the personal rivalries against principled theoretical disagreements and convincingly concludes that "the debate between the two factions was not about Marxism versus non-Marxism, but rather about the appropriate understanding and application of Marxist principles in Bulgarian society."[143] Within such a framework, one can distinguish between prioritizing syndicalist work among the working class (the Geneva group), independent class struggle through a political party without collaboration (the Narrows), and a broad political coalition in the defense of all oppressed (the Broads).[144] If the communist historiography has erred with its condescending attitude toward the not entirely bolshevized Narrows, it has erred gravely toward the Broads, reproducing the venomous language that had purged them from socialism. On the other hand, but understandably, after 1989 there is a tendency to sanctify the Broads, a case of reverse mythologization.[145]

Interestingly, Sakîzov himself in his major work on the split, *Trevoga za Prizratsi* (Ghost Alert), gave more weight to the "personal element" rather than to the theoretical and practical differences.[146] A highly attractive figure, reminiscent of a Doge of Venice with his patrician appearance, Sakîzov advocated "closeness, accord, agreement, joint action of the equally suffering, equally oppressed, equally robbed, equally exploited members of society. Whether workers get together to destroy the machines or raise a revolt, whether they unionize in economic or political organizations—in all these acts the main element is the union, the coming together."[147] Much as Blagoev's later insults were inflated and his tone unacceptable, he may have been right in his early assessment: "For him socialism was a teaching for an ideal order, a socialism of feelings and good wishes; he was altogether a sentimental socialist."[148]

The clearest articulation of the ideas of what would become the BWSDP (b) came, in fact, a couple of years earlier, written by the much younger Dimitîr Dimitrov (1876–1902), recognized on all sides as one of the most promising theoreticians but who, after the split, was maligned for his revisionism and reformism, and forgotten because of

Янко Сакжзовъ,
По случай 70 годишния му юбилей.
1860-1930

Figure 24 Ianko Sakîzov, 1930.

his untimely death from tuberculosis. Dimitrov had studied philosophy and classical literature at the University of Sofia. Before coming to Sofia, he had been a leader of the 1896–97 anarchist group in Ruse, the "group of the communards" under the influence of Gulabchev.[149] In Sofia he was involved in trade union work and journalism. In 1901 he published *Razpra v rabotnishkata partiia* (Quarrel in the Workers' Party), a perspicacious analysis on the eve of the division. Posthumously he was considered the ideologue of the common cause (obshtodelstvo).[150]

Dimitrov wrote *Razpra* in anticipation of the coming party congress, with the conflict between Sakîzov and Blagoev already ripe. He thought it should not be raised at the congress at all since it had little to do with principles and objected specifically to Blagoev's tone. Instead, the congress should focus on the real problems imposed by the current circumstances, namely the attitude of the party toward the agrarian and craftsmen's organizations, to the workers' cooperatives and syndicates, as well as to the Macedonian question.[151] His book came out, of course, a year after the foundation of BANU and at a time of heightened conflicts in Macedonia. Marxism, so Dimitrov, was already so established in all of Europe that it could not be ignored even by mainstream academics. He therefore questioned the need to defend it, let alone a pure form of Marxism in Bulgaria, where in the past decade socialism had already made serious and lasting inroads. He concluded that the accusations of deviation were simply a polemical form of power struggle.[152] But he went further by accusing Blagoev of reducing Marxism to several schematic formulae and fanatically imposing dogmatic thinking: "It is ridiculous to think that Marx is unqualifiedly correct and the bourgeois authors who have written on the same subject are unconditionally wrong. Let us free our thought, let every party member do it, let us question the whole of Marx and not assume that all his opponents are necessarily empty-minded, but that there are honest and sincere thinkers among them."[153] Conditions had changed and there were spheres where Marxist thought was outdated and had only historical significance, recognized even by Marx and Engels.[154]

Dimitrov accordingly raised the question of whether it was mandatory for a member of the social-democratic party to be a Marxist: "Can and should someone who is not a Marxist become a party member?" According to him, "A party member cannot be someone who has violated its program or has committed a dishonorable deed. But nowhere in the party program is it demanded that a party member should swear an oath to Marx."[155] The restricted understanding of the party would prevent it from admitting people who would have accepted its program from a different starting point, "coming from the gospel, from Tolstoy, from the study of bourgeois economists, through disappointment from the other parties, through empirical observation of the current situation, through dissatisfaction in one's social position and so on."[156] Moreover, the division of party members into "conscious" (Marxists) and "unconscious" (non-Marxists) created an internal hierarchy and an "intellectual party aristocracy."[157] The working members of the party were people who came to socialism empirically, by reading the party press and more accessible literature, by participating in meetings and assimilating the demands of the party program, but the "minimal program has no need to be necessarily justified by Marxism." Even the maximal program can be reached without Marxism, which does not mean that Marxism has to be rejected. Party discipline should be exercised on actions, not on thought.[158] His conclusion was programmatic:

> With the bourgeoisie for the development of capitalism, with the peasants and craftsmen for democracy and limiting the appetites of the bourgeoisie! We cannot prefer the fast capitalist development without democracy to the slow capitalist development with democracy. We do not want to deprive the peasants from voting rights because at first they might vote for measures limiting this development. . . . We want democracy first and foremost. The question whether it should be socialism or democracy does not exist for us. Our program and our activities thus far have given the true answer: through democracy toward socialism.[159]

If this all sounds very Bernsteinian, one would not be amiss. Although Dimitrov had translated Eduard Bernstein's *The Preconditions of Socialism and the Tasks of Social Democracy* (Voraussetzungen des Sozialismus und die Aufgaben der Sozialdemokratie) almost immediately after its publication in 1896 in *Die Neue Zeit* and as a separate book in 1899, he was not an epigone. Ideas about the suitability of Marxist ideas in the particular Bulgarian social and economic circumstances had been circulating much before Bernstein (as they had about Russia) and Sakîzov had raised them in his voluminous correspondence with Kautsky.[160] It is completely frivolous to guess what the future evolution of Dimitrov would have been, given the fluctuation of so many of the most cultivated and independently thinking minds between the two camps. What is interesting, however, is that despite the clear closeness to the ideas of Bernstein, Sakîzov disowned any affinity with him and to the end affirmed his loyalty to Kautsky and Marxism, even as Bernstein decades later pointed to him as his most loyal student.[161] Kautsky likewise valued Sakîzov to the point of pronouncing him the best Marxist in the Balkans.[162] Jean Jaurès referred to him as "un esprit large et libre," making the implicit comparison between Blagoev and Sakîzov, and Jules Guesde and himself.[163]

It was not only the debate on party membership that divided the two visions. More important and immediate for the political practice was the debate on private ownership which was linked to the unresolved problem of the attitude of the socialists toward the peasantry. In 1902 both Sakîzov and Blagoev were MPs, among the eight seats for the socialists. The prime minister, Danev, derided the socialists saying that they had no right to speak on behalf of the peasantry since they objected to private property and this for the peasants was sacred domain. Indeed, one of the first tasks of the Bulgarian constitution had been to consecrate the right of property under Articles 67 and 68.[164] Given the accusations against the arbitrariness of Ottoman rule and the insecurity of life and property, the thrill of owning land was one of the great achievements of independence in the eyes of the peasantry. And this, more than the accusations of godlessness, was considered to be the chief threat. When Bozveliev ran an election campaign, his opponent presented him with "Voilà un partageur!"[165]

The risk of alienating the peasantry with the preaching of the abolishment of private property was great and Sakîzov responded that socialists were not against the peasant, or the field, or vineyard that he works with his family and a pair of oxen:

> We consider that humanity will move from private to socialized ownership. The state railways today are not private, but public property.... We think that the large means of production in Bulgaria, like in other countries, will gradually become social property. When we say we are against private property ... this does not mean that we intend to create turmoil in the country in order to destroy private ownership.... So when we say that we are against private ownership, we have to understand simply the following. We are against the private ownership of capital that exploits other people's labor; and further that we are not against it today. At this moment, we desire to avert all evils emanating from it through social measures.[166]

The irony is that this is exactly what the communists after 1944 (before they started the ill-conceived collectivization) maintained and Bozveliev was right to say that were

Blagoev to be alive, "he would loudly reprimand all these communists who . . . in the press and at meetings assure the people that they are not against private property which has been earned with honest labor. For Blagoev such a compromise was impossible. In his negative attitude toward private property he was irreconcilable and remained like this to the end."[167] Indeed, immediately after Sakîzov's intervention, Blagoev took the floor and affirmed that the BSDP objected to any kind of private property and advocated common ownership. Was Blagoev's uncompromising attitude dogmatic and inflexible? Maybe. But he was not alone. It is not simply that he was sticking to the letter of Marx (which he was, incidentally).[168] But a general critique of private property was in the air. It came from the anarchists (Proudhon), implicitly from Christianity (if not from the church institution) and, in the Bulgarian case, most interestingly, from the teachings of Petîr Dînov who had become a popular figure and who was unequivocally and equally uncompromisingly preaching the absolute abolition of private property.[169]

All this was intimately linked to the overall relationship of the workers' party with the peasantry, the overwhelming part of the population. Although this issue was a central point of disagreement between the two factions, it has to be clearly stated that neither the Narrows nor the Broads ever came to a clearly stated philosophy and strategy on the peasant question. In this, they were no more different than the entire international socialist movement, which argued for, and postponed coming out with, a clearly defined position to the agrarian question. In fact, limited and dogmatic that it was, the Narrows had a consistent understanding of the peasantry as an unrevolutionary petty-bourgeois element, although in their program they defended them as an oppressed class. They did argue for the dissemination of socialist propaganda among the peasants but given their makeup, wanted to concentrate on the working class and were afraid that any engagement outside this priority would turn them into a petty-bourgeois party. The Broads, on the other hand, had a clearly stated tactic but not a strategy on the peasant question. The tactic consisted in arguing for a "common cause of all productive classes" in the struggle for broad democratic rights and economic improvements and thus adapting the minimal party program to the interests of the peasants. Yet, Sakîzov himself considered the newly created agrarian movement of Stamboliiski a bourgeois organization.[170]

The one interesting and creative exception was Nikola Gabrovski (1864–1925), a recognized but underestimated socialist leader. Having finished high school in Russia, he studied law in Geneva, and became a lawyer and judge in his home town, Tîrnovo. Already in 1889, when he attended the Inaugural Congress of the Second International in Paris, Gabrovski was of the opinion that a political social-democratic party was needed, and next to Blagoev, he was the person most instrumental in creating the BDSP in 1891. He was especially taken by the agrarian program of the French Workers' Party, in the belief that socialist propaganda could succeed in making the peasantry an ally of the proletariat.[171] Gabrovski objected to the notion of a "common cause" and collaboration with other parties, but what distinguished him strongly from Blagoev was his firm belief in the revolutionary potential of the peasantry. In his article "The Peasants and Socialism" published in *Rabotnik* in 1894, Gabrovski defied the notion that they were "pathological reactionaries," that "in their interests and aspirations peasants are foes of socialism, fierce and rusty conservatives, sworn enemies of any change."[172] He wrote this several years before a peasant organization appeared and believed it was the duty of

> the new party, the socialists, to accomplish what cannot be achieved by the old parties. As the party of the poor, the socialists understand the people's needs. . . . . The socialists seek what is in the interest of the laboring population. Herein lies the panacea for the fast dissemination of socialism in the village. . . . . The peasant, this old slave of land and society is awakening from the historical dream and is becoming conscious of his miserable position. . . . He, along with the city worker—his closest brother in battle—embraces socialism and enters the ranks of the new party.[173]

Gabrovski displayed an intimate and sympathetic knowledge of the village, and wrote about the different peasant categories and about the need of amelioration and modernization. Moreover, he not only wrote but was also a vocal exponent of these ideas as an MP. Since 1894, Gabrovski became the first socialist member of parliament (the second being Sakîzov) and was elected practically every year until the end of the Balkan Wars.[174] One can think of Gabrovski as a less successful Bulgarian Dobrugeanu-Gherea, especially after the creation of BANU in the aftermath of the peasant riots in northeastern Bulgaria. Significantly, at the constituent congress of BANU in Pleven, Dimitîr Dragiev addressed the delegates from other parties thus: "You, gentlemen, representatives of the blood-sucking parties, and you, socialists, who deny the right to private property: you have come as uninvited guests to take over an organization whose representatives have gathered here to judge their own situation and their own great destiny."[175] In 1903, alienated by the domineering role of Blagoev and his centralizing zeal, especially on the issue of the socialist press, Gabrovski joined the Broads but vocally within its left wing. Disappointed with the increasingly collaborationist role of the party that had already been bitten by the bug of nationalism, he left it in 1914 and rejoined the Narrows. Between 1919 and 1923, already as a member of the BCP until its banning, he was again a member of parliament. Gabrovski was shot in his home by hired assassins from the Wrangel army in June 1925.[176]

While Gabrovski has been unjustly and certainly exaggeratedly accused of deviation from socialism, the general accusations of opportunism aimed at the BWSDP (b) were not entirely fabricated. To some extent Sakîzov himself was a tragic figure, trying to keep unified the Broad party torn between a strong right wing and an equally strong left wing that eventually renounced it and quit. Dimitîr Genchev may be correct in seeing the rivalry between the Narrows and Broads as a balancing act, two complementary formations in need of each other, and concluding that in 1924 with the death of Blagoev, not only the Narrows, but Sakîzov's party was also buried.[177] One should be especially careful not to apply retrospectively what became of *some* members of the Broads who, indeed, descended into abject electoral opportunism and eventually into open collaboration with the most reactionary forces, and likewise *some* members of the Narrows who imposed a dogmatic straitjacket and eventually embraced violence, even if these *some* at times were numerous.

5

Socialist Women or Socialist Wives

It is no surprise that socialism, like everything else, was a male enterprise. Only, it was less so. Both socialism and the movement for women's suffrage were contemporaries, having been born from the advent of democracy and mass politics, accompanying the important economic shifts, subsumed under the notion of industrial capitalism. Socialists were the first and for a long time the only political parties that openly advocated women's rights as items on its program agendas.[1] August Bebel's *Die Frau und der Sozialismus*, published in 1879 in Zurich, became not only his own most popular book but next to the *Communist Manifesto*, the most widely read and admired socialist work. It was translated into Bulgarian from the French by Gabrovski in 1893 (Figure 25).[2] For comparison, the English translation came out in 1885 with a US edition in 1897 and was translated by Daniel De Leon in 1904 with the title *Women Under Socialism*.[3] Yet, in this edition De Leon sought to distance himself from Bebel's radical critique on the institution of marriage and strategically endorsed monogamy.[4] Bebel's critique was, of course, based on Marx and Engel's position that women were oppressed in the nuclear family, and he formulated the fate of "woman in the future," something that 150 years later is still in the future:

> In the new society woman will be entirely independent, both socially and economically. She will not be subjected to even a trace of domination and exploitation, but will be free and man's equal, and mistress of her own lot. Her education will be the same as man's. . . . She chooses an occupation suited to her wishes, inclinations and abilities, and works under the same conditions as man. . . . She studies, works, enjoys pleasures and recreation with other women or with men, as she may choose or as occasions may present themselves. In the choice of love she is as free and unhampered as man. She woos or is wooed and enters into a union prompted by no other considerations but her own feelings. This union is a private agreement, without the interference of a functionary, just as marriage has been a private agreement until far into the middle ages. Here Socialism will create nothing new, it will merely reinstate, on a higher level of civilization and under a different social form, *what generally prevailed before private property dominated society* [italics in the original].[5]

Of the four final aims formulated by the Bulgarian Social Democratic Party (BSDP) at its founding congress in 1891, two concerned women: "3. Social and political equality

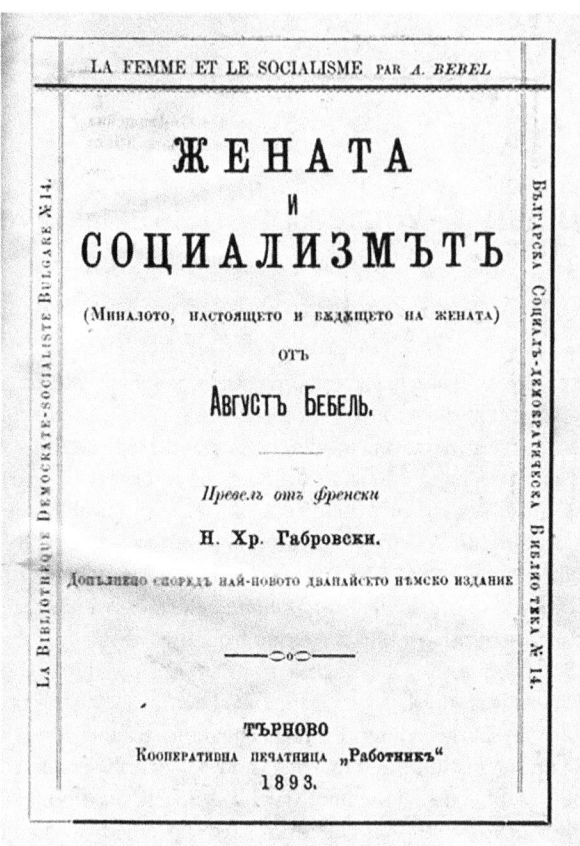

Figure 25 Title page of the Bulgarian translation of Bebel's *Woman and Socialism*.

between the two sexes. 4. Public, free and full scientific upbringing and education for the children of both sexes." The other two were: "1. The transformation of all means of production—the land, mines, machines, tools, communication—to public property; the appropriation of private capitalist wealth should become public and available to each and every one. 2. Decentralization of the state and its transformation into a federative union of free and equal productive communities."[6] Already here, however, one can see the hierarchy of goals that distinguished "bourgeois feminists" from socialists, but also subordinated the socialist women's movement to the general goals of socialism and a delayed prospect for women's priorities. This was a general feature of the socialist women's movement everywhere subsumed in the Marxist juxtaposition between *Hauptwiderspruch* (principal contradiction) and *Nebenwiderspruch* (secondary contradiction), where class contradictions and class struggle were accorded primacy.[7]

With the support of Engels, Bebel initiated the organization of a women's movement as part of the German socialist movement and party. In 1891 a "Women's Office" was founded, led by Clara Zetkin until 1917.[8] While the German socialist women's movement became the role model for the international women socialists, the legal and social position of women in Germany was not necessarily the most progressive. Women in Prussia were legally barred from political meetings until 1902, and the issue of "universal" versus "partial" women's suffrage was a sticking point in the broader women's movement. German women were finally admitted to universities after the turn of the century, but their status was legalized only in 1908.[9] In 1907 Zetkin organized the first international conference of socialist women in Stuttgart, which adopted universal suffrage for all women and men: "But when we demand Woman Suffrage, we can only do so on the ground, not that it should be a right attached to the possession of a certain amount of property, but that it should be inherent in the woman herself. . . . But while we are ready as Socialists to use all our political might to bring about this change, yet we are bound to notice the difference between us and them."[10] One of the most influential social-democratic parties, the Austrian, where women in 1925 comprised close to 30 percent of its membership, adopted universal suffrage only for males in 1906, asking women to participate in strikes and demonstrations in support of manhood suffrage, and keep back demands for female franchise.[11]

By contrast, the BSDP had already called for universal suffrage of all citizens over the age of twenty-one, explicitly emphasizing "irrespective of sex" in its 1893 program, and amended to age twenty in its 1894 program, alongside specific labor demands for the protection of women and children.[12] By 1905 it managed to pass a law in this respect which was the earliest social labor law in the country as well as the earliest in the Balkans.[13] It was the first and until 1906 the only party to advocate full voting rights for women.[14] Still, it is only fair to point out that no socialist representative, either Broad or Narrow, raised the issue of women's political rights in parliament.[15] In 1914 Vela Blagoeva wrote a letter to the social-democratic group to raise the issue of women's voting rights following the example of Finland: "In a proportional system one cannot ignore the voices of female workers, who in some branches of the industry are more numerous than their male counterparts, because in such a way the working class is not represented in parliament."[16]

Patriarchy and Victorian role models in combination with the *Nebenwiderspruch* trumped women. Still, in some ways, the situation in "backward" Bulgaria may have been more conducive to the open articulation of women's emancipation. In a peasant society (around 85 percent) of small proprietors, women took active part in the mainstream of agricultural labor, and this has been abundantly documented by sociological, statistical, agricultural, and ethnographical literature from the nineteenth century till the Second World War.[17] Male and female roles were not so markedly segregated. This tradition of the Bulgarian village had been noticed and described by many foreign observers already during the nineteenth century. They contrasted these relations to other Balkan regions, where the role of women was much more subordinate, and where they were confined almost exclusively to the house. Lucy Garnet, among many others, in her famous *Balkan Home-Life* stressed the relative freedom of Bulgarian country women as compared to their Greek counterparts:

> The Bulgarian women of the peasant class, however, having no opportunities for copying the manners of more "civilized" neighbours, adhere rigidly to their own

national costumes, and circumstances combine to give them more independent position and freer life, not only than that led by the Bulgarian townswomen, but by the generality of Greek peasant women. For the Bulgarian peasant women, taking, as they do, an equal share with the men of the family in field and farm work, are naturally accorded a co-equality with their husbands and brothers. Added to this, the women marry comparatively much later in life than the generality of Orientals, and, subject to the approval of their fathers, themselves select their husbands. For a Bulgarian peasant is in no hurry to get rid of the daughters who take such an active part in all that concerns the welfare of the home.[18]

This specifically Bulgarian tradition of the role of rural women was the result of strategies of survival in a milieu of small and poor land holdings, where women's participation in the labor process was indispensable, and where there was no influence from a hegemonic urban culture. Undoubtedly, this doomed Bulgarian peasant women to a double burden and had as it consequence high mortality and low life expectancy.[19] At the same time, however, it secured for women a particularly respectful place in their immediate nuclear family, in the extended family, in the kinship network, and in the labor process. This perception of a relative independence and freedom of action for women both in the labor process outside the home, and in the decision-making process in the family, should be qualified; it does not imply that it had superseded the male-oriented and male-dominated society. It is important, however, to emphasize these traditions of the Bulgarian village, given the importance of the peasantry in the overall social structure, and the consequent rootedness of the other social strata in the village culture. For all the specific manifestations of male domination, for all the attributes of "Oriental" patriarchy that are the product of a distinctive and complex historical development with a variety of overlapping cultural influences, it would be difficult to describe Bulgaria in terms of what one author has aptly put as "the belt of classic patriarchy," stretching from North Africa to North India.[20]

In more than one way the description of women's life in the Bulgarian village is reminiscent of what Martine Segalen had to say about nineteenth-century women in rural France. Discussing the nature of relationships of labor, authority, and respect, she defied the old cliché of the absolute authority of the "patriarchal" male, showing that by sharing the functions of production, men and women, to a great extent, integrated their activities.[21] It was only the disappearance of women's productive functions that finally relocated and confined them to the home. The role of the bourgeois wife in Western Europe, and her Victorian counterpart in England and the United States became increasingly identified with motherhood and produced the influential and oppressive role model. Professional activity was not needed to establish feminine status. On the contrary, it was considered diverting women from their primary functions and fulfillment. This ideal was emulated by the rising bourgeoisie in Bulgaria but, given its very recent formation as a class and its relative weakness, it did not and could not become the hegemonic role model for other social strata.

Still, with the secession of Bulgaria from the Ottoman Empire and the creation of the modern Bulgarian state after 1878 modeled, as it was, on the pattern of Western Europe, some of the basic functions of women (their socializing roles and tasks as keepers and transmitters of tradition) began to be lost by being transferred to the state. Moreover, the new legal code that superseded customary law institutionalized and legitimized the secondary and subordinate position of women. The Tîrnovo constitution (1879) was ambivalent on the issue of citizenship. While it proclaimed full suffrage for all Bulgarian citizens without specifying males, the interpretation of voters' rights (as well as military service) was confined to them. On the other hand, the law for mandatory and free education, as well as taxing and the right to association was valid for all citizens (boys and girls) without explicitly specifying this. Thus, as Krassimira Daskalova aptly remarks, the concept of "citizen" and "subject" was gender-marked and defined from the point of view of males; it was not clearly explained by the constitution but interpreted through the existing tradition.[22] The general discourse was perpetuating the traditional position of women confined to the home as mothers and keepers of the family but also increasingly, of the nation, with persistent misogynist notes. This was not the preserve merely of conservatives steeped in the Christian tradition but was often shared by the modernizers, the European-educated elites like, for example Stoian Mikhailovski (1865–1927), a leading politician and intellectual whose various and extremely popular literary productions were highly influential. In his poems he specifically targeted the suffragettes who had lost their femininity and were inspired by the "outrageous, bookish lunatic" August Bebel.[23]

On the other hand, one can observe what has been defined as the "literary feminism" of some men of letters, advocating broader education for women. Most did it from a traditionalist but enlightenment viewpoint, embracing Rousseau's idea of the subordination of women, their relegation to the domestic sphere, and defending their right to education but one that should be different, useful, and pleasing to men.[24] Very few others, most notably Liuben Karavelov (1834–79), espoused the view of women's education as a natural right and bitingly criticized a separate education for women, advocating complete equality.[25] Indeed, women's education was the first step toward the emancipation of women. The first schools for girls were opened in the 1840s, and by the 1870s, just before independence, there were ninety of them; in comparison the number of boys' schools was tenfold, 1100.[26] As mentioned, the constitution of 1879 provided for free and mandatory elementary education for all children aged seven to ten, increased in 1908 to age fourteen. Several educational laws in 1891, 1897, 1904, and 1908 broadened the educational system and equalized the number of classes at the high school level for boys and girls, if not entirely the program, so that by 1901, women were admitted to the university (which had opened in 1888).[27]

What is more significant, given the exclusive and influential role of the intelligentsia in Bulgaria, is that women represented a significant share of this social group. The intelligentsia (understood in the prewar context as specialists with university or high school education characterized by their belief in and desire for social transformation through culture, but not necessarily unified and reflecting a diverse set of social and political aspirations) was recruited, unlike its West European counterpart, not from the middle class or aristocratic elites, but from the lower middle class, well-to-do peasants, and quite often from the poor peasantry and the working class. This was only natural in view of the specific social structure of the country characterized by a sizable peasantry and an absence of aristocracy, as well as an emerging bourgeoisie and working class.

Most women were represented in the so-called feminized professions (teachers, and, later, pharmacists, dentists), and their position was incomparably less stable than that of males. Women also formed an important part in the rising industrial working force from the outset and their numbers grew throughout the first half of the century, comprising 22 percent of the industrial labor in 1909, and 36 percent by the 1920s.[28] What was quite unique, however, was the active role of women who transposed the existing traditions to their new social milieu. [29]

The teachers' profession was the only one where women could be employed during the Ottoman period. Of the 4,378 existing teachers, the 415 women comprised roughly 10 percent. Teachers alongside the clergy (3,623) were the most numerous part of the Bulgarian pre-independence intelligentsia (i.e., educated strata).[30] Political independence was accompanied by centralization, regulation, and restrictions of the teachers who were considered state employees. The centralizing 1891 law guaranteed two-thirds of the teacher's salary from state funds, the other third to be paid by local communities, but this came with extending the rights of the trustees, and their close inspection and easy removal of "troublesome" teachers.[31] Dwindling salaries and the fact that female teachers earned 10 percent less than their male counterparts, contributed to the gradual feminization of the profession, despite the fact that married women were banned from teaching.[32]

Women's organizations were first established in Bulgaria in the last decades of Ottoman rule during the 1860s and 1870s.[33] The few women who were the pioneers and driving force of the women's organizations made contributions disproportionate to their numbers to the cause of national liberation. Their associations which set themselves educational and benevolent tasks were inspired first and foremost by the passionate nationalism that was characteristic of the epoch. These women were almost exclusively the wives, daughters, or mothers of educated men who were political and cultural activists. Thus, the initiative for the women's organizations came from the thin crust of educated women from the new middle class in a, usually, small-town setting. This social background and the character of the "modern," "Europeanized" education determined the main goals of these organizations: the education and enlightenment of women for the sake of attaining the highest goal of women's predestination, motherhood, and the extension of maternal duties to the public sphere. This argumentation is clearly reminiscent of the "republican motherhood" discourse.

After the country attained its de facto independence in 1878, the women's press and local women's organizations proliferated, especially with the struggle for educational parity. The concepts "feminist" and "feminism" had entered the socialist press already in the 1880s and in the 1890s they were ubiquitous in the main women's publication of the period, the journal Женски свят (Women's world).[34] According to some authors, it is with the organized protests and petitions to the National Assembly for free access to the university in 1896 that one can speak of the beginning of an authentic feminist movement.[35] The national association *Bŭlgarski Zhenski Sŭyuz* (Bulgarian Women's Union, BWU) was founded in 1901, at a time when, according to one of its contemporary activists "the economic transformations dragged our woman out of the domestic hearth in pursuit of living for herself and her family and when, on the other hand, laws began to be passed, which hampered the free application of feminine labor and the attainment of higher education for women."³⁶ These two problems, the limitation of women's labor and education, became the focus of women's efforts in the 1890s and culminated in the creation of a national organization which by 1931 had seventy-seven local units and a membership of close to 8,400. From the outset socialist ideas predominated within the ranks although there were different views about the strategy and tactics, which eventually led to a split.³⁷

The public debate about the goals of the national women's organization culminated in 1902–03. There were two main currents in the movement, which a contemporary defined as "purely feminist" and "social democratic." The first trend insisted that the organization should have a purely feminist, not a class, character. It should strive to improve women's lot in the present society: "This and this alone: that women be associated with the existing order, sick as it might be."³⁸ Women should be united irrespective of their position in society; "there is no place here for dividing women into bourgeois and not bourgeois."³⁹ The real "question is not of different classes but of a wronged half of humankind."⁴⁰ The aim would be not to concentrate on the consciousness of members of particular classes but on enlightening "the members of this army which is called the female sex, and which has been subjugated throughout the centuries." Realizing that "complete equality of rights" was still not a need internalized by the majority of their followers, and that it was interpreted as a social-democratic slogan, the leaders of this trend formulated and managed to pass as the dominant resolution of the women's congress that its central goal was "to work for the intellectual and moral enlightenment of woman and the improvement of her situation in all respects."⁴¹ As a whole the BWU "remained a mainly urban organization ... [and] its activity was limited chiefly to the sphere of education and did not go beyond the limited charity."⁴² It took another almost two decades to transform the "improvement" to "equal rights" in 1921 while still insisting on the purely feminist "supra-party" and "supra-class" character of the organization.⁴³

The social-democratic trend argued that the social development of the country was leading to the proletarianization of the clear majority of the population regardless of gender. Consequently, the aims of the organization should stress class issues and emphasize its class character, against collaboration with the bourgeoisie. This trend insisted on the formula of "complete equality of rights" with men. In 1903, protesting the adoption of a resolution about the "supra-party" and "supra-class" character of the Union, this group, led by Vela Blagoeva, left the organization:

> Feminists blame working-class women for not agreeing to work together toward gaining equal rights for women. The rights feminists want are meaningless for a working-class woman. Feminists are not going to care about her when she is exhausted from heavy work and poverty. They are interested in their class only and they need the help of a woman worker only in order to have greater gains for themselves. A feminist that belongs to the bourgeoisie will not raise her voice against the exploitation of the labor of women and children because this is not in her interest. Feminism is not going to abolish the trade in women, sanctioned by the law, because most of this commodity consists in women workers for whom this is the only field in which they do not have competitors. For this trade to be abolished, the

Figure 26 Conference of women social democrats, Sofia, July 1914.

working conditions must be fundamentally changed—i.e. the strength of capitalism must be eroded, and one of its most profitable sources taken away, namely the low salaries of obedient women and children. Beautiful words of sentimental religious women cannot destroy brothels but only the strong muscles of workers. . . . A working-class woman should struggle for equal political rights together with her comrades the workers, because only people that belong to the working class will be on her side in the legislature. A conscious woman should never vote for bourgeois MPs, regardless of whether they wear trousers or petticoats. Otherwise she would strengthen her enemies. We point out this contradiction between feminism and socialism in order to protect our comrades from being deluded by the honeyed phrases of the eloquent feminists who want to use working-class women for their own objectives and afterward turn their backs on them.[44]

The subsequent debates between the two trends were acrimonious, although they never reached the spiteful pitch of the confrontation between Broads and Narrows. In 1905, Blagoeva organized a conference of women socialists. While sharing the misgivings of the Narrows about a neutral women's union, she polemicized against many of her male comrades who feared that a separate women's organization could create an opposition of proletarian women against the unified workers' movement. Instead, in the journals she edited—*Delo*, *Women's Labor*, and *Women's Bulletin*—as well as in the general socialist press, she defended the right of socialist women to make their own individual choice on whether they would like to participate in BWU. In 1914 her view for a separate socialist women's association was adopted and under her leadership, the first conference of women's socialist clubs was held in Sofia.[45]

The BWU itself underwent another internal split. The co-founder of the BWU, Anna Karima (1871–1949), who was its chairwoman between 1901 and 1906, left the organization arguing that the BWU was not devoted to attaining political rights for women, and with her "progressive" adherents in 1908 started *Ravnopravie* (Equal Rights), also known as the Union of Progressive Women, which functioned until 1921.[46] In the words of Karima:

> The Union of Progressive Women is completely different from the Bulgarian Women's Union in its membership. As we pointed out earlier, members of the Bulgarian Women's Union are sometimes women who only sympathize with the charitable activity of a specific society. . . . The Union of Progressive Women unites only those Bulgarian women, who before joining it have already assimilated the idea of equal rights and who have promised to work for the success of this idea in our country. In this way, the Union of Progressive Women as a coherent selective entity will be able to follow firmly and insistently a definite course, and as a coherent and selective entity it will be able to influence the society with greater success as well as to educate new women's forces.[47]

Much has been made of the fact that the leadership of both organizations was in the hands of the wives of the leaders of the two socialist formations, Dimitŭr Blagoev and Ianko Sakŭzov. Their disagreements have been seen as a reflection of the opposition between Broads and Narrows, and of the personal competition between their husbands, reinforced by the chronology of the split in 1903. The fact that everywhere socialism in general and the women's movement were divided along the same fault lines is subordinated to the matrimonial argument. Many of the well-known women socialists were, indeed, wives of prominent socialist figures: besides Blagoeva, there was Tina Kirkova (1872–1947), the wife of Kirkov, who became Secretary of the Central Women's Commission of the Women's social-democratic conference, as well as the wives of the Broad socialist leaders Dzhidrov, Bozveliev, and Konov: Maria Dzhidrova, Iordanka Bozvelieva and Kina Konova (1870–1952), respectively. The latter was also the sister of the early socialist Sava Mutafov. While still as Kina Mutafova, she was one of the leaders of the Bulgarian socialist group in Geneva. Later she became an influential teacher, translator, journalist, and cofounder of the BWU.[48] Iordanka Bozvelieva (1872–1940) was the second wife of Bozveliev whom she met when she relocated to Kazanlŭk as a teacher after the death in 1891 of her husband Sava Mustakov, an early socialist. She herself had finished courses in midwifery in Paris and Sofia and was active in the women's and cooperative movements.

Anna Karima, after 1905 the estranged and later divorced wife of Ianko Sakŭzov, was never formally a member of the party but was an important member of this milieu in her social ethic and personal collaborations. Karima was her pen name. Born Anna Todorova Velkova in the family of a wheat merchant and his Ukrainian wife in Russia, the family relocated to independent Bulgaria after 1878, where the father became governor of the Shumen region. A precocious poet, Anna became a teacher and married Ianko Sakîzov at the age of seventeen. They had three children but the marriage was brittle and did not last after 1905. Karima devoted her life to the women's cause; extensive and successful writing of novels, poetry, and drama; editing; and important charity work. After 1925, disgusted with the right-wing regime, she emigrated to Paris and collaborated with anti-fascists, including communists. On the invitation of Rakovski she went to the USSR and upon her return to Bulgaria in 1928 wrote enthusiastically about Soviet women's emancipation but was critical of the regime. She died forgotten in 1949 in Sofia.[49]

It is true that most of these women became well known in the literature and the next generations because of their husbands, but during their lifetime they had their own place and independent influence, even if not acknowledged by many of their male counterparts. In his memoirs Georgi Dimitrov Popov (1872–1948) writes that he became a socialist under the influence of his teachers, the wives of Nikola Gabrovski and Dosiu Chekhlarov, but this was at the time when they were not yet married, and he does not refer to their given names. Maria Khadzhiivanova had been already a

Figure 27 Anna Karima, 1920.

convinced and reputed social democrat, before she met Nikola Gabrovski.[50] This has led to the uncritical acceptance of a characteristic promoted about European social democracy, namely that women were typically attracted to socialist ideas because of their husbands or other male relatives.[51] While this may be true in general, it is difficult to prove as a whole for Bulgaria given the little evidence existing on women, and the little evidence that *does* exist does not make it easily generalizable.

To take the example of the most prominent woman socialist of the period, Vela Blagoeva, it flatly refutes the claim. Born Victoria Atanasova Zhivkova in 1858 in Tîrnovo in a wealthy merchant's family, she received an excellent education for the time. Finishing high school in Gabrovo, she was a teacher in several towns. Tîrnovo itself was the center of educational activism, specifically for girls, and she was as an adolescent, under the influence of Russian *narodniks*. As Daskalova concludes, "it seemed inevitable that she would orient herself toward socialism."[52] Her childhood, as she herself writes, was "melancholy" after the death of her father, as her relations with her dominant but extremely traditional mother were difficult: "My mother did not like her own sex (gender). Her joy and pride were her two sons. . . . The gentle caresses of my father constitute to this day the sweet memories of my innocent childhood."[53]

During the Russo-Turkish war of 1877–78, Victoria volunteered as a nurse in a field hospital and in 1881 with a fellowship from the Slavonic Charitable Society completed the Mariinski high school course in St Petersburg. In 1882–84 she studied at the famous Bestuzhev Courses (the outstanding establishment for women's higher education in Russia).[54] She was involved in the organization *Narodnaya Volya*, in a group organizing escapes of prisoners and exiles.[55] She was also a devoted student of Russian literature and made her own first steps in writing. Turgenev was her favorite writer and on two occasions she visited and spoke to him personally.[56] It is in St. Petersburg and through the revolutionary circles that she met Blagoev and fell in love with him, discreetly and without his knowledge helping him financially. This is what she shared with her diary at the time, addressing it to (Mitia) Dimitîr:

> I keep this diary for you, my heartfelt friend, I devote it to you. I keep nothing from you. I do not deserve your love, but you will not judge me, nor reject the heart that belongs only to you. I cannot be your wife because I cannot give you the full happiness that you deserve. On the other hand, I cannot renounce you. To love and be loved is the highest bliss which is difficult to forsake. It may be a somewhat egotistical emotion, but to renounce my love exceeds my powers. . . . My love is limited to this: to be your friend forever, nothing more. There are some family reasons that have shaped my decision not to marry, but there are others, more important ones, and you understand them well. For to serve my fatherland, I cannot belong to the family. The marriage will hinder my efforts to improve myself, to increase my knowledge. I need to study and learn much more. You, I know, will not hinder my activities and my development. But we both are poor and cannot support a family if I devote myself to housework. What will then become of your life partner (другарка в живота)? Isn't she going to resemble all the limited mothers and wives drowning in trivia? . . . Can you be happy with such a wife? No, let us better stay comrades and friends, rather than husband and wife.[57]

In 1884, Victoria returned from Russia and began teaching in the Sofia Exemplary Girls' School. The following year, after he was expelled from Russia, Dimitîr and she started and co-edited the first socialist journal *Съвременний показател* (*Sîvremennii pokazatel, Contemporary Index*, also translated as *Modern Trends* or *Modern Guide*). It popularized the works of Marx and Engels, David Ricardo, Adam Smith, Chernishevsky, and Lavrov, among others; it also published translations from Balzac, Turgenev, Goethe, Schiller, and Dickens. The two were soon married and had four children: Stella (1887–1954), Natalia (1889–1943), Vladimir (1893–1925), and Dimitîr (1895–1918). Vela Blagoeva died in 1921, very sick and devastated by the death of her youngest son during the war, but at least she was spared the "disappearance" and subsequent murder of her other son by the police in 1925.

Throughout her life and despite her frail health, Vela (as she preferred to be called and is widely known) did not stop working as a teacher in Sofia (1884–1985, 1905–07), Shumen (1886–87), Vidin (1887–90), Tîrnovo (1890–92), Stara Zagora (1892–93), Plovdiv (1893–96, 1902–03), Tulcha (1901–02), and Marashki Trîstenik until her

Figure 28 Vela Blagoeva, 1887.

retirement (1907–12), and de facto supported her husband and the family financially. She was constantly dismissed and transferred from her positions as teacher because of her socialist views. The director of the girls' high school in Tîrnovo wrote a report to the then minister of education Georgi Zhivkov: "The teacher Blagoeva is a wonderful instructor whenever she prepares herself. The lectures I have attended are exemplary. She explains clearly and lively, and makes the students think. . . . Unfortunately, such excellent lectures are rare. Most of times she comes in unprepared and just reads the lesson from the textbook. I know that from students who have complained to me. . . . The teacher also allowed herself to hint in one way or another at the so called 'new ideas'. . . . At the same time students in the higher grades have been divided between 'socialists' and 'non-socialists' and this issue is becoming rather serious; the town is talking that it is the teacher Blagoeva who is preaching socialism to the students and spreads books among them. . . . I have the honor to inform you that I suspect the teacher Vela Blagoeva of disseminating this demoralization, i.e. Bulgarian socialism among the students."[58] His further investigation showed that Blagoeva did not do this in class, but he, nonetheless, asked for her removal the next year. Other reports also tried to diminish her pedagogical skills. In 1892 she was fired and fifteen of her students dismissed from the school for "immoral socialist activity."[59]

The irony is that the minister of education was Vela Blagoeva's own brother. Georgi Zhivkov (1844–99) was one of the heroes of the Bulgarian national movement. Although he had a medical degree, his real vocation was teaching. Suspected by the Ottoman authorities, he had emigrated to Romania and worked in the revolutionary circles. After independence, he held major positions in the Liberal Party, and became minister of education (1887–93) in the government of Stefan Stambolov. It is during his tenure that Sofia University was founded, a new educational law was passed, and a number of progressive educational measures were adopted. He also served as minister of finance and was Speaker of Parliament. Vela Blagoeva adored her brother and wrote a biography and obituary at his death, most likely left unpublished. She defended his legacy and concluded: "Power, as they say, spoils people, but it did not change Zhivkov." He remained, according to her, an honest democrat who was trying to defend teachers whenever possible.[60] She also valued her other brother Nikola Zhivkov (1847–1901), a renowned educational figure, and the author, among many other works, of the national hymn of Bulgaria between 1879 (officially 1886) and 1944, *Shumi Maritsa*.[61] Only with her mother the estrangement was complete. While the brothers tried to advise her to be more prudent, the mother muttered after each firing, "That's what she deserves."[62] Still, Vela sent a wonderful emotional letter to Georgi on the occasion of her mother's death in 1897.[63]

These links to the governing elites were not accidental. As already argued, the BWSDP in both of its wings consisted mostly of intellectuals right until the wars and social provenance does not guarantee similar ideological leanings. Another example is the wife of Gavril Georgiev (1870–1917), a major, but lesser known figure in the BWSDP (n) because of his reclusive and uncompromising character. Known as one of the iron triumvirate, alongside Blagoev and Kirkov, he was the indefatigable editor of the party press. The brother of his wife was Dimitîr Khristov, a former socialist who already in the 1890s had become a member of the Liberal Party. It seems that it was family pressure, besides the incessant conflicts at work that made him retreat from political activity after 1909.[64] Besides her active social life, leading the women's social-democratic movement, Vela was a publisher, editor of numerous journals, translator, and writer of textbooks, novels, dramas, and short stories, mostly on historical and women's themes. Highly articulate, clear, and at the same time nuanced in her language, her belletristic prose was not that successful.[65] When she retired, the ministry did not recognize the years she had been a teacher before Bulgaria's independence and she was denied a pension.[66]

What is revealed from her personal correspondence is a warm and completely selfless person. The family letters to all her children are tender and full of humor, a quality apparently shared by all of them: there are several hilarious ones.[67] Her relations with both her daughters show an enviable trust and friendship, a clear compensation for her own lack of motherly warmth, and both daughters worshiped her.[68] In a letter to her younger daughter Natalia from 1912, already retired, she consoled her over her first disappointment in love and informed her about the family affairs: "Your dad has plumped out, enjoying his third youth (i.e. his sixties) . . ., and Stella has become an excellent housewife, she looks a bit like a spinster, but this only between us."[69] There is an early letter from the sixteen-year-old Stella from Prague in 1903. Stella was an excellent pianist and received a special education in music. In her letter, she thanked her mother for the money she had sent and wrote about her studies in music, French, and the philosophy books she was checking out from the library.

> But I am really tortured by another question. It is the religious question. I do believe in God but not in the way others do. I cannot envisage the Form God takes. I call him the cause of all causes, the thing which has created natural order, the reason mothers are mother. . . . This is what I call God, but it seems to me that I am probably not right, I don't know why. I also ask myself whether Jesus is also God? This is something I cannot explain to myself. Whenever I reach this conundrum, my head become a chaos and I stop thinking. And there is nobody here with whom I can share my thoughts."[70]

That the daughter of the leading social-democratic couple was thinking of religion and Christianity specifically should come as no surprise. Given the enormous influence of Russian literature on the Bulgarian intellectuals, and the practical implementation of Tolstoyism in several communes, the edge of atheism was directed not to Christianity per se, but to the organized church institution from which Tolstoy had also been excommunicated. What is remarkable is that Vela Blagoeva, an avant-garde and atheist woman (as well as the avant-garde couple) did not try to model their children and instill in them their own beliefs. They let them reach their own truths, go their own way. But, of course, they both were powerful role models. No wonder, on his death bed in 1924, three years after his wife had passed away, Dimitŭr Blagoev told his daughter Stella: "I could not have lived with another woman."[71]

One can argue, of course, that Blagoeva was the exception but the evidence points in another direction. As seen from the statistics of the prosopography, women were numerically negligent, comprising slightly over 4 percent of the database (148 entries out of 3448). This is, however, a technical artifact, produced by the underrepresentation of women in general, and socialist women in particular, in the sources. In fact, the remarkable women one encounters as fallouts of casual mentions (like Angelina Boneva portrayed in Chapter 6) never made it to any of the encyclopedias or other synthesizing accounts. On the other hand, membership numbers for women were even lower than the ones in the database, reflecting the fact that socialist activism was not necessarily stamped with formal allegiance. Thus, women in the BWSDP (n) comprised between 1 percent and 2.9 percent of party membership between 1908 and 1912, reaching 4.9 percent only in 1914 with the loss of male membership because of the Balkan Wars.[72]

In a photograph of the crucial Tenth Congress of the BWSDP, which sealed the fateful split, we see the only woman delegate sitting between Blagoev and Kirkov (Figure 29). The back of the photograph gives her name: Anna Stefanova. She is not in any encyclopedia, nor did she leave an archive. We do not know when she was born nor when she died. She is mentioned briefly in the memoirs of her brother Boris Stefanov Mateev who writes that in 1895 his eldest sister Anna was stopped from attending school by their father so that she could help at home. She became the unpaid librarian of the teachers' club *Self-Development* (Samorazvitie) and started learning French on her own so she could finish high school and university. She was apparently instrumental in making him interested in socialism. Anna also appears casually in one line in the memoirs of her younger brother Ivan Stefanov as the first secretary of the Varna organization, but under her married name Anna Ioveva.[73] We also encounter her in the unpublished notes of Koika Tineva and learn that Stefanova was the party secretary of the Varna organization in 1903, that she was one of several women intellectuals in the group, and that she was removed later, after a campaign organized by workers who complained about the leadership of intellectuals. The person who

Figure 29 Tenth Congress of the BWSDP, 1903.

was elected after her was the tailor Todor Dimitrov whom Tineva characterizes as "a virtual lumpen," undisciplined, dishonest, terrorizing his wife, living on loans that he never returned, but ambitious and shrewd, able to find support among the workers with empty revolutionary phraseology, and manipulating their traditional attitudes toward women.[74]

Invisibility in the sources does not correspond to factual invisibility at the time. Often wives would not enter the party formally in order to protect the family: at least one parent should have a guaranteed permanent job. Todor Lukanov (1874–1946), one of the most prominent but forgotten and maligned leaders of the party because of his opposition to 1923, was a member of its CC and organizational secretary after 1921. An early socialist, he had been deprived of teaching rights forever. First studying chemistry at Sofia University, he received a law degree in Geneva in 1900 and subsequently practiced law but mostly was involved in organizational work for the BWSDP (n). During the wars he was sentenced to five years in prison for his anti-war stance and amnestied after the wars. His wife Konstantsa (Kotsa) Lukanova née Basheva (1875–1948) does not appear in any encyclopedia and therefore was not initially included in the initial database, but there is a brief note in the archive of Koika Tineva, which sheds meaningful light. She married Todor young, just after finishing high school, and after he was fired, joined him in Geneva where she completed courses in midwifery. In Pleven she worked as a midwife and at the same time actively propagated socialist ideas, but became a formal party member only in 1910. In 1914, she was elected, together with Tina Kirkova, Anna Maimunkova, Raina Kandeva, and Tsonka Khristova, to the central women's commission of the party. After 1925, the whole family emigrated to the USSR, where she had to live through the humiliation of her husband and his expulsion from the party in 1930 as a "right opportunist," and the death of one of her sons Andrei, a doctor.[75] Todor Lukanov was not even allowed by Georgi Dimitrov to come back to Bulgaria after the war even as his son Karlo Lukanov had become Dimitrov's foreign minister, and died in misery in Moscow in 1946.[76] Kotsa was allowed to return and died in 1948.[77]

Here is another evidence from an invisible woman, the fourteen-year-old girl with whom this book started. In a later 1951 handwritten autobiography, Maria Krusheva explains that she came from a wealthy rural family. Her father had been a soap maker but with the decline of the craft, he became a mill owner, and his mill was nationalized after the Second World War. Her siblings remained with a "bourgeois outlook," although they were never politically active. When she was ten years old, her father was persuaded by the local teachers to send her to the city since she showed remarkable intellectual capabilities. She attended school first in Tîrnovo and later in Ruse.

> When I was 13, I became friends with Stanka Savova . . ., a village girl like myself, who in Tîrnovo chanced into the milieu of teachers social-democrats. I do not remember what we read with her, but we considered ourselves socialists. I only recall that the following year, when the teacher in Bulgarian assigned us an essay about a great personality in world history, Stanka wrote about Karl Marx, and I wrote about Wilhelm Liebknecht. By then, I had already liberated myself from religion and demonstrated it openly, much to the consternation of my mother who chided me for not going to church on Sunday as I used to. During the

Balkan Wars of 1912-1913 we had no school until March because the building in Tîrnovo was occupied as a military hospital. That winter I lived in the village of Vîrbovka with an aunt of mine. She had a tenant, a woman who was a teacher, a Narrow social-democrat. I became very close to her, we read a lot, and since then I considered myself a Narrow [теснячка]. I was a very strong student and read a lot extracurricular literature. I need to emphasize, that the best students during this period tended to be on the left [левееха се] . . . . Thus, early on I shaped myself differently from my background and environment.[78]

Between 1915 and 1918 Maria became a teacher and the only person to whom she felt close was an older cousin and teacher, who also had become a socialist and later an active communist. In 1918 she entered Sofia University with the intention of receiving a degree in chemistry (because there was not yet a medical faculty to fulfill her dream of becoming a doctor), but the following year she was struck by typhus and barely survived. She was introduced to Vîrban Angelov, a leading communist and lawyer, whom she married in 1921. It is only then, she writes, that she entered the organized circles of socialists, became a party member, and was active in the women's group in Ruse, where she delivered lectures to workers. In fact, Angelov was one of the very few who in his memoirs explicitly pointed out the role of socialist wives "who participated in the movement as pronounced figures and their share in the plight and sufferings of their comrade-husbands was in no way lighter."[79] He gave detailed biographical data on seven women who otherwise do not figure in any source. They were all wives of his fellow lawyers: Zlata Tokusheva (1884–1963), Toshka Ruseva (b.1889), Mara Atanasova (1883–1943), Mara Kozlovska, Mariika Kirova, Ivanka Karamincheva, and Maria Angelova, née Krusheva (1896–1981). Most were teachers and activists in the women's and trade union movement.[80]

The process of where and how socialist ideas were encountered is described very clearly in Maria Krusheva's autobiography. It is not through relatives, the influence of a husband, a brother, and so on (although this also certainly happened), but just like young boys and men, in the high schools, and it is worth remembering that in the case of girls, these were all-women schools. Even more telling than these stories are visual materials (Figure 29). There are numerous photos from the period of Marxist circles among women students, a testament to the thriving *Zirkelkultur*.[81]

Figure 30 Marxist circles in women's high schools, Plovdiv 1907 and Shumen 1912.

The principal channels were teachers, both men and women. But, also, the "bacillus" was in the air—socialism, the search for social justice, was displacing nationalism which had betrayed its democratic underpinnings—and the food nurturing this bacillus was books. Evtim Dabev, the first translator of Marx, describes wittily in his memoirs how, as a teacher in the Gabrovo girls' high school he once found a girl reading Engels's *Condition of the Working Class in England* crying bitterly over the plight of the English workers. He had to calm her down and succeeded only after he married her. Who was choosing whom?[82] Some encountered socialism later, once they were out of school. Stefanka Popova (b.1880) became a teacher in Stara Zagora and was exposed to socialism through other teachers. During the vacations she would gather ten to fifteen women colleagues to read socialist literature and sing revolutionary songs. She remembered: "Some of my colleagues married husbands with other political views. For the sake of a harmonious family life they became passive and 'neutral,' but in their souls they retained their sympathies toward socialism."[83] She herself married a socialist colleague.

Mara Ioneva, who was born in Varna and was active in the socialist student circles, studied medicine in Geneva where she probably met Nikola Dimitrov (1883–1943). Both of them came with doctor's diplomas from Geneva (he in 1911, she in 1915) and practiced medicine. It was a harmonious partnership, and the archive contains their numerous, almost daily, correspondence during the war, when Nikola was at the front and where they addressed each other in Bulgarian and French with "sweet child, " "my dear sweet friend," "cheri," "cher gosse," "cher amour," "inoubliable mon gosse," "cher enfant," etc. She died of a crippling disease in 1925; he was arrested and interned and died in 1943.[84]

There were, of course, cases when young women did adopt the political views of their husbands, but their number was neither overwhelming nor should it be generalized. Maria Dzhidrova, née Maria Todorova, was the young teacher-librarian and colleague of Petîr Dzhidrov who recommended socialist books to her, and she "accepted socialism as a teaching for a just social organization."[85] They were married in 1895 when both were twenty, and Maria became one of the recognized leaders of the BWU.[86] Boris Stefanov, the brother of Anna Stefanova, wrote to his future wife Penka Moralieva who thought that public life was hard and preferred to dedicate herself to the home and the children's education: "To think that today a mother can be a good educator without participating in public life, is an immense prejudice."[87]

Many socialist women became socialist wives, rather than socialist wives becoming socialists. Some of these women were dazzling with what they would achieve in their short life. Tsanka (Stoianka) Dragneva Jovanović (1873–1905), born in Ruse, finished high school in Tîrnovo where she encountered socialism, after which she taught for six years. In 1897–1898 she studied natural sciences in Geneva and was an active member of the socialist groups. Back in Bulgaria, she settled in Sliven as a teacher, where she met and married the Serbian engineer and socialist Kosta Jovanović (1875–1930) in 1900. When they moved to Belgrade, she continued her studies and was a prominent figure in Serbian social democracy, being the sole female delegate at the inaugural congress of Serbia's Social Democratic Party in 1903. In the same year she founded the first women's social-democratic organization. On the editorial board of "*Radničke novine*," she prepared a bill for women workers presented in the Skupština. Joining her husband in Germany in 1904, she lost her first-born child and died of cancer at the age of 32.[88]

Not only did all socialist wives not become socialists because of their husbands, but some of them did not even have socialist husbands and some did not even remain socialist, even in their souls. Teofana (Teofano) Popova did not make it into the encyclopedias but has figured in the annals of the women's and charitable movements and some memoirs. Born in 1856 in one of the premier families of Stara Zagora, she was educated broadly and was praised for her intellect at school and her poetic talent, after which she immediately became a celebrated teacher. She was married very early to Vasil Papazoglu (Popov), the son of a wealthy Bulgarian member of the Ottoman *meclis* (town council). Her husband died in a health epidemic in 1878 and Teofana was left a widow at the age of twenty-two with two sons. Already before independence she had organized a women's society in Stara Zagora, and after 1878 she was devoted to her teacher's vocation, although she was not in financial need. She was a teacher in Kazanlŭk and later in Sevlievo where, her niece writes, "she was acquainted with the then fashionable socialist teaching to which she dedicated herself with an idealism typical for her sex."[89]

In Sevlievo she was the soul of the socialist (but not Marxist) circle around Spiro Gulabchev whom she idolized "as a pure angelic creature, a model of moral perfection."[90] In 1889, she was one of the twelve representatives to a clandestine meeting of the network of these secret circles modeled after Gulabchev's ideology of "pauperophilia" (сиромахомилство).[91] They financed Gulabchev's press from their salaries and translated books and pamphlets for free. Despite her reputation as a socialist, with a recommendation from the Bulgarian Exarchate, Teofana Popova was appointed teacher in the Bulgarian girls' high school in Thessaloniki and warden of the girls' boarding house. She needed this to support her son Dimitŭr Popov (1876–96) who was studying medicine in Geneva. Dimitŭr himself had finished the Gabrovo high school and was friends with Georgi Bakalov. According to different sources, he was killed (Bozveliev thought this was a suicide) in 1896 in Svishtov where he had been appointed a teacher of natural history. This loss devastated Teofana completely and she broke off all previous contacts, seeking solace in the church and her friendship with Bishop Metodi Kusevich, one of the fiercest critics of socialism, in the words of Bozveliev "the great socialist-eater (социалистоядец)." She founded the charitable society "The Good Samaritan" to which she bestowed her considerable inheritance, and devoted herself to caring for orphans. Another blow was the criminal killing of her second son, a forester, in 1912. Popova became a mystic, and until her last days in 1929 crisscrossed the country giving talks explaining the gospel and writing articles denouncing her socialist and atheist past as a "lunatic fashionable infatuation."[92] No wonder, her socialist youth has been forgotten, but it leaves a vivid account of the dissemination and pulling force of socialism in this period.

Very few women remained unmarried. Bulgaria was characterized by early and almost universal marriages throughout the whole period of the demographic transition. Even after the Second World War high and relatively early nuptiality was maintained, although the overall fertility declined, especially after the 1960s. It is only after the 1990s that Bulgaria has entered a phase of fewer and late marriages among both men and women. Until the mid-twentieth century delayed marriage and celibacy were a rarity. Bachelors were a tolerated curiosity, but single women were an oddity. This explains how even a woman of the caliber of Vela Blagoeva could utter the abovementioned "she looks a bit like a spinster, but this only between us" apropos of her daughter Stella. As fate would have it, Stella actually married, but just for a year. After finishing her special education in music in Prague, she earned a history degree from Sofia University and became a teacher of history at the First Girls' High School in Sofia while also giving private music lessons. She had become a member of BRSDP (n) in 1915 and in 1924 was fired, without the right to teach anywhere, despite the fact that the documentation collected by the Security Services from the director of the school, other teachers and, even her landlady attested that she was quiet, reliable, correct, and never propagated communist ideas and "most importantly, never missed her work because of a communist celebration."[93]

After the death of her mother, she effectively became Blagoev's secretary. In 1924 she married Kosta Iankov (1888–1925), an army officer (major), who himself came from a legendary patriotic revolutionary family during the nationalist movement against the Ottomans. A member of the Narrows from 1908, and editor-in-chief of *Narodna Armiia* (1920–23), he was elected to the CC, became the leader of the Military Organization, and organized the terrorist act in April 1925 when he was killed.[94] Her brother was assassinated in the police, but Stella was released. In 1926 together with her sister they emigrated to the USSR, where Stella worked at the Comintern. After the war she was briefly in Bulgaria working for the Slavic Committee but between 1949 and 1954 became Bulgarian ambassador in Moscow, where she died. Natalia, on the other hand, never married, and died in Moscow in 1943 from a stroke like the rest of the family (the ones who were not killed). She was remembered as a kind of Mother Teresa by the émigré children.[95]

But all of this explains why, with very few exceptions, most socialist women were married. Angelina Boneva was such an exception, and even in her case, she did conclude a brief formal marriage in order to get out of the Ottoman jail (see Chapter 6). Another "lost" biography is Ekaterina Stoichkova (1876–1902), one of the first women social-democrat teachers. Nikola Vîzharov (1877–1964) himself a teacher in Kiustendil and, later, mayor of the town commune, describes her in his memoirs as tall and thin, wearing her hair short, which was an extreme rarity. Other women would braid their hair, and the "more intelligent" ones like the teachers, would put it in a bun. Active in the socialist teachers' movement, elected to its leadership, she was constantly badmouthed by the other women, and died of tuberculosis in 1902, at the age of only twenty-six. But she too was married, and her married name was Ivanova.[96] Vela Blagoeva also sported short hair in her youth and would run around wearing a man's coat and blue glasses and smoking a cigarette like the Russian nihilists, but quickly domesticated her appearance to the demands of the Bulgarian petty-bourgeois milieu.[97]

All of the above examples are far from denying the influence of family background and male relatives; they only aim at complicating the understanding of how ideas are transmitted and appropriated and reacting against blanket generalizations. For instance, Tina Kirkova was born in the family of Trifon Bogoev, a bookbinder and the

Figure 31 Stella and Natalia Blagoevi in 1914.

founder of the social-democratic group in Stara Zagora. She herself did not finish high school but had to start work as a telegraph operator. She and Georgi Kirkov did not have children. Devoted to party work and respected, she had an austere appearance and several memoirs mention that her nickname among socialists was "the mother-in-law" (свекървата), which, especially in Bulgarian, comes with no exculpating softening.[98] Other memoirs depict her as a warm and completely selfless personality.[99] She knitted gloves and pullovers for sale to add to the family income but most of what she did was given away to poor workers and family members. Kirkov used to joke that they were bankrupt in the knitting department.[100]

Koika Tineva (whose portrait is given in Part III) befriended Tina Kirkova when she came to Sofia. She had great respect for Georgi Kirkov, who was the most popular leader with his sociability and eloquence. Tineva herself came from a progressive, educated, and wealthy milieu and early on was under the influence of her uncle, Christian Rakovski, as well as her older brother. After the Plovdiv Congress in 1904, she was invited often to the home of the Kirkovs and had lively night discussions about the place of women in the movement:

He was very skeptical about their active involvement and would often say: "Fiddlesticks! Don't you see what's happening? They come to the clubs, pretend they are fellow travelers and once they get married are no longer interested in our work." I would object that men are to blame for this. I had many examples when the husband would prefer to have his wife at home and care for his comfort. I had heard a famous comrade of ours saying: "Emancipation for the neighbors. What does it mean to come back home and find your wife rushing to clubs and meetings, instead of meeting you and preparing everything?" [Kirkov] was perfectly aware of this but liked to tease me: "You think I believe you. You will do the same, once you marry. You will hide in the home and will think that you are contributing some important work by caring about the comfort of your husband."[101]

It is true that Kirkov's actions otherwise supported the women's movement in all ways possible and backed Vela Blagoeva's initiative for an independent women's organization of the social democrats, but he could not resist the tease.[102] Much as she resented it, Koika admitted to herself: "I had the chance to observe some of the wives of even some of our leaders consider their participation in the movement creating favorable conditions for their husbands. They were not even conscious of the absurdity and would unapologetically insist that they see their party duty in this."[103] Deep down Koika Tineva herself shared this view, recognizing only the role of the woman activist and did not come to the defense of the "invisible" women. Many of these women were very conscious of their situation and many were not "unapologetic" but, on the contrary, apologized with an unnecessary humility. The same Maria Krusheva who had been active in the movement until 1923, wrote of her position in the interwar period in the same vein. Her husband was interned all the time and she would say "apologetically" about herself: "Until 1939 I did not take direct part in party work, but I never obstructed the work of my husband and helped him in every possible way." There were constant clandestine meetings at her home. Between 1939 and 1944 she herself participated in collecting assistance for prisoners, in demonstrations, hid illegal activists at her home, and supported the work of her university student daughter, an active participant in the underground resistance. "I console myself with the thought that my husband, daughter and son-in-law dedicate themselves to party work. I try to ease them from the petty household chores and in this way I indirectly fulfil my party duty."[104] Whose consciousness was false? "Socialist women" and "socialist wives" should not be seen as a contradiction in terms. Socialist men could afford to be leading and visible because of their invisible socialist wives. That they (and also some socialist women) very seldom acknowledged this says less about the limitations of the socialist idea and more about the rootedness of these men and women in their historical time and place.

The victims of the White Terror were disproportionately men as in any war, but there were also several high-profile assassinations of women. Vela Piskova, née Akhmakova (1889–1925), born in Tîrnovo and the daughter of a teacher, studied in the pedagogical high school in Shumen where she joined the BWSDP (n) in 1907. In 1917 she graduated from Sofia University in mathematics and physics and became a high school teacher. In 1908 she married Peniu Piskov from the Piskov family, where all three brothers were active socialists, but she came to the fore with her leadership. An activist of the teachers' organization, the SDTO, she organized the anti-military women's protests in Shumen, and in 1923 was the first female military commander of the uprising in the town of Biala Slatina. In 1924–25 she was secretary of the district committee in Shumen and leader of the Military Organization in Shumen and Ruse. She was killed in March 1925 in a skirmish with the police. Her husband was arrested and sentenced to ten years in prison. Their fifteen-year-old son at the time, Kamen Piskov, was taken to the USSR where he became an engineer. After 1945 he returned to Bulgaria and became the country's chess champion and a renowned chess coach. Unfortunately, there is no archive of Vela Piskova and one has to deal with dry biographical data.

Luckily, this is not the case with Anna Maimunkova (1878–1925). Born in the wealthy family of a merchant, banker, and mayor of her home town Khaskovo, Anna was the youngest child. She finished the girls' high schools in Stara Zagora and Plovdiv where she had Vela Blagoeva as her teacher in the Russian language, and there she became a socialist, joining the BWSDP in 1897 and the Narrows in 1903. Her father was indulgent toward his daughter's passions and teased her: "When are you going to nationalize my wealth?" Anna prudently responded that it would not be too soon.[105] She was the only woman delegate to the Inaugural Congress of the SDTO in 1907. When she was fired from her teacher's job for her socialist ideas, her father sent her abroad to study for a year but then withdrew the funding in order to support his two sons' medical education in Paris. Anna had chosen to study social and political sciences at the Brussels Free University, her alma mater, a natural choice given the liberal reputation of Belgium. In this year, 1907–08, she also had a brief but intense romance documented in the postcards she was sending to her sister Vesa. Upon her return she was hired again as a teacher and wrote to her sister in 1909 that she had bought a new coat, dress, and hat of "fine-extra" quality. She was excited about her sister's newborn baby and wanted to knit slippers for him. She thought there was nothing more noble than raising a child: "It seems ludicrous, but my luck would have it that I would enjoy and caress other people's children. . . . Today's women push their children in the third place and occupy themselves with empty and foolish things. I am speaking of the wealthy mothers, because working women are forced to leave their children to go work in the factories."[106]

In 1911 she began contributing to *Novo Vreme*, *Rabotnicheski Vestnik*, and *Uchitelska Iskra* under the pen name Anna May. In 1912 she was fired again and during the wars led the anti-war demonstrations in Khaskovo, earning the sobriquet "the Khaskovo Rosa Luxemburg." During a brief stay in Berlin in 1911, she met Red Rosa and kept her autographed photograph as a souvenir. She also met Clara Zetkin with whom she began a continuous friendship. Anna moved to Sofia in 1920 and was elected to the Central Women's Commission at the CC of the BCP, whose secretary was Kirkova. In Sofia she edited two women's newspapers, *Ravenstvo* and *Rabotnichka*, to which she contributed articles such as "Proletarian women in winter," "The widows and orphans of Bulgaria," and "The Muslim woman and communism."[107] In 1921 she was the Bulgarian delegate to the Second Conference of Women Communists in Moscow which coincided with the Third Congress of the *Comintern*, where she met Lenin. In an issue of *Ravenstvo*, she later wrote that Lenin had said: "If the delegates ask me about the revolutionary perspectives I will respond: if the communists behave wisely, the perspectives are good, if they act foolishly, the perspectives are bad."[108] We do not know what Anna considered wise or foolish, but she was instrumental in organizing relief aid during the Russian famine in 1921–22. Her newspaper *Ravenstvo* ceased its publication after June 1923. In September, she organized the strike of tobacco workers in Khaskovo and was arrested. After her release she joined the clandestine struggle. It is unclear whether she was in the leadership of the Military Organization and Dimitŭr Genchev doubts that she knew about the terrorist act on April 16, 1925, judging from her documented behavior that day.[109] What is certain is that she was already a marked target. Arrested the same night in her home, she was tortured and killed in Sofia prison. A couple of months earlier, she had written to her worried sister, full of premonition:

> There is no way back! You should stay calm! You have children and for them you should look after your health and tranquility. History needs its victims and one should not feel sorry and weep for them. I have done no harm to anyone; on the contrary, I sacrificed my youth for my brothers and the family. Now I do not want to shrink as an old woman. What else do I want from life? Mine has been only grief, work and suffering, there is nothing more to covet from life. Really, you should not worry. You know, the end is death. My tired sole craves a rest.[110]

Part III

Structures of Feeling

It has long been an axiom of mine that little things are infinitely the most important.

Arthur Conan Doyle

To Generalize is to be an idiot. To Particularize is the Alone Distinction of Merit.

William Blake

Do emotions have structure? Or is this a complete oxymoron? While reading the memoirs and diaries that form the material for this part, I was struck by how often feelings were spelled out as formative of behavior. Their authors stood out in my imagination not as the Teacher, Lawyer, or Banker, but as the Proud and Willful (teacher), the Love-stricken Graphomaniac (lawyer), and the Romantic Feminist (banker). But how to express this? I was trying to find a phrase that could emphasize that something which at first glance seems inchoate, floating, elusive has a firmness, a configuration that has structure and can structure situations or whole lives, and can be tangible, explicable, and articulable. I thus decided on "structures of feeling."

But this was not a vacant phrase. A confession is due here. While I was aware that Raymond Williams had coined the term, I had never properly studied it, so now was the moment to educate myself. Raymond Williams had introduced it in a brief chapter in *Marxism and Literature* where he was trying to move beyond the determinism of base/superstructure models, especially in art and literary criticism "where the true social content is in a significant number of cases of this present and affective kind" and expressed "a particular quality of social experience and relationship, historically distinct from other particular qualities, which gives the sense of a generation or of a period."[1] Speaking about different historical periods and different groups, he was suggesting that they cannot be methodologically approached only by, and reduced solely to, ideology and class relations. He thus posited a social formation of a specific kind, non-derivative from other social forms and pre-forms "which may in turn be seen as the articulation (often the only fully available articulation) of structures of feeling which as living processes are much more widely experienced."[2] Many critics have found Williams's concept unsatisfactory and problematic and have attempted to subsume it within Bourdieu's notion of habitus, Foucault's episteme, and, especially, Gramsci's concept of hegemony, whose close relationship was recognized by Williams himself.³ While there is consensus that Williams left the notion barely theorized, the impact was momentous. He was emancipating the effective component of social reality by suggesting a third layer—affective infrastructure—alongside the social and material infrastructure.⁴ Yet, the influence of the term remained (and remains) confined almost exclusively to literary studies.

Williams's breakthrough coincided with a general change of the tide of academic interest in the 1970s toward the study of emotion. The psychologists Kurt Fisher and June Price Tangney in 1995 announced a revolution in the past twenty years.⁵ William Reddy, synthesizing the research at the beginning of the twenty-first century, spoke not of a single revolution, but of three revolutions proceeding independently of each other, in cognitive psychology, anthropology, and literary criticism.⁶ The crucial change in cognitive psychology was moving away from the notion that emotions are biologically pre-programmed responses, abandoning linear models of cognition, and forsaking the stark distinction between conscious and unconscious, supraliminal and subliminal, controlled and involuntary, and, as a result, between thought and affect. Based on his clinical research, the neuroscientist Antonio Damasio distinguishes "three stages of processing along a continuum: a state of emotion, which can be triggered and executed non-consciously; a state of feeling, which can be represented non-consciously, and a state of feeling made conscious i.e. known to the organism having both emotion and feeling" where a feeling is the private, mental experience of an emotion, and emotion is "the collection of responses, many of which are publicly observable."⁷ There is a continuing debate between proponents of the view that affect and cognition are indissociable, and those that posit affect and cognition as entirely separate systems.⁸ Some psychologists are speaking of "cogmotions" to express that emotions are indistinguishable from cognition.⁹ Others insist on emotions as practice, especially bodily practice.¹⁰ A consensus is shaping around the notion "that emotions can be regarded as overlearned cognitive habits; they are involuntary (automatic) in the short run in the same sense that such cognitive habits are, but may similarly be learned and unlearned over a longer time frame."¹¹ It is clear at this point that I will be using feeling and emotion, as well as sentiment and affect synonymously, and in this I am following a good part of the literature. Although distinctions can and have been made, especially about feeling and emotion in some of the specialized literature, they oftentimes propose completely opposing definitions.¹²

Anthropologists overwhelmingly treat emotions as socially constructed and ethnographic research from all parts of the world tends to support this constructivist view. Communities in general, in their ultimate goal of attaining a stable emotional regime to underpin a stable political regime, seem "to construe emotion as an important domain of effort" and "provide individuals with prescriptions and counsel concerning the best strategies for pursuing emotional learning."¹³ The emphasis on emotion in anthropology and a variety of other social disciplines has been inseparable, and in many ways set off by feminist concerns over the history and cultural construction of gender. As the anthropologist Catherine Lutz has persuasively argued, "emotion can be viewed as a cultural and interpersonal process of naming, justifying, and persuading by people in relationship to each other."¹⁴ Feminist approaches to emotion with their "attention to the material, institutional, and cultural capillaries of power through which discourses of emotion operate" clashed with normative approaches which restricted the role of emotion.[15]

Finally, emotional expression is analyzed as a type of speech act. Thought material, Reddy observes, exists in many codes, linguistic and extralinguistic. Emotions are among the most important of "the kinds of thought that lie 'outside' of language, yet are intimately involved in the formulation of utterances."[16] He, then, suggests the following definition: "An emotion is a range of loosely connected thought material, formulated in varying codes, that has goal-relevant valence and intensity, that may constitute a 'schema' (or a set of loosely connected schemas); this range of thought tends to be activated together but, when activated, exceeds attention's capacity to translate it into action or into talk in a short time horizon,"[17] or in an abbreviated definition: "Goal-relevant activations of thought material that exceed the translating capacity of attention within a short time horizon."[18] What is also useful is the formulation of an emotional regime as "the set of normative emotions and the official rituals, practices, and emotives that express and inculcate them; a necessary underpinning of any stable political system."[19]

The emotional or affective turn has been announced with much fanfare.[20] In fact, the importance of emotions has always been recognized and their intensive study across a variety of disciplines was present at least since the late-nineteenth century and the first half of the twentieth, inspired by William James's psychology, Max Weber's work on the protestant ethic, Freud's psychoanalysis, Huizinga's and Lucien Febvre's cultural and historicizing approach, and, especially, Norbert Elias's civilizing process. What happened was a hiatus of a couple of decades as a response to the Second World War when emotions, while still having a place in social theory, were marginalized and selected to represent the irrational and premodern. This demotion of emotion had its representatives in different disciplines: logical positivism and utilitarianism in philosophy, rational choice and modernization theory in economics and political science, and behaviorism in psychology, finding its most forceful expression in the works of Jürgen Habermas, John Rawls, Talcott Parsons, B. F. Skinner, and others.[21] When emotion took center stage again in the 1970s, "the field of sociology of emotion might be said to have existed for a long time without a name. But during the nineteenth and first part of the twentieth century, it was a confusing warren of conceptual tunnels and fascinating empirical observations without a sustained focus on emotion as something in and of itself."[22] At present it not only takes center stage; it has also been institutionalized in numerous research centers and as an academic sub-discipline.[23]

The emotional turn, or rather re-turn has also powerfully affected history, although the triumphalist naiveté with which it is heralded as "a fundamentally new direction in history" seems somewhat exaggerated: "History began as the servant of political developments... despite a generation's worth of social and cultural history, the discipline has never quite lost its attraction to hard, rational things."[24] As if soft, irrational things do not serve politics! Mark Steinberg, following Ronald Suny (following Benedict Anderson) has wisely insisted that the whole work on nationalism, that is, on collective identification, is essentially work on an affective tie, involving love and pride, as well as fear, resentment, and hatred.[25] He identifies four broad areas of research on emotions in the modern era for Eastern Europe, although these are also valid outside the region:

emotional identities, especially nationalism; moral emotions, especially around the self and society; the emotional politics of happiness, especially the pursuit of modernity and freedom; and emotional dissent.[26] Another important sphere of research on emotions is religion.[27] As a whole, historians have made significant contributions to the historicization of emotions, what Ute Frevert has aptly described as emotions lost and found: "The historical economy of emotions . . . sees emotions and emotional styles fade away and get lost, but it also witnesses the emergence of new or newly framed emotions."[28] At the same time, scholars warn against overgeneralizations like characterizing whole periods with an emotional regime, especially productive in the work of Barbara Rosenwein who has posited different "emotional communities" available at the same time in any society to a subject who can participate in a number of them.[29]

Much of this work has been executed on the meso- and macrolevel around collective behavior, social movements, nationalism, revolutions, etc. Still, the overwhelming majority is performed on the microlevel because "the history of emotion is in some important way a corollary to a history of personhood."[30] Naturally, emotions are most observable in details about individual lives and subjectivities in the past are most easily approached through biographical material. But what are biographies? The writing of lives: βιο-γραφία? Except that *biography*, this "bastard child of historiography and literature" was baptized under this name only in the late-seventeenth and early eighteenth centuries, but officially only in 1762 by the Academie française.[31] Before it was Life/Lives (vita/vitae, βίος / βίοι), and Plutarch himself would say that he was writing not histories, but Lives.[32] The word "biographia" was used first in the sixth century CE, but "vita" was the dominant term well into the seventeenth century.[33] From the lives of famous military and civic leaders, through church fathers, martyrs and saints, to prominent artists, these Lives were dedicated to people (usually, but not exclusively, men) with exceptional position in society or with exceptional talents, and what was common to all of them was their commemorative character.

With the adoption of a rational-empirical methodology for history supposed to be "objective," biography, by contrast, was considered "a subjective, moral and literary activity."[34] This did not make it less popular with the broad public, but it meant a breach with historiography, and biography was treated exclusively as a literary genre. With the demise of the Great Man Theory, which spanned most of the nineteenth century, historiography concentrated on large-scale historical narratives and a preference for structural and quantitative approaches. The first generation of the Annales school had rejected biography as a historiographical form, although Jacques Le Goff qualified this by saying that they were opposed to its superficial treatment and were even more hostile to its political history.[35] The immensely successful American biographer Deirdre Bair even proclaimed in 2001 that "biography is an academic suicide."[36] She was not entirely correct. By that time, biography had made its way back on legitimate academic ground. This came with the rise of New Historicism, cultural history, *histoire des mentalités, Alltagsgeschichte,* and, in general, the cultural turn in the 1970s and 1980s, with a renewed interest in human experience, in the individual, and subjectivity. Two historiographical trends have been decisive for the biographical turn: Life Writing and microhistory.

Life Writing was propelled by the philosophical and sociological debates about the "subject" and the "self." Michel Foucault's "death of the subject" meant his adherence to the concept of the subject as constituted rather than autonomous and transcendental.[37] Feminist theory was especially important in this respect with Judith Butler's argument about the subject as a performative materialization of its social environment.[38] Crucial in formulating the doubts about the unity of the self was the brief essay by Bourdieu, "The Biographical Illusion."[39] Bourdieu did not renounce biography as such but the belief that life could be understood as a unique and self-sufficient series of events. In his effective and oft cited simile, that was "nearly as absurd as trying to make sense out of a subway route without taking into account the network structure, that is the matrix of objective relations between the different stations."[40] Writing concretely against the methodology of life stories derived from interviews, he questioned the commonsense understanding that life unfolds in a unidirectional and linear way, passing through different stages to "an end, understood both as a termination and as a goal."[41] In this metaphorical understanding of life as a journey, the biographer (and autobiographer) invests life with an artificial coherence by selecting a few significant events and creating causal links between them: "To produce a history of a life, to treat a life like a history, that is to say, like a coherent recital of a meaningful sequence of events, is perhaps to submit to a rhetorical illusion, a common representation of existence, that our literary tradition has not ceased to reinforce."[42]

Bourdieu sees the proper name as "the visible affirmation of its bearer across time and social space, the basis of unity of one's successive manifestations, and of the socially accepted possibilities of integrating these manifestations in official records," a nominal constancy beyond all the biological and social changes. But this is precisely what makes it powerless to "describe properties and conveys no information about that which it names; since what it designates is only a composite and disparate rhapsody of biological and social properties in constant flux, all descriptions are valid only within the limits of a specific stage or place. In other words, it can only attest to the identity of the *personality*, as a socially constituted individuality, at the price of an enormous abstraction."[43] According to Bourdieu, we can follow individuals as they travel through their social trajectories, through the series of positions they successively occupy in social space, rejecting the notion of an essential identity and coherent life, insisting on contingency, emphasizing social and economic conditions but at the same time allowing for personal agency.

The result, in Joanny Moulin's eloquent summary, was: "Exit biography. Enter life writing, or the 'récit de vie', which so far has not felt obliged to take any irrelevant subject concept into consideration but concentrates instead on studying the discursive productions of individuals always necessarily representative of one given community or another. The idea of the self once neutralized, the 'récit de vie' can serve either as sources or as tools of academic discourse."[44] Life Writing has achieved the status of an academic discipline with special interdisciplinary Centres for Life Writing Research at the University of Essex and King's College London. It would seem that it can encompass biographical research and its materials in the broadest sense of the word, including autobiography, biography proper, diaries, memoirs, personal correspondence, travel accounts, testimonies, confessions, and today, also digital sources like emails, blogs, and other social media.[45]

There is, however, a rigorous debate about the foundations of Life Writing. Scholars involved in the theorization of biographical research around the Ludwig Boltzmann Institut für Geschichte und Theorie der Biographie in Vienna observe that Life Writing depends excessively and uncritically on autobiographical sources: "Autobiographica are important in Life Writing research due to the experience which they record, more than as a possible source for illustrating or contextualizing history."[46] The premise on ego-documents as a window to subjectivity is taken too literally, making "this field of scholarship a commemorative and rarely a critical activity" where autobiographical documents are utilized "without reservation as ready-made blocks for the construction of a new perspective on the past."[47] This all stems from the emancipatory ethos of uplifting marginal or oppressed groups (slaves, women, the dispossessed) in the process of which "it offers retrospective justice."[48] They adopt the view that biography (or, rather, the scholarly biography[49]) differs in certain important aspects from Life Writing, and that as a research area it belongs to history. It shares the dedication to the study of the marginals of society who have not been traditionally represented in history but is committed to a rigorous standard of the verifiability of history. Biography thus designates "the study of an individual, based on the methods of historical scholarship, with the goal of illuminating what is public, explained and interpreted in part from the perspective of the personal," something with which many practitioners of Life Writing would also agree.[50] It is based on a narrative technique which "preserves the potential for self-creation, because it conveys the constancy of form within the passage of time."[51]

The second pillar on which the "new biography" is built is microhistory. At first glance, it would be tenuous to assume a direct link between microhistory and biography. "Is it possible," one of its main theoreticians and practitioners Giovanni Levi asked, "to put down in writing an individual's life?"[52] And yet, there are more commonalities if one looks deeper into the methods employed. First, of course, is the scale, the preference for close-ups, the attention to detail. Secondly, there is the interest in the marginal, in the people without voices. Even more important is what Carlo Ginzburg and Giovanni Levi call the "evidentiary paradigm" or "the method of clues." What they mean by this is starting the investigation from something that seems odd, insignificant, and marginal, something that does not quite fit in and needs to be explained.[53] And, unsurprisingly, they resort to biographical material and the description of individuals, although "Ginzburg's *The Cheese and the Worms* was not a peasant biography and not even a history of peasant millers in sixteenth-century Northern Italy," nor are Giovanni Levi's *Inheriting Power* or Natalie Zemon Davis's *The Return of Martin Guerre* biographies.[54] The American historian Jill Lepore well grasped the difference between the two:

> If biography is largely founded on a belief in the singularity and significance of an individual's life and his contributions to history, microhistory is founded upon almost the opposite assumption: however singular a person's life may be, the value of examining it lies not in its uniqueness, but in its exemplariness, in how that individual's life serves as an allegory for broader issues affecting the culture as a whole.[55]

It is not only, and simply, commonalities between the two genres, but also the influence coming from microhistory. Simone Lässig squarely addresses this issue and points out that in contemporary biographies, the "trend is toward discontinuity instead of linear narrative approaches, toward montages and constructions with emphatically multiple perspectives, in which the same life is related and interpreted for different viewpoints."[56] And, as Hans Renders observes, both microhistory and biography are "the sum of a scientific attitude and a penchant for creativity to place a story from the past into a powerful interpretative framework."[57]

6

Dignity and Will

The Odyssey of Angelina Boneva

Imagine a grey autumn day in 1911 in Vratsa, a small town in northwestern Bulgaria, close to the Serbian border. It is easy to imagine a grey autumn day anywhere. Except for a Bulgarian, it is more difficult to map the whereabouts of Vratsa. In the early twentieth century, for someone sitting in the West, say in London, it would not be easy even to map Bulgaria on the European map. For someone well read, who had just laid down *The Prisoner of Zenda*, Anthony Hope's best-selling romance of 1894, his or her Eastern horizons would extend as far as Ruritania (which was unmappable because imagined, but geographically locatable to Kakania). But Bulgaria was even beyond Ruritania. By then, of course, Bulgaria was on the map. In 1878 it had seceded from the Ottoman Empire, under whose rule the Bulgarians had been since the end of the fourteenth century, and having achieved autonomous status, by 1908 it had declared full independence. The year 1911 was off by only one year from the start of the Balkan Wars in 1912, when the Kingdom of Bulgaria and the other small Balkan countries came to the center of international attention with their unexpectedly victorious war against the Ottoman Empire, which pushed the empire practically out of the Balkans and thus out of Europe.

Vratsa in 1911 was a small town of about 15,000 inhabitants, but it was a county center.[1] It boasted a long historical pedigree, but this was not much different from most other towns in this part of the world. It had been an ancient Thracian settlement, then become an important Roman fortress, and retained its military and strategic importance in the Byzantine Empire, and later in the Bulgarian Empire and the early Ottoman Empire. With the further Ottoman conquests in the West, its military importance diminished, but this explains why it retained its Bulgarian character as a small artisanal center. The Muslim population (mostly ethnic Turks) comprised about 10 percent of the population, and almost all emigrated after 1878. During the eighteenth and nineteenth centuries Vratsa was also an important educational center for Bulgarians. It had been the seat of an Orthodox bishopric and the name of the city was immortalized when the Bulgarian bishop Stoiko Vladoslavov, with the clerical name Sophronius (1739–1813), received the sobriquet Sophrony Vrachanski (Sophronius of Vratsa). Sofrony is second only to Paissi Khilendarski as one of the most revered figures of the Bulgarian Revival, the author of a famous autobiography and printed sermons using the Bulgarian vernacular. He was also a political figure, acting on behalf of the Bulgarians in his contacts with the Russian leadership during the Russo-Turkish war of 1806–12.² Vratsa and its environs had a number of monasteries, and from 1822 on there were several secular schools, among them a girls' school, founded in 1843. This explains why the town became one of the centers of attraction for the gradual flow of Macedonian refugees from the Ottoman Empire after 1878, and especially after the demise of the 1903 Ilinden Uprising.³ One of these refugee families—the Miskanov brothers from the town of Veles in Macedonia—settled in Vratsa. Nikola Miskanov was hired as a teacher of French in the local school, and his brother Kotso Miskanov opened a bookstore. The bookstore sold Marxist literature and was a virtual club for the local social democrats, who would gather there and discuss issues for hours on end.

So, it was in this very same bookstore that "a curiosity" happened a grey autumn day in 1911. An old peasant woman entered the bookstore. She was dressed all in black, with a black kerchief over her white hair that was falling over her wrinkled face. She wore simple peasant man's shoes on her feet and, instead of a bag, had a wicker basket hanging from her left arm. Once she entered the bookstore, she reached into her bosom and produced a small cigarette case. Then she rolled a cigarette, took out a pair of glasses, and started looking at the literature spread on a table. Kotso Miskanov, the owner, approached her pointing to the way out: "Grandmother, we don't have the books you are looking for. I know that you are trying to find *The Dreams of the Virgin* or *A Stone Fell From Heaven*." The peasant woman pretended not to have heard him and continued to look at the books. Finally, she asked: "Do you have *Anti-Dühring*?" Miskanov, pop-eyed, stared at her. She continued unruffled by asking him whether he had Kautsky and named a particular book. She finished her cigarette, picked a few other books silently and calmly said: "The bill, please."

This episode was narrated as a small aside under the title "curiosity" (*kurioz*) in the unpublished memoirs of Ivan Draganov Danov (1893–1985), a lifelong social-democrat (Narrow) and, later, a communist.⁴ A native of Vratsa, in 1911 he had just entered university in Sofia, where he studied law. He practiced law in Vratsa and after the Second World War chaired the appellate court in Ruse and was a deputy attorney general of the republic. Curiously, he never made it to the Bulgarian encyclopedia (*Entsilklopedia Bŭlgariia*), which was compiled between 1978 and 1996. In 1967, already retired and back in his hometown, he dictated his memoirs, which were then given for preservation (but never used) in the Central Party Archive (CPA). The little we know of him comes from his autobiographical notes. I encountered his name in the guide to the memoirs on the BCP, kept in the CPA, which was published in 2003.⁵ The memoirs themselves, consisting of 215 pages, were dictated in 1967 in Vratsa.

On the two pages, on which he describes the "curiosity," he gives the name of the old woman and some further details. Angelina Boneva was the oldest teacher in Bulgaria in the village of Pripŭlzhane, in her mid-sixties, and he knew her from around 1910 as a member of the social-democratic teachers' organization. Danov himself, just out of high school, taught for a year in a neighboring village, Sumer. Once a month, on a Saturday, he would go to her village which was about 6-7 kilometers off, and then the two would take the road on foot to Ferdinand (today Montana) to attend a meeting of the organization. "Baba Angelina" (Granny Angelina) had some education and started her teaching career in Macedonia and then in other regions of Bulgaria. Danov specifies that her education corresponded to what today would be considered middle school (either five years, that is, one year after elementary school, or seven years, that is, the third year of middle school). He adds that she had been married but had kicked her husband out. She told him that she was a teacher in Zagorichane, the native village of Dimitîr Blagoev, the future founder of the Bulgarian Social-Democratic Party, and that she would write his parents' letters when he was a student in Russia. Danov concludes: "Overall she was a very interesting person and she retired in 1922, decorated by the then minister of education of the agrarian regime, Stoian Omarchevski."[6] All my efforts to find something more about her at the time I read this excerpt from Danov's memoirs were in vain. I was not even sure I would ever use it, except if utilizing it, in the convention of the new cultural history, as a vignette or telling anecdote. Although I had rebelled against the ubiquity of this convention, I did eventually succumb to it . . .

Later, while speaking to archivists at the Central State Archives in Sofia, I told them the funny story. I was wondering whether there would not be something more from Danov, perhaps in the provincial archive of Vratsa. Perhaps I should make a visit to the archive. Come on, I was told, we are now in the digital age. What digital age? There is not even a detailed published paper catalogue with a proper index on the total holdings of the Sofia archive, let alone something on a small-town archive. Well no, I was told, but there was an internal online catalogue available only to archivists. And, lo and behold, a week later I was called in by my three fairy godmothers[7] and told that they could not find anything on Danov but that a whole file existed on Angelina Boneva! We are lucky that this "small voice of history" in the definition of Ranajit Guha, has been preserved.[8]

The file had been found in the local archive of another small town in northwest Bulgaria, smaller even than Vratsa. Montana is about 40 kilometers (25 miles) from Vratsa, and 30 kilometers (19 miles) from the Serbian border. It is a town that holds pride of place in name-changing, even in the frequent political renaming of Bulgarian settlements. A Thracian settlement, in the second century CE it became a Roman garrison town with the name Civitas Montanensium. During the First and Second Bulgarian Kingdom it was known by its Slavic name Kutlovitsa. The Ottomans preserved this name as Kutlofça. In 1890 it was renamed for the then ruling Prince (after 1908, King/Tsar) Ferdinand. During communist times the town was renamed as Mikhailovgrad to commemorate Khristo Mikhailov (1893–1944), a prominent communist. It was not entirely arbitrary, since the town and the district in general were known for their revolutionary tradition and as a center of the 1923 uprising.

Khristo Mikhailov himself was born in a family of teachers and finished his primary education in Ferdinand. He was sent to a high school in Vidin where he encountered socialist ideas. At the age of eighteen, already a member of the BWSDP (n), he became a village teacher for two years until the outbreak of the Balkan Wars. After the wars, he enrolled as a law student at Sofia University, but was mobilized during the First World War. Captured by the allies in Greece, he was released as a prisoner of war in 1920. He was the secretary of the Communist Party organization in Ferdinand and an important leader of the 1923 uprising. After the crushing of the revolt, he emigrated briefly to Yugoslavia and returned illegally, becoming one of the leaders of the Military Organization. He was captured in 1925 and received a death sentence, which was commuted, and in the general amnesty of 1937 he was released. He became a member of the CC of the BCP and was an organizer of the so-called Sobolev action in 1940, supporting the Soviet offer of a pact for mutual assistance. The offer was declined, but it managed to gather anywhere between 1.5 million (probably exaggerated) and 340,000 (most likely reduced) signatures.⁹ In 1941 Mikhailov went underground and was charged with directing the armed resistance movement. He had become a member of the Politbureau of the CC of the BCP and was caught and killed by the police in February 1944. His younger brother Ivan Mikhailov (1897–1982), born in Ferdinand, joined the socialist movement as a high school student. Enrolled as a law student in 1921, he actively participated in the uprising, and after 1925 emigrated to the USSR where he spent the next twenty years as a high-ranking officer in the Soviet army. After 1945, he became a general and minister of defense, and one of the most high-profile leaders of the country. Thus, the name Mikhailov came with an impeccable communist pedigree, which would tarnish the town's reputation after 1989. Accordingly, and in search of a "neutral" name that would underpin the belonging to the common European home and civilization, the new Roman Empire, Kutlovitsa–Kutlofça–Ferdinand–Mikhailovgrad adopted the Latin name Montana.

In the Montana State Archive the file of Angelina Boneva contains different documentation. There are reminiscences about baba Angelina by her former students and colleagues. One is an attempt at a comprehensive biography. There is the official schoolbook of the school in the village of Pripîlzhane (today Trifonovo, Montana district). Finally, there are the memoirs of Angelina Boneva herself copied by her nephew in 1974. The "Short Biographical Notes" on an official form states that Angelina Bonova (*sic*! elsewhere she is Boneva, and both readings are correct, meaning she is the daughter of Bono, Bone, or Bonio) was born in 1852 in the village of Pripîlzhane, Mikhailovgrad district (Figure 32). The form is written in ink after the Second World War, when an album of teachers in the Pripîlzhane school was produced.¹⁰ At the age of twenty-five she completed her elementary school education (4 grades) in two years in the town of Pirot, and then in Sofia studied for another five years coming out with a pedagogical degree. She first taught in a Sofia school, but in 1884 moved to the village of Zagorichane, in the Kostur district of Macedonia, then in the Ottoman Empire, where she stayed for ten years. She was briefly imprisoned for three months as a "komitka."¹¹ After that she taught for a year in the village of Krushitsa, then for three years in the village of Medkovets, and finally for twenty-three years in Pripîlzhane. Altogether, "she has 37 years of actual employment." At the bottom of the page is added in pencil: "No husband and children." The form has three photographs, when she was thirty-two, seventy, and eighty-two years old.¹²

Remembering Angelina Boneva

These brief biographical notes can be filled with details from the memoirs of her students and colleagues collected most likely when the village was preparing to celebrate the centenary of the school. The school itself was founded in 1858, so the memoirs must have been collected for the centenary of the school in 1958, when the people who had personal memories of the teacher were in their seventies, eighties, and maybe nineties. We know it could not be later than 1958, because Maslina Grîncharova, who was one

Figure 32 "Short Biographical Notes."

of the remembrancers, died the same year at the age of seventy-three. The recollections are undated and seem to be dictated (or taped) during a common discussion, since they have the air of a conversation rather than sustained narratives. The one exception is a signed reminiscence by Spiro Vasilev, from October 1971.

The future teacher and national revolutionary Maslina Grîncharova was a child when Angelina came to Zagorichane in 1885. Maslina was born in 1874, studied first with Angelina Boneva and then finished the Bulgarian high school in Thessaloniki. As a teacher, she became a member of the IMRO in 1895 and participated actively in the Macedonian struggle. She was the flag-bearer, of a flag she had sewed and embroidered herself, for her unit during the Ilinden Uprising. Twice arrested by the Ottoman police and later amnestied, after the Balkan Wars she emigrated to Bulgaria and was a teacher. She settled in Krivodol, halfway between Vratsa and Montana and close to her old teacher. She died in 1958.[13] In the conversation, Maslina recalls how Angelina Boneva had set out from Sofia to Istanbul (Tsarigrad) then the seat of the Bulgarian Exarchate to demand to be sent as a teacher to Ottoman Macedonia. She entered the Ottoman Empire pretending to be the servant of an engineer who obligingly put her on his passport. Once in the city, she was kept for a fortnight during the time of the revolt that resulted in the unification of the Principality of Bulgaria with Eastern Rumelia in 1885. It so happened that representatives from Zagorichane were asking at the same time for a Bulgarian teacher. Once in the village, she lived for a couple of weeks in the house of Blagoev's parents. Every year the school was in the house of a different villager. At first Angelina was teaching, exclusively, girls; she had nearly eighty students. She became well known for her needlework classes, so much so that she attracted all the girls of the village, even the ones who heretofore were attending the classes of the Greek teacher Marigo.

Zagorichane was ethnically Bulgarian (or Bulgarian-speaking), but there was also a large group of the so-called *grikomani* [гръкомани] (literally "Greek maniacs"), Hellenophiles, who identified as Greek and remained members of the Greek patriarchate after the split of the Bulgarians from the *Rum millet* in 1860 and their official recognition as a separate millet with a Bulgarian Exarchate in 1870. Angelina was falsely accused by the Greek priest of participating in a revolutionary plot. Arrested by the Turks, she was sent to prison, but the village hired a Jewish lawyer who proved that the incriminating letter was treacherously placed behind her icon by the Greek priest. Maslina Grincharova thought that Angelina married "someone by the name of Lambo from the family of the former prime minister Andrei Liapchev" but lived with him only for a few months before they separated. The bishop of Berkovitsa exerted pressure on her but she never remarried. Her biggest enemy was Nikola Rangelov from Pripîlzhane.[14]

Kuzman Trifonov remembered her as a student: "She was teaching us beautifully. She was like a second mother to us. Strict and fair, she taught us every day, in the morning and in the afternoon. In good days, she would give us a lump of sugar. In the village sugar was very rare." Angelina had a small first aid kit and would visit the sick in the village: "Once, when Peter the Macedonian was ill, she gave him her bed and stove."[15] Ianaki Panov agreed: "I was in first grade in 1905. She was earnest, had a manly appearance and approached each child depending on his father's trade. If he was a shepherd, she began speaking of sheep." She was apparently not only a very successful teacher but also the first resort for anyone in the village who was sick and needed help or money. "She was loved and respected as teachers in our parts rarely are. . . . She came into the socialist movement in 1908-1910 under the influence of Dimitîr Filipov and Kamen Dimov from the teacher's organization of the Narrows." She was an active and open party member until 1923 and during the uprising hid and encouraged the insurgents: "She was teaching with a revolutionary spirit, she hated the Turks, and the domination of men over women."[16] Nikola Popov chipped in briefly to say that he knew her quite late, from 1927 on. Through her he kept in touch with contacts from other villages: "She would say ten words, but they would be brave and bold. . . . She was a courageous old woman."[17]

Vîlo Lazarov had been a teacher in the village of Lipen from 1904, and the following year was transferred to the village of Stubel. He knew baba Angelina from then: "Her charisma came from her boundless humanity. She was the village judge. She settled all civil disputes. . . . She gave her opinion on marriage unions, and the young women and men listened to her. Parents, who had children of age, came to her for advice."[18] Lazarov also gave detailed information about her political work:

> She would take the floor at teachers' conferences and always spoke very well. She was a Narrow socialist in the real sense of the word. During elections she campaigned for the Party. Her bitter enemy was Nikola Rangelov, who accused her of interfering with the order. He wanted to appoint his own brother as a teacher and drive her away from Pripîlzhane. He warned me not to visit her, because she was allegedly dangerous. The well-known communist Kamen Dimov was with us. We formed circles, organized meetings, read and discussed books and the political

situation in the country. She would regularly go to Sofia and get in touch with our people. She received *Rabotnicheski vestnik* (Worker's gazette) and *Novo Vreme* (New Times). In 1904 the teachers' organization convened a meeting to discuss whether religious education had a scientific value. It was decided to drop it from the school curriculum. The meeting was in hotel "Central," where we have today's bookshop. After our decision Vanko the Lame, the municipality herald, went out with his drum: "Come out, people, the communists drove out the word of God from school." We had to flee so not to get in a street fight with the "tsankovists" [supporters of Dragan Tsankov]. A great number among us were fired for this decision, but this order was revoked, because the schools were left without teachers. In 1907 the "stambolovists" issued a law prohibiting teachers from participating in public life and party work. We teachers assembled for a meeting in Mikhailovgrad. For this, the district chief Ivan Iliev ordered all teachers present to be fired, but again, as the schools were empty, the order was revoked. Angelina Bonova was an active participant at both meetings in 1904 and 1907 and impressed with her speeches and suggestions.[19]

Spiro Vasilev's typed and signed recollections describe the eightieth birth anniversary of Angelina in 1932 and her funeral in 1938. The celebration in 1932 was organized by Macedonian immigrants attached to the "Kostur society" and the "Ilinden society" of Zagorichane. Zagorichane, during communist times chiefly recognized as the birthplace of Blagoev, had been a remarkable village for the rise of Bulgarian education and nationalism in the nineteenth century, so much so that it was known at the time as "Little Sofia." Today the village is in Northern Greece, in the district of Kostur (Kastoria). In the latter decades of the nineteenth century the village had a population of over 3,000 people.[20] By 1905 it topped 4,100.[21] It was a large and comparatively wealthy village known for its dairy produce. Since the arable land was insufficient, seasonal labor was widespread. Passers-by describe it as a Bulgarian village, with some Vlachs and Gypsies.[22] A Bulgarian school was opened in 1869 and, after the creation of the Bulgarian Exarchate, the whole village passed under its jurisdiction in 1897. However, at the time Angelina Boneva came there as a teacher in 1885, the religious affiliation of its inhabitants was disputed as between the Greek Constantinople Patriarchate and the Bulgarian Exarchate. Atanas Shopov, the secretary to the Bulgarian Exarchate, thus described the village, at the time Boneva was a teacher there: "The people of Zagorichane are proud of their huge church and good school buildings for boys and girls but cannot pride themselves on accord and unanimity. Because they lack these two virtues, their schools are divided between *grikomani* and Bulgarians."[23]

The village actively participated in the Ilinden Uprising of 1903 and was entirely burned down. In 1905 Greek bands entered the village and slaughtered a huge number of people. There was an international uproar, but after the massacre the majority of the population emigrated to Bulgaria and North America. After the Balkan Wars the village was incorporated into Greece but dwindled, and after the Treaty of Lausanne, some Pontian Greeks were settled there. The village remained Bulgarian, and during the Civil War supported the communist guerillas. After the war, there was mass emigration to the United States and Canada, and today the village counts three hundred people, entirely Hellenized.[24] Many former inhabitants of Zagorichane, Spiro Vasilev and Maslina Grîncharova among them, gathered for the birthday of baba Angelina in 1932. There were no official government representatives: "Well," Spiro comments, "she was a progressive woman, what would the official ones do here!"[25] It was a joyous meeting, but six years later many of the same people gathered for her funeral.

With its smooth poetic language, Viktor Makaveev's signed recollection, entitled "Our AB . . ." from April 1979 reads like an article prepared for a local anniversary paper. It begins with the white blossoming trees on the eve of the Cyril and Methodius Day, when Bulgarians officially celebrate their education and culture, alphabet and literature. As an official annual celebration this tradition started in the 1850s (1851, 1855, and 1857 are candidates for the official beginning) and it is arguably the most cherished national public holiday to this day.[26] For Makaveev, who had been her student, Angelina Boneva's name was like an acrostic of the beginning of the alphabet and she belonged to those enlightened people whom the "nation entrusted to bring Bulgaria out of the ignorance and assimilation from Anatolians and Phanariotes."[27] The narrative follows her formation as a dedicated teacher and even puts words in her mouth. When asked why she left her teacher's post in Sofia, she would respond: "I cannot calmly live my life, when my brethren in Macedonia need educated people!"[28] Together with her student and future teacher Maslina Grîncharova she sewed and embroidered the flag of Gotse Delchev's *cheta*.

Makaveev's story is the only one that sheds more light on baba Angelina's marital status. While she was in Ottoman prison as a Bulgarian *komitadzhi*, the authorities advised her to marry someone who could ransom her. She, indeed, married someone by the name of Haralampi, wealthy and educated, and obtained her freedom. She was, however, suspicious that this person might have been designated by the authorities and was cautious in her relations with him. She apparently shared with her kith and kin that the marriage was never consummated, and Makaveev refers to her "wedding." After settling in Pripîlzhane, Angelina helped Haralampi to open a store in an adjacent village and they separated (but there is no mention of divorce). She was also instrumental in finding a teacher's position for her former student Maslina Grîncharova in the neighboring village of Krapchene in 1903, and almost every day the two would cross the river Shugla and get together. It was in the first decade of the twentieth century that socialist groups were formed in the villages, and Angelina Boneva was responsible for collecting the membership fees and the subscription to the party organ "Rabotnicheski vestnik."[29]

Finally, there is the aforementioned undated attempt at a comprehensive biography written by Petîr Ivanov, the great-grandson of Angelina Boneva. He does not mention this in the biography, but his signature is identical to the copyist of her memoirs. The biography consists of nineteen typed pages and is based on the recollections of his parents, as well as the two grandsons of Angelina's uncle Ivan, all living in Sumer. Ivanov also used the memoirs of Angelina Boneva, kept in the Museum of the September Uprising in Mikhailovgrad, under inventory number 1023, as well as the schoolbook from the state archive of Mikhailovgrad, Fond 432. He also had the chance to meet and speak to her personally.[30] The biography begins with Angelina's family: "Angelina Bonova Iakimova was born in 1852 in Pripîlzhane, in a poor, but enlightened family." Only the male kin are mentioned. Her grandfather Iakim became a priest in the neighboring village of Sumer. His third son, Bono, stayed in Pripîlzhane. Iakim's first two sons—Pîrvan and Ivan—were literate, but it was not known whether Bono was. Given how much value was given to literacy in those days, we can fairly assume that Bono was, in fact, illiterate. However, the biographer was at pains to emphasize the "enlightened" pedigree of Angelina, so he begins with the extended family.

Although complete literacy was achieved only after the Second World War, and the reading ability was very limited in the countryside where over 80 percent of the population resided, the premium set on education was immense. The political stabilization of the Ottoman Empire in the nineteenth century and the *Tanzimat* reforms created a favorable framework for wealth accumulation in the Bulgarian community. This was accompanied by an intense cultural revival whose culmination fell on the last four decades before Bulgaria seceded from the Ottoman Empire in 1878. There already was a thin stratum of literati educated in Russia, Greece, and Western educational establishments, but it was after the foundation of the Aprilov gymnasium (high school), based on the Bell-Lancaster system, in the industrial town of Gabrovo in 1836 that a veritable modern secular school system took off. A school for girls was opened in 1840 and by mid-century most Bulgarian communities in smaller towns or larger villages had a school teaching in the vernacular. By 1878, Bulgaria had over 2,000 schools and what was remarkable was that all were financed by the local councils or guilds without any support from the Ottoman state. By the time of independence, elementary literacy was widespread but only among the younger generation.[31] By the end of the century, Bulgaria reached a literacy rate of close to 30 percent but literate people lived mostly in the towns.[32] With the coming of independence, the state, in dire need of educated cadres for the growing government bureaucracy, actively intervened to promote public education and implemented a number of progressive reforms aimed at broadening its reach in the most remote rural areas, making high school education affordable and equalizing women's and men's educational programs. The reforms received a special impetus under the 1903-07 tenure of the education minister Professor Ivan Shishmanov. By 1910, there were 4,800 elementary schools, 330 middle schools, twenty-seven high schools, and 113 vocational schools, and many villages had public halls for social gatherings and libraries.[33]

It is in this atmosphere of educational upliftment that Angelina was born. She was six, when a school was opened in Pripîlzhane in 1858, but she was not allowed to attend. Being the youngest child in an orphaned family (her father died when she was still a child), she was sent to work in the fields and at home. At the age of twenty-three, trying to avoid being married and with a desire to learn, she ran away from home. Ivanov's biography follows her through all her peregrinations, from her school years to her teaching career in Macedonia, and finally her settling down in her own village where she taught over the course of twenty-three years, to retire at the age of seventy. This biography really is an "attempt," since most of its narrative consists of verbatim quotes from the autobiography of Angelina Boneva, a kind of half-baked (but admirable) Life Writing.

That all these recollections agree in their main points should come as no surprise. These were coordinated eulogies delivered at a particular commemorating moment. There is no doubt about the facticity of the main events, the "coordination" is, rather, in the tone. They are all praising their subject, but even from their brief accounts it is clear that Angelia Boneva also induced intensive enmity (the *grîkomani* in Zagorichane, the local Greek priest whose deed resulted in her arrest and imprisonment, the influential Nikola Rangelov in Pripîlzhane, who worked intractably to remove her from her teaching post). We can imagine what we could have heard from them, but the important fact is that baba Angelina was not a bland character: she generated strong feelings toward her persona; the least that can be said of her is that she was a maverick.

The recollections are interesting for the ways they reflect the Zeitgeist. There are three dominant facets that emerge in the characterization of Angelina Boneva. First and foremost was her role as a teacher. In the relatively egalitarian Bulgarian society, education was the most valued cultural capital and the principal meritocratic means for advancement. Within this atmosphere, the teachers' vocation was one that inspired enormous public respect, even if its economic position was precarious. It was an especially valued profession in the first decades after Bulgaria's independence when there was also a dearth of teachers. Teachers were considered "makers" of the nation's citizenry, and on the local level, especially in villages, they were the holders of knowledge and wisdom and served as the first legal and medical resort. Angelina Boneva belonged to the pioneering generation of teachers in the independent state.

The second large theme is patriotism or nationalism. In many ways, it is linked to the teacher's vocation, as education is a central pillar of nationalism, but it was more direct than that. Angelina was moved by a desire to learn, but she wanted to put her knowledge in the service of the nation. Again, there should be no surprise given the time when she was born and became an adolescent during a cultural upswing, and the time she matured as a young woman during the national euphoria of building the foundations of a new modern state. Nor was her patriotism bookish and declarative. She relinquished a coveted position in a school in the capital in order to reach Macedonia, the Bulgarian fixation since the Berlin Congress until the Second World War, and a question that still inflames rhetorical passions. By doing this and promoting the Bulgarian cause through education, but clearly also having a share in the armed struggle, she exposed herself to risks, ending up in prison. She was apparently highly valued by the Macedonian refugees who were in the forefront in celebrating her contributions.

The third theme in all recollections are Angelina Boneva's socialist activities. These were naturally emphasized in a socialist setting, given the time when they were gathered after the Second World War. One can say with fair certainty that her dynamic socialist profile would have been downplayed during the celebrations of her eightieth birthday in the 1930s at a time of severe anti-communist repressions. In this environment, anyone with her open espousal of beliefs and activist stance would have been persecuted, but she was spared the humiliation by her nationally recognized aura of a dedicated and long-serving teacher and her gender (she was one of the first women in this profession). As if this was not enough, she was also widely known for her active participation in the national struggles. And then there was her advanced age. All of this would probably not have saved her were it not for the lucky circumstance that she retired in 1922 during the last year of the agrarian regime which decorated her, and before the coup d'état of June 1923 that plunged the country in what was virtually a civil war in the next two decades. The irony was that she was fighting this retirement with all possible means, even filing a protest with the National Assembly.

Was Angelina Boneva an exception? Certainly not as a female teacher, and not as a socialist female teacher either. There were a number of them but mostly seen and seeing themselves as the outside urban modernizer. What raised the eyebrows of the men who witnessed her visit to the socialist bookstore in Vratsa was her appearance of a typical peasant woman. She did not stand out from her village environment. The people who celebrated her treated her not as an exception but as an inspiration, as a role model. Was she then typical? Or representative of some group, so that one can infer some common characteristics?[34] I am inclined to answer defensively that it does not matter. Why do we apply the criterion of typicality only to so-called "ordinary people," a much used and abused, and a thoroughly useless, category?[35] Why are only they subjected to the statistical eye? Do we speak about the untypicality of presidents, generals, princes? I would like to think of Angelina Boneva as an extraordinary "ordinary" person.

Baba Angelina Remembers

There are two items that belong to the so-called group of ego-documents. One is only marginally so, as it is the official school book, but written in the hand of Angelina Boneva until 1922 and occasionally interspersed with her personal comments. Throughout the book she refers to herself in the third person singular. The thirty pages of the schoolbook reaching 1954 (but 1922 in her handwriting) consist mostly of uniform entries. Here is a typical example:

> The 1900/1901 schoolyear begins with the same teacher in the same building. The school is opened on September 1 and ends on May 2. The school library was supplied with the magazine *Uchitelkski pregled* (Teacher's Review). The school has not been closed on account of disease. The school was inspected on 15 November 1900 by the inspector Mr. G. Ivanov. He recommended: 1. The school trustee Pŭrvan Dushkov should leave the room adjacent to the class room, so that the school possessions can be moved there; 2. The same trustee should not tie his horses in the basement under these two rooms because of the bad smell.[36]

Indeed, when Boneva was employed as a teacher in 1899, she had to rent a classroom in the local tavern. The village tavern had belonged to the former mayor who was also the school trustee, but who had mortgaged the tavern and was living in an adjacent room. He opposed any repairs to the decrepit building, which was constantly leaking, in anticipation of buying it back from the bank for a low price. For this reason, he was constantly agitating against her, hoping to close the village school and send the children to the neighboring village. It was only the tenacity of Boneva to maintain a school in her birthplace that saved it from closure.[37]

Most of the other entries document baba Angelina's efforts to improve the school environment. She gradually managed to furnish the room with a few desks, although children continued to bring their little chairs from home to sit. She provided a blackboard, different maps of Asia, Africa, Australia, Europe, North and South America, a separate map of Palestine, a globe, a thermometer, a magnet, an abacus, zoological illustrations, a table and chair, and a wood stove. She even managed to get a

Gravesande's ring to demonstrate thermal expansion. She got the school to subscribe to additional journals, like "Nature" and "Education."

Things were not so eventless after her first two years. There were epidemics that caused students to miss class for weeks on end, and the school itself was closed several times. There was malaria, scarlet fever, influenza, diphtheria, but the most serious and persistent was typhus, which raged every year from 1905 on and especially during the war. Typhus is caused by the bacteria *Rickettsia rickettsii* transmitted by body lice and is linked primarily to wartime, and with the accompanying lack of hygiene, no change of clothes, and overcrowding, malnutrition and stress are ubiquitous. The typhus epidemic infected tens of millions of people and killed millions on the Eastern Front, continuing to Russia where another five million died in 1919–23[38] Pripîlzhane's classroom was meant to hold at the most thirty children but it had fifty-nine in 1915–16, and in the last year of the war 1917–18 the number reached seventy. This was an inadvertently positive result of the war and Angelina Boneva was no less happy for it:

> It came about in this way. The mothers, frightened by the continuous war, scared by the ignorance, wanted their children to learn more. They could not send them to the high school in [the town of] Ferdinand, because they could not afford paying for lodging, food, heat and lighting. So they sent them to me in the same school, to repeat the 4th grade and consolidate their knowledge. Although it was difficult to survive in the narrow room, the consciousness of these women for more education made me so happy that I did not say a word and gladly accepted them all. The stench and constriction seemed easier to handle.[39]

Once the men came back from the war, however, "instead of progress in education, there was regress,"[40] as the students were pulled out of school to help their parents. There was a positive change with the coming of the agrarian government of Alexander Stamboliiski when a law was passed in 1920 to expropriate buildings for village schools. Pripîlzhane's peasants, however, turned a greedy eye on Angelina's small house that she had bought and decided to confiscate it. This was one of the rare moments of emotional crisis that she documented in the schoolbook: "I was so hurt that I lost my spirit and work energy. . . . I thought I was doing them a favor so that their children would not roam about in neighboring villages and they repay me with evil. They kill you, they crush you, they trample mercilessly on you."[41] This decision was eventually reversed and when in 1921 a labor week was introduced, it was used to dig the foundations of a new school building which was finally opened in 1922.

One could understand, if not condone, the envy with which the poor and uneducated peasants were viewing their teacher, a single woman with no family and with a steady income. Teachers were state employees, and their average salary in 1896 was around 1,500 levs. Over half of the state employees (including, besides teachers, all the bureaucracy, around 54 percent) received a salary of under 1,000 levs, 21 percent had an income between 1,000 and 2,000, 13 percent between 2,000 and 3,000, 8 percent between 3,000 and 5,000, and 4 percent (just 800 individuals) over 5,000 levs. Angelina's salary in 1897–98 and 1898–99 was 970 and 940 levs, respectively, but it was raised to 1026 levs in 1900.[42] This was less than the directive from the Ministry of Education, which for 1900 had ordered a fixed salary for teachers in the elementary schools—first degree, 1,680 levs; second degree, 1,428 levs; and third degree, 1,140 levs.[43] The remuneration in the lower ranks was modest, but it still was twice the daily wage of a qualified construction worker, and three times the daily wage of a laborer.[44]

The year 1922 was Angelina Boneva's last as a teacher. Two young teachers were appointed in this year: Mahmud Aliov and Slavka Todorova. Mahmud Aliov, as Angelina notes in the schoolbook, was of Gypsy ethnicity (*по народност циганин*), and of Muslim religion, but signed himself as M. Kovachev. Angelina Boneva was retired by the school board of trustees and she appealed to the National Assembly in Sofia but to no avail. On November 17, 1922, she received her official retirement letter from the Ministry of Education citing her advanced age and thanking her for her long years of service. She copied the texts of the letters notifying her of her retirement and added a final line in her miniscule handwriting: Мижи Асан да ти баям. This is a dialectal phrase, literally translated as "Close your eyes, (H)asan, I'll mumble an incantation" but meaning "Give me a break." A year and a half later, on March 3, 1925, when an inspector looked at the schoolbook, he put a question mark behind the phrase and added with a red pencil: "Such ironies cannot be allowed in official books!" Angelina Boneva seemed to have the last laugh. She continued to be active, both socially and politically, until her death in 1938 at the age of eighty-six.

The other source is a genuine ego-document comprising five notebooks of her unfinished memoirs. These have been preserved in a handwritten copy made by her grandnephew Petîr (Pencho) Ivanov Todorov Popov[45] (the great-grandson of her uncle Ivan, the brother of Angelina's father Bono), handed later to the State Archives of Montana. He made the copy for the family in March and April 1973, having heard from Ivan Danov that these notebooks were kept in the Museum of the September Anti-fascist Uprising under signature N.1023. We do not know what happened to the original. It may have been misplaced, lost, or even destroyed after 1989, when the exhibitions of communist-era museums dedicated to the revolutionary struggle were closed and their buildings privatized. Luckily, however, we can be certain of the authenticity of the text, since all the lengthy quotes in the abovementioned biography by the same Petîr Ivanov were from the original and correspond verbatim to the text in the copy, which was made later. Petîr Ivanov thanks the director of the museum who allowed him to take home the notebooks one by one.[46]

These are strange memoirs, apparently conceived as notes for a future unfinished autobiography, but not ensuing from a preliminary structured plan and obviously following a stream of consciousness. Only the fifth notebook gives a brief summary of her life after Angelina graduated from the Sofia school and started her career. The rest consists of recollections before she adopted her hypostasis as teacher. The text focuses almost entirely on the first year of her Sofia studies and, of the roughly sixty pages, more than half concern events during a couple of months at the end of 1879. There are repetitions of events when she continues the narrative in the next notebook, and she offers more details in some cases, as if she has remembered a certain nuance that she would like to highlight but there are no discrepancies in the account.

The first notebook opens not with Angelina's birth and childhood, but with her leaving her village, clearly the pivotal moment of her life: "I was 23 years old, when

I left my birthplace, the village of Pripîlzhane on 21 November 1874 (new style)[47] for the Bulgarian town of Pirot." Pirot (known as Şehirköy in Ottoman times), a town in the Nish province had a mixed Turkish and Slavic population. Starting as a Roman settlement, after the seventh century it had been part of the First and Second Bulgarian Empires, and its strategic location ensured that it passed through successive rules under the Bulgarians, Byzantines, and Serbs, until in 1386 it was captured by the Ottomans. Sometimes travelers describe its Slav population as Serb, but more often as Bulgarian. In fact, it has a distinct dialect, the Torlak, and some linguists even raise it to the level of an intermediary language between Serbian and Bulgarian. After 1870 the region was part of the Bulgarian Exarchate and for this reason it had several Bulgarian elementary schools, as well as two middle schools (one with four grades for boys; the other with two grades for girls). After completing first grade, Angelina was enrolled with other girls in the boys' school because of the start of the Serbian–Turkish war[48]:

> This was the first time I saw what war is like. Thunder, crash, the town was reverberating. Screams, cries, poor village women in ragged clothes, with bleeding children on their shoulders, held by the legs and with heads hanging on their back, driven by Turkish Gypsies and the bashibozuk, herds of sheep, cattle, horses and mules. Carts filled with grain, clothes and household goods. This was the booty from the villages around Pirot where the war had passed . . . the booty was taken to the gypsy neighborhood.[49]

This may all sound rhetorically like the prejudices of nationalism and anti-Roma sentiment that today's methodological anti-nationalism decries, but there is little doubt about the veracity of what Angelina wrote down. It is a typical picture of war, with atrocities on both sides, and especially well documented during the confrontations of the great Eastern Crisis of 1875–78 (the Bosnian-Herzegovinian and Bulgarian uprisings, the Serbian–Turkish and the ensuing Russo-Turkish war), by countless witnesses and foreign journalists with opposing political sympathies. Things stabilized when the regular Ottoman army entered the town, and during the war Angelina resumed her studies until March 1877 when the Serbian troops entered the town and eventually annexed it to Serbia. Angelina moved to Berkovitsa, the closest town within the future Bulgarian principality. She spent the next year studying there and finishing elementary school. Describing her studies, Angelina's tone becomes romantic and she is given to philosophizing statements: "My work was successful, corresponding to the joy that filled me. What I am saying is that extraordinary joy subtly galvanizes, encourages one's work, and makes the person exceptional."[50]

For lack of a middle-school teacher Angelina could not continue and she called on her previous teacher who promised to teach her privately if she would help in the house. The "teaching" consisted in giving Angelina the history textbook and asking her to learn the first text, which remained unexamined. The "helping" consisted in washing, sewing, mending, looking after the toddler, in a word being treated as the "lowest and simplest maid."[51] When in the fall of 1879 the teacher's family relocated to Sofia, they wanted to keep Angelina exclusively as a servant and, despite her pleas that she would do all the housework only to be allowed to attend school for five hours a day, she was kicked out. Angelina adds as a commentary: "I had no time to think clearly and tell her that I have not abandoned home and youth to be a servant."[52]

At this point begins the most detailed account covering only two months but more than half of the memoirs. Homeless, Angelina made her way to the bishop's residence, thinking that the bishop, "this mutual father of all Orthodox Christians" would recommend her to a family for a couple of nights, before she found a place to live. Her encounter with the Metropolitan Meletius[53] is rendered in dialogue:

> I stood at the side of the table and after a while the bishop came; his head, I thought, was covered with a black cover, like a hood, a servant was holding the back of his long dress. He stopped in front of me and asked me, somewhat haughtily, what I wanted. I don't know how my opinion changed that the bishop is our common father and that I could expect from him something meaningful, so I altered my response and instead of asking for shelter for a day or two, I said that I needed a baptismal record and since my brothers are peasants, they don't know how to proceed. To his question why I needed it, I briefly retorted that I am enrolling in school.
> "You, enrolling in school?"
> "Yes."
> "You should be carding, spinning and weaving, learn housework."
> "I know that."
> "To dig, reap, thresh, gather hay, make bales."
> "I know that too."
> I looked him in the face and for a moment I saw his right moustache move and a white tooth show. As I was standing by the table with a brain on fire, I clutched my fist and slammed it on the table and said to myself: "You dirty old man [пергишин]! And this is supposed to be a father!" The ornamentations on the table jumped, the globes on the lamp clanged, he stared at me: "What is this?"
> "When you laugh at me, your cabman will throw stones on me."
> "No, I am full of joy, I don't ridicule you."
> "I don't want your joy, keep it to yourself."
> And I left. He told the servants to take me back, give my name, so he could secure the baptismal certificate.... Before I left my home for Pirot, I would pray tearfully to God, with specially devised prayers by me, to be merciful and endow me with brains, intelligence and good sense, so I could find the right path. I knew by heart Slavic prayers that my mother would say when we went to bed, got up and ate, but could not take them to heart, unlike the ones that I myself adjusted and recited. Now was the moment to tearfully pour my prayers to God and ask him to curse the bishop's joy.[54]

We can follow here Damasio's three stages: a general emotion of discomfort in a dignified person who has seen and run away from humiliation but is forced to be a supplicant; the formation of a non-conscious feeling of revulsion triggered by what Angelina felt was a haughty attitude and her subconscious decision to change her plea ("I don't know how my opinion changed that the bishop is our common father"); the state of conscious feeling which was also expressed both in deed (slamming her fist on the table) and in words.

Dejected, Angelina reached the metropolitan church "Sveti Kral," where she pleaded with two nuns, "angelic beings," to give her shelter for the night. When they rejected her, she described them as "two dolls wrapped in black with oily faces and hearts of stone."[55] She ended up finally in a smaller church, where the old woman, the caretaker, kindly took her in. Instead of paying rent, she would help around but would provide her own food. Next day she enrolled in the girls' school. Several students did not have their birth certificates, so the teacher asked for their age. One was fourteen, another seventeen, a third nineteen. When Angelina's turn came, the teacher said, "You are twenty" and before she could add another seven, she was registered as a twenty-year-old.[56]

Her relationship with the bishop did not end there. He managed to trace her and called her several times, but she refused to appear before him: "If I would see his photographic image, I would throw at him whatever was at hand: ash, sand, mud."[57] This, as she herself recognized, was excessive, as he simply wanted to see her and give her some money: "I did not ask for the money, he donated it to me, just like the Turks would donate money to us when they stayed in our house."[58] Angelina knew the value of money. When her classmates commented that the bishop was stingy for giving her a mere 20 grosh, she thought: "They should ask the ones like myself who cannot see a single grosh anywhere. How many days would I have to spin wool or hemp for 3 or 4 *grosh* the *oka*?"[59] Throughout, Angelina is painfully aware of her poverty, social class, and subordinate position.

At school she worked hard: "I did not consider myself gifted but I was industrious."[60] Soon the other students were asking for her help, especially in arithmetic, and some of the relatives would occasionally pay her for that. Given that she had no income, this is how she fed herself during the first months. Close to Christmas, the students were given a homework assignment to write a letter home describing their life in the new school. Here is the text of the letter:

My dear and beloved mother,

I have not written to you since we parted. I know your misery, the misery of all poor widows. In such a humiliating situation, what should I write about myself and torment you spiritually. It's useless. Today I feel steadier than ever in what I desire and want to notify you: without a bedspread I spread out, without a cover I cover myself, without fire I heat myself, without food I feed myself, but I am under the roof of honest and good people. Please, my dear mother, do not worry about me, do not think of me, look after yourself. I am filled with joy over my success in the desired studies, which I receive in a good disciplined school from good and conscientious teachers. This joy is my food, heat and lighting. It encourages me to work, work is the very best of health, and health is life.

I greet all the family and relatives. To you, mother, I wish my joy to make you joyful, so that you too can welcome the coming Christmas holidays nourished and cheerful from my joy. Lastly, I embrace you and kiss you sweetly. I remain your dear and kind daughter,

18.XII.1879　　　　　　　　　　　　　　　　　　　　　　　　　　Angelina Boneva[61]

Angelina was mostly concerned by her handwriting and the fact that she was not handy with ink and pen, but to her dismay, the next day the teacher asked her to read her letter aloud. She flatly refused. After class, the teacher called her in and asked:

"Where did you put the notebook to write?"
"On the brick floor in the room."
"How do you heat yourself? How about lighting?"
"Heating and lighting is paid by the other students in the same room."
"Do you have any bedding, blankets?"
"Yes, I have. Peasant stuff. I spread half a rug on the floor and cover myself with the other half."
"Where do you eat and what?"
"For lunch I eat here in the classroom, while the others eat in the boarding house. I toast a slice of bread on the stove, put salt, pepper and some other herbs and drink water. The other students, when they return, reproach me that the room smells of burnt bread. In the evening I eat the same." Here I lied about my dinner. I was eating something cooked from baba Ana.[62]

This last sentence is crucial. Angelina suffered from her poverty but was not sentimental about it. Why did she lie? We can find the answer, although not explicitly stated, in what follows. Immediately after this episode, the teacher spoke to the directress to whom she showed Angelina's letter and it was decided that the latter would offer her warm lunch every day. Angelina's reaction is literally untranslatable. She often wrote (and apparently spoke) in proverbs, and thought: "С чужда пита прави помен," literally: "She is making a memorial service with someone else's bread." She then looked at the teacher and said to herself: "For a piece of bread, I am not becoming dependent." What Angelina had in mind was the internal competition between the teachers and their machinations to win students over to their side. The one who initiated the help would expect gratefulness; so too would the other one who would be giving her food: "You cannot spin and reel at the same time" (да поставя две любеници под една мишница, literally "to put two watermelons under one armpit").[63] So, she refused: "I do not want to oblige private persons; they are not the mayor's office, nor some society."[64] This decision reassured her: "I started breathing calmly. Now no one can claim anything. There is nothing more precious than freedom."[65]

The result was that the very next day the teacher asked her to write a petition to the Ministry of Education, asking for a scholarship. Angelina's initial idea when she met the bishop Meletius the second time had been to ask for a place to live, which essentially meant she was seeking official institutional help but at that point her pride did not allow her to do it given her disgust of him. The petition is very brief and to the point, stating that she is enrolled in the school but cannot rely on family help: "Therefore, I ask, if possible, to be added to the scholarship list, so that I can continue my much-desired studies. 21.XII.1897."[66]

Looking again at the text of the letter to her mother, it is crafted so carefully, unlike the rest of the recollections, that one can be sure that she copied it verbatim from her original notebook. It is a rhetorically savvy letter, and one can hear the prosody of a folk song, especially in the first paragraph, with the inverted phrases starting with "without" and the repetitions of noun and verb. Equally, in the second paragraph the constant repetition of "joy" (радост) in different contexts makes one believe that Angelina instinctively knew how to utilize different figures of speech: palillogy, epibole, epanalepsis, paregmenon. She crafted it so that she would convey a message about her plight, while at the same time praising the school. There is no doubt about the authenticity of her powerful sense of dignity, her almost morbid fear of humiliation, her intense emotions (she often cannot keep back her tears). But there is also a remarkable presence of strategic thinking by first refusing to read her letter aloud, allowing for the tension to build, then slightly exaggerating her malnourishment and, finally, subtly suggesting from which quarters she would accept aid.

Angelina was sent to hand in her petition to the minister of education personally, accompanied by the school attendant. It says much about the state (or lack) of bureaucracy in a brand-new state in the making, when a student can reach the office of a minster and be immediately admitted. She was also lucky. It so happened that at this very moment the minister of education was Bishop Kliment of Tîrnovo, who between December 6 (November 24 old style), 1879 and April 7 (March 26 old style), 1880, was also appointed prime minister of the caretaker government.[67] A highly educated and cultivated personality, he had a reputation of being kind and merciful. Angelina Boneva did receive a scholarship and a place in the girls' boarding house but did not forget to also lobby for her friend in need.

There are other instances when she demonstrated both decency and presence of mind. One of the lengthiest episodes described in the memoirs concerns baba Ana, the woman who took her in. After the happy outcome and during the Christmas holidays that followed, baba Ana had a stroke and Angelina stood firmly by her side. The relatives of the old woman gathered like vultures and were looking only for her money, but Angelina found it and hid it from them. She gave the savings to a priest and secured the hospitalization and eventual recovery of the old woman.[68] The rest of her four-year stay in the school was deemed so uneventful that the memoirs jump to 1884/1885 when she was appointed teacher in a Sofia school. She was thirty-two at the time (Figure 33). She had asked to be sent to Macedonia by the Exarchate, but this was denied with the explanation that since she was born and educated in Bulgaria, she would suffer from the *grîkomani*. This did not deter her and the following year she slipped illegally into the Ottoman Empire without a passport in order to plead her case personally with the Exarchate in Istanbul. When she was asked at the Edirne (Odrin) station to show her passport (*nüfus tezkere*), she showed her teacher's certificate.[69]

The last notebook wraps up her whole biography in three pages and reads like an official CV, from her eleven years in Macedonia of which ten were in Zagorichane, then her return to Bulgaria in 1896, the three years in Medkovets, and, finally, her twenty-three years in Pripîlzhane, where for three years she taught in the tavern and the other twenty in her own room whose mortgage she paid over the course of five years. She finishes the biography with the new school, built entirely from the labor weeks introduced by the agrarians and "perched like a white dove over the village."⁷⁰

The one detail in this lapidarian account is her description of her brief three-and-a-half-month imprisonment by the Ottoman authorities and it is the one instance where her account differs from the recollections of others. Angelina credits her release exclusively to her "tactful and skillful answers" which succeeded in exposing the machinations of her accusers, but she paid a dear price as her face was covered with pimples and deep furrows.⁷¹ She also adds that she was freed against a substantial bail.⁷² This did not mean that Angelina was ungrateful for the efforts of her fellow Bulgarians to free her, but she scrupulously avoids the mention of her marriage, which was apparently decisive in getting her out of prison. While different versions of her marriage (but not controversial ones) are mentioned, the circumstance, let alone the experience, is completely silenced in her own recollections.

Figure 33 Angelina Boneva at 32.

Who Was Angelina Boneva?

With this sole exception, there is fundamental factual agreement between the recollections *about* and *of* Angelina Boneva. And yet, there are significant differences between the style, tone, and emphasis in the description of her public and private persona. The public one has three vectors—teacher, patriot, and socialist. Without denying these, the private one deals only with the first, but is elaborated mostly in the official schoolbook which was expected to be read by the inspectors. The second is mentioned only implicitly, and the third not at all, yet there is no doubt about her political engagements. Why is that? Was she writing strictly for herself? Or did she intend the notebooks for outside eyes?

The format of the notebooks, the arrangement and repetitions of events give the impression that she was jotting down recollections that perhaps might in the future become a coherent autobiography. Yet, in the last notebook there is a very intimate episode that does not tie at all within the rest of her narrative and does not bear on anything about her public self, except to highlight her insecurities. It starts abruptly: "My biggest, intolerable and terrible fear I suffered in Pirot. The reason for the frostbite was my naïve stupidity, and intolerable and terrible fear was foisted on me."[73] What follows is the story of how she almost froze to death. One day a young relative of the family with whom she was staying invited them to an evening party. When she was presented to him, he shook hands and invited her too: "Until this moment I had never experienced something like this. That a man would hold the hand of a man or a woman. I trembled with fear and thought only of how to free my hand. I could not but think that this man was bad." She ran away and confessed to her teacher, who assured her that this was the convention and was called a handshake: "My comedy was over." But still, she decided not to go: "No. I will not go. I did not go to the party, because it was not my place. By my clothing I could not be among the girls, it was not my place to be among the women, and to sit among the grandmothers would be a humiliation." She ended up spending the frosty night in a church and came back with what appears to be a third-degree frostbite. She was twenty-three years old.[74]

This episode sounds like an afterthought that she compulsively jotted down, although it has little place in the eventual narrative. One could let one's imagination loose and hypothesize about what is being silenced. Had Angelina been sexually assaulted as a child? Did this prompt her to run away from home the moment her brothers decided to marry her off? Is that why she never de facto married? There is no interest in the opposite sex in her recollections and for that matter, none toward her own. Yet she was vehement about her incipient feminism. Can we also read some incipient hostility to heterosexuality? Did she sublimate her libido in the service of learning? Did she have a libido at all? Luckily, good historians do not let their imagination go wild without any evidence. In any case, this is hardly an episode that is meant for an outside gaze. On the other hand, all of these thoughts or at least the first about her motivation, seem to have crossed her mind. Directly after the frostbite story, there follows abruptly the following:

> Everyone who would read what I have put down here will probably think that starting my studies so late in life was fortuitous. In my childhood, but also when I was already

grown-up, there has never been talk among my simple folks about some brilliant man or woman who would inspire me. Nothing of the kind influenced me. But I could not stand the harsh treatment from my elder brothers and sisters. Especially when someone among them would push me from my little stool close to the fire and they started to tell wonderful stories. I loved these stories and would freeze in the back only to listen to them. The dominance of the others was unbearable and even as I was playing with my toys, a ray of independence was lurking in. But I still could not work and was hopeless. One day, on the eve of Good Friday, my mother took me to church in Sumer, so we could say we broke our fast with red eggs on Maundy Thursday. We arrived at my uncle Ivan's house, where we found the whole family in front of the iconostasis and he was reading from a book and tears were running from his eyes. I looked at the people and began thinking. Why did uncle Ivan cry? What was the sad story written in this book? He sees it and understands it. How I would like to learn to read and understand what this sad thing is. But the Lord has maybe decided that only men can study and learn how to read. Would the Lord also allow women to read? This thought started to work in my head and wherever I was, with whatever toy, it would pierce me. The injustice of God toward women. No, I must try, even though it might be against his will. I would do that when I grow up and learn all the work a woman should do at home and in the field. Until I turned 18 I did everything that was expected from a peasant maiden. But the thought of learning how to read did not leave me. Not that I was expecting to use it (I never thought I would become a teacher) but I wanted to fulfil my spiritual behest, to learn what God has allowed only to men. Only then would I feel independent. It was precisely then, when I was wondering how to achieve my yearning, that rumors started among the peasants that in the neighboring towns of Vratsa and Berkovitsa little girls went to school, learned how to read, write and count. Their teachers were young women.[75]

This wording may suggest that it may have been meant for an audience. Throughout her narrative, one hears (and mostly feels) the fear of humiliation, her vehement reaction to preserve her dignity. But the Pirot episode as well as a few other instances (like the clash with the bishop or the teachers) sounds almost like a (couch-less) self-psychoanalysis or that her notebooks served as a psychotherapeutic confessional. Another evidence that the notebooks were mostly intended for herself is the use of the dialectal "Ya" instead of "Az" for "I." In a polished version, but also one that would have been written in a self-controlled hypostasis as a teacher, this would have been unacceptable. That the notebooks were written to explore her inner self also accounts for the glaring absence of any mention of her socialist activism. It was something that was part of her public persona, a logical outcome of her striving to emancipate herself as a subaltern and specifically as a woman. Social democracy was the one group that propounded solidarity for the poor but also equality for women, the teaching profession the one that offered some independence for women and socialism was popular among teachers. Angelina would not have second thoughts about this. That she gravitated to socialism was so natural that she did not have to explain that to herself.

Another way to think about all this is to employ Paul Ricoeur's notion of idem- and ipse-identity, developed in his late work *Oneself as Another*, where he addressed the aporia of how ones remain the same throughout all the physical and psychological changes of one's life.[76] These, according to Ricoeur, are aspects of one's personal identity (or of one's self), and they are in a symbiotic and dialectical relationship. Idem-identity (sameness, *mêmeté*) expresses what remains the same in a person (one's name, one's physique despite changes over time, genetics, character, etc.). And importantly, the self can identify the self as self. Both numerical identity, being one and not many, as well as a qualitative identity, being substitutable, are part of sameness. Ricoeur relates them to the "problem of identification: uniqueness versus plurality; resemblance versus difference; continuity versus discontinuity; permanence versus diversity."[77] Idem-identity answers the question "What am I?"

Ipse-identity (selfhood, *ipseité*), on the other hand, is sameness but through change: one *is* and one *is not* what one was a couple of decades ago. It denotes the transformations that one can do on oneself and is strongly linked to memory and imagination, which allows to exert these changes. Through memory and reconstructing one's past one comprehends oneself. It is a reflexive category: "Selfhood denotes the identity which belongs to oneself and not to the other individual. However, this another can be oneself. Therefore, the ipse-identity designates the identity which belongs to oneself as another. Oneself as another is, in fact, a mode of being oneself."[78] The ipse-identity answers the question "Who am I?"

Selfhood cannot be reduced to sameness and *who* one is can never be totally predicted from *what* one is, that is, from one's character or one's habitus:

> Character belongs to idem identity. The awareness that we can take up a stand towards our character, preserving it, strengthening it, and revising it reveals the connection to ipse identity. But these attitudes towards our character are themselves implicated in our character so the dialectical relation between idem-identity and ipse-identity is particularly apparent here. Character is ipse becoming idem, but idem-identity is only recognized as possessing certain traits appearing in certain ways, reflecting certain values, that is, as a product of our character.[79]

It is at this point that Ricoeur introduces the concept of narrative identity as the mediator in the confrontation between these two expressions of identity. It occurs "in the manner of a specific mediator between the pole of character, where idem and ipse tend to coincide, and the pole of self-maintenance, where selfhood frees itself from sameness."[80]

What Angelina Boneva was is not only what she projected with her physical presence, character, and actions and how what she projected was reflected in the eyes of others, but also how she recognized herself as an individual, teacher, patriot, and socialist. But *who* she was emerges from how she shaped the story of herself in her notebooks. Behind the self-assured teacher lurks a traumatized child. It is not merely that she put down information that she had not shared but, remembering different episodes, she created a narrative identity that further helped her to better understand herself. The human need of making oneself intelligible to oneself ultimately equals composing one's own life: "Self-understanding is an interpretation; interpretation of the self, in turn, finds in the narrative, among other signs and symbols, a privileged form of mediation."[81]

7

Love and Internationalism

The Diary of Todor Tsekov

The same year 1911, when Angelina Boneva was buying socialist literature from the socialist bookstore in Vratsa, a Bulgarian socialist newspaper, *Rabotnicheska Prosveta* (Workers' Enlightenment/Education), "devoted to the education of Bulgarian and Macedonian workingmen in America," came out in Granite City, Illinois.[1] This was the organ of the Bulgarian Socialist Labor Federation (BSLF), founded on March 26, 1910, at its First Congress in Madison, Illinois, when it unified seven groups and had a membership of about one hundred persons. By 1918 there were already sixteen local chapters and the membership had quadrupled. There had been a few scattered Bulgarian socialist groups around 1907, and there were two short-lived papers, both in Chicago, *Pabotnicheski Novini* (Workers' News) in 1908 and *Rabotnicheska Zashtita* (Workers' Defense) in 1909, but *Rabotnicheska Prosveta* survived and continued until 1969.[2]

After a few years of discussions on which of the existing American socialist organizations to join, at their Third Congress in Toledo, Ohio, in 1916, the Bulgarian socialists adhered formally to the Socialist Labor Party of America (SLP) under the leadership of Daniel De Leon.[3] They thus began what James Barrett has called their "Americanization from the bottom-up."[4] While the BSLF was the largest and most influential, it was not the only socialist group among Bulgarians. A smaller group was active with the Wobblies (the International Workers of the World, IWW) and a Bulgarian, Georgi Andreichin, was prominent in its leadership.[5]

Bulgarians were latecomers to the New World. They may have been "probably the last of all European nations to send immigrants to America."[6] The first wave began after the turn of the century and reached its height between 1907 and 1910. Bulgarians at the beginning emigrated mostly because of economic reasons. The country, with an overwhelmingly rural population, was experiencing the first phase of its demographic transition, with a serious population explosion, land shortage, and high unemployment. In addition, the young state, attempting to swiftly modernize and, especially, militarize, was heavily taxing the peasantry in the absence of an industry and a sizable wealthy class. In this period, there was practically no political emigration from the Bulgarian Principality (Kingdom after 1908) proper, but after 1903 and the Ilinden Uprising, there was a steady emigration of Bulgarian refugees from Macedonia, still in the Ottoman Empire, and US immigration records showed a doubling of Bulgarian immigrants.[7]

What made Bulgarians unique among other émigré groups was the phenomenon of return migration: an overwhelming majority would return to the old country. Thus between 1910 and 1929 the number of emigrants from the United States (36,671) exceeded the number of immigrants into the United States (35, 786).[8]

Employed mostly in industry—steel mills, foundries, mines, railroad tracks— Bulgarians converged in Illinois, where the tri-city area of Granite City, Madison, and Venice was known as the capital of Bulgarian immigration. The 8,000 to 10,000 Bulgarians in the area in 1905 comprised almost a third of the overall number of Bulgarian immigrants. Another third was in Michigan, mostly Detroit.[9] The influx of Bulgarians coincided with the economic and financial crisis that hit the United States in October 1907, the so-called Knickerbocker Crisis when the New York Stock Exchange crashed and fell 50 percent, starting a chain of bankruptcies and prolonged recession. By the spring of 1908 all industrial activities in Granite City (furnaces and foundries) were halted and 6,000 Bulgarian laborers were laid off. The neighborhood, where Bulgarians lived, Hungary Hollow, became known as Hungry Hollow.[10] It was during these years that the first Bulgarian Orthodox Church, "Saint Cyril and Methodius" in North America was built in Granite City in 1909.[11] By 1910 the economy began recovering, and Granite City alone had a Bulgarian population of close to 10,000, employing almost 8,000 in its twelve factories. Madison, next door, had 5,000 and employed 3,500 men, and Venice was not much behind.[12]

Still, the living and working conditions were miserable, wages comparatively low, and there was a high rate of accidents with little compensation.[13] In 1907, the Federal Immigration Commission revealed that 90 percent of the Bulgarians received less than $300 a year, whereas the average annual earning for immigrants was $455 (and family income $704).[14] "This is one reason why so many Bulgarians formed and joined radical social political movements," concludes Kimball, quite contrary to Altankov's dismissive assertion that "by and large, however, the socialists and radicals were a small minority and had a low reputation among the Bulgarian emigration."[15] In fact, *Rabotnicheska Prosveta* cooperated with *Naroden Glas* (The National Herald), arguably the most successful and popular newspaper of the emigration. *Naroden Glas* had been founded in 1907 in Granite City as an independent paper "devoted to politics, literature and economy."[16] It was mostly mainstream, publishing educational pamphlets, recommending temperance, and extolling the benefits of religion, but it also had a strong social ethic which made it the preferred partner of *Rabotnicheska Prosveta*. The two newspapers controlled the largest Bulgarian bookstores in the United States.[17]

According to Altankov, "the person who was most instrumental in the creation of the socialist groups in this country, Mr. Todor Tsekov" was also a member of the BWSDP (n), the future BCP.[18] Tsekov became secretary of the BSLF and one of the three members of its CC alongside Minko Markov and S. S. Saraliev. He also was the first editor-in-chief of *Rabotnicheska Prosveta*, but after his return to Bulgaria in 1911, Saraliev took up the editorship, and Todor Baev was elected secretary of the organization.[19] Tsekov is mentioned once more in Altankov's work. He had emigrated again to the United States in 1924 and was elected secretary of the Bulgarian communists, which formed a Bulgarian Bureau at the National Committee of the Communist Party of the United States (CPUSA). The CPUSA itself consisted of the

Figure 34 Poster "The Bulgarian–Macedonian Worker Wakes Up." It shows the worker bound in the constricting ropes of "patriotism," "prejudices," "bourgeois ideology," "different societies" and "deception" waking up and looking at the rising sun of socialism under the banner of the first issue of *Rabotnicheska Prosveta*. "Patriotism" stands for chauvinism, "prejudices" for religion.

expelled left wing of the SLP which, after the acrimonious split into several communist sections, was unified under the leadership of John Reed and Charles Ruthenberg. The main issue had been the difference in attitude toward the Bolshevik Revolution. The same problem also hounded the BSLF whose members were split between the so-called "eselpists" (SLP-ists) and "communists." In 1927, Tsekov, "the acknowledged leader of all communist groups" was accused of opportunism and treachery and expelled from the party.[20]

Given his prominence, one would have expected that Todor Tsekov would also figure prominently in other publications, but this is not the case. In 1935, when the BSLF was celebrating its twenty-fifth anniversary, its leadership was mostly represented by "eselpists" exposing the ideology of De Leon and the SLP. It was at odds with the line pursued by the Bulgarian Communist Party and the Comintern, mostly over the notion of the "dictatorship of the proletariat," and the future governance of society after the socialist revolution which they saw in industrial unionism. It also opposed any class cooperation and was against the new line of a "united front" proclaimed by the Comintern in 1935.²¹ For this reason, in its anniversary edition, Tsekov's role was downplayed; he was left either unmentioned or characterized as a "notorious Don Quichotte," although the real wrath was poured on Georgi Andreichin and the IWW.²²

Equally striking is Tsekov's almost complete absence from the earlier copious writings of Georgi Pirinski who lived in the United States from 1923 until 1951 when he was deported to Bulgaria.²³ True, he was of a younger generation, but he was already prominent in the communist circles at the time of Tsekov's dismissal, which he referred to fleetingly as being the result of lack of harmonious work.²⁴ Tsekov fares better in Pirinski's latest book "Summoned by Memory" where he provides portraits of sixteen American communists and/or peace activists and of nine Bulgarians active in the United States: William Foster, Robert Minor, Elizabeth Gurley Flynn, Eugene Dennis, Gus Hall, Henry Winston, Angela Davis, Rockwell Kent, Paul Robeson, and others among the Americans; Todor Tsekov, Minko Markov, Petîr Grigorov, Georgi Andreichin, and others among the Bulgarians. This is a hagiographic collection of portraits and the nine pages dedicated to Tsekov are no exception. They give the essentials of Tsekov's biography but also add a few personal elements. Pirinski had seen Tsekov once delivering a speech in Kiustendil as a communist MP before he had moved to the United States but met him in person only in 1924 at the First Conference of Bulgarian communist groups when Tsekov was sent to unify the emigration.²⁵ There is no mention of the disagreements in 1927; on the contrary, these are completely glossed over and we get a generic image of "a person with a big heart who was sincerely happy that young comrades would follow in his steps."²⁶ They met once more in Sofia in the late 1950s or early 1960s, when Pirinski visited Tsekov after the latter had read one of his reviews of and invited him to his home. They reminisced and Tsekov showed him his diary, replete with photographs: "He was constantly leafing through his diary, which had become his constant companion."²⁷ It is obvious that Pirinski had used it to write his chapter on the "Tireless disseminator of communist ideas."²⁸ Tsekov does get an entry in the Bulgarian Encyclopedia, whose last volume with his biography was published in 1997. It is a typical biography of a regular revolutionary, with a few silences and no mention of the internal factionalism of the leftist movements. Especially strange is the succinct summary of the last thirty years of his life with no party honors (medals, anniversaries, etc.) and only his early work. It is all the more surprising since the abovementioned Georgi Andreichin has received due attention lately, with a special monograph devoted to his colorful (and eventually tragic) life.²⁹

> Tsekov (Todor) (15 November 1882, village of Tavlichevo, Sofia district–1962, Sofia)–party worker, teacher, lawyer. Member of BWSDP (n) from 1904. From June 1907 in the USA where he finished law. Organized Bulgarian social-democratic groups who united in 1910 in Madison (1910); edited the organ *Rabotnicheska prosveta*. Had contacts with BWSDP (n) and contributed to *Rabotnicheski vetsnik* (1897–1939, with interruptions). In 1911 returned to Bulgaria. Director of middle school in the village of Korten, Burgas district. Active in the Teachers' Social-Democratic Organization. Delegate to the XXI Congress of BWSDP (n) in 1915.

Participated in the wars (1912–18) as platoon and company commander; several times rewarded with medals for courage. Lawyer in Kiustendil. Member of the High Party Council (1919–23), of the Regional (1919–21) and Local (1922–23) Council of BCP; also secretary at times. Municipal councilor in the Second Kiustendil commune (1920–921); Member of Parliament in the XVIII (1919–20) and XIX (1920–23) National Assemblies. Arrested on the eve of the September Uprising of 1923. In 1924 re-emigrated to the US. Organized émigrés from the Balkan countries. Secretary of the Bulgarian Bureau and the Balkan Committee of the American Labor Party. In the fall of 1932 returned to Bulgaria; lawyer in Sofia. Supported the antifascist struggle. After 9 September 1944 member of the High Lawyers Council and member-judge of the Supreme Court of the People's Republic of Bulgaria. Author of pamphlets: "The Political assassinations and the bourgeois parties in Bulgaria" (1922) and others.[30]

Writing One's Life

I first came to the name Todor Tsekov not through the above narrative, which I reconstructed only much later. Working my way through the over four-thousand materials classified as "memoir documents" in the Central State Archives in Sofia, I found that most conspicuous were four large bound handwritten volumes comprising more than 1,100 pages.[31] They were classified as "memoirs-diary" and covered the life of Todor Tsekov from his birth until 1932. The volumes are furnished with an explanatory note stating that Tsekov's diary, in fact, consisted of ten separate volumes. Apparently, a scholarly collaborator of the party institute was aware of the diary and Tsekov himself had promised that after his death he would give the volumes to the archives of the institute. However, when he passed away in 1969, his wife and family refused to hand them over. After numerous negotiations, in which they declined any monetary compensation, they agreed to give only the first four volumes to be photocopied and then returned. The note adds that in several instances there were whole pages torn away, either by Tsekov himself or by his relatives.[32] These must have been a substantial number, because the 1,102 pages preserved in the archive follow the archival pagination, which regularly falls short of the original pagination of the diary. Thus, the archive owns xerox copies of not uniformly good quality and the often questionable legibility of what was an ink-pen-written manuscript. It is one of the most valuable documents because it belongs to the class of "naturally occurring" personal documents, different from the multitude of materials provoked by researchers' intervention, such as written life stories, oral histories, and interviews.[33]

The lack of information on Todor Tsekov seems to come from his reticence and attempts to not stand out in the public eye after the 1930s. Indeed, my suspicion is that the entry in the encyclopedia had been compiled by someone in the institute (the above collaborator) who had taken the basic facts from the diary.[34] Tsekov, however, was far from reticent on the page. Indeed, excluding novelists and a few politicians, I have never encountered such graphomania in anyone.[35] I am using the term with tongue in cheek, completely devoid of its medical connotations or derogative use. In fact, the "memoirs-diary" had a specific function and followed specific methods. Let us begin by turning to its genre. It opens with an introduction under the title "Reminiscences": "Today, the 21st of June 1912, I sit down to write about all the most important events in my life, from my birth to the day when I entered life as a free individual, i.e. on 12 September 1904, when I joined the teaching profession. From this date on, I have regularly kept a diary of everything in my life."[36]

Aware that retrospective memory can be tricky, he decided to write only about matters for which he had documentation and about which he was absolutely certain. He had in front of him packages of letters and documents, as well as his exhaustive diary (1900–04), from which he would provide extensive excerpts.[37] We see here a historian at work, someone for whom the reconstruction of the past, even one's own past, had to be verifiable. That poses the question of the purported audience. For whom did he write?

> This task will be pleasant because I will relive again what I experienced in my childhood and adolescence, and in the distant future I will enjoy opening this notebook and contemplating all my past life. . . . Then I will see that I have lived, have seen a lot and will understand my present character and temperament, because I will have in front of me all the circumstances in which I have acted and in which I have lived. Indeed, my life is like a storm. I was like a hurricane who wanted to destroy everything in its way. I have not lived a lot, but I have seen a lot, and have gone through all the stages of our dynamic political-economic life, in which I participated actively. . . . Everywhere I was spirited and was at the center of all movements, and my soul keeps on seething with desire for passion, turbulent life and great deeds. . . . Obstacles do not stop me, I walk boldly forward, with an unflinching faith in attaining my class proletarian ideal—socialism, which has become the flesh and blood of my body. But in order to understand how I became a social-democrat and why today I am a fervent fighter for this great ideal, one should look closely into my life and comprehend the objective circumstances which were reflected in my soul. I passed through a number of fierce struggles and savored patriotism and anarchism until I reached the right teaching and a real understanding of life. Finally, these notes and daily entries in the diaries will serve as a good lesson to my children, so that they would know who I was, how I acted, and why I end like this. . . . These diaries are the mirror and real reflection of my life. In them I have poured my sorrows, joys, tears and happy effusions. . . . Let me now begin from the beginning.[38]

Todor Tsekov began this meditative retrospective as if he was at the closure of his life. He had not turned thirty yet. That this was written in 1912 and not rewritten or edited decades later can be proven by the orthography: the ubiquitous use of the letters "ѣ" and "ѫ" which were removed only after the orthographic reform of 1945.[39] This is the case with the first three volumes. The first volume deals with his youth until 1904 (pages 1–206), the second covers the period of his career as a teacher, 1904–06 (pages 207–753), while the third is devoted entirely to 1906–07, when he was mostly preoccupied with his personal life (pages 561–753). Even if we allow for the unlikely occasion that the text may have been copied and edited once, this would have occurred before the Second World War, because of the abovementioned orthography.

The exception is the fourth volume (pages 754–1102), which is written already in the reformed orthography and details Tsekov's two periods of stay in the United States (1907–11 and 1924–32). He specifies that five bound volumes containing his diaries from the war period as well as the American ones had been given for preservation to his sister-in-law but perished during the American bombardments on Sofia on March 30, 1944, so he was supplying the facts of his life from memory, as well as from correspondence and notes. In fact, the account provides mostly the emigration story, and only the last 100 pages fill in the interim period of the war. These were added in 1950, as the volume ends with the following: "This was written on 30 August 1950 in the village of Bankia, during our vacation. These days I relived the entire World War One and my whole life from 9 September 1915 to 1 November 1918. [signed] T. Tsekov."[40]

These over a thousand pages have not been arranged so as to form the coherent narrative of an autobiography, although at times they approach its tone. Given the inclusion of lengthy excerpts from the diaries and whole letters, the whole exercise looks more like a montage of sources, an aide-mémoire. There are repetitions, and sometimes the narrative jumps back a few years to add some omitted event or state of mind. It might be useful here to distinguish between memoirs, autobiographies, and diaries as ego-documents, the best vehicle for immediate self-expression. As the sociologist Alain Girard remarks, "among all written texts, it is those in the first person that tell us most about the image of the self."[41] And Peter Heehs rightly insists that it is the image of the self and not the thing in itself; it is an image projected by the writer with future readers in mind. These future readers can be others, but they can also be confined to only the writer. First-person writings, according to many, are tools for self-construction or self-creation.[42] For Jerome Bruner, "autobiography is life construction through 'text' construction."[43] And we are reminded by Craig Calhoun that "self-knowledge—always a construction no matter how much it feels like a discovery—is never altogether separable from claims to be known in specific ways by others."[44]

Memoirs have been defined as retrospective narratives about a portion of the writer's life, autobiographies as long memoirs covering most of one's past at the time of writing, and diaries as documents for recording experiences, thoughts, and feelings shortly after they happen. Diaries differ from memoirs in that they are not retrospective and lack an explicit plot, and both differ from autobiographies with their beginning-middle-end structure.[45] The person who classified Tsekov's material as a hybrid, "memoirs-diary," was right on target. Personhood, according to James Rachels and William Redick, is characterized by a distinctly autobiographical consciousness, a set of "self-referring attitudes [that] presuppose a sense of oneself as having an existence spread over past and future time."[46] At times, Tsekov's "memoirs-diary" approach the confessional genre. Most often, though, they remind one of the ancient *hypomnemata* that Foucault saw as a means of establishing a relationship of oneself with oneself, and the writing an act of constituting one's own identity through the recollection of things said:

> They constituted a material record of things read, heard, or thought, thus offering them up as a kind of accumulated treasure for subsequent rereading

and meditation. They also formed a raw material for the drafting of more systematic treatises, in which one presented arguments and means for struggling against some weakness (such as anger, envy, gossip, flattery) or for overcoming some difficult circumstance (a grief, an exile, ruin, disgrace). . . . They constitute a material and a framework for exercises to be carried out frequently: reading, rereading, meditating, conversing with oneself and with others.[47]

Theoretically, Tsekov's notes could have become material for a future autobiography. Autobiography as a field of study has expanded enormously after the 1950s, and not only have its definitions been rethought, but a number of new terms have also appeared: autographies, autre-biographies, nouvelle autobiography, autofiction, faction, égo littérature, and circonfession.[48] Part of its appeal has been explained by its democratic potential and the possibility to enfranchise everyone ready to tell their tale.[49] Writing about autobiography, Leigh Gilmore has suggested that as a genre, it is "characterized less by a set of formal elements than by a rhetorical setting in which a person places herself or himself within testimonial contexts as seemingly diverse as the Christian confession, the scandalous memoirs of the rogue, and the coming-out story in order to achieve as proximate a relation as possible to what constitutes truth in that discourse."[50] Indeed, as already said, there are moments when Tsekov's diary entries approach a confession in tone. But the differences are much more substantial.

Most importantly, what is missing from a diary is the systematic retrospectiveness of the autobiography, which points to a radical distinction. The autobiography is "a review of a life from a particular moment in time, while the diary, however reflective it may be, moves through a series of moments in time."[51] Diary material can be used in an autobiography to give it authenticity, but "autobiographers proceed much more royally with their journals than biographers would dare" and interpret and reinterpret the meaning and significance of the earlier discourse, often altering the direct impression.[52] Authenticity is "far from being the same thing as factual exactitude."[53] There is also a difference in tone: "We expect from the diary all the uncertainties, false starts, momentariness that we find in them. From the autobiography, however, we expect a coherent shaping of the past; and if diary entries or letters are quoted, we need the explanatory, interpretive commentary of the author."[54] No wonder Goethe refused to include letters in his autobiography, because "incoherent *realia* strewn about must necessarily disturb the good effect."[55] It has also been noted that autobiography, even when preserving the truth, suffers from a specific limitation, namely that its author, even when displaying undesirable traits, in the end has to present her/himself in an acceptable and agreeable light.[56]

My impression is that Tsekov never intended to write an autobiography, let alone one for publication. True, the first part—the memoirs of his youth—before he started the regular diary in 1912, is reminiscent of an autobiographical coming of age, but it is too full of the "incoherent *realia*" that Goethe was scrupulously avoiding. In his old age Tsekov did not keep the "memoirs-diary" secret and shared it with his visitors, whenever they would reminisce about some event. Mostly, though, he would spend long hours with it, remembering his past. If there were new interpretations that would come with looking back at different moments, inflected by new experiences or with the wisdom of age, they were not put down. The material was not tampered with but left intact as it was at the moment of writing. This is definitely the case, at least with the first three volumes (and for the most part also the fourth) that we have at our disposal. Tsekov wrote his memoirs-diary with the purpose of self-knowledge and self-construction. He was building what Manuel Castells identified as project identity, "when social actors, on the basis of whatever cultural materials are available to them, build a new identity that redefines their position in society and, by so doing, seek the transformation of overall social structure."⁵⁷

After his pensive introduction, Tsekov provides brief details about his family origins, going back to the late-eighteenth century. His forefathers came from a village priest's family, and they were fairly well-off farmers. Even with that, his grandfather had to supplement the income with *kiradzhiistvo* (driving carts with wheat and other wares to the big centers of the region: Thessaloniki, Bitolia, and Seres). On his mother's side, he came from the richest family in the village. The secret of this wealth was that his poor great-grandfather had found a buried treasure in a place indicated to him by a former bandit. Treasure-hunting was then the lottery of the day (and continues even today in this land of antiquities). This was not impossible, given that the Ottoman Empire, especially in its Balkan provinces, had experienced an unprecedented social disruption in the previous decades, but it mostly tells us about the family mythology. The son (Todor Tsekov's grandfather) inherited this wealth and added to it through trade, agriculture, and keeping the local tavern (which usually indicates the premier position in a village). Tsekov gives these details, not so much to point out the family's social origins but to explain that because of his wealth, his grandfather was well known throughout the region and was elected deputy to the first inaugural Constitutional Assembly of newly independent Bulgaria in 1879 (one of 231 members) and the "whole family was among the more intelligent in the village."⁵⁸

The story then jumps to Tsekov's middle and high school years, during the 1890s. He gives information about his teachers; his favorite subjects, arithmetic and geometry; the school celebrations; the street fights with stones and slings; and the fact that already at the time he had proved his strong-willed nature [буйна натура] and leadership role.⁵⁹ Most of all, Tsekov remembers his friendships and provides detailed portraits of some of his schoolmates or friends outside of school. Two interspersed themes dominate his narrative and hundreds of pages are devoted to them: his ideological evolution and his love life.

From Macedonian Nationalist to Socialist Internationalist

Ivan Iliev had been hired by Todor's father to work as a servant in the *han* (the hostel next to the tavern). In 1897 he started living in the house of the Tsekovs and exerted the first strong influence on young Todor. Iliev is described as intelligent, agile, courageous, a fiery patriot of the Macedonian cause, and an atheist [безбожник]. He never stepped into the church, was a constant scoffer, and tore all the icons in the house. "The first thing that he achieved was that I left my religiosity and became an atheist."⁶⁰ Iliev was in contact with some of the most pronounced *komitadhi*, leaders of the Bulgarian guerilla bands operating in Macedonia who often would stay in their house, and Todor could converse with them. These were mostly the men around Boris Sarafov and the Supreme Macedonian Committee, which operated from Bulgaria with the support of the crown and the army and was the rival organization of the IMRO. Young educated men, ready to give their life for the liberation of Macedonia, would pass through their house and would leave to fight the Ottoman forces and the Greek bands.

> All this acted upon my soul and reorganized all my outlook on life. From the meditative figure that I was, which found delight solely in nature's beauties and the sensationalist stories in books, I abruptly turned into a serious young man who was seeking his life goal. I started thinking how I could aid my fatherland and my people. Have I been created only to read and lie around or to act for the improvement of humanity? Of course, one should act, but how? This was the big question whose answer I was seeking. . . . In no time I became a fiery Macedonian patriot.[61]

Todor Tsekov was a teenager at the time and spent three years in thrall of the Macedonian idea, so much so that "I nearly would have perished as a *komitacdzhi* in Macedonia and now I could have filled a ravine in the Macedonian mountains, just like Ivan Iliev."[62] At first he moved among the friends of Iliev who had founded an anarchist circle. Its members would gather secretly around midnight, present reports, speak quietly, and discuss society: "I heard 'bourgeois,' 'tyranny,' 'death to the bourgeoisie,' but could not understand anything." They were all sworn to secrecy. Todor's presence

Figure 35 Todor Tsekov (in the middle) with his friends Kosta Nikolaev (left) and Georgi Goranov (right), 1900 (ЦДА, С-2060 Б, 24/об).

was vouched for by Iliev but after three or four meetings the circle either dispersed or sidetracked the young man: "I don't know.... The important thing was that I had entered an organization and learned order, discipline and confidentiality."[63] The next few months he was in the clutch of less disciplined friends of Iliev, who made him steal from his father's wine and made him drink. Ten years later, when Tsekov started his memoirs-diary and was armed with a new Marxist vocabulary, he added at the end of this episode: "I am glad that soon I corrected myself and life pushed me in another direction—toward patriotism and love—and through them I could preserve myself ideologically and morally and not sink to the level of the *lumpen*."[64]

The year 1900 was one of deep transformations for Todor: "I was filled with great ideas; my soul had found a meaning in life . . . and I directed my energy toward a conscious struggle to serve the greatest ideal of liberty. . . . I saw the slaves stretching their arms for liberty and I was the one who could help them. The great ideal of Macedonian liberation conquered my head and heart."[65] He was already in the pedagogical high school in Kiustendil and entered the secret youth society "Liberation" (Освобождение), one of a number of such societies under the auspices of the Supreme Committee. The society had all the trappings of a masonic lodge, with a solemn oath taken over a dagger and a revolver, a detailed statute, and a strict criminal code. Todor took on the pseudonym of "Gladstone," the society's chairman's alias was "Byron."[66] The best students, "the cream of the school," entered the society and within a year it

Figure 36 The Board of Trustees of the "Liberation" Society–February 25, 1901. Todor Tsekov is standing to the right.

had seventy-seven members.[67] He was one of the most active members of the circle and was elected as its secretary and librarian. The same year he initiated and organized on the side a secret circle in the girls' school, but "never had any ulterior motive to think about love."[68] He was also authorized by both the Supreme Committee and the IMRO to organize groups in the villages and to collect money and other support for the Macedonian cause.[69]

Yet, the activities of the circle were confined to recruitment and there were constant quarrels among the members. In some ways this youthful society was a mirror image of the constant bickering, recriminations, and assassinations that characterized the different Macedonian organizations. In a long excerpt from his school diary from February 16, 1902, which he had written in a secret code and transcribed verbatim in his memoirs, Tsekov describes how he and his friend Iordan Levkov were expelled from the organization. Todor had long been critical of the fact that the group was not engaging in meaningful activities and had shared his desire for reform with his friends. On the fateful night, Levkov and Tsekov were charged with not being sincere adherents of the Supreme Committee and secretly helping IMRO. The specific accusation against Todor Tsekov was that he was arrogant and kept sneering sarcastically during the sessions [че съм стоял нахално в време на събранията, като съм се с хумор смеял].[70] Levkov was blamed for wanting to push the society in a socialist direction.

Todor's close friendship with Levkov, but especially with their other friend Dimitŭr Lazov, who was already a social democrat, strengthened his interest in socialist ideas: "I was already inclined toward socialism, but could not yet get rid of the *komitadhii* cause and the stupid patriotism."[71] He adds: "this was a stage of my development through which I had to pass, in order to reach my new vocation, no longer as a patriot and Macedonian revolutionary, but as a social-democrat and internationalist proletarian revolutionary."[72] During the next two years, Todor immersed himself fervently in self-education. He dropped the novels which until then he had absorbed with passion hoping to emulate its protagonists: Alexandre Dumas' *The Three Musketeers* and *The Count of Monte Cristo*, Eugène Sue's *The Wandering Jew* and *The Mysteries of Paris*, and the sentimental love stories of Émile Richebourg. Now he was reading books on Darwin's evolutionary theory, on scientific materialism through Ludwig Büchner's *Force and Matter*, and on socialism with Nikolai Chernyshevsky's *What is to Be Done* and the works of the Serbian socialist Vasa Pelagić.[73]

Dimitŭr Lazov, in particular, was credited as being "my first teacher in socialism." He was described as "more intellectually developed than myself, with a clear and determined socialist outlook who, either in person or through his letters, cleaned the fog in my consciousness and influenced me a lot to become a social-democrat."[74] Todor was an obsessive letter writer and during the two-and-a-half-month period after finishing school (from July to September 1902) he wrote 128 letters and received eighty-seven. He was writing several letters a day (or, rather, a night, since he was working during the day), often over fifty pages each: "This is a deep passion of mine and I am patient with the writing. The benefit from letter writing for me is huge, most importantly I create the conditions where I feel close to my friends, and the letters also contribute mightily to my self-improvement."[75] His chief correspondent was Dimitŭr Lazov. On several pages Todor cites several of Lazov's letters where he shared his love insecurities and defeats, asking Todor to send him the notes for several violin waltzes, "so as to kill the time of my solitude."[76] Mostly, however, they were full of advice and philosophizing. Here is one of Lazov's letters of November 25, 1903 (an amazingly wise missive written by a teenager or, at most, a twenty-year-old):

> You say that you have many ideals, but do not know what road to take. This shows that these ideals are not clear for you in their totality, because if you know this, a general ideal will be generated, i.e. your path in life. . . . One can assume at first that education is an ideal, but if you look deeper, it is a means to a goal. Educating yourself means forming yourself, receiving the ideals, striving for truth and real life. The first partial ideal is to know yourself, the second—to comprehend nature, the third—to seek the truth, the fourth—to live in the spirit of truth. . . . Once you know your place in nature, you will realize your responsibilities. . . . What is the social question then? To determine your place and responsibilities. If you achieve this, your path will be clear. . . . This is the answer to the question to what you should aspire, and this is education. We are still too young to act (in the sense that we cannot yet creatively act to lift the general welfare). Now we should follow the older ones in raising the socialist ideal. . . . First, we should study social sciences. We are going to learn the basic things that will prepare us for the bigger ones. . . . We will be able to fight successfully for the common welfare after we learn to care for ourselves without impairing the interest of others, to work for the common accord. . . . The socialist ideal must be common, because it brings common well-being, it guarantees the common existence. If everyone is protected, everybody will try to educate oneself and all humanity to seek the truth.[77]

The letter is followed by concrete reading advice: Johannes Rehme's and Wilhelm Windelband's histories of philosophy (in Russian translation) as well as the Brockhaus Encyclopedia, "and for literary pleasure the works of the contemporary geniuses Ibsen and Sudermann."[78] Todor Tsekov started his military service in February 1903 and spent seven months in the Reserve Officers' School in Kniazhevo near Sofia, coming out as a second lieutenant. During these months he wrote more than 300 letters and received some 200. He would often go to Sofia and meet Lazov, and he continued his avid reading.[79] Upon his retirement from the military, he took his state exams in the summer of 1904 and in the autumn of 1904 he took a job as a teacher, spending the next three years at his post in a village. His initial culture shock was immense. Page after page, he describes his constant hunger. His disappointment with the crude relations in the village depressed him and he would spend long hours among his diaries and photo albums. And, of course, he was continuing his self-education.[80] Still looking for his path in life, he wrote a seven-page letter to Georgi Bakalov, one of the leaders of the BWSDP (n) and editor of the popular socialist journal *Rabotnishko delo* asking for his advice and recommendations for reading. While waiting for Bakalov's response, Todor wrote in his diary on October 19, 1904:

> This is the day of the great transformation. From now on I reject all novels and stories that fill one's fantasy and arouse desires. I will read and buy only scientific

books for my library. From this day on I become a SOCIALIST. Yes, I will become one and will devote all my efforts to the spread of this idea and the road to the morning star which will illuminate the whole world. I will study the causes for the social ills and find the ways to cure them. I will know myself. I will find the truth and will apply this truth to life.[81]

The gesture in the letter to his friend Lazov is unmistakable. On the next page, Todor printed a seal with five intertwined circles: one with the text "Liberty, Equality, Fraternity," the other four with the images of Karl Marx, Friedrich Engels, Wilhelm Liebknecht, and Ferdinand Lassalle. He added: "These are my real teachers and leaders in life. Their ideal becomes my ideal! Fedia." "Fedia" is the Russian diminutive of the name Todor (Fiodor) which Todor Tsekov would adopt.

The "Pleasures of Amor" or Taming the Testosterone

However, the reading of novels had left its lasting imprint and so had nature: "I was taken by the love scenes in the books and cried over *The Sorrows of Young Werther*. . . . I was already 18 years old, completely devoted to nature, entertainment, reading and patriotism, but my sexual life was in a lethargic state. . . . Yet, time passes, one matures, and everything evolves, and my feelings also evolved." The first stirring of love was documented on October 10, 1900, toward Miss Elenka Nikolaeva with whom he was collecting grapes on a rainy day. We do not find what exactly happened because the archivist who was photocopying the diary left a penciled note: "Text without any significance has been skipped. Trifonov, December 29, 1969."[82] Luckily, Todor Tsekov was a passionate soul and he passionately poured his feelings about "insignificant" events (love) next to "significant" ones (ideas) on the same page, often in the same sentence, so we have a detailed, sometimes steamy, picture of his intellectual and physical cravings. Altogether, some seventy pages of his daily diary entries were skipped at this point and when the "significant" events resume, Todor Tsekov had finished school in the summer of 1902 and was preparing to do his military service, while having already reached a profound love crisis with another girl, his "ideal love" Katerina Ivanova (Katia).[83]

Among the 300 letters that he sent from the military school, the longest one—160 pages—was to Katia. It was meant to be the final letter to her but remained unsent (a shorter one sealed the break). Todor started writing it on June 18, 1903, and his last entry in it was on August 8, 1903, but he considered it unfinished. Forty pages of it make their way into the diary.[84] Already when leaving for the military school, he felt the crisis coming. He knew that Katia's parents disapproved of him and while he bombarded her with pleading letters every day, he received no answer. So deep was his consternation that he lost his sleep and appetite and had to be hospitalized for a few days, "unconscious" and with high fever[85] Amazingly, even in his deep melancholy, he never lost his pedantic streak and kept copies of all his sent letters, each with its consecutive number. In March, barely a month after he had left, he sent a letter under the number 98! Finally, in May, he received a sentimental letter from Katia, in which she explained her silence, and reassured him of her love. It is a curious letter, in which she alternated between "ti" and "Vi," the intimate and polite form of address. The reasons she gave were that before leaving, she had asked him to get officially engaged to her or speak to her parents of his serious intentions, but he had refused, and she was shamed by her mother who told her that "he was only looking for . . ."[86] She also had heard that he had another love affair with Iordanka Nikolova.

Todor was dismayed and reacted fiercely. Iordanka Nikolova was his cousin "of the same blood" with whom he would share his longings for Katia: "Jealousy is one of the greatest sores of humanity. It destroys spousal life. . . . How will you be able to love sincerely when you doubt my love? Is it possible that jealousy can disappear? This is the important and difficult question. Read Tolstoy's *The Kreutzer Sonata* and you will see that jealousy cannot disappear."[87] It bears the reminder that *The Kreutzer Sonata* was published in 1889 and promptly censored in Russia and in other countries, including the United States where Theodore Roosevelt called Tolstoy a "sexual moral pervert."[88] It was, however, immediately published in France and Britain, as well as in Russian (in Geneva), and many Russian mimeographed versions had appeared. It was arguably the most talked about work of Tolstoy outside of his great novels, where he denounced carnal love and marriage. While Todor Tsekov never explicitly stated that he was a Tolstoyian, the influence of Tolstoy's teachings in Bulgaria was enormous.[89] One can see this influence also in his constant insistence on his "ideal" love and on his chastity: "I had no other intentions with my love, but the alignment of our characters that would be the basis of our shared life. . . . I have been chaste until now and have loved you for two years, so how could you suspect me of ulterior motives?"[90] The most they had come to was holding hands while attending performances, most notably of Lessing's *Emilia Galotti,* and he was regretting that he would never again feel her hand which drove electricity through his whole body and made him incapable of thinking of anything but the "pleasures of Amor." And then there was her present, a kiss: "Can I ever forget it? Oh, never. My lips are still burning. I feel it each moment."[91] While he dismissed the negative versions of Katia's behavior that he received from his friends, he broke off their relationship, even as he was vacillating for several months.

> I decided to reject you as unworthy of my heart. . . . Yes, I have rejected you from my mind and no longer hope to unite with you forever, but this is caused by my pride, my conscience, not by my heart. My heart will always remain loyal and will always belong to you. . . . My conscience and my heart waged a fierce and long struggle . . . and finally the conscience subdued the heart which remains loyal to its queen. But the victory over the heart was caused by you only. No bad news diverted it, it was convinced that these were lies and you will refute them. But you did not do that and mocked it and so my heart was defeated in the struggle with the sole consolation that it stays true to its ideal.[92]

What is remarkable about this overwrought prose is that it uses the same vocabulary about love and socialism. Citing Shakespeare on how "the greater glory dims the less," he wished Katia would find solace elsewhere, but this was impossible for him.[93] This is what he thought and wrote in 1903. Ten years later, already married to another Katia, he commented on this letter:

> It is the epic poem of my love. It reflects all my feelings at the time and today I am laughing over many of them. Today I have different views on life and love. Then I was a kid, an idealist, a romantic, entering life for the first time and expecting it to be ideal. . . . I did not know the effects of the social environment on the individual. . . . I was not thinking about the ideals in life, about the struggles in it, I was not concerned about my economic status, and much less about the role of my life companion. . . . Others loved, and I had to love too. . . . Today it is clear to me that love without the proper economic, social, and ideological foundations, will collapse sooner or later. And it did. . . . Love too is a product of social relationships and it requires physiological, ideological and economic harmonization and a final goal which should stimulate reciprocity. . . . My past conclusions that I can no longer be happy and love another, are completely stupid. Life demonstrated the opposite. Once I oriented myself in life and chose an ideal, I was able to find a worthy companion for my heart. With her I strengthened my love, was and continue to be completely happy.[94]

Before Todor reached this stage of bliss, he had several more amorous disappointments. On September 15, 1904, the beginning of the school year, he started his career as a teacher, but only fifty of the registered students appeared, something that was a predicament for village schools during harvest time.[95] The misery around depressed him but led to his epiphany a month later when he embraced socialism not simply as a bookish ideal, but as an organized social democrat. He was active in the social-democratic teachers' organization, where the most discussed issue seemed to be the social position of the teachers' class, that is, the intelligentsia, and whether teachers should be considered part of the proletariat or the petty bourgeoisie.[96]

He started correspondence with a young woman, Teofana Georgieva, who did not approve of his socialist beliefs and anti-militaristic stance. He responded first with a sixteen-page letter in which he recommended that she read some literature before judging socialism. He also told her his opinion about marriage as it was existent then. As for love, "it can console only the ones who share at least part of their worldview and have common convictions about the world and life."[97] Teofana was a beauty and sent him her portrait which he recorded under incoming Number 159. He politely thanked her in a letter under outgoing Number 180, this time on twenty pages, in which he explained the significance of ideas, the economic interests that move people, the situation of women in present society, and how she should commiserate and help her sisters, the reasons for prostitution, and his conviction that today's bourgeois society should be removed. He also told her that the impression he had made on her was only a fleeting inflammation of the senses that would disappear, and recommended that she read, read, and read. He disagreed with her that one should just "sing, laugh and love":

> I too want to love, but a woman pure of debauchery, who is not a hypocrite, far from meanness and deception, who despises coquetry and directs her thoughts

to the realization of a new social order. . . . I want a woman whose ideas are superior to her feelings, and only then, backed by ideals, shall we be able to lead a completely happy life. Only a woman with a progressive spirit can be a true companion to man.[98]

At the end of this excerpt, Todor added in larger letters: "I had a pollution and was very excited" (Figure 37). By then he was already captivated by Elena Antonova, a young fellow teacher, and well over a hundred pages are full of sentimental outpourings about his love anguish. His insomnia came back, he was waiting for letters and tried to kill his suffering with reading. In January 1905 he finished the first volume of Chekhov's works, *Historical Materialism* by Mikhail Tugan-Baranovsky, and the books *Tolstoy and Socialism* and the *Agrarian Question*, a collection of socialist articles.[99] Later he added the short stories of Leonid Andreyev which Elena had sent him. The correspondence with Elena was tense, because he had shared his feelings, but his love was unrequited. He was tortured by suspicions that his best friend Levkov was also courting Elena, but finally she refused them both. Even though Todor had already embraced the lofty socialist ideal, love and desire clearly proved to be the dominant force: "Why should I live? Death is dearer to me than life. Death brings solace, it is the only way out of my ordeal. If nobody loves you, it is senseless to live."[100]

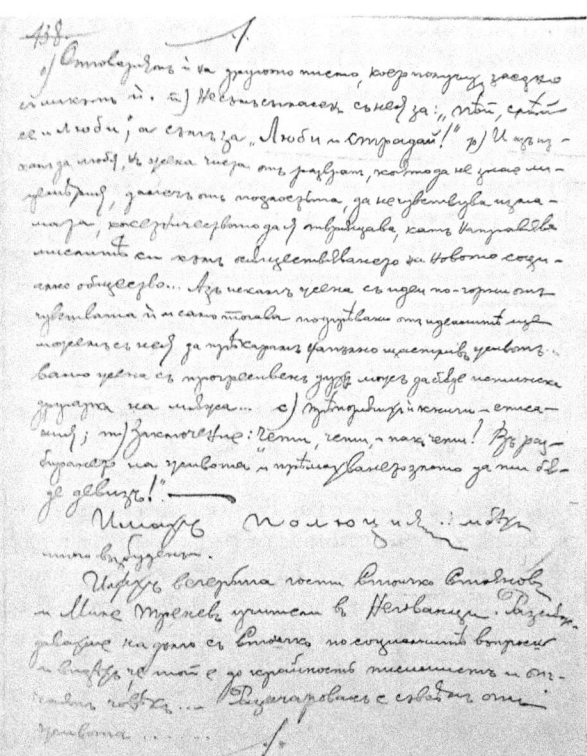

Figure 37 Manuscript page.

But a new life was on the horizon. In August 1905 he met a high school student in her last year, Katerina Vasileva who was four or five years his junior: "I liked her a lot and immediately decided to test her and if I were to find in her good ground for my ideas, I will offer her my services and will want to spend all my life with her."[101] It took them only a couple of weeks to swear an oath of faithfulness, and Todor "had now something to live for. I have no other desire but to raise her to my level and lead her on my path."[102] There was soon a first kiss, embraces, dreams, and more oaths. Mostly, however, this was Todor's Pygmalionite work-in-progress. He was tutoring her for long hours, as well as in his long letters, about the social environment, class theory, bourgeois, petty-bourgeois and proletarian ideology, competition and exploitation, human evolution and, of course, love: "Love is the free, rational and sincere union of two individuals, harmonized with liking based on physical, moral and intellectual qualities" and it is "a moment in the human evolution long prepared by the evolution of other emotions."[103]

Once Katia finished school and started work as a teacher, he subscribed to several progressive pedagogical journals for her, and made her read his own socialist subscriptions: "Whatever money I have, I will assign it for books, so as to enrich Katia's mental baggage and raise her to the level of complete freedom and independence. Only strong convictions bring complete independence. . . . Ah, when will the time come when we shall converse with you, Katia, about all the questions that excite us! When are we going to become so close as to share all the most minute flutters of our souls and hearts? Future, come soon!"[104] He held strong opinions and directly interfered with her appearance and style, when she came dressed up at a party:

> Katia made a strange and poor impression on me with her aristocratic suit and bourgeois hat. . . . I noticed that this girl is leaning more toward the "bourgeois harmful fashion" rather than to a bodily hygiene. This is especially evident in the wearing of a corset. She also had adopted the twisted high heels which are extremely unhygienic. I do not object to the fulfillment of one's personal taste, but only when it does not go against hygiene and is not harmful to the body. Naturalness is much more pleasing than artificialness. Ah! I will have to work harder on her, so that this aristocratic air would disappear. I had a completely different notion of her and it turned the opposite. If she loves me, she will uproot her desire to doll up, to dress sumptuously and to sprain her body with corsets.[105]

They were enjoying each other's company and went together to the theater to see Gogol's *The Government Inspector* whose performance Todor disliked, but he relished sitting close to Katia. On the other hand, he was hugely impressed by Hermann Sudermann's play *The Battle of the Butterflies* which was staged at the "Slavianska beseda" theater. Sudermann was popular among the progressive youth, because of his celebration of moral freedom and his critique of petty-bourgeois philistinism. They also went to the opera and loved Verdi's *La Traviata*, much more than Gounod's *Faust*.[106] Galatea-Katia was weathering the modeling well, but Pygmalion-Todor often did not heed his own moralizing advice. He was tormented by her inhibitions and suffered from unfounded jealousies, punctuated by tears and melodramatic verbal gush, both oral to his friends and written in his diary. Whenever he was disappointed by Katia's reserve or had doubts about her behavior, he tended to explain it in socioeconomic terms: "Woman seems to me today . . . like a parasite . . . looking only for the economic position of man and starts life wherever she has found a good ground. . . . She cannot rise to the level of giving her heart to where nature commands."[107] One of the reasons was that he was forcing her to enter her letters in the common diary and she was reticent. She did concede later, and there is a long, day-by-day, even hour-by-hour, account in her own writing of how she spent her Christmas vacation.[108] Another reason was that she wanted to use her family ties to secure a teaching position in a city, while he needed her constant presence. Finally, one of his friends gave up his place, so both Katia and Todor could be appointed in the same village.[109]

They started living together and these were the most blissful moments of his life (and writing). He was complaining only that he had entirely neglected his own self-education but left it for the future.[110] It was not easy for them, especially for Katia, with the pressure exerted by her mother who was concerned about Katia's reputation and the rumors of neighbors who saw them openly "a la braccia" (алабраца, hand in hand).[111] Socialists in this period were not only considered godless but also with loose morals by the philistine public opinion. Katia was especially interested in the physiology of males and females and the "sexual question" and he lectured to her: "We study together but mostly we are devoted to the Amor! . . . We live the ideal life (in the complete sense)!!"[112] While in the "illegal wedding bed" (Katia's nomenclature), he usually would develop a theme from political economy. Katia was laughing all the time and when he would fall asleep among caresses, she would tease him that he forgot his theme. She called him "the lovely baby" and they developed a child's chatter for their lovemaking sprinkled with politically incorrect vocabulary: "Ah! What perfect forms her body has! My 'private property' i.e. her breasts fill me with admiration!"[113] The testosterone was not entirely tamed, but it was channeled.

Katia and Todor in America

There was no more sentimental introspection and love insecurities in the diaries, but there were difficulties. Todor was in debt, to the tune of almost the whole amount of his yearly salary. He sent a quarter of his salary to his father, who demanded more, and supported his sister in school.[114] The young people dreamed of continuing their education at the university, their only salvation from their stressful situation as village teachers in an environment "where everything progressive can be stifled," but their means did not allow it.[115] Socialism continued to be their leading light. All in all, purely quantitatively, at least until his marriage, Todor's love life takes more pages than his ideology, but what is remarkable is that the two were intimately linked together. He was active in the teachers' organization, attended meetings and talks, himself delivered lectures, and became the secretary of the Radomir teachers' organization.[116] (Figure 38)

One of the topics that excited him and was the object of animated debates with his friends was the confluence of aesthetics and political views. Todor firmly defended the idea that there should be complete consonance, whereas his friend Iordan Levkov

Figure 38 The Radomir social-democratic teachers' group, 1904/05. Todor Tsekov is reclining in front, on the left.

allowed for the appreciation of beauty even if it espoused ideas contrary to one's belief: "I thought his attitude individualistic and philistine, because one's worldview becomes one's flesh and blood, and when appreciating a work of art, you cannot excise your worldview, and if you do, this means that you do not share the genuine socialist proletarian view."[117] If this sounds a little doctrinaire, let us not forget that the debate over *l'art pour l'art* was a century-old one and had involved thinkers as diverse as Edgar Allen Poe and John Ruskin, Théophile Gautier and Charles Baudelaire, Friedrich Nietzsche and Stefan George, not to speak of later ones like Walter Benjamin and György Lukács.

When Todor Tsekov became an organized socialist in October 1904 at the age of twenty-two, he had joined the Narrows to whom he was leaning already in the military school but his was not a blind allegiance. Especially interesting are his thoughts on the dispute about the status of the Social-Democratic Teachers' Organization (SDTO, the Bulgarian acronym УСДО) vis-à-vis the party in 1905. The SDTO had been formed in 1905 by socialist teachers who had left the Bulgarian Teachers' Union (BTU, Bulgarian acronym БУС), itself created in 1895 and representing the largest professional group in Bulgaria at the time.[118] The BTU had been a staunch supporter of teachers' interests in the preceding decade, pressing for higher salaries, insisting on the public and secular character of education, which should encompass the whole population regardless of nationality and religion, protesting against the decision to deprive married women of their teaching rights, against the arbitrary political and professional control of inspectors and municipal authorities, and, especially, against the ban on teachers to participate individually and openly in political organizations, arguing that teachers were citizens and as such their rights were guaranteed by the constitution. Most of its activities were in the form of petitions to the Ministry of Education and to the National Assembly.[119] While it helped out teachers who were unjustly laid off, it had a negative attitude toward strikes, given their consequences.[120]

The SDTO was against the political neutrality of the trade union movement represented by the BTU and its conciliatory collaboration with the Ministry of Education. The SDTO required a free range for the expression and propagation of their socialist ideas. When the General Federation of Trade Unions (GFTU) was formed in 1904 under the initiative and auspices of the Narrows, it forsook its organizational independence (its leadership was appointed by the party). The Broads, on the other hand, consistently defended the independence and neutrality of the trade union movement that was supposed to unify people according to their professional and economic interests, irrespective of their political and religious allegiance. The so-called "anarcho-liberals" shared with the Narrows their stance against neutrality but were against the dilution of its autonomy vis-à-vis the party. Eventually, the SDTO conformed to the party line but this diminished its potential for growing and attracting teachers from a diverse background and with diverse views. In 1921 it was separated from the Communist Party and joined the GFTU.[121] The party line of the disciplined and centralizing BWSDP (n) professed that the SDTO should not be accepted and considered as a trade union within the GFTU but should simply be an educational society under the control of the party and without a special delegate voice. To Todor this made little sense. Trade unions united people with similar economic interests and they had the means to fight for these interests through strikes. By delegating this right to the party and remaining only an educational society, the organization was essentially emasculating itself.

> For now, I am inclined for us to stay as a trade-union. This may be considered somewhat "liberal," but I cannot help thinking that our place is only among the trade unions.... I may be wrong as we consider ourselves social-democrats but do not accept the decision of the party. However, I cannot allow the party to dismiss our goal which was adopted after a year-long struggle at our inaugural meeting when the party disgracefully did not say a word and now, maybe because of some "private ambitions" takes the opposite view. I think that this issue should remain open. It should be discussed in all our circles and be decided only at our congress, which has the right to change the statutes.[122]

The year 1905 was a crucial one in the evolution of the Narrows. After the 1903 split of the BWSDP into Broads and Narrows over the issue of collaboration with bourgeois parties, there was internal critique within the BWSDP (n) over what was seen as the obsessive centralization of the party leadership under Blagoev and the lack of democratic tolerance. The main leaders of this critique, Georgi Bakalov and Nikola Kharlakov were disparagingly called "liberals" or more often "anarcho-liberals" and the whole group was expelled in December 1905. They created their own Bulgarian Social-Democratic Union "Proletarii" which in 1908 was unified with the Broads and comprised its left wing, and they referred to themselves as "proletartsi." After the wars, they left the Broad party and entered the Communist Party in 1920.[123] An additional issue was the success of Bakalov's journal *Rabotnishko delo* which, according to the party leadership, was competing with the party organ *Rabotnicheski vestnik* and *Novo vreme*. The problem of control of the party press and mostly of the allocation of the limited resources became a central issue of the party's politics.[124]

Todor Tsekov, for whom the influence of Bakalov, a CC member from 1903 until his expulsion in 1905, was crucial for his embrace of socialism; he was appalled over several letters from his friend Lazov, a devoted Narrow, castigating Todor for distributing Bakalov's journal and his other publications, and claiming that he was working for the cause of the "liberals." He had also listened with admiration to Kharlakov's lecture on "Nationalism and Socialism."[125] He was so torn that he even considered the possibility of going over to the "liberals" if he did not understand the party logic.[126] The fateful decision was delayed because of a series of personal crises. First came his father's angry and accusatory letter. Then came the death of his close friend Georgi Goranov (1882–1905), a talented composer, and the author of some of the most popular Bulgarian songs, among them "You are beautiful, my forest" (Хубава си, моя горо) and the "Labor Song" (Песен на труда или Дружна песен). Born in Kiustendil, Goranov was Todor's classmate and participated in the secret Macedonian "Liberation" society. He later entered the workers' educational society "Class Consciousness," and the "Labor Song" was composed to the lyrics of Georgi Kirkov. He started a musical academy in Zagreb in 1902, but died of tuberculosis, the plague of the time.

In addition, the political situation was growing tenser. In the decade spanning the turn of the century, but especially after 1903, Bulgaria saw a remarkable economic growth, but this came at a political price. Following the fall and assassination of Stefan Stambolov, the new government after 1894 adopted a systemic program for the modernization of the country. Home industry, chiefly mining, metallurgy, construction, and textiles, received state encouragement, although the Bulgarian economy continued to be dominated by food and textile production. In the ensuing decade, factories and the work force in the encouraged industries quintupled (from 72 factories in 1894 to 345 in 1911). Commerce and railway construction were stimulated. This went hand in hand with protectionist measures and the adoption of huge government foreign loans, a lion's share of which went to armament and reforms in the military.[127] It also immensely extended the centralizing hand of executive power which, together with the personal ambitions of Prince Ferdinand (king after 1908) who wanted to extend the role of the crown, seriously curtailed parliamentary and, in general, democratic rights. Despite the impressive electoral system (universal male suffrage), elections were manipulated, government offices trafficked, and opposition suppressed. The foreign loans needed to be paid for and this necessitated an increase in internal revenues with the tax burden falling disproportionately on the peasantry. Discontent was widespread not only in the villages but also in the cities with the rise in the cost of living. The response was numerous strikes, of which the biggest one, by the railway workers (December 1906–February 1907), ended with a victory for the workers. In December 1906 a law was passed that threatened employees of the state (of which teachers were the largest part) with firing for participation in a strike. In addition, this was the time of acute conflict between Greece and Bulgaria over the future of Macedonia and this was accompanied by anti-Greek pogroms.[128] Students were rioting too, first emboldened by the Russian Revolution of 1905 and then in support of the railway workers. The culmination came in early January 1907 when, at the opening of the new National Theater, Ferdinand was booed and pelted with snowballs by university students. The reaction was immediate and excessive. The university was closed, the whole faculty laid off, a new law took away university autonomy, and students were forbidden from participating in political organizations. Of the 1,350 students, many went abroad, as did a number of professors, and the popular and enlightened minister of education Ivan Shishmanov resigned. The crisis ended only at the beginning of 1908.[129]

All of this was reflected in Todor Tsekov's diary. During the anti-Greek riots he wrote that "people became barbarians" and he blamed the government for its perfunctory reaction.[130] His entries on the university crisis were detailed and he was anticipating with trepidation the reorganization of schools: "Let us see how far this reaction will go and will it not stumble in the face of the resistance of the organized teachers? Will teachers be able to defend their honor and freedom, even in the face of long-term deprivation?"[131] It was in this atmosphere that Todor began considering emigration. The trigger came from a letter from his old friend and classmate Georgi Efremov who invited him to come to Battle Creek and described the university where he had been studying medicine for the past two years. Efremov was close to the Tolstoyan movement, a young man of great integrity and broad culture.[132] America seemed to be the only salvation from their insecurity and on March 6, 1907, a Tuesday, the two took the firm decision to emigrate.[133] Todor who until then had put his efforts to mastering French, started learning English. Katia and Todor began preparing their documents and collecting money and decided to get married. They left Bulgaria on June 20, 1907. Their emigration came at the high point of Bulgarian emigration to the United States, reaching the figure of 17,000 in 1907 and just before the passing of the restrictive emigration law in December of the same year.[134] The one thing that made Todor feel guilty was that his family and aging father were relying on his help and now they seemed to be destined to greater hardship and poverty. He was torn between this sorrow and the promise of something new: "Farewell past! Tomorrow I start a new life."[135]

They were on the road for a whole month: first on a train through Europe, and then on board a transatlantic ship. The travel notes are lively.[136] They were impressed by Belgrade as an industrial center, and Zagreb and Ljubljana, which had the look of European cities. Todor was especially struck by the beauty of the women in Austria and Hungary: "blond, blue eyed, with red cheeks, gracious."[137] His poetic side was awoken by the Alps. What bothered him were the long tunnels and ceaseless crosses and churches on every peak and meadow: "This mocks the Alpine natural beauty."[138] He was envious of the many tourists he was observing: "And Katia and I will be just hired workers who are seeking their chance not in the clean air of beautiful nature, but among the stifled air of factories and hard labor."[139] Germany and Switzerland struck him with their many castles, out of the Middle Ages.

As already noted, Tsekov's last volume reconstructed his stay in the United States from separate notes and letters but mostly from memory, because the diaries had perished in the bombardments. They are very interesting but what is absent, of course, is the direct impression which is mediated through the additional filter of time. Upon

Figure 39 Katia and Todor Tsekov, 1907.

their arrival, Katia and Todor began work in the Battle Creek Sanatorium of Dr. Kellog together with a whole group of other Bulgarians. Katia worked in the kitchen and Todor worked in the restaurant and the men's bath where he cleaned the floor. It was difficult at the beginning because he was not used to physical labor. They were paid little but were grateful for receiving lodging and food (vegetarian, following the Sanatorium's diet). They were also advancing in their language acquisition, in which Katia was excelling, and were preparing to enter university.[140]

Unfortunately for the young people, the Knickerbocker Crisis struck in the fall of 1907 and what followed was a protracted depression, in which they were laid off. Luckily, they were allowed to live in the dormitory and for six months Todor worked for free as a masseur. They were also studying to get the American high school diploma so that they could enroll in the university. While in Bulgaria, Todor was very critical of the educational program but here he concluded that "our Bulgarian schools offer much better and broader knowledge in every respect, while the American ones do not give even half of it." The only thing that they had to learn anew was Latin.[141] They enrolled in medicine in the Seventh-day Adventist Battle Creek College (the future Andrews University) without tuition but on the promise that they would become missionaries. They were happy with their lectures in anatomy, chemistry, biology, and hydrotherapy but hated the biblical lessons. After a laboratory seminar with the microscope, when the biology professor marveled at God's creation, Todor decided to quit. Yet, fortune smiled on him. Todor continued to work as a masseur and had up to eight patients a day. One of them happened to be the president of Valparaiso University, one of the largest American universities, known as "The poor man's Harvard." He offered him lodging, food, and free education if Todor would give him free massages.[142]

In October 1908 Todor entered the School of Law at Valparaiso University and the following semester Katia joined him to study natural history. They were especially moved by the gift of a female employer at the Sanatorium who was not wealthy but gave Katia $50 to pay her tuition fees, a considerable sum at the time.[143] Todor received his Bachelor of Law diploma (LL.B.) in 1910 and passed the bar for Indiana. He was especially proud of Katia's achievements. She earned her Bachelor of Sciences (B.S.) with distinction and her geology professor said that she was his best student during his fifteen-year teaching career. He wrote her a recommendation to continue her education at Washington University of St. Louis, MO.[144] After spending the summer in Battle Creek, they relocated to Madison, IL. Katia started her master's degree in zoology and in her spare hours worked for her bed and food, taking care of her professor's child.[145]

These notes do not provide the day-by-day emotions of a diary, but Todor gives the impression of someone enamored of his appearance and confident of his masculine appeal. While reading in the library in Valparaiso, he noticed a girl who was constantly observing him instead of reading. Todor shared this with Katia and brought her to the library. After she left, the girl, who happened to be a student of literature from the southern states, approached him and asked who Katia was. Upon hearing that she was his wife, she started crying and told him that she was deeply in love with him. "American love!" he condescendingly observes.[146] Even as he preferred the "naturalness" in Katia, he was always dressed up, often like a dandy and at Katia's graduation, he took four photographs of himself in different poses "to remember how I looked at the time."[147] They show him with a trendy hairstyle and hat, and a carefully trimmed moustache. Regrettably, the wonderful photographs of their student life have been preserved only as very faded xerox copies and cannot be reproduced here.

All throughout, Todor sought out socialist sympathizers, organized the Bulgarian–Macedonian workers, gave lectures, and was instrumental in creating the BSLF. For over a year he was its soul, the secretary of the organization and the editor-in-chief of *Rabotnicheska Prosveta* (from January to August 1911) as well as the manager of the bookstore.[148] There was also a typical dose of self-conceit. All the first fifteen issues during his tenure as editor-in-chief have his name in the masthead, in English, "Managing Editor Theo. Tsekoff" and in Bulgarian: "Редакторъ: Т. Цековъ."[149] After his departure, the paper never gave the name of the editor. Issue Number 3 even published his personal advertisement on the front page: "Theodore Tsecoff, lawyer. Offers guidance, settles disputes, helps withdraw money left in the companies, gives information for American citizenship, etc." And in bold: "Gives free advice to the organized workers of the Bulgarian–Macedonian Social-Democratic Enlightenment Union in America. P. O. Box 146, Granite City, IL."[150] Todor was especially proud that Blagoev had published his article "In the land of dollars and swift enrichment" in the journal *Novo Vreme*.[151] When Katia received her MA and was urged to continue for a PhD, they decided that they felt tired of the United States and yearned for home. They had no money for the way back, so Katia started work in a chocolate factory and Todor was paid for representing the family of a worker who had died in a mining accident. On August 1, 1911, they left from St. Louis for Bulgaria.[152]

The rest of Todor Tsekov's reminiscences are briefer and sketchier. They are partial, covering only the war years and the second emigration to the United States (1924–32), with nothing on the interim period (1918–24), which was crucial in the political development of Bulgaria. We know from his biographical entry in the encyclopedia that he was in the leadership of the legal Communist Party, active in the Kiustendil commune and MP throughout the period from 1919 to 1923. Arrested briefly on the eve of the September Uprising, he subsequently left for the United States in 1924. These notes are also not chronologically arranged, with the account of the war years following the second stay in America. Upon their return from the United States in 1911, the young family relocated to Sofia where Todor became a lawyer. He was terrified by the extent of prostitution and venereal disease, and on the request of Blagoev started to research the reasons.[153] His mother died of typhoid fever and in 1913 their first child, Florence, was born.[154] During the wars he was mobilized and decorated twice for courage. A photograph from 1916 shows him, cigarette in hand, among officers from the 13th Rilski regiment. After the war's end, he was appointed prosecutor in Vratsa and later in Gorna Dzhumaia.[155]

The family, now also with a son Lori (Laurence), arrived in the United States in May 1924 and settled in Detroit. On their return after thirteen years, their biggest surprise was the disappearance of horse carriages and the ubiquity of cars and trucks.[156] Todor worked in a greenhouse and Katia first in a kitchen and later in a night shift in the Square D manufacturing company for electrical equipment. Tsekov was preoccupied with his work among the immigrant Bulgarian and Macedonian community which, according to his data, counted between 60,000 and 100,000 for all of the Americas and Australia.[157] He became secretary of the communist organization in Detroit and his main task was to propagate the idea of a Balkan Federative Soviet Republic among the South Slavs.[158] He was secretary of the Bulgarian Bureau and the Balkan Committee of the American Labor Party. He was also editor-in-chief of the weekly newspaper *Siznanie* (Suznanie, Съзнание), the organ of the Bulgarian section of the Workers' Party of America. As mentioned, the Bulgarian social-democratic movement in America was split, and *Rabotnicheska Prosveta* had become the organ of the "eselpists" (SLP-ists), while the "communists" were organized around *Siznanie* and there was no love lost between the two publications; but Tsekov does not dwell on this. Moving paragraphs are dedicated to the Sacco and Vanzetti trial. In 1928 Florence entered high school, and looking at his photograph, Todor wrote: "I am 46 and am still filled with energy for work and firm belief in the socialist idea. I boldly go ahead and there is not a single day that I am not working for the cause."[159] (Figure 40)

Yet, time was moving on. The 1929 crisis was devastating and Todor himself became a victim of unemployment: "In America the whole life of the worker consists of work or looking for work."[160] Unused to physical labor, he found temporary work in the Briggs Automotive Company but was laid off in 1931. He had to pull out his teeth and wear dentures. He organized a consumer community with a free soup kitchen.[161] He was arrested at the May Day demonstration in 1931 and accused of illegally entering the United States but proved his legal status and was released.[162] By then he was already sidelined from the communist organization, but says little about the reasons, except that he later learned that he had been accused of "Macedonian deviation" which he does not explain. Depressed and disappointed—"The ultimate individualism disgusts me"—they decided to return to Bulgaria in July 1932.[163]

It is a pity that the lively diary entries finish before the First World War and the later memoirs based on notes and correspondence end in the early 1930s so that we cannot

Figure 40 In the editorial office of *Sīznanie*, 1928. On the wall there is a portrait of Blagoev.

follow Todor Tsekov's further ideas about social democracy, communism, and party affairs. Especially conspicuous is the absence of the early 1920s and Tsekov's opinion on the party line vis-à-vis the agrarian government and the 1923 uprising. We know from the critique of *Rabotnicheska Prosveta* against *Sīznanie* (personally mentioning Tsekov) that he represented the party line in defense of the 1923 uprising and the Comintern position, but we do not know whether his ideas evolved, especially after his expulsion in 1927. If at times, when he discusses politics, his language approaches the characteristics of the *langue de bois* as Soviet speech has been characterized, one should be careful about positing a causal link.[164] Mary Jo Maynes points out that nineteenth-century working-class autobiographies are characterized by their high commitment to self-improvement through education and a tendency to militancy.[165] It would be forcing the evidence to count Tsekov's memoir-diary as a working-class one. He was a self-styled, but not class-crossing intellectual [интелигент], and was viewed by others as one. He definitely shared the characteristic of self-improvement but less so militancy. What he did not share with these autobiographies was another characteristic, that they "often denied their individuality and emphasized how similar their story was to others."[166]

Granted, both socialist and communist narratives partook in what Jochen Hellbeck describes as the disposition of a socialist subjectivity "with its triple valuation of self-expression, collective action, and historical purpose" but I would like to emphatically distinguish Tsekov's prose from the genre of communist autobiographies, memoirs, and diaries where, according to Hellbeck, the distinction between the private and public domain was obliterated and personhood was "markedly illiberal in the sense that it lacked a positive evaluation of autonomy and private values."[167] These narratives, as Diane Koenker points out, describing the corpus of Soviet autobiographical writing, reflected Soviet Russia's unique position as the first socialist society: "Autobiographies written after 1917 were written with the knowledge of the happy ending of the story of struggle."[168] A great number among them were also part of a ritualized procedure.[169] This was also valid for American communist autobiographies (as a subgenre of working-class ones) that "seemed to shape their own personal narratives with Soviet models in mind."[170] One should also emphasize here the difference between power and authority. Marxist vocabulary and speech in the USSR and among communists elsewhere after the triumph of the Bolshevik revolution was no longer serving the language of utopia, it had become the discourse of power, even when it may have been accepted voluntarily and with conviction. Power demands submission, while authority does not need to affirm itself through authoritarian means.[171]

Tsekov's is a highly individualistic account, at times even egocentric. His devotion to a shared ideal is dominant but not such as to subordinate himself to the collective or dissolve his subjectivity. What emerges is an individual with strongly held but not rigid opinions. There is no trace of self-censorship in the texts that we have, and most likely, there would not have been any trace of self-censorship in the ones that were withheld by his family after his death. Clearly, the family was concealing not personal indiscretions but most likely critical policy assessments, although probably these were not so severe, given that Tsekov had agreed to give his volumes to the archive. This speaks not only to his scholarly approach, seeing himself as a professional remembrancer, whose writings would serve future historians, but also to someone who did not think his materials would jeopardize seriously the well-being of his family. But we are not to know this definitively. What we do know is that in his last years, Todor Tsekov was a man who seemed content with how he had spent his life following his ideal, even if reality did not always conform to the ideal.

8

Romanticism and Modernity

Koika Tineva and Nikola Sakarov

In March 1911, the same year that *Rabotnicheska Prosveta* was launched in Illinois and Angelina Boneva was buying socialist books in Vratsa, a marriage that seemed made in heaven was falling apart. Koika Tineva left her husband of four years, Nikola Sakarov, while he was in Rome as an employee of the Ministry of Finance. In 1907 the two had translated *Anti-Dühring* which Boneva purchased in 1911. They had been married on September 10, 1906, but the divorce came only in October 1922, when the marriage was annulled. The procedure for divorce had to be initiated by one of the spouses, and Nikola Sakarov accordingly sent an application to His Eminence Metropolitan Stefan. He had shown the application to his lawyer who approved of it. Sakarov's archive holds a note in pencil next to the wedding and divorce certificates. (Figure 41):

> Today, 5 September 1922, I spoke to Deian. He approved of the text. I asked him to communicate this to Koika's lawyer, Dr. Mikhailov. He should tell him that I want to make it easy for her. I will not suggest anything about adultery, so her reputation would not be tarnished but mostly so that Kharlakov's presence does not stand out. She lives with him at present and, given the Statutes of the Exarchate, she would not be able to wed him. I would like her to marry him. For me everything between us is finished forever. I do not wish to benefit from the privileges that the law bestows on men. I am against these rights and privileges. Against the restrictions on women. A marriage should be based on love. If there is no love, there is no marriage. Eleven and a half years I did not undertake anything against her. If she thinks that she is following her heart, let her do it. I do not have such feelings toward her any longer. The past is in the past and it has been forgotten. I would like to lead my life faithful to my beliefs about the relations between men and women.[1]

Koika Tineva's response to Sakarov's chivalry was brief and curt: "I found it impossible to live with him and therefore left the house in March 1911. I have nothing against the divorce that I myself desire."[2] The resolution faulted Tineva for the dissolution of the marriage but allowed both spouses to remarry. There are no diaries, no written evidence of their romance, no letters of the two from the time they were dating and the early years of the marriage, although the archives contain numerous documentation on both. Sakarov's fund is especially big, encompassing 3,053 archival units, but they

Figure 41 The wedding and divorce certificates.

are almost exclusively on his political and professional activities. Tineva's fund is smaller, but it contains a few photographs that attest to the beginning of a romantic and harmonious relationship.

In June 1903, Koika sent a photograph of her university friends in Berlin, inscribed "To my dear parents." She is sitting on the far right, and Nikola Sakarov, her future husband, is standing behind her with his hand over her shoulder. Both are wearing pince-nez, which was not a sign of affectation since in all their later photographs they needed their glasses. Next to Sakarov, in the middle, stands another Nikola, Kharlakov, Koika's future life-partner. (Figure 42) With hindsight, it looks as if this is more than a marriage made in heaven, this is a picture of a future love triangle.

On another photograph from 1902, the two Nikolas and two other friends are posing, and on the back, Sakarov has inscribed the photo to Koika in French with a quote from Victor Hugo: "Bien lire l'univers, c'est bien lire la vie; Le monde est l'oeuvre ou rien ne ment et ne dévie."[3] We can see here what Monique Scheer has described as the communicating category of emotional practices, where "the success of an emotional performance depends on the skill of the performer as well as that of its recipient(s) to interpret it."[4] Koika and Nikola were speaking the language of European high culture in its main vernaculars of the time, French and German, and sharing in its main sensibilities and perhaps also affectations. They were a studious couple but not excessively stern and humorless. In two undated photographs from the studio of D. Joseph in Istanbul, they are dressed up as Turks, reclining on an ottoman holding hands, with a hookah in front of them. It is the only photograph of Koika without her pince-nez. (Figure 43)

Romanticism and Modernity 231

Figure 42 Berlin, June 1903.

Figure 43 In Istanbul as newlyweds.

The Making of a Modern (Female) Socialist Feminist

These photographs, and many more, are all in the Tineva archive but, as already mentioned, lacking a "verbal illustration." Her archive contains memoirs and autobiographical notes, but exclusively on her political activism. They are unfinished and unpublished and consist of several notebooks with extensive notes on different topics written in pencil after the Second World War.[5] She was born in what may be closest to the Bulgarian progressive elites of the time. Her father was a wealthy landowner and banker: he was the cashier of the People's Bank in Varna., but he frequented the social-democratic clubs and was excommunicated from the Orthodox Church. Both her parents were non-believers.[6] Her mother was the sister of Christian Rakovski. This uncle had an enormous influence on her throughout his life (and even after his death). Whenever Christian would come home from his studies during the summer months, "we, the children, were more and more imbued with a spirit of protest against the capitalist system, a drive to become as courageous and decisive and be true to our principles." As a high school student, she decided she was for socialism and despised her rich classmates, "although I belonged to the same social group" but with a Spartan upbringing at home.[7] (Figure 44)

In 1898, suffering from consumption, the eighteen-year-old Koika was sent to a sanatorium in Tyrol and she left poignant observations on how the rich treated the poor. Back in Bulgaria, she witnessed the peasant protests in northeast Bulgaria in 1900 in which hundreds of peasants were killed and wounded. She became active in the Sunday school organized by the Teachers' Union and, especially, in the women's courses which at first were simply courses for literacy, but then broadened to cover literature, chemistry, and other disciplines.[8] In 1900, she travelled to Lausanne and enrolled at the university, but found the professors mediocre. She moved in socialist circles, among both Bulgarians and Russian students, and listened to Plekhanov's lectures. She was deeply impressed by the Russian community, which was open and free of prejudice, especially its female body. Indeed, in 1906–07, of the 1,823 women registered in Swiss universities, 1,696 were foreigners and only 197 Swiss. Of the foreigners, 89 percent or 1,545 were Russian, the remainder mostly other Slavs and Central Europeans (Bulgarians, Serbs, Romanians, and Germans).[9] By contrast, the Bulgarian students were of two kinds. One group spent their time in cafes and bars; the other seemed progressive and leaning toward socialism but Koika writes that many simply used socialist phraseology, neither having read Marx, nor knowing French, but pronouncing themselves confidently on all social issues.[10]

Finding Lausanne unsatisfying and against her doctors' advice, she moved to Berlin and enjoyed the completely new atmosphere: "The torpid, philistine Switzerland with its petty life expectations changed to the big city, boiling with life in every aspect."[11] She had already read August Bebel's *Women and Socialism*, but now could listen in person to his lectures, and the speeches of Rosa Luxemburg and Clara Zetkin. She was very impressed by the discipline of German workers, so unusual compared to the Bulgarians. Rosa Luxemburg she admired for her energy and consistency, but found her a poor speaker, using a high style, difficult to understand. Clara Zetkin, on the other hand, exerted a real influence over Koika.[12] She and her friends moved in Russian

Figure 44 Koika standing with her parents and younger siblings, Varna 1893.

circles and were aware of the hot disputes among Bolsheviks and Mensheviks, but were unclear about the issues and "traditionally, we were on the side of Plekhanov." Their heroes were August Bebel, Rosa Luxemburg, and Karl Liebknecht in Germany, Jules Guesde and Paul Lafargue in France, and Georgi Plekhanov, Pavel Axelrod, and Vera Zasulich in Russia. "Lenin's ideas were alien to us. We believed that, as the Russian revolution was bourgeois-democratic, the bourgeoisie would advance with the revolutionary movement."[13]

On the other hand, Berlin struck her with its negative attitude toward women. German women were not admitted at the university; even the ones who had completed the classical gymnasium were allowed only to audit without the right to sit for exams. In general, Germany admitted women later than Switzerland, Belgium, or France, the pioneer being the University of Heidelberg in 1900. Prussian universities, however, legalized the status of women students only in 1908. At one point, a notification was issued that the university would not accept Russian women any longer on the pretext

Figure 45 With her brother Tiniu Tinev in Berlin 1902.

that the Russian Revolution was becoming contagious to the German students. When Koika Tineva went to enroll, she was first told that Russian women were not accepted. Upon her insistence that she was Bulgarian, the secretary reacted that Bulgaria was Russia's Danubian province. She was still registered but had difficulties finding lodging, landlords presuming that these young women were prostitutes. Often when women entered the auditoria, they were met with hissing and stamping on the floor.[14]

Koika was struck by the Russian women, and not only the revolutionaries: "They were completely liberated of the petty-bourgeois philistinism which was dominant in our [i.e., Bulgarian] midst. I was amazed by the relations between men and women: complete mutual respect, perfect equality, free from all kinds of prejudices. We were encountering the people of the future, and when I compared them to the prejudices in our dear country, I had to conclude how remote we were from the progressive understanding of the relations between men and women."[15] It was in Berlin, in 1903, that she formally became a member of the Bulgarian student social-democratic group.[16] She could not finish her studies, and had to return because of her poor health. This prevented her from sustaining a permanent profession, like a teacher or employee, but she was economically secure and lived with her parents. What could not be curbed was her desire to be useful through social work.[17] Varna had several big factories, the cotton factory having 600 workers. The first trade unions had appeared in the 1890s and they organized regular strikes for better working conditions, most effective among them being the union of printers. Especially dismal was the situation in the yarn factory, which had an Englishman as director. Mostly women and children worked a twelve-hour shift, the environment was unhygienic, there was constant harassment, and one girl was seduced and became pregnant by an English overseer. He was replaced and returned to England, but the girl received no compensation.[18]

When Koika's name was put up for the position of the secretary of the Varna party organization of the Narrows, a worker objected: "Women should stay next to the stove and should talk less." Koika, who had just come back from the huge meetings at which Lily Braun, Rosa Luxemburg, and Clara Zetkin spoke, was so shocked that she almost quit.[19] The party group conducted mostly educational activities. They organized a Sunday school where they discussed Kautsky's brochures. The most popular writer was Maxim Gorky whom they recited. The workers were mostly interested in the history of revolution: the French Revolution of 1789, the 1848 revolutions, the 1871 Paris Commune. They organized celebrations, first and foremost Labor Day, and gave political and art talks. An interesting detail is the advice that Vasil Kolarov, then a lawyer and popular speaker, gave them. Seeing that Koika's brother, who was well educated and cultivated, was gluing slogans on the walls, he told them that they should specialize in their efforts, not wasting their time, and focus on further educating themselves.[20]

At first the Varna party group had not a single factory worker; it consisted of intellectuals and craftsmen (shoemakers, tailors). Factory workers were cautious since they were warned that they would be fired if they were in contact with socialists, but by the time Koika Tineva joined, there were already some members who were factory workers. Initially, writes Tineva, the intellectuals were leading, but later they began sharing this role with the rising number of conscious and intelligent workers. This resulted in conflicts, especially over the election of delegates to the national party congresses. The intelligentsia could not properly understand its role, and the workers overestimated theirs.[21] It came to acrimonious complaints, and an official team from the Sofia CC was sent to investigate the issue.[22]

It was at this time, in 1905, that the aforementioned split and expulsion of the so-called "anarcho-liberals" occurred. Georgi Bakalov was the most prominent figure in the Varna organization with a national profile as member of the CC and with enormous influence due to his publishing activities. Tineva describes the conflict in a neutral tone, but it is clear where her sympathies lie. She writes that the accusations against the intelligentsia were based neither on theory nor on practical issues but were entirely personal. She gives the example of the complaint that the party calendars had been dispatched to the address of an intellectual and not to a worker. She was personally attacked for underestimating the proletariat. While she takes no stand on

Figure 46 Koika Tineva in Varna, 1904.

the problem of control of the party press which cost Bakalov his party membership, she gives brief and altogether positive portraits of the "liberals."[23] The result was the disbanding of the Varna organization and the formation of an educational group as part of the Narrows, with some twenty-seven members: twenty-one were workers, and four were women, among them Koika Tineva. Despite her closeness to the Bakalov group (of which Nikola Kharlakov was a member), she and her comrades refused to organize a common celebration with the "liberals."[24] By then, her romance with Sakarov was heading toward her wedding in 1906, but Tineva does not mention it at all. She relocated to Sofia where Sakarov was based.

Her subsequent memoirs of the Sofia organization, of which she was a member between 1906 and 1908, are written in an official jargon, describing strikes and propaganda, full of newspaper articles and official documents.[25] Given the central role Tineva played in the faction of the "progressists," which was expelled from the party in 1908, it may be startling that she has little to say about it. And again, there is no mention of Sakarov, one of the leaders of the so-called "progressists." However, keeping in mind that her reminiscences and other notes were penned after the Second World War, when she was supposed to have already adopted the "correct" worldview, it should come as no surprise. In her brief autobiography, she sums up these years, which are not at all mentioned in her extended notes: "I was under the influence of west European social-democratic parties who had preserved their unity, despite some internal serious contradictions. At that time, not clearly cognizant of tactical and organizational issues and thinking that in a common party these contradictions could be solved, I became part of this group, which defended the union with the 'Broads.' This group, and I with it, was kicked out of the party."[26] "Anarcho-liberals" and "progressists" shared more in common than some minor differences. They both had a principled stand for allowing factions within the party against the tendency of centralization. "Minimum unanimity, maximum unity of action" was their slogan, and they championed freedom of opinion and the press, free from the control of the CC.[27] Their main goal was to bring the unification of the socialist movement after the 1903 split. They were the ones supported by Rakovski and Trotsky in their bid to unite the Bulgarian socialists in 1910–11. Both factions joined the Broads but as an autonomous left faction (*levichari*), and the majority of both factions left the Broad party and joined the communists in the early 1920s. The small differences concerned their attitude toward trade unionism, most of the "anarcho-liberals" sharing with the Narrows the stand against syndical neutrality and the progressists, as a whole, sharing the Broads' view of neutrality.[28]

The one exception from the Sofia period, where she displays emotion and gets into personal memories concerns the women's movement. In general, Tineva was taken aback by the attitude to the "Woman Question." On the one hand, she shared the view of the party that gender solidarity should not trump social and political allegiance, but, on the other hand, she was critical of the party's line toward women, something that continued to bother her in the 1950s when she penned her reminiscences:

> In our country, not a single socialist defended the view that women should be organized in a single united association for the attainment of their civic and political rights. No one shared the feminist view that women's first task, irrespective of their social class, should be to win these rights and after that as citizens with full rights, determine their place in political life. In a word, our party, from its very beginning did have a correct general attitude to this question but paid little attention to actual work among women and this in the face of numerous women filling the factories and enterprises as cheap labor.[29]

This underestimation was especially flagrant in 1908 when, at the Pleven congress a delegate was to be elected to the Stuttgart Congress and another to the International conference of women. Tineva was proposed for the latter since she would be in Stuttgart anyway at her own expense, but Blagoev forcefully countered the suggestion. They could have authorized Tina Kirkova, who was also to be there with her husband Georgi Kirkov, if the candidacy of Koika was objectionable, but no one was appointed. "It was clear that our comrades did not sufficiently value the significance [of the conference], so much so as this would not have incurred any expenses."[30] The condescension was shared by the leaders of the party. Tineva was teased by Kirkov about the involvement of women who, according to him, were interested in the party work only until they got married: "You will do the same, once you marry. You will hide in the home and will think that you are contributing some important work by caring about the comfort of your husband."[31] The sad thing is that Tineva actually accepted this verdict and never stood for these derided women: "I had the chance to observe some of the wives of even some of our leaders consider their participation in the movement in creating favorable conditions for their husbands. They were not even conscious of the absurdity and would unapologetically insist that they see their party duty in this."[32]

The decade between 1908 and 1917 remains "unremembered" and there is only one mention in the brief autobiography that the "progressives" entered the Broad party but left in 1915 disappointed at the Broad's support of the war. Tineva does not even mention her work as editor of the progressists' journal *Nachalo*; this is known from other sources.[33] For a few years she worked as an independent and was active in the trade unions. In 1917 she travelled to Stockholm (for the Third Zimmerwald conference—the final anti-war conference of the Second International) as a delegate of the Syndical Committee of the Bulgarian Trade Unions. It is the Stockholm episode that is described in some detail in her notes, as well as her subsequent travel to Russia with her uncle Christian Rakovski.

She went to Stockholm with Kharlakov and spent most of her time in the company of Rakovksi. She was thus present when one of her former idols—Axelrod—stormed into Rakovski's room the morning of October 26 (i.e., the day after the Bolshevik October revolution of the 25th) and shouted, "Russia is falling into the abyss!" maintaining that Lenin's policies were fatal for the country. By that time, however, Rakovski, a very close friend of Trotsky, had embraced the Bolshevik cause.[34] Rakovski was also visited by Parvus with whom they had been close friends. Parvus, who had become an advocate for the German side, restrained himself from speaking against the Russian Revolution and the conversation was on different international issues. What struck Koika most was Parvus's bragging about his wealth: "I thought it bizarre that at such an important, even fateful, moment for civilization, one could speak of petty insignificant issues. . . . When the whole world is shaking under the war, when so many victims are falling due to German imperialism, this person boasted of his millions that he had made at the expense of the German working class." He even offered Rakovski money, which the latter refused.[35]

Koika followed Rakovski to Petrograd where she had a brief encounter with Lenin and had warm reminiscences about Angelica Balabanoff who "was like a sister to me, and a mother to all arriving helpless ones."[36] The next nearly half a century of Tineva's life (she died in 1964) is covered by little more than a page in her short autobiography. After two years in Petrograd, she was back and in 1920 their group, that is, the "progressists," returned to the Narrows (after 1921, the Communist Party). In 1923 she travelled to an economic exhibition in the USSR with the permission of the CC and was there when the September Uprising took place. Not being able to return, she became a member of the Russian Communist Party and started work in the Bulgarian section of the Comintern. From 1925 to 1933 she was a referee in the International Women's Secretariat of the Executive Committee of the Comintern; from 1933 to 1935 she lectured in the Communist University of the West, and in 1936–37 worked as a translator and editor. In 1937 she was "dismissed from the party in connection with the arrest of my uncle, Christian Rakovski. This derailed me, and I had a nervous breakdown." She received a certificate for disability and worked in the Association of Invalids as a knitter. With the beginning of the war, she pleaded with the Bulgarian communists to put her to use and in 1943 was hired as a translator at the Institute for foreign languages. After 1946 she went back to Bulgaria "to devote myself to the full democratization of my country."[37]

There is no mention of Kharlakov (1874–1927) with whom she shared her political views and spent her life until his untimely death in Moscow. Kharlakov was a major but forgotten figure in the party. He had studied natural sciences in Kiev and participated in the Russian revolutionary movement in the 1890s. In 1902 he became a member of the CC of the SDP and after the 1903 split, sided with the Narrows. By 1905, however, he and Bakalov were expelled as leaders of the "anarcho-liberals" and in 1909 they joined the Broads as their left faction. Kharlakov edited *Proletarii*, *Delo,* and *Nachalo* (with Tineva) and by 1915 the group had left the Broad party. Between 1915 and 1919, he was a member of parliament as an independent socialist. He emigrated after 1923 to Moscow with Tineva, but after 1924 was sent to Vienna where he edited the organ of the Balkan Communist Federation *La fédération balkanique* and also became a member of the left-wing IMRO (united), which cooperated with the Comintern. A photograph with Koika in Moscow one year before his death is the only evidence in her memoirs about her association with him. (Figure 47)

Figure 47 Kharlakov and Tineva, Moscow 1926.

Strangely, Tineva does not mention Bakalov (1873–1939) during his Soviet period despite her closeness to him and his extremely prominent role in the movement. Arguably one of the (maybe the) most cultivated of socialist intellectuals, Bakalov had studied natural sciences in Geneva, was very close to the Plekhanov circle, and his great passion was literature and literary criticism. His career as a teacher in Bulgaria ended in a ban for life because of his political activities. His subsequent career, aside from his political leadership of, first, the Narrows, then, the "anarcho-liberals," and, later, the communists, was mostly literary. Bakalov emigrated in 1925, first to Vienna, and then to the Soviet Union where he became a member of the Russian Communist Party. Between 1926 and 1929, he worked in the Soviet trade mission in Paris, and between 1928 and 1932 in the "Marx–Engels–Lenin" Institute, He became a corresponding member of the Soviet Academy of Sciences, a rare distinction for a foreigner. He died in Sofia in 1939, where he spent his last seven years. By the end of his life, he had written more than seventy books, authored over 1,300 articles, and had translated 700 works.[38] A fellow "anarcho-liberal," Petko Velichkov (1880–1969) who remained a Broad socialist, gives an almost saintly portrait of Bakalov as someone coming from a wealthy family, elegant, with an aristocratic air, but completely dedicated to the cause of the working class. He was extremely modest, generous, broad-minded, systematic, and a complete workaholic.[39] Kharlakov he characterized as very gifted, original, and passionate, but undisciplined and argumentative. Trotsky delivered a eulogy at Kharlakov's funeral.[40]

In Bulgaria Koika Tineva was reinstated in the party and worked as editor in the publishing house of the BCP. She published numerous articles on different revolutionaries and a book about Gavril Georgiev, whom she specially admired since he was the favorite of her father who thought the other socialists around his brother-in-law Rakovski were too immodest and self-assured.[41] She reconnected with her siblings, both of whom had been socialists. Tiniu, the older brother, had withdrawn from the movement but was always progressive; the younger Georgi was an active communist but honest and highly critical, so ended up as a janitor in the workers' club in Varna. Her sister Maria was active in the anti-fascist resistance but was very modest and never became a formal party member.[42] Koika Tineva died in 1964 in Sofia.

The Shaping of a Romantic (Male) Feminist

In many ways, Nikola Sakarov (1881–1943) was luckier than Koika, having never experienced the realities of utopia. He donated his enormous library to the Bulgarian Academy of Sciences and left a vast archive housed today at the Central State Archives, much of which postdates the First World War. There are, however, a number of documents that shed light on his youth. Five years before his death at sixty-five, Sakarov decided to write his memoirs. Both his parents had passed away at age sixty-seven, and Sakarov thought that his father, who died from stomach ulcer (most likely cancer) could have lived another ten years had he not smoked and drunk so much. Sakarov himself was a teetotaller and non-smoker.[43] His autobiography is penned in an orange notebook, written in several types of ink. It is unfinished and twenty-five

Figure 48 Koika Tineva, 1960s.

pages later ends abruptly in half a sentence. It is unclear whether it was ever copied or typed but it had been clearly intended for future publication. It begins with Sakarov's credo about how to write memoirs: "16 February 1938. I decided to write down a brief autobiography of my life and of my social-political and educational-cultural activities. To state, admit and even consciously emphasize the facts of my activity. First and foremost, the historical truth. It is this truth which has to lead the author of memoirs, whatever they are."[44] He was fond of reading memoirs but was hugely irritated by the tendency to hide mistakes, as well as outright lies: "Only people who don't act, don't struggle, don't work make no mistakes." He was disgusted by Mikhail Madzharov, who was eighty-five at the time and did not acknowledge a single mistake in his long life but "writes constantly about morality in politics and life, yet he is worthy of his sobriquet of the Byzantine and Beelzebub."[45]

Nikola Sakarov was born in Sofia on September 4, 1881. His father, Ilia Sakarov, had prospered as an artisan and merchant, maker of fur caps (*kalpakchia*), and furrier. He had a reputation of being an honest businessman, but his reputation was based more on his ebullient character. He left his business to be taken care of by relatives and friends, became a well-known public figure, and for ten years was a municipal councilor and vice-mayor. Being a lifelong member of the Liberal Party, after 1886 the People's Liberal Party, he was a staunch follower of Stambolov and shared the prime minister's nationalism and Russophobia. Very sociable, he would attend political meetings of different formations, including the socialist ones. He respected Blagoev, Sakîzov, Dzhidrov, and, especially, Kirkov whom he called "the wisecracker." Socialists would tease him: "Come on, uncle Ilia, we'll make you a socialist." "No," he would respond, "I am a stambolovist. Just to hear what you are saying." When his socialist son Nikola was about to speak, he would quip: "I know, he will bark too."[46]

There are comparatively few letters and documentation of the prewar period, among them a letter sent by the fifteen-year-old Nikola to his father in 1896, from the elite Commercial High School in Svishtov. Written in a highly official style, typical for the patriarchal relations of the time, it gives thanks for the clothes and money Nikola was sent and gives information on the curriculum: "Here, father, they pay greatest attention to the acquisition of languages, so I study a lot of French and German."[47] This training served him well when young Nikola went to Berlin and enrolled in the philosophical faculty of the Friedrich-Wilhelm University, where he studied political economy, finance, and statistics. He graduated in 1904 with a dissertation on the industrial development of Bulgaria.[48] The work was divided in two parts with an overview of the period before and after independence, and had separate chapters on the decline of handicrafts, the development and decline of home industry, on the reform policies, and the rise of industry. The dissertation is dedicated to his fiancée: "Meiner Braut." This is the only mention of Koika Tineva (without her name) in Sakarov's archive, aside from the divorce papers.

Were it not for one item in his archive that was luckily deposited alongside the hundreds of pages describing his political views and dozens of books and articles on economic and social issues, one would remain with the impression of an extremely thoughtful, upright, and disciplined human being, completely in control of his emotions, even to the point of suppressing them. One could then perhaps dare speculate about the reasons Koika left him for the dashing Kharlakov. But this item certainly belies any hasty supposition of lack of emotion or even inability to express it. It is a handmade tiny little album, in fact a herbarium, of about forty pages, around 8 to 10 cm (3 by 4 inches) with pressed flowers. (Figure 49) Half the pages are inscribed with poems by Heinrich Heine, the other half with entries in Bulgarian about the meaning of love. While not dated, the little album clearly stems from Nikola's student years in Berlin. The Bulgarian texts are not expressly referenced. They could be translations, or unacknowledged quotes, or Sakarov's own musings. One entry proclaims, "When love is strong and has united two creatures in a sacred and angelic union, they have found the secret of life; they have become the two sides of one and the same fate; the two wings of the same spirit. Love and fly!" Another reads, "You, who suffer because of love, love even stronger! To die from love means to live from it." A third

Figure 49 Pages from the herbarium.

concludes philosophically: "If no one in this world would love, the sun would expire."⁴⁹ Sentimentality was the twin of the socialist sentiment.

Sie sprechen eine Sprache,	Ich glaub nicht an den Himmel,
Die ist so reich, so schön;	Wovon das Pfäfflein spricht;
Und keiner der Philologen	Ich glaub nur an dein Auge,
Kann diese Sprache verstehn.	Das ist mein Himmelslicht.
They speak a language,	I don't believe in the sky
Rich and lovely,	that the preacher speaks about.
And no philologist	I only believe in your eye,
Can understand it.	It is my heavenly light.

In Berlin Sakarov was the secretary of the Bulgarian social-democratic group. His encyclopedia biographies mention that he became a member of the BWSDP (n) in 1904, but in a one-page handwritten note from 1939 Sakarov states that he has preserved all the eleven cards (booklets) of his party membership from 1902 until 1923. He entered the social-democratic party as a student in Berlin in 1902; after the split in 1903, joined the Narrows; from 1908 until 1920 was in the united social-democratic party (the Broads); from 1920 to 1922 was independent, and from 1922 until the middle of 1923 was a member of the Communist Party. After 1923 he did not have any party affiliation.⁵⁰ A typed "authorized" biography from 1938, but amended by Sakarov, summarizes his career. Upon his return from Berlin, he was immediately employed by the Ministry of Finance as vice-head and later head of the department for state and personal accounting. He left the ministry in 1911 (coinciding with the break with Koika) and dedicated himself to public life. In the course of fourteen years, from 1911 to 1925, he was regularly elected as a municipal councilor and beginning in 1913 was an MP (in 1914, 1919, 1920, 1923, and 1938). He had the reputation of an excellent orator and was considered the fastest speaker in Parliament since the creation of independent Bulgaria in 1878.[51] His hobbies were reading works in sociology, philosophy, history, and economic geography. The biographer ended with a description of Sakarov as being "modest, honest, cordial and an abstainer, who does not know the atmosphere of taverns and coffee bars." To which Sakarov added in ink "and he does not smoke."[52]

Sakarov authored and co-authored works on economic, social, and political problems. Besides his dissertation, published in Germany but not translated into Bulgarian, he wrote a work on the Bulgarian state finances (1918).[53] Many of his hour-long speeches in parliament were issued in separate brochures, such as on taxing policies and on budget issues, in which he advocated for the nationalization

Figure 50 Nikola Sakarov, 1917.

of banks and insurance as well as higher taxes on share capital.[54] So were his lectures and articles on the five-year plan of the USSR, in which he offered a balanced analysis of Soviet policies in industry, agriculture, and commerce, admiring the achievements but critical of the methods, and skeptical specifically of the possibility of socialism on a national basis.[55] There were books on the tactics of social democracy and the position of the International toward the war.[56] And a crucial work was the co-authored polemical *Attempts to Illuminate the Ideological Muddle* (1929), which took stock of the workers' movement.[57]

But all was not only work. Sakarov sent numerous postal cards and notes to his second wife Elena Sakarova, née Pîntova. The first ones are from 1919 and the last from 1940; they are regular but very brief. Most give concise information on his lectures in Bulgaria, his travels in France, Germany, Italy, the United States, Greece, Turkey, Poland, Czechoslovakia, Austria, and Switzerland.[58] Especially interesting are his cards from Moscow and Kiev during his 1939 visit to the USSR. Sakarov was staying at the hotel "National," and sent a card on October 20, 1939, after a visit to the Volga-Moscow Canal: "A spectacular technical achievement. I was on a luxury steamer. It was rather chilly but warm inside. Last night I went to see the opera 'Boris Godunov.' A majestic performance. Twice I went to the theater. Divine performances. Visited Lenin's museum and his mausoleum. The mausoleum has a magnificent architecture, with assorted marble plates."[59] A couple of notes sent by courier attest to a warm relationship: "Lenichka, if you are well, come 5 or 10 minutes after 7 pm, between the palace and the military club; we'll go to the theater to listen to *The Gypsy Baron*." Another tells her to wait for him at home. He'll fetch her at 7:30 and they will visit a friend. Elena, who was a consummate pianist, should choose what she would play and take along her sheets of music.[60] Sakarov was a great speaker and gentle soul, but far from a verbose epistolographer.

Sakarov's archive is invaluable for shedding close and direct light on the motives of the internal critique within the Narrow party that is usually obfuscated in the condescending and defensive party literature upholding the official party line.[61] More importantly, his own views were articulated during the interwar period when these frictions were ongoing but were not censored. In a letter he published in the newspaper *Zora* in 1926 he stated:

> The struggles in the socialist movement interest me passionately, because I know well not only the issues but also the individuals in the opposing camps. I have my convictions about both but am not taking sides. Whenever I have been asked about my opinion from both sides, I have advised them to avoid splits at any cost. The regrouping must occur within the party. The debates about ideas and tactics must be confined within the party. I have lived through four splits in this movement since 1903. During the first one I was abroad and so my participation was academic. During the splits of 1905, 1908 and 1920 however, I was an active participant. I know both my own sins and the sins of others. I know the role of the painfully ambitious leaders, I know how you burn a house to get rid of the mouse, I know and see the ruin of the workers movement.[62]

While the serious differences concerned the understanding of intra-party democracy and centralization, particularly the consent to the existence of factions, what is most surprising is the extent to which the notions of "intellectual" (интелигентски) and "intelligentsia" are used as terms of abuse by both opposing camps. In a leaflet from December 2, 1905, the Narrows were characterized as "a tightly fused intellectual bureaucracy which, having taken the leading positions in the party, has placed its own individualistic aspiration higher than the interests of the party. The weak presence of workers has allowed the development of these authoritarian ambitions among this handful of individualists."[63] This corresponded to the ideology of the group around *Proletarii* (the "anarcho-liberals") who had sided with the Narrows in 1903 but now found that with the strengthening of the workers' movement, their excessive organizational rigidity limited workers' access to the party.[64] They were also critical of the Broads and their organizational looseness but thought that their work among the labor classes had been a positive corrective. Therefore, Bakalov concluded that "both the philosophy of the common cause [the codeword for the Broads–MT] and the intellectual socialism [the codeword for the Narrows–MT] were equally harmful for the workers' movement. . . . The party has to be transformed from an intellectual (*inteligentska*) party to a workers' one."[65] Accordingly, they saw their mission in creating an authentic proletarian party not by forming a third socialist party but by working for the unification of the Broads and Narrows.[66] The 1905 leaflet announced that the group would leave the Sofia organization which had "numbed the brains of the intellectual bureaucrats (интелигенти бюрократи)" with its anti-workers activity "typical of all intellectual (интелигентска) dictatorship."[67]

> The conflict between the working class and the party, between the workers' intelligentsia and the individualistic intelligentsia of the party bureaucracy is not a conflict between the working class and socialism but between proletarian discipline and intellectual bureaucratism, a conflict between the bottom-up trust and the top-down trust, a struggle between the authentic dictatorship of the proletariat and the intellectual dictatorship. Down with the coterie! Down with the intellectual dictatorship.[68]

Naturally, the response of Blagoev was symmetrical, that these accusations were the result of the ambitions of a few intellectuals (интелигенти).[69] All of this may be downplayed as just the typical rhetorical bickering between intellectuals, all of whom genuinely desired to become a workers' party like their inspiring German model, but it laid the grounds for the future anti-intellectualism and they became their own gravediggers.[70] There are relatively few materials about Sakarov's own activities as a leader of the "progressists." At a meeting in which he was speaking in front of an overfilled auditorium, skirmishes followed the attempt by activists of the Narrows to disrupt the meeting.[71] There are also a number of letters from Christian Rakovski about the Balkan Wars, the parliamentary elections, and about the publication of *Napred*, which Rakovski sponsored financially.[72] Most of the left wing of the Broads had left the party at the beginning of the war in 1915, but Sakarov stayed as their MP until 1920. For a year there was speculation that he would form a new party but in December 1920, he wrote a letter in *Rabotnicheski vestnik* explaining that the revolutionary movement of the proletariat was in no need of new parties but needed to be united:

> Today I do not belong organizationally to the Communist Party. Ideologically, however, I wholeheartedly belong to it. The sooner the forces of the proletariat unite under the banner of the Third International, the closer will be its decisive victory. Today, participating or helping directly or indirectly any other bloc in the decisive battle against capitalism and imperialism, for the triumph of revolutionary socialism, would mean a fight against the proletarian revolution.[73]

A month later he was already a member of the BCP. His decision was reinforced by his understanding that the party was entirely dedicated to only legal forms of struggle. At a moment when Russia had adopted the New Economic Policy (NEP) after the disaster of war communism, when the country felt the consequences of the imperialist intervention and civil war, when there was talk of cooperation with the democratic forces within the bourgeoisie, "the party started to understand that the world revolution, such as they imagined it in 1919, and such as was propagated by the decisions and manifestos of the Third International, is impossible."[74] After the coup of June 9, 1923, which toppled the agrarian government of Stamboliiski, he sided with the decision of the party to observe "neutrality" and avoid a military clash:

> After June 9, the leaders of the party always told me that we should in no way take up arms. Vasil Kolarov, who was then in Sofia, was of the same opinion. He seems to have wavered after Zinoviev, then the leader of the Communist International, condemned the party for not supporting Stamboliiski and not participating in revolutionary actions. . . . I was asked by the Central Committee and personally by Kolarov to intercede with the government and allow him to go back to Russia, in order to explain the situation in Bulgaria and insist on legal actions. I did so in good faith. It turned out that I was misled, or rather, that some [of the leaders] were ready to satisfy Moscow's instructions despite their inner conviction against revolutionary actions.[75]

Georgi Dimitrov and Khristo Kabakchiev too had defended the stand of the party immediately after June 9 but eventually altered their position, wanting "to save the party's prestige in front of the Moscow International."[76] The result was the fiasco of the September Uprising. Participants told Sakarov later how Dimitrov and Kolarov deserted from the battlefield and emigrated to Yugoslavia, "leaving thousands of victims with the hope that the movement would intensify."[77] Sakarov believed, and this belief was widely shared, that any revolutionary move would be reckless, now that the government had stabilized itself: "Whoever shared the view not to act after June, is committing a crime by the decision to act in September."[78] He was arrested on September 12, ten days before the uprising, with hundreds of other communists, among them the old and ailing Blagoev, Kabakchiev, Bakalov, Muletarov, and others.

None of them had been aware of the "revolutionary instructions."[79] As Sakarov later reminisced:

> Arrested were the most moderate, high minded and judicious activists that had heretofore led the party. Deprived of its leadership, the party members were in the hands of lesser, but younger and adventurous elements. Adherents of the "audacious actions," they now had the free hand and executed a coup not only in the Communist party but in the tactics of the Bulgarian workers' movement. These elements were led by some members of the Central Committee: Vasil Kolarov, Georgi Dimitrov and Todor Petrov. The reckless and disastrous September uprising, to which acceded almost exclusively the rural party organizations and groups, was the first act of these extreme elements who, led by Kolarov and Dimitrov, had seized the party leadership.[80]

After the bloody quashing of the revolt, the arrested communists were released and during the parliamentary election in November, the communists won eight seats. Seven of them, led by Sakarov, decided to create an independent labor group within the parliament as party representatives. They all came with mandates from their electorate to continue the legal struggle. On December 24 Sakarov gave a speech in which he dissociated himself and the whole group from the uprising and from conspiratorial activities.[81] Before this he had met representatives of the new CC in which they insisted that he accept the decisions of the Comintern and not denounce the uprising. Two days after his speech, on December 26, Sakarov was expelled from the party.[82] Two days before his speech, Sakarov had visited Blagoev on December 22 to consult with him. Blagoev was bedridden and he would pass away a few months later, on May 7, 1924. Sakarov asked him three questions:

1. Would he still support his view that the revolution in Bulgaria depended three-quarters on external circumstances, and only one-quarter on internal ones? He responded nervously, "Yes, yes, yes, and now even more than before." I added, now the three-quarters had become four-fifths. He agreed.
2. Can we allow communists who emigrated to Yugoslavia to become, even unintentionally, instruments of a foreign country, moreover a country which had quashed its own communist movement in 1920-1921? Isn't this a betrayal? Immediately and trembling, he answered: "it is a betrayal, yes, it is a betrayal."
3. Since it is clear, that the party will be banned, would it not be wise to assemble the scattered workers in a legal party that would start from the beginning? Unhesitatingly, he said: "You have to create such a party, but make sure not to split and most importantly, gather the old ones and do not allow the young ones to meddle too much."[83]

Following the tragic bombing of 1925, in which 128 people of the political and military elite were killed, Sakarov added:

> The September events in 1923 and the villainy at "Sveta Nedelia" [Cathedral] were the crowning acts of a reckless policy. They devastated me to such extent that I am

still overwhelmed. My belief in legal, upright, honest work, against the poisonous demagogy and against conspiratorial work... was not heard. Everything collapsed, and I was desolate, because I saw and felt what was being destroyed in the souls of the decent idealists.... Many values of our past struggles and tactics have to be reevaluated. I have done that for myself. I wish both friends and opponents to do the same in the interest of the people and the state.[84]

Iordan Panov, a member of the Military Organization, was surprised by the April bombing and wrote that in Sofia no communist believed that this was ordered by the BCP; they thought it was an anarchist act. Panov felt that it was the lack of coordination between the political and military branch of the party that led to the fatal decision and the subsequent decimation of the party.[85] But the decision was definitely taken by the leadership of the Military Organization which by that time had completely sidelined the CC; indeed, the Military Organization was "not a party within the party: it was the party."[86] Sakarov himself was spared the tragic fate of many communists and leftists because he took refuge in the house of his brother-in-law, Ianko Stoianov, a cabinet minister who despite the pressure did not give him up. General Protogerov came personally to ask for him and declared he would slaughter 2,000 communists, guilty or innocent, because of the terrorist attack.[87] After 1925 Sakarov withdrew from political life, and until 1931 gave public lectures on different economic issues as an independent public figure. Critical as he was of the decisions of the party, his clear-eyed verdict was that "with the strengthening of the prospects for a socialist victory, it is not the proletariat, but the bourgeoisie that abandoned the legality that it had established itself, and began to refute democracy and parliamentarism, by turning to different forms of dictatorship and violence against the victorious progress of the proletariat."[88] In 1931 he was appointed Governor of the Bulgarian Agricultural Bank (after 1934, the Bulgarian Agricultural and Cooperative Bank), where he tried to mitigate the effects of the crisis in agriculture by extending cheap credit and encouraging the cooperative movement. All through his later years, he was active as a journalist, mostly in the socialist press (*Novo vreme, Rabotnicheski vestnik, Napred, Nachalo, Delo, Borba, Narod, Sotsialdemokrat, Rabotnichesko delo,* and *Obshtestvena misîl*), and, after 1925, writing on economic problems (*Ikonomicheski zhivot,* the *Journal of the Bulgarian Economic Society, Samoupravlenie,* and others).[89]

In his unpublished memoirs from the 1950s, Kiril Dramaliev (1892–1961), communist minister of education (1947–52), and, later, ambassador to Poland (1942–54) and the German Democratic Republic (1956–58), gave a patronzing (if not arrogant) assessment of Nikola Sakarov as a living encyclopedia with a phenomenal power of memory but "a vacillating, unsatisfied and unsteady individual who could not find his place." If he had lived through 1944, Dramaliev mused, he could have become an excellent minister of finance: "When there was a firm and respected hand to lead him, like the legal party, his knowledge could be creatively employed. But left without control, at a crossroads, he was rambling between the two irreconcilable sides."[90] Sakarov may have been lucky to have died in 1943. He was just sixty-two, five years younger than his father, the hefty smoker and drinker, had been when he passed away. One particular engagement merits emphasis. Sakarov was active in the "High School for Social Studies" (Висша социална школа) as part of the Bulgarian Women's

Union. This school operated throughout the period between its foundation in 1933 and 1944 and was inspired and supported by the German Academy for Women's Social and Education Work, founded in 1925 by Alice Salomon in Berlin. It was recognized by the Ministry of Education in 1936 as a college (*poluvisshe zavedenie*). Sakarov read lectures on contemporary social and economic problems.[91] He remained a "feminist" until his end, although probably less romantic.

Coda

This book seems to be ending on a melancholy note. Most of the lives I was trying to recover from oblivion were inspired by a "utopia of the future" and were attempting to live their lives according to its ideals. Insofar as they conformed to these ideals, one can simply define them as idealists. Many of the older ones among this political generation completed their voyage through life in the interwar decades, before the advent of "utopia on earth." Many, especially among the younger generation (born after the turn of the century) who grew up in the interwar period, gave their lives for it, others survived and tasted the utopia of state socialism. Again, some were persuaded by it, whereas others were disappointed and paid with their lives. Still others reserved a skepticism toward the praxis but preserved their belief in the ideal with the proverb "Because of our John, let us not blame Saint John." By confining my narrative and analysis to the first generation (the cohorts born before 1900), I do not wish to pass judgment on how they conducted their lives and least of all to posit that there existed liberal, tolerant, legal socialists who were displaced by intolerant and terrorist communists. As George Lichtheim wisely observed, "the principle that men make their history under definite conditions, imposed upon them by their surroundings and by the structure of their society, holds good for us all, including those of us who believe that acceptance of this truth paradoxically offers a means of evading its full consequences."[1]

All generations that were pursuing some kind of socialist ideal imagined a better future and a better human being creating a better society. This is the place where I am bound to explain my use of "imagining" in the title. It was not a concept I worked with from the outset and I avoided it as a central concept not because it was not apposite. On the contrary, it has been profitably used in a newly published collective volume on *Socialist Imaginations* that I liked very much. The volume works with this concept in order to "emphasize the collective and dynamic aspect of socialism's creativity, which has not been fully explored in work on 'political imaginaries' and socialist utopianism."[2] Juxtaposing it to ideology, which "connoted systemic and disciplined thought," imagination was meant "to conjure its unruly, exuberant, and unpredictable side," to bring in "the warm current that besides the cold current of critical analysis makes up Marxist socialism."[3] Interestingly, practically all contributions in this volume scrupulously avoid the concept of "emotion," while freely working with "dream," "fantasy," "wish," "desire," "passion," "aspiration," "anticipation," and "hope," to me all a rich array of powerful emotions. I cannot explain the hostility to (or at least the painstaking avoidance of) emotion, but at least I can explain my preferences. In Part III, I very consciously wanted to engage with the literature on the emotional turn, precisely because in its most sophisticated iterations it avoids binaries and does not oppose "emotion" to "ideology," the warm to the cold, the fluid to the structured. In addition, "imagination" itself can be organized, planned, logical, and even dogmatically overstructured.

If I have sparingly used, but not avoided, the concept of imagination, it is not because I have a quarrel with the concept. Once clearly explained, any concept can be successfully applied. I was shying away from the gerund "imagining," especially in the title, in order to avoid the obvious parallel to my previous work "Imagining the Balkans." In fact, my initial title was "Living utopia" which I meant as "to live one's utopia." But I could not insist on the use of "living" as a verb, without at the same time acknowledging the alternate reading as an adjective, with its implication of an actualized, living utopia, a subject in its own right that would have displaced or at least overshadowed the human subjects of my work. Settling on "imagining" gave me the opportunity to disentangle the meanings but it also forced me to reflect on the trajectory of my work from "imagining the Balkans" to "imagining Utopia." My desire to distinguish between the projects should not obscure the similarities, however. *Imagining the Balkans* was incubated within resentment against the ghettoization of the region and a sense of ethical outrage against the debilitating effects of discursive essentializations. It operated on the level of a metadiscourse, historicizing and problematizing the discursive practices that generated and reproduced understandings of the Balkans. Individual contributions within such an approach accrete and disappear within a structural framework which analytically can be traced through its imbedded logics. The last chapter on realia and *qu'est-ce qu'il y a hors de texte* notwithstanding, that work's power remains its discursive exegesis.

The elevation/excavation of the life of the early socialists is a similarly motivated emancipatory project that, at its most inductive limit, problematizes generalized ideological descriptions that rely on the silencing and erasure of the liminal. Yet, in between these projects one can insert another of the themes that has preoccupied my thinking, namely the concept of scaling. Within the present work discursive imagination is individualized, with all the resultant consequences. It is a difference in the level and character of analysis which requires a different set of tools. The top-down examination of interpellation to the individual level is reversed/foregone in favor of individual close-ups, emphasizing how thought/emotion shapes one's individual agency, in turn contributing to the habitus of utopia. The grounding in individuals, in the scale of the particular, is a methodology that provides a constant reminder against inference and terminological slippage. Different scales of analysis require different methods and are based on different sources. Working on a small scale, essentially producing a historical ethnography from the archive, inflects also the questions being asked and comes with specific implications. A central one is the possibility to fracture sweeping generalizations about ideology, to demonstrate the power dynamics between and within different ideological currents. The concrete empirical grounding highlights multiplicity and dissonance. It also allows to sweep away the generalizing hegemony of the dominant and showcase the significance of the liminal both on a regional and on the social and individual level. It moreover argues for a creative dialogue with the liminal in which it often has constitutive power. My socialists were imagining a world in which they wanted to live. For at the same time as one speaks of discursive frameworks being imagined, of a socialist imagination of think/feel, one necessarily has to account for the fact that for the Marxists among the socialists especially, socialism was not utopia. Even someone like Kołakowski, who was adamant about the desirable demise of utopia, still left the door open for socialism:

> This does not mean that socialism is a dead option. I do not think so. . . . And when I say "socialism" I do not mean a state of perfection but rather a movement trying to satisfy demands for equality, freedom and efficiency, a movement that is worth trouble only as far as it is aware not only of the complexity of problems hidden in each of these values separately but also of the fact that they limit each other and can be implemented only through compromises. We make fools of ourselves and of others if we think (or pretend to think) otherwise. All institutional changes have to be treated entirely as means at the service of these values and not as ends in themselves and be judged correspondingly, taking into account the price we pay in one value when we reinforce another one.[4]

Some forty years ago, when I lived under "real socialism" in Bulgaria, but especially after the crushing of the Prague Spring in 1968, I was taking seriously Max Weber's much cited adage from 1919 that the audacious Russian experiment would bereave socialism of its reputation and authority for a hundred years.[5] Whether Weber's dictum was borne out by reality can be a matter of debate, but even as someone who disliked and feared socialism, he pointed out its pivotal place and role as a social alternative in Europe before the First World War. Weber died in 1920 and could not foresee the peregrinations of socialism and witness the different moments at which believers acceded to his doubts: 1925, 1937, 1949, 1953, 1956, and 1968. Later, but especially after 1989, I began to realize the impoverishing nature of Weber's dictum. Not only was it presumptuous and dismissive of human agency, but it was also as monolithic as its Soviet foil. They both closed off the possibility of multiplicity. Now that we have reached and passed the centenary of "the audacious experiment," I think it is worth trying to rescue this multiplicity and argue for the groundedness of divergent "horizons of expectation."

I wish I had not read Zygmunt Bauman and could finish this book with my own words, but he expressed it best. So, here is the Gospel via Bauman:

> The body of utopian criticism is bound to remain, as before, inherently fissiparous. Men climb, as it were, successive hills only to discover from their tops virgin territories which their never-appeased spirit of transcendence urges them to explore. Beyond each successive hill they hope to find peacefulness of the end. What they do find is the excitement of the beginning. Today as two thousand years ago, 'hope that is seen is not hope. For who hopes for what he sees?' (Paul to the Romans, 8.24)[6]

Notes

Introduction

1 Jacques Attali, *Fraternités. Une nouvelle utopie* (Paris: Fayard, 1999), 132.
2 Ibid., 132–34.
3 Bernard Chavance, *Marx en perspective* (Paris: Editions de l'Ecole des hautes études en sciences sociales, 1985), 255, cited in Geoffrey M. Hodgson, *Economics and Utopia: Why the Learning Economy Is Not the End of History* (London and New York: Routledge, 1998), 5; Terry Eagleton, "Utopia and Its Opposites," *Socialist Register 2000: Necessary and Unnecessary Utopias*, vol. 36, 34, explains that Marxism did not reject the idea of a transfigured society but premised it on an interrogation of the present that reveals the alternative already implicit in it. See also Terry Eagleton, *Why Marx Was Right* (New Haven: Yale University Press, 2011), 64–106.
4 Private archive.
5 Michael D. Gordin, Helen Tilley, and Gyan Prakash, eds., *Utopia/Dystopia: Conditions of Historical Possibility* (Princeton: Princeton University Press, 2010), 2.
6 Enzo Traverso, *Left-Wing Melancholia: Marxism, History, and Memory* (New York: Columbia University Press, 2017), 61.
7 Stephen K. Kotkin, *Magnetic Mountain: Stalinism as a Civilization* (Berkeley: University of California Press, 1887).
8 Ernst Bloch, *The Spirit of Utopia*, trans. Anthony A. Nassar (Stanford: Stanford University Press, 2000) (this is the translation of the second revised edition from 1923: *Geist der Utopie: Bearbeitete Neuaufgabe der zweiten Fassung von 1923* (Frankfurt am Main: Suhrkamp Verlag, 1964).
9 Karl Marx, *The German Ideology* (Moscow: International Publishers, 1972), 65–67, https://www.marxists.org/archive/marx/works/1845/german-ideology/ch01a.htm.
10 Ernst Bloch, *The Principle of Hope*, trans. N. Plaice, S. Plaice, and P. Knight. 3 vols. (Cambridge, MA: The MIT Press, 1986) (original *Das Prinzip Hoffnung* [Berlin: Aufbau Verlag, 1954–1959], later multiple editions Suhrkamp).
11 Ernst Bloch, *Geist der Utopie* (München und Leipzig: Verlag Von Duncker & Humblot, 1918), 276, 372, 424, 443.
12 "Something's Missing: A Discussion Between Ernst Bloch and Theodor W. Adorno on the Contradictions of Utopian Longing," in Ernst Bloch, *The Utopian Function of Art and Literature: Selected Essays*, trans. Jack Zipes and Frank Mecklenburg (Cambridge, MA: The MIT Press, 1988), 16–17.
13 Bloch, *The Principle of Hope*, 445–46. See also Leo Panitch and Sam Gindin, "Transcending Pessimism: Rekindling Socialist Imagination," *Socialist Register 2000: Necessary and Unnecessary Utopias*, vol. 36, 1–29.
14 Ruth Levitas, "Marxism, Romanticism and Utopia: Ernst Bloch and William Morris," *Radical Philosophy*, 51, 1989, 28. See also Levitas, *The Concept of Utopia* (Syracuse: Syracuse University Press, 1990), especially chapter 5, and Levitas, "Educated Hope: Ernst Bloch on Abstract and Concrete Utopia," *Utopian Studies*, 1, no. 2, 1990, 13–26.

15　Bloch, *The Principle of Hope*, Introduction, 3–18, here 17–18.
16　Peter Thompson, "The Frankfurt School, part 6: Ernst Bloch and the Principle of Hope," *The Guardian*, April 29, 2013, https://www.theguardian.com/commentisfree/belief/2013/apr/29/frankfurt-school-ernst-bloch-principle-of-hope
17　Hodgson, *Economics and Utopia*, 4–12.
18　Written first in Hebrew in 1945 and published in 1946, the English translation appeared as Martin Buber, *Paths in Utopia*, trans. R. F. C. Hull (London: Routledge, 1949), 134, 148–49.
19　Thomas Nipperdey, "Die Funktion der Utopie im politischen Denken der Neuzeit," *Archiv für Kulturgeschichte*, 44, no. 3 (1962).
20　Adam Ulam, "Socialism and Utopia," in Frank E. Manuel, ed., *Utopias and Utopian Thought* (Boston: Beacon Pres, 1967), 134.
21　"Something's Missing: A Discussion Between Ernst Bloch and Theodor W. Adorno," 12–13.
22　Leszek Kołakowski, *The Death of Utopia Reconsidered* (The Tanner Lectures on Human Values, delivered at the Australian National University, June 22, 1982), 229–41, https://tannerlectures.utah.edu/_documents/a-to-z/k/kolakowski83.pdf
23　Ibid., 247.
24　Ralf Dahrendorf, *Reflections on the Revolution in Europe: In a Letter Intended to Have Been Sent to a Gentleman in Warsaw* (New York: Random House, 1990), 71.
25　François Furet, *The Passing of an Illusion: The Idea of Communism in the Twentieth Century*, trans. Deborah Furet (Chicago: University of Chicago Press, 1999) (original *Le passé d'une illusions: essai sur l'ideé communiste au XXe siècle* [Paris: Calmann-Lévy/Robert Laffont, 1995]); Fredric Jameson, *Archaeologies of the Future: The Desire Called Utopia and Other Science Fictions* (London: Verso, 2005). *What's Left? Prognosen zur Linken*. Rotbuch Taschenbuch 78 (Berlin: Rotbuch Verlag, 1993), especially the contributions of Norbersto Bobbio, Antje Vollmer, and Tony Judt; Slavoj Žižek, "From Revolutionary to Catastrophic Utopia," in Jörn Rüsen, Michael Fehr, and Thomas W. Rieger, eds., *Thinking Utopia: Steps into Other Worlds* (New York and Oxford: Berghahn Books, 2005), 247–62.
26　Traverso, *Left-Wing Melancholia*, xiv, 2–3.
27　Beverley Best, "The Problem of Utopia: Capitalism, Depression, and Representation," *Canadian Journal of Communication*, 35 (2010), 498. Susan Buck-Morss, *Dreamworld and Catastrophe: The Passing of Mass Utopia in East and West* (Cambridge: MIT, 2000) makes a similar point, explaining the collapse of utopian innovation in Soviet Russia with the decision of Stalin to strive for Western materialism and compete with the anti-utopian capitalist West on Western terms. Already in 1976 Zygmunt Bauman had argued that the Soviet system had abandoned socialism as a critical utopia once it came to measure its own progress with a bourgeois measuring-rod—*Socialism: The Active Utopia* (Routledge Revivals) (New York: Routledge, 2010), first published in New York: Holmes and Meier Publishers, 1976, 47–62.
28　Lyman Tower Sargent, "The Necessity of Utopian Thinking: A Cross-National Perspective," in Rüsen, Fehr, and Rieger, *Thinking Utopia*, 1–14.
29　Jörn Rüsen, "Rethinking Utopia: A Plea for a Culture of Inspiration," in Rüsen, Fehr, and Rieger, *Thinking Utopia*, 280. For an interesting take on Chinese utopian vision, including socialist utopia, see Zhang Longxi, "The Utopian Vision, East and West," in Rüsen, Fehr, and Rieger, *Thinking Utopia*, 207–29. For other positive views, see David Harvey, *Spaces of Hope* (Berkeley: University of California Press, 2000); Rudolf Maresch and Florian Rötzer, *Renaissance der Utopie. Zukuftfiguren des 21. Jahrhunderts* (Frankfurt am Main: Suhrkamp Verlag, 2004); Krishnan Kumar,

Utopianism (Minneapolis: University of Minnesota Press, 1991). See also Arnhelm Neusüss, Hg. *Utopie: Begriff und Phänomen des Utopischen* (Frankfurt am Main and New York: Campus Verlag, 1986); Gregory Claeys and Lyman Tower Sargent, eds., *The Utopia Reader* (New York: New York University Press, 1999); Jay Winter, *Dreams of Peace and Freedom: Utopian Moments in the Twentieth Century* (New Haven: Yale University Press, 2008); Кирил Нешев, Сотирис Теохаридис. *Философия на утопиите* (София: Фабер, 2008).

30 Karl Mannheim, *Ideology and Utopia: An Introduction to the Sociology of Knowledge*, translated from the German by Louis Wirth and Edward Shils (New York: A Harvest Book-Harcourt, Brace and Company, 1936) (reprint in 1985), 192–211, 262–63. German original *Ideologie und Utopie* (Berlin: F. Cohen, 1929).

31 Levitas, *The Concept of Utopia*, 74–75; Mannheim, *Ideology and Utopia*, 205–11; George Lichtheim, *The Concept of Ideology and Other Essays* (New York: Vintage Books, 1967), 3–46.

32 Rowan Wilken, "Mannheim's Paradox: Ideology, Utopia, Media Technologies, and the Arab Spring," *The Fibreculture Journal*, no. 20 (2012), 179–80.

33 Paul Ricoeur, *Lectures on Ideology and Utopia* (New York: Columbia University Press, 1986), 258, cited in Wilken, "Mannheim's Paradox," 181.

34 Ricoeur, *Lectures on Ideology and Utopia*, 265–66, 299–300, cited in Wilken, "Mannheim's Paradox," 182.

35 Ricoeur, *Lectures on Ideology and Utopia*, 312, cited in Wilken, "Mannheim's Paradox," 183.

36 Lyman Tower Sargent, "In Defense of Utopia," *Diogenes*, 53, no. 1 (February 2006), 12. See also idem., *Contemporary Political Ideologies: A Comparative Analysis* (Belmont, CA: Wadsworth/Thomson Learning, 2006).

37 Ruth Levitas, *Utopia as Method: The Imaginary Reconstitution of Society* (New York: Palgrave Macmillan, 2013), xi, xix.

38 Bloch, *The Spirit of Utopia*, 237, italics in the original. Žižek also locates the utopian potential in a dream: "The easiest way to detect the ideological surplus enjoyment in an ideological formation is to read it as a dream and analyse the displacement at work in it" (Žižek, "From Revolutionary to Catastrophic Utopia," in Rüsen, Fehr, and Rieger, *Thinking Utopia*, 259).

39 As noted by Norberto Bobbio, "Die Linke und ihre Zweifel. Eine Bestandaufnahme," in *What's Left? Prognosen zur Linken*, 223, while in the past the Left might not have been entirely Marxist, it was wholly socialist. The decoupling from socialism is a later phenomenon of the end of the twentieth century with the coming of new challenges and new historical agents, primarily from the Third and Fourth Worlds.

40 Walter Benjamin, *Selected Writings*, ed. Marcus Bullock and Michael W. Jennings, vol. 1 (1913–926) (Cambridge, MA: The Belknap Press of Harvard University Press. 1996), 254.

41 Patrick Lagrange, an invented historian in Julian Barnes, *The Sense of an Ending* (New York: Vintage Books, 2012), 18.

Part I

1 Jacques Revel, ed. *Jeux d'échelles. La microanalyse à l'expérience* (Paris: Seuil, 1998). See also Bernhard Struck, Kate Ferris, and Jacques Revel, "Introduction: Space and Scale in Transnational History," *Size Matters: Scales and Spaces in Transnational and*

Comparative History, Special Issue, *International History Review*, 33, no. 4 (2011), 573–84.
2 Sebouh David Aslanian, Joyce E. Chaplin, Ann McGrath, and Kristin Mann, "How Size Matters: The Question of Scale in History," *American Historical Review*, 118, no. 5 (December 2013), 1431–72.
3 David G. Christian, "Macrohistory: The Play of Scales," *Social Evolution & History*, 4, no. 1 (March 2005), 22–59. See also David G. Christian, *Maps of Time: An Introduction to Big History* (Berkeley: University of California Press, 2004).
4 Jürgen Osterhammel, *The Transformation of the World: A Global History of the Nineteenth Century* (Princeton: Princeton University Press, 2014) (German original, 2009); Emily Rosenberg, ed. *A World Connecting, 1870-1945* (Cambridge, MA: The Belknap Press of Harvard University Press, 2012).
5 Braudel (1902–1985) and James (1901–1989) were contemporaries, and even their major and most influential works were conceived in the late 1930s. C. L. R. James, *The Black Jacobins: Toussaint L'Ouverture and the San Domingo Revolution* was first published in London by Secker & Warburg, 1938. Its revised edition came out in New York: Vintage Books/Random House, 1963. Braudel began research on the Mediterranean in 1937 but the war delayed his doctorate, and *La Méditerranée et le Monde Méditerranéen a l'époque de Philippe II*, appeared in Paris: Colin, 1949.
6 Michel Espagne, *Les transfers culturels franco-allemand* (Paris: PUF, 1999); Michel Espagne and Michael Werner, eds., *Transfers. Les relations interculturelles dans l'espace franco-allemand (XVIIIe et XIXe siècle)* (Paris: Editions recherches sur les civilisations, 1988); Heinz-Gerhard Haupt und Jürgen Kocka, eds., *Geschichte und Vergleich. Ansätze und Ergebnisse international vergleichender Geschichtsschreibung* (Frankfurt: Campus Verlag, 1996); Matthias Middell, *Kulturtransfer und Vergleich* (Leipzig: Leipziger Universitäts Verlag, 2000); Michael Werner and Bénédicte Zimmermann, "Histoire Croisée and the Challenge of Reflexivity," *History and Theory*, 45, no. 1 (February 2006). For an exhaustive bibliography on these trends, see Pekka Hämäläinen, "Crooked Lines of Relevance: *Europe and the People Without History* by Eric R. Wolf," *American Historical Review*, 123, no. 3 (June 2018), 875–85, especially notes 4, 5, 6, 7, and 8. In the literature entangled and connected histories are most often used synonymously to differentiate them from comparative history, but all three reflect global approaches. Connectedness, in particular, relies on transfers and connections, and gives precedence to mobility over place (see James Belich, John Darwin, Margret Frenz, and Chris Wickham, eds., *The Prospect of Global History* [New York: Oxford University Press, 2016], 13).
7 Eric J. Hobsbawm, *The Age of Revolution: 1789-1848* (New York: Vintage, 1996 [1962]); *The Age of Capital: 1848-1875* (New York: Vintage, 1996 [1975]); *The Age of Empire, 1875-1914* (New York: Vintage, 1996 [1987]).
8 Jeremy Friedman and Peter Rutland, "Anti-Imperialism: The Leninist Legacy and the Fate of World Revolution," *Slavic Review*, 76, no. 3 (Fall 2017), 593.
9 Patrizia Dogliani, "The Fate of Socialist Internationalism," in Glenda Sluga and Patricia Clavin, eds., *Internationalisms: A Twentieth-Century History* (Cambridge, UK: Cambridge University Press, 2017), 38.
10 Ibid., 59.
11 Ibid., 40–41.
12 Moira Donald, "Workers of the World Unite? Exploring the Enigma of the Second International," in M. H. Geyer and J. Paulmann, eds., *The Mechanics of Internationalism* (Oxford: Oxford University Press, 2001), 177–201.

13 Leszek Kołakowski, *Main Currents of Marxism* (Oxford: Clarendon Press, 1976), Vol. II. *The Golden Age*, 1. Patrizia Dogliani, by contrast, considers all the fifty years "from 1889 to 1939 as the *golden age* of the socialist international" (Dogliani, "The Fate of Socialist Internationalism," 49). For Albert S. Lindemann, *The 'Red Years': European Socialism vs. Bolshevism, 1919-1921* (Berkeley: University of California Press, 1974), 1, this was the "classic age" of European socialist parties.
14 James Joll, *The Second International, 1889-1914* (New York: Routledge, 1966), 5.
15 Stephen Bronner, *Imagining the Possible: Radical Politics for Conservative Times* (New York: Routledge, 2001), 181. See especially Georges Haupt, *La Deuxième Internationale 1884-1914. Étude critique des sources. Essai bibliographique* (Paris: Mouton, 1964).
16 This list is compiled, with some additions, from Geoff Eley, *Forging Democracy: The History of the Left in Europe, 1850-1900* (Oxford: Oxford University Press, 2002), 63. Gareth Stedman Jones gives 1884 for the English Social Democratic Federation and 1888 for the Austrian Social Democratic Party (*Karl Marx: Greatness and Illusion* [Cambridge, MA: The Belknap Press of Harvard University Press, 2016], 557).
17 Joll, *The Second International*, 122. See also Jacques Droz, ed. *Histoire générale du socialisme. Tome II: De 1875 à 1918* (Paris: Presses Universitaires de France, 1974), 459-504; Jack Ross, *The Socialist Party of America: A Complete History* (Lincoln, NE: Potomac Books, 2015); Paul Buhle, *Marxism in the United States: A History of the American Left* (London: Verso, 2013), first published in 1987.
18 Droz, *Histoire Générale*, Tome II, 513-29.
19 Ibid., 531-37.
20 Savkar Ghose, *Socialism and Communism in India* (Bombay: Allied Publishers, 1971), 1-8; Droz, *Histoire générale*, Tome II, 541-43.
21 Mete Tunçay and Erik Zürcher, *Socialism and Nationalism in the Ottoman Empire, 1876-1923* (London: British Academic Press in association with the International Institute of Social History, Amsterdam, 1994). In the late Ottoman Empire, socialist groups were mostly active among the minorities: Armenians, Bulgarians, and Jews. See also Paul Dumont, *Du socialism ottoman à l'internationalisme anatolien* (Paris: Gorgias Pr., 2011).
22 Cosroe Chaqueri, *Origins of Social Democracy in Modern Iran* (Seattle: University of Washington Press, 2001).
23 Emily Rosenberg, ed. *A World Connecting*, 154. To be fair, the mention of the "primitive and dark" forces comes from a lively and informative chapter on "The Human Zoo" by Charles Maier in which he ironically describes the evolution of states and governments from the 1870s to the First World War and how they mastered the "primitive forces of humanity," in this case the peasants of Eastern Europe. Yet, these peasant masses do not find any further mention in the narrative and are thus present only in this allegorical form. The Second International, on the other hand, is mentioned in a brief paragraph on page 207 (the author is again Maier).
24 Emily Rosenberg, ed. *A World Connecting*, 857 about the otherwise fascinating figure of Jean Jaurès and "his Second International" (author Emily Rosenberg).
25 Osterhammel, *The Transformation of the World*, 907.
26 Enzo Traverso, "Rethinking the Nineteenth Century. On Jürgen Osterhammel," *The Transformation of the World*," *Constellations*, 21, no. 3 (2014), 430.
27 *The Modern World System* (New York: Academic Press, 1974); *The Capitalist World-Economy* (Cambridge: Cambridge University Press, 1979); "World System Analysis: Theoretical and Interpretative Issues," in Terence Hopkins, Immanuel Wallerstein, and

Associates, eds., *World-Systems Analysis: Theory and Methodology* (Beverly Hills: Sage Publications, 1982).
28 Wallerstein, *World-Systems Analysis*, 17.
29 Christopher Chase-Dunn, "Comparing World-Systems: Toward a Theory of Semiperipheral Development," *The Comparative Civilizations Review*, 18 (1988), 29–66; Christopher Chase-Dunn, "Resistance to Imperialism: Semiperipheral Actors," *Review (Fernand Braudel Center)*, 13, no. 1 (1990), 1–31; Anna Klobucka, "Theorizing the European Periphery," *symplokē*, 5, no. 1/2 (1997), 119–35.
30 Chase-Dunn, "Comparing World-Systems," 31.
31 Osterhammel, *The Transformation of the World*, 78.
32 Susan Gal, "A Semiotics of the Public/Private Distinction," *Differences: A Journal of Feminist Cultural Studies*, 13, no. 1 (2002), 80.
33 Henrik Stenius, "Concepts in a Nordic Periphery," Willibald Steinmetz, Michael Freeden, and Javier Fernandez-Sebastian, eds., *Conceptual History in the European Space* (New York: Berghahn, 2017), 264.
34 Pamela Ballinger, "Whatever Happened to Eastern Europe? Revisiting Europe's Eastern Peripheries," *East European Politics and Societies and Cultures*, 31, no. 1 (February 2017), 61. Ballinger emphasizes that peripherality is an important concept in its various meanings and deployments, particularly the economic. She adds: "Likewise, the asymmetries of power inherent in the notion of periphery underscore the various forms of political, economic, and legal control, exercised by the EU over its borderlands. The periphery concept thus offers a particularly powerful lens through which to consider the recombinations and intersections of old distinctions— North versus South, East versus West—shaping the landscape of contemporary Europe."
35 Anna Lowenhaupt Tsing, "On Nonscalability: The Living World Is Not Amenable to Precision-Nested Scales," *Common Knowledge*, 18, no. 3 (2012), 505.

Chapter 1

1 Julius Braunthal, *Geschichte der Internationale* (Hannover: Dietz, 1961–1971) (3 volumes, of which the first is on the First and Second International, 1864–1914); Albert S. Lindemann, *A History of European Socialism* (New Haven: Yale University Press, 1983); William Smaldone, *European Socialism: A Concise History with Documents* (Lanham: Rowman & Littlefield, 2014); Eley, *Forging Democracy*; Joll, *The Second International, 1889-1914*. A "quantitative" exception is actually the most impressive and comprehensive history of socialism, initiated and published under the direction of Jacques Droz. True to the French tradition, it is a huge collaborative, but exclusively French, rather than a transnational undertaking. Published in four volumes between 1972 and 1978, it covers, respectively, the periods until 1875; 1875–1918; 1919–1945; and 1945 to the present. The Second International is the subject of volume 2 (674 pages). While explicitly recognizing the German hegemony in the International, the chapter on France is twice as big as that on Germany. Similarly, G. D. S. Cole, in his seven-volume *A History of Socialist Thought* (London: Macmillan, 1953–1960), who has a slightly different emphasis on intellectual history, gives disproportionate attention to Britain and Fabian socialism in the two parts of volume 3 on the Second International.

2 Joll, *The Second International*, 2–3, 11–13 and passim; Droz, ed. *Histoire générale, Tome II*, chs.1, 2, 3, 7, 8, 10, 11; Georges Haupt, "Model Party: The Role and Influence of German Social Democracy in South-East Europe," in *Aspects of International Socialism, 1871-1914: Essays by Georges Haupt*, trans. Peter Fawdett, with a Preface by Eric Hobsbawm (Cambridge: Cambridge University Press, 1986), 48–80; Georges Haupt, "Internationale Führungsgruppen in der Arbeiterbewegung," in *Herkunft und Mandat: Beträge zur Führungsproblematik in der Arbeiterbewegung* (Frankfurt-Köln: Europäische Verlagsanstalt, 1976).

3 Lars T. Lih, *Lenin Rediscovered: What Is to Be* Done? *In Context* (Chicago: Haymarket Books, 2008) (first published in Leiden: Brill, 2006): "I have coined the term Erfurtian to describe the bundle of beliefs, institutional models and political strategies that constituted orthodox Marx-based Social Democracy" (6).

4 Marek Waldenberg, *Il papa rosso Karl Kautsky* (Roma: Editori Riuniti, 1980). This is the Italian translation of *Wzlot i upadek Karola Kautsky Ego: Studium z historii myśli społecznej i politycznej* (Warszawa: Wydawn Literackié, 1972).

5 Georges Haupt, *Socialism and the Great War: The Collapse of the Second International* (Oxford: The Clarendon Press, 1972), 18 and passim.

6 This was the sense imparted by Thucydides in his History of the Peloponnesian War (see Perry Anderson, *The H-Word: The Peripeteia of Hegemony* [London: Verso, 2017], 1–3).

7 Anderson, *The H-Word*, 94. For an earlier critical interpretation of Gramsci, see Perry Anderson's "The Antinomies of Antonio Gramsci," first published in *New Left Review* in 1976, and published again in a reworked and expanded version as *The Antinomies of Antonio Gramsci: With a New Preface* (London: Verso, 2017), 90–97.

8 Annie Kriegel, "Le IIe Interntanionale (1889-1924)," in *Histoire générale du socialisme. Tome II*, 555.

9 Tony Judt, *Socialism in Provence, 1871-1914: A Study in the Origins of the Modern French Left* (Cambridge: Cambridge University Press, 1979), 306.

10 Ibid., 307.

11 Shahid Amin and Marcel van der Linden, eds., *"Peripheral" Labour? Studies in the History of Partial Proletarianization* (New York: Cambridge University Press, 1997, 1–3; Peter Worsley, *The Three Worlds: Culture & World Development* (Chicago: University of Chicago Press, 1984); Robin Cohen, "Workers in Developing Societies," in Hamza Alavi and Teodor Shanin, eds., *Sociology of "Developing Societies"* (London: Palgrave, 1982).

12 Balázs Trencsényi, Maciej Janowski, Mónika Baár, Maria Falina, and Michal Kopeček, *A History of Modern Political Thought in East Central Europe. Volume I. Negotiating Modernity in the "Long Nineteenth Century"* (Oxford, UK and New York: Oxford University Press, 2016), 446, 448. Tellingly the twenty pages devoted to socialist thought in an almost 700-page tome, is under the title "Socialism and Underdevelopment" (446–69).

13 Smaldone, *European Socialism*, 104.

14 Eley, *Forging Democracy*, 66.

15 G. D. S. Cole, *History of Socialist Thought*, vol. 3, part II, 586, 588.

16 Augusta Dimou, *Entangled Paths Toward Modernity: Contextualizing Socialism and Nationalism in the Balkans* (Budapest: Central European University Press, 2009), 13.

17 Droz, "Introduction," *Histoire générale, Tome II*, 12–14.

18 Ibid., 14. This "general consensus" is reproduced unerringly in Madelaine Ribérioux, "Le socialism et la première guerre mondiale (1914-1918)" in *Histoire générale*

du socialisme, 632 ff. who speaks of "European socialism and bolshevism" as if Bolshevism was not European and antedating by a good decade the appearance of "Western socialism" (but not yet European socialism) in the nomenclature. It occurs also in Dimou, *Entangled Paths*, who speaks of "an eastern variant of socialism" (19), and of a "Russian model" to be emulated (39). Equally, Trencsényi, Janowski, Baár, Falina, and Kopeček, *A History of Modern Political Thought in East Central Europe*, 466 neatly divide the influence of socialism in the 1870s and 1880s into "east" (read Russia) and "west," thereby reproducing and strengthening the fault lines between the Balkans and Habsburg Central Europe.

19 Karl Marx, *Capital*, vol. 1, Preface to the First German Edition, 1867, here cited from Karl Marx and Friedrich Engels, *Basic Writings on Politics and Philosophy*, ed. Lewis D. Feuer (New York: Anchor Books, 1959), 135.

20 Theodore Shanin, ed. *Late Marx and the Russian Road: Marx and the Peripheries of Capitalism* (New York: Monthly Review Press, 1983), 124. Plekhanov was critical of this stance of Marx. In his conversations with Stoian Nokov in 1893 he thought that Marx was unfamiliar with the Russian situation but never put it in writing: Central State Archive, Sofia (*Централен Държавен Архив*) further ЦДА, Фонд 186 Б, оп. 1, а.е. 212, л. 94–99.

21 Eley, *Forging Democracy*, 42, lists the main figures who alongside Kautsky, "the faithful mouthpiece" of Marx's authority, labored to systematize historical materialism and validate Marxism as a philosophy of history—Eduard Bernstein, Victor Adler, Georgy Plekhanov, Antonio Labriola— and finds them less dogmatic but sharing the same commitment.

22 Otto Brunner, Werner Conze, and Reinhart Koselleck, *Geschichtliche Grundbegriffe: Historisches Lexicon zur politisch-sozialen Sprache in Deutschland* (Stuttgart: Klett-Cotta, 1972–1997). See also Raymond Williams, *Keywords: A Vocabulary of Culture and Society*, Revised ed. (New York: Oxford University Press, 1983).

23 Wolfgang Schieder, "Kommunismus," *Geschichtliche Grundbegriffe*, Bd.3, 1982, 477, 488–94.

24 Schieder, "Kommunismus," 496.

25 Williams, *Keywords*, 288.

26 Ibid., 74, 288. For a view challenging the neglect of the religious dimension of Owenism, ascribing it to Engels, see Edward Lucas, "Religious Dreams of a Socialist Future: The Case of Owenism," in Stefan Arvidsson, Jakub Beneš, and Anja Kirsch, eds., *Socialist Imaginations: Utopias, Myths, and the Masses* (New York: Routledge, 2019), 41–61.

27 Schieder, "Kommunismus," 507.

28 Ibid., 510–11.

29 Schieder, "Sozialismus," *Geschichtliche Grundbegriffe*, Bd.5, 1984, 934–39, quote on p. 939.

30 Ibid., 940.

31 Williams, *Keywords*, 286.

32 Lorenz Stein, *Der Sozialismus und Communismus des heutigen Frankreichs. Ein Beitrag zur Zeitgeschichte* (Leipzig: Otto Wigand, 1842).

33 Schieder, "Sozialismus," 958.

34 Ibid., 965.

35 Ibid., 968–70.

36 Ibid., 994.

37 Otto Weininger, *Sex and Character: An Investigation of Fundamental Principles* (Bloomington, IN: Indiana University Press, 2005), 277.

38 Schieder, "Kommunismus," 516.
39 Ibid., 522.
40 Ibid., 529.
41 For a comparative synthesis of communism in the twentieth century, see Michel Dreyfus, Bruno Groppo, Caudio Sergio Ingerflom, Roland Lew, Claude Pennetier, Bernard Pudal, and Serge Wolikow, eds., *Le siècle des communismes* (Paris: Les Éditions ouvrières, 2000).
42 Thus, in response to Engels' attack, Dühring spoke of Marxocracy, Marxist scholastics, Marxotheocracy, Marxist authoritarian state despotism, Marxist social rabbinism, Marxist gadgetries, etc. Eugen Dühring, *Kritische Geschichte der National ökonomie und des Sozialismus* (Leipzig, 1979), cited in Rudolf Walther, "Marxismus," *Geschichtliche Grundbegriffe*, Bd.3, 1982, 948.
43 The book was published in 1878 as *Herrn Eugen Dührings Umwälzung der Wissenschaft*. The first complete English translation came out in 1907: *Herr Eugen Dühring's Revolution in Science*.
44 On the important differences between Marx, who tolerated but rarely endorsed the system-building ambitions of Engels, especially concerning *Anti-Dühring*, see Terrell Carver, *Engels: A Very Short Introduction* (New York: Oxford University Press, 2003), 55–60, 88–91.
45 Karl Kautsky, "Franz Mehring," *Die Neue Zeit*, 22, I, 1903/1904, 104; Carver, *Engels*, 56. Mehring was the author of perhaps the most influential biography of Marx published at his centenary in 1918, and on which he had worked for many years: *Karl Marx: The Story of His Life*, translated by Edward Fitzgerald and New Introduction by Max Shachtman (Ann Arbor: The University of Michigan Press, 1962). The literature on Marx is, of course, enormous, the latest addition being Michael Heinrich. *Karl Marx und die Geburt der modernen Gesellschaft* (Stuttgart: Schmetterling Verlag, 2018) (the English translation appeared in 2019 with Monthly Review Press, 2019).
46 It is known in two versions stemming from Engels in 1882: "Tout ce que je sais, c'est que moi, je ne suis pas marxiste" and "Ce qu'il y a de certain c'est que moi, je ne suis pas marxiste" (see Walther, "Marxismus," 950).
47 Walther, "Marxismus," 953.
48 Ibid., 954–55. See Haupt, "From Marx to Marxism," in *Aspects of International Socialism*, 1–22.
49 Droz, *Histoire Générale, Tome II*, 9.
50 Interestingly, Kautsky had started to work on a synthesis of Marxism and Darwinism, but between 1890 and 1914 he abandoned and even criticized the project as problematic, only to return to it again during his closing years.
51 *Marxism versus Social Democracy: The Revisionist Debate 1896-1898*, edited and translated by H. Tudor and J. M. Tudor, with an Introduction by H. Tudor (Cambridge: Cambridge University Press, 1988), 37. This conclusion is based on an extensive analysis and juxtaposition of the views of Marx and Engels, as well as the critiques from Parvus, Luxemburg, Bebel, and Kautsky, to those of Bernstein toward the revolution, democracy, the final goal of the socialist movement, class struggle, the tactics of legality, political collaboration, etc. Bernstein's standpoint is characterized as "not fundamentally Marxist. It was, rather, a form of socialism which drew its inspiration from the broader tradition of nineteenth-century radicalism to which (in Bernstein's view) Marx along with many other Socialists belonged" (36).
52 Lih, *Lenin Rediscovered*, 111 and passim. In Lih's definition "An Erfurtian is someone who accepts the SPD as a model party, accepts the Erfurt Program as an authoritative statement of the Social-Democratic mission, and accepts Karl Kautsky's

tremendously influential commentary on the Erfurt Program as an authoritative definition of Social Democracy" (6). He goes on to later speak of "Lenin's Erfurtian Drama" (387).
53 Lindemann, *The "Red Years,"* 1 and 11.
54 Karl Korsch, *Marxismus und Philosophie* (Frankfurt am Main: Europäische Verlagsanstalt, 1966), 42–50. Bizzarely, George Lichtheim attributes Lukács' (and also Gramsci's) views to an intuitive affinity between the Russian and Hungarian and Italian national traditions that were "a little outside the West European mainstream" (*Marxism: An Historical and Critical Study* [New York: Praeger, 1965], 368–69).
55 Maurice Merleau-Ponty, *Adventures of the Dialectic* (Evanston, IL: Northwestern University Press, 1973); Perry Anderson, *Considerations on Western Marxism* (London: New Left Books, 1976); Martin Jay, *Marxism and Totality: The Adventures of a Concept from Lukacs to Habermas* (Berkeley: University of California Press, 1984); Marcel Van der Linden, *Western Marxism and the Soviet Union* (Leiden: Brill, 2007); Korsch, *Marxismus und Philosophie*, 50, speaks of "west-European" communists, using inverted commas.
56 To his credit (and being by far the sole exception), Eley, *Forging Democracy*, speaks of Stalinism (not Eastern Marxism) and Western Marxism (249 ff.), and locates the split in the 1920s.
57 Lindemann, *The "Red Years,"* xiv, 300.
58 Ibid., xiv.
59 Joseph Rothschild, *The Communist Party of Bulgaria: Origins and Development, 1883-1936* (New York: Columbia University Press, 1959), 1. One should also add Nissan Oren's continuation of Rothschild's work *Bulgarian Communism: The Road to Power, 1934-1944* (New York: Columbia University Press, 1971) which adopts the same perspective (p. 3). John Bell's *The Bulgarian Communist Party from Blagoev to Zhivkov* (Stanford: Hoover Press, 1986) is a brief survey of 200 pages, which spends a mere 50 pages on the history until the Second World War as against the 350 of Rothschild's account until 1936. Nonetheless, it offers the most balanced and informed of all existing analyses.
60 Rothschild, *The Communist Party of Bulgaria*, 1–2. Gymnasium is used in the European sense of high school.
61 Петър Цанев, "Георги Кирков в Николаев, Русия (1879-1886)," *Известия на Института по История на БКП (ИИИ)*, 33 (1975), 369.
62 Rothschild is actually aware of this and adds that Sakîzov attended Huxley's lectures in London and Taine's in Paris, but this comes only on pages 11–12 to explain why Sakîzov became the main antagonist of the dogmatic and Russian-formed Blagoev.
63 Трендафил Митев, "Възникване и същност на 'широкия социализъм' в България," in Евгений Кандиларов, Таня Турлакова, ред. *Изследвания по история на социализма в България, 1891-1944*, том I. София: Фондация "Фридрих Еберт," Център за исторически и политилогически изследвания (2008), 78–79.
64 Rakovski's Bulgarian given name was Krîstiu but he has been known in the literature by this "westernized" rendition. The Romanian rendering of his name is Cristian. Further, I will follow the common usage of Christian.
65 Rothschild, *The Communist Party of Bulgaria*, 2–3.
66 For the internal splits, see more in Parts II and III.

67 Димитър Генчев, "Теоретичното и програмно развитие на българската социалдемокрация (1891-1919 г.)," in *Изследвания по история на социализма в България, 1891-1944*, том I, 31. Blagoev was expelled from the university in Russia. Unfortunately, the program perished when a fire burnt Blagoev's whole library.

68 Howard Quint, *The Forging of American Socialism: Origins of the Modern Movement: The Impact of Socialism on American Thought and Action, 1886-1901* (Columbia: University of South Carolina Press, 1953), 145–46.

69 Coined by Michel Espagne, "cultural transfer" was utilized first in the study of the circulation of knowledge between France and Germany: Michel Espagne, *Les transfers culturels franco-allemand* (Paris: PUF, 1999); Michel Espagne and Michael Werner, eds., *Transfers. Les relations interculturelles dans l'espace franco-allemand (XVIIIe et XIXe siècle)* (Paris: Editions recherches sur les civilisations, 1988). On comparative history, see Heinz-Gerhard Haupt und Jürgen Kocka, eds., *Geschichte und Vergleich. Ansätze und Ergebnisse international vergleichender Geschichtsschreibung* (Frankfurt: Campus Verlag, 1996). On the comparison between the two methods, see Matthias Middell, *Kulturtransfer und Vergleich* (Leipzig: Leipziger Universitäts Verlag, 2000).

70 Eric Hobsbawm, *How to Change the World: Tales of Marx and Marxism, 1840-2011* (London: Little, Brown, 2011), 235–36.

71 Marin Pundeff, "Marxism in Bulgaria Before 1891," *Slavic Review*, 30, no. 2 (September 1971), 523–50; Cyril Black, "Russia and the Modernization of the Balkans," in Barbara and Charles Jelavich, eds., *The Balkans in Transition: Essays on the Development of Balkan Life and Politics since the Eighteenth Century* (Berkeley: University of California Press, 1963).

72 Dimou, *Entangled Paths*, 19.

73 Eley, *Forging Democracy*, 43.

74 This and the following tables are adapted from Georges Haupt, "'Führungspartei'? Die Ausstrahlung der deutschen Sozialdemokratie auf den Südosten Europas zur Zeit der Zweiten Internationale," *Internationale Wissenschaftliche Korrespondenz zur deutschen Arbeiterbewegung* (IWK), Bd.15, 1979, 16–20 and from Leo van Rossum, "Einleitung," in Georges Haupt, Janos Jemnitz, Leo van Rossum, Hg. *Karl Kautsky und die Sozialdemokratie Südosteuropas. Korrespondenz 1883-1938* (Frankfurt: Campus Verlag, 1986), 17, 24.

75 It came from a dispatch written by Lazar Iovchev, the future Exarch (head of the Orthodox Church) of Bulgaria between 1877 and 1915. He had been a student in Paris between 1864 and 1870 and wrote about the goals of the First International. While not necessarily sympathetic, the dispatch was surprisingly evenhanded and leaves it to the reader to make up his mind (Лазар Йовчев „Интернасионал," *Читалище*, г. II, 3, 1871, 97–109; кн. 4, 144–55).

76 Георги Младжов, "Карл Маркс в България," *ИИИ* 50, 1983, 14.

77 *Каталог на книгите в Областната библиотека, постъпили до 1885*. Пловдив, 1885, 171.

78 Albert Resis, "*Das Kapital* Comes to Russia," *Slavic Review*, 29, no. 2 (June 1970), 219–37.

79 Младжов, "Карл Маркс в България," 21–22.

80 For an excellent comparison of the terminology used in both translations and how this reflects their ideological foundations, see Георги Найденов, "Ценност или стойност – Г.Бакалов срещу Д.Благоев," *Икономически и социални*

алтернативи, бр.3, 2017; see also "Димитър Зашев за превеждането на Маркс," *Философски алтернативи* 3/2018 (selections from *Философска мисъл*, 12/1983, 94–98), https://www.unwe.bg/uploads/Alternatives/12_Alternativi%20br3%202 017_BG.pdf); http://philosophical-alternatives.com/wp-content/uploads/2018/07/ Philosophical-Alternatives_2018_3__41.pdf.

81 Ursula Ratz, "Perspektiven über Kautsky. Neuerscheinungen zur Geschichte der Arbeiterbewegung anläßlich des 50. Todestages des 'Chefideologien'," *Neue politische Literatur*, Bd.33, 1988, 7.

82 Michael Werner and Bénédicte Zimmermann, "Histoire Croisée and the Challenge of Reflexivity," *History and Theory*, 45, no. 1 (February 2006), 37.

83 Leon Trotsky, *The War Correspondence of Leon Trotsky: The Balkan Wars 1912-13*, trans. Brian Pearce (New York: Monad Press; Australia: Pathfinder Press) (first published in 1980, reprinted in 1993), 38.

84 Ibid., 39.

85 Ibid., 157.

86 *Кратка история на Българската Комунистическа Партия* (под редакцията на Борис Боев, Боян Григоров, Стефан Радулов) (София: Партиздат, 1986), 67; Димитър Генчев. *Първоапостолите на идеала*. София: (Фондация „Ново време", Издателска къща „Христо Ботев", 2006), 23; Йордан Йотов. *Из борбите на тесните социалисти против опортюнизма на Втория интернационал* (София: БКП, 1964), 63–82. The last work bears the heavy imprint of the time it was written but is the most detailed empirically.

87 Blagoev was widely known by the sobriquet Granddad or Grandfather (Дядото), already acquired when he was young, because of one of the pseudonyms he used: Dr. Senex (Стефчо Кирин, "Малко известно: как и кога Димитър Благоев станал Дядото", http://www.nabore.bg/statia/kak-i-koga-blagoev-stanal-dyadoto-1853-14).

88 *The War Correspondence of Leon Trotsky*, 42–43, 45. Trotsky developed his analysis in further articles in which he wrote about the "lag in Bulgaria's historical development and the low level of social differentiation," the "primitive social basis of Bulgarian democracy," and its embryonic bourgeoisie that "had not yet managed to throw off its Asiatic features" [sic] (49, 53, 54).

89 Димитър Благоев, "Статията на др. Троцки," *Работнически вестник*, September 7, 1910, cited in Leo van Rossum, "Einleitung," in *Karl Kautsky und die Sozialdemokratie Südosteuropas*, 26. On the relationship between Bulgarian and German social democracy, see Мария Маринова, *Българските марксисти и германското работническо движение, 1900-1912* (София: Партиздат, 1979).

90 Йотов, *Из борбите на тесните социалисти*, 71.

91 *Социализмът в България (Отчет на централния комитет до международния социалистически конгрес в Щутгарт)* (София, 1907), 15. The Liberation refers to 1878, when Bulgaria seceded from the Ottoman Empire.

92 Letters of Ivan Klincharov, Georgi Bakalov, and Krum Tikhchev in ЦДА, Фонд 1Б, оп.2, а.е. 21. Eighteen letters from Bulgaria have been published in Russian translation in *Философско-литературное наследие Г. В. Плеханова. Том II. Г. В. Плеханов и международное рабочее движение*. Под ред. М. Т. Йовчук, И. Н. Курбатова, Б. А. Чагин (Москва: Наука, 1973), 90–103.

93 Cited in Георгий Чернявский, Михаил Станчев, Мария Тортика (Лобанова). *Жизненный путь Христиана Раковского, 1973-1941. Европеизм и Большевизм: Неоконченная дуэль*. Москва: Центрполиграф, 2014, 66. On the unification mission and the publication of *Napred*, see pp. 46–66.

94　The personal archive of Pavel Deliradev contains a letter from 1907 addressed to the Stuttgart Congress of the Socialist International, explaining their ideas and the reasons for forming a separate party. It claimed that they had 22 political groups with 425 members, 4 study groups with 118 members, and 35 syndicalist groups with 969 members, thus a total of 1,512 members (ЦДА, Фонд 251 Б, оп.1, а.е. 12, л.51).

95　Bell, *The Bulgarian Communist Party*, 14–15. See also Здравка Константинова. *Бунтът на "анархолибералите". Бакалов срещу Благоев.* София: Университетско издателство "Св.Климент Охридски," 1995.

96　Владимир Топенчаров, *Българската журналистика, 1903-1917* (София: Наука и изкуство, 1981), 303–10.

97　Bell, *The Bulgarian Communist Party*, 12.

98　Rothschild, *The Communist Party of Bulgaria*, 1. In the words of Bertrand Patenaude, "most of the American *Trostkysants* of the 1930s had become Cold War liberals" (*The Cambridge History of Communism*, Silvio Pons and Stephen A. Smith. Vol. 1 [Cambridge: Cambridge University Press, 2017], 208).

99　Пол Дюмон, "Българската социалдемокрация в архивите на Международното Социалистическо Бюро (1900-1918)," *ИИИ*, 46 (1982), 352. The best account of the 1903 split belongs to Dimou, *Entangled Paths*, 164–74.

100　Stefan Troebst, "'Hochverehrter Meister und Genosse': Karl Kautsky und die sozialistische Bewegung in Bulgarien (1887-1933)," in Wolfgang Gesemann, Kyrill Haralampieff, Helmut Schaller, Hg. *Bulgaristik-Symposium Marburg*. Südosteuropa-Studien Heft 43 (München: Hieronymus, 1990). Reprinted in Stefan Troebst. *Zwischen Arktis, Adria und Armenien. Das östliche Europa und seine Ränder. Aufsätze, Essays und Vorträge 1983-2016* (Köln, Weimar, Wien: Böhlau Verlag, 2017), 93.

101　György Lukács, "Bernstein's Triumph: Notes on the Essays Written in Honor of Karl Kautsky's Seventieth Birthday," *Die Internationale*, VII, no. 22 (1924). See http://the charnelhouse.org/2014/12/30/lukacs-on-the-rapprochement-between-bernstein-and-kautsky-after-world-war-i-democracy-reformism-and-the-dialectic/

102　Карл Кауцки, "Социалистите в икономически изостаналите назад страни," in *Янко Сакъзов-Юбилеен сборник*. София: Издателство "Обществена мисъл" (1930), 17–19, cited in Dimou, *Entangled Paths*, 161–62.

103　Trencsényi, Janowski, Baár, Falina, Kopeček, *A History of Modern Political Thought in East Central Europe*, 466.

104　See Peter Gay, *The Dilemma of Democratic Socialism: Eduard Bernstein's Challenge to Marx* (New York: Columbia University Press, 1952); Manfred B. Steger, *The Quest for Evolutionary Socialism: Eduard Bernstein and Social Democracy* (Cambridge, UK: Cambridge University Press, 1997); H. Kendall Rogers, *Before the Revisionist Controversy: Kautsky, Bernstein, and the Meaning of Marxism, 1895-1898* (London: Routledge, 2015).

105　Bell, *The Bulgarian Communist Party*, 10. On the efforts of the International to restore socialist unity in these parties, see Haupt, *Socialism and the Great War*, 133.

106　"Уводна статия на в. Работник за характера и задачите на БСДП, 1 ноември 1892," *Българска комунистическа партия. Документи на централните ръководни органи*, т.I. (София: Партиздат, 1972), 41–42.

107　Stephen Kotkin, *Stalin, Volume I: Paradoxes of Power, 1878-1928* (New York: Penguin, 2015), 79.

108　Bulgarian governments changed thirty-four times between 1879 and 1913 (some cabinets were reconstituted): Roumiana Preshlenova, "Liberation in Progress:

Bulgarian Nationalism and Political Economy in a Balkan Perspective, 1878-1912," in Timothy Snyder and Katherine Younger, eds., *The Balkans as Europe, 1821-1914* (Rochester: University of Rochester Press, 2018), 62.

109 On the debates around the character of the Bulgarian constitution, see *История на България*, том 7, София: Издателство на БАН, 1991, 65–68.

110 The phrase comes from Jakub Beneš, *Workers and Nationalism: Czech and German Social Democracy in Habsburg Austria, 1890-1918* (New York: Oxford University Press, 2017), 101.

111 *The War Correspondence of Leon Trotsky*, 260–61.

112 Ibid., 277.

113 Ibid., 278. To his credit, Trotsky saw the Balkan War as having "more in common with the Italian war of liberation of 1859 than it has ... with the Italian-Turkish War of 1911-1912" (152). In a remarkable article "Bulgaria's Crisis" he even agreed with the analysis of a Bulgarian officer, who admonished Trotsky that "the duty of Russian journalists, and especially of those who are combating the reactionary nonsense of the Slavophiles, is to explain the role and significance of a free, independent, and strong Bulgaria for the destiny of Southeastern Europe" (346–47).

114 Ibid., 278.

115 Ibid., 279. Trotsky was, in fact, very effective in denouncing the atrocities committed by the Bulgarian army and the complicity of the Bulgarian intelligentsia, concluding that "elementary political and moral concepts have as yet not been established among you" (284–85). Only five years later, however, he decisively forgot about these precepts as the leader of the Red Army. On this, see Maria Todorova, "War and Memory: Trotsky's War Correspondence from the Balkan Wars," *Perceptions – Journal of International Affairs*, Special Issue – From the Balkan Wars to Balkan Peace (Spring 2013), 5–27.

116 Antoinette Burton, *The Trouble with Empire: Challenges to Modern British Imperialism* (Oxford: Oxford University Press, 2015), 8.

117 Sanjay Subrahmanyam, "Connected Histories: Notes Towards a Reconfiguration of Early Modern Eurasia," *Modern Asian Studies*, 31, no. 3 (1997), 760.

118 Върбан Ангелов, *Неизвестни страници от миналото, 1919, 1923, 1925, 1944, 1956, 1968.* София: Военноиздателски комплекс "Св. Георги Победоносец" (1993), 42.

119 Димитър Благоев, "'Тесни социалисти' с анархистически глави," *Съчинения*, Т.18 (София: БКП, 1962), 552.

120 Генчев, "Теоретичното и програмно развитие," 64–65.

121 Bell, *The Bulgarian Communist Party*, 24;

122 ЦДА, Фонд 361 К, оп. 1, а.е. 9, л.7, cited in Alex Toshkov, *Agrarianism as Modernity in 20th-Century Europe: The Golden Age of the Peasantry* (London: Bloomsbury, 2019), 6, 38.

123 Христо Кабакчиев, "После переворота," *Коммунистический интернационал* 28–29 (1923): 7695–96, cited in Bell, *The Bulgarian Communist Party*, 34.

124 Ангелов, *Неизвестни страници*, 48; Rothschild, *The Communist Party of Bulgaria*, 128–30.

125 Citing Nissan Oren, John Bell speaks of between two and three thousand people as the scope of the Bulgarian emigration to the USSR (Bell, *The Bulgarian Communist Party*, 42).

126 Георги Бакалов, "Старая 'Искра' среди болгар," *Пролетарская революция*, no. 91–92 (1929): 67–95; Георги Бакалов, "Когда и как болгарские рабочие впервые

познакомились с В. И. Лениным," *Пролетарская революция*, no. 93 (1929), cited in Шнитман, А. „К вопросу о влиянии русского революциюнного движения 1885-1903 годов на революционное движение в Болгарии," *Вопросы истории*, no. 1 (1949): 39; Христо Кабакчиев, "Ленин и болгарские тесняки," *Историк-марксист*, no. 35 (1934): 173-88.

127 Милен Куманов, "Левият политически спектър в България (1918-1934 г.)," in *Изследвания по история на социализма в България, 1891-1944*, том I, 2008, 348. On this, see also the memoirs of Raicho Karakolov ЦДА, Сп 2220 Б.

128 ЦДА, Фонд 147 Б, оп.2, а.е. 449, cited in Ангел Веков, "Васил Коларов в историята на българския социализъм," Васил Коларов. *Статии, дневници, речи, писма, спомени*, Т.1 (1877-1919) (София: Христо Ботев, 2001), 21.

129 *Кратка история на Българската Комунистическа Партия*, 74.

130 Friedrich Engels, "The Program of the Blanquist Fugitives from the Paris Commune, 1873," first published in *Der Volksstaat*, no. 73 (June 26, 1874), English translation in the *International Socialist Review*, IX (August 2, 1908), https://www.marxists.org/archive/marx/works/1874/06/26.htm.

131 Stalin's letter "Some questions from the history of bolshevism" was published in the journal *Proletarskaia revoliutsia* and reprinted in *Kommunisticheskii internatsional*, cited in Веков, "Васил Коларов в историята," 229.

132 Веков, "Васил Коларов в историята," 21; Георги Чанков, *Равносметката* (София: Христо Ботев, 2000), 280.

133 *Восточная Европа в документах российских архивов 1949-1953. Том 2.* Москва-Новосибирск (1998), 193, cited in Веков, "Васил Коларов в историята," 21.

134 Веков, "Васил Коларов в историята," 19.

135 Коларов, *Статии, дневници, речи, писма, спомени*, 226.

136 ЦДА, Фонд 147 Б, оп.2, а.е. 449, cited in Веков, "Васил Коларов в историята," 21.

137 Julia Richers, "Zimmerwald als sowjetischer Erinnerungsort," in Bernard Degen, Julia Richers, Hg., *Zimmerwald und Kiental: Weltgeschichte auf dem Dorfe* (Zurich: Chronos Verlag, 2015), 174.

138 Two honorable exceptions in this respect are the inspired works of Filip Panaiotov and Dimitǐr Genchev, written in a journalistic style for a broad audience: Филип Панайотов, *Съвременници на бъдещето* (София: Народна младеж, 1971) (another edition, *Чучулигите* [София: Народна младеж, 1981], is absolutely identical, with a different layout and very slightly changed pagination but does not indicate that it is actually a reprint, not even a reworked edition); Димитър Генчев, *Профили от кафене "Ландолт"* (София: Партиздат, 1990); Димитър Генчев, *Първоапостолите на идеала*.

139 А.Шнитман, „К вопросу о влиянии русского революциюнного движения 1885-1903 годов на революционное движение в Болгарии, *Вопросы истории*, no. 1 (1949), 55.

140 Ibid., 42.

141 Ibid., 52-53.

142 Harry Harootunian, *Marx After Marx: History and Time in the Expansion of Capitalism* (New York: Columbia University Press, 2015), 73.

143 Gerassimos Moschonas, "European Social Democracy, Communism, and the Erfurtian Model," in William Outhwaite and Stephen Turner, eds., *The SAGE Handbook of Political Sociology* (London: Sage Publicatoions, 2018), 518.

144 Stefan Berger, "Democracy and Social Democracy," *European History Quarterly*, 32, no. 1 (2002), 23.

145 George Lichtheim, *A Short History of Socialism* (New York: Praeger, 1970), cited in Moschonas, 12.
146 Moschomas, "European Social Democracy," 11–14.
147 "Работническата класа е революционна," *Работнически вестник*, no. 4 (October 2, 1898), in Георги Кирков, *Избрани произведения*, т. I. (София: Партиздат, 1989), 96; also Георги Кирков, *Публицистика*. София: Фондация Арете, Университетско издателство "Св. Климент Охридски" (2006), 62–64.
148 Most likely written by Blagoev in 1893, cited in Генчев, "Теоретичното и програмно развитие," 34–36.
149 Таня Турлакова, "Някои необходими акценти в новия прочит на историята на социализма в България (1891-1944)," in *Изследвания по история на социализма*, I, 13; Генчев, "Теоретичното и програмното развитие," 48.
150 Йордан Йотов, Кирил Василев, Стоянка Поборникова, and Татяна Колева, *Димитър Благоев. Биография* (София: Партиздат, 1979), 69–71 and passim. This is true also for the otherwise moving laudatory biography in English by Mercia McDermott. *Lone Red Poppy: A Biography of Dimiter Blagoev, Founder of the First Marxist Circle in Russia and of the Bulgarian Communist Party* (Croydon: Manifesto Press, 2014), translated to Bulgarian as Мерсия Макдермот, *Ален мак самотен. Биография на Димитър Благоев* (София: ИК "Синева," 2018).
151 Генчев, "Теоретичното и програмното развитие," 46–54. On the ideology of the Broad party, see Dimou, *Entangled Paths*, 224–78.
152 Janko Sakasoff, "Die Bedeutung der Lebensarbeit Karl Kautskys für die Entwicklung des Sozialismus in Bulgarien," *Karl Kautsky dem Wahrer und Mehrer der Marxschen Lehre. Zum 70-ten Geburtstage* (Berlin, 1932) (Unveränderter Neudruck, Frankfurt/Main: Verlag Sauer & Auvermann, 1968), 112.
153 Генчев, "Теоретичното и програмното развитие," 63.
154 Веселин Янчев, "Апология на българската социалдемокрация (1891-1944)," in *Изследвания по история на социализмя*, т. I, 172–73; On the inner debates within the Broad party see Трендафил Митев, "Възникване и същност на 'широкия социализъм' в България," in *Изследвания по история на социализма*, т. I, 136–41.
155 Петър Джидров, *Пред прага на социализма* (София: Работническа кооперативна печатница "Напред," 1919), 14–17.
156 Ibid., 80.
157 Ibid., 82.
158 Ibid., 21–28; Петър Джидров, *Социализмът и неговите методи* (София: Издателско кооперативно дружество "Просвета," 1921), 37, 44–45.
159 Д-р Петър Джидров и Асен Цанков, *Империализъм, болшевизъм и социализъм. Речи държани в София на 17 април 1921 в салона на Градското Казино* (София: Издателско кооперативно дружество "Просвета," 1921), 18–19, 26, 35.
160 Ibid., 26–27.
161 Ibid., 29. The same accusation of the agrarians as a semi-Bolshevik regime is in Петър Джидров, *Безпомощна България. Проблеми и перспективи* (София: Издателско кооперативно дружество "Просвета," 1927), 40.
162 Реч на Асен Цанков, in *Империализъм, болшевизъм и социализъм*, 7. Asen Tsankov (1883–1964) was a lawyer, and member of the BWSDP (b) who after 1923 joined his brother's Democratic Alliance. His brother, Alexander Tsankov (1879–1959), a university professor of economics, had been a member

of the Broad party until 1907. A leader of the People's Alliance, he participated in the 1923 coup against Stamboliiski. A founder of the Democratic Alliance that effectively ruled Bulgaria between 1923 and 1934, Tsankov was prime minister and presided over the bloody suppression of communists and agrarians, which made him an international pariah. A nationalist and believer in the strong state, he was close only to Mussolini and in 1932 created the National Social Movement. Pro-German, but not an anti-Semite, in 1944 he emigrated to Nazi Germany where he created an anti-communist Bulgarian government abroad. Captured by the Americans, he was released and ended his life in exile in Buenos Aires. His death sentence in absentia by the People's Court was revoked in 1991 and his academic titles reinstated, in a controversial move that rehabilitated everyone tried by the overzealous people's courts, including outright fascists, anti-Semites, and criminals, alongside simply opponents of the communists. The move to étatism and/or fascism, primarily because of the nationalism of many right-wing Broad socialists was not an exception, like Tsoniu Brîshlianov (1876–1947) or Sotir Yanev (1891–1943). Asen Tsankov managed to emigrate and died in France. Dzhidrov was less lucky: sentenced first to seven and then, as a "chauvinist" to eleven years, he died in prison in 1952 and was rehabilitated in 1994. Most amazing were the vacillations of Dimo Kazasov (1886–1980), a teacher, prominent journalist, and leader of the Broad socialists, who was a member of the Tsankov government after 1923 as minister of railways, posts and telegraphs. He was expelled from the BWSDP (b) together with Asen Tsankov in 1926 (Петър Кузманов; Москов, Атанас, *Коста Лулчев. Един живот в служба на социалдемокрацията* [София: Христофор Христов, 1998], 175–77). One of the founders of *Zveno*, he left it and joined Tsankov's National Social Movement, and was ambassador to Yugoslavia in the 1930s. From 1936 to 1944, however, he chaired the anti-fascist committee for amnesty and support of political figures and became a member of the Popular Front. In 1944–1947 he was minister of propaganda and until 1953 the main director of the publishing houses and book trade. He wrote several volumes of memoirs well into the 1970s.

163 Eley, *Forging Democracy*, 83–84.
164 In 1903, BWSDP (n). had 1,174 members, of whom only 480 were classified as proletarians; by 1910, the ratio had changed in favor of the working-class members: they were 1,519 of a total membership of 2,126 (Rothschild, *The Communist Party of Bulgaria*, 41). In 1912 the general membership had risen to 2,923, mostly in the big industrial centers ("Годишен отчет на ЦК за 1911-12 година на XIX конгрес," *Българска комунистическа партия. Документи на централните ръководни органи, 1911-1912*. Т.6. [София: Партиздат, 1984], 355).
165 Introduction to Енгелс, Фридрих, *Развитие на научния социализъм*. Превод: Евтим Дабев (Габрово, 1890), 6, cited in Генчев, "Теоретичното и програмно развитие," 32. Rothschild, *The Communist Party of Bulgaria*, 45, makes the same point citing the self-description of Bulgarian communists looking back at their history: Vasil Kolarov, "Die Taktik der K.P. Bulgariens im Lichte der Ereignisse," *Die Kommunistische Internartionale*, no. 31–32 (1924), 255; Христо Кабакчиев, Б. Бошкович, Х.Д. Ватис. *Коммунистические партии балканских стран* (Москва: Московский рабочий, 1930), 54.
166 *Работнически вестник*, no. 1 (September 5, 1897), in Кирков, *Избрани произведения*, 96.

Chapter 2

1. Gerhart Niemeyer, "The Second International: 1889-1914," in Milorad Drachkovitch, ed., *The Revolutionary Internationals, 1864-1943* (Stanford: Stanford University Press (Hoover Institution Publications), 1966), 119 and 120. One cannot but agree with this verdict, even if the rest of the article is a venomous and rather predictable, but erudite, diatribe written at the height of the Cold War by a committed anti-communist.
2. Joll, *The Second International*, 114.
3. Ibid., 115–16.
4. Ibid., 117.
5. Ibid., 118.
6. Words used by Josef Seliger, one of the leaders of the Austrian party at the first congress of the socialist parties of the Habsburg monarchy, when they assembled as a united party, a *Gesamtpartei*, composed of national sections (Arthur Kogan, "The Social Democrats and the Conflict of Nationalities in the Habsburg Monarchy," *Journal of Modern History*, 21 (1949), 207).
7. Стефан Аврамов, "Ленин за българските тесни социалисти, за догматизма, сектантството и пр. (Спомени)," ЦДА, ЧП 11 Б, л. 235–36 (pp. 16–17 of the report).
8. Bernstein at the 1907 congress, cited in Richard Day and Daniel Gaido, eds. *Discovering Imperialism: Social Democracy to World War I* (Chicago: Haymarket Books, 2012), 25.
9. Day and Gaido, *Discovering Imperialism*, 23, 26.
10. Gerhard Sandner and Mechthild Rössler, "Geography and Empire in Germany, 1871-1945," in Anne Godlewska and Neil Smith, eds., *Geography and Empire* (Oxford: Blackwell, 1994), 121.
11. Day and Gaido, *Discovering Imperialism*, 29. Already in 1896, Bernstein had argued that "races who are hostile to or incapable of civilization cannot claim our sympathy when they revolt against civilization.... We will condemn and oppose certain methods of subjugating savages. But we will not condemn the idea that savages must be subjugated and made to conform to the rules of higher civilization" (ibid., 11). See also Eduard Bernstein, "Social Democracy and Imperialism (May 1900)," in Day and Gaido, *Discovering Imperialism*, 211–30.
12. Joll, *The Second International*, 126.
13. Friedrich Engels, "The Magyar Struggle" (1849), cited in Dragan Plavšić, "Introduction," *The Balkan Socialist Tradition: Balkan Socialism and the Balkan Federation, 1871-1915* (*Revolutionary History*, 8, no. 3) (London: Porcupine Press, 2003), 31.
14. Roman Rosdolsky, *Engels and the "Nonhistoric" Peoples: The National Question in the Revolution of 1848* (Glasgow: Critique Books, 1987) (published first in *Critique*, no. 18/19, 1986; translation of "Friedrich Engels und das Problem der 'Geschichtslosen' Völker (Die Nationalitätenfrage in der Revolution 1848–1849 im Lichte der 'Neuen Rheinischen Zeitung')" *Archiv für Sozialgeschichte*, 4 (1964), 87–276); Francé Klopčič, "Friedrich Engels und Karl Marx über der 'Geschichtslosen' Slawischen Nationen 1847-1895," *Geschichte der Arbeiterbewegung* (ITH Tagunsberichte, Band 19) (Wien: Europaverlag, 1984), 217–49; Ephraim Nimni, *Marxism and Nationalism: The Theoretical Origins of a Political Crisis* (London: Pluto Press, 1991); Jules Townshend,

The Politics of Marxism: The Critical Debates (London: Leicester University Press, 1996); Traverso, *Left-Wing Melancholia*, 158–60. In English, the views of Marx and Engels have been compiled in Paul Blackstock and Bert Hoselitz, *The Russian Menace to Europe by Karl Marx and Friedrich Engels* (Glencoe, Ill.: Free Press, 1952); Kevin Anderson, *Marx at the Margins: On Nationalism, Ethnicity, and Non-Western Societies* (Chicago: The University of Chicago Press, 2010), 44–56, 196, 224–36, 261 is a particularly poignant attempt to attribute the particular anti-Slav animus solely to Engels, even when Marx approved and even agreed that some of his explicit racist pieces be published under his name. Marx's views on Russia and the Slavs seem to have begun to change slowly after 1858 and he started learning Russian in 1869, and Engels by the 1870s.

15 Stefan Troebst, "'Hochverehrter Meister und Genosse,'" in *Bulgaristik-Symposium Marburg. Südosteuropa-Studien* Heft 43 (München: Hieronymus, 1990), 232; also in Troebst, *Zwischen Arktis, Adria und Armenien*, 90.
16 Letters of Engels in the *Commonwealth* magazine in 1866, cited in Bertram Wolfe, "Nationalism and Internationalism in Marx and Engels," *The American Slavic and East European Review*, 17, no. 4 (December 1958), 412–13 (quotes on p. 413).
17 Ibid., 414.
18 Marx to Liebknecht, February 4, 1878, cited in Plavšić, "Introduction," *The Balkan Socialist Tradition*, 31.
19 Quoted in Plavšić, "Introduction," *The Balkan Socialist Tradition*, 32.
20 Carl E. Schorske, *German Social Democracy, 1905-1917: The Development of the Great Schism* (New York: Harper Torchbooks, 1972), 67–68.
21 Tucović to Lapčević, February 20, 1908, in *The Balkan Socialist Tradition*, 139–40. What Bernstein wrote comes from his 1907 article "Kulturrecht und Kolonialfrage," in *Vorwärts* (October 4, 1907): "Austria in Bosnia and Herzegovina, England in Egypt, or France in Tunis, have accomplished real cultural work that is very beneficial to the population of these lands."
22 Ibid., 140 [italics mine].
23 One of the best syntheses of the relationship between Marxism and nationalism belongs to Shlomo Avineri, "Marxism and Nationalism," *Journal of Contemporary History*, 26, no. 3/4 (September 1991), 637–57.
24 Karl Marx, "Draft of an Article on Friedrich List's Book *Das nationale System der politischen Ökonomie*," Collected Works, 4, 280. Cited in Roman Szporluk, *Communism and Nationalism: Karl Marx versus Friedrich List* (New York: Oxford University Press, 1988), 35.
25 *Marx & Engels on Ireland* (London: Lawrence & Wishart Ltd., 1971); *Ireland and the Irish Question: A Collection of Writings by Karl Marx & Friedrich Engels* (New York: International Publishers, 1972); For online texts of Marx and Engels on the Irish Question: https://www.marxists.org/archive/marx/works/subject/ireland/index.htm; http://www.politicalworld.org/showthread.php?10967-Marx-and-Engels-on-Irelnd#.Wr0icmcsB1s (last visited March 29, 2018).
26 Карл Маркс, Фридрих Енгелс. *Съчинения*, т.35, 221. The German original is in Karl Marx, Friedrich Engels, *Werke*, Bd.35, Berlin, 1973, 272. An English translation of the letter is in *Marx-Engels Collective Works*, vol. 46, 194.
27 Ibidem.
28 Engels to August Bebel, November 17, 1885, cited in Troebst, "Hochverehrter Meister und Genosse," 232.

29 Карл Маркс, Фридрих Енгелс, *Съчинения*, т.36, 452, cited in Георги Първанов. *Българската социалдемокрация и македонският въпрос (От края на XIX век до 1918 година)* (София: Графимакс, 1997), 62.
30 Ibidem.
31 Георги Боршуков, "Данни за някои социалистически групи до основаването на БСДП," *ИИИ*, 6 (1956), 240–41.
32 ЦДА, Фонд 186 Б, оп.1, а.е. 212, л.14–15.
33 Nokov's life can be partly reconstructed from his archive found in the Central State Archive, Sofia and particularly his manuscript memoirs ЦДА, Фонд 186 Б, оп.1, а.е. 212.
34 ЦДА, Фонд 186, Б оп.1, а.е. 93, л.1, also in Живка Велева, "Фридрих Енгелс и първите български социалисти," *ИИИ*, 24 (1970), 354.
35 ЦДА, Фонд 186 Б, оп.1, а.е. 93, л.2, also in Велева, "Фридрих Енгелс и първите български социалисти," 354–55.
36 ЦДА, Фонд 186 Б, оп.1, а.е. 93, л.3, also in Велева, "Фридрих Енгелс и първите български социалисти," 358.
37 Bulgaria was recognized as an autonomous principality after the Russo-Turkish war of 1877–78 and achieved formal independence as a kingdom in 1908. However, 1878 has been traditionally accepted as the restoration of its statehood (Liberation—Освобождение) and March 3, 1878, as the National Independence Day. In this text, I will refer to the post-1878 period as independent Bulgaria, unless I want to specify the political significance of 1908.
38 ЦДА, Фонд 186 Б, оп.1, а.е. 212. л. 59–60.
39 Benedikt Kautsky (Hg.), *Erinnerungen und Erörtungen von Karl Kautsky* ('s-Gravenhage: Mouton & Co, 1960), 454–56.
40 P. Argyriadès and P. Lagarde, *Solution de la question d'Orient. La confédération balkanique; compte-rendu de la conférence tenue au Grand-Orient de France sur cette question: et La Macédoine; relation sur ce pays* (Paris, 1896); Stavrianos, *Balkan Federation*, 151. On Paul Argyriadès (Παύλος Αργυριάδης), see Δημητρίου Μιχάλης, *Το Ελληνικό Σοσιαλιστικό Κίνημα*. Αθήνα: Πλέθρον, 1985 and https://rassias.wordpress.com/article/ παύλος-αργυριάδης-gnmodo87aoe9-78/. Socialist federations were only some of the plethora of federative visions as solutions to the Eastern Question: see John A. Mazis, "The Idea of an Eastern Federation: An Alternative to the Destruction of the Ottoman Empire," in Lucien J. Frary and Mara Kozelsky, eds., *Russian-Ottoman Borderlands. The Eastern Question Reconsidered* (Madison, WI: University of Wisconsin Press, 2014), 251–79.
41 П. Аржириадис, П. Лагард, *Разрешението на Източния въпрос. Балканската конфедерация и Македония (превод от френски)* (Габрово: Заря, 1902).
42 Leften S. Stavrianos, *Balkan Federation: A History of the Movement Toward Balkan Unity in Modern Times* (Hamden, CT: Archon Books, 1964).
43 Георги Първанов, *Българската социалдемокрация*, 13.
44 Ibid., 16–17.
45 Димитър Благоев, *Съчинения*, т. 1 (София: БКП, 1957), 67–8.
46 Първанов, *Българската социалдемокрация*, 34, 49.
47 Christian Rakovsky, "An Autobiography," in Gus Fagan, ed., *Selected Writings on Opposition in the USSR, 1923–30* (London and New York, 1980), 68–69, cited in Plavšić, "Introduction," *The Balkan Socialist Tradition*, 35.
48 An English translation of these articles is published in *The Balkan Socialist Tradition*, 64–66.

49 Christian Rakovsky, "Die Bulgarische Sozialdemokratie und die Orientfrage," *Die Neue Zeit*, XV (1896-97), 820-24; Първанов, *Българската социалдемокрация*, 67.
50 The Armenian Question was one of the central issues discussed in numerous articles in *Социалист*, the organ of the BWSDP between 1894 and 1897, after the merger of *Rabotnik* and *Drugar* and the BSDP and BSDU. See Владимир Топенчаров, *Българската журналистика, 1885-1903* (София: Наука и изкуство, 1963), 288 ff.
51 Marwan R. Buheiry, "Theodore Herzl and the Armenian Question," *Journal of Palestinian Studies*, 7 (Autumn 1977), 75-97. Herzl initiated a campaign to publish favorable opinions of the Ottoman Empire and unsuccessfully mediate between the Sultan and the Armenians. "Under no circumstances," he wrote, "are the Armenians to learn that we want to use them in order to erect a Jewish state." (Margaret Anderson, "'Down in Turkey, Far Away': Human Rights, the Armenian Massacres, and Orientalism in Wilhelmine Germany," *Journal of Modern History*, 79 (March 2007), 88).
52 "Арменският въпрос пред френския парламент," *Социалист*, no. 5 (November 22, 1896), 4, cited in Първанов, *Българската социалдемокрация*, 69.
53 "Circulaire communiquant les réponses des Partis socialistes sur les questions suivantes: Intervention du B.S.I. dans les événements de Macédoine, 26.3.1903," in *Bureau socialiste International. Comptes rendus des reunions. Manifestes et circulaires, vol. I.1900-1907, réunis par G. Haupt* (Paris: Mouton, 1969), 65-72, quote on p. 66, n. 4.
54 "Circulaire, 20.7.1903," in *Bureau socialiste International*, 89.
55 Ibid., 105. This seems to have been achieved most likely because of Plekhanov who insisted on "independence" for Macedonia.
56 Ibid., 104-5.
57 Първанов, *Българската социалдемокрация*, 131-32, quote on page 132.
58 Ibid., 132.
59 Георги Тошев, *Балкански митнически съюз (Balkanzoll - verein). Политикономическо изследване* (Пловдив: книж. Антим I на Р. Милков, 1907).
60 Павел Делирадев, *Балканската конфедерация* (Татар Пазарджик: Печатница Търговска, 1909).
61 Първанов, *Българската социалдемокрация*, 132.
62 It came out as a separate article "Die nationalen Aufgaben der Sozialisten unter den Balkanslawen," *Der Kampf*, no. 2 (December 1, 1908), 105-12. In Bulgaria it was published under a slightly different title, "The National Tasks of the Socialists in the Slavic States in the Balkans" (Националните задачи на социалистическите балкански славянски държави), *Съвременник*, no. 4 (1908), 193-99, before it came out as a preface: К. Кауцки, *Републиката във Франция и социалдемокрацията* (София: Партийна социалистическа книжарница, 1909). An English translation is published in *The Balkan Socialist Tradition*, 157-64.
63 The Broads under Sakîzov rejected the federative idea: Armando Pitassio, "Janko Sakazov e Karl Kautsky. Un socialista balcanico di fronte al Papa Rosso," *Annali del Dipartimento di Studii dell' Europa Orientale*, IV-V (1982-83), 269-328.
64 "La question d'Orient et les puissances," *Revue de la Paix*, XIII, no. 11 (1908), 245-52; "Vers l'entente balkanique," *Revue de la Paix*, XIII, no. 12 (1908), 287-303. The correspondence between Kautsky and Rakovski on this issue is in *Karl Kautsky und die Sozialdemokratie Südosteuropas*, 363-67. See also Живка Дамянова, "Карл Кауцки и социалдемокрацията в Югоизточна Европа," *ИИИ*, 59 (1988), 343-52; Mariana Hausleitner, "Christian Rakovskis Bedeutung für die international

Arbeiterbewegung und seine Lösungsvorschläge der Nationalitetätenprobleme Rückständiger Länder," *Internationale Wissenschftliche Korrespondenz*, Bd.18, 3 (1982), 298-310.
65 This exchange is reproduced in *The Balkan Socialist Tradition*, 37-63.
66 Кауцки, *Републиката*, v-vi.
67 Ibid., vi-vii.
68 Ibid., x-xi.
69 Ibid., xii.
70 Kriegel, "Le IIe Interntanionale," 574. John Schwarzmantel, "Nationalism and Socialist Internationalism," in John Breuilly, ed. *The Oxford Handbook of the History of Nationalism*, Oxford University Press, 2013, 635-54, while correctly emphasizing the intertwinement of nationalism and socialism with the achievement of political and social rights in the context of the nation-state, reduces his coverage exclusively to Germany, France and Austria-Hungary.
71 Tom Bottomore and Patrick Goode, *Austro-Marxism* (Oxford: Clarendon Press, 1978); Mark E. Blum, *The Austro-Marxists 1890-1918: A Psychobiographical Study* (Lexington: The University of Kentucky Press, 1985); Norbert Leser, *Zwischen Reformismus und Bolschewismus. Der Austromarxismus als Theorie und Praxis* (Wien: Europa Verlag, 1968).
72 Otto Bauer, *The Question of Nationalities and Social Democracy*, trans. Joseph O'Donnell (Minneapolis: University of Minnesota Press, 2000), 98.
73 Ibid., 577-78.
74 Eley, *Forging Democracy*, 92.
75 Jeremy Smith, *The Bolsheviks and the National Question, 1917-1923* (New York: Macmillan, 1999).
76 On Luxemburg's views, published in 1909 in Polish, see *The National Question–Selected Writings by Rosa Luxemburg*, edited and introduced by the late Horace B. Davis (New York: Monthly Review Press, 1976). Also available at https://www.marxists.org/archive/luxemburg/1909/national-question/index.htm (last visited March 29, 2018).
77 Dimitrije Tucović to Kautsky, February 2, 1909, in *Karl Kautsky und die Sozialdemokratie Südosteuropas*, 237-80. See also Enver Redžić, *Austromarksizam i jugoslovensko pitanje* (Beograd: Narodna knjiga i Institut za savremenu istoriju, 1977); Haupt, *Socialism and the Great War*, 70-71. The articles and whole exchange between Bauer, Tucović, and Renner has been published in *The Balkan Socialist Tradition*, 123-50.
78 Georges Haupt, "'Führungspartei," 25.
79 Leo van Rossum, "Einleitung," in *Karl Kautsky und die Sozialdemokratie Südosteuropas*, 26.
80 Vladimir Claude Fišera, *Les peoples slaves et le communism de Marx à Gorbatchev* (Paris: Berg, 1992), 90-91.
81 *Karl Kautsky und die Sozialdemokratie Südosteuropas* includes the correspondence with Kautsky from Bulgaria (78 letters), Hungary (141 letters), Romania (57 letters), and Yugoslavia (91 letters).
82 Haupt, "Führungspartei," 27.
83 Werner and Zimmermann, "Histoire Croisée," 38.
84 Ibid., 39.
85 Blagovest Njagulov, "Early Socialism in the Balkans: Ideas and Practices in Serbia, Romania and Bulgaria," in Roumen Daskalov and Diana Mishkova, eds., *Entangled*

Histories of the Balkans, Volume Two: Transfers of Political Ideologies and Institutions (Leiden: Brill, 2014), 267.

86 *Кратка история на Българската Комунистическа Партия*, 71–72; Първанов, *Българската социалдемокрация*, 132.
87 *The Balkan Socialist Tradition*, 165–66.
88 Dimitŭr Blagoev, "The Revolution in Turkey and Social Democracy" (1908), *The Balkan Socialist Tradition*, 112.
89 Ibid., 111.
90 *Работническа искра*, March 15, 1909, in *The Balkan Socialist Tradition*, 117. See also the letter of the BWSDP (n) to the ISB from May 3, 1907: фонд 1Б, оп.2, а.е.60, 1–10. On Glavinov, see also Fikret Adanir, "The National Question and the Genesis and Development of Socialism in the Ottoman Empire: The Case of Macedonia," Mete Tunçay and Erich Zürcher, eds., *Socialism and Nationalism in the Ottoman Empire, 1876-1923* (London: I. B. Tauris, 1994), 33–35.
91 Dimo Hadzhidimov, "Our Political Standpoint: The Principle of Autonomy, Regional Self-Government and the Balkan Federation," *The Balkan Socialist Tradition*, 116 was published first in *Конституционна заря*, August 29–September 1, 1908.
92 Adanir, "The National Question," 41.
93 Ibid., 175, n. 40 quotes Georgi Pîrvanov's comment that Hadzhidimov's proposed structure was unjustified because of the numerical preponderance of Bulgarians, but he (Pîrvanov) was specifically addressing the federative structure of the organization, not the territory.
94 Adanir, "The National Question," 41.
95 Ibid., 41, 48.
96 Janko Sakasoff, "Neoslawismus, Balkanföderalismus und Sozialdemokratie," *Der Kampf*, 4, no. 5 (February 1, 1911), 212, cited in Troebst, "Hochverehrter Meister und Genosse," 238. It was in the aftermath of this difference that Kirkov substituted for Sakîzov as Kautsky's chief informer on things Bulgarian. See also Първанов, *Българската социалдемокрация*, 176–77, 184–87, 212–13.
97 William Maehl, "The Triumph of Nationalism in the German Socialist Party on the Eve of the First World War," *The Journal of Modern History*, 24, no. 1 (March 1952), 30.
98 Yura Konstantinova, "The Role of Bulgarians for the Spread of National, Anarchist and Socialist Ideas in Ottoman Salonica," *Etudes balkaniques*, LIV (2018), 3, 522.
99 See Димо Хаджидимов, *Публицистика, писма и документи* (София: Партиздат, 1989), 185–94.
100 Дечо Добринов, "Македоно-одринска социалдемократическа група," in *Национално-освободителното движение на македоните и тракийските българи (1878-1944). Том 3, Освободителното движение след Илинденско-Преображенското въстание 1903-1919* (София: Македонски научен институт, 1997), 139–40.
101 Abraham Benaroya, "A Note on 'the Socialist Federation of Saloniki," *Jewish Social Studies*, XI, no. 1 (January 1949), 70–71.
102 Апостолос Христакудис, "Аврам Бенароя (1997-1979) – живот и дейност," *Алманах за история на евреите в България*, XXX (1998/1999), 241–47; Dobrinka Parusheva, "Social Democracy and the Jewish Working Class in Bulgaria (Late 19th–Early 20th Century)," *Annual of the Organization of Jews in Bulgaria "Shalom,"* XXVII (1993/1994), 62–75.
103 Добринов, "Македоно-одринска социалдемократическа група," 141.

104 See https://bg.wikipedia.org/wiki/Работнически_вестник_(солунски_вестник).
105 Gila Hadar, "Jewish Tobacco Workers in Salonica: Gender and Family in the Context of Social and Ethnic Strife," in Amila Butirović and Irvin Cemil Schick, eds., *Women in the Ottoman Balkans: Gender, Culture, and History* (London: I.B. Tauris, 2007), 128.
106 Αβραάμ Μπεναρόγια. *Η πρώτη σταδιοδρομία του ελληνικού προλεταριάτου*. Κομμούνα, 1986, 46–47, 51–52; Benaroya, "A Note on 'the Socialist Federation of Saloniki,'" 69–72; Yura Konstantinova, "The Role of Bulgarians," 523–24, 526. See also https://www.solunbg.org/en/razkajete/drugi/119-otkasi-kniga-avram-benaroya-sazdavane-na-rabotnicheska-federacia.html.
107 All issues of the paper have been digitized: www.strumski.com/books/Работническа искра.pdf.
108 Rapport au Bureau Socialiste International. Movement Socialiste en Turquie d'Europe, in Георги Първанов, Валери Русанов, "Документ на Васил Главинов за ранното социалистическо движение в Европейска Турция," *ИИИ*, 51 (1984), 444–58, also published in Georges Haupt, "Le debut du movement socialiste en Turquie," *Le movement socialiste*, no. 45 (October–December, 1963), 129–35.
109 See Mercia MacDermott, *For Freedom and Perfection: The Life of Yane Sandanski* (London: Journeyman, 1988), https://bg.wikipedia.org/wiki/Народна_федерат ивна_партия_(българска_секция).
110 The Ottoman Socialist Party was founded in 1910 as a group of intellectuals under the leadership of Hüseyin Hilmi (1885–1922). Its main support in parliament were the Armenian and Bulgarian groups. After the arrest in 1913 of Hilmi, who was imprisoned until 1918, the party ceased to exist. An attempt was made in 1911 to join the Second International but the party was not admitted, https://en.wikipedia.org/wiki/Ottoman_Socialist_Party.
111 See Christian Rakovski's articles of 1908 and 1909, "The Turkish Revolution," "The Eastern Question and the Great Powers," "Towards a Balkan Entente," "Constitutional Turkey," "Revolution and Counter Revolution in Turkey" all in the Marxists' Internet Archive: https://www.marxists.org/archive/rakovsky/. Първанов, *Българската социалдемокрация*, 153–55, 164–65, 185–87. On *Napred*, see Топенчаров, *Българската журналистика, 1903-1917*, 303–10.
112 Njagulov, "Early Socialism in the Balkans," 268.
113 Haupt, *Socialism and the Great War*, 60–61.
114 Andreja Živković, "The Revolution in Turkey and the Balkan Federation," *The Balkan Socialist Tradition*, 105–6.
115 https://en.wikipedia.org/wiki/Avraam_Benaroya.
116 Abraham Benaroya, "A Note on 'The Socialist Federation of Saloniki,'" *Jewish Social Studies*, 11, no. 1 (January 1949), 71.
117 Първанов, *Българската социалдемокрация*, 196. During the war, socialists continued the anti-war campaign in all possible venues, the military front included.
118 Trotsky, *The War Correspondence of Leon Trotsky: The Balkan Wars*, 325.
119 Groh, "The 'Unpatriotic Socialists,'" 159.
120 Maehl, "The Triumph of Nationalism," 41.
121 Quoted in Niemeyer, "The Second International," 110.
122 Quoted in Wolfe, "Nationalism and Internationalism," 417.
123 Niemeyer, "The Second International," 110–11. See also Dieter Groh, "The 'Unpatriotic Socialists' and the State," *Journal of Contemporary History*, 1, no. 4 (October 1966), 157.

124 Maehl, "The Triumph of Nationalism," 28.
125 Groh, "The 'Unpatriotic Socialists,'" 157.
126 Maehl, "The Triumph of Nationalism," 29. In the aftermath of the resolution, Hervé exclaimed that the Germans gave the International a new motto: "Working men of the world, massacre each other!" As Maehl convincingly shows, not only was the SDP "bitten by the bug of nationalism" but a substantial number in the party were also becoming social imperialists, dreaming of a greater Germany on par with England and France with respect to markets and colonies (ibid., 30).
127 The text of the manifesto is in Georges Haupt, ed., *Congrès international extraordinaire* (Bâle, 24–25 novembre 1912); *Congrès international socialiste de Stockholm 1917* (Genève: Minkoff Reprint, 1980), 43–45.
128 Христо Кабакчиев, *Към Балканската федерация* (София: Партийна социалистическа книжарница, [1913]).
129 Haupt, *Socialism and the Great War*, 72. The quote is from the unpublished manuscript note of Dušan Popović, the secretary of the Serbian party, sent to the secretariat of the ISB on August 1, 1912.
130 Cited in Maehl, "The Triumph of Nationalism," 40–41.
131 Haupt, *Socialism and the Great War*, 245.
132 Иван Орманов, "Непримиримата класова борба и международната солидарност на пролетариата," *Ново време*, no. 1 (January 15, 1915), 9.
133 Haupt, "Führungspartei," 28. As Haupt observes, neither of these missions has been thoroughly researched. More has been written on Parvus because of his connection to German intelligence and possible ties with Lenin, but almost nothing on his mission outside the reaction of the Bulgarian socialists in the Bulgarian literature. For a refutation of the link with Lenin, see Ehrenfried Pößneck, *Lenin als Kontrahent von Parvus im Jahre 1917* (Leipzig: Leipziger Gesellschaft für Politik und Zeitgeschichte, 1997). The hagiographic memoir of Konrad Haenisch, *Parvus: Ein Blatt der Erinnerung* (Berlin: Verlag für Sozialwissenschaft, 1925), 30–35, glosses over Parvus's wealth accumulation and politics in the Ottoman Empire and in Balkan affairs, notably Bulgaria and Romania, as a chapter of his attempts to create a viable socialist party and his struggle against Tsarist Russia. Even more adulatory and uncritical is M. Asim Karaömerlioğlu, "Helphand-Parvus and the Impact on Turkish Intellectual Life," *Middle Eastern Studies*, 40, no. 6 (2004), 145–65. See also Heinz Schurer, "Alexander Helphand-Parvus – Russian Revolutionary and German Patriot," *Russian Review*, 18, no. 4 (1959), 313–31.
134 Winfried Scharlau and Zbynek Zeman, *Freibeuter der Revolution: Parvus-Helphand. Eine politische Biographie* (Köln: Wissenschaft und Politik, 1964), 151. Scharlau and Zeman also claim that Rakovski, through Parvus, was also linked to German intelligence, but the evidence is cursory (152, n. 1).
135 Благоев. *Съчинения*, т. 16, 401.
136 *Ново време*, no. 16 (August 1914), 483, cited in Първанов, *Българската социалдемокрация*, 222. *Ново време* (Novo vreme) was the theoretical journal of the Narrows, and this article was contributed before the news of the German socialists' vote for the war credits had arrived (Rothschild, *The Communist Party of Bulgaria*, 62).
137 *Ново време*, no. 23–24, 1924.
138 Благоев. *Съчинения*, т. 16, 493–95. See also Ангел Веков, "Д. Благоев и Г. В. Плеханов," *ИИИ*, 36 (1977), 85–119 and Ангел Веков, "Г. В. Плеханов и българската социалдемокрация," *ИИИ*, 31 (1974), 283–16. A much weaker article

is Ангел Христов, "Г. В. Плеханов и българските социалисти," *ИИИ*, 1–2 (1957), 399–427.
139 Scharlau and Zeman, *Freibeuter der Revolution*, 153.
140 Димитър Благоев, *Избрани съчинения в два тома*, Т.2. (София: БКП, 1951), 673.
141 Kirkov to Huysmans, 18/31 March 1915, cited in Haupt, "Führungspartei," 28–29.
142 Rothschild, *The Communist Party of Bulgaria*, 63.
143 *Manifesto of the Socialist Parties of the Balkans, Bucharest, 19-21 July 1915*, published in *The Balkan Socialist Tradition*, 242–43.
144 Декларация на БРСДП (о) относно Втората балканска социалистическа конференция, ЦДА, фонд 11, оп.1, а.е. 50, л. 28–29, cited in Йордан Йотов, *Центризмът в българското социалистическо движение*, 1905–1920 (София: Издателство на БКП, 1969), 260.
145 *Narod*, no. 255 (November 8, 1914), cited in *История на България*, том 8 (София: ГАЛ-ИКО, 1999), 245.
146 Rothschild, who in general is more benign toward the Broads, characterized them as "chauvinistic" and "rabid war supporters" (Rothschild, *The Communist Party of Bulgaria*, 70–71).
147 Madeleine Rebérioux, "Le socialism et la première guerre mondiale (1914-1918)," in *Histoire générale du socialism. Tome II*, 599.
148 Lindemann, *The "Red Years,"* 14.
149 Lenin developed the idea of workers or labor aristocracy in his *Imperialism, the Highest Stage of Capitalism* (1916), but he had prefigured it already at the 1907 Stuttgart Congress where he lamented the "negative feature in the European labor movement," where "even the proletariat has been somewhat infected with the lust of conquest" and the privileged position of European workers in relation to the "practically enslaved natives in the colonies" (cited in Day and Gaido, *Discovering Imperialism*, 29). He also refereed to Cecil Rhodes who, in 1895, had argued that "my cherished idea is a solution for the social problem, that is, in order to save the 40,000,000 inhabitants of the United Kingdom from a bloody civil war, we colonial statesmen must acquire new lands to settle the surplus population, to provide new markets for the goods produced in the factories and mines. The Empire, as I have always said, is a bread and butter question. If you want to avoid civil war, you must become imperialists" (Day and Gaido, 97).
150 ЦДА, Сп 1332 Б, 1–2.
151 Dimou, *Entangled Paths*, 424. Bell, *The Bulgarian Communist Party*, 20 [italics in the original], gives them credit that they never wavered, but immediately weakens this by saying that their opposition to the war had an abstract, theoretical character. While it was, indeed, the Agrarians of Stamboliiski who took the brunt of the government's repression during the war, this is to minimize the practical anti-war activities of the social democrats.
152 This stemmed primarily from the fact that the Bulgarian communists adopted the *Comintern* directive from 1934 to recognize a separate Macedonian nation. After the Second World War, they arduously implemented this policy until the Tito–Stalin split of 1948.
153 In many ways, Rakovski already belonged, avant la lettre, to what Brigitte Studer has aptly defined as *The Transnational World of the Cominternians*, trans. Davydd Rees Roberts (Palgrave Macmillan, 2015). In her book, she describes the generation of cosmopolitan international cadres, not even transnational but supra- or postnational,

who were centered in Moscow in the Hotel Lux between 1919 and 1943. Despite the asymmetrical relationship between representatives of mostly clandestine parties and one hegemonic party which was holding state power, at least during the first decade of its existence until the advent of Stalin and the subsequent Great Terror, the *Comintern* was the "embodiment of romantic hopes of proletarian emancipation" and a "distinctive transnational cultural and political space" (Studer, *The Transnational World*, 147, 150).

154 C. L. R. James, *World Revolution, 1917-1936: The Rise and Fall of the Communist International*, edited and introduced by Christian Høgsbjerg (Durham: Duke University Press, 2017), 93.
155 Haupt, *Socialism and the Great War*, 2; Eley, *Forging Democracy*, 125.
156 Eley, *Forging Democracy*, 114.
157 Annoyingly, Eley keeps on writing about Rakovski as the "Romanian-born future Bolshevik." Is Kautsky by the same token" the Czech-born," Luxemburg "the Russian-born," or Hobsbawm "the Egyptian-born"? On top of it, Rakovski was born in 1873 near Kotel, at the time in the Ottoman Empire, and after 1878 a town in Bulgaria in the Balkan Mountains. True, because his family estates were in Dobrudzha, which was lost to Romania, he also became a Romanian subject. He studied in Bulgaria and became an active participant in the Bulgarian socialist movement. He was also one of the founders of the Social Democratic Party of Romania, and one of the leaders of the Balkan Social-Democratic Federation. On the other hand, Rakovski himself would probably not have objected, since he was an authentic cosmopolitan and would not have cared how he would be ethnically described.
158 Sabine Rutar, *Kultur-Nation-Milieu. Sozialdemokratie in Triest vor dem Ersten Weltkrieg* (Essen: Klartext Verlag, 2004), 345–46.
159 *Karl Kautsky und die Sozialdemokratie Südosteuropas*, 168.
160 Ibid., 168.
161 ЦДА, Сп 655 Б, l.3. This comes from the unpublished memoirs of Dimitîr Ivanov Zahariev.
162 ЦДА, Фонд 368 Б, оп.1, а.е.43, л.5.
163 Симеон Радев, *Погледи върху литературата и изкуството и лични спомени* (София: Български писател, 1965), 148–49, cited also in Симеон Правчанов, *Майстора в Народното събрание* (София: Партиздат, 1987).
164 *Karl Kautsky und die Sozialdemokratie Südosteuropas*, 169.
165 Émile Vandervelde (1866–1938) became minister in the war cabinet of Belgium and was a prominent statesman in the interwar period.
166 *Karl Kautsky und die Sozialdemokratie Südosteuropas*, 169–70.
167 Ibid., 171–72.
168 Kautsky's brief thanking letter of May 8, 1917, speaks of the fate of the eggs (*Karl Kautsky und die Sozialdemokratie Südosteuropas*, 173). Interestingly, despite the fact that these letters have been known since 1986, and the "reproach" has been quoted by Haupt and Troebst and mentioned by Damianova, there is no mention of the eggs which, of course, raises the question of what we consider significant. Kirkov and Kautsky met in Berlin shortly before the Third and final Zimmerwald conference in Stockholm in September 1917. See Живка Дамянова, "Третата Цимервалдска конференция," *ИИИ*, 41 (1979), 129–77.
169 Frank Trentmann, "Materiality in the Future of History: Things, Practices, and Politics," *Journal of British Studies*, 48 (April 2009), 284.
170 Ibid., 297.

171 "Tuberculosis in Europe and North America, 1800-1922," *Historical Views on Diseases and Epidemics*, Harvard University Library Open Collection Program, http://ocp.hul.harvard.edu/contagion/tuberculosis.html.
172 The expression "multiscopic approach" has been used by Paul-André Rosental, "Construire le 'macro' par le 'micro': Frederik Barth et la microstoria," in Revel, ed. *Jeux d'échelles*, 142–43 to juxtapose it methodologically to the Italian practice of microhistory.
173 See especially Dipesh Chakrabarty, *Provincializing Europe: Postcolonial Thought and Historical Difference* (Princeton and Oxford: Princeton University Press, 2000); Gayatri Spivak, *A Critique of Postcolonial Reason: Toward a History of the Vanishing Present* (Cambridge, MA: Harvard University Press, 1999); Harry Harootunian, *Overcome by Modernity: History, Culture and Community in Interwar Japan* (Princeton and Oxford: Princeton University Press, 2000).
174 Max Weber, "The Methodological Foundations of Sociology," in *Sociological Writings* (London: Bloomsbury, 1994), https://www.marxists.org/reference/subject/philosophy/works/ge/weber.htm.
175 "Les Révélations d'un ancient conseiller de Carter: "Oui, la CIA est entrée en Afghanistan avant les Russes . . ." *Nouvel Observateur* (January 15–21, 1998), http://dgibbs.faculty.arizona.edu/brzezinski_interview.
176 Eugen Weber, *Movements, Currents, Trends: Aspects of European Thought in the Nineteenth and Twentieth Centuries* (Lexington, MA: D.C. Heath, 1992), 7.
177 Saul Kripke, *Naming and Necessity* (Cambridge, MA: Harvard University Press, 1980).

Part II

1 Д-р Кръстьо Кръстев, *Млади и стари. Критически очерки върху днешната българска литература* (Тутракан: Мавродинов, 1907 [2004]).
2 Милен Куманов, "Левият политически спектър в България (1918-1934 г.)," 324–54, here 339–40. See also Сава Арабаджиев, "Борбата на БКП против догматизма на сектантство на 'левите' комунисти през периода 1919-1922 г.," *ИИИ*, 11 (1964), 90–99; Жак Натан, "Борбата на БКП против 'лявото' сектантство," ibid., 125–44.
3 Благоев, "'Тесни социалисти' с анархистически глави," 547–48; *Кратка история на Българската Комунистическа Партия*, 94. See also Йордан Йотов, *Водителят, съвременник на бъдещето* (София: Издателство "Булгарика," 2000), 103–8 (this is an abbreviated version of the collective biography *Димитър Благоев. Биография*).
4 Bell, *The Bulgarian Communist Party from Blagoev to Zhivkov*, 42–53.
5 Stephen Lovell, "From Genealogy to Generation: The Birth of Cohort Thinking in Russia," *Kritika: Explorations in Russian and Eurasian History* 9, no. 3 (2008), 567, 590. See also Ben Ekloff and Tatiana Saburova, *A Generation of Revolutionaries: Nikolai Charushin and Russian Populism from the Great Reforms to Perestroika* (Indiana: Indiana University Press, 2017), as well as Philip Pomper, *The Russian Revolutionary Intelligentsia* (Northbrook, IL: AHM Publishing, 1970).
6 Ulrike Jureit and Michael Wildt, *Generationen: Zur Relevanz eines wissenschaftlichen Begriffes* (Hamburg: Hamburger Edition, 2005). For a sophisticated cautionary

approach to the concept, see Alan B. Spitzer, "The Historical Problem of Generations," *The American Historical Review*, 78, no. 5 (December 1973), 1353–85.
7   Martin Kohli, "Aging and Justice," in R. H. Binstock and L. K. George, eds., *Handbook of Aging and the Social Sciences* (Amsterdam: Elsevier, 2006), 458. See also Peter Laslett, "Interconnections over Time: Critique of the Concept of Generation," *Journal of Classical Sociology*, 5, no. 2 (2005), 205–13.
8   Shmuel N. Eisenstadt and Bryan S. Turner, "Sociology of Generations," *International Encyclopedia of Social & Behavioral Sciences (IESBH)*, 2nd ed., vol. 9 (2015), 866–70.
9   Gerhard Kleining, "Heuristik zur Erforschung von Biographien und Generationen," in Gerd Jüttemann and Hans Thomae, Hrsg. *Biographische Methoden in den Humanwissenschaften* (Weinheim: Beltz, Psychologie Verlags Union, 1998), 188–90.
10 Steven Mintz, "Reflections on Age as a Category of Analysis," *The Journal of the History of Childhood and Youth*, 1, no. 1 (Winter 2008), 93.
11 Bernd Weisbrod, "AHR Conversation: Each Generation Writes Its Own History of Generations," *The American Historical Review*, 123, no. 5 (December 2018), 1537.
12 Josef Ehmer, "Generationen in der historischen Forschung: Konzepte und Praktiken," in Harald Künemund and Marc Szydlik, Hrsg. *Generationen. Multidisziplinäre Perspektiven* (Wiesbaden: Verlag für Sozialwissenschaften, 2009), 59.
13 Marc Szydlik and Harald Künemund, "Generationen aus Sicht der Soziologie," in Künemund and Szydlik, *Generationen*, 9; see also Ehmer, "Generationen in der historischen Forschung," 60.
14 Anthony Esler, "Generations in History," *IESBH*, 2nd ed., vol. 9 (2015), 859.
15 Ehmer, "Generationen in der historischen Forschung," 61–64.
16 Ibid., 71–74.
17 Ibid., 64–68, 72.
18 Szydlik and Künemund, "Generationen aus Sicht der Soziologie," 10–11; Ehmer, "Generationen in der historischen Forschung," 60.
19 Paul R. Abramson, "Political Generations," *IESBH*, 2nd ed., vol. 9 (2015), 861. For a critique of the reliance on election results and survey data for the study of political generations, see Klaus R. Allerbeck, "Political Generations: Some Reflections on the Concept and Its Application to the German Case," *European Journal of Political Research*, 5 (1977), 119–34. For valuable surveys of the concept, see the above-cited Ehmer, "Generationen in der historischen Forschung," 59–80, as well as Ulrich Hermann, "Was ist eine 'Generation'? Methodologische und begriffsgeschichtiliche Explorationen zu einem Idealtypus," in Annegret Schüle, Thomas Ahbe, und Rainer Gries, Hg. *Die DDR aus generationsgeschichglicger Perspektive. Eine Inventur* (Leipzig: Universitätsverlag, 2006), 23–39; Peter Wienand, "Revoluzzer und Revisionisten. Die 'Jungen' in der Sozialdemokratie vor der Jahrhundertwende," *Politische Vierteljahresschrift*, XVII (1976), 208–41.
20 See, for example, Thomas Welskopp, "Die 'Generation Bebel,'" in Klaus Schönhoven und Bernd Braun, Hg., *Generationen in der Arbeiterbewegung* (München: Oldenbourg, 2005), 51–67.
21 Erdmute Alber, Sjaak van der Geest, and Susan Reynolds Whyte, eds. *Generations in Africa: Connections and Conflicts. Beitrage zur Afrikaforschung 33* (Berlin, etc.: Lit Verlag, 2008), cited in Sarah Lamb, "Generation in Anthropology," *IESBH*, 2nd ed., vol. 9 (2015), 859.
22 Ehmer, "Generationen in der historischen Forschung," 76. For a critique of the undertheorization of intergenerationality, see Alan France and Steven Roberts, "The Problem of Social Generations: A Critique of the New Emerging Orthodoxy in Youth

Studies," *Journal of Youth Studies*, 18, no. 2 (2015), 221–22; Fredric Jameson, *The Valences of the Dialectic* (London: Verso, 2010), 524–25; Heinz Bude, "Die Erinnerung der Generationen," in Helmut König, Michael Kohlstruck, and Andreas Wöll, Hrsg. *Vergangenheitsbewältigung am Ende des zwanzigsten Jahrhunderts* (Wiesbaden: Westdeutscher Verlag, 1998), 69–85; Pierre Nora, "La generation," in idem. *Les lieux de mémoire* (vol. 3.1) (Paris: Gallimard, 1992), 931–71.
23 Karl Mannheim, "The Problem of Generations," in idem. *Essays*, ed. Paul Kecskemeti (London and New York: Routledge, 1952), republished in 1972, 292 (original "Zum Problem der Generationen," *Kölner Vierteljahrschrifte für Soziologie*, 7, 1928, Heft 2, 157–85, Heft 3, 309–30. For an in-depth analysis of Mannheim, see Lutz Niethammer, "Generation und Geist: Eine Station auf Karl Mannheims Weg zur Wissenssoziologie," in Schüle, Ahbe, Gries, *Die DDR aus generationsgeschichtlicher Perspektive*, 47–64.
24 Ibid., 311.
25 Ibid., 282.
26 Ibid., 292.
27 Ibid., 306.
28 Ibid., 298.
29 Ibid., 300.
30 Ibid., 304.
31 Ibid., 307–8.
32 Ibid., 309.
33 Ibid., 313.
34 Ibid., 314.
35 Esler, "Generations in History," 857–58; Jennifer Cole, *Sex and Salvation: Imagining the Future in Madagascar* (Chicago, IL: University of Chicago Press, 2010), xii; "Generation," https://en.wikipedia.org/wiki/Generation; Szydlik and Künemund, "Generationen aus Sicht der Soziologie," 10–11; Ehmer, "Generationen in der historischen Forschung," 60, 71.
36 Tamara K. Hareven, "Aging and Generational Relations: A Historical and Life-Course Perspective," *Annual Review of Sociology*, 20, no. 4 (1994), 440–41.
37 Eisenstadt and Turner, "Sociology of Generations," *IESBH*, 866; Abramson, "Political Generations," *IESBH*, 861–65; Ehmer, "Generationen in der historischen Forschung," 74.
38 Constellations, in particular, defined as "social formations, in which individuals are linked by a specific interdependence," have become the object of systematic research: Martin Mulsow, "Qu'est-ce qu'une constellation philosophique?," *Annales. Histoire. Sciences Sociales*, 64, no. 1 (2009), 81–109 (here 88); Martin Mulsow and Macelo Stamm, Hg. *Konstellationsforschung* (Frankfurt am Main: Suhrkamp, 2005). On community, see Gerald Creed, ed. *The Seductions of Community: Emancipations, Oppressions, Quandaries* (Santa Fe, New Mexico: School of American Research Press, 2006).
39 Jürgen Kocka, "Reformen, Generationen und Geschichte," *Neue Gesellschaft/ Frankfurter Hefte*, 8 (2004), 34.
40 The literature on the effects of the Great War is immense, especially after its recent centenary. I am mentioning here only a few titles, beginning with the pioneering work of Jay Winter, *The Experience of World War I* (New York: Oxford University Press, 1989); *Sites of Memory, Sites of Mourning: The Great War in European Cultural History* (Cambridge, UK: Cambridge University Press, 1995); *Remembering War: The Great War Between History and Memory in the 20th Century* (New Haven: Yale University

Press, 2006); *War Beyond Words: Languages of Remembrance from the Great War to the Present* (Cambridge, UK: Cambridge University Press, 2017). See also Paul Fussel, *The Great War and Modern Memory* (New York: Oxford University Press, 1975 [2013]); Robert Wohl, *The Generation of 1914* (Cambridge: Harvard University Press, 1979); Neil Howe and William Strauss, *Generations: The History of America's Future, 1584 to 2069* (New York: William Morrow, 1991) define the "Lost Generation" as the cohorts born from 1883 to 1900, who came of age during the First World War I; Jay Winter and Emmanuel Sivan, eds. *War and Remembrance in the Twentieth Century* (Cambridge, UK: Cambridge University Press, 1999); Stéphane Audoin-Rouzeau, and Annette Becker, *14-18, retrouver la Guerre* (Paris: Éditions Gallimard, 2002) in English *1914-1918: Understanding the Great War* (New York: Hill and Wang, 2002); Jay Winter and Antoine Prost, *The Great War in History: Debates and Controversies, 1914 to the Present* (New York: Cambridge University Press, 2005); Jay Winter, ed. *The Legacy of the Great War Ninety Years On* (Columbia, MI: University of Missouri, 2009); Jason Crouthamel and Peter Leese, eds. *Psychological Trauma and the Legacies of the First World War* (London: Palgrave Macmillan, 2016); Konrad Jarausch, *Out of Ashes: A New History of Europe in the Twentieth Century* (Princeton: Princeton University Press, 2016); Ian Andrew Isherwood, *Remembering the Great War: Writing and Publishing the Experiences of World War I* (London: I. B. Tauris, 2017).
41 Sofia's population had increased tenfold from 20,000 in 1880 and reached 230,000 in 1929. T. Tchitchovsky, "Political and Social Aspects of Modern Bulgaria," *The Slavonic and East European Review*, 7, no. 21 (March 1929), 595. http://pogled.info/avtorski/Hristo-Georgiev/mersiya-makdermot-poslednite-dni-na-dimitar-blagoev-200-000-s e-stekoha-na-pogrebenieto-mu-v-karvavata-1924-g.90383; http://pogled.info/avtors ki/Hristo-Georgiev/mersiya-makdermot-poslednite-dni-na-dimitar-blagoev-200-000-se-stekoha-na-pogrebenieto-mu-v-karvavata-1924-g.90383
42 Heinz Bude, "Die 'Wir-Schicht' der Generation," *Berliner Journal für Soziologie*, 2 (1997), 197–204.
43 Kevin Morgan, "A Family Party? Some Genealogical Reflections on the CPGB," in Kevin Morgan, Gidon Cohen, and Andrew Flinn, eds., *Agents of the Revolution: New Biographical Approaches to the History of International Communism in the Age of Lenin and Stalin* (Bern: Peter Lang, 2005), 190.

Chapter 3

1 In 2011–12, the seven-volume encyclopedia had a new twelve-volume edition (*Голяма енциклопедия "България"* (София: Труд), with some additional materials and re-editing. While in many ways the general articles have been improved, I am sticking to the seven-volume version for the biographical data on individuals, some of whom have been left out in the new version.
2 I am immensely grateful to Gavril Lazov, a prominent archaeologist at the NHM who, against all odds, prevented the annihilation of this catalog. I also thank the leadership of the museum, which allowed me to work with it.
3 "Province" here means people from rural or small-town locales. It is a notoriously imprecise but ubiquitous concept that deserves rigorous scholarly theorizing. To my knowledge, the only valuable analytical approach to date has been a conference held in Ljubljana in 2013 dealing with this notion in the former Habsburg space: *Provinz*

als Denk- und Lebensfrom: Der Donau- und Karpatenraum im langen 19. Jahrhundert. Komission für Geschichte und Kultur der Deutschen in Südosteuropa (KGKDS) (Tübingen: Institut für Germanistik, Universität Ljubljana, September 26–28, 2013). Reviewed by Karl-Peter Krauss (H-Soz-u-Kult, December 2013) and a follow-up 2015 conference in Graz, published as Ulrike Tischler-Hofer/Karl Kaser, Hrsg. *Provincial Turn: Verhältnis zwischen Staat und Provinz im südlichen Europa vom letzen Drittel des 17. Bis ins 21. Jahrhundert* (Frankfurt am Main: Peter Lang, 2017).

4   I insist on using the Russian term instead of the usual English translation into populist (*narodnik*) and populism (*narodnichestvo*) since it obscures the socialist appurtenance of the movement and creates an infelicitous ideological comparison and classification, especially with today's overuse of "populism." Even the English title of the justly admired classic of Franco Venturi, *Roots of Revolution: A History of the Populist and Socialist Movements in Nineteenth-Century Russia* (New York: Knopf, 1960) makes this explicit opposition between "socialists" and "populists," but not the Italian original *Il populismo russo* (1952).

5   Tsanko Bakalov Tserkovski (1869–1926), a poet and teacher, was a member of the BWDSP until 1901, and then one of the leaders of the agrarian movement, and minister of culture in the government of Alexander Stamboliiski (1918–23).

6   Bell, *The Bulgarian Communist Party from Blagoev to Zhivkov*, 13.

7   Ibid., 12; Rothschild, *The Communist Party of Bulgaria*, 55.

8   Bell, *The Bulgarian Communist Party*, 26; Кратка история на Българската Комунистическа Партия, 96, 105.

9   Bell, *The Bulgarian Communist Party*, 26–27.

10 The incomplete database in an ACCESS table is at the readers' disposal and can be augmented at the Bloomsbury Companion Website.

11 Daniel Bertaux, "The Life Story Approach: A Continental View," *Annual Review of Sociology*, 10 (1984), 215–37, cited in Mary Jo Maynes, "Autobiography and Class Formation in Nineteenth-Century Europe: Methodological Considerations," *Social Science History*, 16, no. 3 (Autumn 1992), 531.

12 This comes from the memoirs of Blagoev, cited in Филип Панайотов. *Чучулигите*, 55.

13 On the initial reception, see Ibid., 156; Димитър Генчев, *Профили от кафене "Ландолт,"* 7; *Зараждане и развитие на социалистическото движение в Габровски окръг. Материали и документи.* (София: Партиздат, 1975), 238.

14 Панайотов, *Чучулигите*, 55.

15 Panaiot Pipkov (1871–1942) was a celebrated composer, professor of music, and opera conductor, who conducted police, military, and church choruses and orchestras as well. He left an amazing choral heritage, among them perhaps the most beloved hymn in Bulgaria, sung on May 24, the official national celebration of education and culture: Върви, народе възродени. A patriot, he was closely attached to the Macedonian cause, but had no contact to socialism. https://bg.wikipedia.org/wiki/Панайот_Пипков.

16 The writer Stoian Chilingirov, cited in Димитър Генчев, *Първоапостолите на идеала*, 54.

17 ЦДА, Сп 1038 Б (recollections by Dimitîr Iliev).

18 Besides Iordan Kînev, the other two born in the 1880s were Alexander Sokolov (1883–1903) who became a member of the BWSDP and was killed as a participant in the Macedonian Ilinden Uprising in 1903, and Strashimir Dimitrov Krinchev

(1884–1913) who was expelled from school for socialist ideas, became a writer and was killed in the Balkan Wars.
19 Mentioned in the memoirs of Todor Marinov, *ЦДА, Сп* 2827 Б, л. 13–20.
20 Панайотов, *Чучулигите*, 146.
21 Константин Бозвелиев, *Моите спомени*. Съст. и ред. Тихомир Тихов. София: Военноиздателски комплекс „Св. Георги Победоносцев," Университетско издателство "Св. Климент Охридски," (1993), 60.
22 Ibid., 73–74. Bozveliev presents one of the rare cases of persistent and successful self-education. Never getting outside Bulgaria and rarely outside his home town of Kazanlik, whose mayor he was between 1913 and 1927, he earned the respect of socialists of both wings with his honesty and decent behavior. A lifelong social democrat, and one of the leaders of the Broads until 1919, he nevertheless preserved good relations and respect for Blagoev. After 1934 he gradually retreated from political life. His phenomenal memory makes his memoirs a rare portrait gallery of early socialism, in which he does not spare the weaknesses of his contemporaries but always with goodwill.
23 Трендафил Митев, "Възникване и същност на 'широкия социализъм' в България," in *Изследвания по история на социализма*, т. I, 84–85.
24 Ibid., 85.
25 Rothschild, *The Communist Party of Bulgaria*, 46–47. Tchitchovsky, "Political and Social Aspects of Modern Bulgaria," 598–99 calculates that in 1920 Bulgaria had approximately 1,200,000 people (including dependents out of a total 4,850,000) living apart from agriculture, consisting of 485,000 in handicrafts and larger businesses; 103,000 in transport; 202,000 in commerce; and 250,000 employees, in the army and liberal professions. The official figure for wage-workers in 1920, 436,000, comprises 223,000 in agriculture; 132,000 in industry and handicrafts; 25,000 in transport; 27,000 in commerce and banking; 19,000 in domestic service; and 9,000 in other occupations.
26 *История на България*, том 7, 100.
27 М. А. Бирман, *Формиране и развитие на българския пролетариат, 1878-1923* (София: Партиздат, 1983), 108.
28 *История на България*, том 7, 231.
29 М. А. Бирман, "Численост и структура на работническата класа в началото на XX век," *ИИИ*, 37, 1977, 160.
30 Йотов, *Водителят*, 56.
31 Rothschild, *The Communist Party of Bulgaria*, 15.
32 Димитър Благоев, *Що е социализъм и има ли той почва у нас?* in *Съчинения*, т. 1 (София: БКП, 1957), 519. See also Йотов, *Водителят*, 57; *Димитър Благоев. Биография*, 76. Blagoev's conclusion about the differentiation of the population is altogether borne out by subsequent scholarly analysis, although he may have been too sanguine about the tempo: *История на България*, том 7, 99–101, 230–33.
33 Трендафил Митев, "Възникване и същност на 'широкия социализъм' в България," in *Изследвания по история на социализма*, т. I, 90–91.
34 Карл Кауцки, "Социалистите в икономически изостаналите назад страни," in *Янко Сакъзов-Юбилеен сборник* (София: Издателство "Обществена мисъл," 1930), 18–19, cited in Dimou, *Entangled Paths*, 162.
35 Mirjana Gross, "Ideologija socialističkog pokreta u Hrvatskoj do prvog svjetskog rata," in Ivan Kampuš, Igor Karaman and Bogdan Krizman, eds. *Kulturnohistorijski*

simpozij "Mogersdorf 74": Radnički pokreti id početaka do svršetka prvoga svjetskog rata (Zagreb: Republički savjet za naučni rad SR Hrvatske,, 1976), 13–14.
36 Благоев, *Що е социализъм и има ли той почва у нас?*, 439, also in Йотов, *Водителят*, 62.
37 Vlado Oštrić, "Radnički pokret u jugoslovenskim zemljama od svojih početaka do 1918/1819. godine," *Povijesni prilozi*, br.1 (1982), 28–31; Witscho Rainoff, *Die Arbeiterbewegung in Bulgarien* (Grüningen, 1909), 87 (Reprint from the collections of the University of California Libraries); Rothschild, *The Communist Party of Bulgaria*, 48.
38 Журнал *Съвременний показател*, I, 1885, no. 1, 4–5; *Димитър Благоев. Биография*, 72.
39 Димитър Благоев, "Защо няма щастие и как то може да се достигне," (Why there is no happiness and how can one achieve it), cited in Йотов, *Водителят*, 46.
40 Никола Сакаров, Найден Николов, *Опити за разсейване на идейната безпътица* (София: Печатница Гладстон, 1929), Addendum "Към социализма!," 1.
41 Ibid., 2.
42 Ibid.
43 Ibid., 2–3.
44 Rothschild, *The Communist Party of Bulgaria*, 39, 41–42. Rothschild had compiled the figures from the publications of both parties, especially their reports to the Second International.
45 "Rapport du Parti Ouvrier Social Democrate Bulgare (Unifié) au Bureau Socialiste International," *Rapports sur le movement ouvrier et socialiste soumis au Congrès Socialiste International de Copenhagen*, no. 21 (1910), 7, cited in Rothschild, *The Communist Party of Bulgaria*, 42.
46 *Годишен отчет на Централния комитет на Работническата социалдемократическа партия за 1913/1914 година*, 8 in ЦДА, Фонд 1Б, оп.2, а.е.219, л.5. The category "owners" would encompass shopkeepers, master artisans, etc.; "state employees" would include teachers, and liberal professions—lawyers, doctors, etc.
47 Ibid.
48 Панайотов, *Чучулигите*, 147.
49 ЦДА, Сп 1462 Б.
50 Dimitrov's place in the Bulgarian historiography before 1989 is enormous, including the publication of his collected works. In Western languages, see Marietta Stankova, *Georgi Dimitrov: A Life* (London: I.B. Tauris, 2010); Mona Foscolo, *Georges Dimitrov: une biographie critique* (dissertation, 2006), translated into Bulgarian Мона Фосколо, *Георги Димитров: една критическа биография* (София: Просвета, 2013); Ivo Banac, ed. *The Diary of Georgi Dimitrov, 1933-1949* (New Haven: Yale University Press, 2003); Veselin Chadzinikolov, *Georgi Dimitroff: Biographischer Abriss* (Berlin: Dietz, 1972).
51 Rothschild, *The Communist Party of Bulgaria*, 51. On the labor movement, see pp. 46–57, 305–11.
52 ЦДА, Сп 2934 Б, л. 41.
53 Rothschild, *The Communist Party of Bulgaria*, 52.
54 ЦДА, Фонд 368, оп.1, а.е.28, л. 38–39.
55 ЦДА, Фонд 196 Б, оп.1, а.е.3, л. 1.
56 Панайот Панайотов, *Приносът на българи за победата на Октомврийската революция (1917-1920)* (София: Издателство на БКП, 1967).

57 Ibid., 196–200.
58 ЦДА, Фонд 196 Б, оп.1, а.е. 4, 5. *Пътеводител по фондовете на БКП*, 252.
59 ЦДА, Фонд 196 Б, оп.1, а.е. 2, л. 1–7.
60 ЦДА, Фонд 368, оп.1, а.е.28, л. 45.
61 Mark Steinberg, *Proletarian Imagination: Self, Modernity, and the Sacred in Russia, 1910-1925* (Ithaca, NY: Cornell University Press, 2002); ЦДА, Фонд 196 Б, оп.1, а.е. 11, 12, 13, 14, 16. Amazingly, а.е. 15, consisting of over 1,000 pages including Dhorov's thoughts on Marxism and the village as such, has a two-page review from 1957, recommending that this work should be returned as a memento to Dhorov's heirs, since it is of no value to the archive.
62 ЦДА, Сп 240 Б, л. 10.
63 ЦДА, Сп 2060 Б, 137, 268–70, 296–300.
64 *Selections from the Prison Notebooks of Antonio Gramsci*, edited and translated by Quentin Hoare and Geoffrey Nowell Smith (London: Lawrence & Wishart, 1971), 5. The *Prison Notebooks* were written between 1929 and 1935.
65 Ibid., 9.
66 Robert J. Brym, "Intellectuals, Sociology Of," *International Encyclopedia of Social & Behavioral Sciences (IESBH)*, 2nd ed., vol. 12 (2015), 277–82; Christophe Charle, "Intellectuals: History of the Concept," *(IESBH)*, 2nd ed., vol. 12 (2015), 273–76. The following is a brief but by no means exhaustive list of some of the most important works: Michel Trebitsch and Marie-Christine Granjon, eds., *Pour une histoire comparée des intelectuels* (Brussels, Belgium: Complexe, 1998); Dietz Bering, *Die Intellektuellen. Geschichte eines Schimpfwortes* (Stuttgart: Klett, 1978); Stefan Collini, *Public Moralists: Political Thought and Intellectual Life in Britain, 1850–1930* (Oxford, UK: Clarendon Press, 1991); Ingrid Gilcher-Holthey, *Das Mandat des Intellektuellen: Karl Kautsky und die Sozialdemokratie* (Siedler, Berlin: Siedler, 1986); Jerzy Jedlicki, ed. *A History of the Polish Intelligentsia* (Frankfurt am Main: Peter Lang, 2014); Mark Raeff, *Origins of the Russian Intelligentsia: The Eighteenth-Century Nobility* (New York: Houghton-Mifflin, 1966), followed by numerous works on the Russian intelligentsia by Barbara Alpern Engel, Jane Burbank, Richard Pipes, Victoria Frede, Christopher Read, and many others. Of the sociological works: Talcott Parsons, "The Intellectual: A Social Role Category," in Paul Rieff, ed., *On Intellectuals* (Garden City, NJ: Anchor, 1963), 3–24; Jerome Karabel, "Towards a Theory of Intellectuals and Politics," *Theory and Society*, 25, no. 2 (1996), 205–33; Lawrence Peter King and Iván Szelényi, *Theories of the New Class: Intellectuals and Power* (Minneapolis: University of Minnesota Press, 2004); Georg Konrad and Iván Szelényi, *The Intellectuals on the Road to Class Power: A Sociological Study of the Role of the Intelligentsia in Socialism* (New York: Harcourt Brace Jovanovich, 1979); Randall Collins, *The Sociology of Philosophies: A Global Theory of Intellectual Change* (Cambridge, MA: Harvard University Press, 1998); Robert J. Brym, *The Jewish Intelligentsia and Russian Marxism: A Socio- logical Study of Intellectual Radicalism and Ideological Divergence* (London: Macmillan, 1978); Robert J. Brym, *Intellectuals and Politics* (London: Routledge, 1980 [2010]); Alex Demirović and Peter Jehle, "Intellektuelle," *Historisch-kritisches Wörterbuch des Marxismus*. Bd. 6/II (Berlin, Hamburg: Argument, 2004), 1267–86.
67 Karl Mannheim, "The Sociological Problem of the 'Intelligentsia,'" in *Ideology and Utopia: An Introduction to the Sociology of Knowledge*, translated from the German by Louis Wirth and Edward Shils (New York: A Harvest Book-Harcourt, Brace and Company, 1936) (reprint in 1985), 156.

68 Ibid., 157.
69 Ibid., 155.
70 Ibid., 158.
71 Любен Беров, "Аграрният преврат в Северна и Южна България," *История на България*. Том 7 (София: Издателство на БАН, 1991), 79–86; Христо Христов, *Аграрният въпрос в българската национална революция* (София: Наука и изкуство, 1976), 267–72; Michael Palairet, *The Balkan Economies, c1800-1914: Evolution Without Development* (Cambridge: Cambridge University Press, 1997), 175–86; John R. Lampe and Marvin R. Jackson, *Balkan Economic History, 1550-1950* (Bloomington: Indiana University Press, 1982), 184–86. See also Anna M. Mirkova, *Muslim Land, Christian Labor: Transforming Ottoman Imperial Subjects into Bulgarian Citizens,* 1878–1939 (Budapest: CEU Press, 2017).
72 *Годишен отчет,* 8 in ЦДА, Фонд 1Б, оп.2, а.е.219, л.5.
73 Rothschild, *The Communist Party of Bulgaria*, 42.
74 Върбан Ангелов, *Живот за партията* (София: Партиздат, 1972), 188–90.
75 Ibid., 191.
76 Иван Танчев, *Учението на българи в чужбина, 1879-1892* (София: Академично издателство "Марин Дринов," 1994), 5–6. These figures are based on the research of Николай Генчев. *Българска възрожденска интелигенция* (София: Университетско издателство "Св. Климент Охридски," 1991).
77 Ibid., 69–70, 93–95.
78 Ibid., 80.
79 Ibid., 90–92.
80 Ibid., 70.
81 *Спомени на д-р Петър Джидров* (съставител Богдан Джидров) (София: Университетско издателство "Св.Климент Охридски," 1996), 74–83.
82 According to the memoirs of Iordan Panov (Shemsheto), this was decided at a secret conference of about forty communists. There was a secret list of about 200 people involved in the secret intelligence activities: ЦДА, Сп 1427 Б, л. 1–5.
83 *Кратка история на Българската Комунистическа Партия*, 90–93.
84 ЦДА, Сп 1728 Б, 1.
85 Ibid., 8.
86 Благоев, "'Тесни социалисти' с анархистически глави," 547-548.
87 *The Cambridge History of Communism*. Vol.1, 475, 477.
88 Филю Христов, *Военно-революционната дейност на българската комунистическа партия, 1912-1944* (София: Държавно военно издателство, 1959), 70–77. While the span of the book covers 1912–44, the period until 1919 is dedicated exclusively to the socialist theory of war and work in the army, and to the anti-militarist propaganda of the party.
89 Ангелов, *Неизвестни страници*, 47–48; Rothschild, *The Communist Party of Bulgaria,* 128–30.
90 Иван Клинчаров, *Димитър Благоев, история на неговия живот* (София: n.p., 1926), 276–77 (italics in the original). Klincharov (1877–1942) had been a student of Blagoev in high school, entered BWSDP in 1898, became a Narrow after 1903, and a communist in 1919. He studied literature at Sofia University (1902–06), finished a law degree in Lyon (1910), and obtained a doctorate from the University of Brussels in 1915. A high school teacher and, later, lawyer, he was a member of the BCP leadership in 1919. While he criticized the politics of neutrality, he was opposed to

the September Uprising and the subsequent illegal activities of the party. In 1932 he was expelled from the then legal Workers' Party for attempting to create an alternative legal formation. His mission was the defense of the legacy of the Narrow socialists. After his death, he was posthumously declared in 1948 to be a Trotskyist, left sectarian and his fundamental works on Botev, Karavelov, Levski, Blagoev, and pop Bogomil were not reissued and practically banned.

91 Rothschild, *The Communist Party of Bulgaria*, 122–26.
92 Report of Karl Radek, June 23, 1923, published in *Internationale Presse-Korrespondenz*, no. 117, July 17, 1923, in ЦДА, Фонд 366 Б, оп.1, а.е. 673.
93 Bell, *The Bulgarian Communist Party*, 35.
94 Ibid., 36.
95 Rothschild, *The Communist Party of Bulgaria*, 142–43; Ангелов, *Неизвестни страници*, 51–52.
96 For a scathing and sober analysis of the strategy or rather lack thereof of the leaders of the uprising, see Ангелов, *Неизвестни страници*, 67–73, 87–89.
97 The concept of "permanent revolution" developed by Trotsky (and Parvus) first for Russia already in his early writings from 1905 but then extended to the so-called "undeveloped countries" (he wrote specifically about China, India, and Spain) argued that the social-democratic perspective was a utopian fantasy as these countries' weak bourgeoisie would never be able to carry out what was achieved by the bourgeoisies of the advanced countries. He accordingly advocated a direct proletarian revolution with an alliance with the peasantry but under the hegemony of the working class and against the two-stage theory of revolution (first bourgeois-democratic, then proletarian). It was adamantly opposed to Stalin's (and Bukharin's) theory of socialism in one country. In the 1929 introduction to *The Permanent Revolution* Trotsky wrote: "The socialist revolution begins on national foundations—but it cannot be completed within these foundations. The maintenance of the proletarian revolution within a national framework can only be a provisional state of affairs, even though, as the experience of the Soviet Union shows, one of long duration. In an isolated proletarian dictatorship, the internal and external contradictions grow inevitably along with the successes achieved. If it remains isolated, the proletarian state must finally fall victim to these contradictions." The permanent revolution was understood globally also as the task of the "the first victorious revolution to operate as the yeast of revolution on the world arena" in the words of Saumyeandranath Tagore (see Leon Trotsky, *The Permanent Revolution: Results and Prospects*. https://www.marxists.org/archive/trotsky/1931/tpr/index.htm; *La Teoría de la Revolucion Permanente*. Buenos Aires: Centro de Estudios y publicaciones León Trotsky (CEIP), 2000; https://en.wikipedia.org/wiki/Permanent_revolution; "The Development and Extension of Leon Trotsky's Theory of Permanent Revolution," http://www.icl-fi.org/english/wv/901/permrev.html). Ангелов directly speaks of "permanent revolution" as advocated by Trotsky over the warnings that Lenin gave the Bulgarian communists in 1921 and 1922 (*Неизвестни страници*, 49, 52, 60–63, 78). In his memoirs, Iurdan Rashenov also shares the information given to him by Naiden Kirov who as a delegate to the congress of the Comintern heard Lenin's warnings against the hasty actions of the "left" that would only produce pointless victims and weaken the communist parties (ЦДА, Сп 1647 Б, 34). The concept of "socialism on one country" was already promoted by Stalin by the end of 1924, theorized by Bukharin in April 1925, and adopted as the official state policy of the USSR in January 1926.

98 According to Reviakina, after 1925 the BCP had less than 1,000 members: Луиза Ревякина, "БКП и селското движение в България: теория, практика (май 1919-септември 1944)," in *Изследвания по история на социализма*, т. I, 376.
99 Клинчаров, *Димитър Благоев*, 278.
100 Blagoev to Krum Tikhchev after the uprising, cited in Ангелов, *Неизвестни страници*, 49. This has been recorded in many other memoirs of the older generation. An additional slightly different version comes from the memoirs of Matei Ikonomov, who was very close to Blagoev as he had adopted the child of his deceased brother Khristo, and therefore was not careful in the choice of words. Blagoev told him about Georgi Dimtrov, "What I had built in the course of 38 years, this *пичлеме* has destroyed" and started crying (ЦДА, Сп 2686 Б, 4). *Пичлеме* or *пишлеме* is practically untranslatable. It comes from the Turkish pişlemek (to smear, to dirty) and carries all the meanings of a flunky, conjuror, operator, etc.
101 Cited in Anderson, *The Antinomies of Antonio Gramsci*, 106.
102 *Архив на МВР*, ОБ (Общо дело) 280, Vol. 1, 70/ob – 71.
103 ЦДА, Сп 934 Б, 32–35. Ангелов, *Неизвестни страници*, 53, 113, also uses "young" and "old" as demographic terms.
104 Ivan Kamenov, "A Small History and the September Uprising of 1923 in the Ruse District," *ЦДА*, Сп 807 Б. Likewise, Dragan Kodzheikov, a supporter of the armed uprising, speaks of the reservations among party members and paints a detailed picture of its impossibility after the September 12 arrests, without criticizing the decision, ЦДА, Сп 911 Б.
105 ЦДА, Фонд 265 Б, оп.1, а.е.36, л.18.
106 ЦДА, Сп 2565 Б.
107 Трифон Митев, "Септемврийското въстание (1923 г.) и паметта за него в българската литература," https://stzagora.net/2013/09/26/септемврийското-въстание-1923-г-и-паметт/.
108 Rothschild, *The Communist Party of Bulgaria*, 144.
109 ЦДА, Сп 3049 Б, 376.
110 *Архив на МВР*, ОБ 4744, л.106.
111 *Архив на МВР*, ОБ 280, vol. 3, 38–39.
112 Димитър Косев, *Септемврийското въстание през 1923 г* (София, 1953).
113 Георги Марков, *Покушения, насилие и политика в България 1878-1947* (София: Военно издателство, 2003), 221.
114 Bell, *The Bulgarian Communist Party*, 37.
115 Ангелов, *Неизвестни страници*, 134. A well-known critic of 1923, in this instance he was speaking of the partisan movement. The memoirs were written in the 1950s.
116 Ангелов, *Неизвестни страници*, 77. To this day one can encounter positive accounts of the uprising as inspirational and the first anti-fascist one in the world: http://alexsimov.blogspot.com/2008/09/blog-post_7491.html; http://pogled.info/a vtorski/Nako-Stefanov/septemvriiskoto-vastanie-prez-1923-godina-parvoto-antifash istko-vastanie-v-sveta.57927.
117 ЦДА, Сп 683 Б. For obituaries, see *Работник*, I, 1 (November 1, 1892), no. 4 (November 21, 1892) and many others. One can add here Nikola Stefanov (1872–1910), the elder brother of the greatest interwar writer Iordan Iovkov, who died of TB and mental disturbance (М. Христов, "Биографични сведения за Никола Стефанов, брат на писатля Йордан Йовков," *ИИИ*, 6 [1959]).
118 Панайотов, *Чучулигите*, 73–75.
119 Ibid., 76–77.

120 *Anthology of Bulgarian Poetry*, translated by Peter Tempest (Sofia: Sofia Press, 1980), 251.
121 Филип Панайотов. Йосиф Хербст: *Живот и смърт* (София: Партиздат, 1981).
122 *Flame* (Plamîk, Пламък) came out with the financial support of the Federation of anarcho-communists and personally from the charismatic anarchist Georgi Sheitanov (1896–1925). It published Sheitanov's poetry, and Kropotkin's and other anarchists' works: https://bg.wikipedia.org/wiki/Георги_Шейтанов_(анархист), https://bg.wikipedia.org/wiki/История_ на_анархическия_печат_в_България.
123 Светлозар Игов. *Кратка история на българската литература* (София: Издателство "Захарий Стоянов," Университетско издателство "Св.Климент Охридски," 2005), 380-83; Никита Нанков, "Баснята за блудния син: Гео Милев, европейският модернизъм и българската лява критика," *Литературна мисъл*, 47, no. 1–2 (2003), 85–111, https://liternet.bg/publish13/n_nankov/kritika/basniata.htm.
124 Following are excerpts from the poem "Septemvri," in *Anthology of Bulgarian Poetry*, 211–27. For an interesting analysis of crowd theory and the terminological shift from the "crowds" of Marx and Engels to the "multitudes" of Hardt and Negri, see William Mazzarella, "The Myth of the Multitude, or, Who's Afraid of the Crowd?," *Critical Inquiry*, 36, no. 4 (Summer 2010), 697–727.

Chapter 4

1 Кръстю Кръстев, "Отворено писмо до г-н Велчо Велчев," *Народни права*, no. 137 (February 28, 1896), cited in Николай Попптеров, "Личността на Георги Кирков като възможност/повод за многостранна историческа реконструкция," in Максим Мизов, Таня Турлакова, (ред.) *Георги Кирков и нашето съвремие. Материали от конференцията, посветена на 140 години от рождението му.* (София: Център за исторически и политилогически изследвания, 2007), 40.
2 ЦДА, Фонд 177 К, оп.1, а.е. 111, л. 113–14.
3 Ibid., а.е. 299, л. 12/об -13.
4 Ibid., а.е. 110, л. 91–92.
5 Ibid., а.е. 45, л. 9/об -10.
6 Иван Друмев, *Социализма в България* (Стара Загора: Печатница "Светлина," 1922), 4–6.
7 *Цариградски вестник*, no. 61 (November 17, 1851); no. 74 (February 16, 1852).
8 *Цариградски вестник*, no. 46 (April 30, 1849); no. 48 (May 14, 1849); no. 56 (July 9, 1849).
9 *Македония*, IV, no. 32 (March 10, 1870); no. 34 (March 17, 1870); no. 35 (March 21, 1870) (*sic*! no. 33 never came out).
10 *Турция*, VI, no. 6 (March 28, 1870); no. 7 (April 4, 1870); no. 8 (April 11, 1870); no. 10 (April 26, 1870); no. 11 (May 2, 1870).
11 *Дунав*, XI, no. 1001 (August 27, 1875) (September 8, 1875).
12 *Ден*, I, no. 21 (June 30, 1875), 2.
13 *Ден*, I, no. 15 (May 19, 1875), 7.
14 Лазар Йовчев, "Интернасионал," *Читалище*, II, no. 3 (November 1, 1871), 97–109; no. 4 (November 15, 1871), 145–54.
15 *Читалище*, II, no. 3 (November 1, 1871), 99.

16 *Читалище*, II, no. 4 (November 15, 1871), 152.
17 Ibid., 153.
18 Ibid., 154.
19 This is even the case in the otherwise exemplary history of Bulgarian literature by Svetlozar Igov: Игов. *Кратка история на българската литература*, 236–47.
20 Илия Тодоров, "Символ-верую на българската комуна," *Летописи*, бр. 1 (1991). Botev's welcome and defense of the Paris Commune is in his feuilleton "Ridiculous lament" (Смешен плач) published in n. 2 of *Дума на българските емигранти*, the paper he edited in 1871 and of which only five issues came out. Ilia Todorov's article can be accessed at http://clubs.dir.bg/showthreaded.php?Board=politics&Number=1 939666704. Beyond this serious publication, most of the rest belong to the tabloid press.
21 М. И. Йосько, *Николай Сурзиловский -Руссель. Жизнь, революционная деятельность и мировозрение* (Минск: Издательство БГУ им. В. И. Ленина, 1976), 97–100. Sudzilovsky had personally met Marx and Engels in 1875 (ibid., 73).
22 Христо Ботев, "Народът вчера, днес и утре," *Дума на българските емигранти*, бр.1–2 (1871), http://www.litclub.bg/library/bg/botev/publ/narodut.htm
23 Йосько, *Николай Сурзиловский -Руссель*, 78–79.
24 *Знаме*, no. 16 (May 17, 1875) and no. 17 (May 23, 1875).
25 For one of the latest iterations, see Илия Стоянов, "Христо Ботев начело на революционното движение," in Илия Стоянов, *История на българското Възраждане* (Велико Търново: Абагар, 1999). A rare exception is Людмил Стоянов. *Христо Ботев*, written in the 1920s where Stoianov credits Nechayev with informing Botev about the national and revolutionary struggles in Europe and thus broadening his horizon: "Nechayev could give him nothing else" (*Библиотека "Български писатели." Живот - творчество - идеи*. Т. III. Под ред. на М. Арнаудов [София: Факел, 1929]; https://liternet.bg/publish5/lstoianov/hbotev.htm).
26 Йосько, *Николай Сурзиловский -Руссель*, 95.
27 Игов, *Кратка история на българската литература*, 296.
28 Ibid., 84–85, 94–96.
29 Dimou. *Entangled Paths*, 59.
30 Ibid., 59–60, 65–69; Latinka Perović, *Srpski socijalisti 19. veka: prilog istoriji socijalističke misli* (Beograd: Izdavačka radna organizacija "Rad," 1985); Đorđe Tomić and Krunoslav Stojaković, "Aus der Geschichte der jugoslawischen Linken. Von den Anfängen im 19. Jahrhundert bis zum Ausbruch des Zweiten Weltkrieges – Desideratsskizze(n)," *Südosteuropäische Hefte*, 1, no. 1 (2012), 86–88. The literature on Marković is enormous. To the topic, see Vitomir Vuletić, *Svetozar Marković i ruski revolucionarni demokrati* (Beograd: Matica Srpska, 1964); also Walter Daugsch. *Internationalismus und Organisation. Studien zur Entstehung und Entwicklung der serbishen Sozialdemokratie*. Herne: Gabriele Schäfer Verlag, 2008, 207-211.
31 Dimou, *Entangled Paths*, 21–22, 284, 300, 330–31; Jochen Schmidt, *Populismus oder Marxismus. Zur Ideengeschichte der radikalen Intelligenz Rumäniens* (Tübingen: Verlag der Tübinger Gesellschaft, 1922); Dietmar Müller, *Agrarpopulismus in Rumänien. Programmatik und Regierungspraxis der Bauernpartei und der Nationalbäuerlichen Partei Rumäniens in der Zwischenkriegszeit* (St. Augustin: Gardez Verlag, 2001); Йосько, *Николай Сурзиловский -Руссель*, 108–16, 120–22.
32 Dimou, *Entangled Paths*, 22.
33 Ibid., 23.
34 Ibid., 39.

35 Ibid., 175. Even Russian revolutionary democrats were not all *narodniks*.
36 Йосько, *Николай Сурзиловский -Руссель*, 124–25.
37 Ibid., 126–30, 136.
38 Ibid., 130–34.
39 Ibid., 135.
40 Ibid., 136. These were Vladimir Lutskii, Yakim Tranen, and Miron Ignatiev.
41 Ibid., 123.
42 Dimou, *Entangled Paths*, 185–90.
43 https://en.wikipedia.org/wiki/Natalie_de_Bogory and https://en.wikipedia.org/wiki/Harris_A._Houghton
44 В. К. Дебогорий-Мокриевич, *Воспоминания* (Санкт Петербург: Книгоиздательство "Свободный Труд," 1906), 596–97, cited in Йосько, *Николай Сурзиловский -Руссель*, 122; W. Debogory-Mokriewitwsch, *Erinnerungen eines Nihilisten* (Stuttgart: Verlag von Robert Lutz, 1905), 324–27.
45 http://sitebulgarizaedno.com/index.php?option=com_content&view=article&id=722:sr&catid=29:2010-04-24-09-14-13&Itemid=61
46 There exists no separate monographic treatment of Bulgarian anarchism. The following section is compiled from the relatively small file existing in the Central State Archives (*ЦДА*, Фонд 272 Б Анархистко движение), as well as the article of Дончо Даскалов, "Анархизмът в България по време на революционната криза (1918-1925)," *ИИИ*, 26 (1971), 111–41.
47 Панайотов, *Чучулигите*, 154.
48 Ivanka Boteva studied social sciences in Geneva and was active in the socialist anarchist and Macedonian movements. She died very young after an unsuccessful operation, most likely from sepsis. https://bg.wikipedia.org/wiki/Иванка_Христова_Ботева.
49 The first anarchist newspaper is considered to be *Borba*, edited by Dimitîr Boiknov in Plovdiv in 1894, but little is known about it. Other short-lived papers were *Anarchy* (Sofia, 1901) and *Free Thought* (Vidin): https://bg.wikipedia.org/wiki/История_на_анархическия_печат_в_България.
50 Tomić, Stojaković, "Aus der Geschichte der jugoslawischen Linken," 91–94.
51 Даскалов, "Анархизмът в България," 113.
52 Михаил Герджиков, *Спомени, документи, материали* (София: Наука и изкуство, 1984); https://bg.wikipedia.org/wiki/Михаил_Герджиков. After 1923, Gerdzhikov lived in emigration mostly in Vienna and was instrumental in the Istanbul conference of the IMRO in 1930 which reconciled the Macedonian communist and nationalist wings. He returned to Bulgaria in 1931 and as an antifascist at first welcomed 1944 but retreated from political life and died in 1947.
53 *Работническа мисъл*, January 19, 1923, cited in Даскалов, "Анархизмът в България," 123.
54 Даскалов, "Анархизмът в България," 136. The list of anarchists is in *ЦДА*, Фонд 370, оп.1, а.е. 515. After 1923 many went underground, joined guerila groups, and emigrated. By 1926 the movement effectively ended its organized existence. Bulgarian anarchists were active in the Spanish Civil War but did not join the popular front and were banned in 1945, with a few scattered acts in the following decades (*ЦДА*, Фонд 272 Б, оп.1а.е. 56, 61, 63). Anarchist press, however, continued to be published: https://bg.wikipedia.org/wiki/История_ на_анархическия_печат_в_България.
55 Панайотов, *Чучулигите*, 30.

56 Георги Константинов, "Лев Толстой в България," *Българска мисъл*, no. 7–8 (1928), 12, cited in М.Т.Терзиева, "Летописцы толстовского движения в Болгарии," *Перспективы Науки и Образования*, 2, 20 (2016). Международный электронный научний журнал https://pnojournal.files.wordpress.com/2016/03/pdf_160214.pdf. He agreed that compared to the communists, the followers of Tolstoy in Bulgaria were negligent but, according to him, Marxism was a foreign and superficial influence, whereas Tolstoyism was organic.

57 Keith Hitchins, "Balkan Identity and Europe Between the Two World Wars in the Thought of Yanko Yanev," *Revue des Études Sud-Est Eropéennes*, 41, nos. 1–2 (2003), 65–74; Ivan Elenkov and Mila Koumpilova, "On the History of Rightist Thought in Interwar Bulgaria: The Existential Dimensions of 'Crisis' in the Writings of Yanko Yanev," *Studies in East European Thought*, 53, no. 1–2 (June 2001), 47–59; Balázs Trencsényi, "Balkans Baedecker for Übermensch Tourists: Janko Janev's Popular Historiosophy," in Stefan Berger, Chris Lorenz, and Billie Melman, eds., *Popularizing National Pasts* (New York: Routledge, 2012), 149–68; Nicholas Huzsvai, "Revolt Against Europe: An Introduction to the Radical Occidentalism of Janko Janeff," https://historikerkreis.wordpress.com/2017/09/12/revolt-against-europe-an-introduction-to-the-radical-occidentalism-of-janko-janeff/

58 https://bg.wikipedia.org/wiki/ Димо_Кьорчев

59 Married to a Russian, Taushanov was involved in illegal transactions under the guise of commerce. In 1917 he joined the Bolsheviks and in 1932 was sent to Bulgaria to promote trade relations with the USSR. He was quite active in this respect and well connected but in 1838 was warned to stop his Soviet links. His memoirs say nothing about the period 1919–1932 and it seems that he was a spy. The memoirs were typed in 1965.

60 *ЦДА*, Сп 2686 Б.

61 https://bg.wikipedia.org/wiki/Матей_Икономов.

62 *ЦДА*, Сп 1826 Б, л. 18.

63 Виктория Георгиева, "Толстой и България: как учението на великия хуманист намира последователи у нас," *Култура* (September 30, 2017), https://bg.rbth.com/culture/325672-толстой-българия-учение-последователи; https://bg.wikipedia.org/wiki/Йордан_Ковачев; https://bg.wikipedia.org/wiki/Толстоизъм; Маргарита Терзиева, Неля Иванова, Тинка Иванова, *Поглед върху толстоизма в България* (Бургас: Диамант, 2006).

64 Йордан Йорданов, "За България ли е тръгнал Лев Толстой?" http://www.svobodata.com/page.php?pid=11296.

65 Игов, *Кратка история на българската литература*, 280. This is the place to address the much cited essay on the Bulgarian intelligentsia by the celebrated literary critic Boian Penev. Written in the early 1920s as part of his "Introduction to the Bulgarian Literature after the Liberation," it was printed posthumously in 1942 (Боян Пенев, "Увод в българската литература след Освобождението," *Годишник на Софийския Университет, Историко-филологически факултет*, 38, no. 4 (1942), 1–56; Боян Пенев, *Студии, статии, есета* (София: Български писател, 1985), 159–220; http://www.librev.com/index.php/scribbbles-essays-publisher/864-2). Written inspiringly, with undoubted insights, but also full of errors and overgeneralizations, it hastily explains the overall intellectual through to the literary trends.

66 Игов, *Кратка история на българската литература*, 282.

67 М. Христов, "Неизвестно писмо на Димитър Благоев," *ИИИ*, 9 (1962), 383–85; https://bg.wikipedia.org/wiki/Найчо_Цанов.

68 The best assessment of Anton Strashimirov belongs to the writer Dimitîr Kirkov https://dimkirkov.wordpress.com/2015/06/17/антон-страшимиров/; see also Игов, *Кратка история на българската литература*, 292–95, 344–45.
69 Игов, *Кратка история на българската литература*, 314–18.
70 Ibid., 296.
71 Крумка Шарова, "Идейният път на Спиро Гулабчев," *ИИИ*, 9 (1962), 106–8.
72 Ibid., 110–12. Dragomanov's daughter, Lidia (1866–1937) married Ivan Shishmanov (1862–1928), the future Bulgarian minister of education, diplomat, and major writer and humanist scholar, in 1888 in Geneva. She herself was a prominent writer, journalist, and music critic with a significant role in the Bulgarian women's movement.
73 Dragomanov coined the slogan "Cosmopolitanism in the ideas and the ends, nationality on the ground and the forms." http://www.encyclopediaofukraine.com/display.asp?AddButton=pages\D\R\DrahomanovMykhailo.htm.
74 Шарова, "Идейният път на Спиро Гулабчев," 113–14.
75 The Bogomil connection was proposed first by Blagoev, already in 1906, cited in Генчев, *Профили от кафене "Ландолт"*, 18. Panaiotov even suggests that he chose the name of his teaching, *siromakho-mili* (loving the poor) by analogy to *bogo-mili* (loving of God or loved by God): Панайотов, *Чучулигите*, 85.
76 Шарова, "Идейният път на Спиро Гулабчев," 124–26. Sharova contests Evlogi Buzhashki's conclusion that there was a whole network of *siromakhomil* societies by showing that in other places these were educational circles preceding, and not part of, Gulabchev's activities.
77 Панайотов, *Чучулигите*, 86; Клинчаров, *Димитър Благоев*, 127–29; Шарова, "Идейният път на Спиро Гулабчев," 132–35.
78 Панайотов, *Чучулигите*, 87–88; Генчев, *Профили от кафене "Ландолт"*, 23–25. Bozveliev, who knew Gulabchev personally, attributed this to a direct transfer of Russian conspiratorial tactics (Бозвелиев, *Моите спомени*, 32).
79 Бозвелиев, *Моите спомени*, 28–29.
80 Панайотов, *Чучулигите*, 87.
81 ЦДА, ЧП 18 Б, л. 90–111.
82 Ibid., л. 45, 73.
83 Ibid., л. 77.
84 Ibid., л. 84–84/ об.
85 Ibid., л. 83.
86 Шарова, "Идейният път на Спиро Гулабчев," 130–32.
87 The whole issue of 2,000 was destroyed on the insistence of the collaborators and a sole copy, today a bibliographical rarity, was discovered in a private library in 1954 (Панайотов, *Чучулигите*, 120–21).
88 Шарова, "Идейният път на Спиро Гулабчев," 141–42.
89 Едуард Белами, *След 100 години*, прев. Константин Бозвелиев Русе: изд. Спиро Гулабчев, 1892; Бозвелиев, *Моите спомени*, 33. Unlike the popularity it reached in Western Europe and the fierce debates it engendered, there is little to speak about its influence in Bulgaria. Philipp Reick, "'If *that* is socialism, we won't help its advent': the impact of Edward Bellamy's utopian novel *Looking Backward* on socialist thought in late-nineteenth-century Western Europe," in Arvidsson et al., *Socialist Imaginations*, 93–115.
90 Interestingly, the twenty-year-old Slavi Balabanov had visitied Gulabchev in 1892 in Ruse during his summer vacation as a student in Geneva. He wrote in a letter to Stoian Nokov from July 29, 1892, that Gulabchev "now declares he is an anarchist,

although he has no understanding of anarchism. He will continue to work alone as he has done so far" (*ЦДА*, Фонд 186 Б, оп.1, а.е.88, л.1–4).

91 Шарова, "Идейният път на Спиро Гулабчев," 143–44.
92 Димтър Благоев, *Кратки бележки из моя живот* (София: Издателство на БКП, 1971), 140. The most detailed account of the early evolution of Marxist ideas in Blagoev is Евлоги Бужашки, *Д.Благоев и победата на марксизма в българското социалистическо движение 1885-1903* (София: Издателство на БКП, 1960).
93 Much as I was eager to find more cobblers among my "early socialists" in order to add to the proverbial radicalism of nineteenth-century shoemakers, I did not succeed. Eric J. Hobsbawm and Joan Wallach Scott, "Political Shoemakers," *Past & Present*, 89, no. 1 (November 1980), 86–114, https://doi.org/10.1093/past/89.1.86.
94 Цоньо Петров, "Първият социалистически вестник в България - 'Росица,'" *ИИИ*, 57 (1987), 252–55, here 253. Petrov rejects the suggestion that the channels were Russian *narodniks*, immigrants to Bulgaria (252). Andrei Konov finished law in Geneva and was a founder of the BSDP at Buzludzha in 1891. An MP in 1902, he joined the BWSDP (b)) after 1903.
95 *Росица*, no. 5 (July 2, 1886), cited in Генчев, *Профили от кафене "Ландолт,"* 10.
96 *ЦДА*, Сп 1647 Б, 1–5. The memoirs were written in 1957–1958 and copies given to the Ruse archive and the Sofia House of Jurists in 1962 by the author.
97 *ЦДА*, Сп 579 Б, 14.
98 Michel de Certeau, *The Practice of Everyday Life*, trans. Steven Rendall (Berkeley: University of California Press, 2011), xiv–xv.
99 Ibid., 174.
100 Robert Darnton, "Readers Respond to Rousseau: The Fabrication of Romantic Sensitivity," in *The Great Cat Massacre and Other Episodes in French Cultural History* (New York: Basic Books, 2009), 215–56.
101 *ЦДА*, Фонд 186 Б, оп.1, а.е.212, л.4–6.
102 *ЦДА*, Фонд 186 Б, оп.1, а.е.18, л. 28–9.
103 Йотов, *Водителят*, 23.
104 Милен Куманов, "Янко Сакъзов - жизнен и обществен път," in Янко Сакъзов. *Интелигецията и нейната роля в обществото* (София: Издателска къща "Христо Ботев," 1993), 8.
105 Ibid., 10–12.
106 Иван Маринов, "По тайната пътека към забранените науки," *ЦДА*, Сп 1128 Б, 3.
107 Ibid., 4–7.
108 Ibid., 9–15.
109 Victoria Frede, *Doubt, Atheism and the Nineteenth-Century Russian Intelligentsia* (Madison: The University of Wisconsin Press, 2011), 149, 192. On atheism in Russia, see also William B. Husband, *"Godless Communists": Atheism and Society in Soviet Russia, 1917-1932* (De Kalb: Northern Illinois University Press, 2000), 3–35.
110 Dimou, *Entangled Paths*, 27–28. Dimou also notes the absence of religiously affiliated syndicalist movements typical for Western Europe and concludes that "the Orthodox church did not function as a secular forum either for the political or the corporatist organization of the working class" (56). For a comparison with Germany, see Sebastian Prüfer, *Sozialismus statt Religion: Die deutsche Sozialdemokratie vor der religiösen Frage 1863-1890* (Göttingen: Vandenhoeck & Ruprecht, 2002).
111 Бозвелиев, *Моите спомени*, 144, 158, 162–64.
112 Генчев, *Профили от кафене "Ландолт,"* 10.

113 On Bakalov, see Веселина Петрова-Чомпалова, *Георги Бакалов. Обществено-политическа и културна дейност (1891-1903)* (Пловдив: ИК "Глас," 2002); Георги Бакалов, *Избрани произведения* (София: Фондация Арете-Фол, Университетско издателство "Св. Климент Охридски," 2007); Веселина Петрова, "Из кореспонденцията на Георги Бакалов с полските социалисти в края на век," *ИИИ*, 46 (1982), 342–48.
114 ЦДА, Фонд 186 Б, оп.1, а.е. 212, л.10–13, 34–39. This is Nokov's manuscript original. There also exists a typed copy in ЦДА, Сп 1378 Б.
115 ЦДА, Фонд 186 Б, оп.1, а.е. 212, л.14–15. The other Bulgarian students were organized in the nationalist organization *Bratstvo*.
116 Ibid., л.16–27.
117 Ibid., л.79–157. Nokov left especially warm memoirs on Bakalov whom he valued highly, ЦДА, Сп 1377 Б, л. 3–4; ЦДА, Фонд 186 Б, оп.1, а.е.48.
118 Генчев, *Първоапостолите на идеала*, 119–20. Bakalov and Nokov were categorical that this was because of a stomach (most likely cancer) disease that completely unnerved him (ЦДА, Фонд 186 Б, оп.1, а.е. 212, л.73).
119 ЦДА, Фонд 186 Б, оп.1, а.е. 88, л.1–4.
120 Ibidem.
121 Two important members of the Geneva group who, however, have been left out of posterity's and historians' attention are Todor Stoianov, b.1866 and Dimitîr Atanasov (1873–1945). Stoianov studied social sciences and was a cofounder of the group. A teacher of, among others, Khristo Kabakchiev and Vasil Kolarov, he later was a lawyer who joined the Broads in 1903, but nothing is known about his later life. Atanasov finished the Stara Zagora high school where he became a socialist. In Geneva, newly married to another student Maria, Plekhanov became the godfather of their daughter Lila. A lawyer in Stara Zagora and Ruse, Atanasov sided with the Narrows, and in the interwar period was a prominent defense lawyer in political cases (Ангелов, *Живот за партията*, 165–67).
122 ЦДА, Фонд 186 Б, оп.1, а.е. 213, draft of a letter of Nokov to Mikhail Kremen, л. 2–11.
123 ЦДА, Фонд 186 Б, оп.1, а.е. 82.
124 ЦДА, Фонд 186 Б, оп.1, а.е. 109/6. Unsigned postcard to Nokov, March 14, 1939.
125 Here only a few works will be mentioned: Francis Conte, *Un révolutionnaire – diplomate: Christian Rakovski: l'Union soviétique et l'Europe (1922-1941)* (Paris: Mouton, 1978) (translated from the French by A. P. M. Bradley as *Christian Rakovski (1873-1941): A Political Biography* (Boulder, Co: East European Monographs, 1989), no. 256; Georges Haupt and Jean-Jacques Marie, *Makers of the Russian Revolution: Biographies* (New York: Routledge 1974 [2017]). The latest work is in Russian: Чернявский, *Жизненный путь Христиана Раковского*; Георгий Чернявский, Михаил Станчев. *В борьбе против самовластия: Х. Г. Раковский в 1927-1941 гг.* Харківський державний інститут культури, 1993. In Bulgarian, see Филип Панайотов, *Животът и смъртта на Кръстю Раковски* [София: Издателство Захари Стоянов, 2003], Лиляна Гевренова, *Спомени за моя вуйчо Кръстю Раковски* (София: Български писател, 1989) and Ангел Веков, "Към въпроса за участието на Кръстю Раковски в руското революционно движение (1891–1912 г.)," *ИИИ*, 53 (1985). There are also numerous articles in Romanian. Rakovski himself also left an enormous written legacy. See online: https://www.marxists.org/archive/rakovsky/

126　Nonchev's enormous correspondence is in the Sofia archives (ЦДА, Фонд 157 Б, оп.1, altogether 374 items). His reminiscence about the encounter between Plekhanov and Lenin is in ЦДА, Фонд 157 Б, оп.1, а.е.5. There are a few pieces in the Kalofer archives, and Nonchev's private archive is still in the hands of his son from his second marriage in Plovdiv. Nonchev was first married to the sister of Rakovski, Anna, and they had a son Valentin.

127　Cited in Генчев, *Първоапостолите на идеала*, 136.

128　ЦДА, Фонд 160 Б, оп.1, а.е.52. See also other critical letters from Bakalov: ЦДА, Фонд 160 Б, оп.1, а.е. 45, 46, 47, 49, 50, 53, 54.

129　ЦДА, Фонд 160 Б, оп.1, а.е. 45. Bakalov was particularly disappointed by the lack of theoretical sophistication among the party leaders, with the exception of Blagoev, Kirkov, Gavril Georgiev, and Kharlakov (ibid., а.е. 75).

130　ЦДА, Фонд 160 Б, оп.1, а.е. 10.

131　https://bg.wikipedia.org/wiki/Роман_Аврамов indicates 1938 as the year of his death and that he was rehabilitated after 1954. Other sources give 1937: Генчев, *Първоапостолите на идеала*, 140; *Пътеводител по фондовете на БКП*, 236–37. The introduction to the publication of his articles and correspondence from 1985 intimates that he just died peacefully at his post in 1937: Роман Аврамов, *Публицистика и кореспонденция* (София: Партиздат, 1985), 58. Avramov's file contains two official autobiographies in Russian from 1926 and 1932 (ЦДА, Фонд 160 Б, оп.1, а.е.2 and 3), and his correspondence with Gorky, Lenin, Kautsky, Sakarov, Todor Petrov, Bakalov, Kabakchiev, and Zinoviev.

132　ЦДА, Сп 1590 Б.

133　ЦДА, Сп 1409 Б, 126–36.

134　ЦДА, Сп 2652 Б, 3–5, 24–25.

135　ЦДА, Сп 1996 Б. His memoirs were apparently written immediately after 1944 because he had a stroke at the end of the year and died in 1946.

136　ЦДА, Сп 1522 Б, 1–2.

137　ЦДА, Фонд 265 Б, оп.1, а.е.2, л. 9–14. Kostov's autobiography had been given orally to the writer Orlin Vasilev after 1944, written down, and typed on thirty-eight pages and given to the archive in 1967. Kostov was rehabilitated in 1956, but there is still no definitive biography on him. On his death see Мито Мито Исусов, *Последната година на Трайчо Костов* (София: Издателско дружество „Христо Ботев", 1990). For his memoirs and his writings see Трайчо Костов, *Избрани произведения*, 1944-1948 (София: Партиздат, 1978); Трайчо Костов, *Публицистика, кореспонденция и спомени за него в два тома* (София: Партиздат, 1987); Борис Христов, *Изпитанието: спомени за процеса и съдбата на Трайчо Костов и неговата група* (София: Университетско издателство "Св. Климент Охридски", 1995); *Процесът и зад процеса "Трайчо Костов": 1949-1997, 48 години след процеса* (София: Макон-S, 1998); Петър Япов, *Трайчо Костов и Никола Гешев: съдебните процеси през 1942 и 1949 г.* (София: Факел, Изток-Запад, 2003).

138　ЦДА, Фонд 265 Б, оп.1, а.е.36, л. 2–4 (July 22, 1916).

139　Ангелов, *Живот за партията*, 5–7.

140　Ibid., 9–13, 16–17.

141　Ibid., 18–21.

142　Dimou, *Entangled Paths*, 157–300. Other important contributions are Клара Пинкас, *Реформистката социалдемокрация в България. Идеология, политика, организация 1903-1917* (София: Партиздат, 1981); Sina Maria Dubowoj, *The*

Schism in the Bulgarian Socialist Movement and the Second International, 1900-1914 (Unpublished PhD, University of Illinois at Urbana-Champaign, 1981).

143 Ibid., 174.
144 The framework is premised, of course, on accepting that Bernstein's revisionism was an intra-Marxist dispute, a question which is still open and depends on how one defines "real, authentic" Marxism. As a whole, the general consensus accepts Bernstein as a Marxist theoretician but there are also serious analyses against this, among them Rosa Luxemburg. See, in particular *Marxism versus Social Democracy: The Revisionist Debate 1896-1898*.
145 This is especially prominent in Веселин Янчев, "Апология на българската социалдемокрация (1891-1944)," in *Изследвания по история на социализма*, т. I, 142–243; also Марин Калинов, *Един дух широк и свободен. Щрихи към портрета на Янко Сакъзов* (Шумен: Антос, 2000). It is less so in Трендафил Митев, "Възникване и същност на 'широкия социализъм' в България," in *Изследвания по история на социализма*, т. I, 70–141.
146 Янко Сакъзов, *Тревога за призраци (нашето отстъпничество или тяхното недомислие)* (София: Фондация "Янко Сакъзов," 1991), 10 (First edition, София: печатница Б.Зилберт, 1903).
147 Ibid., 80–81. The comparison to a Venetian doge comes from Simeon Radev, cited in Генчев, *Първоапостолите на идеала*, 80.
148 Димитър Благоев, *Принос към историята на социализма в България* (София, 1906), cited in Генчев, *Първоапостолите на идеала*, 82.
149 Шарова, "Идейният път на Спиро Гулабчев," 144.
150 Димитър Димитров, *Разпра в работнишката партия* (Шумен: Издание на П.Байнов, 1901).
151 Ibid., 4, 6.
152 Ibid., 10–13.
153 Ibid., 15–16, 21, 23, 30, quote on 20.
154 Ibid., 30–31, 33–34.
155 Ibid., 22, 24.
156 Ibid, 26.
157 Ibid, 27.
158 Ibid., 32, 41–42.
159 Ibid., 58.
160 Bozveliev in his memoirs insists that Sakîzov explicitly made the parallel to Russia as two backward agrarian countries and in this particular case was under the influence of the Russian *narodniks* doubting that capitalism can develop and that a strong bourgeoisie would appear (Бозвелиев, *Моите спомени*, 283).
161 Генчев, *Първоапостолите на идеала*, 104.
162 The lawyer Stefan Avramov (1883–1959) was a dedicated Narrow and delegate to the ISB in Brussels in 1908. In conversation with Kautsky, he gave a negative portrait of the Broads, but Kautsky interrupted him and referred to Sakîzov as "the best Marxist, not only in Bulgaria, but in the whole Balkans." When Avramov reported this to Blagoev and told him he had voted with the minority (including Lenin) on a particular issue against Kautsky, Blagoev scolded him: "How could you forget yourself to the point of voting with Lenin against Kautsky? Who are you and who is Kautsky?" (ЦДА, ЧП 11 Б, л. 174-5, 237-40). This forced Avramov to rethink his allegiance and he left the party formally in 1911 but continued his contacts and in

the interwar period was interned several times. The Avramov file contains his high school students' album from 1901–1902 of almost 100 pages where his schoolmates had written down personal messages and a lot of poems by Vazov, Iavorov, Polianov, Tserkovski, Andreichin, and Mihailovski, translations from Hugo, Byron, the Italian poet Ada Negri, and even a few original ones. His album is prefaced with a strophe by Paul Verlain: "Et toi, dis donc, que voilà, qu'a tu fait de ta jeunesse?" (ЦДА, ЧП 11 Б, л. 178–219).

163 Kalinov took this characterization as the title for his hagiographic book Калинов, *Един дух широк и свободен*.
164 Tchitchovsky, "Political and Social Aspects of Modern Bulgaria," 596.
165 "Here is one of the distributors, sharers." Бозвелиев, *Моите спомени*, 129.
166 Sakîzov's speech in parliament was printed as a separate brochure, Янко Сакъзов, *Належащите реформи* (София: Печатница Ив. Цучев, 1902), here cited from Dimou, *Entangled Paths*, 257.
167 ЦДА, Сп 174 Б, л. 4.
168 The Communist Manifesto had posited that "the theory of the Communists may be summed up in the single sentence: Abolition of private property." See also *The Economic and Philosophic Manuscript of 1844*, https://www.marxists.org/archive/marx/works/1844/manuscripts/comm.htm. The literature interpreting Marx on this issue is endless and controversial. For an analysis of Marx's attitudes to various forms of property, see Thomas Keyes, *Karl Marx on Property* (Unpublished dissertation, Marquette University, 1981). George G. Brenkert, "Freedom and Private Property in Marx," *Philosophy and Public Affairs* 8, no. 2 (1979), 122–47 makes the interesting point that the Marxian attitude was not simply a redistributive measure and on the grounds of justice but was argued very broadly on the grounds of freedom.
169 *Петър Дънов за частната собственост* (София: Издателство Хелиопол, n.d.), especially the part on private property with its two chapters "Should there be private property?" and "The abolition of private property," 5–14. The book is compiled by a "patriotic Bulgarian" and distributed freely. A graduate of the Drew Theological Seminary and the Boston University School of Theology, Petîr Dînov (1864–1944) returned to Bulgaria in 1895. Already the following year he had published *Science and Education*, and crisscrossed the country giving talks on the new culture he was preaching. By 1900 he had established a transreligious, eclectic, and esoteric spiritual community which made serious inroads in intellectual circles in Bulgaria and abroad. While the peak of his activities fell on the interwar period when the movement flourished as the *Universal White Brotherhood* and had a broad social reception, his views on private property were spelled out from the beginning. Today there is a revival of the dînovist movement and Dînov was voted in public polls the second most venerated Bulgarian figure after Vasil Levski.
170 Ревякина, "БКП и селското движение в България," 356–57; Владислав Топалов, "Основаване на Българския Земеделски Съюз," *ИИИ*, 8 (1960), 153–208; *Кратка история на Българската Комунистическа Партия*, 39.
171 Георги Братанов, "Никола Габровски," *ИИИ*, 49 (1983), 396; Филип Гинев, *Никола Габровски* (София: Отечествен фронт, 1982) is the only existing biography of Gabrovski.
172 *Работник*, no.15 (February 5, 1894), cited in Митев, "Възникване и същност на 'широкия социализъм' в България," 106.
173 *Работник*, no. 16 (February 12, 1894), cited in Dimou, *Entangled Paths*, 213–14.
174 Братанов, "Никола Габровски," 398.

175 Cited in John Bell, *Peasants in Power: Alexander Stamboliiski and the Bulgarian Agrarian National Union 1899-1923* (Princeton: Princeton University Press, 1977) (Princeton Legacy Library, 2019), 37. This continues to be the best exposition on BANU. For the agrarian alternative in a comparative European framework, see Alex Toshkov. *Agrarianism as Modernity*.
176 Братанов, "Никола Габровски," 401.
177 Генчев, *Първоапостолите на идеала*, 108.

Chapter 5

1 Marylin Boxer and Jean Quataert, eds., *Socialist Women: European Feminism in the Nineteenth and Early Twentieth Century* (New York: Elsevier Science Ltd., 1978), 2.
2 Август Бебел, *Жената и социализмът*. Превел Н. Хр. Габровски (Търново: Печатница "Работник," 1893).
3 August Bebel, *Women Under Socialism*, trans. Daniel De Leon (New York: Labor News Press, 1904). The next translation omitted De Leon's Introduction: August Bebel, *Woman and Socialism*, trans. Meta L. Stern (Hebe) (New York: Socialist Literature Co., 1910).
4 *Women Under Socialism* (1904), vi.
5 *Woman and Socialism* (1910), 466–67.
6 "Програма на БСДП приета на Бузлуджанския конгрес, 20 юли 1891," *Българска комунистическа партия. Документи на централните ръководни органи*, т.I. (София: Партиздат, 1972), 29.
7 Boxer and Quataert, eds., *Socialist Women: European Feminism*, 6–7.
8 Clara Zetkin (1857–1933) became a cofounder of the Spartacist League in 1916, a member of the Communist Party in 1919, and one of the leaders of the Comintern.
9 Natalia Tikhonov, "Student Migrations and the Feminization of European Universities," *L'étudiant étranger*. Préactes dela journée d'études du 8 février 2002, http://barthes.enssib.fr/clio/revues/AHI/articles/english/tiko.html).
10 Clara Zetkin, "Social-Democracy & Woman Suffrage," paper read at the Women's Conference in Mannheim before the Stuttgart Congress of German Social-Democracy, https://www.marxists.org/archive/zetkin/1906/xx/womansuffrage.htm.
11 Ingrun Lafleur, "Five Socialist Women: Traditionalist Conflicts and Socialist Visions in Austria, 1893-1934," in Boxer and Quataert, eds., *Socialist Women: European Feminism,* 216, 232.
12 "Програма на БСДП приета на I партиен конгрес, София, 3-7 юли 1894," *Българска комунистическа партия. Документи*, 118.
13 Красимира Даскалова, *Жени, пол и модернизация в България, 1878-1944* (София: Университетско издателство "Св. Климент Охридски," 2012), 401.
14 Dobrinka Parusheva, "Emancipation Between Feminism and Socialism (A Bulgarian Example of the Turn of the Century)," *Etudes balkaniques* (1997), 1–2, 127.
15 Даскалова, *Жени, пол и модернизация*, 304. There were also other parties that advocated greater rights for women, like the Radical-Democratic Party, the Democratic Party, and the Agrarian Union, but only gradually.
16 ЦДА, Фонд 197 Б, оп.1, а.е.20, also in Елена Богданова, "Документи от и за Вела Благоева," *ИИИ*, 19 (1968), 180.

17 Мария Динкова, *Социален портрет на българската жена* (София: Профиздат, 1980); Любен Беров, "Социална струтура на селото в балканските страни през периода между двете световни войни," *Трудове на ВИИ Карл Маркс*, IV (1977), 43–76; Анастас Тотев. *Статистическа характеристика на българското земеделско стопанство*. (София : М-во на земеделието и държ. имоти, 1940).
18 Lucy Garnett, *Balkan Home-Life* (New York: Dodd, Mead & Co, 1917), 177–78.
19 Maria Todorova, *Balkan Family Structure and the European Pattern: Demographic Development in Ottoman Bulgaria*, 2nd ed. (Budapest and New York: CEU Press, 2006), 20–27, 55, 79–98. See also Maria Todorova, "Historical Tradition and Transformation in Bulgaria: Women's Issues, Feminist Issues," *Journal of Women's History*, 5, no. 3 (Winter 1994), 129–43.
20 Deniz Kandiyoti, "Bargaining with Patriarchy," *Gender and Society*, 2 (September 1988), 274–90.
21 Martine Segalen, *Love and Power in the Peasant Family: Rural France in the Nineteenth Century* (Chicago: The University of Chicago Press, 1983).
22 Даскалова, *Жени, пол и модернизация*, 295–96.
23 Ibid., 97–98.
24 Ibid., 125–27.
25 Ibid., 128–30.
26 Ibid., 126, 130.
27 Ibid., 141–51, 161–65. Between 1888 and 1838, 45,503 students (31,852 men and 10,651 women) enrolled at the University of Sofia; 14,626 completed their education (11,732 men and 3,094 women).
28 Roger Whitaker, "Social Structure," in Klaus-Detlev Grothusen (ed.), *Bulgarien. Südosteuropa-Handbuch*, Vol. VI (Göttingen: Vandenhoeck & Ruprecht, 1990), 463–64; Даскалова, *Жени, пол и модернизация*, 401, citing Ярослав Йоцов, "Социално-икономически облик на България, 1919-1923," *Известия на Института по История*, т.20 (1968).
29 Динкова, *Социален портрет*, 59–60. At the end of the nineteenth century there were less than 14 percent of literate women, but their share rose to 46 percent in 1926 and to 57 percent by 1934. In 1937, 22.7 percent of the students in higher education were women which compared favorably to the somewhat lower percentage in Czechoslovakia (17.3 percent) and Hungary (14.7 percent), closer to the figures for the other East European countries: Yugoslavia (23.3 percent), Romania (26.0 percent), and Poland (28.3 percent). By 1946, 21 percent among the specialists with higher education (16 percent being economically active), and close to 40 percent among the specialists with high school education were women. See also *Women, State, and Party in Eastern Europe*, ed. Sharon L. Wolchik and Alfred G. Meyer (Durham: Duke University Press, 1985), 33–34.
30 Даскалова, *Жени, пол и модернизация*, 134, 200, 351–52.
31 Петко Кандев, "Зараждане и развитие на учителското движение в България (до 1895 г.)," *Известия на Института по История на БКП*, т.7 (1960), 252.
32 Даскалова, *Жени, пол и модернизация*, 141, 148, 356–59. The ban on married women was lifted and re-imposed several times. By 1929 women comprised 48.5 percent of teachers, and by 1940 they were in the majority, overwhelmingly in the younger school grades.
33 Виржиния Пакалева, *Българката през Възраждането* (София: Отечествен фронт, 1984 [1964]).
34 Даскалова, *Жени, пол и модернизация*, 175, 202–4.

35 Parusheva, "Emancipation," 127; Даскалова, *Жени, пол и модернизация*, 141–42.
36 *Български женски съюз (по случай 30-годишнината от неговото основаван), 1901-1931)*. София: Бълг. женски съюз, 1931, 1.
37 Даскалова, *Жени, пол и модернизация*, 175, 206.
38 *Женски глас*, III, 5 (November 15, 1901), cited in Parusheva, "Emancipation," 128.
39 *Женски глас*, III, 6 (December 15, 1901), cited in Parusheva, "Emancipation," 128.
40 *Женски глас*, III, 7 (January 1, 1902), cited in Parusheva, "Emancipation," 128.
41 *Bulgarski Zhenski Suyuz*, 15–17; *Женски глас*, II, 21–22 (August 1, 1901), 1–9.
42 Parusheva, "Emancipation," 130.
43 Даскалова, *Жени, пол и модернизация*, 206–13.
44 Vela Blagoeva, "Class Consciousness and Feminism," *Женски труд* 1, no. 2 (1904–1905), 1–2, in Krassimira Daskalova and Karen Offen, "The Tensions Within the Early-Twentieth-Century Bulgarian Women's Movement," *Aspasia*, 9 (2015), 115.
45 Даскалова, *Жени, пол и модернизация*, 237–38, 271.
46 Ibid., 274.
47 Anna Karima, "Do We Divide the Union?" *Равноправие*, 1, no. 3 (1908), 1–2, in Daskalova and Offen, "The Tensions within the Early-Twentieth-Century Bulgarian Women's Movement," 122.
48 *ЦДА*, ЧП 15 Б.
49 Даскалова, *Жени, пол и модернизация*, 272–76.
50 *ЦДА*, Сп 1569 Б, 2. Popov studied law in Geneva and was a Narrow and communist MP from Iambol (1913–1923). He emigrated to the USSR (1923–1936). Maria Khadzhiivanova is mentioned in Панайотов, *Чучулигите*, 97.
51 Jean Quataert, "Unequal Partners in an Uneasy Alliance: Women and the Working Class in Imperial Germany," in Boxer and Quataert, eds., *Socialist Women: European Feminism*, 121; Даскалова, *Жени, пол и модернизация*, 241.
52 Ibid., 270. On Blagoeva, see Елена Богданова, *Вела Благоева* (София: Издателство на БКП, 1969), the only extant book-length biography. In English, Krassimira Daskalova, "Vela Blagoeva," in Francisca de Haan, Krassimira Daskalova, and Anna Loutfi, eds., *A Biographical Dictionary of Women's Movements and Feminisms: Central, Eastern and South Eastern Europe, 19th and 20th Centuries* (Budapest: Central European University Press, 2006), 62–65. Probably the best emotional essay on Blagoeva is the chapter "Mother Courage" of Dimitŭr Genchev (Генчев, *Първоапостолите на идеала*, 45–58).
53 *ЦДА*, Фонд 197 Б, оп.1, а.е.7.
54 The certificate is in *ЦДА*, Фонд 197 Б, оп.1, а.е.1.
55 Генчев, *Първоапостолите на идеала*, 50. Since Vela Blagoeva did not leave memoirs, we know that from her daughter's memoirs. Blagoev himself only mentions that when he first met her, she was a *narodovolka*.
56 Генчев, *Първоапостолите на идеала*, 48–49.
57 Панайотов, *Съвременници на бъдещето*, 24. The diary is also quoted in Генчев, *Първоапостолите на идеала*, 51.
58 Ст.Д. Стойчев, "Нови документи за живота и дейността на в. Благоева като учителка в гр. Търново – 1890-1892," *ИИИ*, 3–4 (1958), 427, 436–38.
59 Генчев, *Първоапостолите на идеала*, 55–56.
60 *ЦДА*, Фонд 197 Б, оп.1, а.е.6; *ЦДА*, Фонд 197 Б, оп.2, а.е.31.
61 Nikola Zhivkov wrote the text in 1876 and after many redactions, a final one by Vazov was adopted in 1912.
62 Генчев, *Първоапостолите на идеала*, 54.

63 ЦДА, Фонд 197 Б, оп.2, а.е.4.
64 Генчев, *Първоапостолите на идеала*, 61–68; Топенчаров, *Българската журналистика, 1903-1917*, 209.
65 Her archive has thirty files with her published and unpublished fiction and poetry: ЦДА, Фонд 197 Б, оп.1, а. е. 33 to 62.
66 Богданова, *Вела Благоева*, 119–20; Богданова, "Документи от и за Вела Благоева," 169–76.
67 ЦДА, Фонд 197 Б, оп.1, а.е.77.
68 Чавдар Драгойчев, *Дъщерите на Дядото (Спомени)* (София: [s.n.], 1997), 16.
69 ЦДА, Фонд 197 Б, оп.1, а.е.72.
70 Ibid., а.е.76.
71 Генчев, *Първоапостолите на идеала*, 45.
72 *Годишен отчет,* 8 in ЦДА, Фонд 1Б, оп.2, а.е.219, л.5.
73 ЦДА, Фонд 285, оп.1, а.е.134, л. 5, 21. Boris Stefanov Mateev (1883–1969) was a member of BWSDP (n) since 1904 and a member of the Romanian SDP since 1913. He was a leading figure in the Romanian socialist and communist movements, member of the CC of the RCP and its general secretary from 1936; after 1938 he was in exile in Moscow. After 1944 he settled in Bulgaria. Close to the views, and under the influence of, Dobrugeanu-Gherea, he was denounced by the RCP in the 1950s and 1960s. (Трендафила Ангелова, "Борис Стефанов," *ИИИ*, 51 (1984), 341–58). The younger brother and future academician Ivan Stefanov Mateev (1899–1980), a prominent economist and statistician, defended his doctorate in Berlin and was a member of the BCP from 1919, the German SDP (1920–1925), and the French CP (1924–1927). After 1927 he worked in the Main Statistical Bureau, was a professor of statistics and insurance, and became the author of outstanding works. Between 1929 and 1931 he was a member of the CC of the BCP. After 1944 he was director of the national bank (1944–1946) and minister of finances (1946–1949). He was sentenced to life in prison during the show trial against Traicho Kostov, and released and rehabilitated after 1956. The memoirs which he deposited in the archive in 1974 had the label "Strictly Confidential" (ЦДА, Сп 2234 Б, 2.).
74 ЦДА, Фонд 368, оп.1, а.е.28, л. 34, 38, 44–45.
75 Lukanov was accused of boycotting the September Uprising, although contemporary sources are categorical that, as a disciplined communist, he obeyed the decision: memoirs of Ivan Kamenov, ЦДА, Сп 807 Б; Ангелов. *Неизвестни страници*, 71–72, 83, 85–86. He was compelled to write a humiliating petition in December 1935 addressed to Georgi Dimitrov and Vasil Kolarov in which he repented for his sins and begged to be reinstated in the party but to no avail (ЦДА, Фонд 263, оп.1, а.е.47, л.1–6).
76 Ангелов, *Неизвестни страници*, 57.
77 ЦДА, Фонд 368, оп.1, а.е.16, л.1–6.
78 Private archive.
79 Ангелов, *Живот за партията*, 180.
80 Ibid., 180–85.
81 The German term for the mostly urban phenomenon of the eighteenth and nineteenth centuries whereby intellectuals would gather in clubs and *circles* to discuss the problems of the day, usually modeled after French and British examples.
82 Генчев, *Първоапостолите на идеала*, 56.
83 ЦДА, Сп 2012 Б, 350.
84 ЦДА, ЧП 75 Б.

85 *Спомени на д-р Петър Джидров*, 52–54.
86 Мария Джидрова, *Искания на българката (Сказка)* (София: Печатница "Гражданин," 1912).
87 ЦДА, Фонд 285, оп.1, letter from February 24, 1919, cited in Ангелова, "Борис Стефанов," 345.
88 Елена Атанасова, "Видна деятелка на сръбското социалистическо движение," *ИИИ*, 17 (1967), 233–59.
89 "Биографически бележки за Теофано В. Попова по баща Ненова (1931)," https://www.samaritans.bg/dnes/2011/teofano-popova-primer-za-dobriyat-samar yanin
90 Панайотов, *Съвременници на бъдещето*, 89. Бозвелиев, *Моите спомени*, 48.
91 Bell, *The Bulgarian Communist Party from Blagoev to Zhivkov*, 6.
92 Бозвелиев, *Моите спомени*, 48–9.
93 Report of the State Security Service, April 24, 1924: ЦДА, Фонд 141 Б, оп.1, а.е.2, 16.
94 The literary scholar Vladislav Todorov, in a spirited essay about the terrorist act, has advanced the hypothesis that Kosta Iankov conceived of the act not as a prelude to a mass uprising but as one leading to an internal coup d'état under the leadership of General Zhekov and to the eventual legalization of the party, after removing the existing right-wing elite and opening the way for a centrist government in agreement with Dimitrov, Kolarov, and the Comintern (Владислав Тодоров, *Хаотичното махало* [София: Фондация "Пространство Култура," 2005]); the essay can also be accessed in http://www.librev.com/index.php/--/1183-2011-03-24-13-30-03)
. In her equally spirited and engagingly written book but from a different political premise from Todorov's, the journalist Velislava Dîreva supports this explanation but depicts the act as a response to the preceding White Terror (Велислава Дърева, *Атентатът '1925: Денят, в който се отвориха портите Адови* [София: Синева, 2019]). Both authors implicitly accept the official version that Kolarov and Dimitrov had taken down the Comintern policy of armed uprising already in the summer and fall of 1924 by sending several letters from Vienna. This, indeed, has been the mainstream version in the communist historiography, lifting the responsibility from Dimitrov/Kolarov (Дончо Даскалов, *Васил Коларов и Георги Димитров и революционните събития в България, 1923-1925* [София, 1978]; Георги Наумов, *Атентатът в катедралата "Света Неделя"* [София: Партиздат, 1989]). This version, however, was contested already during communist times and there was an interesting debate, criticizing these works from the 1970s (see the critical the reviews of Tatiana Koleva in *ИИИ* 42, 1980, 471–84 and Petko Boev in *ИИИ*, 67 (1990), 361–64, as well as Татяна Колева, "Политическата линия в началото на 1925 г. и Априлският атентат," *ИИИ*, 65 (1989), 471–84). In her biography of Dimitrov, based on a detailed perusal of documentary sources, the French political scientist Mona Foscolo has carefully weighed all the versions around the terrorist act of 1925 and has concluded that both Dimitrov and the Comintern share the prime responsibility, if not for the act itself, then for the whole militant atmosphere, including active armament and financing, feeding the so-called "armed course" (Фосколо, *Георги Димитров*, 80–96; this is the Bulgarian translation of Foscolo's unpublished dissertation in French). The version that the terrorist act may have been linked to the planned coup d'état, including the King, General Zhekov, agrarians and the Military Organization of the BCP is in Foscolo's narrative "not entirely to be dismissed" (p. 92) but becomes a firm fact for Todorov and Dîreva.
95 Драгойчев, *Дъщерите на Дядото*, 12.

96 ЦДА, Сп 322Б, 14, 28; *Юбилеен сборник на Българския Учителски Съюз (по случай 10-годишнината от основаването му), 1895-1905* (София: Печатница "Св. София," 1905), 137–38.
97 Генчев, *Първоапостолите на идеала*, 47.
98 Dimitîr Zakhariev guiltily acknowledges that he would call her "svekîrvata"—*ЦДА*, Сп 655 Б, 2; equally, Nasta Isakova—*ЦДА*, Сп 768 Б.
99 Асен Кантаржиев, "Спомени за Тина Киркова," *ИИИ*, 18 (1968), 379–86.
100 *ЦДА*, Сп 829 Б.
101 *ЦДА*, Фонд 368 Б, оп.1, а.е.43, л.9–10. An abbreviated version is also in Tineva's unpublished memoirs on Kirkov: *ЦДА*, Сп 1880 Б, л.7.
102 Таня Турлакова, "Георги Кирков за правата на жените в Булгария," Мизов and Турлакова, *Георги Кирков и нашето съвремие.*, 49–55.
103 *ЦДА*, Фонд 368 Б, оп.1, а.е.43, л.10.
104 Private archive.
105 Генчев, *Първоапостолите на идеала*, 160.
106 *ЦДА*, Фонд 153 Б, оп.1, а.е.7, letter to Vesa Angelova, November 24, 1909.
107 Генчев, *Първоапостолите на идеала*, 162–63.
108 Ibid., 163–64.
109 Ibid., 166.
110 *ЦДА*, Фонд 153 Б, оп.1, а.е.7, letter to Vesa Angelova, February 28, 1925.

Part III

1 Raymond Williams, *Marxism and Literature* (Oxford: Oxford University Press, 1977), 131, 133.
2 Williams, *Marxism and Literature*, 133.
3 Paul Filmer, "Structures of Feeling and Socio-Cultural Formations: The Significance of Literature and Experience to Raymond Williams's Sociology of Culture," *British Journal of Sociology*, 54, no. 2 (June 2003), 199–219.
4 Devika Sharma and Frederik Tygstrup, eds., *Structures of Feeling: Affectivity and the Study of Culture* (Berlin, Munich and Boston: Walter de Gruyter, 2015), 2.
5 Kurt W. Fisher and June Price Tangney, "Introduction: Self-Conscious Emotions and the Affect Revolution: Framework and Overview," in June Price Tangney and Kurt W. Fisher, eds., *Self-Conscious Emotions: The Psychology of Shame, Guilt, Embarrassment, and Pride* (New York: The Guilford Press, 1995), 3, cited in William M. Reddy, *The Navigation of Feeling: A Framework for the History of Emotions* (Cambridge, UK: Cambridge University Press, 2001), ix.
6 Reddy, *The Navigation of Feeling*, x.
7 Antonio Damasio, *The Feeling of What Happens: Body and Emotion in the Making of Consciousness* (London: William Heinemann, 2000), 37, cited in Jack Barbalet, "Consciousness, Emotions and Science," Debra Hopkins, Jochen Kleres, Helena Flam, and Helmut Kuzmics, eds., *Theorizing Emotions: Sociological Explorations and Applications* (Frankfurt and New York: Campus Verlag, 2009), 56.
8 Ruth Leys, "The Turn to Affect: A Critique," *Critical Inquiry*, 37 (Spring 2011), 434–72.
9 Douglas Barnett and Hilary Horn Ratner, "Introduction: The Organization and Integration of Cognition and Emotion in Development," *Journal of Experimental Child Psychology*, 67 (1997), 303–16.

10 Monique Scheer, "Are Emotions a Kind of Practice (and Is That What Makes Them Have a History)? A Bourdieuian Approach to Understanding Emotion," *History and Theory*, 51 (May 2012), 193-220.
11 Reddy, *The Navigation of Feeling*, 31-32. Reddy cites especially the research of Alice M. Isen and Gregory Andrade Diamond, "Affect and Automaticity," in J. S. Uleman and John A. Bargh, eds., *Unintended Thought: Limits of Awareness, Intention and Control* (New York: The Guilford Press, 1989).
12 Some neuroscientists define emotions as lower level responses in the subcortical regions of the brain and the neocortex that trigger neurological reactions. Feelings, on the other hand, are sparked by emotions and colored by experience, belief, memories, and thoughts, that is, feelings are the side product of the brain perceiving emotions and assigning meaning to them (https://imotions.com/blog/difference-feelings-emotions/). Quite to the contrary, Jenefer Robinson, *Deeper than Reason: Emotion and Its Role in Literature, Music and Art* (Oxford: Clarendon Press, 2005), 5-27 assigns the lower level to feeling as an immediate physiological response (like hunger, tickling etc.) while emotions add several more levels of complexity: "It just seems wrong to reduce such a lofty emotion as love to an inner feeling such as butterflies in the tummy" (5).
13 Reddy, *The Navigation of Feeling*, 54-55.
14 Catherine Lutz, *Unnatural Emotions: Everyday Sentiments on a Micronesian Atoll and Their Challenge to Western Theory* (Chicago: The University of Chicago Press, 1988), 5.
15 Catherine Lutz, "Feminist Theories and the Science of Emotion," Frank Biess and Daniel M. Gross, eds., *Science and Emotions after 1945: A Transatlantic Perspective* (Chicago: The University of Chicago Press, 2014), 342-64 (here p. 24).
16 Reddy, *The Navigation of Feeling*, 64.
17 Ibid., 94.
18 Ibid., 128.
19 Ibid., 129. "Emotives" for Reddy are "a type of speech act different from both performative and constative utterances, which both describes (like constative utterances) and changes (like performatives) the world, because emotional expression has an exploratory and self-altering effect on the activated thought material of emotion" (128).
20 Most scholars use affect and emotion synonymously, and I am following this convention. Psychology, however, pointedly distinguished between the two, considering affect the experience of a feeling or emotion (Frank Biess and Daniel M. Gross, "Emotional Returns," *Science and Emotions after 1945*, 6).
21 Biess and Gross, "Emotional Returns," 2-3. For a thorough review of the theoretical and empirical work, see Jonathan H. Turner and Jan E. Stets, *The Sociology of Emotions* (Cambridge: Cambridge University Press, 2005).
22 Arlie Russell Hochschild, "Introduction: An Emotions Lens on the World," in Hopkins, Kleres, Flam, and Kuzmics, *Theorizing Emotions*, 29.
23 To name just a few of the most prominent research centers: The Max Planck Institute for Human Development in Berlin, the Yale Center for Emotional Intelligence, King's College London, the Emotional Brain Institute, the Australian Research Council for the History of Emotions, alongside scores of departments and laboratories at universities.
24 Susan J. Matt and Peter N. Stearns, "Introduction," Susan J. Matt and Peter N. Stearns, eds., *Doing Emotions History* (Urbana: University of Illinois Press, 2014), 1.

25 Mark Steinberg, "Emotions History in Eastern Europe," *Doing Emotions History*, 77. Nationalism has also been highlighted by Nicole Eustace, "Emotion and Political Change," *Doing Emotions History*, 170–80.
26 Steinberg, "Emotions History in Eastern Europe," 76–77. See also Mark D. Steinberg and Valeria Sobol, eds., *Interpreting Emotions in Russia and Eastern Europe* (DeKalb: Northern Illinois University Press, 2011).
27 John Corrigan, "Religion and Emotions," *Doing Emotions History*, 143–62; see also Miri Rubin speaking of "world of affect" in her *Emotion and Devotion: The Meaning of Mary in Medieval Religious Cultures* (Budapest: Central European University Press, 2009).
28 Ute Frevert, *Emotions in History – Lost and Found* (Budapest: Central European University Press, 2011), 12.
29 Barbara H. Rosenwein, *Emotional Communities in the Early Middle Ages* (Ithaca: Cornell University Press, 2006).
30 Biess and Gross, "Emotional Returns," 18.
31 Binne de Haan and Hans Renders quote Samuel Johnson, the subject of what is accepted as the first modern biography—Boswell's *The Life of Samuel Johnson*, 1791— as considering biography positioned between historiography and the novel. ("Towards Traditions and Nations," in Hans Renders and Binne de Haan, eds., *Theoretical Discussions of Biography: Approaches from History, Microhistory, and Life Writing* [Lampeter: The Edwin Mellen Press, 2013], 16, 21).
32 Joanny Moulin, "Introduction: Towards Biography Theory," *Cercles: Revue Pluridisciplinaire du Monde Anglophone* (2015), 1, https://hal.archives-ouvertes.fr/hal-01078127v2.
33 Haan and Renders, "Towards Traditions and Nations," 17.
34 Ibid., 21.
35 Ibid., 32. Jacques Le Goff, "Comment écrire une biographie historique aujourd'hui?" *Le Débat* (1989), no. 2, 49.
36 Deirdre Bair, "Die Biographie ist Akademischer Selbstmord," *Literaturen*, Heft 7/8 (2001), 38–39.
37 Daniel Whitcomb Ambord, "Wrong Turns on the Way to the Graveyard: The Death of Man and the Status of the Subject in Foucault Studies," *Minerva - An Internet Journal of Philosophy* 13 (2009), 53–66 (here 64), http://minerva.mic.ul.ie/vol13/Foucault.pdf.
38 Noela Davis, "Subjected Subjects? On Judith Butler's Paradox of Interpellation," *Hypatia: A Journal of Feminist Philosophy*, 27, no. 4 (November 2012), 881–97; see also Volker Depkat, "The Challenges of Biography: European-American Reflections," *Bulletin of the German Historical Institute* (Fall 2014), 39–48.
39 Pierre Bourdieu, "L'illusion biographique," *Actes de la recherche en sciences sociales*, 62–63 (June 1986), 69–72. English translation first published in Working Papers and Proceedings of the Center for Psychological Studies, ed. R. J. Parmentier and G. Urban (Chicago, 1987), 1–7 and reprinted as "The Biographical Illusion (1986)" in Wilhelm Hemecker and Edward Saunders, eds., *Biography in Theory: Key Texts with Commentaries* (Berlin: De Gruyter, 2017), 210–16.
40 "The Biographical Illusion (1986)," 215.
41 Ibid., 210.
42 Ibid., 211.
43 Ibid., 213.
44 Moulin, "Introduction: Towards Biography Theory," 5.

45 Christian Klein, ed. *Grundlagen der Biographik. Theorie und Praxis des biographischen Schreibens* (Stuttgart: Verlag J. B. Metzler, 2002). See also Ханс Ерих Бьодекер, "Биографията: Изследване на частен случай," Ивайло Знеполски, ред. *Между макроисторията и микроисторията или историята в множествено число* (София: Дом на науките за човека и обществото, 2010), 155–82.
46 Hans Renders and Binne de Haan, "Introduction: The Challenges of Biography Studies," in *Theoretical Discussions of Biography*, 3.
47 Ibid., 4; Hans Renders, "Biography in Academia and the Critical Frontier in Life Writing: Where Biography Shifts into Life Writing," in *Theoretical Discussions*, 257.
48 Renders, "Biography in Academia," 257.
49 I am insisting on scholarly biography, because biographies can also be fictional, and as Arnaldo Momigliano has observed, biography has an ambiguous role in history: "It can be an instrument for social research or offer precisely the possibility of escaping from this research" (Arnaldo Momigliano, *Lo sviluppo della biografia greca* [Turin: Einaudi, 1974], 8, cited in Giovanni Levi, "The Uses of Biography," *Theoretical Discussions*, 90).
50 Renders and de Haan, "Introduction: The Challenges of Biography Studies," 2.
51 Heinz Bude, "Lebenskonstruktionen als Gegenstand der Biographieforschung," in Gerd Jüttemann and Hans Thomae, Hrsg. *Biographische Methoden in den Humanwissenschaften* (Weinheim: Beltz, Psychologie Verlags Union, 1998), 256.
52 Giovanni Levi, "The Uses of Biography," in *Theoretical Discussions*, 89.
53 Matti Peltonen, "What Is Micro in Microhistory?" in *Theoretical Discussions*, 158–59.
54 Ibid., 172–73.
55 Jill Lepore, "Historians Who Love Too Much: Reflections on Microhistory and Biography," *The Journal of American History* 88, no. 1 (2001), 129–44, cited in Renders and de Haan, "Introduction: The Challenges of Biography Studies," 9.
56 Simone Lässig, "Introduction: Biography in Modern History – Modern Historiography in Biography," Volker Berghahn and Simone Lässig, eds., *Biography Between Structure and Agency: Central European Lives in International Historiography* (New York and London: Berghahn Books, 2008), 10, cited in Peltonen, "What Is Micro in Microhistory?",174.
57 Hans Renders, "The Limits of Representativeness: Biography, Life Writing and Microhistory," in *Theoretical Discussions*, 207.

Chapter 6

1 It became a district center in 1934, after which its population began increasing, but it rose drastically only with the modernization after the Second World War. By 1976 it was a town of 63,000 people.
2 Sofrony Vrachanski was canonized by the Bulgarian Orthodox Church in 1964.
3 The biggest flow of hundreds of thousands of Macedonian refugees came after the Balkan Wars and the First World War, when most of them settled in Sofia and the areas adjoining the territories that were conquered by, and included in, Serbia and Greece.
4 ЦДА, Сп-517 Б, 10–11.
5 *Пътеводител по мемоарните документи за БКП*, 127.

6 *ЦДА*, Сп-517 Б, 10–11.
7 My everlasting gratitude to Marietta Tzanova, Ivanka Gezenko, and Virban Todorov, who not only found the whereabouts of the file but secured a wonderful copy of the materials and did all this with an endless sense of humor.
8 Ranajit Guha, "The Small Voice of History," in Shahid Amin and Dipesh Chakravarty, eds. *Subaltern Studies IX: Writings on South Asian History and Society* (Delhi: Oxford University Press, 1994).
9 *История на антифашистката борба в България*, т. I 1939/1943 г. София, 1976; Стефан Цанев, *Български хроники*. Т.3. (София: Издателство Труд; Жанет-45, 2008), 552. See also https://bg.wikipedia.org/wiki/Соболева_акция.
10 *Държавен архив (ДА) Монтана*, Фонд 432К, оп.1, а.е.2, л.3.
11 "Komitka" is the Bulgarian feminine form for komitadzhi (in Turkish *komitaci*), the name the Ottoman authorities gave to the Bulgarian guerilla bands operating in Macedonia.
12 The age is specified in *ДА Монтана*, Фонд, 1074, оп.1, а.е.13, л.4.
13 *Македонска енциклопедија, том I. Скопје: Македонска академија на науките и уметностите*, 2009, 401.
14 *ДА Монтана*, Фонд 1074, оп.1, а.е.13: Спомени от Маслина Грънчарова, Никола Попов, Кузман Трифонов, Янаки Панов и Вълко Георгиев Лазаров за учителката Ангелина Бонова от с. Припължане (Трифоново), родена 1852 г. Умира 1938 г., л.1–3.
15 Ibid., л.4–5.
16 Ibid., л.5–6. The hatred of Turks (as oppressors) and love for Russia (as liberator) were central code phrases of Bulgarian nationalism.
17 Ibid., л.3.
18 Ibid., л.7.
19 Ibid., л.7–8.
20 It had 3,300 people in 1900. (Васил Кънчов, *Македония. Етнография и статистика* [София: Държавна печатница, 1900], 265).
21 D. M. Brankoff, *La Macédoine et sa population chrétienne* (Paris, 1905), 180–81.
22 Верковичъ, С.И., *Топографическо-этнографическій очеркъ Македоніи* (Санкт Петербургъ: Военная Типографія,-1889), 145–46.
23 Атанас Шопов, *Из живота и положението на българите във вилаетите* (Пловдив: Търговска печатница, 1893), 239–40.
24 There is an excellent entry on Zagorichane in both the Bulgarian and Greek Wikipedia: https://bg.wikipedia.org/wiki/Загоричани; https://el.wikipedia.org/wiki/Βασιλειάδα_Καστοριάς.
25 *ДА Монтана*, Фонд 1074, оп.1, а.е.13: Спиро Василев-Загоричанин. Спомени за учителствуването на Ангелина Бонова от с. Припължане, Михайловградско в Загоричани, Костурско (Трифоново), л.2.
26 Krassimira Aleksova, "24 May – The Day of Slavonic Alphabet, Bulgarian Enlightenment and Culture," *BalkanFolk*, May 24, 2013, http://www.balkanfolk.com/news.php?id=23.
27 *ДА Монтана*, Фонд 1074, оп.1, а.е.13: Виктор Макавеев. Нашето АБ..., 1 (28). Anatolians and Phanariotes are code words for Ottomans and Greeks, "the double yoke," referring to Bulgaria's church emancipation from the Constantinople Patriarchate and to the national struggle for independence.
28 Ibid., 2 (29).
29 Ibid., 4–5 (21–32).

30 *ДА Монтана* and Петър Иванов, *Ангелина Бонева Якимова–баба Ангелина. Бележита българка,* л. 2.
31 Richard Crampton, *A Concise History of Bulgaria* (Cambridge: Cambridge University Press, 1997), 60–63.
32 Kiril Popov, *La Bulgarie économique 1879-1911: Étude statistique* (Sofia: Imprimerie de la Cour, 1920), gives 23.9 percent but not excluding the population under six years of age; Г. Чанков, "Грамотност на населението в България," *Училищен преглед,* 1–2 (1926), 7 gives 29.8 percent, both cited in Roumiana Preshlenova, "Liberation in Progress," 59, 74.
33 Елена Стателова and Стойчо Грънчаров, *История на Нова България (1878-1944)* (София: Издателска къща „Анубис," 1999), 193–95; Nedyalka Videva and Stilian Yotov, "European Moral Values and Their Reception in Bulgarian Education," *Studies in East European Thought,* 53, no. ½ (March 2001), 119–28; T. Tchitchovsky, "Political and Social Aspects of Modern Bulgaria," *The Slavonic and East European Review,* 7, no. 21 (March 1929), 601–2.
34 Edouard Machery, *Philosophy Within Its Proper Bounds* (Oxford: Oxford University Press, 2017), 109 warns that while it is considered that inductive conclusions from untypicality are unreliable, this can also be true about conclusions from typicality.
35 Ianni Kotsonis, "Ordinary People in Russian and Soviet History," *Kritika: Explorations in Russian and Eurasian History,* 12, no. 3 (Summer 2011), 740 noted that "with the concept of the ordinary, we risk losing sight of the category's usefulness: to show that the people we term ordinary are in fact extraordinary when viewed through the right lens with creative imagination on the part of the historian."
36 *ДА Монтана,* Фонд 432К, оп.1, а.е.1, л.5.
37 *Inid.,*, л.7–7 гръб.
38 *Typhus in World War I,* https://microbiologysociety.org/publication/past-issues/world-war-i/article/typhus-in-world-war-i.html; *Epidemic Typhus,* https://en.wikipedia.org/wiki/Epidemic_typhus.
39 *ДА Монтана,* Фонд 432К, оп.1, а.е.1, л.22.
40 Ibidem.
41 *ДА Монтана,* Фонд 432К, оп.1, а.е.1, л.14 – 14 гръб.
42 Ibid., л.4 гръб.
43 *ЦДА,* Фонд 177 К, оп.1, а.е.85, л.6–8. Directive from January 18, 1900. Two-thirds of these salaries were to be paid by the state and one-third by the municipalities. The salaries of high school teachers were higher: first degree–1,740 levs, second degree–1,440 levs, and third degree–1,140 levs.
44 Любен Беров, "Промени в класовата структура на населението," *История на България.* Том 7, 231–32.
45 It is unusual to cite so many family names, but Petîr wanted to stress that they came from a priest's family, that is, they were educated. Petîr's father was Ivan, his grandfather Todor, his great-grandfather Ivan, but the founder of the clan was Iakim who became a priest, and that usually became the family name Popovi (from *pop,* priest).
46 *ДА Монтана,* Фонд 1074, оп.1, а.е.13, л.2.
47 Bulgaria adopted the Gregorian calendar in 1916. The Orthodox Church continued to use the Julian calendar until 1968, when together with the Greek and Romanian church it switched to the Gregorian. The Russian and Serbian church still follow the Julian calendar.
48 Angelina mistakenly sets the beginning of the war in the summer of 1875 whereas it began in the next year, in 1876.

49 ДА Монтана, Фонд 1074, оп.1, а.е.13, л.44. The bashibozouk are irregular troops, and "Turkish Gypsies" refers to the Muslims within the group.
50 ДА Монтана, Фонд 1074, оп.1, а.е.13, л.3.
51 Ibid., л.6.
52 Ibid., л.8.
53 Meletius (1832–91) was the first metropolitan of the Bulgarian Exarchate in Sofia, 1872–83. Born in Strumitsa, Macedonia, he received his theological education in Athens, Vienna, Berlin, Kishinev, and St. Petersburg. He was a teacher and preacher in different Bulgarian towns, before being elected by the newly established Bulgarian Exarchate as a metropolitan. He actively supported the Bulgarian national movement and was arrested several times by the Ottoman authorities, and with the beginning of the Russo-Turkish war unilaterally joined the Russian troops. A fiery conservative and Russophile, he was an MP in the Constituent Assembly, meddled in political life, and was forced to abdicate in 1883. He was a founder of the National Library to which he donated his valuable manuscript and book collection and a member of the Bulgarian Literary Society (i.e., an academician of what became the future Bulgarian Academy of Sciences).
54 ДА Монтана, Фонд 1074, оп.1, а.е.13, л.9–10.
55 Ibid., л.11–12.
56 Ibid., л.17. This error had important consequences, as Angelina herself used it to pass for a younger teacher and in the official schoolbook she gives her age at the moment of employment in Pripilzhane during 1899/1900 as forty-one (ДА Монтана, Фонд 432К, оп.1, а.е.1, л.3).
57 Ibid., л.15.
58 Ibid., л.17.
59 Ibid., л.17. The oka is a little over 1.2 kilograms.
60 Ibid., л.18.
61 Ibid., л.24.
62 Ibid., л.22.
63 Ibidem.
64 Ibid., л.23.
65 Ibid., 46.
66 Ibid., л.25.
67 Kliment of Tîrnovo (also known as a writer by his secular name Vasil Drumev, 1840–1901) was a prominent cleric, man of letters, and politician. Having joined the revolutionary nationalist struggle in his youth as part of Rakovski's Bulgarian Legion, he later emigrated to Russia in 1862 where he studied in the Kiev seminary, and in 1873 was ordained as a bishop. He was a deputy in Bulgaria's Grand National Assembly in 1879 and is considered the father of the modern Bulgarian (short) novel and drama.
68 ДА Монтана, Фонд 1074, оп.1, а.е.13, л.27–40.
69 Ibid., 48.
70 Ibid., 52.
71 Ibid., 50–51.
72 Ibid., 60.
73 Ibid., 52.
74 Ibid., 52–56.
75 Ibid, 56–57.

76 Paul Ricoeur, *Oneself as Another* (Chicago: University of Chicago Press, 1992). This is the English edition, translated by Kathleen Blamey of *Soi-même comme un autre*, Paris: Seuil, 1990.
77 Andrew Wiercinski, "Hermeneutic Notion of a Human Being as an Acting and Suffering Person: Thinking with Paul Ricoeur," *Ethics in Progress*, 4 (2013), 22.
78 Ibidem.
79 David Vessey, "The Polysemy of Otherness: On Ricoeur's Oneself as Another," (http://www.davevessey.com/), also cited in Shaun Gallagher and Stephen Watson, *Ipseity and Alterity: Interdiscipinary Approaches to Intersubjectivity* (Rouen: Publications de l'Université de Rouen, 2014), 18.
80 Ricoeur, *Oneself as Another*, 119, cited in Wiercinski, "Hermeneutic Notion of a Human Being," 23.
81 Ricoeur, *Oneself as Another*, 114, cited in Gérôme Truc, "Narrative Identity Against Biographical Illusion: The Shift in Sociology from Bourdieu to Ricoeur," *Études Ricoeuriennes/ Ricoeur Studies*, 2, no. 1 (2011), 155.

Chapter 7

1 A full run of the newspaper is in the library of Western Reserve Historical Society, Cleveland, Ohio: http://norton.wrhs.org/starweb/d.skclmarc-opac/servlet.starweb?path=d.skclmarc-opac/skclmarcfastlink.web&search1=001=ocm12309011
2 The paper had regular subscribers, at the outset 150–200, who had reached over 400 already in its first year, despite the fact that not all were necessarily members of the organization. See С. С. Саралиевъ, "Страница изъ историята на нашия вѣстник," *25-годишенъ юбилей на Българския Социалистически Работнически Съюзъ и В-къ "Работническа Просвѣта" (Сборник статии)* (Granite City, IL: Bulgarian Socialist Labor Federation, 1935), 116–17; Ст. Колевъ, "Интересни възпоменания," *25-годишенъ юбилей*, 190–91; Nikolay G. Altankov, *The Bulgarian-Americans* (Palo Alto, CA: Ragusan Press, 1979), 59–60.
3 Т. Баевъ, "Четвъртъ столѣтие," *25-годишенъ юбилей*, 31–32; Стоянъ Колевъ, "Лутахме се, но налучкахме пѫтя," *25-годишенъ юбилей*, 83.
4 James R. Barrett, "Americanization from the Bottom-Up: Immigration and the Remaking of the Working Class in the United States, 1880-1930," in James R. Barrett, ed., *History from the Bottom Up & the Inside Out* (Durham: Duke University Press, 2017), 122–44, especially 130–36.
5 Altankov, *The Bulgarian-Americans*, 61.
6 Ibid., viii. Altankov's is the first and to date the only extensive scholarly account about the Bulgarian emigration in the twentieth century.
7 Костадин Гърдев, *Българската емиграция в Канада* (София: Академично издателство „Марин Дринов," 1994), 15–20; Altankov, *The Bulgarian-Americans*, viii, 4–7; David E. Cassens, "The Bulgarian Colony of Southwestern Illinois, 1900-1920," *Illinois Historical Journal*, 84, no. 1 (1991), 16. The rough estimate is about 36,000 Bulgarians in the United States in the first decade of the century (1900–09) (Altankov, 12). Гърдев, *Българската емиграция*, 22, puts the combined figure for the United States and Canada at 50,000 in 1907, and 80,000 in 1911.
8 Altankov, *The Bulgarian-Americans*, xiv, no. 3. The US immigration official who worked through the papers of Bulgarians who had arrived in New York City in 1912

told them that Bulgarians work for two to three years, earn some money, and then return. Less than 5 percent of them become US citizens and the country does not need such immigrants (Гърдев, *Българската емиграция*, 30).

9 Cassens, "The Bulgarian Colony," 15–16; Altankov, *The Bulgarian-Americans*, 23.
10 Cassens, "The Bulgarian Colony," 21.
11 Ibidem; Георги Иванов, *Българските църковни общини в Америка и Чикаго* (Документална хроника). Чикаго, 2004–2011, 36–37, http://otzvuk.com/Knigi/T SURKOVNI%20OBSHTINI.pdf.
12 Cassens, "The Bulgarian Colony," 21.
13 Altankov, *The Bulgarian-Americans*, 34–40.
14 Stanley B. Kimball, *East Europeans in Southwestern Illinois: The Ethnic Experience in Historical Perspective,* Research Report #14. Coordinator of Area Development, SIUE (Southern Illinois University at Edwardsville, May 1981), 25; Altankov, *The Bulgarian-Americans*, 33.
15 Kimball, *East Europeans*, 25; Altankov, *The Bulgarian-Americans*, 45. See also George J. Prpic, *South Slavic Immigration in America* (Boston: Twayne, 1978) who writes that socialism found a special receptive audience among Bulgarian and Slovenes.
16 Altankov, *The Bulgarian-Americans*, 84–85.
17 Cassens, "The Bulgarian Colony," 24; Kimball, *East Europeans*, 25.
18 Altankov, *The Bulgarian-Americans*, 59.
19 Ibid. Stoyan Kolev, in his reminiscences written in 1935, mentions that the three members of the Board or CC were Todor Tsekov, S. S. Saraliev, and D. Ikonomov, the latter sympathizing with Georgi Bakalov's faction and later expelled as an "anarcho-liberal" (Стоянъ Колевъ, "Лутахме се, но налучкахме пѫтя," *25-годишенъ юбилей*, 82). Saraliev, without mentioning Tsekov by name, writes that when in August 1911, the secretary and treasurer, "who was one of the so-called intelligentsia" decided to return to Bulgaria, it was difficult to find a substitute, because most members were workers without any education and only a few had attended middle school (С. С. Саралиевъ, "Страница изъ историята на нашия вѣстникъ," *25-годишенъ юбилей*, 117).
20 Altankov, *The Bulgarian-Americans*, 62.
21 К. Ловачевъ, "Максизма и нашия съюзъ," *25-годишенъ юбилей*, 142–43; П. Матеевъ, "Съюзътъ и нашитѣ учители," *25-годишенъ юбилей*, 198.
22 Т.Граматиковъ, "Единъ ретроспектъ," *25-годишенъ юбилей*, 93–94.
23 Georgi Nikolov Zaikov, known by his pen name Pirinski (1901–92, and therefore not figuring in my cohort born before 1900) had emigrated to the United States on July 2, 1923, mostly for economic reasons, to join his brother there, although he had been close to the communist circles. The Wikipedia entry of his son heroically but wrongly claims that he had participated in the September Uprising (https://en.wikipedi a.org/wiki/Georgi_Pirinski_Jr.), which is belied by Pirinski's own memoirs (Георги Пирински, *Двата свята в моя живот* [София: Народна младеж, 1981], 5). A green card holder, he worked in the mining industry, a wagon factory in Madison, where he became a member of the CPUSA, and in General Motors in Pontiac. He became a leader of the Macedono–American People's Union, the left wing of the Macedonian Bulgarians in the United States, and by the 1930s was a journalist and professional functionary, close to the Comintern. In 1941 he created the American Slavic Committee. He was arrested and expelled as an undesirable alien in 1951 when he came back to Bulgaria as a hero and headed the National Committee for the Protection of Peace. He left several books of memoirs, written in a highly romantic tone and rather obsequious toward the party leadership, especially Todor Zhivkov.

His son, Georgi Pirinski, b.1948 in New York, is a politician and was the candidate of the Bulgarian Socialist Party for president in 1996.
24 Георги Пирински, *Какво видях и преживях Америка* (София: Издателство на Отечествения Фронт, 1970), 84. He does, however, mention, also briefly, that Tsekov was the main founder of the BSLF (p. 52) and that he had been elected secretary of the Bulgarian communists in 1924 (p. 71). Tsekov is not mentioned at all in Пирински, *Двата свята в моя живот*.
25 Георги Пирински, *Извикани от спомена. Портрети на американски и български борци за мир и демокрация в САЩ* (София: Партиздат, 1986), 157.
26 Ibid., 159.
27 Ibid., 161.
28 Ibid., 152–61.
29 Йордан Баев and Константин Грозев, *Българинът Джордж. Одисея в два свята* (София: Труд, 2008). Georgi Andreichin (George Andreytchine) (1884–1950), was a refugee from Ottoman Macedonia to Bulgaria in 1903. Orphaned, he was supported by the state and finished high school in Samokov where he encountered socialist ideas. He volunteered for the Balkan Wars, but after he was wounded, he emigrated to the United States in 1913. He worked as a miner in Minnesota where he joined the Industrial Workers of the World (IWW) and edited its organ "Solidarity." Arrested for organizing anti-war strikes, he was sentenced in 1917 in Chicago to twenty years in prison. Freed after a year thanks to the intervention of American workers organizations, he joined the Communist Labor Party of America as a member of its CC. He was a prominent figure, close to John Reed and with personal ties to Theodore Dreiser, Dudley Field Malone, Art Young, and Charlie Chaplin. He edited the Bulgarian language papers *Rabotnichesko delo* (1918–19) and *Rabotnicheska misil* (1920). In 1921 he travelled to Soviet Russia as the American delegate to the Profintern congress in Moscow and was elected to its leadership. He became a Soviet citizen and joined the Bolshevik Party. A friend of Trotsky, he was expelled from the party and exiled in Kazakhstan in 1927, but later pardoned. He worked in foreign trade and tourism until his second arrest and exile to Siberia. Released in 1941, he spent the war years in the ministry of propaganda. At the end of 1945 he came to Bulgaria and was head of the Office of the Interim Presidency of the Republic. He participated in the 1946 Paris peace conference and was chargé d'affaires (1948–49). Arrested in 1949, he was sent to the USSR and executed in 1950 by the NKVD. He was rehabilitated after Stalin's death. See also https://bg.wikipedia.org/wiki/Георг и_Андрейчин and Бойка Асиова, "Обратите на съдбата. Безпощаден разказ за невероятния живот на българина Джордж – Георги Андрейчин," *Земя* March 31, 2008 (http://library.belitsa.com/andreichin.php). The first book devoted entirely to Andreichin was by Georgi Pirinski: Георги Пирински, *Георги Андрейчин, пламенен революционер и деец на българското и международното комунистическо движение* (Благоевград: Научно-производствена дирекция "Културно-историческо наследство," 1984).
30 *Енциклопедия България* (София: Академично издтаелство "Проф. Марин Дринов," 1997), 351.
31 ЦДА, Сп – 2060 Б.
32 Трифон Трифонов, "Бележки към спомените-дневник на Тодор Цеков," *ЦДА*, Сп – 2060 Б, 1–2.
33 George Steinmetz, "Reflections on the Role of Social Narratives in Working-Class Formation: Narrative Theory in the Social Sciences," *Social Science History*, 16, no. 3 (Autumn 1992), 490.

34 The above-cited chapter by Pirinski (Пирински, *Извикани от спомена*, 152–61) also worked from the diary and also was apparently not given access to the later volumes, as Tsekov's later career is summarized in a couple of general sentences that after September 1944 Tsekov went from village to village to organize party and youth groups. Pirinski does add, though, the oral account of Tsekov's daughter Florence, who remembered a brief and warm encounter between her father and Georgi Dimitrov.

35 The famous diary of Marie Bashkirtseff (1887) which is celebrated as the first literary life document, was explicitly meant to be published, as the twenty-year-old who died of tuberculosis and had written the diary for a decade, wanted to reach fame with it and leave an indelible mark on posterity: *The Journal of Marie Bashkirtseff: I Am the Most Interesting Book of All* (Volume I), *Lust for Glory* (Volume II), trans. Katherine Kernberger (Stroud, UK: Fonthill Press, 2013).

36 ЦДА, Сп – 2060 Б, 6.

37 Ibid., 93.

38 Ibid., 7–8.

39 The Bulgarian orthography was standardized only in 1899 with the so-called Drinov orthography and a thirty-two-letter alphabet. It was simplified once during the rule of the Agrarian Party between 1921–23, but then restored and finally, in 1945, a thirty-letter alphabet and reforms, like the ones under the agrarian regime, were adopted. Tsekov, on the other hand, does not use the letter "ъ" as a back vocal, which was also removed in 1921–23 and again in 1945, but this seems to have been widespread, judging from other people's letters from the period. This may also have been an individual choice, as discussions over the simplification and democratization of the orthography were widespread and passionate, and Tsekov, as a progressive teacher, would have sided with the reforms.

40 ЦДА, Сп – 2060 Б, 755–56, 1098.

41 Alain Girard, *Le journal intime* (Paris: Presses Universitaires de France, 1963), xix, cited in Peter Heehs, *Writing the Self: Diaries, Memoirs, and the History of the Self* (London: Bloomsbury Academic, 2013), 6.

42 Heehs, *Writing the Self*, 6.

43 Jerome Bruner, "The Autobiographical Process," in Robert Folkenflik, ed., *The Culture of Autobiography: Constructions of Self-Representation* (Stanford, CA: Stanford University Press, 1993), 55; see also David C. Rubin, *Remembering Our Past: Studies in Autobiographical Memory* (Cambridge: Cambridge University Press, 1996), especially Martin A. Conway, "Autobiographical Knowledge and Autobiographical Memories," (67–93).

44 Craig Calhoun, "Social Theory and the Politics of Identity," in Calhoun, ed., *Social Theory and the Politics of Identity* (Oxford: Blackwell, 1994), 10.

45 Calhoun, ibidem; Steinmetz, "Reflections on the Role of Social Narratives," 490.

46 James Rachels and William Redick, "Lives and Liberty," in John Christman, ed., *The Inner Citadel: Essays on Individual Autonomy* (New York: Oxford University Press, 1898), 227, cited in Paul John Eakin, *How Our Lives Become Stories: Making Selves* (Ithaca: Cornell University Press, 1999), 167.

47 Michel Foucault, "L'écriture de soi," *Corps écrit*, no. 5. *L'autoportrait* (February 1983), 7–8. English translation https://foucault.info/documents/foucault.hypomnemata.en/. On the distinction between memoirs, autobiographies and diaries, see James S. Amelang, *The Flight of Icarus: Artisan Autobiography in Early Modern Europe* (Stanford, CA: Stanford University Press, 1998), 28–46. See also Philippe Lejeune, *On Autobiography* (Minneapolis: University of Minnesota Press, 1989).

48 Kerstin W. Shands, Giulia Grillo Mikrit, Dipti R. Pattanik, and Karen Ferreira-Meyers, eds., *Writing the Self: Essays on Autobiography and Autofiction* (Flemingsberg: Södertörns högskila, 2015), 26.
49 Robert Folkenflik, "Introduction: The Institution of Autobiography," in Folkenflik, ed., *The Culture of Autobiography*, 13.
50 Leigh Gilmore, *The Limits of Autobiography: Trauma and Testimony* (Ithaca: Cornell University Press, 2001), 3 cited in Shands et al., eds. *Writing the Self*, 9.
51 Roy Pascal, *Design and Truth in Autobiography* (New York: Routledge, 2017 [1960]), 3.
52 Ibid., 4.
53 Lydia Ginzburg, *On Psychological Prose*, trans. and ed. Judson Rosegrant (Princeton, NJ: Princeton University Press, 1991), 6.
54 Ibid., 5.
55 Cited in Pascal, *Design and Truth*, 5.
56 Malina Stefanovska, "Donner un noble sujet de rire à la bonne compagnie: *Histoire de ma vie* de Casanova," in Jean-Pierre Castellani, ed., *Écriture de soi et autorité* (Tours: Presses universitaires François-Rabelais, 2016), 55.
57 Manuel Castells, *The Power of Identity*, 8. The other two types identified by Castells are legitimizing identity (which generates civil society), and resistance identity (which leads to the formation of communities).
58 ЦДА, Сп – 2060 Б, 9–11.
59 Ibid., 12–15.
60 Ibid., 25–26.
61 Ibid., 27–28.
62 Ibid., 30.
63 Ibid., 34–35.
64 Ibid., 36.
65 Ibid., 38.
66 Ibid., 40–46.
67 Ibid., 48. Tsekov provides the full list with names, and ages between seventeen and nineteen (49–53).
68 Ibid., 78–79.
69 Ibid., 68.
70 Ibid., 69–75.
71 Ibid., 90. Under the "*komitadzhi* cause" [komitadzhilî] is understood as the armed struggle in Macedonia.
72 Ibid., 32, 75.
73 Ibid., 89, 94, 109.
74 Ibid., 173.
75 Ibid., 172–73.
76 Ibid., 177.
77 Ibid., 178–79.
78 Ibid., 179.
79 Ibid., 110–20.
80 Ibid., 207–21.
81 Ibid., 239.
82 Ibid., 93.
83 We know the size of this omission because the archival page 93 corresponds to the diary page 138, page 94 to 175, and page 104 to 205. There are discrepancies before and after, but usually smaller ones. We can assume that some of them were taken out

by the family. Only in this instance is there an explicit note by the archivist. By "ideal love" is meant platonic love (pp. 127, 165).

84 ЦДА, Сп – 2060 Б, 132–71.
85 Ibid., 129.
86 Ibid., 130.
87 Ibid., 136, 138–38/об.
88 https://en.wikipedia.org/wiki/The_Kreutzer_Sonata#Censorship.
89 Терзиева, *Поглед върху толстоизма*.
90 ЦДА, Сп – 2060 Б, 137, 155–56.
91 Ibid., 159–60.
92 Ibid., 164–64.
93 Ibid., 161–62.
94 Ibid., 164–67.
95 Ibid., 262.
96 Ibid., 268–70, 296–300.
97 Ibid., 320.
98 Ibid., 335–36.
99 Ibid., 321–32.
100 Ibid., 370.
101 Ibid., 444.
102 Ibid., 447.
103 Ibid., 486.
104 Ibid., 536.
105 Ibid., 577.
106 Ibid., 483–84, 518, 588.
107 Ibid., 563, 566–67.
108 Ibid., 643–57.
109 Ibid., 586.
110 Ibid., 611, 662.
111 Ibid., 641.
112 Ibid., 610–11.
113 Ibid., 621–22.
114 Ibid., 537–38, 607, 640, 663. His monthly salary was 85 levs, after two years as a teacher his debt was 770 levs and by 1907 their common debt had risen to over 900 levs, despite their efforts at frugality.
115 ЦДА, Сп – 2060 Б, 663, 675, 681.
116 Ibid., 662.
117 Ibid., 565.
118 Петко Кандев, "Зараждане и развитие на учителското движение в България (до 1895 г.)," *Известия на Института по История на БКП*, т.7 (1960), 241–62.
119 ЦДА, Фонд 200 К, оп.2, л. 5–23, various petitions 1901–05.
120 ЦДА, Фонд 200 К, оп.3, л. 78–79, Protokol N. 26, February 25, 1901.
121 *Кратка история на Българската Комунистическа Партия*, 65.
122 ЦДА, Сп – 2060 Б, 497–502, here 500–501.
123 See Йордан Йотов, *Централизмът в българското социалистическо движение*.
124 For two opposing interpretations, see Топенчаров, *Българската журналистика, 1903-1917*, 125–46 and Константинова, *Бунтът на "анархолибералите."* Topencharov defends the dominant communist view on the so-called "debate on the press" that the proliferation of so many socialist publications hampered

the targeted and planned expenditure and the concentrated efforts for socialist propaganda. *Rabotnishko delo* was seen as too popular and entertaining and was becoming redundant. Konstantinova, on the other hand, whose whole book analyzes this debate, sees it as the imposition of the authoritarian personality of Blagoev and commencement of the stifling of inner party democracy which would see its culmination after the wars with the creation of a Leninist communist party.

125 ЦДА, Сп – 2060 Б, 464.
126 Ibid., 505–8.
127 Richard J. Crampton, *A Concise History of Bulgaria* (Cambridge: Cambridge University Press, 1997), 120–22; Стателова and Грънчаров, *История на Нова България*, 180–93; Цветана Тодорова, *Дипломатическа история на външните заеми на България 1888-1912* (София: Наука и изкуство, 1971); Цветана Тодорова, "Индустриализация и структурни промени в България през Първата световна война," *Исторически преглед*, 5 (1991), 22-43.
128 Crampton, *A Concise History*, 122–29.
129 Стателова and Грънчаров, *История на Нова България*, 203–12. The university, first opened as a pedagogical school in 1887, was renamed as a university in 1904 with three departments: history and philology, physics and mathematics, and law.
130 ЦДА, Сп – 2060 Б, 599–600.
131 Ibid., 669–74 (here 672). Todor Tsekov credits him with being their main support while in America to whom they owed their education and future stable life (810).
132 Ibid., 674, 758–59.
133 Ibid., 626.
134 Ulf Brunnbauer, "Emigrants and Countries of Origin: The Politics of Emigration in Southeastern Europe Until the First World War," in Timothy Snyder and Katherine Younger, eds., *The Balkans as Europe, 1821-1914* (Rochester: University of Rochester Press, 2018), 93–94.
135 ЦДА, Сп – 2060 Б, 714–15.
136 Ibid., 715–53.
137 Ibid., 729.
138 Ibid., 732.
139 Ibid., 736.
140 Ibid., 757–71.
141 Ibid., 772–75.
142 Ibid., 776–78.
143 Ibid., 784–87.
144 Ibid., 805–8.
145 Ibid, 809–12.
146 Ibid., 789–90.
147 Ibid., 822.
148 Ibid., 779–81, 790–91, 796–804, 814–19.
149 *Rabotnicheska Prosveta (Работническа просвѣта)*, Granite City, vol. 1, no. 1 (January 1, 1911) to no. 15 (August 1, 1911).
150 *Rabotnicheska Prosveta*, vol. 1, no. 1 (February 1, 1911).
151 ЦДА, Сп – 2060 Б, 780.
152 Ibid., 820–21.
153 On prostitution, see Даскалова, *Жени, пол и модернизация*, 453–84.
154 Ibid., 1007, 1053, 1077.
155 Ibid., 1063, 1071.

156 Ibid., 832–34.
157 Ibid., 835–47.
158 Ibid., 853–78.
159 Ibid., 915.
160 Ibid., 949.
161 Ibid., 943–69.
162 Ibid., 981–84.
163 Ibid., 987–96.
164 Françoise Thom, *La Langue de bois* (Paris: Julliard, 1987). This is most obvious in Tsekov's discussion of the 1903 split which comes early on, already in the first volume, where he uses all the invectives against the Broads, like "intellectual riffraff," careerism and the like. It is clearly, however, a later interpolation, but one made before the wars, judging from the simplified but not reformed orthography (the "ѣ" is there, but the back vocal "ъ" has disappeared) (ЦДА, Сп – 2060 Б, 121–26). The wooden language is also present in the last pages of volume 4 (ЦДА, Сп – 2060 Б, 1096–98) written in 1950, where he describes the hopes that the victory of the Bolshevik revolution raised in his heart, using much later communist shibboleths.
165 Mary Jo Maynes, "Autobiography and Class Formation," 520.
166 Ibid., 528.
167 Jochen Hellbeck, *Revolution on My Mind: Writing a Diary Under Stalin* (Cambridge, MA: Harvard University Press, 2006), 5, 350. Helbeck may be partly right for some of the communist writing under Stalinism but this is a vast overgeneralization. There is a similar critique in the review of Malte Griesse in *Cahiers du monde russe*, 43, no. 4 (October–December 2002), 739–43.
168 Diane Koenker, "Scripting the Revolutionary Worker Autobiography: Archetypes, Models, Inventions, and Markets," *International Review of Social History*, 49, no. 3 (December 2004), 377.
169 Igal Halfin, *Terror in My Soul: Autobiographies on Trial* (Cambridge, MA: Harvard University Press, 2003), 59.
170 James R. Barrett, "Was the Personal Political? Reading the Autobiography of American Communism," *International Review of Social History*, 53, no. 3 (December 2008), 402.
171 Myriam Revault D'Allonnes, *Le Pouvoir des commencements. Essai sur l'autorité* (Paris: Le Seuil, 2006), 12, cited in Stefanovska, "Donner un noble sujet de rire," 53.

Chapter 8

1 ЦДА, Фонд 366 Б, оп.1, а.е.19, л.9 а-10.
2 Ibid., 3.
3 From Hugo's "Les Contemplations": "To read the universe well is to read life well; The world is a creation where nothing lies, and nothing strays."
4 Scheer, "Are Emotions a Kind of Practice?," 214. Scheer distinguished between four categories of emotional practice: mobilizing, naming, communicating, and regulating.
5 The one exception is a brief autobiography in Russian, written after 1946, surprisingly with lots of grammatical and orthographic mistakes given the long time she had spent in Russia ЦДА, Фонд 368 Б, оп.1, а.е.1, л.1–5. There are also biographies of socialist figures, both Bulgarian and foreign, as well as some personal documents and correspondence.

6   ЦДА, Фонд 368 Б, оп.1, а.е.1, л.1, 11.
7   Ibid., 12–16, 57 a.
8   Ibid., 17–18. On the peasant riots, see *История на България*, том 7, 333–39.
9   Tikhonov, "Student Migrations and the Feminization of European Universities."
10 ЦДА, Фонд 368 Б, оп.1, а.е.1, л.63.
11 Ibid, 20–21.
12 Ibid., 22–28.
13 Ibid., 33–34, 62 a.
14 Ibid., 34–34 a, 69–70; Tikhonov, "Student Migrations and the Feminization of European Universities."
15 ЦДА, Фонд 368 Б, оп.1, а.е.1, л. 69.
16 She names some other members of the group: Strashimir Dechkov, Toni Angelov, St. Draganov, Velichka Giulgelieva, Nikola Sakarov, K. Kunev, B. Balevski, Petko Todorov, Khristo Vlakhov, St. Girzdhikov, D. Gavriiski, Dzhena (Zhana) Bozhilova Panteva, and V. Kostov (Ibid., 36 б).
17 ЦДА, Фонд 368 Б, оп.1, а.е.28, л.17.
18 Ibid., 19–29.
19 Ibid., 46.
20 Ibid., 47–49, 110.
21 Ibid., 26, 34–38.
22 Ibid., 71–73.
23 Ibid., 73–96.
24 Ibid., 96–105.
25 ЦДА, Фонд 368 Б, оп.1, а.е.43.
26 ЦДА, Фонд 368 Б, оп.1, а.е.1, л.2–3.
27 The Bulgarian "Минимум единомислие, максимум единодействие" makes the point even more eloquently. *Пролетарий*, бр.24–24, 25.VIII.1906, cited in Йордан Йотов, "Борбата на тесните социалисти против анархолибералите и прогресистите," *Известия на Института по История на БКП*, т.11, 1964, 63.
28 *Кратка история на Българската Комунистическа Партия*, 65. On the position of this left wing, see the 1909 brochure of Mihail (Mancho) Vodenicharov, a close friend of Sakarov, who in 1912 returned то the Narrows. In 1913 he left for Germany, and nothing is known about his later fate: Михаил Воденичаров. *Борбата на левите течения в "обединената" социалистическа партия*. София, 1909 (The struggle of the left currents in the "united" socialist party"). Also see the appeals of several of the local organizations of the left factions (levichari) for a conference to coordinate their tactics in ЦДА, Фонд 368 Б, оп.1, а.е.661.
29 ЦДА, Фонд 368 Б, оп.1, а.е.1, л. 67–67 а.
30 Ibid, 67 a.
31 ЦДА, Фонд 368 Б, оп.1, а.е.43, л.9–10. An abbreviated version also in Tineva's unpublished memoirs on Kirkov: ЦДА, Сп 1880 Б, л.7. See the details and the whole quote in chapter 5. On Russian women revolutionaries, see Barbara Engel and Clifford Rosenthal, *Five Sisters: Women Against the Tsar* (New York: Alfred Knopf, 1975).
32 ЦДА, Фонд 368 Б, оп.1, а.е.43, л.10.
33 On *Nachalo*, see Топенчаров, *Българската журналистика, 1903-1917*, 287–29.
34 ЦДА, Фонд 368 Б, оп.1, а.е.31, л. 2–3, 8.
35 Ibid., 5–6.
36 Ibid., 12–15 (here 15); the meeting with Lenin (20–23).
37 ЦДА, Фонд 368 Б, оп.1, а.е.1, л.5. Rakovski was shot in the Soviet Gulag in 1941.

38 Георги Бакалов, *Избрани произведения* (София: Фондация Арете-Фол, Университетско издателство "Св.Климент Охридски," 2007), 5–22.
39 ЦДА, Сп 2934 Б, л. 79–91. Velichkov's very intelligent and balanced memoirs are written at the end of 1940 (as he mentions the then prime minister Dimitrov who died in 1949), most likely before the final suppression of the political opposition by the communists. It is unclear how they made their way into the party archives. He is happy with the transformation of Bulgaria after 1944 but adds that the freedom of speech and press is essential: "I don't see anything bad and dangerous about it" (155–56).
40 Ibid., 69.
41 ЦДА, Фонд 368 Б, оп.1, а.е.1, л.13–14. Койка Тинева, *Гаврил Георгиев. Биографичен очерк* (София: Издателство на БКП, 1964). Peko Velichkov characterized Georgiev as a profound thinker but an alcoholic, something that was considered a public secret (ЦДА, Сп 2934 Б, л. 58 ff).
42 ЦДА, Фонд 368 Б, оп.1, а.е.1, л.57.
43 ЦДА, Фонд 366 Б, оп.1, а.е.1, л.16; ЦДА, Фонд 366 Б, оп.3, а.е.1, л.6.
44 ЦДА, Фонд 366 Б, оп.1, а.е.1, л.2.
45 Ibid., 3–5. Mikhail Madzharov (1854–1944) was one of the major figures in Bulgarian political life, a member and leader of the conservative People's Party, a diplomat and formidable journalist. He died after having been fatally wounded in the Anglo-American bombings over Sofia in January 1944.
46 ЦДА, Фонд 366 Б, оп.1, а.е.1, 10–14.
47 ЦДА, Фонд 366 Б, оп.1, а.е. 85.
48 Nikola Sakaroff, *Die industrielle Entwicklung Bulgariens. Inaugural Dissertation zur Erlagung der Doktorwürde geheimigt von der philisophischen Fakultät der Friedrich-Wilhelms-Universität zu Berlin* (August 18, 1904).
49 ЦДА, Фонд 366 Б, оп.1, а.е. 1750. The English translations from Heine are mine. For a professional poetic translation, see Hal Draper (https://www.oxfordlieder.co.uk/song/839) and https://lyricstranslate.com/en/ich-glaube-nicht-den-himmel-i-dont-believe-heven.html.
50 ЦДА, Фонд 366 Б, оп.1, а.е.2.
51 ЦДА, Фонд 366 Б, оп.1, а.е. 3, л.1–3; a copy is also in the personal archive of Roman Avramov, ЦДА, Фонд 160 Б, оп.1, а.е. 32.
52 Ibid., 4–6. There are also hagiographic interviews with Sakarov in *Literaturen glas* (probably from 1929) and *Misil* (from 1930) in ЦДА, Фонд 366 Б, оп.1, а.е.6.
53 Никола Сакаров, *Българските държавни финанси от Освобождението до Световната война* (София: Издава Българската Академия на Науките, 1918).
54 Никола Сакаров, *Капиталът трябва да плаща* (София: Книгоиздателство Знание, 1920); Никола Сакаров, *Железопътното и телеграфопощенското дело в България* (София: Издателство на Българския Железничарски съюз, 1919).
55 Никола Сакаров, *Петилетния стопански план на Русия* (София: Книгоиздателство Азбука, 1931 [5 brochures]); Никола Сакаров, "Руският социален опит и неговите близки изгледи," *Философски преглед*, кн. 1, 1931.
56 Никола Сакаров, *Социалистическият интернационал и войната* (София: Напред, 1919); Никола Сакаров, *Тактика на социалната демокрация* (София: Напред, 1920).
57 Сакаров and Николов, *Опити за разсейване на идейната безпътица*.
58 ЦДА, Фонд 366 Б, оп.1, а.е. 62, а.е. 64, а.е. 65, а.е. 66, а.е. 68.

59 ЦДА, Фонд 366 Б, оп.1, а.е. 67. There is also a small notebook about his visit, with addresses and very laconic – ЦДА, Фонд 366 Б, оп.1, а.е. 50.
60 ЦДА, Фонд 366 Б, оп.1, а.е. 63.
61 This literature can be at times very informative but is as a whole mired by a negative *parti pris*: Йотов, *Централизмът в българското социалистическо движение*; Йотов, "Борбата на тесните социалисти против анархолибералите и прогресистите"; Топенчаров, *Българската журналистика, 1903-1917*; Георги Борисов, "Борбата на Българската работническа социалдемократическа партия против анархолибералите," *Известия на Висшата Партийна Школа при ЦК на БКП*, отдел "История," 1962, кн.14. The only academic "rehabilitation" of these factions after 1989 belongs to Константинова. *Бунтът на "анархолибералите*, focused on the debate on the press.
62 *Зора,*, VII, no. 2030 (April 2, 1926), in ЦДА, Фонд 366 Б, оп.1, а.е. 627.
63 ЦДА, Фонд 366 Б, оп.1, а.е. 569, л.1.
64 Никола Харлаков, "Изказване пред русенската сбирка," *Пролетарий*, бр.12, 30.IV.1906, 16, cited in Йотов, *Централизмът в българското социалистическо движение*, 84. See also Топенчаров, *Българската журналистика, 1903-1917*, 272–80.
65 Георги Бакалов, "Работническото движение у нас и задачите на пролетарското течение (доклад изнесен пред Учредителния конгрес на съюза 'Пролетарий')," *Пролетарий*, бр.7, 15.VIII.1906, 13, cited in Йотов, *Централизмът в българското социалистическо движение*, 86.
66 Георги Бакалов, "Към обединение," *Пролетарий*, бр.17, 30.XII.1906, cited in Йотов, *Централизмът в българското социалистическо движение*, 87.
67 ЦДА, Фонд 366 Б, оп.1, а.е. 569, л.7–8.
68 Ibid., л.11–12. The leaflet had twenty-two signatures: Petko Velichkov. A. Sabetaev, Ia. D. Markov, P. D-ov [Dzhidrov], St. Popova, G. Bakalov, V. Zarkov, P. Charîkchiev, M. Rafaelov, N.K Harlakov, Dramchev, T. I. Semerdzhiev, Sht. Bozukovam, A. Benaroi, M. Graovski, B. Popov, M. Geraskov, Vasil Nikolov, Petko Ralev, Radi Vasilev, N. Nikolov, and Al. Antonov.
69 Йотов, *Централизмът в българското социалистическо движение*, 187.
70 In the interwar period, one of the oldest socialists, Evtim Dabev, lamented the low theoretical level of workers. In a poll he conducted, out of 100 workers sixty-eight knew the name of Marx, thirty-five had heard of Engels, but all knew details about Trotsky and some maintained that Marxism has to be corrected with the views of Lenin. Only twelve had heard about surplus value, and only two understood what it meant: Евтим Дабев, "Разколът в работническото движение," *Бележник на един социалдемократ (непериодично издание)*, no. 1 (February 1928), 8.
71 ЦДА, Фонд 366 Б, оп.1, а.е.562.
72 ЦДА, Фонд 366 Б, оп.1, а.е. 306; 307; а.е.308; а.е.309.
73 *Работнически вестник*, бр.135, 16.XII.1920 - ЦДА, Фонд 366 Б, оп.1, а.е. 6. The letter from Sakarov was followed by a vicious editorial commenting on his past and accepting his declaration with great reservation.
74 ЦДА, Фонд 366 Б, оп.1, а.е.1, л. 25.
75 Ibid., 21.
76 Ibid., 22.
77 Ibid., 22-23, citing the testimony of Velislav Kozharov, a lawyer from Berkovitsa, the center of the uprising.

78 Ibid., 23.
79 Ibid., 20. Kabakcheiv's fate is especially poignant. An accomplished intellectual who had studied law in Geneva and Sofia, independently thinking but highly disciplined, he sided with Blagoev after 1903 and served as an MP between 1914 and 1923. He became the political secretary of the BCP. Arrested on September 12, 1923, he spent two years in prison. Rearrested in 1925, he was later freed and emigrated to Vienna (1926) and to Moscow (1927) where he became a member of RCP (b). Subjected to all the humiliations that the Narrows received from the "young" bolshevized Bulgarian left, he nonetheless defended a doctorate in history and worked at the Institute for History of the Soviet Academy of Sciences. Arrested in 1938 he disappeared and with Dimitrov's intervention he was found in 1939 in the Sukhanovsky convent, one of the strictest Moscow prisons, and released. Physically and morally wrecked, he died in 1940 of his third heart attack (see the memoirs of Blagoi Popov, ЦДА, Фонд 321 Б, оп.1, а.е.48).
80 Сакаров and Николов, *Опити за разсейване на идейната безпътица*, 69.
81 Bell, *The Bulgarian Communist Party*, 39. In fact the declaration that Sakarov read, was signed by six MPs, since the seventh was still in prison (Сакаров and Николов, *Опити за разсейване на идейната безпътица*, 46–47).
82 Сакаров and Николов, *Опити за разсейване на идейната безпътица*, 47–49.
83 Ibid., 50–51.
84 *Зора*, VII, no. 2030 (April 2, 1926), in ЦДА, Фонд 366 Б, оп.1, а.е. 627.
85 ЦДА, Сп-1427 Б. л. 55, 73.
86 Bell, *The Bulgarian Communist Party*, 41–42; Rothschild, *The Communist Party of Bulgaria*, 259–64. The quote comes from Дърева, *Атентатът '1925*, 96.
87 ЦДА, Фонд 366 Б, оп.1, а.е. 1, л. 14А.
88 Сакаров and Николов, *Опити за разсейване на идейната безпътица*, Addendum "Към социализма!," 5.
89 ЦДА, Фонд 366 Б, оп.1, а.е. 3, л. 4–6.
90 ЦДА, Сп 625 Б, 33–35. These are bound memoirs of about 100 pages mostly on events of the later 1930s. Dramaliev also left another two typed, bound volumes which were reviewed positively by the institute but with suggestions for abbreviations that he did not accept (ЦДА, Сп 619 Б, ЦДА, Фонд 215 Б, оп.1, а.е. 36).
91 Даскалова, *Жени, пол и модернизация*, 158.

Coda

1 George Lichtheim, *The Origins of Socialism* (London: Weidenfeld and Nicolson, 1969), 217.
2 Arvidsson et al., *Socialist Imaginations*, 1.
3 Ibid., 2, 8.
4 Leszek Kołakowski, "My Correct Views on Everything: A Rejoinder to Edward Thompson's 'Open Letter to Leszek Kolakowski,'" *Socialist Register*, 11 (1974), 19–20.
5 Ferenc Feher, Agnes Heller, and Gyorgy Markus, *Dictatorship over Needs: An Analysis of Soviet Societies* (Oxford, UK: Basil Blackwell, 1983), 299.
6 Bauman, *Socialism: The Active Utopia*, 90.

Bibliography

Archives

Архив на МВР, ОБ (Общо дело) 280, Vol. 1, 3; 4744.

Държавен архив (ДА) Монтана
  Фонд 432К, оп.1, а.е.1, 2; Фонд, 1074, оп.1, а.е.13.
  Петър Иванов, *Ангелина Бонева Якимова–баба Ангелина. Бележита българка*

Централен Държавен Архив (ЦДА)

  Фонд 1Б, оп.2, а.е. 21, 219, 601; Фонд 11, оп.1, а.е. 50; Фонд 141 Б, оп.1, а.е.2; *ЦДА*, Фонд 147 Б, оп.2, а.е. 449; Фонд 153 Б, оп.1, а.е.7; Фонд 157 Б, оп.1, а.е.5; Фонд 160 Б, оп.1, а.е. 2, 3, 10, 32, 45, 52; Фонд 177 К, оп.1, а.е. 45, 85, 110, 111, 299; Фонд 186 Б, оп.1, а.е. 18, 48, 82, 88, 93, 109/6, 212, 213; Фонд 196 Б, оп.1, а.е.2, 3, 4, 5, 11, 12, 13, 14, 15, 16; Фонд 197 Б, оп.1, а.е.1, 6, 7, 20, 72, 76, 77; оп.2, а.е. 4, 31, 33-62; *ЦДА*, Фонд 200 К, оп.2, оп.3; Фонд 215 Б, оп.1, а.е. 36; Фонд 251 Б, оп.1, а.е. 12; Фонд 263, оп.1, а.е.47; Фонд 265 Б, оп.1, а.е.2, 36; Фонд 272 Б, оп.1, а.е. 56, 61, 63; Фонд 285, оп.1, а.е.134; Фонд 321 Б, оп.1, а.е.48; *ЦДА*, Фонд 361 К, оп. 1, а.е. 9; Фонд 366 Б, оп.1, а.е. 1, 2, 3, 6, 19, 50, 62, 63, 64, 65, 67, 68, 306, 307, 308, 309, 562, 569, 627, 673, 1750; оп.3, а.е.1; Фонд 368 Б, оп.1, а.е. 1, 16, 28, 31, 43, 661; Фонд 370, оп.1, а.е. 515.

  Unpublished memoirs: Сп 174 Б; Сп 240 Б; Сп 322Б; Сп-517 Б; Сп 579 Б; Сп 619 Б; Сп 625 Б; Сп 655 Б; Сп 683 Б; Сп 768 Б; Сп 807 Б; Сп 829 Б; Сп 911 Б; Сп 934 Б; Сп 1038 Б; Сп 1128 Б; Сп 1332 Б; Сп 1377 Б; Сп 1378 Б; Сп 1409 Б; Сп 1427 Б; Сп 1462 Б; Сп 1522 Б; Сп 1569 Б; Сп 1590 Б; Сп 1647 Б; Сп 1728 Б; Сп 1826 Б; Сп 1880 Б; Сп 1996 Б; Сп 2060 Б; Сп 2012 Б; Сп 2220 Б; Сп 2234 Б; Сп 2565 Б; Сп 2652 Б; Сп 2686 Б; Сп 2827 Б; Сп 2934 Б; Сп 3049 Б; ЧП 11 Б; ЧП 15 Б; ЧП 18 Б; ЧП 75 Б.

Contemporary Newspapers and Journals

Българска мисъл
Drugar
Ден
Дума на българските емигранти
Дунав
Женски глас,
Женски труд
Журнал Съвременний показател
Знаме,
Зора
Историк-марксист

Коммунистический интернационал
Македония
Напред
Народни права
Ново време
Пролетарий
Пролетарская революция
Работник
Работническа искра
Работническа мисъл
Работническа просвѣта
Работнически вестник
Равноправие
Росица
Социалист
Съвременник
Турция
Училищен преглед
Философски преглед
Цариградски вестник
Читалище

Encyclopedias and Catalogs

Brunner, Otto, Werner Conze, and Reinhart Koselleck. *Geschichtliche Grundbegriffe: Historisches Lexicon zur politisch-sozialen Sprache in Deutschland*. Stuttgart: Klett-Cotta, 1972–1997.
International Encyclopedia of Social & Behavioral Sciences (IESBH), 2nd ed., 2015.
Голяма енциклопедия "България." София: Труд, 2011–2012.
Енциклопедия България. София: Академично издтаелство „Проф. Марин Дринов", 1997.
Каталог на книгите в Областната библиотека, постъпили до 1885. Пловдив, 1885.
Пътеводител по мемоарните документи за БКП, съхранявани в Централния Държавен Архив. София: ЦДА, 2003.
Пътеводител по фондовете на БКП, съхранявани в Централния държавен архив, София, 2006.

Published Documents and Memoirs

Banac, Ivo, ed. *The Diary of Georgi Dimitrov, 1933–1949*. New Haven: Yale University Press, 2003.
Benaroya, Abraham. "A Note on 'the Socialist Federation of Saloniki,'" *Jewish Social Studies* XI, no. 1 (1949): 70–71.
Debogory-Mokriewitwsch, W. *Erinnerungen eines Nihilisten*. Stuttgart: Verlag von Robert Lutz, 1905.

Engel, Barbara and Clifford Rosenthal. *Five Sisters: Women Against the Tsar*. New York: Alfred Knopf, 1975.
Haupt, Georges, ed. *Congrès international extraordinaire, Bâle, 24–25 novembre 1912; Congrès international socialiste de Stockholm 1917*. Genève: Minkoff reprint, 1980.
Haupt, Georges, Janos Jemnitz, and Leo van Rossum, Hg. *Karl Kautsky und die Sozialdemokratie Südosteuropas. Korrespondenz 1883–1938*. Frankfurt: Campus Verlag, 1986.
Kautsky, Benedikt, Hg. *Erinnerungen und Erörtungen von Karl Kautsky*. 's-Gravenhage: Mouton & Co, 1960.
The Balkan Socialist Tradition. Balkan Socialism and the Balkan Federation, 1871–1915 (Revolutionary History 8, no. 3). London: Porcupine Press, 2003.
Trotsky, Leon. *The War Correspondence of Leon Trotsky: The Balkan Wars 1912–13*, trans. Brian Pearce. New York: Monad Press, 1980.
Аврамов, Роман. *Публицистика и кореспонденция*. София: Партиздат, 1985.
Ангелов, Върбан. *Живот за партията*. София: Партиздат, 1972.
Ангелов, Върбан. *Неизвестни страници от миналото, 1919,1923,1925,1944, 1956, 1968*. София: Военноиздателски комплекс "Св. Георги Пебедоносец," 1993.
Благоев, Димтър. *Кратки бележки из моя живот*. София: Издателство на БКП, 1971.
Бозвелиев, Константин. *Моите спомени*. Съст. и ред. Тихомир Тихов. София: Военноиздателски комплекс „Св. Георги Победоносцев," Университетско издателство "Св. Климент Охридски," 1993.
Българска комунистическа партия. Документи на централните ръководни органи. София: Партиздат, 1972–1984, 1–6.
Гевренова, Лиляна. *Спомени за моя вуйчо Кръстю Раковски*. София: Български писател, 1989.
Герджиков, Михаил. *Спомени, документи, материали*. София: Наука и изкуство, 1984.
Дебогорий-Мокриевич, В. К. *Воспоминания*. Санкт Петербург, 1906.
Джидров, Богдан, съст. *Спомени на д-р Петър Джидров*. София: Университетско издателство "Св.Климент Охридски", 1996.
Коларов, Васил. *Статии, дневници, речи, писма, спомени*, Т.1 (1877-1919). София: Христо Ботев, 2001.
Радев, Симеон. *Погледи върху литературата и изкуството и лични спомени*. София: Български писател, 1965.
Социализмът в България (Отчет на централния комитет до международния социалистически конгрес в Щутгарт). София, 1907.
Чанков, Георги. *Равносметката*. София, 2000.

Secondary Literature

Adanir, Fikret. "The National Question and the Genesis and Development of Socialism in the Ottoman Empire: The Case of Macedonia," in Mete Tunçay and Erich Zürcher (eds.), *Socialism and Nationalism in the Ottoman Empire, 1876–1923*. London: I. B. Tauris, 1994, 27–48.
"AHR Conversation: Each Generation Writes Its Own History of Generations," *The American Historical Review* 123, no. 5 (2018): 1505–46.
Alavi, Hamza and Teodor Shanin, eds. *Sociology of "Developing Societies."* London: Palgrave, 1982.

Allerbeck, Klaus R. "Political Generations: Some Reflections on the Concept and Its Application to the German Case," *European Journal of Political Research* 5 (1977): 119–34.
Altankov, Nikolay G. *The Bulgarian-Americans*. Palo Alto, CA: Ragusan Press, 1979.
Ambord, Daniel Whitcomb. "Wrong Turns on the Way to the Graveyard: The Death of Man and the Status of the Subject in Foucault Studies," *Minerva – An Internet Journal of Philosophy* 13 (2009): 53–66.
Amelang, James S. *The Flight of Icarus: Artisan Autobiography in Early Modern Europe*. Stanford, CA: Stanford University Press, 1998.
Amin, Shahid and Marcel van der Linden, eds. "Peripheral," *Labour? Studies in the History of Partial Proletarianization*. New York: Cambridge University Press, 1997.
Anderson, Kevin. *Marx at the Margins: On Nationalism, Ethnicity, and Non-Western Societies*. Chicago: The University of Chicago Press, 2010
Anderson, Margaret, "'Down in Turkey, Far Away': Human Rights, the Armenian Massacres, and Orientalism in Wilhelmine Germany," *Journal of Modern History* 79, no. 1 (2007): 80–111.
Anderson, Perry. *Considerations on Western Marxism*. London: New Left Books, 1976.
Anderson, Perry. *The Antinomies of Antonio Gramsci: With a New Preface*. London: Verso, 2017.
Anderson, Perry. *The H-Word: The Peripeteia of Hegemony*. London: Verso, 2017.
Anthology of Bulgarian Poetry, trans. Peter Tempest. Sofia: Sofia Press, 1980.
Argyriadès, P. and P. Lagarde. *Solution de la question d'Orient. La confédération balkanique; compte-rendu de la conférence tenue au Grand-Orient de France sur cette question: et La Macédoine; relation sur ce pays*. Paris, 1896.
Arvidsson, Stefan, Jakub Beneš, and Anja Kirsch. *Socialist Imaginations: Utopias, Myths, and the Masses*. New York: Routledge, 2019.
Aslanian, Sebouh David, Joyce E. Chaplin, Ann McGrath, and Kristin Mann, "How Size Matters: The Question of Scale in History," *American Historical Review* 118, no. 5 (2013): 1431–72.
Attali, Jacques. *Fraternités. Une nouvelle utopie*. Paris: Fayard, 1999.
Audoin-Rouzeau, Stéphane Annette Becker. *1914-1918: Understanding the Great War*. New York: Hill and Wang, 2002.
Avineri, Shlomo. "Marxism and Nationalism," *Journal of Contemporary History* 26, no. 3/4 (1991): 637–57.
Bair, Deirdre. "Die Biographie ist Akademischer Selbstmord," *Literaturen* 7, no. 8 (2001): 38–39.
Ballinger, Pamela. "Whatever Happened to Eastern Europe? Revisiting Europe's Eastern Peripheries," *East European Politics and Societies and Cultures* 31, no. 1 (2017): 3–10.
Barnes, Julian. *The Sense of an Ending*. New York: Vintage Books, 2012.
Barnett, Douglas and Hilary Horn Ratner. "Introduction: The Organization and Integration of Cognition and Emotion in Development," *Journal of Experimental Child Psychology* 67 (1997): 303–16.
Barrett, James R. "Was the Personal Political? Reading the Autobiography of American Communism," *International Review of Social History* 53, no. 3 (December 2008): 395–423.
Barrett, James R. *History from the Bottom Up & the Inside Out*. Durham, NC: Duke University Press, 2017.
Bauer, Otto. *The Question of Nationalities and Social Democracy*, trans. Joseph O'Donnell. Minneapolis: University of Minnesota Press, 2000.

Bauman, Zygmunt. *Socialism: The Active Utopia*. New York: Routledge, 2010 (1976).
Bebel, August. *Women under Socialism*, trans. Daniel De Leon. New York: Labor News Press, 1904.
Belich, James, John Darwin, Margret Frenz, and Chris Wickham, eds. *The Prospect of Global History*. New York: Oxford University Press, 2016.
Bell John. *Peasants in Power: Alexander Stamboliski and the Bulgarian Agrarian National Union 1899-1923*. Princeton: Princeton University Press, 1977.
Bell John. *The Bulgarian Communist Party from Blagoev to Zhivkov*. Stanford: Hoover Press, 1986.
Beneš, Jakub. *Workers and Nationalism: Czech and German Social Democracy in Habsburg Austria, 1890-1918*. New York: Oxford University Press, 2017.
Benjamin, Walter. *Selected Writings*. Vol. 1. 1913-1926, edited by Marcus Bullock and Michael W. Jennings. Cambridge, MA: The Belknap Press, 1996.
Berger, Stefan. "Democracy and Social Democracy," *European History Quarterly* 32, no. 1 (2002): 13-37.
Berghahn, Volker and Simone Lässig, eds. *Biography Between Structure and Agency: Central European Lives in International Historiography*. New York and London: Berghahn Books, 2008.
Bering, Dietz. *Die Intellektuellen. Geschichte eines Schimpfwortes*. Stuttgart: Klett, 1978.
Bertaux, Daniel. "The Life Story Approach: A Continental View," *Annual Review of Sociology* 10 (1984): 215-37.
Best, Beverley. "The Problem of Utopia: Capitalism, Depression, and Representation," *Canadian Journal of Communication* 35 (2010): 497-513.
Biess, Frank and Daniel M. Gross. *Science and Emotions after 1945: A Transatlantic Perspective*. Chicago: The University of Chicago Press, 2014.
Binstock, R. H. and L. K. George, eds. *Handbook of Aging and the Social Sciences*. Amsterdam: Elsevier, 2006.
Blackstock, Paul and Bert Hoselitz. *The Russian Menace to Europe by Karl Marx and Friedrich Engels*. Glencoe: The Free Press, 1952.
Bloch, Ernst. *The Principle of Hope*, trans. N. Plaice, S. Plaice and P. Knight. Cambridge, MA: The MIT Press, 1986.
Bloch, Ernst. *The Spirit of Utopia*, trans. Anthony A. Nassar. Stanford: Stanford University Press, 2000.
Bloch, Ernst. *The Utopian Function of Art and Literature: Selected Essays*, trans. Jack Zipes and Frank Mecklenburg. Cambridge, MA: The MIT Press, 1988.
Blum, Mark E. *The Austro-Marxists 1890-1918: A Psychobiographical Study*. Lexington: The University of Kentucky Press, 1985.
Bottomore, Tom and Patrick Goode. *Austro-Marxism*. Oxford: Clarendon Press, 1978.
Bourdieu, Pierre. "L'illusion biographique," *Actes de la recherche en sciences sociales* 62-63 (1986): 69-72.
Boxer, Marylin and Jean Quataert, eds. *Socialist Women: European Feminism in the Nineteenth and Early Twentieth Century*. New York: Elsevier Science Ltd, 1978.
Brankoff, D. M. *La Macédoine et sa population chrétienne*. Paris, 1905.
Braunthal, Julius. *Geschichte der Internationale*. Vols. 1-3. Hannover: Dietz, 1961-1971.
Brenkert, George G. "Freedom and Private Property in Marx," *Philosophy and Public Affairs* 8, no. 2 (1979): 122-47.
Bronner, Stephen. *Imagining the Possible: Radical Politics for Conservative Times*. New York: Routledge, 2001.

Brunnbauer, Ulf. "Emigrants and Countries of Origin: The Politics of Emigration in Southeastern Europe until the First World War," in Timothy Snyder and Katherine Younger (eds.), *The Balkans as Europe, 1821–1914*. Rochester: University of Rochester Press, 2018, 78–109.

Brym, Robert J. *Intellectuals and Politics*. London: Routledge, 1980.

Brym, Robert J. *The Jewish Intelligentsia and Russian Marxism: A Sociological Study of Intellectual Radicalism and Ideological Divergence*. London: Macmillan, 1978.

Buber, Martin. *Paths in Utopia*, trans. R. F. C. Hull. London: Routledge, 1949.

Buck-Morss, Susan. *Dreamworld and Catastrophe: The Passing of Mass Utopia in East and West*. Cambridge, MA: MIT Press, 2000.

Bude, Heinz. "Die Erinnerung der Generationen," in Helmut König, Michael Kohlstruck, and Andreas Wöll, Hrsg. *Vergangenheitsbewältigung am Ende des zwanzigsten Jahrhunderts*. Wiesbaden: Westdeutscher Verlag, 1998, 69–85.

Bude, Heinz. "Die 'Wir-Schicht' der Generation," *Berliner Journal für Soziologie* 2 (1997): 197–204.

Bude, Heinz. "Lebenskonstruktionen als Gegenstand der Biographieforschung," in Gerd Jüttemann and Hans Thomae, Hrsg. *Biographische Methoden in den Humanwissenschaften*. Weinheim: Beltz, Psychologie Verlags Union, 1998, 247–58.

Buheiry, Marwan R. "Theodore Herzl and the Armenian Question," *Journal of Palestinian Studies* 7 (1977): 75–97.

Buhle, Paul. *Marxism in the United States: A History of the American Left*. London: Verso, 2013.

Bureau socialiste International. *Comptes rendus des reunions. Manifestes et circulaires, vol. I. 1900–1907, réunis par G. Haupt*. Paris: Mouton, 1969.

Burton, Antoinette. *The Trouble with Empire: Challenges to Modern British Imperialism*. Oxford: Oxford University Press, 2015.

Calhoun, Craig, ed. *Social Theory and the Politics of Identity*. Oxford: Blackwell, 1994.

Carver, Terrell. *Engels: A Very Short Introduction*. New York: Oxford University Press, 2003.

Cassens, David E. "The Bulgarian Colony of Southwestern Illinois, 1900–1920," *Illinois Historical Journal* 84, no. 1 (1991): 15–24.

Castellani, Jean-Pierre, ed. *Écriture de soi et autorité*. Tours: Presses universitaires François-Rabelais, 2016.

Certeau, Michel de. *The Practice of Everyday Life*, trans. Steven Rendall. Berkeley, CA: University of California Press, 2011.

Chadzinikolov, Veselin. *Georgi Dimitroff: Biographischer Abriss*. Berlin: Dietz, 1972.

Chakrabarty, Dipesh. *Provincializing Europe: Postcolonial Thought and Historical Difference*. Princeton, NJ: Princeton University Press, 2000.

Chaquer, Cosroe. *Origins of Social Democracy in Modern Iran*. Seattle, WA: University of Washington Press, 2001.

Chase-Dunn, Christopher. "Comparing World-Systems: Toward a Theory of Semiperipheral Development," *The Comparative Civilizations Review* 18 (1988): 29–66.

Chase-Dunn, Christopher. "Resistance to Imperialism: Semiperipheral Actors," *Review* (Fernand Braudel Center) 13, no. 1 (1990): 1–31.

Chavance, Bernard. *Marx en perspective*. Paris: 'Ecole des hautes études en sciences sociales, 1985.

Christian, David G. "Macrohistory: The Play of Scales," *Social Evolution & History* 4, no. 1 (2005): 22–59.

Christian, David G. *Maps of Time: An Introduction to Big History*, Berkeley, CA: University of California Press, 2004.
Christman, John, ed. *The Inner Citadel: Essays on Individual Autonomy*. New York: Oxford University Press, 1898.
Claeys, Gregory and Lyman Tower Sargent, eds. *The Utopia Reader*. New York: New York University Press, 1999.
Cole, George Douglas Howard. *A History of Socialist Thought*. London: Macmillan, 1953–1960.
Cole, Jennifer. *Sex and Salvation: Imagining the Future in Madagascar*. Chicago: University of Chicago Press, 2010.
Collini, Stefan. *Public Moralists: Political Thought and Intellectual Life in Britain, 1850–1930*. Oxford: Clarendon Press, 1991.
Collins, Randall. *The Sociology of Philosophies: A Global Theory of Intellectual Change*. Cambridge, MA: Harvard University Press, 1998.
Conte, Francis. *Un révolutionnaire – diplomate: Christian Rakovski: l'Union soviétique et l'Europe (1922–1941)*. Paris: Mouton, 1978.
Crampton, Richard. *A Concise History of Bulgaria*. Cambridge: Cambridge University Press, 1997.
Creed, Gerald, ed. *The Seductions of Community: Emancipations, Oppressions, Quandaries*. Santa Fe: School of American Research Press, 2006.
Crouthamel, Jason and Peter Leese, eds. *Psychological Trauma and the Legacies of the First World War*. London: Palgrave Macmillan, 2016.
Dahrendorf, Ralf. *Reflections on the Revolution in Europe*. New York: Random House, 1990.
Damasio, Antonio. *The Feeling of What Happens: Body and Emotion in the Making of Consciousness*. London: William Heinemann, 2000.
Darnton, Robert. *The Great Cat Massacre and Other Episodes in French Cultural History*. New York: Basic Books, 2009.
Daskalov, Roumen and Diana Mishkova, eds. *Entangled Histories of the Balkans, Volume Two: Transfers of Political Ideologies and Institutions*. Leiden: Brill, 2014.
Daskalova, Krassimira and Karen Offen. "The Tensions within the Early Twentieth-Century Bulgarian Women's Movement," *Aspasia* 9 (2015): 115–25.
Daugsch, Walter. *Internationalismus und Organisation. Studien zur Entstehung und Entwicklung der serbishen Sozialdemokratie*. Herne: Gabriele Schäfer Verlag, 2008, 207–11.
Davis, Noela. "Subjected Subjects? On Judith Butler's Paradox of Interpellation," *Hypatia: A Journal of Feminist Philosophy* 27, no. 4 (November 2012): 881–97.
Day, Richard and Daniel Gaido, eds. *Discovering Imperialism: Social Democracy to World War I*. Chicago: Haymarket Books, 2012.
Degen, Bernard and Julia Richers, Hg. *Zimmerwald und Kiental: Weltgeschichte auf dem Dorfe*. Zurich: Chronos Verlag, 2015.
Demirović, Alex and Peter Jehle. "Intellektuelle," in *Historisch-kritisches Wörterbuch des Marxismus*. 6/II. Berlin and Hamburg: Argument, 2004, 1267–86.
Depkat, Volker. "The Challenges of Biography: European-American Reflections," *Bulletin of the German Historical Institute* 55 (2014): 39–48.
Dimou, Augusta. *Entangled Paths Toward Modernity: Contextualizing Socialism and Nationalism in the Balkans*. Budapest: CEU Press, 2009.
Drachkovitch, Milorad. *The Revolutionary Internationals, 1864–1943*. Stanford: Stanford University Press, 1966.

Dreyfus, Michel, Bruno Groppo, Caudio Sergio Ingerflom, Roland Lew, Claude Pennetier, Bernard Pudal, and Serge Wolikow, eds. *Le siècle des communismes*. Paris: Les Éditions ouvrières, 2000.
Droz, Jacques, ed. *Histoire générale du socialisme. Tome II: De 1875 à 1918*. Paris: Presses Universitaires de France, 1974.
Dubowoj, Sina Maria. *The Schism in the Bulgarian Socialist Movement and the Second International, 1900-1914*. Unpublished PhD, University of Illinois at Urbana-Champaign, 1981.
Dumont, Paul. *Du socialism ottoman à l'internationalisme anatolien*. Paris: Gorgias Press, 2011.
Eagleton, Terry. "Utopia and Its Opposites," *Socialist Register: Necessary and Unnecessary Utopias* 36 (2000): 31–40.
Eagleton, Terry. *Why Marx Was Right*. New Haven: Yale University Press, 2011.
Eakin, Paul John. *How Our Lives Become Stories: Making Selves*. Ithaca, NY: Cornell University Press, 1999.
Ehmer, Josef. "Generationen in der historischen Forschung: Konzepte und Praktiken," in Harald Künemund and Marc Szydlik, Hrsg. *Generationen. Multidisziplinäre Perspektiven*. Wiesbaden: Verlag für Sozialwissenschaften, 2009, 59–80.
Ekloff, Ben and Tatiana Saburova. *A Generation of Revolutionaries: Nikolai Charushin and Russian Populism from the Great Reforms to Perestroika*. Bloomington: Indiana University Press, 2017.
Elenkov, Ivan and Mila Koumpilova. "On the History of Rightist Thought in Interwar Bulgaria: The Existential Dimensions of 'Crisis' in the Writings of Yanko Yanev," *Studies in East European Thought* 53, nos. 1–2 (2001): 47–59.
Eley, Geoff. *Forging Democracy: The History of the Left in Europe, 1850–1900*. Oxford: Oxford University Press, 2002.
Engels, Friedrich, "The Program of the Blanquist Fugitives from the Paris Commune, 1873," *International Socialist Review* IX, no. 2 (August 1908). https://www.marxists.org/archive/marx/works/1874/06/26.htm.
Espagne, Michel. *Les transfers culturels franco-allemand*. Paris: PUF, 1999.
Espagne, Michel and Michael Werner, eds. *Transfers. Les relations interculturelles dans l'espace franco-allemand (XVIIIe et XIXe siècle)*. Paris: Editions recherches sur les civilisations, 1988.
Feher, Ferenc, Agnes Heller, and Gyorgy Markus. *Dictatorship over Needs: An Analysis of Soviet Societies*. Oxford: Basil Blackwell, 1983.
Filmer, Paul. "Structures of Feeling and Socio-Cultural Formations: The Significance of Literature and Experience to Raymond Williams's Sociology of Culture," *British Journal of Sociology* 54, no. 2 (2003): 199–219.
Fišera, Vladimir Claude. *Les peoples slaves et le communism de Marx à Gorbatchev*. Paris: Berg, 1992.
Folkenflik, Robert, ed. *The Culture of Autobiography: Constructions of Self-Representation*. Stanford, CA: Stanford University Press, 1993.
Foucault, Michel. "L'écriture de soi," *Corps écrit*, no. 5. *L'autoportrait* (1983): 3–23.
France, Alan and Steven Roberts, "The Problem of Social Generations: A Critique of the New Emerging Orthodoxy in Youth Studies," *Journal of Youth Studies* 18, no. 2 (2015): 215–30.
Frede, Victoria. *Doubt, Atheism and the Nineteenth-Century Russian Intelligentsia*. Madison: The University of Wisconsin Press, 2011.
Frevert, Ute. *Emotions in History – Lost and Found*. Budapest: CEU Press, 2011.

Friedman, Jeremy and Peter Rutland. "Anti-Imperialism: The Leninist Legacy and the Fate of World Revolution," *Slavic Review* 76, no. 3 (2017): 591-99.
Furet, François. *The Passing of an Illusion: The Idea of Communism in the Twentieth Century*, trans. Deborah Furet. Chicago: University of Chicago Press, 1999.
Fussel, Paul. *The Great War and Modern Memory*. New York: Oxford University Press, 1975.
Geyer, M. H. and J. Paulmann, eds. *The Mechanics of Internationalism*. Oxford: Oxford University Press, 2001.
Gal, Susan. "A Semiotics of the Public/Private Distinction," *Differences: A Journal of Feminist Cultural Studies* 13, no. 1 (2002): 77-95.
Gallagher, Shaun and Stephen Watson. *Ipseity and Alterity: Interdisciplinary Approaches to Intersubjectivity*. Rouen: Publications de l'Université de Rouen, 2014.
Garnett, Lucy. *Balkan Home-Life*. New York: Dodd. Mead & Co, 1917.
Gay, Peter. *The Dilemma of Democratic Socialism: Eduard Bernstein's Challenge to Marx*. New York: Columbia University Press, 1952.
Ghose, Savkar. *Socialism and Communism in India*. Bombay: Allied Publishers, 1971.
Gilcher-Holthey, Ingrid. *Das Mandat des Intellektuellen: Karl Kautsky und die Sozialdemokratie*. Berlin: Siedler, 1986.
Gilmore, Leigh. *The Limits of Autobiography: Trauma and Testimony*. Ithaca, NY: Cornell University Press, 2001.
Ginzburg, Lydia. *On Psychological Prose*, trans. and ed. Judson Rosegrant. Princeton, NJ: Princeton University Press, 1991.
Godlewska, Anne and Neil Smith, eds. *Geography and Empire*. Oxford: Blackwell, 1994.
Gordin, Michael D., Helen Tilley, and Gyan Prakash, eds. *Utopia/Dystopia: Conditions of Historical Possibility*. Princeton, NJ: Princeton University Press, 2010.
Groh, Dieter. "The 'Unpatriotic Socialists' and the State," *Journal of Contemporary History* 1, no. 4 (1966): 151-77.
Gross, Mirjana. "Ideologija socijalističkog pokreta u Hrvatskoj do prvog svjetskog rata," in Ivan Kampuš, Igor Karaman and Bogdan Krizman (eds.), *Kulturnohistorijski simpozij "Mogersdorf 74": Radnički pokreti id početaka do svršetka prvoga svjetskog rata*. Zagreb: Republički savjet za naučni rad SR Hrvatske, 1976, 9-28.
Guha, Ranajit. "The Small Voice of History," in Shahid Amin and Dipesh Chakravarty (eds.), *Subaltern Studies IX: Writings on South Asian History and Society*. Delhi: Oxford University Press, 1994.
Haan, Francisca de, Krassimira Daskalova, and Anna Loutfi, eds. *A Biographical Dictionary of Women's Movements and Feminisms: Central, Eastern and South Eastern Europe, 19th and 20th Centuries*. Budapest: CEU Press, 2006.
Hadar, Gila. "Jewish Tobacco Workers in Salonica: Gender and Family in the Context of Social and Ethnic Strife," in Amila Butirović and Irvin Cemil Schick (eds.), *Women in the Ottoman Balkans: Gender, Culture, and History*. London: I. B. Tauris, 2007, 127-52.
Haenisch, Konrad. *Parvus. Ein Blatt der Erinnerung*. Berlin: Verlag für Sozialwissenschaft, 1925.
Halfin, Igal. *Terror in My Soul: Autobiographies on Trial*. Cambridge, MA: Harvard University Press, 2003.
Hämäläinen, Pekka. "Crooked Lines of Relevance: *Europe and the People without History* by Eric R. Wolf," *American Historical Review* 123, no. 3 (2018): 875-87.
Hareven, Tamara K. "Aging and Generational Relations: A Historical and Life-Course Perspective," *Annual Review of Sociology* 20, no. 4 (1994): 437-61.

Harootunian, Harry. *Marx After Marx: History and Time in the Expansion of Capitalism.* New York: Columbia University Press, 2015.

Harootunian, Harry. *Overcome by Modernity: History, Culture and Community in Interwar Japan.* Princeton, NJ: Princeton University Press, 2000.

Harvey, David. *Spaces of Hope.* Berkeley, CA: University of California Press, 2000.

Haupt, Georges. *Aspects of International Socialism, 1871–1914,* trans. Peter Fawdett. Cambridge: Cambridge University Press, 1986.

Haupt, Georges. "'Führungspartei'? Die Ausstrahlung der deutschen Sozialdemokratie auf den Südosten Europas zur Zeit der Zweiten Internationale," *Internationale Wissenschaftliche Korrespondenz zur deutschen Arbeiterbewegung* 15 (1979): 1–30.

Haupt, Georges. "Internationale Führungsgruppen in der Arbeiterbewegung," in *Herkunft und Mandat: Beträge zur Führungsproblematik in der Arbeiterbewegung.* Frankfurt-Köln: Europäische Verlagsanstalt, 1976.

Haupt, Georges. *La Deuxième Internationale 1884–1914. Étude critique des sources. Essai bibliographique.* Paris: Mouton, 1964.

Haupt, Georges, "Le debut du movement socialiste en Turquie," *Le movement socialiste* 45 (1963): 129–35.

Haupt, Georges. *Socialism and the Great War: The Collapse of the Second International.* Oxford: The Clarendon Press, 1972.

Haupt, Georges and Jean-Jacques Marie. *Makers of the Russian Revolution: Biographies.* New York: Routledge 1974.

Haupt, Heinz-Gerhard und Jürgen Kocka, eds. *Geschichte und Vergleich. Ansätze und Ergebnisse international vergleichender Geschichtsschreibung.* Frankfurt: Campus Verlag, 1996.

Hausleitner, Mariana. "Christian Rakovskis Bedeutung für die international Arbeiterbewegung und seine Lösungsvorschläge der Nationalitetätenprobleme Rückständiger Länder," *Internationale Wissenschftliche Korrespondenz* 18, no. 3 (1982): 298–310.

Heehs, Peter. *Writing the Self: Diaries, Memoirs, and the History of the Self.* London: Bloomsbury Academic, 2013.

Heinrich, Michael. *Karl Marx und die Geburt der modernen Gesellschaft.* Stuttgart: Schmetterling Verlag, 2018.

Hellbeck, Jochen. *Revolution on My Mind: Writing a Diary Under Stalin.* Cambridge, MA: Harvard University Press, 2006.

Hemecker, Wilhelm and Edward Saunders, eds. *Biography in Theory: Key Texts with Commentaries.* Berlin: De Gruyter, 2017.

Hermann, Ulrich. "Was ist eine 'Generation'? Methodologische und begriffsgeschichtliche Explorationen zu einem Idealtypus," in Annegret Schüle, Thomas Ahbe, und Rainer Gries (Hg.), *Die DDR aus generationsgeschichglicger Perspektive. Eine Inventur.* Leipzig: Universitätsverlag, 2006, 23–39.

Hitchins, Keith. "Balkan Identity and Europe Between the Two World Wars in the Thought of Yanko Yanev," *Revue des Etudes Sud-Est Eropéennes* 41, no. 1–2 (2003): 65–74.

Hobsbawm, Eric J. *How to Change the World: Tales of Marx and Marxism, 1840–2011.* London: Little, Brown, 2011.

Hobsbawm, Eric J. *The Age of Capital: 1848–1875.* New York: Vintage, 1975.

Hobsbawm, Eric J. *The Age of Empire, 1875–1914.* New York: Vintage, 1987.

Hobsbawm, Eric J. *The Age of Revolution: 1789–1848.* New York: Vintage, 1962.

Hobsbawm, Eric J. and Joan Wallach Scott. "Political Shoemakers," *Past & Present* 89, no. 1 (1980): 86-114.
Hodgson, Geoffrey M. *Economics and Utopia. Why the Learning Economy Is Not the End of History*. New York: Routledge, 1998.
Hopkins, Debra, Jochen Kleres, Helena Flam, and Helmut Kuzmics, eds. *Theorizing Emotions: Sociological Explorations and Applications*. Frankfurt and New York: Campus Verlag, 2009.
Hopkins, Terence, Immanuel Wallerstein and associates. *World-Systems Analysis: Theory and Methodology*. Beverly Hills: Sage Publications, 1982.
Howe, Neil and William Strauss. *Generations: The History of America's Future, 1584 to 2069*. New York: William Morrow, 1991.
Husband, William B. *"Godless Communists": Atheism and Society in Soviet Russia, 1917-1932*. De Kalb, IL: Northern Illinois University Press, 2000.
Isen, Alice M. and Gregory Andrade Diamond, "Affect and Automaticity," in J. S. Uleman and John A. Bargh. *Unintended Thought: Limits of Awareness, Intention and Control*. New York: The Guilford Press, 1989, 124-54.
Isherwood, Ian Andrew. *Remembering the Great War: Writing and Publishing the Experiences of World War I*. London: I. B. Tauris, 2017.
James, C. L. R. *World Revolution, 1917-1936: The Rise and Fall of the Communist International*, ed. and introduced by Christian Høgsbjerg. Durham, NC: Duke Univerdsity Press, 2017.
Jameson, Fredric. *Archaeologies of the Future: The Desire Called Utopia and Other Science Fictions*. London: Verso, 2005.
Jameson, Fredric. *The Valences of the Dialectic*. London: Verso, 2010.
Jarausch, Konrad. *Out of Ashes: A New History of Europe in the Twentieth Century*. Princeton, NJ: Princeton University Press, 2016.
Jay, Martin. *Marxism and Totality: The Adventures of a Concept from Lukacs to Habermas*. Berkeley, CA: University of California Press, 1984.
Jedlicki, Jerzy, ed. *A History of the Polish Intelligenstia*. Frankfurt am Main: Peter Lang, 2014.
Jelavich, Barbara and Charles Jelavich, eds. *The Balkans in Transition: Essays on the Development of Balkan Life and Politics Since the Eighteenth Century*. Berkeley, CA: University of California Press, 1963.
Joll, James. *The Second International, 1889-1914*. New York: Routledge, 1966.
Judt, Tony. *Socialism in Provence, 1871-1914: A Study in the Origins of the Modern French Left*. Cambridge: Cambridge University Press, 1979.
Jureit, Ulrike und Michael Wildt. *Generationen: Zur Relevanz eines wissenschaftlichen Begriffes*. Hamburg: Hamburger Edition, 2005.
Kandiyoti, Deniz. "Bargaining with Patriarchy," *Gender and Society* 2 (1988): 274-90.
Karabel, Jerome. "Towards a Theory of Intellectuals and Politics," *Theory and Society* 25, no. 2 (1996): 205-33.
Karaömerlioğlu, M. Asim. "Helphand-Parvus and the Impact on Turkish Intellectual Life," *Middle Eastern Studies* 40, no. 6 (2004): 145-65.
Keyes, Thomas. *Karl Marx on Property*. Unpublished dissertation, Marquette University, 1981.
Kimball, Stanley B. *East Europeans in Southwestern Illinois: The Ethnic Experience in Historical Perspective*. Research Report no.14. Coordinator of Area Development, SIUE, 1981.
King, Lawrence Peter and Iván Szelényi. *Theories of the New Class: Intellectuals and Power*. Minneapolis, MN: University of Minnesota Press 2004.

Klein, Christian, ed. *Grundlagen der Biographik. Theorie und Praxis des biographischen Schreibens*. Stuttgart: Verlag J. B. Metzler, 2002.
Kleining, Gerhard. "Heuristik zur Erforschung von Biographien und Generationen," in Gerd Jüttemann, Hans Thomae (Hrsg.), *Biographische Methoden in den Humanwissenschaften*. Weinheim: Beltz, Psychologie Verlags Union, 1998, 185–92.
Klobucka, Anna. "Theorizing the European Periphery," *symplokē* 5, 1/2 (1997): 119–35.
Klopčič, Francé. "Friedrich Engels und Karl Marx über der 'Geschichtlosen' Slawischen Nationen 1847–1895," in *Geschichte der Arbeiterbewegung* (ITH Tagunsberichte, Band 19), Wien: Europaverlag, 1984, 217–49.
Kocka, Jürgen. "Reformen, Generationen und Geschichte," *Neue Gesellschaft/Frankfurter Hefte* 8 (2004): 34–37.
Koenker, Diane. "Scripting the Revolutionary Worker Autobiography: Archetypes, Models, Inventions, and Markets," *International Review of Social History* 49, no. 3 (2004): 371–400.
Kogan, Arthur. "The Social Democrats and the Conflict of Nationalities in the Habsburg Monarchy," *Journal of Modern History* 21, no. 3 (1949): 204–17.
Kolakowski, Leszek. *Main Currents of Marxism*. Oxford: Clarendon Press, 1976.
Kolakowski, Leszek. "My Correct Views on Everything. A Rejoinder to Edward Thompson's 'Open Letter to Leszek Kolakowski,'" *Socialist Register* 11 (1974): 1–20.
Kolakowski, Leszek. *The Death of Utopia Reconsidered* (The Tanner Lectures on Human Values). Canberra: Australian National University, 1982.
Konrad, Georg and Iván Szelényi. *The Intellectuals on the Road to Class Power: A Sociological Study of the Role of the Intelligentsia in Socialism*. New York: Harcourt Brace Jovanovich, 1979.
Konstantinova, Yura. "The Role of Bulgarians for the Spread of National, Anarchist and Socialist Ideas in Ottoman Salonica," *Etudes balkaniques* 54, no. 3 (2018): 3, 508–34.
Korsch, Karl. *Marxismus und Philosophie*. Frankfurt am Main: Europäische Verlagsanstalt, 1966.
Kotkin, Stephen. *Magnetic Mountain: Stalinism as a Civilization*. Berkeley, CA: University of California Press, 1887.
Kotkin, Stephen. *Stalin, Volume I: Paradoxes of Power, 1878–1928*. New York: Penguin, 2015.
Kotsonis, Ianni. "Ordinary People in Russian and Soviet History," *Kritika: Explorations in Russian and Eurasian History* 12, no. 3 (2011): 739–54.
Kripke, Saul. *Naming and Necessity*. Cambridge, MA: Harvard University Press, 1980.
Kumar, Krishnan. *Utopianism*. Minneapolis, MN: University of Minnesota Press, 1991.
Lampe, John R. and Marvin R. Jackson. *Balkan Economic History, 1550–1950*. Bloomington: Indiana University Press, 1982.
Laslett, Peter. "Interconnections over Time: Critique of the Concept of Generation," *Journal of Classical Sociology* 5, no. 2 (2005): 205–13.
La Teoría de la Revolucion Permanente. Buenos Aires: Centro de Estudios y publicaciones León Trotsky (CEIP), 2000.
Le Goff, Jacques. "Comment écrire une biographie historique aujourd'hui?" *Le Débat* 54, no. 2 (1989): 48–53.
Lejeune, Philippe. *On Autobiography*. Minneapolis, MN: University of Minnesota Press, 1989.
Lepore, Jill. "Historians Who Love Too Much: Reflections on Microhistory and Biography," *The Journal of American History* 88, no. 1 (2001): 129–44.

Leser, Norbert. *Zwischen Reformismus und Bolschewismus. Der Austromarxismus als Theorie und Praxis*. Wien: Europa Verlag, 1968.
Levitas, Ruth. "Educated Hope: Ernst Bloch on Abstract and Concrete Utopia," *Utopian Studies* 1, no. 2 (1990): 13–26.
Levitas, Ruth. "Marxism, Romanticism and Utopia: Ernst Bloch and William Morris," *Radical Philosophy* 51 (1989): 27–36.
Levitas, Ruth. *The Concept of Utopia*. Syracuse: Syracuse University Press, 1990.
Levitas, Ruth. *Utopia as Method: The Imaginary Reconstitution of Society*. New York: Palgrave Macmillan, 2013.
Leys, Ruth. "The Turn to Affect: A Critique," *Critical Inquiry* 37 (2011): 434–72.
Lichtheim, George. *A Short History of Socialism*. New York: Praeger, 1970.
Lichtheim, George. *Marxism: An Historical and Critical Study*. New York: Praeger, 1965.
Lichtheim, George. *The Concept of Ideology and Other Essays*. New York: Vintage Books, 1967.
Lichtheim, George. *The Origins of Socialism*. London: Weidenfeld and Nicolson, 1969.
Lih, Lars T. *Lenin Rediscovered: What Is To Be Done? In Context*. Chicago: Haymarket Books, 2008.
Lindemann, Albert S. *A History of European Socialism*. New Haven: Yale University Press, 1983.
Lindemann, Albert S. *The 'Red Years': European Socialism vs. Bolshevism, 1919–1921*. Berkeley, CA: University of California Press, 1974.
Lovell, Stephen. "From Genealogy to Generation: The Birth of Cohort Thinking in Russia," *Kritika: Explorations in Russian and Eurasian History* 9, no. 3 (2008): 567–94.
Lukács, György. "Bernstein's Triumph: Notes on the Essays Written in Honor of Karl Kautsky's Seventieth Birthday," *Die Internationale* VII, no. 22 (1924). http://thecharn elhouse.org/2014/12/30/lukacs-on-the-rapprochement-between-bernstein-and-ka utsky-after-world-war-i-democracy-reformism-and-the-dialectic/.
Lutz, Catherine. "Feminist Theories and the Science of Emotion," in Frank Biess and Daniel M. Gross, *Science and Emotions after 1945: A Transatlantic Perspective*. Chicago: The University of Chicago Press, 2014, 342–64.
Lutz, Catherine. *Unnatural Emotions: Everyday Sentiments on a Micronesian Atoll and Their Challenge to Western Theory*. Chicago: The University of Chicago Press, 1988.
MacDermott, Mercia. *For Freedom and Perfection: The Life of Yane Sandanski*. London: Journeyman, 1988.
MacDermott, Mercia. *Lone Red Poppy: A Biography of Dimiter Blagoev, Founder of the First Marxist Circle in Russia and of the Bulgarian Communist Party*. Croydon: Manifesto Press, 2014.
Machery, Edouard. *Philosophy Within Its Proper Bounds*. Oxford: Oxford University Press, 2017.
Maehl, William. "The Triumph of Nationalism in the German Socialist Party on the Eve of the First World War," *The Journal of Modern History* 24, no. 1 (1952): 15–41.
Mannheim, Karl. *Essays*, ed. Paul Kecskemeti. New York: Routledge, 1952.
Mannheim, Karl. *Ideology and Utopia: An Introduction to the Sociology of Knowledge*, trans. Louis Wirth and Edward Shils. New York: Harcourt, Brace and Company, 1936.
Maresch, Rudolf and Florian Rötzer. *Renaissance der Utopie. Zukuftfiguren des 21. Jahrhunderts*. Frankfurt am Main: Suhrkamp, 2004.
Marx, Karl. *The German Ideology*. Moscow: International Publishers, 1972.
Marx, Karl and Friedrich Engels. *Basic Writings on Politics and Philosophy*, ed. Lewis D. Feuer. New York: Anchor Books, 1959.

Marx, Karl and Friedrich Engels. *Ireland and the Irish Question: A Collection of Writings by Karl Marx & Friedrich Engels*. New York: International Publishers, 1972.

Marx, Karl and Friedrich Engels. *Marx & Engels on Ireland*. London: Lawrence & Wishart Ltd, 1971.

Marxism versus Social Democracy: The Revisionist Debate 1896–1898, ed. and trans. H. Tudor and J. M. Tudor, with an introduction by H. Tudor. Cambridge: Cambridge University Press, 1988.

Matt, Susan J. and Peter N. Stearns, eds. *Doing Emotions History*. Urbana, IL: University of Illinois Press, 2014.

Maynes, Mary Jo. "Autobiography and Class Formation in Nineteenth-Century Europe: Methodological Considerations," *Social Science History* 16, no. 3 (1992): 517–37.

Mazzarella, William. "The Myth of the Multitude, or, Who's Afraid of the Crowd?", *Critical Inquiry* 36, no. 4 (2010): 697–727.

Mazis, John A. "The Idea of an Eastern Federation: An Alternative to the Destruction of the Ottoman Empire," in Lucien J. Frary and Mara Kozelsky (eds.), *Russian-Ottoman Borderlands. The Eastern Question Reconsidered*. Madison, WI: University of Wisconsin Press, 2014, 251–79.

Mehring, Franz. *Karl Marx: The Story of His Life*, trans. Edward Fitzgerald. Ann Arbor, MI: The University of Michigan Press, 1962.

Merleau-Ponty, Maurice. *Adventures of the Dialectic*. Evanston, IL: Northwestern University Press, 1973.

Middell, Matthias. *Kulturtransfer und Vergleich*. Leipzig: Leipziger Universitäts Verlag, 2000.

Mintz, Steven. "Reflections on Age as a Category of Analysis," *The Journal of the History of Childhood and Youth* 1, no. 1 (2008): 91–94.

Mirkova, Anna M. *Muslim Land, Christian Labor: Transforming Ottoman Imperial Subjects into Bulgarian Citizens, 1878–1939*. Budapest: CEU Press, 2017.

Morgan, Kevin, Gidon Cohen, and Andrew Flinn, eds. *Agents of the Revolution: New Biographical Approaches to the History of International Communism in the Age of Lenin and Stalin*. Bern: Peter Lang, 2005.

Moschonas, Gerassimos. "European Social Democracy, Communism, and the Erfurtian Model," in William Outhwaite and Stephen Turmer (eds.), *The SAGE Handbook of Political Sociology*. London: SAGE Publicatoions, 2018, 516–47.

Moulin, Joanny. "Introduction: Towards Biography Theory," *Cercles: Revue Pluridisciplinaire du Monde Anglophone*, 2015, 1. https://hal.archives-ouvertes.fr/ha l-01078127v2.

Müller, Dietmar. *Agrarpopulismus in Rumänien. Programmatik und Regierungspraxis der Bauernpartei und der Nationalbäuerlichen Partei Rumäniens in der Zwischenkriegszeit*. St. Augustin: Gardez Verlag, 2001.

Mulsow, Martin. "Qu'est-ce qu'une constellation philosophique?", *Annales. Histoire. Sciences Sociales* 64, no. 1 (2009): 81–109.

Mulsow, Martin and Macelo Stamm, Hg. *Konstellationsforschung*. Frankfurt am Main: Suhrkamp, 2005.

Neusüss, Arnhelm, Hg. *Utopie: Begriff und Phänomen des Utopischen*. Frankfurt am Main and New York: Campus Verlag, 1986.

Niethammer, Lutz. "Generation und Geist: Eine Station auf Karl Mannheims Weg zur Wissenssoziologie," in Annegret Schüle, Thomas Ahbe und Rainer Gries (Hg.), *Die DDR aus generationsgeschichglicger Perspektive*. Eine Inventur. Leipzig: Universitätsverlag, 2006, 47–64.

Nimni, Ephraim. *Marxism and Nationalism: The Theoretical Origins of a Political Crisis*. London: Pluto Press, 1991.
Nipperdey, Thomas. "Die Funktion der Utopie im politischen Denken der Neuzeit," *Archiv für Kulturgeschichte* 44, no. 3 (1962): 357–78.
Njagulov, Blagovest. "Early Socialism in the Balkans: Ideas and Practices in Serbia, Romania and Bulgaria," in Roumen Daskalov and Diana Mishkova (eds.), *Entangled Histories of the Balkans, Volume Two: Transfers of Political Ideologies and Institutions*. Leiden: Brill, 2014, 199–280.
Nora, Pierre. *Les lieux de mémoire*. Paris: Gallimard, 1992.
Oren, Nissan. *Bulgarian Communism: The Road to Power, 1934–1944*. New York: Columbia University Press, 1971.
Osterhammel, Jürgen. *The Transformation of the World: A Global History of the Nineteenth Century*. Princeton, NJ: Princeton University Press, 2014.
Oštrić, Vlado. "Radnički pokret u jugoslovenskim zemljama od svojih početaka do 1918/1819. godine," *Povijesni prilozi* 1 (1982): 12–61.
Palairet, Michael. *The Balkan Economies, c1800–1914: Evolution without Development*. Cambridge: Cambridge University Press, 1997.
Panitch, Leo and Sam Gindin, "Transcending Pessimism: Rekindling Socialist Imagination," *Socialist Register: Necessary and Unnecessary Utopias* 36 (2000): 1–29.
Parsons, Talcott. "The Intellectual: A Social Role Category," in Paul Rieff (ed.), *On Intellectuals*. Garden City, NJ: Anchor, 1963, 3–24.
Parusheva, Dobrinka. "Emancipation between Feminism and Socialism (A Bulgarian Example of the Turn of the Century)," *Etudes balkaniques* 1–2 (1997): 125–30.
Parusheva, Dobrinka. "Social Democracy and the Jewish Working Class in Bulgaria (late 19th – early 20th Century)," *Annual of the Organization of Jews in Bulgaria "Shalom"* XXVII (1993/1994): 62–75.
Pascal, Roy. *Design and Truth in Autobiography*. New York: Routledge, 2017.
Perović, Latinka. *Srpski socijalisti 19. veka: prilog istoriji socijalističke misli*. Beograd: Izdavačka radna organizacija "Rad", 1985.
Pitassio, Armando. "Janko Sakazov e Karl Kautsky. Un socialista balcanico di fronte al Papa Rosso," *Annali del Dipartimento di Studii dell' Europa Orientale* IV–V (1982–1982): 269–328.
Pößneck, Ehrenfried. *Lenin als Kontrahent von Parvus im Jahre 1917*. Leipzig: Leipziger Gesellschaft für Politik und Zeitgeschichte, 1997.
Pomper, Philip. *The Russian Revolutionary Intelligentsia*. Northbrook, IL: AHM Publishing, 1970.
Pons, Silvio and Stephen A. Smith, eds. *The Cambridge History of Communism*. Vol. 1. Cambridge: Cambridge University Press, 2017.
Popov, Kiril. *La Bulgarie économique 1879–1911: Étude statistique*. Sofia: Imprimerie de la Cour, 1920.
Preshlenova, Roumiana. "Liberation in Progress: Bulgarian Nationalism and Political Economy in a Balkan Perspective, 1878–1912," in Timothy Snyder and Katherine Younger (eds.), *The Balkans as Europe, 1821–1914*. Rochester, NY: University of Rochester Press, 2018, 54–77.
Provinz als Denk- und Lebensfrom: Der Donau- und Karpatenraum im langen 19. Jahrhundert. Komission für Geschichte und Kultur der Deutschen in Südosteuropa (KGKDS), Tübingen: Institut für Germanistik, Universität Ljubljana, September 26, 2013–September 28, 2013.
Prpic, George J. *South Slavic Immigration in America*. Boston: Twayne, 1978.

Prüfer, Sebastian. *Sozialismus statt Religion: Die deutsche Sozilademokratie vor der religiösen Frage 1863–1890*. Göttingen: Vandenhoeck & Ruprecht, 2002.
Pundeff, Marin. "Marxism in Bulgaria before 1891," *Slavic Review* 30, no. 2 (1971): 523–50.
Quint, Howard. *The Forging of American Socialism: Origins of the Modern Movement: The Impact of Socialism on American Thought and Action, 1886–1901*. Columbia, SC: University of South Carolina Press, 1953.
Raeff, Mark. *Origins of the Russian Intelligentsia: The Eighteenth-Century Nobility*. New York: Houghton-Mifflin, 1966.
Rainoff, Witscho. *Die Arbeiterbewegung in Bulgarien*. Grüningen, 1909.
Rakovsky, Christian. "Die Bulgarische Sozialdemokratie und die Orientfrage," *Die Neue Zeit* XV (1896–1897): 820–24.
Rakovsky, Christian. "La question d'Orient et les puissances," *Revue de la Paix* XIII, no. 11 (1908): 245–52.
Rakovsky, Christian. "Vers l'entente balkanique," *Revue de la Paix* XIII, no. 12 (1908): 287–303.
Ratz, Ursula. "Perspektiven über Kautsky. Neuerscheinungen zur Geschichte der Arbeiterbewegung anläßlich des 50. Todestages des 'Chefideologien'," *Neue politische Literatur* 33 (1988): 7–24.
Reddy, William M. *The Navigation of Feeling: A Framework for the History of Emotions*. Cambridge: Cambridge University Press, 2001.
Redžić, Enver. *Austromarksizam i jugoslovensko pitanje*. Beograd: Narodna knjiga i Institut za savremenu istoriju, 1977.
Renders, Hans and Binne de Haan, eds. *Theoretical Discussions of Biography: Approaches from History, Microhistory, and Life Writing*. Lampeter: The Edwin Mellen Press, 2013.
Resis, Albert. "*Das Kapital* Comes to Russia," *Slavic Review* 29, no. 2 (1970): 219–37.
Revault D'Allonnes, Myriam. *Le Pouvoir des commencements. Essai sur l'autorité*. Paris: Le Seuil, 2006.
Revel, Jacques, ed. *Jeux d'échelles. La microanalyse à l'éxperience*. Paris: Seuil, 1998.
Ricoeur, Paul. *Lectures on Ideology and Utopia*. New York: Columbia University Press, 1986.
Ricoeur, Paul. *Oneself as Another*, trans. Kathleen Blamey. Chicago: University of Chicago Press, 1992.
Robinson, Jenefer. *Deeper than Reason: Emotion and Its Role in Literature, Music and Art*. Oxford: Clarendon Press, 2005.
Rogers, H. Kendall. *Before the Revisionist Controversy: Kautsky, Bernstein, and the Meaning of Marxism, 1895–1898*. London: Routledge, 2015.
Rosdolsky, Roman. *Engels and the 'Nonhistoric' Peoples: The National Question in the Revolution of 1848*. Glasgow: Critique Books, 1987.
Rosenberg, Emily, ed. *A World Connecting, 1870–1945*. Cambridge, MA: Belknap Press, 2012.
Rosenwein, Barbara H. *Emotional Communities in the Early Middle Ages*. Ithaca, NY: Cornell University Press, 2006.
Ross, Jack. *The Socialist Party of America: A Complete History*. Lincoln, NE: Potomac Books, 2015.
Rothschild, Joseph. *The Communist Party of Bulgaria: Origins and Development, 1883–1936*. New York: Columbia University Press, 1959.
Rubin, David C. *Remembering Our Past: Studies in Autobiographical Memory*. Cambridge: Cambridge University Press, 1996.

Rubin, Miri. *Emotion and Devotion: The Meaning of Mary in Medieval Religious Cultures*. Budapest: CEU Press, 2009.
Rüsen, Jörn, Michael Fehr, and Thomas W. Rieger, eds. *Thinking Utopia: Steps into Other Worlds*. New York: Berghahn, 2005.
Rutar, Sabine. *Kultur-Nation-Milieu. Sozialdemokratie in Triest vor dem Ersten Weltkrieg*. Essen: Klartext Verlag, 2004.
Sakaroff, Nikola. *Die industrielle Entwicklung Bulgariens*. Inaugural Dissertation *zur Erlagung der Doktorwürde geheimigt von der philisophischen Fakultät der Friedrich-Wilhelms-Universität zu Berlin*, August 18, 1904.
Sakasoff, Janko. "Die Bedeutung der Lebensarbeit Karl Kautskys für die Entwicklung des Sozialismus in Bulgarien," in *Karl Kautsky dem Wahrer und Mehrer der Marxschen Lehre. Zum 70-ten Geburtstage* (Rudolf Hilferding, ed. *Internationale Revue für Sozilaismus und Politik. Ein Sonderrheft zu Kartl Kautskys 70. Geburtstag*). Berlin: Dietz, 1932, 110–13.
Sargent, Lyman Tower. *Contemporary Political Ideologies: A Comparative Analysis*. Belmont, CA: Wadsworth/Thomson Learning, 2006.
Sargent, Lyman Tower. "In Defense of Utopia," *Diogenes* 53, no. 1 (2006): 11–17.
Scharlau, Winfried and Zbynek Zeman, *Freibeuter der Revolution: Parvus-Helphand. Eine politische Biographie*. Köln: Wissenschaft und Politik, 1964.
Scheer, Monique. "Are Emotions a Kind of Practice (and Is that What Makes them Have a History)? A Bourdieuian Approach to Understanding Emotion," *History and Theory* 51 (2012): 193–220.
Schmidt, Jochen. *Populismus oder Marxismus. Zur Ideengeschichte der radikalen Intelligenz Rumäniens*. Tübingen: Verlag der Tübinger Gesellschaft, 1922.
Schorske, Carl. *German Social Democracy, 1905–1917: The Development of the Great Schism*. New York: Harper Torchbooks, 1972.
Schurer Heinz. "Alexander Helphand-Parvus – Russian Revolutionary and German Patriot," *Russian Review* 18, no. 4 (1959): 313–31.
Schwarzmantel, John. "Nationalism and Socialist Internationalism," in John Breuilly (ed.), *The Oxford Handbook of the History of Nationalism*. Oxford: Oxford Universioty Press, 2013, 635–54.
Segalen, Martine. *Love and Power in the Peasant Family: Rural France in the Nineteenth Century*. Chicago: The University of Chicago Press, 1983.
Selections from the Prison Notebooks of Antonio Gramsci, ed. and trans. Quentin Hoare and Geoffrey Nowell Smith. London: Lawrence & Wishart, 1971.
Shands, Kerstin W., Giulia Grillo Mikrit, Dipti R. Pattanik, and Karen Ferreira-Meyers, eds. *Writing the Self: Essays on Autobiography and Autofiction*. Flemingsberg: Södertörns högskila, 2015.
Shanin, Theodore, ed. *Late Marx and the Russian Road: Marx and the Peripheries of Capitalism*. New York: Monthly Review Press, 1983.
Sharma, Devika and Frederik Tygstrup, eds. *Structures of Feeling: Affectivity and the Study of Culture*. Berlin, Munich and Boston: Walter de Gruyter, 2015.
Sluga, Glenda and Patricia Clavin. *Internationalisms: A Twentieth-Century History*. Cambridge: Cambridge University Press, 2017.
Smaldone, William. *European Socialism: A Concise History with Documents*. Lanham: Rowman & Littlefield, 2014.
Smith, Jeremy. *The Bolsheviks and the National Question, 1917–1923*. New York: Macmillan, 1999.

Spitzer, Alan B. "The Historical Problem of Generations," *The American Historical Review* 78, no. 5 (1973): 1353–85.
Spivak, Gayatri. *A Critique of Postcolonial Reason: Toward a History of the Vanishing Present*. Cambridge, MA: Harvard University Press, 1999.
Stankova, Marietta. *Georgi Dimitrov: A Life*. London: I. B. Tauris, 2010.
Stavrianos, Leften S. *Balkan Federation: A History of the Movement Toward Balkan Unity in Modern Times*. Hamden, CT: Archon Books, 1964.
Stedman Jones, Gareth. *Karl Marx: Greatness and Illusion*. Cambridge, MA: The Belknap Press of Harvard University Press, 2016.
Steger, Manfred B. *The Quest for Evolutionary Socialism: Eduard Bernstein and Social Democracy*. Cambridge: Cambridge University Press, 1997.
Stein, Lorenz. *Der Sozialismus und Communismus des heutigen Frankreichs*. Ein Beitrag zur Zeitgeschichte. Leipzig: Otto Wigand, 1842.
Steinberg, Mark. *Proletarian Imagination: Self, Modernity, and the Sacred in Russia, 1910-1925*. Ithaca, NY: Cornell University Press, 2002.
Steinberg, Mark and Valeria Sobol, eds. *Interpreting Emotions in Russia and Eastern Europe*. DeKalb, IL: Northern Illinois University Press, 2011.
Steinmetz, George. "Reflections on the Role of Social Narratives in Working-Class Formation: Narrative Theory in the Social Sciences," *Social Science History* 16, no. 3 (1992): 489–516.
Steinmetz, Willibald, Michael Freeden, and Javier Fernandez-Sebastian. *Conceptual History in the European Space*. New York: Berghahn, 2017.
Struck, Bernhard, Kate Ferris, and Jacques Revel. "Introduction: Space and Scale in Transnational History," *Size Matters: Scales and Spaces in Transnational and Comparative History*, Special Issue, *International History Review* 33, no. 4 (2011): 573–84.
Studer, Brigitte. *The Transnational World of the Cominternians*, trans. Davydd Rees Roberts. London: Palgrave Macmillan, 2015.
Subrahmanyam, Sanjay. "Connected Histories: Notes towards a Reconfiguration of Early Modern Eurasia," *Modern Asian Studies* 31, no. 3 (1997): 735–62.
Szporluk, Roman. *Communism and Nationalism: Karl Marz versus Friedrich List*. New York: Oxford University Press, 1988.
Szydlik, Marc and Harald Künemund, "Generationen aus Sicht der Soziologie," in Harald Künemund and Marc Szydlik (Hrsg.), *Generationen. Multidisziplinäre Perspektiven*. Wiesbaden: Verlag für Sozialwissenschaften, 2009, 7–22.
Tangney, June Price and Kurt W. Fisher, eds. *Self-Conscious Emotions: The Psychology of Shame, Guilt, Embarrassment, and Pride*. New York: The Guilford Press, 1995.
Tchitchovsky, T. "Political and Social Aspects of Modern Bulgaria," *The Slavonic and East European Review* 7, no. 21 (1929): 595–603.
The National Question: Selected Writings by Rosa Luxemburg, ed. and introduced by the late Horace B. Davis. New York: Monthly Review Press, 1976.
The Journal of Marie Bashkirtseff, trans. Katherine Kernberger. Stroud: Fonthill Press, 2013.
Thom, Françoise. *La Langue de bois*. Paris: Julliard, 1987.
Tikhonov, Natalia. "Student Migrations and the Feminization of European Universities," *L'étudiant étranger*. Préactes dela journée d'études du 8 février 2002. http://barthes.enssib.fr/clio/revues/AHI/articles/english/tiko.html.
Tischler-Hofer, Ulrike and Karl Kaser, Hrsg. *Provincial Turn: Verhältnis zwischen Staat und Provinz im südlichen Europa vom letzen Drittel des 17. Bis ins 21. Jahrhundert*. Frankfurt am Main: Peter Lang, 2017.

Todorova, Maria. *Balkan Family Structure and the European Pattern: Demographic Development in Ottoman Bulgaria*. Budapest and New York: CEU Press, 2006.

Todorova, Maria. "Historical Tradition and Transformation in Bulgaria: Women's Issues, Feminist Issues," *Journal of Women's History* 5, no. 3 (1994): 129–43.

Todorova, Maria. "War and Memory: Trotsky's War Correspondence from the Balkan Wars," *Perceptions* —Journal of International Affairs, Special Issue—*From the Balkan Wars to Balkan Peace* (2013): 5–27.

Tomić, Đorđe and Krunoslav Stojaković. "Aus der Geschichte der jugoslawischen Linken. Von den Anfängen im 19. Jahrhundert bis zum Ausbruch des Zweiten Weltkrieges – Desideratsskizze(n)," *Südosteuropäische Hefte* 1, no. 1 (2012): 84–114.

Toshkov, Alex. *Agrarianism as Modernity in 20th-Century Europe: The Golden Age of the Peasantry*. London: Bloomsbury, 2019.

Townshend, Jules. *The Politics of Marxism: The Critical Debates*. London: Leicester University Press, 1996.

Traverso, Enzo. *Left-Wing Melancholia: Marxism, History, and Memory*. New York: Columbia University Press, 2017.

Trebitsch, Michel and Marie-Christine Granjon, eds. *Pour une histoire comparée des intelectuels*. Brussels: Complexe, 1998.

Trencsényi, Balázs. "Balkans Baedecker for Übermensch Tourists: Janko Janev's Popular Historiosophy," in Stefan Berger, Chris Lorenz, and Billie Melman (eds.), *Popularizing National Pasts*. New York: Routledge, 2012, 149–68.

Trencsényi, Balázs, Maciej Janowski, Mónika Baár, Maria Falina, and Michal Kopeček. *A History of Modern Political Thought in East Central Europe, Volume I: Negotiating Modernity in the "Long Nineteenth Century."* New York: Oxford University Press, 2016.

Trentmann, Frank. "Materiality in the Future of History: Things, Practices, and Politics," *Journal of British Studies* 48 (2009): 283–307.

Troebst, Stefan. "'Hochverehrter Meister und Genosse': Karl Kautsky und die sozialistische Bewegung in Bulgarien (1887–1933)," in Wolfgang Gesemann, Kyrill Haralampieff, and Helmut Schaller (Hg.), *Bulgaristik-Symposium Marburg*. Südosteuropa-Studien Heft 43. München: Hieronymus, 1990, 231–46.

Trotsky, Leon. *The Permanent Revolution: Results and Prospects*. https://www.marxists.org/archive/trotsky/1931/tpr/index.htm.

Truc, Gérôme. "Narrative Identity against Biographical Illusion: The Shift in Sociology from Bourdieu to Ricoeur," *Etudes Ricoeuriennes/ Ricoeur Studies* 2, no. 1 (2011): 150–67.

Tsing, Anna Lowenhaupt. "On Nonscalability: The Living World Is Not Amenable to Precision-Nested Scales," *Common Knowledge* 18, no. 3 (2012): 505–24.

Tunçay, Mete and Erik Zürcher. *Socialism and Nationalism in the Ottoman Empire, 1876–1923*. London: British Academic Press, 1994.

Turner, Jonathan H. and Jan E. Stets. *The Sociology of Emotions*. Cambridge: Cambridge University Press, 2005.

Ulam, Adam. "Socialism and Utopia," in Frank E. Manuel (ed.), *Utopias and Utopian Thought*. Boston: Beacon Press, 1967, 116–34.

Uleman, J. S. and John A. Bargh. *Unintended Thought: Limits of Awareness, Intention and Control*. New York: The Guilford Press, 1989.

Van der Linden, Marcel. *Western Marxism and the Soviet Union*. Leiden: Brill, 2007.

Venturi, Franco. *Roots of Revolution: A History of the Populist and Socialist Movements in Nineteenth-Century Russia*. New York: Knopf, 1960.

Vessey, David. "The Polysemy of Otherness: On Ricoeur's Oneself as Another," http://www.davevessey.com/.
Videva, Nedyalka and Stilian Yotov. "European Moral Values and their Reception in Bulgarian Education," *Studies in East European Thought* 53, no. 1/2 (2001): 119–28.
Vuletić, Vitomir. *Svetozar Marković i ruski revolucionarni demokrati*. Beograd: Matica Srpska, 1964.
Waldenberg, Marek. *Il papa rosso Karl Kautsky*. Roma: Editori Riuniti, 1980.
Wallerstein, Immanuel. *The Capitalist World-Economy*. Cambridge: Cambridge University Press, 1979.
Wallerstein, Immanuel. *The Modern World System*. New York: Academic Press, 1974.
Weber, Eugen. *Movements, Currents, Trends: Aspects of European Thought in the Nineteenth and Twentieth Centuries*, Lexington: D.C. Heath, 1992.
Weber, Max. *Sociological Writings*. London: Bloomsbury, 1994.
Weiningher, Otto. *Sex and Character: An Investigation of Fundamental Principles*. Bloomington: Indiana University Press, 2005.
Welskopp, Thomas. "Die 'Generation Bebel,'" in Klaus Schönhoven und Bernd Braun (Hg.), *Generationen in der Arbeiterbewegung*. München: Oldenbourg, 2005, 51–67.
Werner, Michael and Bénédicte Zimmermann. "Histoire Croisée and the Challenge of Reflexivity," *History and Theory* 45, no. 1 (2006): 30–50.
What's Left? Prognosen zur Linken. Berlin: Rotbuch Verlag, 1993.
Whitaker, Roger. "Social Structure," in *Bulgarien. Südosteuropa-Handbuch*. Vol. VI, ed. Klaus-Detlev Grothusen. Göttingen: Vandenhoeck & Ruprecht, 1990, 458–73.
Wienand, Peter. "Revoluzzer und Revisionisten. Die 'Jungen' in der Sozialdemokratie vor der Jahrhundertwende," *Politische Vierteljahresschrift* XVII (1976): 208–41.
Wiercinski, Andrew. "Hermeneutic Notion of a Human Being as an Acting and Suffering Person: Thinking with Paul Ricoeur," *Ethics in Progress* 4 (2013): 18–33.
Wilken, Rowan. "Mannheim's Paradox: Ideology, Utopia, Media Technologies, and the Arab Spring," *The Fibreculture Journal* 20 (2012): 176–95.
Williams, Raymond. *Keywords: A Vocabulary of Culture and Society*. New York: Oxford University Press, 1983.
Williams, Raymond. *Marxism and Literature*. New York: Oxford University Press, 1977.
Winter, Jay. *Dreams of Peace and Freedom: Utopian Moments in the Twentieth Century*. New Haven, CT: Yale University Press, 2008.
Winter, Jay. *Remembering War: The Great War between History and Memory in the 20th Century*. New Haven, CT: Yale University Press, 2006.
Winter, Jay. *Sites of Memory, Sites of Mourning: The Great War in European Cultural History*. Cambridge: Cambridge University Press, 1995.
Winter, Jay, ed. *The Legacy of the Great War Ninety Years On*. Columbia, MO: University of Missouri, 2009.
Winter, Jay. *War Beyond Words: Languages of Remembrance from the Great War to the Present*. Cambridge: Cambridge University Press, 2017.
Winter, Jay. *The Experience of World War I*. New York: Oxford University Press, 1989.
Winter, Jay and Antoine Prost. *The Great War in History: Debates and Controversies, 1914 to the Present*. New York: Cambridge University Press, 2005.
Winter, Jay and Emmanuel Sivan, eds. *War and Remembrance in the Twentieth Century*. Cambridge: Cambridge University Press, 1999.
Wohl, Robert. *The Generation of 1914*. Cambridge, MA: Harvard University Press, 1979.
Wolchik, Sharon L. and Alfred G. Meyer, eds. *Women, State, and Party in Eastern Europe*. Durham, NC: Duke University Press, 1985.

Wolfe, Bertram. "Nationalism and Internationalism in Marx and Engels," *The American Slavic and East European Review* 17, no. 4 (1958): 403–17.
Worsley, Peter. *The Three Worlds: Culture & World Development.* Chicago: University of Chicago Press, 1984.
Žižek, Slavoj. "From Revolutionary to Catastrophic Utopia," in Jörn Rüsen, Michael Fehr, and Thomas W. Rieger (eds.), Thinking Utopia: *Steps into Other Worlds.* New York: Berghahn, 2005, 247–62.
25-годишенъ юбилей на Българския Социалистически Работнически Съюзъ и В-къ "Работническа Просвѣта" (Сборник статии). Published by the Bulgarian Socialist Labor Federation. Granite City, 1935.
Аржириадис, П., П. Лагард. *Разрешението на Източния въпрос. Балканската конфедерация и Македония (превод от френски).* Габрово: Заря, 1902.
Асиова, Бойка, "Обратите на съдбата. Безпощаден разказ за невероятния живот на българина Джордж – Георги Андрейчин," *Земя* 31 March 2008. http://library.belitsa.com/andreichin.php.
Ангелова, Трендафила. "Борис Стефанов," *ИИИ*, 51 (1984): 341–58.
Арабаджиев, Сава. "Борбата на БКП против догматизма на сектантство на 'левите' комунисти през периода 1919–1922 г.," *ИИИ* 11 (1964): 90–99.
Баев, Йордан, Константин Грозев. *Българинът Джордж. Одисея в два свята.* София: Труд, 2008.
Бакалов, Георги. *Избрани произведения.* София: Фондация Арете-Фол, Университетско издателство "Св. Климент Охридски," 2007.
Бебел, Август. *Жената и социализмът.* Превел Н. Хр. Габровски. Търново: Печатница "Работник," 1893.
Белами, Едуард. *След 100 години,* прев. Константин Бозвелиев. Русе: изд. Спиро Гулабчев, 1892.
Беров, Любен. "Социална струтура на селото в балканските страни през периода между двете световни войни," *Трудове на ВИИ Карл Маркс* IV (1977): 43–76.
Бирман, М. А. "Численост и структура на работническата класа в началото на XX век," *ИИИ* 37 (1977): 155–96.
Бирман М. А. *Формиране и развитие на българския пролетариат, 1878–1923.* София: Партиздат, 1983.
Благоев, Димтър. *Съчинения.* София: Издателство на БКП, 1957-.
Благоев, Димтър. *Принос към историята на социализма в България.* София: Издателство на БКП, 1906.
Благоев, Димтър. *Избрани съчинения в два тома.* София: Издателство на БКП, 1951.
Богданова, Елена. *Вела Благоева.* София: Издателство на БКП, 1969.
Братанов, Георги. "Никола Габровски," *ИИИ* 49 (1983): 395–401.
Бужашки, Евлоги. *Д.Благоев и победата на марксизма в българското социалистическо движение 1885–1903.* София: Издателство на БКП, 1960.
Български женски съюз (по случай 30-годишнината от неговото основаване), 1901–1931. София: Бълг. женски съюз, 1931.
Бьодекер, Ханс Ерих. "Биографията: Изследване на частен случай," Ивайло Знеполски, ред. *Между макроисторията и микроисторията или историята в множествено число.* София: Дом на науките за човека и обществото, 2010, 155–82.
Веков, Ангел. "Г. В. Плеханов и българската социалдемокрация," *ИИИ* 31 (1974): 283–316.
Веков, Ангел. "Д. Благоев и Г. В. Плеханов," *ИИИ* 36 (1977): 85–119.

Веков, Ангел. "Към въпроса за участието на Кръстю Раковски в руското революционно движение (1891–1912 г.)," *ИИИ* 53 (1985): 287–307.

Велева, Живка. "Фридрих Енгелс и първите български социалисти," *ИИИ* 24 (1970): 352–66.

Верковичъ, С.И. *Топографическо-этнографическій очеркъ Македоніи*. Санкт Петербург: Военная Типографія, 1889.

Воденичаров, Михаил. *Борбата на левите течения в "обединената" социалистическа партия*. София, 1909.

Восточная Европа в документах российских архивов 1949-1953. Том 2. Москва-Новосибирск, 1998.

Генчев, Димитър. *Профили от кафене "Ландолт"*. София: Партиздат, 1990.

Генчев, Димитър. *Първоапостолите на идеала*. София: Фондация „Ново време", Издателска къща „Христо Ботев", 2006.

Генчев, Димитър. "Теоретичното и програмно развитие на българската социалдемокрация (1891–1919 г.)," in Евгений Кандиларов, Таня Турлакова (ред.), *Изследвания по история на социализма в България, 1891–1944*, том I. София: Фондация "Фридрих Еберт," Център за исторически и политилогически изследвания, 2008, 30–60.

Генчев, Николай. *Българска възрожденска интелигенция*. София: Университетско издателство "Св. Климент Охридски," 1991.

Георгиева, Виктория. "Толстой и България: как учението на великия хуманист намира последователи у нас," *Култура*, 30 September 2017. https://bg.rbth.com/culture/325672-толстой-българия-учение-последователи.

Гинев, Филип. *Никола Габровски*. София: Отечествен фронт, 1982.

Гърдев, Костадин. *Българската емиграция в Канада*. София: Академично издателство „Марин Дринов," 1994.

Дабев, Евтим. "Разколът в работническото движение," *Бележник на един социалдемократ (непериодично издание)*, 1, 1928.

Дамянова, Живка. "Третата Цимервалдска конференция," *ИИИ* 41 (1979): 129–77.

Дамянова, Живка. "Карл Кауцки и социалдемокрацията в Югоизточна Европа," *ИИИ* 59 (1988): 343–52.

Даскалов, Дончо. "Анархизмът в България по време на революционната криза (1918–1925)," *ИИИ* 26 (1971): 111–41.

Даскалов, Дончо. *Васил Коларов и Георги Димитров и революционните събития в България, 1923-1925*. София: Партиздат, 1978.

Даскалова, Красимира. *Жени, пол и модернизация в България, 1878-1944*. София: Университетско издателство "Св. Климент Охридски," 2012.

Дебогорий-Мокриевич, В. К. *Воспоминания*. Санкт Петербург: Книгоиздательство "Свободный Труд", 1906,

Делирадев, Павел. *Балканската конфедерация*. Татар Пазарджик: Печатница Търговска, 1909.

Джидров, Петър. *Пред прага на социализма*. София: Работническа кооперативна печатница "Напред," 1919.

Джидров, Петър. *Социализмът и неговите методи*. София: Издателско кооперативно дружество "Просвета," 1921.

Джидров, Петър и Асен Цанков. *Империализъм, болшевизъм и социализъм. Речи държани в София на 17 април 1921 в салона на Градското Казино*. София: Издателско кооперативно дружество "Просвета," 1921.

Джидров, Петър. *Безпомощна България. Проблеми и перспективи.* София: Издателско кооперативно дружество "Просвета," 1927.

Джидрова, Мария. *Искания на българката (Сказка).* София: Печатница "Гражданин," 1912.

Динкова, Мария. *Социален портрет на българската жена.* София: Профиздат, 1980.

Димитров, Димитър. *Разпра в работнишката партия.* Шумен: Издание на П.Байнов, 1901.

Драгойчев, Чавдар. *Дъщерите на Дядото (Спомени).* София: s.n., 1997.

Друмев, Иван. *Социализма в България.* Стара Загора: Печатница "Светлина," 1922.

Дърева, Велислава. *Атентатът '1925: Денят, в който се отвориха портите Адови.* София: Синева, 2019.

Дюмон, Пол. "Българската социалдемокрация в архивите на Международното Социалистическо Бюро (1900–1918)," *ИИИ* 46 (1982): 349–55.

Енгелс, Фридрих. *Развитие на научния социализъм.* Превод: Евтим Дабев. Габрово: s.n., 1890.

Зараждане и развитие на социалистическото движение в Габровски окръг. Материали и документи. София: Партиздат, 1975.

Иванов, Георги. *Българските църковни общини в Америка и Чикаго.* (Документална хроника). Чикаго, 2004–2011. http://otzvuk.com/Knigi/TSURKOVNI%20OBSHTINI.pdf.

Игов, Светлозар. *Кратка история на българската литература.* София: Издателство "Захарий Стоянов," Университетско издателство "Св.Климент Охридски," 2005.

История на антифашистката борба в България. София: Партиздат, 1976.

История на България. Том 7. София: Издателство на БАН, 1991.

История на България, Том 8. София: ГАЛ-ИКО, 1999.

Исусов, Мито. *Последната година на Трайчо Костов.* София: Издателско дружество "Христо Ботев," 1990.

Йорданов, Йордан. "За България ли е тръгнал Лев Толстой?" http://www.svobodata.com/page.php?pid=11296.

Йосько, М. И. *Николай Сурзиловский -Руссель. Жизнь, революционная деятельность и мировозрение.* Минск: Издательство БГУ им. В. И. Ленина, 1976.

Йордан Йотов. *Из борбите на тесните социалисти против опортюнизма на Втория интернационал.* София: БКП, 1964.

Йотов, Йордан. "Борбата на тесните социалисти против анархолибералите и прогресистите," *ИИИ* 11 (1964): 60–66.

Йотов, Йордан. *Центризмът в българското социалистическо движение, 1905–1920.* София: Издателство на БКП, 1969.

Йотов, Йордан. *Водителят, съвременник на бъдещето.* София: Издателство "Булгарика," 2000.

Йотов, Йордан, Кирил Василев, Стоянка Поборникова, and Татяна Колева, *Димитър Благоев. Биография.* София: Партиздат, 1979.

Йоцов, Ярослав. "Социално-икономически облик на България, 1919–1923," *Известия на Института по История* 20 (1968): 5–52.

Кабакчиев, Христо. *Към Балканската федерация.* София: Партийна социалистическа книжарница, 1913.

Кабакчиев, Христо, Б. Бошкович, and Х. Д. Ватис. *Коммунистические партии балканских стран.* Москва: Московский рабочий, 1930.

Калинов, Марин. *Един дух широк и свободен. Щрихи към портрета на Янко Сакъзов*. Шумен: Антос, 2000.
Кандев, Петко. "Зараждане и развитие на учителското движение в България (до 1895 г.)," *Известия на Института по История на БКП* 7 (1960): 241–62.
Кандиларов, Евгений, and Таня Турлакова, ред. *Изследвания по история на социализма в България, 1891–1944*, Том I. София: Фондация "Фридрих Еберт," Център за исторически и политилогически изследвания, 2008.
Кантаржиев, Асен. "Спомени за Тина Киркова," *ИИИ* 18 (1968): 379–86.
Кауцки, К. *Републиката във Франция и социалдемокрацията*. София: Партийна социалистическа книжарница, 1909.
Кирин, Стефчо. "Малко известно: как и кога Димитър Благоев станал Дядото." http://www.nabore.bg/statia/kak-i-koga-blagoev-stanal-dyadoto-1853-14.
Кирков, Георги. *Избрани произведения*, т. I. София: Партиздат, 1989.
Кирков, Георги. *Публицистика*. София: Фондация Арете, Университетско издателство "Св. Климент Охридски," 2006.
Клинчаров, Иван. *Димитър Благоев, история на неговия живот*. София: s.n., 1926.
Колева, Татяна. "Политическата линия в началото на 1925 г. и Априлският атентат," *ИИИ* 65 (1989): 471–84.
Константинова, Здравка. *Бунтът на "анархолибералите". Бакалов срещу Благоев*. София: Университетско издателство "Св.Климент Охридски", 1995.
Косев, Димитър. *Септемврийското въстание в 1923 г.* София: БАН, 1954.
Костов, Трайчо. *Избрани произведения, 1944–1948*. София: Партиздат, 1978.
Костов, Трайчо. *Публицистика, кореспонденция и спомени за него в два тома*. София: Партиздат, 1987.
Кратка история на Българската Комунистическа Партия (под редакцията на Борис Боев, Боян Григоров, Стефан Радулов). София: Партиздат, 1986.
Кръстев, Д-р Кръстьо. *Млади и стари. Критически очерки върху днешната българска литература*. Тутракан: Мавродинов, 1907.
Кузманов, Петър; Москов, Атанас. *Коста Лулчев. Един живот в служба на социалдемокрацията*. София: Христофор Христов, 1998.
Куманов, Милен. "Левият политически спектър в България (1918–1934 г.)," in Евгений Кандиларов and Таня Турлакова (ред.), *Изследвания по история на социализма в България, 1891–1944*, Том I. София: Фондация "Фридрих Еберт," Център за исторически и политилогически изследвания, 2008, 324–54.
Кънчов, Васил. *Македония. Етнография и статистика*. София: Държавна печатница, 1900.
Макдермот, Мерсия. *Ален мак самотен. Биография на Димитър Благоев*. София: ИК "Синева," 2018.
Македонска енциклопедија. Скопје: Македонска академија на науките и уметностите, 2009.
Маринова, Мария. *Българските марксисти и германското работническо движение, 1900–1912*. София: Партиздат, 1979.
Марков, Георги. *Покушения, насилие и политика в България 1878–1947*. София: Военно издателство, 2003.
Маркс, Карл and Фридрих Енгелс. *Съчинения в 25 тома*. София: Издателство на БКП, 1975 -.
Мизов, Максим and Таня Турлакова, ред. *Георги Кирков и нашето съвремие. Материали от конференцията, посветена на 140 години от рождението му*. София: Център за исторически и политилогически изследвания, 2007.

Митев, Трендафил. "Възникване и същност на 'широкия социализъм' в България," in Евгений Кандиларов and Таня Турлакова (ред.), *Изследвания по история на социализма в България, 1891–1944*, Том I. София: Фондация "Фридрих Еберт," Център за исторически и политилогически изследвания, 2008, 70–141.

Митев, Трифон. "Септемврийското въстание (1923 г.) и паметта за него в българската литература." https://stzagora.net/2013/09/26/септемврийското-въстание-1923-г-и-паметт/.

Младжов, Георги. "Карл Маркс в България," *ИИИ* 50 (1983): 7–37.

Нанков, Никита. "Баснята за блудния син: Гео Милев, европейският модернизъм и българската лява критика," *Литературна мисъл* 47, nos. 1–2 (2003): 85–111.

Найденов, Георги. "Ценност или стойност – Г.Бакалов срещу Д.Благоев," *Икономически и социални алтернативи* 3 (2017): 127–39.

Натан, Жак. "Борбата на БКП против 'лявото' сектантство," *ИИИ* 11 (1964): 125–44.

Наумов, Георги. *Атентатът в катедралата "Света Неделя"*. София: Партиздат, 1989.

Националнo-освободителното движение на македонските и тракийските българи (1878 – 1944). Том 3. Освободителното движение след Илинденско-Преображенското въстание 1903 –1919. София: Македонски научен институт, 1997.

Нешев, Кирил. Сотирис Теохаридис. *Философия на утопиите*. София: Фабер, 2008.

Орманов, Иван. "Непримиримата класова борба и международната солидарност на пролетариата," *Ново време* 1 (January 15, 1915).

Панайотов, Панайот. *Приносът на българи за победата на Октомврийската революция (1917–1920)*. София: Издателство на БКП, 1967.

Панайотов, Филип. *Съвременници на бъдещето*. София: Народна младеж, 1971.

Панайотов, Филип. *Чучулигите*. София: Народна младеж, 1981.

Панайотов, Филип. *Йосиф Хербст: Живот и смърт*. София: Партиздат, 1981.

Панайотов, Филип. *Животът и смъртта на Кръстю Раковски*. София: Издателство Захари Стоянов, 2003.

Пакалева, Виржиния. *Българката през Възраждането*. София: Отечествен фронт, 1984.

Пенев, Боян. "Увод в българската литература след Освобождението," *Годишник на Софийския Университет, Историко-филологически факултет* 38, no. 4 (1942): 1–56.

Пенев, Боян. *Студии, статии, есета*. София: Български писател, 1985.

Петров, Цоньо, "Първият социалистически вестник в България – 'Росица,'" *ИИИ* 57 (198): 243–67.

Петрова, Веселина. "Из кореспонденцията на Георги Бакалов с полските социалисти в края на век," *ИИИ* 46 (1982): 342–48.

Петрова-Чомпалова, Веселина. *Георги Бакалов. Обществено-политическа и културна дейност (1891–1903)*. Пловдив: ИК "Глас," 2002.

Петър Дънов за частната собственост. София: Издателство Хелиопол, n.d.

Пинкас, Клара. *Реформистката социалдемокрация в България. Идеология, политика, организация 1903–1917*. София: Партиздат, 1981.

Пирински, Георги. *Какво видях и преживях Америка*. София: Издателство на Отечествения Фронт, 1970.

Пирински, Георги. *Георги Андрейчин, пламенен революционер и деец на българското и международното комунистическо движение*. Благоевград: Научно-производствена дирекция "Културно-историческо наследство," 1984.

Пирински, Георги. *Извикани от спомена. Портрети на американски и български борци за мир и демокрация в САЩ.* София: Партиздат, 1986.
Попптеров, Николай. "Личността на Георги Кирков като възможност/повод за многостранна историческа реконструкция," in Максим Мизов and Таня Турлакова (ред.), *Георги Кирков и нашето съвремие. Материали от конференцията, посветена на 140 години от рождението му.* София: Център за исторически и политилогически изследвания, 2007, 37–48.
Правчанов, Симеон. *Майстора в Народното събрание.* София: Партиздат, 1987.
Процесът и зад процеса "Трайчо Костов": 1949–1997, 48 години след процеса. София: Макон-S, 1998.
Първанов. Георги. *Българската социалдемокрация и македонският въпрос (От края на XIX век до 1918 година).* София: Графимакс, 1997.
Първанов, Георги and Валери Русанов. "Документ на Васил Главинов за ранното социалистическо движение в Европейска Турция," *ИИИ* 51 (1984): 444–58.
Ревякина, Луиза. "БКП и селското движение в България: теория, практика (май 1919-септември 1944)," in Евгений Кандиларов and Таня Турлакова (ред.), *Изследвания по история на социализма в България, 1891–1944,* том I. София: Фондация "Фридрих Еберт," Център за исторически и политилогически изследвания, 2008, 355–400.
Сакаров, Никола. *Българските държавни финанси от Освобождението до Световната война.* София: Издава Българската Академия на Науките, 1918.
Сакаров, Никола. *Железопътното и телеграфопощенското дело в България.* София: Изд. на Българския Железничарски съюз, 1919.
Сакаров, Никола. *Капиталът трябва да плаща.* София: Книгоиздателство Знание, 1920.
Сакаров, Никола. "Руският социален опит и неговите близки изгледи," *Философски преглед* 1 (1931): 46–61.
Сакаров, Никола. *Петилетния стопански план на Русия.* София: Азбука, 1931.
Сакаров, Никола. *Социалистическият интернационал и войната.* София: Напред, 1919.
Сакаров, Никола. *Тактика на социалната демокрация.* София: Напред, 1920.
Сакаров, Никола. *Петилетния стопански план на Русия.* София: Азбука, 1931.
Сакаров, Никола and Найден Николов. *Опити за разсейване на идейната безпътица.* София: Печатница Гладстон, 1929.
Сакъзов, Янко. *Належащите реформи.* София: Печатница Ив. Цучев, 1902.
Сакъзов, Янко. *Тревога за призраци (нашето отстъпничество или тяхното недомислие).* София: Фондация "Янко Сакъзов," 1991.
Сакъзов, Янко. *Интелигецията и нейната роля в обществото.* София: Издателска къща "Христо Ботев," 1993.
Стателова, Елена and Стойчо Грънчаров. *История на Нова България (1878–1944).* София: Издателска къща „Анубис," 1999.
Стойчев, Ст.Д. „Нови документи за живота и дейността на в. Благоева като учителка в гр. Търново – 1890-1892," *ИИИ* 3–4 (1958): 426–43.
Стоянов, Илия. *История на българското Възраждане.* Велико Търново: Абагар, 1999.
Танчев, Иван. *Учението на българи в чужбина, 1879–1892.* София: Академично издателство "Марин Дринов," 1994.
Терзиева, Маргарита, Неля Иванова, and Тинка Иванова. *Поглед върху толстоизма в България.* Бургас: Диамант, 2006.

Терзиева, М. Т. "Летописцы толстовского движения в Болгарии," *Перспективы Науки и Образования* 2, no. 20 (2016). Международный электронный научний журнал. https://pnojournal.files.wordpress.com/2016/03/pdf_160214.pdf.

Тодоров, Владислав. *Хаотичното махало*. София: Фондация "Пространство Култура," 2005.

Тодоров, Илия. "Символ-верую на българската комуна," *Летописи* 1 (1991). http://clubs.dir.bg/showthreaded.php?Board=politics&Number=1939666704.

Тодорова, Цветана. *Дипломатическа история на външните заеми на България 1888-1912*. София: Наука и изкуство, 1971.

Тодорова, Цветана. "Индустриализация и структурни промени в България през Първата световна война," *Исторически преглед* 5 (1991): 22-43.

Топалов, Владислав. "Основаване на Българския Земеделски Съюз," *ИИИ* 8 (1960): 153-208.

Топенчаров, Владимир. *Българската журналистика, 1885-1903*. София: Наука и изкуство, 1963.

Топенчаров, Владимир. *Българската журналистика, 1903-1917*. София: Наука и изкуство, 1981.

Тотев, Анастас. *Статистическа характеристика на българското земеделско стопанство*. София : М-во на земеделието и държ. имоти, 1940.

Тошев, Георги. *Балкански митнически съюз (Balkanzoll - verein). Политикономическо изследване*. Пловдив: книж. Антим I на Р. Милков, 1907.

Турлакова, Таня. „Георги Кирков за правата на жените в Булгария," in Максим Мизов and Таня Турлакова (ред.), *Георги Кирков и нашето съвремие. Материали от конференцията, посветена на 140 години от рождението му*. София: Център за исторически и политилогически изследвания, 2007, 49-55.

Турлакова, Таня. "Някои необходими акценти в новия прочит на историята на социализма в България (1891-1944)," in Евгений Кандиларов and Таня Турлакова (ред.), *Изследвания по история на социализма в България, 1891-1944*, том I. София: Фондация "Фридрих Еберт," Център за исторически и политилогически изследвания, 2008, 9-29.

Философско-литературное наследие Г. В. Плеханова. Том II. Г. В. Плеханов и международное рабочее движение. Под ред. М. Т. Йовчук, И. Н. Курбатова, Б. А. Чагин. Москва: Наука, 1973.

Фосколо, Мона. *Георги Димитров: една критическа биография*. София: Просвета, 2013.

Хаджидимов, Димо. *Публицистика, писма и документи*. София: Партиздат, 1989.

Христакудис, Апостолос. „Аврам Бенароя (1997-1979) - живот и дейност," *Алманах за история на евреите в България* XXX (1998/1999): 241-47.

Христов, Ангел. "Г. В. Плеханов и българските социалисти," *ИИИ* 1-2 (1957): 399-427.

Христов, Борис. *Изпитанието: спомени за процеса и съдбата на Трайчо Костов и неговата група*. София: Университетско издателство "Св. Климент Охридски," 1995.

Христов, М. "Биографични сведения за Никола Стефанов, брат на писатля Йордан Йовков," *ИИИ* 6 (1959): 275-77.

Христов, М. "Неизвестно писмо на Димитър Благоев," *ИИИ* 9 (1962): 383-85.

Христов, Филю. *Военно-революционната дейност на българската комунистическа партия, 1912-1944*. София: Държавно военно издателство, 1959.

Христов, Христо. *Аграрният въпрос в българската национална революция*. София: Наука и изкуство, 1976.

Цанев, Петър. "Георги Кирков в Николаев, Русия (1879–1886)," *ИИИ* 33 (1975): 361–69.
Цанев, Стефан. *Български хроники*. Т.3. София, Издателство Труд; Жанет-45, 2008.
Чанков, Георги. *Равносметката*. София: Христо Ботев, 2000.
Чанков, Георги. "Грамотност на населението в България," *Училищен преглед* 1–2 (1926).
Чернявский, Георгий, Михаил Станчев, and Мария Тортика (Лобанова). *Жизненный путь Христиана Раковского, 1973–1941. Европеизм и Большевизм: Неоконченная дуель*. Москва: Центрполиграф, 2014.
Чернявский, Георгий and Михаил Станчев. *В борьбе против самовластия: Х. Г. Раковский в 1927–1941 гг.* Харківський державний інститут культури, 1993.
Шарова, Крумка. "Идейният път на Спиро Гулабчев," *ИИИ* 9 (1962): 103–51.
Шнитман, А. „К вопросу о влиянии русского револююционного движения 1885–1903 годов на революционное движение в Болгарии," *Вопросы истории*, no. 1 (1949): 39–55.
Шопов, Атанас. *Из живота и положението на българите във вилаетите*. Пловдив: Търговска печатница, 1893.
Юбилеен сборник на Българския Учителски Съюз (по случай 10-годишнината от основаването му), 1895–1905. София: Печатница „Св. София," 1905.
Янко Сакъзов-Юбилеен сброник. София: Издателство "Обществена мисъл," 1930.
Янчев, Веселин. "Апология на българската социалдемокрация (1891–1944)," in Евгений Кандиларов and Таня Турлакова (ред.), *Изследвания по история на социализма в България, 1891–1944*, том I. София: Фондация "Фридрих Еберт," Център за исторически и политилогически изследвания, 2008, 142–243.
Япов, Петър. *Трайчо Костов и Никола Гешев: съдебните процеси през 1942 и 1949 г.* София: Факел, Изток-Запад, 2003.

Index

Abdul Hamid II   55
Adanir, Fikret   62, 277
Adler, Friedrich   71
Adler, Victor   49, 56, 58, 70, 71, 262
Africa   18, 150, 189, 283
anarchism   8, 12, 14, 19, 23, 25, 31, 54, 69, 88, 91, 120, 123-9, 134, 142, 145, 206, 210, 249, 277, 293, 295, 297-8
"anarcho-liberals"   8, 28, 63-4, 99, 131, 136, 138, 221, 235-40, 246
Andreichin, Georgi   72, 201, 204, 302, 317
Andreyev, Leoniv   217
Angelov, Vîrban   72, 103, 140, 163, 268, 290-2, 299, 300, 306
Anti-Dühring   23, 180, 229, 263
Aprilov High school   52, 117, 131, 134, 187
Arbore-Ralli, Zamfir   121
Argyriadès, Paul   54, 274
Armenia, Armenians   13, 31, 54-5, 60, 90, 141, 259, 275, 278
Asia   18, 23, 47, 189
Asia Minor   54, 56
Atanasov, Aleksandîr   72
Atanasov, Dimitîr   299
atheism   21, 33, 89, 131, 133-4, 139, 144, 160, 165, 209, 219
Attali, Jacques   1, 255
Austria-Hungary   13, 19, 26, 39, 45, 49, 50-1, 55-6, 58-60, 70-2, 103-6, 112, 122-3, 133, 149, 223, 245, 259, 272, 273, 276, 303
Austro-Marxism   24, 35, 58, 65, 76, 276
autobiography   9, 54, 162-3, 175-6, 179-80, 187, 191, 198, 207-8, 227-8, 232, 237-8, 240-1, 274, 286, 300, 318-19, 322
Avramov, Roman   72, 137-8, 300, 324
Avramov, Stefan   49, 301
Axelrod, Pavel   122, 233, 238

Bakalov, Georgi   26-7, 33, 42, 54, 134-6, 138, 165, 213, 221-2, 235-6, 239-40, 246-7, 266, 299-300
Bakîrdzhiev, Dimitîr   112
Bakunin, Mikhail   12, 120, 124, 129
Balabanov, Slavi   134-6, 297
Balamezov, Gavril   91, 126
Balkan federation   8, 37, 54-67
Balkan Question, *see* Eastern Question
Balkans   19, 30-1, 35, 51, 56, 59, 65, 67, 76, 101, 104, 121, 123, 134, 144, 149, 179, 252, 261, 262
Balkan wars   40, 62, 64, 65, 67, 85, 105, 110, 112, 146, 161, 163, 179, 181, 183, 185, 246, 266, 268, 287, 311, 317
Ballinger, Pamela   260
Battenberg, Alexander   104, 122
Baudelaire, Charles   220
Bauer, Otto   58, 276
Bauman, Zygmunt   253, 256
Bavaria   41
Bebel, August   46, 48-9, 66, 81, 147-8, 151, 232-3, 263, 273, 283, 303
Belgium   13, 18, 19, 68, 70, 103, 105, 112, 122, 169, 233, 281
Belgrade   60, 164, 223
Belinsky, Vissarion   131, 132
Bellamy, Edward   129, 297
Benaroya, Avram   63-5, 277-8
Benjamin, Walter   9, 220, 257
Berlin   40, 105, 109, 110, 130, 138, 141, 169, 230, 232-4, 242-3, 250
Berlin Congress, 1878   130, 188
Bernstein, Eduard   17, 23-4, 38-9, 46, 49, 51-2, 57, 59, 70, 72, 144, 262-3, 267, 272-3, 301
Berrett, James   201, 228
biography   19, 159, 166, 174-7, 182, 186-7, 191, 196, 204, 243, 263, 270, 310-11

Blagoev, Dimitîr   25, 27–9, 33, 35–6, 41–4, 53–54, 56, 60, 63, 68–9, 80, 85, 91–4, 106–7, 109, 123–4, 126–7, 131, 133–4, 138, 142–6, 155, 157, 159–61, 181, 185, 221, 225–7, 237, 242, 246–8, 264–6, 270, 287, 290, 292, 297, 298, 300, 301, 305, 321, 326
Blagoev, Khristo   125
Blagoeva, Natalia   158, 160, 166–7
Blagoeva, Stella   72, 158, 160, 166–7
Blagoeva, Vela   91, 149, 153–4, 157–60, 166, 168–9, 305
Blanc, Louis   133
Blanqui, Louis-August   42–4
Bloch, Ernst   2, 4–7, 24, 255
Bobchev, Stefan   118
Bogdanov, Alexander   33, 133, 141
Bogoev, Georgi   91
Bogoev, Trifon   91, 188
Bohemia, *see* Czechoslovakia
Bolshevik Revolution   2, 7, 14, 24–5, 41, 46, 69, 85–6, 95, 99, 105–6, 109, 124, 203, 228, 238, 322
bolsheviks   38, 42–4, 47, 58, 70, 99, 124–5, 138, 233, 238, 270, 281, 296, 317
Boneva, Angelina   9, 90, 161, 166, 179–200
Bordiga, Amedeo   109
Bosnia-Hercegovina   51, 54, 58–9, 65, 273
Botev, Khristo   119–21, 123–4, 128, 130–1, 294
Boteva, Ivanka   124, 295
Bourdieu, Pierre   101, 175, 310, 315
Bozveliev, Konstantin   92, 129, 134, 144, 155, 165, 287, 297
Bozvelieva, Iordanka   155
Braun, Lily   235
Bruner, Jerome   207, 318
Brussels   13, 49, 52, 169, 290, 301
Brzezinski, Zbigniew   77
Buber, Martin   4, 256
Bucharest   67–9
Büchner, Ludwig   132, 212
Bulgaria
    education   26, 47, 101, 151–3, 159, 220–1, 185–91, 223, 304, 313
    emigration   110–11, 179, 185, 201–5, 223, 247–8
    Liberal party   73, 91, 123, 126, 159, 242
    People's party   73, 118, 324
    social structure and economy   39, 80, 93, 107, 150–1, 222–3, 304
    unification, 1885   54, 62, 104, 122–3, 130, 183
Bulgarian Agrarian National Union (BANU)   41, 47, 88, 107, 109, 124, 125–6, 143, 146, 303
Bulgarian Communist Party (BCP)   28, 41–4, 80, 87–8, 91, 98, 105–7, 112, 124–5, 127, 131, 138–9, 146, 169, 180–2, 202, 240, 247, 249, 290, 292, 306, 326
    Military Organization   99, 106, 109, 166, 169–70, 181, 249, 307
Bulgarian Social Democratic Party (BSDP)   27, 147, 181
    socialist education   24, 28, 88, 95, 100–5, 133–7, 147–8, 151, 157, 213, 220
Bulgarian Social Democratic Union (BSDU)   53, 136, 275
Bulgarian Socialist Labor Federation (BSLF)   201–3, 225, 317
Bulgarian Teachers' Union (BTU)   126, 220–1
Bulgarian Women's Union (BWU)   152–5, 164
Bulgarian Workers' Social Democratic Party (BWSDP, broads)   28, 37–9, 41, 44, 46–7, 53, 56, 61–2, 68–71, 88, 95, 102, 136, 141–6, 154, 221, 237, 246, 275, 280, 287
Bulgarian Workers' Social Democratic Party (BWSDP, narrows)   28, 35–9, 41–4, 46–7, 56, 60–4, 67–72, 85, 88, 91, 95–6, 98, 106, 141, 145–6, 154–5, 161–2, 168, 221, 271, 326
Burton, Antoinette   40
Butler, Judith   175
Buzludzha congress   91, 98, 130–1, 134, 298

Calhoun, Craig   207
Carpenter, Edward   133

Certeau, Michel de   132
Chekhov, Anton   125, 217
Chernopeev, Khristo   64
Chernyshevsky, Nikolai   44, 54, 120, 122, 131–2, 212
China   22, 123, 291
Christianity   119, 131, 145, 160
Christian socialism   22
Codreanu, Nicolae Zubcu   121
colonialism   17, 49, 71, 280
Comintern   8, 19, 22, 24, 41–4, 80, 98–9, 106–11, 137, 166, 169, 203–4, 227, 239, 247–8, 280–1, 291, 303, 307, 316
communism   3–7, 19–23, 25–6, 42–6, 52–3, 106–9, 111–12, 118–20, 137–8, 141, 166, 169, 202–4, 221, 226–8, 247–9, 302, 306–7, 320–2
Communist Manifesto   21–3, 31, 66, 93, 133–4, 147
Comte, Auguste   133
Constantinople   54, 185, 312
Croatia   13, 31–2, 50, 60, 94, 124
Czechoslovakia, Czechs   13, 18, 31, 49, 54, 55, 141, 268, 281

Dabev, Evtim   130–1, 134, 164, 325
Dahrendorf, Ralf   5
Damasio, Antonio   172, 193
Danov, Ivan   180–1, 191
Darnton, Robert   132
Darwin, Charles   44, 120, 133, 141, 212
Daskalova, Krassimira   151, 157
Debogory-Mokrievich, Vladimir   123–4, 295
Delchev, Gotse   124, 186
De Leon, Daniel   29, 147, 201, 203
Deliradev, Pavel   63, 267
Denmark   13, 70
Deutsch, Lev   122, 131
diaries   9, 129, 157, 171, 175, 201, 204–9, 212–14, 219, 223, 225–7, 229, 318, 322
Dickstein, Szymon   131
Dimchev, Vladimir   132
Dimitrov, Dimitŭr   141–4
Dimitrov, Georgi   139, 156, 162, 247–8, 288, 306–7, 324
Dimitrov, Nikola   164

Dimou, Augusta   19, 30–1, 121–2, 141
Dimov, Georgi   139
Dînov, Petîr   145, 302
Dobrogeanu-Gherea, Constantin   121
Dobroliubov, Nikolai   128, 131
Dorosiev, Iako   109
Draganov, Petîr   91
Dragiev, Dimitîr   146
Dragomanov, Mikhail   127, 297
Dramaliev, Kiril   249, 326
Drumev, Ivan   118
Drumev, Vasil, *see* Kliment of Tîrnovo
Dumas, Alexandre   132, 212
Dzhidrov, Petîr   46–7, 105, 155, 164, 242, 271
Dzhidrova, Maria   155, 164
Dzhorov, Stoian   98–100

Eastern Europe   8, 14–15, 17–18, 22, 31, 44, 61, 71, 173, 259–60
Eastern Question   51, 54–7, 61, 66–7, 71, 143, 274–5, 278
Eastern Rumelia   54, 62, 90, 104, 122–3, 127, 183
Ebert, Friedrich   72, 81
Eley, Geoff   31, 47, 71, 259, 262, 264, 281
Elin Pelin   127
emotions   74, 171–4, 196, 218, 225, 242–3, 251, 308–10, 322
Engels, Friedrich   17, 21–3, 31, 33, 42, 50, 139, 143, 148, 158, 164, 214, 262–3, 294, 325
England   13, 18, 21, 26, 33, 68, 86, 103, 138, 150, 164, 235, 279
Exarchate   165, 183–5, 192, 196–7, 229, 314

Fabianism   45
feminism   151–4, 198, *see also* women
Finland   18–19, 149
First International   12–13, 25, 50, 120, 265
First World War   2, 8, 13–14, 19, 22–3, 25, 30, 38, 45, 50, 72, 78, 85, 105, 181, 207, 226, 240, 253, 259, 284–5
Flammarion, Camille   133
Foucault, Michel   171, 175, 207
Fourier, Charles   21, 118

France 13, 18–20, 22, 26–7, 33, 38–9, 45, 49, 54, 56, 66, 68, 70, 99, 103–6, 112, 118, 122–3, 127, 137–8, 150, 215, 233, 245, 260, 265, 279
French Revolution 1, 129, 235
Frevert, Ute 174
Fridman, Marko 109
Fromm, Erich 24

Gabrovo 26, 52, 92, 117, 124, 127–8, 130–1, 134, 137, 157, 164–5, 187
Gabrovski, Nikola 25–6, 94, 122, 145–7, 156–7
Ganchev, Ivan 80
Gautier, Théophile 220
Genchev, Dimitîr 146, 170, 269
generation 8, 35, 79–8, 91, 102, 106, 111, 127, 132, 136, 156, 171, 174, 187–8, 204, 251, 283–5, 326
Geneva 22, 26–7, 29, 33, 43, 52, 103, 105, 119, 121–4, 131–2, 145, 162, 164–5, 215, 240, 295, 297–8, 305, 326
Geneva circle 28, 52, 124, 134–7, 141, 155, 299
George, Henry 126, 133
George, Stefan 220
Georgiev, Gavril 159, 240, 324
General Federation of Trade Unions (GFTU) 88, 98, 221
Gerdzhikov, Mikhail 124, 295
Germany 13, 17–23, 25–6, 31–6, 38–9, 45, 48–55, 58–9, 62, 66–76, 80–1, 83, 85, 103–6, 112–13, 119–20, 123, 125, 127, 138, 148–9, 165, 223, 230, 232–4, 238, 242, 244–6, 271, 279
Gilmore, Leigh 208
Ginzburg, Carlo 176
Glavinov, Vasil 62–4
Goethe, Johann Wolfgang 158, 208
Gogol, Nikolai 132, 218
Goranov, Georgi 112
Gorky, Maxim 40, 125, 131, 138, 235, 300
Gradovskii, Alexander 129
Gramsci, Antonio 17, 24–5, 100
Granite City 201–2, 225
Grave, Jean 129
Great Britain, *see* England

Greece 39, 54, 62, 64, 104, 181, 185, 187, 222, 245, 311
Grimm, Robert 43
Grincharova, Maslina 182–4, 186
Guesde, Jules 23, 25, 33, 53–5, 133, 135, 144, 233
Gulabchev, Spiro 91, 127–9, 142, 165, 297

Haase, Hugo 72
Habsburg Empire, *see* Austria-Hungary
Hadzhidimov, Dimo 62–3
Hadzhistoianov, Nenko 139
Haupt, Georges 59, 67, 71
Heehs, Peter 207
Heine, Heinrich 33, 232
Hellbeck, Jochen 227, 322
Herbst, Iosif 112
Hervé, Gustave 66, 279
Herzen, Alexander 120
Herzl, Theodore 293
histoire croisée 12, 59–60
Hobsbawm, Eric 12, 30, 71, 281
Hungary 31–2, 41, 50, 70, 223, 276, 304
Huxley, Thomas 120, 133, 264
Huysmans, Camille 69

Iankov, Kosta 109, 166, 307
Iasenov, Khristo 112
Iavorov, Peiu 127, 302
Ibsen, Henrik 125, 127, 213
identity 6, 81–2, 175, 199–200, 207, 209
Ikonomov, Matei 125, 292
Ilinden Uprising 56, 124, 180, 183, 185, 201, 286
intelligentsia 19, 28, 35–6, 54, 94–8, 100–5, 120, 125, 151–2, 216, 235, 246, 268, 289, 296, 316
Internal Macedonian Revolutionary Organization (IMRO) 62–5, 88, 110, 124–5, 183, 210, 212, 239, 295
internationalism 9, 12, 15, 48, 50, 58, 71–2, 78, 123, 201, 276
International Workers of the World (IWW) 201, 204, 317
International Workingmen's Association, *see* First International
Ioneva, Mara 165
Iovchev, Lazar (Exarch Iosif) 119, 139, 265
Iskrov, Petîr 109

Ismian, Tigran   90–1
Italy   13, 18–20, 32, 39, 58, 67, 70, 77,
    103, 134, 176, 245, 264, 268
Ivanov, Petîr   186–7, 191

Japan   48, 137
Jaurès, Jean   14, 33, 40, 54–5, 65–6, 137,
    144, 259
Jovanović, Kosta   164
Jovanović, Tsanka Dragneva   164–5

Kabakchiev, Khristo   25, 27, 41, 67,
    106–7, 247, 299
Kalchev, Tsonio   89
Kandeva, Raina   162
Karavelov, Liuben   120, 130, 151
Karavelov, Petko   112, 126
Karev, Nikola   63
Karima, Anna   155–6
Kautsky, Karl   17, 20, 23–5, 31, 33–4,
    38–9, 46, 49, 52–3, 55–9, 67–8,
    70–4, 76–7, 94, 144, 180, 235,
    262–3, 301
Kazanlîk   92, 98, 117, 124, 134, 137, 155,
    165, 287
Khadzhiivanova, Maria   156–7
Kharlakov, Nikola   25, 28, 63, 138, 221,
    230, 236, 238–40, 242
Khilendarski, Paissi   179
Khristov, Dimitîr   159–60
Khristov, Kiril   127
Khristova, Tsonka   162
Kiev   25, 28, 127, 239, 245, 314
Kinchov, Vasil   126
Kiorchev, Dimo   125
Kîrdhiev, Georgi   91, 125–6
Kirkov, Georgi   25–6, 35, 45, 47, 69,
    72–5, 91, 106, 139, 159, 161, 167–8,
    222, 237–8, 242, 277, 283
Kirkova, Tina   155, 162, 166–7, 169, 237
Kirov, Naiden   291
Kiustendil   166, 204–5, 211, 222, 226,
Kliment of Tîrnovo, Bishop   118, 196, 314
Klincharov, Ivan   80, 107–8, 266
Kocka, Jürgen   84
Koenker, Diane   227–8
Kołakowski, Leszek   5, 13, 253
Kolarov, Vasil   27, 42–3, 70, 72, 90,
    106–7, 235, 247–8, 307

Konov, Andrei   131, 155, 298
Konova, Kina   155
Konstantinov, Georgi   125
Korsch, Karl   24
Kostov, Traicho   109–10, 139, 300, 306
Kovachev, Iordan   126
Krestintern   43
Krîstev, Krîstiu   117
Kropotkin, Peter   33, 124, 126, 129
Krusheva, Maria   1, 3, 162–3, 168
Kun, Bela   106
Kusevich, Metodi   165
Kutev, Ivan   134

Lafargue, Paul   23, 31, 33, 233
Lambrev, Georgi   109
Lapčević, Dragiša   51
Lassalle, Ferdinand   1, 21, 33, 120
Lässig, Simone   177
Latin America   14, 18, 23, 189
Lausanne   124–5, 185, 232
Lavrov, Petr   54, 120–2, 158
Lazarov, Vilo   184–5
Lazov, Dimitîr   212–14, 222
League of Nations   48
Lenin, Vladimir   58, 70, 74, 137–8,
    169–70, 238, 263, 279–80, 291, 301
Lepore, Jill   176
Lermontov, Mikhail   128
Lessing, Gotthold Ephraim   215
Levi, Giovanni   176
Levitas, Ruth   4, 6
Levkov, Iordan   212, 217, 219
Levski, Vasil   120, 131, 302
Lichtheim, George   251, 264
Liebknecht, Karl   24, 57, 69, 72, 74, 233
Liebknecht, Wilhelm   1, 21, 31, 46, 50,
    53, 135, 162, 214
Life Writing   174–6, 187, 205–9,
    310–11
Lukács, György   24, 38, 220, 264
Lukanov, Karlo   162
Lukanov, Todor   107, 162, 306
Lukanova, Konstantsa   162
Lutskii, Vladimir   122
Lutz, Catherine   172
Luxemburg, Rosa   20, 24–5, 49, 53, 57–8,
    69, 71, 74, 112, 135, 169, 232–3,
    235, 301

Macedonia 30, 41, 54–7, 61–3, 71, 88, 124, 126–7, 132, 143, 179–80, 182–5, 186–8, 196, 201, 203, 209–12, 222, 225–6, 275, 280, 286, 295, 311–12, 314, 316–17
macrohistory 11
Madison 201–2, 204, 225, 316
Madzharov, Mikhail 241, 324
Maehl, William 66, 279
Maier, Charles 259
Maimunkova, Anna 162, 169–70
Maksimov, Khristo 126
Malatesta, Errico 124
Mandzhukov, Petîr 124
Manev, Ivan 109
Mannheim, Karl 6, 82–4, 101
Marinov, Ivan 133
Marković, Svetozar 121
Marx, Karl 30, 33–4, 125, 128, 131, 133, 139, 143, 145, 147, 158, 162, 164, 214, 232
Marxism 1, 4–5, 18–20, 23–5, 29–30, 33, 35, 39, 44, 51, 58–9, 76, 112, 120–1, 129–31, 141, 143–4, 171, 255, 262, 296, 301, 325
Mateev, Boris Stefanov 161, 306
Mateev, Ivan Stefanov 306
Mehring, Franz 23, 69
Meletius, metropolitan 193, 195, 314
memoirs 87–8, 171, 175, 205–9
Mensheviks 38, 70, 233
microhistory 11, 174, 176–7
Mikhailov, Ivan 182
Mikhailov, Khristo 181–2
Mikhailovski, Stoian 127, 151
Milev, Geo 113–16
Mill, John Stuart 128
Mintses, Boris 93, 123
Miskanov, Kotso 180
Miskanov, Nikola 180
Montana 180–3, 191
Morgan, Lewis H. 133
Moscow 4, 43–4, 125–7, 162, 166, 169, 239, 245, 247, 281, 317
Most, Johann 124
Moulin, Joanny 175
Muletarov, Vasil 247

multilingualism 72
Mutafov, Sava 134, 155

narodniks 88, 91, 93–4, 121–3, 125–7, 130, 134, 157, 295, 298, 301
nationalism 12, 51, 58, 62, 66, 76–8, 129–30, 146, 152, 164, 173–4, 185, 188, 192, 222, 242
Nechayev, Sergey 120, 294
Netherlands 13, 18–19, 70
Nietzsche, Friedrich 125, 220
Nokov, Stoian 52–3, 132, 134–7, 262
Nonchev, Pavel 137, 300

October revolution, *see* Bolshevik Revolution
Omarchevski, Stoian 181
Ortega y Gasset, José 81
Orthodoxy (Christian) 35, 134
Osterhammel, Jürgen 14–15
Ottoman Empire/Turkey 8, 39, 50, 52, 55–6, 62, 64–5, 67, 179, 184, 187, 192, 194, 196–7, 201, 209–10, 275, 278–9, 281, 312, 314
Owen, Robert 21–2

Pandov, Dimitîr 138–9
Panov, Iordan 249, 290
Pan-Slav congress 35, 40
Paris 120, 122–3, 125, 133, 137, 139, 145, 155–6, 169, 212, 240
Paris Commune 119–20, 235
Parvus, Alexander 59, 67–9, 238, 279, 291
patriotism, *see* nationalism
Penev, Boian 98
Penev, Nikola 98
periphery 7–8, 14–15, 48, 76–7, 260, 285–6
permanent revolution 108, 291
Petersburg/Petrograd 25, 138, 157, 238
Petrov, Khristo 139
Pipkov, Panaiot 89, 286
Pirinski, Georgi 204, 316–18
Pirot 182, 192–3, 198–9
Pîrvanov, Georgi 71
Pisarev, Dmitry 128, 131–3
Piskova, Vela 168–9

Plekhanov, Georgy   20, 26–9, 31, 33,
    35–6, 38, 42–4, 48, 53, 66, 68–9,
    120, 122–3, 125, 131, 134–5, 137,
    232–3, 240, 299, 300
Pleven   124, 146, 162, 237
Poe, Edgar Allen   220
Poland   5, 13, 38, 48–50, 55, 120, 131,
    245, 249, 304
Popov, Dimitîr   165
Popova, Stefanka   164
Popova, Teofana   91, 165
Poprusinov, Konstantin   138
populists, *see narodniks*
Postompirov, Todor   91, 134
Pripîlzhane   180, 182, 184, 186–8, 192,
    196
"progressives"   37, 238
proletariat, *see* working class
Protogerov, Aleksandîr   249
Proudhon, Pierre-Joseph   118–19, 124,
    128, 133, 145

Quelch, Harry   55–6

Radek, Karl   107
Radev, Simeon   37, 73
Radomir rebellion   41, 86
Rakovski, Christian   28, 35, 37, 53–5,
    57, 59–60, 64–5, 71–2, 100, 128,
    130, 134–8, 156, 167, 232, 237–40,
    246, 281
Rakovski, Georgi Sava   130
Rashenov, Iurdan   131, 291
Reclus, Jacques Élisée   124, 129
Reddy, William   172–3
Renders, Hans   177
Renner, Karl   58–9
Revel, Jacques   11
revolution   2, 7, 18, 22, 24, 38–47,
    60–1, 68–9, 95, 105–9, 129, 235,
    247–8
Riabova, Elisaveta   135, 137
Ricardo, David   158
Richebourg, Émile   212
Ricoeur, Paul   6, 200
Romania   31–3, 54, 60, 62, 103–4, 121–2,
    133, 137, 159, 281, 304
Rosenwein, Barbara   174
Rothschild, Joseph   25–6, 28, 38, 98

Ruse   1, 92, 124, 129, 140, 142, 161–4,
    169, 180
Ruskin, John   22, 220
Russel, Nicholas, *see* Sudzilovsky
Russia   4, 13, 19, 25–6, 28, 30–40, 44–6,
    48, 50–6, 58, 66–72, 74, 76–7, 80,
    85–6, 91, 93–5, 99, 103–6, 109–10,
    112, 118, 120–38, 144–5, 155,
    157–8, 160, 166, 169–70, 179, 181,
    187, 190, 213–15, 223, 228, 232–4,
    238–40, 247, 253, 262, 273, 279, 301
Russophobia   50, 53, 242
Rutar, Sabine   72

Saint-Simon, Henri de   21, 118–19
Sakarov, Nikola   9, 72, 94, 229–30, 236–7,
    240–50
Sakîzov, Ianko   26–8, 46, 53, 62, 70, 133–4,
    136, 141–2, 144–6, 155, 242, 264, 301
Sandanski, Iane   64
Sarafov, Boris   210
scale   8, 11–12, 15, 176, 252, 257–8
Scheer, Monique   230, 322
Schiller, Friedrich   132, 137, 158
Second International   50–4, 65, 122, 137,
    145, 238, 259–6
    Amsterdam congress   48
    Basel congress   66
    Copenhagen congress   59, 64, 66
    Kienthal Conference   70
    London congress   54
    Paris congress   122
    Stuttgart congress   36, 49, 66, 237,
        267, 280
    Zimmerwald conference   42–4, 238,
        281
    Zurich congress   52–3
Second World War   4, 22, 24, 44, 92,
    98, 138, 149, 162, 165, 173, 180–1,
    187–8, 207, 232, 237
Segalen, Martine   150
September Uprising   43, 95, 108, 111,
    186, 205, 226, 238, 247–8, 291, 306
Serbia   13, 31–3, 39, 50–1, 54–5, 58–60,
    62, 64, 69–70, 77, 103, 108, 110,
    121–2, 125, 164, 179, 181, 192, 212
Shakespeare, William   125, 132, 215
Shelgunov, Nikolai   128, 132
Shishmanov, Ivan   187, 223, 297

Slaveikov, Petko   118
Slavophilism (Slavophil)   20, 35, 52, 268
Smilov, Petko   106
Smirnenski, Khristo   112
Smith, Adam   128, 158
Social-Democratic Teachers' Organization (SDTO)   220-1
Social-Democratic Union "Proletarii," *see* "anarcho-liberals"
socialist circles   25, 35, 52, 124, 129, 131-2, 134, 139, 157, 159, 163-5, 184, 204, 214, 221, 232-3, 297
Socialist Labor Party of America (SLP)   201, 203, 226
Sofia   134, 139, 141-2, 154-6, 158-9, 162-3, 166-70, 180-6, 191-2, 196, 204-5, 207, 213, 226, 235-7, 240, 242, 246-7, 249, 290
Spencer, Herbert   120, 128, 133
Stalin   2, 4, 5, 24, 42-4, 58, 80, 109, 256, 264, 291
Stamboliiski, Alexander   41, 126, 145, 190, 247, 271, 280
Stambolov, Stefan   53, 92, 104, 126, 159, 222, 242
Stefanova, Anna   98, 161, 164
Steinberg, Mark   100, 173
Stere, Constantin   121
Stockholm   238
Stoianov, Zakhari   93, 122-3, 131
Stoichkova, Ekaterina   166
Strashimirov, Anton   126
Strashimirov, Todor   126
Strike   20, 25, 45, 66, 95, 124, 132, 138-9, 149, 170, 221-2, 235-6, 317
Subjectivity   9, 74, 174, 176, 227-8
Südekum, Albert   67
Sudzilovsky, Nikolai   120-4, 294
Sue, Eugène   212
Suny, Ronald   173
Supreme Macedonian Committee   210-12
"Sveta Nedelia" bombing   108, 242, 248-9, 307
Sweden   13, 70
Switzerland   13, 18-19, 28, 39, 70, 103-5, 120, 122-3, 127, 134, 223, 232-3, 245

Taushanov, Petîr   125, 296
Thessaloniki   63-5, 124, 165, 183, 209
Third International, *see* Comintern

Third World   18, 76
Tineva, Koika   9, 72, 98, 100, 161-2, 168, 229-42
Tîrnovo   1, 127-8, 131, 134, 140, 145, 157-9, 162-4, 168
Tîrnovo constitution   39, 151
Todorov, Petko   39-40, 126-7
Todorov, Sider   80
Tolstoyism   125-6, 143, 160, 215, 217, 296
Toshev, Georgi   56
transfer studies   8, 12, 15, 30-1, 33-4, 59, 265
Traverso, Enzo   5, 14
Troebst, Stefan   38, 50
Trotsky, Leon   35, 37-40, 65, 100, 237-8, 240, 266, 268, 291, 317
Tsankov, Alexander   113, 270-1
Tsankov, Asen   47, 270-1
Tsankov, Dragan   185
Tsanov, Naicho   126
Tsekov, Todor   9, 132, 201-28, 316-21
Tsekova, Katia   216, 218-19, 223-6
Tserkovski, Tsanko   126, 286, 302
tuberculosis   40, 74-5, 90, 111-12, 127, 139, 142, 166, 222, 318
Tucović, Dimitrije   51, 59, 273, 276
Turgenev, Ivan   131-2, 157-8
Turkey (Modern)   14, 230, 245
typhus   163, 190

Ukraine   13, 31, 41, 127, 137, 155
United States   11-12, 14, 23, 29-30, 38, 48-9, 84, 103, 139, 150, 174, 176, 185-6, 201-2, 204-5, 207, 215, 219, 223-6, 228, 245, 315-17
utopia   1-7, 39, 119, 228, 240, 251-3, 256

Vaillant, Édouard   54-5, 66
Vandervelde, Emile   31, 110, 281
Varna   91-2, 98, 100, 127, 131, 161, 164, 232-3, 235-6, 240
Vazov, Ivan   121, 132, 302, 305
Vienna   26, 35, 70, 91, 105, 108, 123, 176, 239-40, 295, 307, 326
Vlahov, Dimitîr   64-5
Vlaikov, Todor   126
Vrachanski, Sophrony   180, 311
Vratsa   179-81, 183, 189, 199, 201, 226, 229

Wallerstein, Immanuel   15
Weber, Eugen   77
Weber, Max   6, 40, 76, 173, 253
White Terror   53, 108, 110, 168, 307
Williams, Raymond   171–2
women   89, 105, 147–70
working class   2, 7–8, 17–19, 24–5, 36, 43–8, 51, 56, 58, 60–1, 64, 66–9, 73–4, 76, 81, 85, 88, 92, 94–6, 100, 106–7, 109, 119, 124, 141, 145, 149, 151, 153–4, 164, 203, 216, 227–8, 235, 238, 240, 246–7, 249, 271, 280
Wrangel army   146

Yankov, Yanko   125
Young Turks   56, 61, 63–5

Zagorichane   181–5, 187, 196
Zagubanski, Ivan   112
Zasulich, Vera   122, 135, 233
Zeitgeist   7, 83–4, 188
Zemon Davis, Natalie   176
Zetkin, Clara   24, 31, 148–9, 169, 232, 235, 303
Zhivkov, Georgi   159
Zhivkov, Nikola   159, 305
Zurich   52–3, 66, 91, 112, 125, 147

www.ingramcontent.com/pod-product-compliance
Lightning Source LLC
Chambersburg PA
CBHW072119290426
44111CB00012B/1706